The Science of Debugging

Matt Telles

Yuan Hsieh

President and CEO
Keith Weiskamp

Publisher
Steve Sayre

Acquisitions Editor
Kevin Weeks

Product Marketing Manager
Tracy Rooney

Project Editor
Tom Lamoureux

Technical Reviewer
Bob Arnson

Production Coordinator
Peggy Cantrell

Cover Designer
Laura Wellander

Layout Designer
April E. Nielsen

The Science of Debugging

Limits of Liability and Disclaimer of Warranty
The author and publisher of this book have used their best efforts in preparing the book and the programs contained in it. These efforts include the development, research, and testing of the theories and programs to determine their effectiveness. The author and publisher make no warranty of any kind, expressed or implied, with regard to these programs or the documentation contained in this book.

The author and publisher shall not be liable in the event of incidental or consequential damages in connection with, or arising out of, the furnishing, performance, or use of the programs, associated instructions, and/or claims of productivity gains.

Trademarks
Trademarked names appear throughout this book. Rather than list the names and entities that own the trademarks or insert a trademark symbol with each mention of the trademarked name, the publisher states that it is using the names for editorial purposes only and to the benefit of the trademark owner, with no intention of infringing upon that trademark.

The Coriolis Group, LLC
14455 North Hayden Road
Suite 220
Scottsdale, Arizona 85260

(480) 483-0192
FAX (480) 483-0193
www.coriolis.com

Library of Congress Cataloging-in-Publication Data
Telles, Matthew A.
     The science of debugging / by Matt Telles and Yuan Hsieh.
        p.   cm.
     Includes index.
     ISBN 1-57610-917-8
     1. Debugging in computer science.   I. Hsieh, Yuan. II.   Title.

QA76.6.T4412 2001
005.1'4 — dc21   2001028385
                                                                        CIP

Printed in the United States of America
10 9 8 7 6 5 4 3 2 1

CORIOLIS™

The Coriolis Group, LLC • 14455 North Hayden Road, Suite 220 • Scottsdale, Arizona 85260

Dear Reader:

Coriolis Technology Press was founded to create a very elite group of books: the ones you keep closest to your machine. Sure, everyone would like to have the Library of Congress at arm's reach, but in the real world, you have to choose the books you rely on every day *very* carefully.

To win a place for our books on that coveted shelf beside your PC, we guarantee several important qualities in every book we publish. These qualities are:

- *Technical accuracy*—It's no good if it doesn't work. Every Coriolis Technology Press book is reviewed by technical experts in the topic field, and is sent through several editing and proofreading passes in order to create the piece of work you now hold in your hands.

- *Innovative editorial design*—We've put years of research and refinement into the ways we present information in our books. Our books' editorial approach is uniquely designed to reflect the way people learn new technologies and search for solutions to technology problems.

- *Practical focus*—We put only pertinent information into our books and avoid any fluff. Every fact included between these two covers must serve the mission of the book as a whole.

- *Accessibility*—The information in a book is worthless unless you can find it quickly when you need it. We put a lot of effort into our indexes, and heavily cross-reference our chapters, to make it easy for you to move right to the information you need.

Here at The Coriolis Group we have been publishing and packaging books, technical journals, and training materials since 1989. We're programmers and authors ourselves, and we take an ongoing active role in defining what we publish and how we publish it. We have put a lot of thought into our books; please write to us at **ctp@coriolis.com** and let us know what you think. We hope that you're happy with the book in your hands, and that in the future, when you reach for software development and networking information, you'll turn to one of our books first.

Keith Weiskamp
President and CEO

Jeff Duntemann
VP and Editorial Director

Look for these related books from The Coriolis Group:

Software Project Management: From Concept to Deployment
by Kieron Conway

Data Modeling Essentials, 2nd Edition
by Graeme C. Simsion and Graham C. Witt

Also published by Coriolis Technology Press:

C++ Black Book
by Steven Holzner

Designing Visual Basic.NET Applications
by David Vitter

Visual Basic 6 Black Book
by Steven Holzner

XML Black Book, 2nd Edition
by Natanya Pitts

This book is dedicated to my wife, Dawnna, my three children, Jenny, Rachel, and Sarah, and to my best friend Carol, who kept me sane throughout the writing of this tome. Thank you all.

—Matt

ह

This book is dedicated to my Dad, my brother, and my friends. You all helped make this possible.

—Y'

ह

About the Author

Matt Telles is a 15 year veteran of the software development wars. In his time, he has seen FORTRAN, COBOL and other dinosaur languages come and go. Currently a senior software engineer for Microsoft Corporation, his days are spent finding and fixing bugs that other people have created. Besides trying to be tactful, he also enjoys working with other developers to teach the techniques he has mastered over his career. With expertise in programming, designing, documenting, and debugging applications, he has reached the pinnacle of a programmer's existence: the ability to write his own bio blurbs for books. The author of five other programming books, Matt lives in Lakewood, Colorado and pines away for his beloved DEC 10.

Yuan Hsieh remembers the day when it was still possible to read every single newsgroup on the Internet. He had spent the last 12 years creating bugs out of thin air. He had also spent the same 12 years fixing those bugs. He got rather good at doing the latter. But he no longer has to do either himself. He is currently the Director of Software Development at InfoNow Corporation. Instead of making and fixing bugs, he gets to watch others make and fix bugs. Now he spends most of his time getting the development group working as a lean, mean, coding machine so they can create bug-free software on time and under budget. He currently lives in Lone Tree, Colorado, and spends most of his free time falling: falling off the side of a mountain, falling off a mountain bike and falling into champagne-powder snow.

Acknowledgments

The author would like to acknowledge his employer, Microsoft Corporation, for allowing him the time and space to work on this book. In addition, he would like to acknowledge his wife, Dawnna, and his three children for ignoring the ranting and raving that came out of his office from time to time. Finally, no book could be written without a considerable amount of behind-the-scenes work. Tom Lamoureux, Kevin Weeks, Peggy Cantrell, Jodi Winkler, Quentin Correll, Bob Arnson, and Anne Marie Walker worked tirelessly to turn the inane words I wrote into something vaguely resembling English.
—Matt

They said that an artist usually performs best when he is emotionally disturbed. Even though this is a technical book, muses are still desirable and inspirations needed. For a bachelor like me, what better way to become emotionally disturbed than to go through the dating rituals. Therefore, I would like to thank all the past and present members of the opposite sex that came in and out of my life, for all the angst, inspirations and sleepless nights (What better time to write, then when venting alone in the dark, spewing forth words of wisdom).

Seriously, there are a few people that I would like to acknowledge. I would like to thank Kim Wright for helping me proofread some of the earlier chapters. I would also like to acknowledge Stephen Shiller, for kindly providing some hair-raising examples used in this book. I would like to thank the people at Coriolis: Kevin Weeks, Tom Lamoureux, Peggy Cantrell, Jodi Winkler, and the technical reviewer, Quentin Correll, and the copy editor, Anne Marie Walker, for their help and assistance. Also, there are all the people that I have worked with and the companies and places that I had worked at. The experiences have been invaluable.

Finally, I would like to thank Matt for providing me with an opportunity to write this book with him.
—Y'

Contents at a Glance

Chapter 1   Introduction to Debugging   1

Chapter 2   Case Studies of Famous (and Not So Famous) Bugs   13

Chapter 3   What Are Bugs?   53

Chapter 4   Life Cycle of a Bug   77

Chapter 5   A Bug Taxonomy   109

Chapter 6   Detective Work   165

Chapter 7   Debugging Tools and When to Use Them   187

Chapter 8   The General Process of Debugging   205

Chapter 9   Debugging Techniques   241

Chapter 10   Debugging Different Application Types   287

Chapter 11   Post Debugging   309

Chapter 12   Prebugging   325

Chapter 13   Testing   393

Chapter 14   Maintenance   423

Chapter 15   Debugging as a Profession   447

Appendix A   Bug Puzzle Solutions   467

Appendix B   Additional Reading   477

Table of Contents

Chapter 1 Introduction to Debugging 1

What This Book Is about 3

Why Care about Bugs? 4

What Is a Bug? 5

Who Is This Book for? 5

Organization of this Book 7

A Brief History of Debugging 8

Summary 11

Bug Puzzle 11

Chapter 2 Case Studies of Famous (and Not So Famous) Bugs 13

Scenarios 14

A Buggy Vignette #1 26

A Buggy Vignette #2 30

A Buggy Vignette #3 33

A Buggy Vignette #4 38

Summary 48

Bug Puzzle 51

Chapter 3 What Are Bugs? 53

What Is a Bug? 53

Why Worry about Bugs? 60

The Nature of Bugs 64

Summary 74

Bug Puzzle 74

Chapter 4 Life Cycle of a Bug 77

Why Are Bugs Created? 77

How Are Bugs Created? 89

How Do Bugs Slip through Testing? 103

Summary 107

Bug Puzzle 107

Chapter 5 A Bug Taxonomy 109

Classes of Bugs   111
Severity   122
The Bug Taxonomy   123
The Bug Classes   124
Why Is Classification Important?   161
Summary   161
Bug Puzzle   162

Chapter 6 Detective Work 165

Holistic Debugging   166
Debugging Methods   173
Tricks of the Trade   176
Reproducible Cases   180
Summary   185
Bug Puzzle   185

Chapter 7 Debugging Tools and When to Use Them 187

Testing and Debugging Environments   187
Middle Level Debugging Techniques   192
Summary   203
Bug Puzzle   203

Chapter 8 The General Process of Debugging 205

Identify the Problem   205
Gather Information   211
Form a Hypothesis   223
Test Your Hypothesis   230
The Case of the Crashing Web Server   231
Iterate until a Proven Hypothesis Is Found   234
Propose a Solution   235
Test the Solution   237
Iterate until Solution Is Proven   237
Regression Test   238
Summary   238
Bug Puzzle   239

Chapter 9 Debugging Techniques 241

Intrusive vs. Non-intrusive Debugging   242
Short-Term vs. Long-Term Debugging Techniques   243
Compromises for Production Environments   244

The Techniques   245
Summary   286
Bug Puzzle   286

Chapter 10   Debugging Different Application Types 287
Small-Scale Standalone Applications   288
Mid-Size Standalone Applications   292
Mid-Size Client/Server Applications   293
Large-Scale Applications   295
Real-Time Systems   297
Embedded Systems   299
Distributed Systems   301
Simulated Systems   305
Summary   306
Bug Puzzle   307

Chapter 11   Post Debugging 309
Did I Make the Same Mistake Elsewhere?   310
What's Hiding Behind This Bug?   312
How Can I Prevent this Bug?   313
How Can I Make this Kind of Bug Easier to Find?   315
Am I Getting Better?   320
Summary   323
Bug Puzzle   324

Chapter 12   Prebugging 325
What Is Prebugging?   326
General Techniques   328
Prebugging in Requirement   362
Prebugging in Design   367
Prebugging in Implementation   378
Summary   389
Bug Puzzle   390

Chapter 13   Testing.. 393
Unit Testing   393
Verification Testing   395
Quality Assurance Testing   396
Testing Methods   398
Summary   419
Bug Puzzle   420

Chapter 14 Maintenance 423

What Is Software Maintenance?   424
Creating a Maintainable Software System   427
Maintaining Existing Software   438
When Do You Give Up?   443
Summary   444
Bug Puzzle   445

Chapter 15 Debugging as a Profession 447

Learning to Be a Debugger   447
Where Can Professional Debuggers Be Used?   451
Traits of a Good Professional Debugger   455
A Day in the Life   461
Summary   464
Bug Puzzle   464

Appendix A Bug Puzzle Solutions 467

Appendix B Additional Reading 477

Index 481

Chapter 1

Introduction to Debugging

Matt Telles

As Benjamin Franklin said, "in this world, nothing is certain but death and taxes." If you are in the software development business, however, you can amend that statement. Nothing in life is certain except death, taxes, and software bugs. If you cryogenically freeze yourself, you can delay death indefinitely. If you move to a country with no income tax, you can avoid paying taxes by not buying anything. If you develop software, however, no remedy known to mankind can save you from the horror of software bugs.

This book is about software bugs—big bugs, little bugs, ugly bugs, and famous bugs. Bugs of all sorts are discussed. If you have ever written a program that contained a bug (in other words, if you've ever written a software program), you will likely find a version of your bug herein. Within these pages, you will not only learn what bugs are and how to find and fix them, but also how to detect them before they escape into production code.

One of the things that most programmers find most frustrating about software development books is the fact that they assume that with a perfect design, perfect code, and a perfect test plan there would be no bugs in the software world. You can be assured that this is far from the truth. Even "perfect" code will contain bugs, if only in the fact that it may not do what the user wants it to do. This is not to say that it doesn't work; it most certainly does, but it doesn't do what is desired.

Software bugs can be amusing. For example, one such bug in an early version of the Calculator program that shipped with Microsoft Windows calculated the square root of 2 as an almost infinite number. That would certainly make a small difference in your checkbook calculations! Bugs like this often make the news and are treated with the derision and laughter that they deserve. They also tend to give the programmers who wrote the applications a bad reputation. No real harm is done by such bugs, but it does call into question other, more serious, applications written by the same developers. For example, suppose that the developer who made the error in the square root function also made a similar (but more serious) error in the file system code for the operating system? It would hardly be as amusing to have all of your files suddenly disappear from your hard drive!

Other types of bugs may be somewhat amusing, at least to programmers, but can cost users real money. For example, a "glitch" in software made by Sun Microsystems resulted in a 22 hour system crash for the online auctioneer, eBay.[1] Not only was the revenue from the 22 hour period entirely lost to the company, but their reputation was also severely damaged. There is no telling how much money a bug like this could cost in the long run. In this case, Sun acknowledged that such a bug existed, but also stated that a "patch" (software fix) was available to fix the bug and had not been installed. Of course, to eBay users it hardly mattered which company was at fault, they simply knew that they could not use the system.

Software can cost more than just money. It can cost you your credibility and reputation in the eyes of the world. For example, Northeastern University unintentionally admitted 25 percent more freshmen to their fall classes than they could handle. Earlier, the university had been chagrined to admit that hundreds of potential applicants had been lost when its new software system was first installed. This loss forced the university to go on an aggressive recruiting campaign to enroll the students who had initially been accepted, which resulted in the secondary problem of too many students. How do you suppose students who were not admitted felt? Northeastern certainly suffered a blow to their reputation with this fiasco.[2]

Software has become increasingly pervasive in our society. Systems that once ran with pure human intervention are now run entirely by software systems. This means that life and death situations can, and do, rely on the software performing exactly as it is supposed to. A software bug, or defect, will result in a program doing something unexpected or doing something wrong. In a worst case scenario, this can result in death. As an example, between the years 1985 and 1987, faulty software in a Therac-25 radiation treatment machine resulted in the deaths of several cancer patients from lethal doses of radiation.[3] Although it is certainly ironic that a machine intended to help save people from a life-threatening disease ended up killing them, it is also a tragedy of epic proportions. Although the number of bugs found in software for medical equipment is extremely low, it illustrates what the results can be when software bugs occur in production code.

---

[1] Ginty, Maura. "Cost Of eBay's 22-Hour Outage Put At $2 Million." http://www.internetnews.com/ec-news/article/ 0,,4_137251,00.html.

[2] Abel, David. "Admissions Mixup Leaves NU Struggling." *Boston Globe*, August 10, 2000.

[3] Leveson, Nancy, and Clark S. Turner. "An Investigation of the Therac-25 Accidents", *IEEE Computer*, July 1993, Vol. 25, No. 7, pp. 18–41.

What This Book Is about

In a nutshell, this book is about software bugs—how to detect bugs, how to fix bugs, and how to eliminate the root causes of bugs. When you finish reading this book, you should know why bugs occur, what you can do to help stop them from occurring, and how to find and fix bugs in your existing code. Mostly, however, this book is "bug-centric." We approach the problem from the perspective that bugs have always existed, still exist, and will exist in the future. It is easy to talk about "bug-free" software, but because it is nonexistent, we focus on what does exist—buggy software.

In the history of software development books, much time and space has been dedicated to talking about better ways to design software, better ways to write code, and better ways to deploy systems. In all of these approaches, debugging was always considered an afterthought. Debugging was the software industry's dirty little secret, the one that was ignored and kept in the back closet in the basement. It is time that we take debugging out of the closet, and treat it as what it is—a natural part of the software development life cycle.

Bugs can creep into applications at any level of the software life cycle. We will examine how bugs occur in the requirements phase of development, an area where bugs cost very little to fix but can result in bugs that are enormously expensive when they are found in the finished product. Likewise, we will examine how bugs can occur due to extraneous portions of the development cycle, which is often called "feature creep." Software bugs often slip through the testing phase of the development life cycle for a variety of reasons. By understanding why this happens, you can better design, implement, and test your systems.

One theme that will continually crop up throughout this book is the idea that to avoid bugs, fix them, or verify your bug fixes, you need to understand the system's "big picture." We will examine how you can better understand software systems by including information on how to better document your own code and ideas on how to approach a system you have had little or no experience with. Although we often consider the role of debugging to be done by the original developer, it is quite normal for new developers to be brought onto an existing system to debug problems.

Additionally, we will examine the role of a "professional debugger" in today's software engineering world. Despite the importance of debugging in the software development world, debugging is still considered a routine task of a software engineer. It is becoming more and more obvious that this must change. Debugging must be considered in the same way that design and requirements gathering are considered: that is, as a profession unto itself. It doesn't make sense to have a specialized position for writing the design for systems, but not have a specialized position for maintaining and fixing the code for systems. It is time that our industry began to understand this issue.

We will also look at the traits that make a good debugger and explain how you can emphasize those traits while you are working in a debugging role. We will look at the tasks that you can perform to make yourself a better debugger including techniques you can use when no problems are being worked on, or in the space before bugs exist in a system.

Why Care about Bugs?

Earlier this year, the state of New York admitted that due to a problem with the way it assigned numbers to fingerprints stored in its database, it would run out of numbers by the end of the year. In order to fix this "bug," the state would begin recycling numbers starting from one.[4] Imagine, for a moment, that you were fingerprinted in a criminal investigation at some point in the past in New York. Or perhaps your fingerprints were on file because you visited the Capitol building and allowed them to be taken. No problem? Not really.

When crimes are committed and fingerprints are stored, the identification of the fingerprint is used to keep track of who was investigated, charged, and so forth. Suppose that one of your fingerprints happened to have the same identifying number as a new fingerprint, which matched that of a crime. Because the two database systems are not synchronized due to the recent duplication of numbers, you could find yourself dragged into court to defend yourself.

Still not convinced that bugs are important? Consider this: In 1972, a software journal (no longer published, sadly) called *EDP Analyzer*, determined that 50 percent of the total data processing budget in most organizations is devoted to maintenance and debugging.[5] During the late 1980s, some organizations saw that number climb as high as 80 percent of the budget (also from *EDP Analyzer*). Considering that the budget of an average IT department is mostly used for equipment and salaries, this means that money that could be spent for raises and new cutting-edge equipment and tools is, instead, used to fix problems. If it makes you feel any better, later studies by Capers Jones, Howard Rubin, and Larry Putnam tell us that at present the number has dropped back to that 50 percent level.[6]

Another interesting piece of information that came from the Jones et al study is that approximately 20 percent of the maintenance budget is spent to fix defects that were introduced during the original development of the system. What does this tell us? If you are in the business of fixing software problems, it means that you are likely to stay employed for the remainder of your life. The infamous Y2K problem should have proved that. Future problems, already on the horizon, will likely put the Y2K problem to shame. We will look at a few of these problems in this book.

Another important reason to consider bugs is the "silver bullet" problem. In a nutshell, people believe there is some simple magic formula that can be applied to software development that will eradicate all bugs before they ever make it into the field. This is simply

---

[4] Wilson, Greg. "State's Running out of Fingers to Count IDs on." *New York Daily News*, August 25, 2000.

[5] Canning, R.G. "The Maintenance Iceberg." *EDP Analyzer*, October 1972. Volume 10, Number 10, pp 1–4.

[6] Jones, Capers, Howard Rubin, and Larry Putnam. *Assessment and Control of Software Risks*, Yourdon Press, 1994. Prentice Hall; ISBN: 0137414064.

nonsense. Programmers haven't really changed all that much in the last 30 years. Basic problems that existed when the software industry was in its infancy still exist. The same basic kinds of software bugs show up in software today as they did in the beginning. The magnitude of the problems has changed, however. Where most problems were isolated to a single user or group of users in the past, they now apply to the entire world. Problems that would have once meant going over a report by hand and reentering data now can mean the life or death of an organization.

If all of these issues haven't convinced you that software bugs are a serious problem and need to be addressed, it's probably not possible to convince you. For further evidence, we invite you to read Chapter 2 to see just what kinds of problems have occurred in the "real world" and what they have cost the industry in dollars and reputation. If, after reading all of these case studies, you still don't believe that software bugs are a problem, please go ahead and close the book. But don't be surprised when you have to work seven days a week fixing problems that have reached the crisis stage.

What Is a Bug?

We call them by many names: software defects, software bugs, software problems, and even software "features." Whatever you want to call them, they are things the software does that it is not supposed to do (or, alternatively, something the software doesn't do that it is supposed to). Software bugs (the term we will use in this book) range from program crashes to returning incorrect information to having garbled displays.

For the purpose of this book, a software bug is a case in which the software fails to do what it is supposed to. We will discuss this in more detail in Chapter 2. The severity of a bug is considered to be how badly it misbehaves. We consider the "cost" of a bug to be the severity of the damage it causes to the user, added to the amount of time and effort it will take on the part of the debugger or developer to fix the problem.

Other terms we will use in this book to describe bugs include category, reproducibility, side effects, and scalability. We will discuss each term as it is introduced. We will also discuss the issue of "bug fixing." We will talk about how to find a bug, how to fix a bug, and how to determine if the bug is really fixed or not. One of the points that cannot be stressed enough in debugging is that it doesn't do any good to "fix" a bug if you cannot verify that it will not reoccur.

Who Is This Book for?

Although it would appear that this book would mostly appeal to developers, this is certainly not the only group that should be reading it. Developers will certainly benefit from understanding what sorts of bugs can occur in applications, how to detect them, and how to prevent them in the first place. Likewise, debuggers will learn how to classify and identify the types of problems that they find and how to scientifically root out and destroy bugs in applications they are responsible for.

Management should also be reading this book. Without understanding the processes and problems that create software bugs and encouraging processes that are designed to minimize software bugs, these problems most likely will never go away. People will generally do what management stresses as most important. If all you want is faster and cheaper software, brace yourself for bigger, more complex bugs. If you want happy customers, be willing to balance the needs of better error detection and diagnostic tools in the application core against more aggressive schedules. This is not a coding book. Although there are certainly code examples listed in many chapters, there are also nontechnical examples as well.

Testers are certainly going to be interested in the book. Testers build test cases based on the kinds of problems that people have experienced in the past. As a result, by studying the kinds of bugs that have been found and determining the root causes for those bugs, testing people can build more effective test cases. Testing does not eliminate bugs, it simply prevents some of them from escaping into the production code and in turn appearing to the end user. Too many people believe that testing is synonymous with bug prevention. Bug prevention can only be done at the system design and implementation levels.

Obviously, software developers can use this book. By understanding the problems that have cropped up in other people's software, you stand a better chance of not having similar problems in your own. As George Santayana said, "Those who do not remember the past are condemned to repeat it." In addition to preventing bugs, developers can also use this book to understand what the best strategies are to find and fix bugs in production code. Although the emphasis in the book is on the role of a professional debugger, it is understood that most often it is the original development staff (or the entry level people hired thereafter) that will have to fix the problems. By understanding the proper strategies and techniques that are available to you, you will reduce the amount of time needed to find and fix problems.

One of the groups that is likely to discount this book is the system architects camp, although they are the ones that are most likely to be aided by understanding the root causes of bugs and how they can be avoided. Too often, we blame poorly written code for problems in the software development industry. In fact, a large percentage of bugs are written directly into the system design for applications. If you have poor requirements or poor design plans, you will end up with a poor system. The code can be brilliantly written, but it won't have the slightest effect if the underlying design is poorly thought out or poorly understood by those implementing the software.

In addition, we will discuss the novel concept of a "professional debugger" as a real profession. This particular role may never be granted an "open requisition" in a corporate hiring sheet, but we will argue that it should be. Debugging is an important part of the development and delivery process, and it should be treated as one.

Organization of this Book

This book is organized into three distinct sections. Chapters 2 through 5 cover diagnosis and taxonomies of bug types and their symptoms. Chapters 6 through 10 discuss strategies for dealing with bugs and includes the tools you have available to you and how you can use them most effectively in various situations. Chapters 11 through 16 contain an explanation of the profession of debugging and how you can become a more effective debugger even if it is not your primary position in your company.

Because Chapters 2 through 5 contain the diagnosis and taxonomy tools for the book, we refer to this section as the "detective" section. These chapters primarily involve determining what is a bug and what is not, determining the root cause of a bug from the symptoms, and building the necessary hypotheses to fix the problem. Once you have determined exactly what the real cause of the symptoms you are observing in the application are, solving the problem is usually more of a matter of figuring out how you want the application to work.

Diagnosis work encompasses the majority of the work we do in debugging, and as such, consumes the majority of this book. Although you may have thought that debugging was a simple matter of being told what is going on and fixing it, it is rarely that simple. What we call "bugs" reported by testers and users are often simple symptoms that mask the underlying root case. For example, consider a program that crashes whenever procedures A, B, and C are run in the order specified by the user manual. It might appear that the problem is created by some interaction between A, B, and C. However, further analysis of the problem might show that simply doing A and C in any order causes the problem. This could easily indicate an unhandled error condition between the two, a memory corruption error, or perhaps simply an uninitialized memory address that is used in process A and later reused in process B. Problems like this are often easy to find, but difficult to fix, because the root cause has nothing to do with the apparent symptoms. These are the kinds of bugs we will examine in this first section.

Chapters 6 through 10 contain strategies and techniques for dealing with bugs you encounter and diagnosing these bugs using the information you found in the detective stage. In this section of the book, we begin to examine some of the ways you can use the diagnostics and symptoms you have discovered to look at ways to actually fix the problem. Obviously, it is impossible to discuss every kind of bug and way to fix it because many bugs are application-specific. But general techniques for finding and fixing bugs work in almost any operating system, programming language, and application type.

Debugging and bug-fixing techniques are the "black art" of the computer-programming world. Although unintentional, most programmers do not think to share the ways in which they fix the problems that they encounter. This lack of communication and scientific method results in a hundred inefficient and overly complex methodologies being used in each group of developers. If we approach debugging in the same way that we approach design and implementation, we will find that software bugs, although certainly not a thing of the past, will consume a vastly smaller percentage of our time in the field. This will result in more robust applications and more user-friendly features, as the time saved not doing bug fixing will be used for more productive endeavors (from the end user's perspective, of course).

Chapters 11 through 16 discuss what the role of a professional debugger should be. If there is one area in our profession where we need to consider assigning a "specialist" to each project team, debugging is certainly that area. We will show you how, if debuggers were standard members of development teams, the entire software development process would improve. Debuggers can apply their skills to much more than simply fixing problems. They can also apply the skills they have to design, requirements gathering, testing, and documentation. All of these skills are essential to most parts of software development, but debugging combines them all into a single package. We will look at what makes a good debugger and how you can enhance the individual skills that you have in other areas by concentrating on techniques you learn while debugging.

A Brief History of Debugging

It would appear that as long as there have been computers, there have been computer bugs. However, this is not exactly true. Even though the earliest known computer programs contained errors, they were not, at that time, referred to as "bugs." It took a lady named Admiral Grace Hopper to actually coin the term "bug."

Grace Brewster Murray Hopper was born in New York City on December 9, 1906. She was the oldest of three children and spent most of her childhood playing with gadgets. At the age of seven, she dismantled seven alarm clocks to determine exactly how they worked. Such skills would serve her well in the future of the computer world.

After graduating from Vassar in 1928 (Phi Beta Kappa), she went to Yale to receive her master's degree in mathematics. After graduating from Yale, she worked at the university as a mathematics professor. Leaving Yale in 1943, Grace made a decision that would change her future as well as the future of the computer world. With the onset of World War II, Mrs. Hopper decided to work for the Navy. Due to her age (34) and weight (105 pounds) she was deemed inappropriate for the Navy regime. In addition, the government had, at that time, determined that mathematicians such as Mrs. Hopper were essential to the war effort. Grace asked for, and received, a waiver for all of these issues, and enlisted in the Naval Reserve in December 1943.

Mrs. Hopper's first assignment was under Commander Howard Aiken at Harvard University, working at the Bureau of Ordinance Computation. She was a programmer on the Mark II, the world's first automatically sequenced digital computer. The Mark II was used to determine shooting angles for the big guns in varying weather conditions during wartime. It was considered one of the most important programs of its time (second, perhaps, to a project being done in White Sands, New Mexico—the atomic bomb).

It was during her term with the Mark II that Hopper was credited with coining the term "bug" for a computer problem. The first "bug" was actually a moth, which flew through an open window and into one of the Mark II's relays. At that time, physical relays were used in computers, unlike the digital components we use today. The moth shorted out across two contacts, temporarily shutting down the system. The moth would later be removed (de-bugged?) and pasted into the log book of the project. From that point on, if her team was not producing numbers or working on the code, they claimed to be "debugging" the system.

From that auspicious beginning, computer debugging developed into something of a hit-or-miss procedure for quite a few years. Early debugging efforts mostly centered around either data dumps of the system or used output devices, such as printers and display lights, to indicate when an error occurred. Programmers would then step through the code line by line until they could determine the location of the problem.

After computer programs moved past the punch card stage, and as paper line-writers and finally CRT terminals became available, debugging took something of a quantum leap. Computer programs, too, were changing at this point. Rather than batch-oriented programs that were run at night (or over successive days), programs were becoming user interactive, requiring actual input from the user at startup or even during the program run. The program output could also be seen as the program was running rather than waiting until the program had finished. This was considered by many to be a major leap forward in computer programming. Little did they know...

The next step in the evolution of debugging came with the advent of command-line debuggers. These simple programs were an amazing step forward for the programmer. No longer did he or she have to guess what the values of the memory addresses in the program contained. The debugger could now "dump" the values at given memory locations. This allowed a programmer working in an assembler to look directly at the registers and the memory blocks that contained the addresses of the local variables in the program. Although difficult to use, even at the time, these programs represented the first real attempt to turn debugging from a hit-or-miss proposition into a reproducible process. Being able to reproduce something is the first step toward making it a scientific or engineering process.

Once the debugger became a part of the programmer's arsenal, the software world began to consider other ways that programs could be more easily debugged. Software projects started getting bigger, and the same techniques that worked well for small projects no longer worked when the program reached a certain size. Scalability, it seems, was an issue even at the beginning of the software complexity curve. Compiler vendors discovered that the information they had while they were parsing higher level languages, such as C, FORTRAN, and COBOL, could be kept in a separate file, called a symbol map, which would "map" the variable names in the programs to the actual memory addresses into which they would be loaded at runtime. The ability to look at the variable names and map them to memory addresses allowed the programmer to dump memory by name. These debuggers were called "symbolic debuggers" because they worked from symbols to allow the developer to view data.

Another huge improvement at this stage was the ability to set breakpoints. The term breakpoint means the ability to "break" into the code and stop the program execution at a given point. The program would still be loaded into memory, it just would not be running at the time the breakpoint was encountered. This improvement allowed programmers to set breakpoints when certain critical areas of the code were reached and allowed them to view the contents of the variables (symbols) before the program crashed or did whatever it was that it was not supposed to do. Prior to the use of breakpoints, programs could really only be looked at in two states: the initial state of the application, before it ran, and the final state of the application, when it had completed or crashed. If something happened in the middle of the run, programmers could only guess at its cause. With the ability to set breakpoints at critical junctures of code, programmers could then see exactly why something happened. It wasn't the perfect solution, of course, as they still needed to know when they wanted the program to stop, but it was a big step forward for those of us programming at the time.

The debugging process, much like that of the software world itself, began to move forward faster and faster. The ability to see the original lines of code in order to set breakpoints was added. Better ways to dump memory and look at changes in that memory were added. And, conditional breakpoints were also added to many debuggers. Conditional breakpoints allowed you to set a condition, such as when a given variable became equal to zero, under which the program would stop as if you had set a breakpoint at that particular line. Debuggers joined the visual age along with many of the Integrated Development Environments (IDEs) when Borland introduced Turbo Pascal in the early 1980s. In this amazing environment, you could edit, compile, link, and debug code all within the same system. There was no need to run separate programs and no need to load special symbol tables or use special compiler options. Turbo Pascal signified the dawn of the modern age of debugging.

When Microsoft Windows was introduced in the mid- to late-1980s, there was a need for a new kind of debugger. In the past, especially in the MS-DOS world, debuggers worked only on single programs doing single tasks. Microsoft Windows changed all of that. Although multithreaded debuggers already existed in the Unix world, they were clunky and hard to use in a true multithreaded, multitasking system. Although Microsoft Windows applications were not truly multitasking at the beginning, they emulated the concept well. Developers needed to be aware not only of their own applications, but also of all of the other applications running on the machine at the same time. Although previous application debuggers could handle text-based applications, Microsoft Windows was a graphical user interface (GUI). This required some additional thought for debugging. After all, if the output of the application was graphic, you needed to be able to see it to know whether or not it was working properly. Existing debuggers did not permit this. You could flip back and forth between the application and the debugger screen, but this was of little help when it was your application that "painted" the screen. If the application was not running, the screen would be blank.

All of these features only applied to the physical debugging application. Yet, in other ways, we were also learning considerably more about the profession of debugging and the art of "prebugging," that is, removing bugs before they reach the final code. The techniques you will learn in this book are all built upon the years of sweat and pain of thousands of programmers before you. Take the time to read through these pages and understand why the debugging techniques are the way they are, and how you can fix the bugs in your software using these techniques. It will be worth your time and effort.

Summary

In this chapter, you learned all about the mysterious world of bugs. You were given a taste of the kinds of problems we will be looking at in this book, as well as a small sample of the techniques used in solving those problems.

Bugs are a major problem in the software development industry. They continue to plague us due to poor development processes, poor understanding of systems, and poor requirements definitions. By reading through the remainder of this book, you will learn not only how to identify and solve problems when you encounter them, but also how to prevent those bugs from ever happening in the first place.

Bug Puzzle

In order to better understand what bugs are and how you should approach them, we have decided to add a simple bug example to each chapter. The "answers" to these bugs will be found in Appendix A. Although some of the examples will contain code, many will simply describe the situation that led up to the reported problem. It is up to you to use the clues presented, as well as your own detective skills, to determine what is happening in each example. In that spirit, let's look at a real-world bug.

In an Internet shop somewhere in the wilds of the software world, there was a system that ran to keep customers updated with stock quotes. This particular system ran most of the time, but would regularly stop updating the user's quote requests and would simply return invalid or outdated data. The programmers spent considerable time trying to determine why the system would spontaneously start and stop. Meanwhile, the operations people spent considerable amounts of time figuring out workarounds to the problem. Eventually, the problem grew so severe that the system started crashing several times a day. The programmers were stumped, and the operations people were livid.

In the end, however, the solution turned out to be not only simple, but one that required almost no work on either side to fix. Before you turn to the end of the book for the solution, ask yourself what process you would have followed to find out what was happening if you were the programmer. Then ask yourself what process you would have followed if you were the operations person. Finally, imagine yourself in the position of a professional debugger trying to solve the mystery.

The actual answer to this problem isn't entirely contained in the clues. But the process you should have followed, if done correctly, would have gotten you to the solution quickly and easily. Think through this example both before and after you read the "real" solution. Then move on to the first section of the book where you will learn how you might have seen this problem coming long before it became a serious issue.

Keep in mind that this book encompasses the "science" of debugging. Science involves reproducible cases that can be explained using rules. Debugging is no different. Bugs don't just spontaneously appear, they either exist or they don't. We will provide you with the tools and the techniques you will need to understand why the bug appears in the code and how to eliminate it without breaking the application.

Chapter 2

Case Studies of Famous (and Not So Famous) Bugs

Yuan Hsieh

Imagine the year is 1986. And, imagine that you are the late Richard Feynman. The phone rings and you pick it up. It's a call from William R. Graham, NASA's acting administrator. You know it can't be a social call because the space shuttle *Challenger* blew up a few days prior on January 28, 1986. You are right. He is calling to ask you to be part of a commission to investigate the cause of the *Challenger* disaster. In effect, NASA is asking you, the renowned Nobel Laureate, to become a high profile professional debugger for one of the most infamous NASA accidents in recent history.[1] You accept the job with trepidation. After all, you might be a Nobel Prize winner, but you are no rocket scientist. You were not involved in designing the space shuttle. You are not familiar with the components and systems of the space shuttle. You have no idea what kind of data was recorded on the fateful *Challenger* flight. You don't know the state or usefulness of the documentation. The only clue you have to start your investigation is your observation from the video that the flame seemed to originate from the right fuel tank. How do you go about the task of finding the cause of the accident?

In reality, Dr. Feynman discovered the cause of the accident by flying nationwide to speak with engineers and operational staffs, while not succumbing to political pressure. He eventually performed

---

[1] Gleick, James. *Genius, The Life and Science of Richard Feynman*. Vintage Books, New York, New York, 1992.

his famous table-top experiment with a sample from one of the shuttle's O-rings and a cup of ice water to prove his theory during a live press conference. [2]

Thankfully, our jobs as debuggers for software systems are a lot easier than the task Dr. Feynman faced. In most cases, we can attempt to replicate the bug to ensure that we have totally understood its causes and effects. NASA scientists had no such luxury. After all, they couldn't very well reproduce the bug by blowing up another space shuttle. Furthermore, Dr. Feynman had to submit a formal report detailing his findings and analyses for public scrutiny and, worse yet, had to fight political pressure from NASA officials. When was the last time we had to do any of that when fixing a bug? In the software industry, we do very little in terms of postmortem analysis of bugs. We don't ask questions like how the bug was discovered, how the bug occurred, and what can we do to prevent the bug? If we do perform a postmortem, very seldom do we document our findings so that our knowledge can be shared.

In many ways, this book is the cumulation of many years of postmortem analyses of bugs that we have known and experienced. In Chapter 12, we will show you how to analyze bugs, how to increase your collective knowledge about your bug formation processes, and how this knowledge can help you avoid the same mistakes and produce better software in the future. Does postmortem analysis of bugs help us produce a better product? We believe the answer is yes! In 1981, NEC implemented a plan to help software engineers and project managers learn from bugs. The project cataloged bugs from many of the corporate projects where they originated. The software engineers were encouraged to find the cause of a software failure and prevent its recurrence. In the 10 years since the origination of the project, they learned many lessons and were able to apply these lessons to increase their productivity and reduce the bug introduction rates. [3]

The NEC initiative started by cataloging problems and solutions. Then, by learning to work out the cause and effect relationships between problems, software engineers were able to formulate countermeasures to solve these problems. We will start the same way.

Scenarios

In this chapter, we have collected a set of bugs to study. Most of these bugs are rather well known and typically well documented because their occurrences were public events, and many had grave consequences. However trite and overused, these bugs do make for perfect case studies. The problem is that not everyone is involved in these kinds of large scale and safety-critical software projects, so the difficulties those developers ran into might seem somewhat unrelated to your daily tasks. Therefore, we have also included a few examples from our tenures as software engineers. These personal bugs are more down-to-earth and do

---

[2] Feynman, Richard P. *The Pleasure of Finding Things Out*. Perseus Books, Cambridge, Massachusetts, 1999.

Gleick, James. *Genius, The Life and Science of Richard Feynman*. Vintage Books, New York, New York, 1992.

✱ [3] Kajihara, J., Amamiya, G., and Saya, T. "Learning from Bugs," *IEEE Software*, pp 46–54, September 1993.

not involve explosions and multibillion dollar expenses. Furthermore, throughout the book, we present bugs written by others to illustrate various points. We do not present these bugs to ridicule. Our focus is to study the events surrounding these famous and not-so-famous bugs to see what we can learn from these mistakes.

Distributed Computing Systems from Real Life

The bug parade starts with examples from two of my previous jobs. The first bug lasted a few hours and was quickly resolved. It was an instructive lesson for the second bug. Nine months later, shortly after I started another job, I encountered a similar bug. However, in the new company, the problem manifested itself two months prior to my involvement. The severity of the first bug was such that it crippled the entire system. The second bug, although persistent, was not a showstopper; it was merely a minor annoyance and not a total disaster.

The Story: Company Y

It was late 1999, and I was working for an Internet company that serves financial reports on the Internet. Let's call it company Y. The architecture of the system that serves financial reports is very simple; the Web requests come in via one of many Web servers. The Web server hands the request to a load manager, and the load manager delivers the request to one of four reporting servers in a round-robin fashion. The report servers then fetch information from a database to generate the report.

One day, the alarms started going off left and right. The report servers were crashing one after another. A report server would crash, restart a few minutes later, and crash yet again a few minutes later; this was happening to all of the servers. The request rate wasn't particularly high nor was it abnormal. Rebooting the machine did not seem to help. The network operation personnel were at a loss as to what was causing this chaos, and the development team was summoned. Because I designed and implemented the communication infrastructure used by the internal servers, I was asked to help. The development team suspected that the load-balancing module in the communication infrastructure was faulty, and the report servers were crashing because they were overloaded.

The communication infrastructure had built-in logging and tracing capabilities that were normally deactivated in the production environment. The first thing I did was to turn on the logging and tracing output to observe what the systems were doing. The log produced by the reporting server didn't make much sense to me. There were a lot of errors and warning messages in the log, and none of the messages were descriptive. However, in every instance, just before the report server would crash and restart, there was a log entry noting that the reporting server was terminating. I asked an engineer about the meaning of the log entry, but his response was somewhat cryptic; it was something to the effect that the program was designed to restart itself when it thought there was a problem. During that time, as I was looking at the log files from the load manager, I saw that it was hitting one server at a time. My immediate assumption was that the load-balancing mechanism wasn't working correctly, and the load manager was overloading the reporting server, causing it to restart itself.

I informed the team of my speculations and went back to my desk to inspect the code, looking for potential faults. Nothing leaped out, and I thought of the engineer's comments that the reporting server was designed to restart itself when it thought that there was a problem. I decided to find out exactly what kind of problems would cause the reporting server to restart itself. Basically, the reporting server maintained 20 threads, and each request to the reporting server occupied 1 thread. Normally, each thread was expected to finish processing within one or two seconds. The reporting server had a history of fault-proneness and was not considered stable. So a "safety" logic was built into the server so that when all 20 threads were busy and the 21st request came in, the 21st request would wait up to 5 seconds for a thread to open up. If the 21st request timed out, the reporting server would assume that something was wrong and that all 20 processing threads had hung. As a result, the only course of action would be to terminate and restart the server.

Upon hearing this, I went back to my desk to mull it over. A few minutes later, it all clicked. I validated my speculation with the log and tracing files and outlined my hypothesis to the report server team.

♦ The reason that the load manager was using only one server at a time was not because the load-balancing algorithm was faulty. It was using only one server at a time because other report servers were not available; they were being restarted. This was easily verified by looking at the time stamp of the log files on the load managers and the report servers.

♦ The log file from the reporting server indicated that the "safety" logic had been triggered, which implied that every report server must contain 21 concurrent requests. This meant that at some point there were 84 requests in the system because there were 4 report servers in operation at the time of the incident.

♦ Ultimately, one of the report servers would restart due to the violation of the "safety" logic. This, in effect, reduced the capacity of the system to 63 requests. However, the input request rate remained constant. This further increased the load on the remaining three report servers, and eventually, the other servers restarted due to the "safety" logic. The capacity of the system was then reduced to 42 requests. By the time the first report server had finished restarting, the third report server would crash and restart. This effect would persist as long as nothing else changed; the input rate and the response rate of the system remained constant.

This hypothesis corresponded with the observation that the servers were crashing consistently, and that they simply were not able to stay functional. However, we still needed to determine the original cause of the backlog of 84 requests. We had already checked that the load wasn't extremely heavy. There was only one possibility left. The problem had to be related to the assumption that each request be processed within a second or two and that the 21st request can only wait for up to 5 seconds. The values selected seemed to have a sufficient margin of error. However, this assumption is valid under normal operating conditions.

In the beginning of this description, I stated that the report server relied on the database to generate its reports. In this case, the database was suffering some kind of meltdown. We were never able to determine the cause of the meltdown. A simple SELECT statement, instead of taking a few tenths of a second, was taking up to 10 seconds to complete. The dramatic performance degradation in the database triggered the design flaw, and the situation quickly deteriorated. Because every report server that crashed would, in effect, reduce the available capacity, more stress was placed on the remaining operational servers. Left alone, the problem would simply go away when the load was reduced to less than 20 concurrent requests in the entire system.

Once it was determined that the database server was at fault, rebooting the SQL server solved the problem.

The Story: Company X

In mid-2000, I started a job with another Internet company that serves mapping and business information and e-commerce. Let's call it company X. The system infrastructure of company X is similar to that of company Y: Web servers talk to load managers that talk to back-end agents that talk to the databases. However, there is a slight complication in that company X also provides an Interactive Voice Response (IVR) interface that allows customers to access the system through normal telephones. The infrastructure that implements the IVR solution merely replaces the Web server with an IVR server and communicates with the load manager in exactly the same fashion as the Web servers. Another difference is that company X employs two completely separate data centers. Typically, the IVR server uses one data center as its primary and active system. When there are complications with the active data center, the IVR server switches to the backup data center.

One day, the CTO of company X came to my cubicle to ask me to talk to the IVR team and help them investigate a recent service outage. Apparently, a few days prior, the IVR system was out for over eight hours. When I went to talk to the IVR team, it didn't have a lot of information to go on. There were log files from the IVR server at the time of the outage, but they were deleted due to a miscommunication with the Network Operation center. The maintainers of the system suspected that it was related to some obscure network problem with one data center. However, this didn't explain why the backup data center wasn't used. After further inquiry, it turned out that the IVR server had a problem staying connected to one of the data centers. This problem had been persistent for the prior two months.

Because I wasn't familiar with the system, I asked the team if they could show me the log files that were generated. I wanted to be able to capture the system behavior when and if the outage occurred again. The log file, although useful for showing errors, was not helpful in describing the system activities. It only showed the status of each request after it had been completed. If a particular request was causing the failure, the log would never show the state of the IVR server at the time of the crash. Furthermore, the IVR server did not crash during the outage; there was no core file that we could use. However, the log file did show a relatively large number of events when the IVR server switched from one data center to another. Each data center switching event was correlated with a series of three requests with status of error code −3, a code that means that a request had timed out when the IVR server was attempting to communicate with the load manager. In company X, every request had a unique request ID that was logged at every server that the request had visited, so it was possible to track the request in the entire system. However, the IVR server was not recording request IDs in its log, so we could not investigate why the request was timing out.

Learning from my experience at company Y, I asked the team about the fail-over strategy of the IVR server. It turned out that the IVR had a performance requirement—unlike using a Web site, people didn't like to wait on the phone, so the IVR had to return within a specific amount of time. The IVR server was set to retrieve data from the load manager with a time out of three seconds. After three consecutive failed attempts, the IVR server would automatically switch to the backup data center. At the backup data center, the IVR server would attempt to reconnect to the primary data center after two hours. If successful, it would reestablish its connection with the primary data center.

At this point, I had two rather reasonable hypotheses that would cover all the observations. (1) Because the IVR server was having problems staying connected to one of the data centers, the IVR server was essentially running without a backup. If the data center that it was connected to suffered any problem, IVR service would be unavailable. And (2) the reason that the IVR server was not able to stay connected to the data center was recorded precisely in the existing log file. It was timing out on its requests. In order to determine why it was timing out so frequently, we would need to track the requests that were causing the timeout in the system.

However, there were no logs or other information to validate my hypothesis, so I worked with the IVR team to generate a more useful log for debugging. Once we were able to track the flow of requests through the system, it was easy to see where the bottleneck was. One of the back-end servers was taking an unusually long time to process a request. This back-end server made a few SQL calls to a database that resided on the same machine as the server. The duration of the database calls was longer than expected. Because the back-end server was seeing some unusually heavy CPU load, one conjecture made was that the machine was too heavily loaded and additional hardware might be necessary. Another conjecture was that the SQL statements as implemented were inefficient; this needed to be investigated. A few more days of investigation revealed that the database had been updated two months prior to the incident. But the database administrator forgot to reindex the database, and every request was taking 10 times as long as usual to process. The heavy CPU load merely reflected the execution of the SQL statements on an unindexed database. The database in the "functional" data center was updated and reindexed, so it wasn't having any trouble. We were never able to properly explain the outage because there was no information available to perform the investigation. However, the lack of a backup data center was a major contributing cause for the outage.

The Lessons

The similarities between the previous two cases are striking. Both cases involved systems that were operational for a long time. Both systems were operating as designed, and there were no implementation bugs. The fixes in both cases (at least in the short term) were simply to restart or reindex the database. Both problems manifested because the database responses were taking longer than anticipated. The causes for the problems were plainly shown in the log files. However, it was still difficult to sift through the logs and fully understand the implications. Why?

♦ *Component thinking*—In both cases, the original engineers involved mainly concentrated on the components; they never evaluated the observations in the context of the entire system. Debugging in a distributed computing environment requires holistic thinking. Every component in the system can affect the behavior of another component and of the system itself. The inter-relationships between components in the system can be highly complex and are often nonintuitive. When you are wondering why a component is failing, it might be useful to ask the question, "What other component in the system could cause this component to fail?"

♦ *Second guessing the clue*—A few years ago, I took an avalanche training class. One of the subjects in the class was conducting a beacon search. The idea behind a beacon search is that when a victim is buried, his avalanche beacon is supposed to send out a radio signal that another avalanche beacon can receive. The radio signal is converted to audio signal on the receiving beacon. The proximity between the two beacons is signified by the loudness of the audio signals; the louder it sounds, the closer the victim is. Initially, I had some problems with the search. Instead of listening and following the audio signals, I would look around for visual clues. Once I was able to discard all my other senses and focus on the audio signal, my time to recovery sped up dramatically. The same advice can be useful in debugging applications. In both of our examples, the original engineers ignored the clues that were presented by their systems. Instead of following the clues, they chose to second guess the clues and created incorrect hypotheses that were not consistent with all observations. All clues and observations must be considered when creating a hypothesis.

♦ *Ignoring clues*—Important clues were ignored. In company X, the heavier than normal CPU load on the back-end server should have been investigated because the machine input request rate was not heavier than normal. The unacceptable processing times of the back-end server to process a request and make database calls were recorded in the log file during the two months when the problem persisted. There were plenty of warnings that something bad would potentially happen. However, due to lack of resources, time, and infrastructure, these warnings were not heeded until a catastrophic event occurred.

These two incidents did not involve bugs in the traditional sense, even though the developers were summoned. The problems that were faced at companies X and Y might have been preventable if the operation staff had been better informed. How?

♦ *Better monitoring tools*—In both cases, if the operation staff had been able to detect and notice the unusual behavior of the database server, they might have been able to take actions to correct the database server. The problems that were encountered might have never surfaced.

♦ *Following the procedures*—In company X, the standard procedure was to reindex the database when the database was updated. In this case, the reindexing step was not performed, and there was no knowledge nor record of the update. The lack of a record made it difficult to determine the changes in the environment and the system to aid the debugging process.

Therac-25

The Therac-25 bug was perhaps one of the costliest bugs in recent history. Between June 1985 and January 1987, six patients were known to be overdosed by Therac-25, resulting in three deaths. For this account, we rely heavily on a report published by Leveson and Turner in 1993 after several years of detective work. This report arguably contains the most detailed and thorough account of the causes and effects of the Therac-25 incidents and covers all aspects of system safety issues. However, because this book is about software bugs, we will restrict our presentation and analysis to software-related issues.[4]

The Story

Therac-25 was a computerized radiation therapy machine built by Atomic Energy of Canada, Limited (AECL). The lineage of the Therac-25 included Therac-6, which was a six million electron volt (MeV) accelerator capable of only producing X rays, and Therac-20, a 20MeV X ray and electron accelerator. All three machines used a DEC PDP 11 minicomputer for their software operations. Therac-6 and Therac-20 both employed hardware features to prevent unsafe operations. Some software modules from Therac-6 were reused in Therac-20 and Therac-25. In addition, Therac-25 also reused software modules from Therac-20 for the electron mode.

Therac-25 was an enhancement of Therac-20. It was capable of delivering 25MeV photons or electrons at multiple energy levels. It was smaller, had more features, and was easier to use. It had also been designed to incorporate computer control more fully than its predecessors. The software written for Therac-25 was designed to monitor and control the hardware. Therefore, it was decided to remove the hardware safety features and rely on the software to maintain system safety.

Therac-25 was commercially available in late 1982, and 11 Therac-25 machines were installed in North America, 5 in the U.S., and 6 in Canada. Six accidents involving massive overdoses by Therac-25 occurred between 1985 and 1987.[5]

---

[4] Leveson, Nancy, and Turner, Clark S. "An Investigation of the Therac-25 Accidents," *IEEE Computer*, Vol 26, No. 7, pp 18–41, July 1993.

[5] ibid.

Kennestone Regional Oncology Center, Marietta, Georgia, June 1985

A 61-year-old woman was sent to the oncology center for follow-up treatment on Therac-25 after lumpectomy surgery. The patient was believed to have received one or two doses of radiation in the range between 15,000 to 20,000-rads (radiation absorbed dose). For comparison, typical single therapeutic doses were in the 200-rad range. The Kennestone facility had been using Therac-25s since 1983, apparently without incident, and the technicians and AECL did not believe that her problem could have been caused by Therac-25. Eventually, the patient lost a breast due to radiation burns, and she lost the use of her shoulder and arms.

Ontario Cancer Foundation, Hamilton, Ontario, Canada, July 1985

The Hamilton facility had been using Therac-25 for about six months before the overdose incident. A 40-year-old woman came to the clinic for her 24th Therac-25 treatment. Therac-25 shut down five seconds after the operator activated the machine. Apparently, Therac-25 operators had become accustomed to frequent malfunctions of the machine; these malfunctions appeared to have no bad consequences for the patient. Because the machine indicated that no dose was delivered, the operator attempted to deliver the dose again. The operator attempted five times. After the fifth attempt, the technician was called, but no problem with the machine was found.

The incident was reported to AECL, but they could not reproduce the malfunction and had no conclusive explanation for the behavior of the Therac-25. However, due to the report, AECL did discover some design weakness and potential mechanical problems that involved the turntable positioning of the Therac-25, and modifications were made to address these issues. The patient died five months later. The autopsy determined that her death was caused by cancer, and not from the overdose. However, the autopsy also revealed substantial damage to the patient's hip as result of radiation over-exposure, and it was later estimated the patient had received between 13,000 and 17,000 rads. [6]

Yakima Valley Memorial Hospital, Yakima, Washington, December 1985

After a treatment on the Therac-25, a woman developed excessive reddening of the skin in a parallel striped pattern. The hospital staff suspected that the Therac-25 could have caused this pattern. However, they were not able to reproduce the hardware configuration that was used during her treatment in order to match the observed pattern. The hospital staff informed AECL of the potential overexposure. AECL again felt that it was impossible for the Therac-25 to overdose a patient. The hospital staff was not aware of the two prior incidents and lacked the ability to investigate the incident, so they did not pursue the matter after AECL's response. The patient apparently had a lower dosage delivered than the previous two, and she did not develop significant problems as the result of the overexposure. [7]

---

[6] ibid.
[7] ibid.

East Texas Cancer Center, Tyler, Texas, March 1986

The East Texas Cancer Center had been using Therac-25 since 1984 and had treated more than 500 patients. On March 21, 1986, a male patient came in for follow-up treatments as instructed. The operator who treated this male patient was familiar with the Therac-25 and was proficient with its features and usage. When she was entering the patient and prescription data, she made a mistake that she quickly fixed, and then began the treatment. A moment later, the machine shut down and the console displayed error messages. As is typical with software systems, the error message was in a code that no one could decipher; "Malfunction 54" on the console was translated as a "dose input 2" error on a sheet of paper. The East Texas Cancer Center had no other documentation to explain the meaning of "dose input 2". But the console showed a substantial underdose, and because the operator was used to the quirks and malfunctions of the Therac-25, she immediately requested that the Therac-25 attempt treatment again. Again, the machine shut down with the same error messages.

AECL was contacted in response to this problem. The AECL technicians dispatched to the East Texas Cancer Center were not able to reproduce the malfunction, and the AECL still believed that it was impossible for Therac-25 to overdose a patient. The patient died from complications of the overdose five months after the accident. [8]

East Texas Cancer Center, Tyler, Texas, April 1986

Three weeks later, another male patient came in to be treated on the Therac-25. The same operator that was involved in the previous accident was again responsible for the treatment. Similar to the previous time, she made the same mistake in entering the data, and just as quickly, she fixed her mistake and proceeded with treatment. The machine responded with a "Malfunction 54" message and shut down. However, the patient had already been overdosed, and the operator immediately went for help. The Therac-25 was taken out of service, and the hospital informed AECL that a second overexposure had occurred.

The hospital physicist, Fritz Hager, working with the operator, learned to reproduce the "Malfunction 54" message at will. Apparently, if the prescription data was edited at a fast pace, the overdose occurred. AECL was finally able to reproduce the error and admitted that overdosing by a Therac-25 was possible. [9]

How was it possible that rapid editing changes caused an overdose? Therac-25 was able to operate in either photon or electron mode. In the electron mode, the operator was forced to enter the energy level; however, if the photon mode was selected, the default energy for the photon mode was 25MeV. The mistakes made by the operator were the same in both cases. The two patients that received the overdose required electron mode for their treatments. However, because most patients required photon mode, the operator was accustomed to

---

[8] ibid.
[9] ibid.

selecting the photon mode. In these two incidents, the operator initially selected the photon mode, and then corrected her mistake. The physical calibration and setting of the magnets took about eight seconds. The software module that checked for the completion of data entry would proceed with magnet calibration as soon as the mode and energy parameter had been set. Another software module had the responsibility of monitoring for any data entry changes, so that when a change occurred, the magnet was reset and calibration would start again with the new data. However, a logic error in this module caused it to be unable to recognize editing changes if they were done within eight seconds after the mode and the energy level had been entered initially. (This is an extreme simplification of the software algorithm. The reader is advised to refer to Leveson and Clark's report for additional detail.) In these two cases, when the operator selected the photon mode the first time, the machine prepared to deliver an energy level of 25MeV in photon mode. However, when the operator changed the mode to electron mode within eight seconds, the magnet was not reset and incorrect dosages were delivered.

When it understood the bug, AECL immediately sent a letter to the user community recommending a temporary fix, which was to disable editing during the data entry phase of the operation.

The patient died three weeks after the accident due to extreme radiation overdose.[10]

Yakima Valley Memorial Hospital, Yakima, Washington, January 1987

By this time, the problems with Therac-25 were well publicized, at least in the user community. The operators knew not to make editing changes. During this time, AECL was actively engaged in submitting a corrective action plan with the FDA when the sixth incident occurred. In this incident, the patient was to receive three doses. The first two doses required exposures of four and three rads. The third dose was a 79-rad photon treatment. The first two doses apparently proceeded without complications. After the second dose, the operator entered the treatment room to rotate the turntable in order to verify the beam position with respect to the patient's body. The operator pressed the "set" button near the turntable to indicate that the position had been verified. After the turntable had been set, the operator proceeded to start the treatment. The machine paused after five or six seconds, so the operator proceeded to start the treatment again. And again, the machine paused and displayed the "flatness" reason for the shut down. It was suspected that the patient had been overdosed; however, the console displayed a total exposure of only seven rads from the first two exposures.

About a week later, AECL discovered a flaw in the software that could explain this behavior. The software defect that caused this accident differed from the East Texas Cancer Center accident in detail. However, both defects were caused by unanticipated race-conditions in software modules. In this incident, there was a shared variable called Class3 that was a one

---

[10] ibid.

byte value. This variable indicated whether the machine parameters were consistent with the treatment. If the value of Class3 was nonzero, then inconsistency existed, and the beam was inhibited. The Class3 variable was initialized in the software module that set up the machine for treatment. However, the initialization was accomplished by incrementing the Class3 variable. Because the variable was one byte in size, on every 256th iteration, this value rolled over to zero. The software module that performed this initialization was executed continuously depending on other events in the system. When the "set" button was pressed at the precise time the Class3 variable rolled over to zero, the inconsistency check was not performed, and the machine was allowed to dose the patient with a full 25MeV of electron beam.

The patient died in April 1987 from complications resulting from the overdose. And the machine was recalled shortly thereafter. [11]

The Lesson

There were two software defects that were uncovered in the short life span of Therac-25.

◆ A logic error that failed to update the machine parameters when the operator changed the state of the machine.

◆ Safety checks were bypassed whenever a particular 8-bit counter overflowed and reached zero once every 256 iterations.

However, from a system safety perspective, the biggest flaw was the reliance on software to maintain safety. Apparently, the same software error that existed in Therac-25 also existed in Therac-20. The same fault that caused overdoses on Therac-25 also caused the Therac-20 to shut down without overdosing the patient because Therac-20 had independent hardware safety devices that prevented radiation overexposure.

Bugs that are results of race-conditions are notoriously difficult to identify and reproduce. In the first case, two precise events were required to trigger the bug:

1. The operator must make changes to the mode and energy level of the machine parameters.

2. The operator must accept the changes within eight seconds.

In the second case, luck comes into play; the bug is triggered only when a button is pressed at the same time the counter reaches zero. This is why, despite inherent defects in the product, only six cases were uncovered and noted. If the bug had been obvious and easier to trigger, there is no doubt in our minds that AECL would have detected it in its normal testing and quality assurance process, and the bug would have never made it to the public. The fact that the bug was difficult to trigger also made it difficult to detect in a normal testing process. It's hard to find bugs when you can't reproduce them.

---

[11] ibid.

Note
Most accidents are system accidents; that is, they stem from complex interactions between various components and activities. To attribute a single cause to an accident is usually a serious mistake. [12]

In addition to the two major flaws described earlier, there are numerous issues that we have observed in the account of the story that could have contributed to the prolonged existence of the bugs.

- Therac-25 had a history of malfunctions that appeared to cause no harm, so operators had learned to ignore the quirks. This is similar to the story about the boy who cried wolf—the townspeople learned to ignore the boy. The frequent shut down and pausing of the machine were inconvenient to the operators. The operators never observed any ill effects on the patients due to these shutdowns, so they learned to ignore them. Something that might have serious consequences was ignored. The constant malfunctions also demonstrated the inherent instability and unsafeness of the machine.

- When a malfunction occurred, Therac-25 produced incomprehensible messages that provided the operational staff no clues as to the cause and effect of the system error. The system design did not provide adequate feedback to allow the operational staff to know exactly what was occurring. The information went from the operator to the software to the hardware. When there was a disconnect, the user had no way of knowing what the state of the hardware was because the software was not designed to query the hardware. The data entry bug was a clear example of a consequence resulting from a lack of feedback. For example, instead of simply allowing the operator to turn the beam on after making changes to the parameters, the software could have been designed so that the treatment could not begin until after the software had queried the hardware about its status and reported the hardware configuration back to the operator for verification.

- When the hospitals contacted AECL regarding potential problems, AECL did not take the problems seriously. Because AECL could not reproduce the problem, it felt that the machine could not be the problem. Furthermore, because Therac-25 was based on Therac-20 and Therac-6, both of which had proven field records, AECL became complacent about potential hazards. The bugs were hard to detect and reproduce, but given enough commitment, it would have been possible to identify them. The Yakima incidents of 1985 and 1987 are clear examples. When a problem was reported in 1985, a cursory examination was performed by AECL. AECL informed the hospital that the bug was not reproducible, hence there was no problem. However, in 1987, AECL took the report seriously, and discovered the probable cause for the erroneous behavior in a matter of weeks. Once AECL was willing to accept that its product might contain defects, it was able to look at the problem report with a different mentality.

---

[12] ibid.

♦ When the data entry bug was uncovered, there did not seem to be any attempt to evaluate the safety of the entire system. There were a total of five cases reported at that time, and the data entry bug was able to explain only two of them, both at the East Texas Cancer Center. The first three overdose cases could not be explained by this bug. This implies that there were additional defects in the system that were not accounted for, and the machine was likely to overdose another patient at a later time for a completely different reason. Eight months later, the second Yakima case surfaced.

♦ Therac-25 reused software modules from its predecessors. Software reuse helped AECL bring Therac-25 to market faster, but it also provided a false complacency about the robustness of the system. Software reuse has been hailed by the industry gurus as a way to enhance productivity and decrease the number of defects. This is true, but on the other hand, software reuse also means that the bugs and defects are recycled. In addition, software reuse will create new interactions between previously unconnected usage of software components in the new environment. The new interactions can expose hidden defects and introduce new bugs. A defect that doesn't exhibit itself in one usage may suddenly blow up in your face under another environment. Furthermore, software is usually not well documented, and it is difficult for the user to understand all the nuances of the reused modules. Forced reuse of software modules can also lead to awkward and dangerous designs.

A Buggy Vignette #1

In April 2000, a sensitive nine page NATO document dated December 23, 1999, found its way to a London publishing company. Apparently, during the Kosovo conflict, NATO computers were under virus attack by the Serbs. NATO scientists, seeking to protect themselves from further virus attacks, created viruses to simulate various attack modes. But the experiment went wild. The experimental virus did exactly what it was designed to do. It retrieved documents from the hard drives of the infected computer, sent these documents as invisible attachments in an email, and the sensitive documents were released. [13]

The bug in this case was not the virus that the NATO scientists designed and implemented. The bug was in NATO's network environment and the testing process that allowed the document to be released. Don't you hate it when the computer does what you tell it to do?

Intel Pentium Processor FDIV Bug

In 1993, Intel Corporation introduced a new Pentium TM chip that promised to be the meanest chip in the PC market at the time. A year after the chip was released, a bug was discovered and reported to Intel by Professor Thomas Nicely of Lynchburg College. It became a full-fledged publicity nightmare for Intel, and eventually, Intel agreed to replace

---

[13] Nathan, Adam. "NATO Creates Computer Virus That Reveals Its Secrets," *The Sunday Times*, June 18, 2000. www.thetimes.co.uk/news/pages/sti/2000/06/18/stinwenws01024.html.

chips automatically by request. The popular press would have you believe that the bug was caused by the stupidity of the Intel engineers and testers—after all, how hard is it to test every value in a lookup table? As usual, reality is far more complex than the blurbs outlined in newspaper clippings.

The Story

Professor Thomas Nicely is a mathematician. Between 1993 and 1994, he was doing a research project in an area called computational number theory. One of his objectives was to demonstrate the utility of desktop PCs. For his study, he had set up a large number of PCs to enumerate the primes, twin primes, prime triplets, and prime quadruplets for all positive integers up to 6×10^{12}. Primes are integers that are only divisible by one and themselves (e.g., 3). Twin primes are two consecutive odd integers that are also prime (e.g., 3, 5). Prime triplets are three consecutive odd integers that are also prime (e.g., 3, 5, 7). During the computation, his program also performed a number of checks in which known published values were computed in order to validate the correctness of the computation performed. A Pentium machine was added in March 1994, and on June 13, 1994, a check came up with an unexpected value. After about four months of debugging, Professor Nicely was able to trace the problem to the Pentium's floating point unit (FPU). In a public posting made on December 9, 1994, he described his trials and tribulations in determining the cause of his errors.[14]

After he was certain of his analysis, Professor Nicely sent a bug report to Intel technical support on October 24, 1994. After Intel failed to respond, on October 30, 1994, Professor Nicely wrote a letter to several of his colleagues stating the discovery of an apparent floating point division bug in the Intel Pentium chip. In the email, he described his observation:

> In short, the Pentium FPU is returning erroneous values for certain division operations. For example,
>
> 1/824633702441.0
>
> is calculated incorrectly (all digits beyond the eighth significant digit are in error). [15]

Soon, the bug report was circulating among CompuServe's forum and Internet news groups. Alexander Wolfe, a reporter from the *EE Times*, picked up the story and wrote an article that appeared in the November 7, 1994, issue of the *EE Times*. Responding to Alexander Wolfe's query, Intel stated that they had discovered the bug during the summer of 1994, and it was fixed in a later release of the Pentium chip. However, Intel was unable to determine the number of defective Pentium chips that were shipped, and they attempted to downplay the significance of the bug.

> Intel's Smith emphasized that the anomaly would not affect the average user. Speaking of Nicely, Smith said: "He's the most extreme user. He spends

---

[14]Nicely, Thomas R. Pentium FPU Bug, Memo available on **acavax.lynchburg.edu**.
[15]Nicely, Thomas R. Letter to Intel, October 30, 1994.

round-the-clock time calculating reciprocals. What he observed after running this for months is an instance where we have eight decimal points correct, and the ninth not showing up correctly. So you get an error in the ninth decimal digit to the right of the mantissa. I think even if you're an engineer, you're not going to see this. [16]

CNN broadcasted the story on November 22, 1994, and soon it was all over other mainstream news outlets, such as the *New York Times* and the Associated Press. When interviewed, Intel reiterated its earlier stance that the bug was insignificant for average users.

Intel said Wednesday that it did not believe the chip needed to be recalled, asserting that the typical user would have but one chance in more than nine billion of encountering an inaccurate result as a consequence of the error, and thus there was no noticeable consequence to users of business or home computers. Indeed, the company said it was continuing to send computer makers Pentium chips built before the problem was detected. [17]

On November 28, 1994, Tim Coe of Vitesse Semiconductor published an article to the **comp.sys.intel** newsgroup where he reverse engineered the algorithm and proposed a model of the behavior of the Pentium chip. A few days later, a software and hardware workaround for the Pentium FDIV bug appeared. On December 3, 1994, Vaughan R. Pratt of Stanford University published a letter to the **comp.arch** and **comp.sys.intel** newsgroup in which he took issue with Intel's position that the probability of the bug being encountered was "once in every 27,000 years." He was able to demonstrate that he could trigger the bug once every three milliseconds in a plausible scenario, and that an innocuous looking division, 4.999999/14.999999, resulted in an error of 0.00000407 using the faulty Pentium chip. [18]

On December 12, 1994, IBM published a report in which they also questioned Intel's analysis that the chance of detecting the error would be one in nine billion. [19]

On December 14, 1994, Intel made available a white paper that was dated November 30, 1994. [20]

This white paper examined the bug and discussed its impacts, and apparently was the source of many of Intel's claims. In this report, it was determined that the probability of a bug encounter was "one in nine billion" and average mean time to failure for this bug was "once every 27,000 years." Furthermore, Intel described the cause for the bug and the algorithm of the FPU. Intel engineers chose a radix 4 SRT algorithm for the Pentium processor's divide algorithm, so that a Pentium chip could double the rate of division compared to an Intel

---

[16] Wolfe, Alexander. *EE Times*, Issue 822, pp 1, November 7, 1994.

[17] Markoff, John. "Circuit Flaw Causes Pentium Chip to Miscalculate, Intel Admits," *New York Times.* November 24, 1994.

[18] Pratt, V. R. "A natural scenario with high FDIV bug probability (was: In Intel's Defense...)," comp.arch newsgroup, December 3, 1994, 15:20:17 UTC.

[19] IBM, Pentium Study, IBM Memo, December 12, 1994.

[20] Sharangpani, H. P., and Barton, M. L. "Statistical Analysis of Floating Point Flaw in the Pentium Processor (1994)," Intel White Paper, November 30, 1994.

486 processor. A full description of the SRT algorithm used in the Pentium chip is beyond the scope of this book, and a more detailed description of the SRT algorithm can be found in Edelman, Sharangpani, and Bryant. [21]

However, the crux of this bug is that the SRT algorithm required a lookup table to be used to determine quotient result. The value in the lookup table was numerically generated and downloaded into a Programmable Lookup Array. A defect in the script resulted in a few entries in the lookup table being omitted. When a division that required these entries was executed, an incorrect value was retrieved, and the computed quotient result resulted in reduced precision.

Finally, Intel announced on December 20, 1994, that it would begin to replace Pentium chips on a per request basis, which essentially extinguished the Pentium bug furor. However, this did not stop people from analyzing the Pentium bug. On September 19, 1995, Alan Edelman published a report where he performed a detailed analysis of the Pentium FDIV bug. [22]

In this report, he determined that there were only two ways the buggy entries in the lookup table could be reached and used during the computation. The flawed table entry could only be reached if the divisor had six consecutive bits of ones from bit 5 to bit 10. Furthermore, the bad lookup table entries could not be reached uniformly at random, a proper test would have to perform smarter than random testing in choosing the test cases. He also showed that the maximum absolute error of the bug could be no larger than 0.00005.

The Lesson

The Intel Pentium FDIV bug resulted from an error that is easy to make but difficult to catch for two reasons. First, the error in the result of a division computed by the flawed Pentium chip has a maximum error of 0.00005. How many of us would quibble over the differences between 0.33332922 and 0.33333329? Furthermore, if we used it in an application that automatically rounds the values to two significant figures, we would not even be aware of the minor differences. As Vaughn Pratt wrote in his correspondence:

> This bug is maximally insidious: It is about as large as it could possibly be without actually triggering warning bells when people review their columns of data. In this way, tiny errors of one part in a hundred thousand can, over a long period of time, sneak into the trillions of calculations done around the

---

[21] Bryant, R. "Bit-level analysis of an SRT circuit", CMU technical report, CMU-CS-95-140, 1995.
Edelman, Alan. "The Mathematics of the Pentium Division Bug," 1995. Available from **www-math.mit.edu/-edelman/**. Also appears in *SIAM Review*, March 1997.
Sharangpani, H. P., and Barton, M. L. "Statistical Analysis of Floating Point Flaw in the Pentium Processor (1994)," Intel White Paper, November 30, 1994.
[22] Edelman, Alan. "The Mathematics of the Pentium Division Bug," 1995. Available from **www-math.mit.edu/-edelman/**. Also appears in *SIAM Review*, March 1997.

world, and there is no practical way to spot them short of doing a massively detailed audit of a kind that would have to be tailored to the Pentium FDIV bug and would be entirely unnecessary for a reliable floating point unit. [23]

The second reason that the bug is hard to catch is that the defect is hard to reach. [24]

The chance of reaching the defective table entry in a random test is fairly low. Intel independently identified the bug in its random testing about a year after it released the faulty Pentium chip. This speaks volumes to the difficulty of testing and detecting this defect.

For Professor Nicely, the bug identification process started because he noticed a minor inconsistency. But the reason that he was in the position to notice the inconsistency was that he placed checks in his code to validate his computations. He provided scaffoldings in his program to allow him to monitor the correctness of his program. Without these checks, he might not have noticed the problem as early as he did, and his enumeration of prime numbers might be erroneous. Once he realized that a problem existed, he began to systematically eliminate possible causes of the bug and narrow it down to the Pentium's FPU.

The lessons that we can learn at Intel's expense are many:

♦ Not only does testing have to follow the specification, it also needs to account for algorithms used to ensure maximal completeness.

♦ We should provide scaffolding in programs to continually monitor program correctness. This gives us the opportunity to identify potential bugs as early as possible.

♦ All unexpected results need to be questioned and probed until we can explain the reason for them. There could be a bug in hiding.

♦ Finding the potential root cause of a bug is a systematic process. A potential cause is first hypothesized, and experiments are set up to validate the hypothesis.

♦ Creating a simplistic reproducible case can sometimes make all the difference. The fact that Professor Nicely was able to trigger a bug with a simple division allowed him to test other systems and configurations that helped him eliminate a false hypothesis.

A Buggy Vignette #2

According to legend, early torpedo designs had a fail-safe device to prevent the torpedo from damaging the submarine after the torpedo had been launched. After launch, torpedoes were designed to self-destruct if they turned 180 degrees. The theory behind this design was that the torpedo had a chance of hitting the submarine that fired it if it turned 180 degrees.

---

[23]Pratt, V. R. "A natural scenario with high FDIV bug probability (was: In Intel's Defense...)," comp.arch newsgroup, December 3, 1994, 15:20:17 UTC.

[24]Edelman, Alan. "The Mathematics of the Pentium Division Bug," 1995. Available from **www-math.mit.edu/-edelman/**. Also appears in *SIAM Review*, March 1997.

One day, a submarine captain decided to fire a torpedo. However, the torpedo got stuck in the firing chamber and could not be dislodged. The submarine captain decided to return to port so that it could be repaired. When the submarine performed its 180-degree maneuver, the torpedo self-destructed and took the submarine with it.

The bug in this case was in the design of the torpedo safety design. At some point, someone thought it was a good idea to put some kind of fail-safe device into the torpedo so that it could not destroy the submarine that launched it. The concept was sound, but the design was not. The designer failed to consider the error scenario that sunk a submarine. However, it's not clear to us if this incident showed a real bug that manifested itself back in the early day of submarine weaponry design or if the incident was just an urban legend. But it was amusing and realistic enough that we thought we would include it.

Ariane 5 Operand Error

The short story of the *Ariane 5* accident is that the accident was caused by an unhandled exception during the conversion from a 64-bit floating point value to a 16-bit signed integer value. The floating point value that caused the exception (or operand error, as it was called in the official inquiry report) was larger than the value that could possibly be represented by the 16-bit integer value. However, the longer version of the story is infinitely more interesting and educational.[25]

The Story

Ariane 5 was the answer to the European Space Agency's attempt to become the dominant launcher in the commercial space market. Costing $7 billion and taking over 10 years to build, *Ariane 5* was capable of carrying two 3-ton satellites into orbit.

On its maiden flight, the *Ariane 5* launcher exploded 40 seconds after lift-off on the morning of June 4, 1996. Analysis of the flight data quickly showed that the *Ariane 5* launcher was behaving normally up until the moment when it suddenly veered off its flight path and self-destructed. The weather on the morning of the test flight was acceptable; so, weather was not a factor. The flight data also showed that the active and primary Inertial Reference System that affected the control of the nozzle of the solid booster both failed more or less simultaneously just prior to the destruction of the launcher.

After the accident, an inquiry board was formed to investigate the failure. The inquiry board had the telemetry data of the launcher, trajectory data from the radar stations, optical observations of the launch and the recovered debris, and the recovered Inertial Reference Systems to assist it with its bug finding tasks. Additionally, the inquiry board had the individual components and software systems on the launcher available for testing and review. Given this information, it was able to reconstruct the sequences of events on June 4, 1996.

[25] Lions, J. L., et al. "ARIANE 5 Flight 501 Failure," Report by the Inquiry Board. Paris, July 19, 1996. Available at **www.csrin.esa.int/htdocs/tidc/Press/Press96/ariane5rep.html**.

1. The software module where the fault eventually occurred was reused from the *Ariane 4* launcher. This module performs alignment of the inertial platform so that the precision of the computations performed in the Inertial Reference System can be estimated. After lift-off, this module serves no purpose for *Ariane 5*. However, on *Ariane 4*, this module was required to operate for a full 50 seconds. The early part of the flight trajectory of *Ariane 5* is significantly different from Ariane 4, and this software module was never properly tested.

2. Shortly after lift-off, the faulty software module attempted to compute a value based on the horizontal velocity of the launcher. Because this value for *Ariane 5* was significantly larger than the value expected for *Ariane 4*, an operand error occurred on both the backup and active Inertial Reference System. The validity of this conversion was not checked because it was never expected to happen.

3. The specification for error handling of the system indicated that the failure context should be stored in EEPROM memory before shutting down the processor. After the operand error, the Inertial Reference System set the failure context as specified, which was read by the onboard computer. Based on these values, the onboard computer issued a command to the nozzle of the solid boosters and the main engine. The command called for a full nozzle deflection, which caused the launcher to take on an extreme trajectory.

4. The new trajectory caused the launcher to be under extreme aerodynamic load, and the launcher started to disintegrate. The boosters separated from the main rocket, which triggered the self-destruction system of the launcher.

Admittedly, a dumb mistake, but the interesting question is: How did this mistake slip through testing? The aerospace industry typically has very strict standards and elaborate processes and procedures to ensure safety, due to the high cost of failures. The inquiry board asked the same question, and the *Ariane 5* team offered the following rationale:

♦ The *Ariane 5* team decided not to protect certain variables from a potential operand error because they felt that the value of these variables were either physically limited or that there was a large margin of safety.

♦ The *Ariane 5* team decided not to include the trajectory data as part of the functional requirements for the Inertial Reference System. Therefore, trajectory data for *Ariane 5* was not used during the test.

♦ It is difficult to perform a realistic flight test using the Inertial Reference System due to physical laws. During the functional simulation testing of the flight software, it was decided not to have the actual Inertial Reference System in the test mainly for the reason that the Inertial Reference System should have been validated at the equipment testing level, and that it would have been difficult to achieve the desired accuracy during the simulation test if the real Inertial Reference System was used.

The Lesson

As with other bugs that we have discussed, the failure of the *Ariane 5* was not caused by a single event. There were many stages in the entire development and testing process where the defect could have been identified.

♦ A software module was reused in a new environment where the operating condition was different from the original requirement of the software module. These requirements were not reviewed.

♦ The system caught and recognized the fault. Unfortunately, the specification of the error-handling mechanism was inappropriate and caused the eventual destruction.

♦ The faulty module was never properly tested in the new environment—not at the equipment level, not at the system integration level. Therefore, the faulty design and implementation was never exposed.

The inquiry board report contained the following observation that we believe to be highly appropriate for the entire software industry, not just for the *Ariane 5* software designers.

> An underlying theme in the development of *Ariane 5* is the bias towards the mitigation of random failure. … The exception which occurred was not due to random failure but a design error. The exception was detected but inappropriately handled because the view had been taken that software should be considered correct until it is shown to be at fault. … The board is in favour of the opposite view, that software should be assumed to be faulty until applying the currently accepted best practice methods can demonstrate that it is correct.[26]

However, one of the reasons that the inquiry board could successfully identify the culprits was due to the collection of measurement data, simulation environments, and documentation. Without meteorological data, it might have been difficult to rule out weather effects. Without telemetry and flight data, it might have been hard to determine the timing of the trajectory change and the faulty Inertial Reference Systems, which allowed the board to quickly narrow down the potential defects. Post-flight simulations were performed using the actual trajectory data from the *Ariane 5* flight and the simulation faithfully reproduced the chain of events leading to the failure of system. The inquiry board was able to reproduce the bug!

A Buggy Vignette #3

The Internet is a great source of information. Unfortunately, the word "great" is not used as an adjective to describe the quality of information. Rather, "great" denotes the quantity of information—too much information, which in some circumstances is unwanted information

---

[26] Lions, J. L., et al. "*ARIANE 5* Flight 501 Failure," Report by the Inquiry Board. Paris, July 19, 1996. Available at **www.csrin.esa.int/htdocs/tidc/Press/Press96/ariane5rep.html**.

that we call *spam*. In other cases, the access to some specific form of information, such as pornography, is intentionally blocked and censored for any number of reasons. Either way, there are a number of tools whose job is to act as filters to remove potentially unwanted emails and block questionable Web sites. These tools can be a source of great annoyance. For example:

> Just heard a report on CBS network radio that net-savvy football fans around the country are being stymied in their efforts to learn about this Sunday's Super Bowl. Seems the Web filtering software installed on browsers, e.g., in certain public libraries, spots the "XXX" in "Super Bowl XXXIV" and interprets this to mean it's an adult porn site. [27]

In another example, over-zealous censoring of potentially offensive words can make an otherwise innocent message incomprehensible and funny. For example, an Internet service of the BBC censored the sentence:

"I hope you still have your appetite for scraps of dickens when I bump into you in class in Scunthorpe, Essex, on Saturday"

to:

"I hope you still have your appetite for s****s of dickens when I ***p into you in class in S****horpe, Es***, on Sa****ay" [28]

But the biggest potential annoyance is with anti-spam software that can delete important emails because the software erroneously classifies these emails as spam.

> I recently upgraded (?) to MS Office 2000, which, among other things, lets you have more than 8 email filters active at once. In my glee, I started turning things on, including junk mail filtering. Surprise! I found 8–10 important messages—all replies to a query I sent out to a personal mailing list—all dumped into the Junk Mail folder.
>
> What was it? I'm riding in a charity bicycle ride, and I needed to tell my pledgees that I needed their money now. So I sent them an email updating my training status and asking them to send their checks. Obviously, this message had at least one dollar sign "$" in it—and because I'm an excitable guy it had at least one multiple exclamation mark "!!", and since, at the end, I chided my manager to make good on my exaggerated version of his pledge:
>
> >> Mark, didn't you promise $5,000 or something like that?
>
> ...we also hit the magic phrase ",000".

---

[27] Wharton, J. "Super Bowl XXXIV Web-Filtered: Adult Porn?," *Risk Digest*, Vol 20, No. 77. January 26, 2000. **catless.ncl.ac.uk/Risks**.

[28] McWilliams, P. "BBC Censorship," rec.humor.funny, December 3, 1999. **www.netfunny.com/rhf/jokes/99/Dec/censorship.html**.

Now, the fine folks in Redmond have determined that if these three elements converge, you have received spam. The actual rule (from their Web site) is:

Body contains ",000" AND Body contains "!!" AND Body contains "$"

Who'd have guessed? In fact, even looking at their filter list, it took me a long time to figure out which rule I'd hit. (OK, I'm slow sometimes.) [29]

Are these bugs or user errors? In all three cases, the software functioned exactly as prescribed by the algorithm, and the software manufacturers would not consider these cases to be bugs. However, sometimes the effect of the algorithm is not what is desired by an end user. So as end users, do we turn off the filtering and anti-spam software in order to do what we want, or do we find ways to work around the faulty algorithm? In Chapter 3, we explore the nature of bugs, which might help us determine exactly what a bug is.

Mars Climate Orbiter

Mars Climate Orbiter is part of the Mars Surveyor program to explore and map out Mars. The Mars Surveyor program is expected to last a decade and launch an average of one mission per year. The first two missions included the launching of *Mars Pathfinder* and *Mars Global Surveyor* in 1996. *Mars Climate Orbiter* was launched on December 11, 1998, which was followed by the *Mars Polar Lander* on January 3, 1999. Both *Mars Climate Orbiter* and *Mars Polar Lander* were lost shortly after their arrival on the red planet. These two spacecraft cost NASA about $327.6 million to build and operate. Their failures caused NASA to reassess its objectives, procedures, and processes of the Mars program in order to ensure the success of its future missions. The cause of the *Mars Polar Lander* failure still cannot be determined; however, the error that caused the *Mars Climate Orbiter* to be lost was identified. We therefore focus our case study on the *Mars Climate Orbiter*.

The Story

Mars Climate Orbiter was launched on December 11, 1998, atop a *Delta 11* launch vehicle from Cape Canaveral Air Station in Florida. After nine-and-a-half months of space flight, it was scheduled to go into orbit around Mars on September 23, 1999. However, when the designated time came, something went wrong.

> Early this morning at about 2:00 A.M. Pacific Daylight Time the orbiter fired its main engine to go into orbit around the planet. All the information coming from the spacecraft leading up to that point looked normal. The engine burn began as planned, five minutes before the spacecraft passed behind the planet as seen from Earth. Flight controllers did not detect a signal when the spacecraft was expected to come out from behind the planet. [30]

---

[29] Cattarin, G. "Junk-Mail Filters," *Risks Digest*, Vol. 20, No. 89. **catless.ncl.ac.uk/Risks**.

[30] Media Relations Office, Jet Propulsion Laboratory. "NASA's Mars Climate Orbiter Believed to Be Lost." NASA Press Release. September 23, 1999.

The *Mars Climate Orbiter* was developed by a joint team of scientists and engineers in two locations: the Jet Propulsion Laboratory (JPL), located in Pasadena, California, and the Lockheed Martin Astronautics (LMA) facility, located in Denver, Colorado. LMA was responsible for the design and development of the *Mars Climate Orbiter* for flight system integration and testing and for the support of launch operations. JPL had the responsibilities of project management, spacecraft and instrument development management, project system engineering, mission design, navigation design, mission operation system development, ground data system development, and mission assurance. [31]

During its nine-and-a-half months' journey, the ground crew tracked and compared the observed trajectory of the vehicle and the expected trajectory. Furthermore, the ground crew also tracked all events that were occurring aboard the *Mars Climate Orbiter*. One of these events was the Angular Momentum Desaturation (AMD) event. An AMD event occurred when the Orbiter fired its thrusters to remove the angular momentum built-up in its flywheels. Basically, it is a calibration maneuver to keep system components operating within an expected range. When an AMD event occurred, the following sequence of actions were to take place:

1. The *Orbiter* sends the relevant data to the ground station.

2. The data is processed by a software module called SM_FORCE.

3. The result of SM_FORCE is placed into a file called the AMD file.

4. The data from the AMD file is then used to compute the change in velocity of the *Orbiter*.

5. The computed velocity change is used to model the trajectory of the *Orbiter*.

According to the specification, the SM_FORCE module should produce the data that it placed into the AMD file using metric units, that is, Newton-seconds. However, for one reason or another, the SM_FORCE module in the ground station output data used English units, that is, pound-seconds (the official report did not state a reason, so we'd rather not speculate). The software module that computed the velocity change using data in the AMD file expected it to be in metric units, according to the specification. However, on board the Orbiter, the module that created the AMD file used metric units; this resulted in a difference between the trajectory computed by the spacecraft and the ground station. Specifically, the trajectory computed by the ground station was too small by a factor of 4.45, because 1 pound-second is equal to 4.45 Newton-seconds.

The spacecraft periodically transmitted its computed trajectory model to the ground station for comparison. Theoretically, a quick comparison between the spacecraft model and the ground station model should have raised a red flag. However, a few complicating factors prevented the ground crew from realizing the error:

---

[31] Mars Climate Orbiter Mishap Investigation Board, Phase 1 Report, November 10, 1999.

- There were a few bugs in the ground station software, so the ground crew was not able to use the SM_FORCE module to compute the *Orbiter* trajectory. The bugs were not fixed until four months into the flight, around April 1999.

- The ground crew in charge of the spacecraft navigation was not aware that velocity change data from the spacecraft was available for comparison until long after the launch.

- The line of sight between the spacecraft and Earth prevented the ground crew from accurately modeling the spacecraft trajectory using observation.

If the AMD events had occurred infrequently, the factor of 4.45 might not have had such a dramatic effect. However, due to the shape of the spacecraft, AMD events occurred 10 to 14 times more frequently than expected. Furthermore, when the discrepancy between the ground station model, the spacecraft model, and the observation was uncovered, these observations were informally reported using email instead of following the project's standard procedure. Ultimately, these discrepancies were not resolved until after the loss of the spacecraft.

On September 8, 1999, the ground crew computed a maneuver to put the *Orbiter* into Mars' orbit. This computation was done using the incorrect model. The purpose of this maneuver was to adjust the trajectory of the *Orbiter* such that the point of closest approach to Mars would be at a distance of 226 kilometers. On September 23, the maneuver was executed. The engine start occurred at 09:00:46 coordinated universal time (UTC), formerly known as Greenwich mean time (GMT). Four minutes and six seconds later, the ground station lost its signal from the *Orbiter*. The loss of signal was caused by the fact that the Orbiter was behind the planet, but this occurrence was 49 seconds earlier than predicted by the trajectory model. Because the faulty trajectory model was used, the spacecraft was actually closer to the planet surface than expected. The actual closest point of the spacecraft to Mars' surface was more like 57 kilometers. This altitude was judged to be too low for the *Orbiter* to survive.

The Lesson

"People sometimes make errors," said Dr. Edward Weiler, NASA's Associate Administrator for Space Science. "The problem here was not the error, it was the failure of NASA's systems engineering, and the checks and balances in our processes, to detect the error. That's why we lost the spacecraft."[32]

One mistake was made in one part of the software. However, a series of mistakes in the span of nine-and-a-half months ultimately caused the demise of the *Mars Climate Orbiter*. To call the original mistake the root cause undermines the fact that this accident was not the result of a single mistake. There are three main contributions to the failure of the *Mars Climate Orbiter*:

- If proper testing had been performed, this kind of error could have been quickly detected and corrected.

---

[32] Isbell, Douglas; Hardin, Mary; and Underwood, Joan. "Mars Climate Orbiter Team Finds Likely Cause of Loss," NASA Press Release 99-113, September 30, 1999.

- However, because ground station software was not properly tested, additional bugs manifested after the launch of the spacecraft. These bugs delayed the observation of the problem. Instead of having nine months to identify the bug, the additional bugs reduced the amount of time the ground crew had available to track down the discrepancy to five months.

- When the discrepancy was finally observed, it was never properly explained. The original bug was never identified, which would have informed the crews of the impending accident.

The investigation board's phase 1 report also cited the following factors for the mishap and made some additional recommendations.[33] These factors and recommendations are mostly related to the procedure and processes of the project that might be appropriate for terrestrial software systems.

- *Communication*—Communication is a major problem in any large-scale project, software or otherwise. In the case of the *Mars Climate Orbiter*, teams on the project did not communicate effectively with each other. The operation team did not communicate its concern for the trajectory discrepancy to the spacecraft operation team and project management. Critical knowledge from one team was not adequately transferred or shared with another team, which partially contributed to the failure.

- *Training and transition from development to operations*—One reason that the discrepancy in the trajectory model was never fully explained until after the accident is that the operational staff was not fully trained; the transition from the development project to the operations project was not carefully planned or executed. In a software project environment, this equates to the software development team tossing the finished system over the wall to the network operation team without providing the adequate tools and training needed by the operational staff on the characteristics and behavior of the system.

- *Analyze what could go wrong*—The investigators felt that prior analyses of the failure conditions of the system could help prevent future accidents. This is akin to performing fail-over, fault-tolerant, and capacity planning analyses for the distributed computing environment commonly seen in an Internet system.

- *Complacency*—The investigation board found that the project personnel believed that the task of sending a spacecraft into orbit around Mars was easy because the JPL had 30 years of interplanetary navigation experience with no history of navigational failures. This complacency might explain the lack of proper testing of the software modules.

A Buggy Vignette #4

This incident does not relate a software bug of any sort. In fact, the story does not involve software at all. However, it is amusing and instructive and deserves a place in this chapter. The short version of the story involves a subcontractor who was working on laying fiber

---

[33] Mars Climate Orbiter Mishap Investigation Board, Phase 1 Report, November 10, 1999.

optic cable for the local telephone company. Prior to the incident, the subcontractor had disabled the phone line and was using a trenching machine to cut a trench in the ground. However, the ground was wet from morning dew and the trenching machine slid down the side of the road into a ditch, knocking the subcontractor 10 to 15 feet into the ditch. Upon seeing the accident, one observer ran to the closest house to call 911, but the phone didn't work. Why? Because the phone line was disabled by the subcontractor in order to do his work. To make the incident even more ludicrous, a cell phone was in the subcontractor's truck, but coworkers of the injured man had totally forgotten about the cell phone at the time of the accident. Eventually, another observer was able to call 911 from another house, and the incident resulted in a happy ending. The injured man was sent to the hospital with no major injuries. The trenching machine was towed out of the ditch, and the community got fiber optic cables. [34]

What kind of lesson can we learn from this incident that we can apply to software debugging? The main lesson is—always have a backup. Often, in the heat of fixing and changing code, we feel so confident about our changes that we make these changes, committing them without proper testing. Committing changes are modifications that are difficult to roll back, and we are stuck if there is a problem. This is like the subcontractor disabling the phone line while installing the new line without thinking about the possibility that something could go wrong, and when it did, ending up with no phone at all.

Making a backup copy of the source code, commenting out the codes that you are replacing instead of deleting them, making a copy of the old function and calling it a different name, and using configuration management tools are some tips that you can use to keep a backup until you have sufficiently tested your changes. But a backup is useless if you don't remember that you have it. In the story, help could have been summoned earlier if someone had remembered the cell phone in the truck. In our work, the danger is not in forgetting that we have a backup, but rather, in trying to figure out which version of the backup (or combination of versions from different modules) comprises the last known working system.

AT&T Phone Outages

In the telecommunications industry, loss of service is known as an outage. For most of us, when an outage occurs, we lose our telephone service; we cannot make calls and we cannot receive calls. Outages are accepted and expected hazards in the industry. Hurricanes can knock down telephone lines, underground cables can be severed due to human error or earthquakes, or there can be bugs in the software that manages the network.

On January 15, 1990, AT&T had a nationwide telephone system outage that lasted for nine hours. The cause was due to a program error in the software that was meant to make the system more efficient. Eight years later, on April 13, 1998, AT&T suffered another massive failure in its frame-relay network, which affected ATM machines, credit card transactions,

---

[34] Cook, Michael. "A Self-Referential Risky Accident," *Risks Digest*, Vol 20, No. 95.

and other business data services. This failure lasted 26 hours. Again, the bug was introduced during a software upgrade.

Did AT&T make the same mistake twice? Or was there more to these bugs?

The Story: The 1990 Outage

In 1990, the AT&T telephone network consisted of 114 interconnecting 4ESS toll switching systems (this is a simplification). For our discussion, we will conceptually model the AT&T network as a graph. In the graph, there are 114 nodes, and each node represents one of the 4ESS switches. The lines that are drawn between nodes represent conduits of communication between the nodes.

In this telephone network, when any one of the nodes experiences a problem, the faulty node sends a "do not disturb" message to all the nodes that are connected to it. This message informs the neighboring node that the faulty node cannot process new calls and asks the neighboring node to identify the faulty node as out of service. Meanwhile, the faulty node activates a fault recovery process that lasts between four to six seconds. At the end of the fault recovery process, the faulty node sends a message, known as an Initial Address Message (IAM), to its neighboring nodes to inform them of its new status and asks them to start forwarding calls to the "now-working" node.

In mid-December 1989, AT&T upgraded the software in the 4ESS switches to enhance network performance and enable faster fail-over procedures when problems were encountered in the network. At approximately 2:30 P.M. EST on January 15, 1990, the 4ESS switch in New York suffered a minor hardware problem, so it started its fault recovery process as previously described. After the New York switch had fixed its problems, it sent out an IAM to notify its neighboring switches that it was ready to resume service. However, the software upgrade that was done in mid-December introduced a flaw. This flaw manifested itself when a switch received two IAMs within an interval of $1/100^{th}$ of a second—some data in the switch became corrupted and the switch was taken out of service to be reinitialized. When the neighboring switches were removed from service, they performed the same recovery procedure. Because all switches were the same, the same sequence of events cascaded from one switch to another and took down the entire network.

Throughout the day, AT&T engineers were able to stabilize the network by reducing the load on the network. By 11:30 P.M. EST, they were able to clear up all the links in the network, and the system was essentially back to normal.

On Tuesday, January 16, 1990, the AT&T engineers were able to identify and isolate the bug, which was traced to a set of faulty codes. The faulty codes were activated in the switch recovery procedure. The code snippet that caused the outage is illustrated as follows:[35]

---

[35] Neumann, Peter. "Risks to the Public in Computers and Related Systems," ACM *SIGSOFT* *Software Engineering Notes*, Vol. 15, No. 2, pp 11ff, April 1990.

```
1. do {
2.     ...
3.     switch (expression) {
4.         case (value 0): {
5.             if (logical_test) {
6.                 ...
7.                 break;
8.             } else {
9.                 ...
10.             }
11.             ...
12.             break;
13.         }
14.         ...
15.     }
16.     ...
17. } while (expression);
```

In this case, the break statement on line 7 was the culprit. As implemented, if the logical_test on line 5 was successful, the program should have proceeded to line 6 to execute those statements. When the program stepped to line 7, the break statement caused the program to exit the "switch" block between line 3 and line 15, and proceeded to execute the codes in line 16. However, this path of execution was not the intention of the programmer. The programmer intended the break statement in line 7 to break the if-then clause; so, after the program executed line 7, it was supposed to continue execution in line 11. Table 2.1 shows the differences in the program path as implemented and as intended.

The Lesson: 1990 Outage

The programming mistake that contributed to the 1990 outage was a typical rookie mistake. But we all make mistakes, and even a 20-year veteran can produce stupid mistakes on occasion. If mistakes are inevitable, the question is, what can we do to ferret out the error before it becomes a public spectacle? We do not have any first-hand knowledge of the

Table 2.1   The intended and implemented instruction sequence that lead to AT&T 1990 outage.

Flow	Implemented	Intended
Step 1	Line 2	Line 2
Step 2	Line 3	Line 3
Step 3	Line 4	Line 4
Step 4	Line 5	Line 5
Step 5	Line 6	Line 6
Step 6	Line 7	Line 7
Step 7	Line 16	Line 11 (incorrect)
Step 8	Line 17	Line 12 (incorrect)
Step 9	-	Line 16 (incorrect)

internal AT&T software development processes and procedures during 1990; therefore, we are not in the position to evaluate other contributing causes. The official AT&T report stated that:

> We believe the software design, development, and testing processes we use are based on solid, quality foundations. All future releases of software will continue to be rigorously tested. We will use the experience we've gained through this problem to further improve our procedures. [36]

We do not believe we can fault AT&T's software development process for the 1990 outage, and we have no reason to believe that AT&T did not rigorously test its software update. In hindsight, it is easy to say that if the developers had only tested the software, they would have seen the bug. Or that if they had performed a code inspection, they would have found the defect. Code inspection might have helped in this case. However, the only way the code inspection could have uncovered this bug is if another engineer saw this particular line of code and asked the original programmer if that was his or her intention. The only reason that the code reviewers might have asked this question is if they were familiar with the specifications for this particular code block.

Bugs of this nature are usually not easy to test and uncover in a normal testing environment. The bug can be reproduced once you understand it and can create the sequence of events necessary to trigger it. However, the chance of producing the correct sequence of events at random is very small, especially when the system will be used in a real-time, high-volume environment that is difficult to simulate in the laboratory. Furthermore, the new software performed correctly for about a month, which translates to billions of completed calls. The software had a defect, but this defect required a set of specific events and factors to bring it to life.

♦ The bug required a sustained load on the network. When the load on the network dwindled, the effect of the bug essentially disappeared. [37]

♦ The bug was timing dependent. Two IAM messages from the same switch needed to be received within 10 milliseconds in order for the defect to be triggered.

♦ The fact that all the switches had the same software made the system scalable. However, the risk was that all the switches had the same defect, and were susceptible to the same bug.

The Story: The 1998 Outage

On April 13, 1998, at about 2:30 P.M., a technician was dispatched to upgrade trunk cards on a Cisco Stratacom BPX frame-relay switch. A Stratacom BPX frame-relay switch hosts a pair of redundant trunk cards, one of which is active, whereas the other is on standby and

---

[36] Neumann, Peter. "Risks to the Public in Computers and Related Systems," ACM SIGSOFT *Software Engineering Notes*, Vol. 15, No. 2, pp 11ff, April 1990.

[37] Neumann, Peter G. *Computer Related Risks*. Addison-Wesley, New York, New York, 1995.

serves as a backup. AT&T employed two procedures for trunk card upgrades. One of the procedures assumed the switch was currently active and connected to the network, whereas the other procedure assumed the switch was isolated and not connected to the network.

In the first scenario, where the switch was assumed to be on the network, the procedure required the technician to replace the standby card first. Once it was clear that the new card was stable, the old active card was placed on standby, and the new card became the active card. Once this process was performed, the technician was then allowed to upgrade the remaining card (now the standby card). The second procedure assumed the switch was not connected to the network, and the technician was free to replace both cards at the same time.

When the technician arrived at the facility to perform the upgrade, the technician assumed the switch that needed to be upgraded was not on the network because it didn't seem to carry any network traffic. However, the switch was connected to the network and was active. Unfortunately for the technician and AT&T, both upgrade cards had flaws on them. After the trunk cards were installed and active, they immediately sent out a stream of error messages to the switch. These error messages from the trunk cards triggered a defect in the software module of the switch. This defect caused the error messages to be propagated to other switches on the network, all 145 of them. The volume of error messages was large enough that all switches were quickly overloaded with error messages, which effectively took down the entire network at approximately 3:00 P.M. [38]

There wasn't a lot of information regarding the software faults in the trunk cards or the Cisco switch. Alka Jarvis, manager of software quality engineering at Cisco Systems, commented at a May 29, 1998, International Software Quality Week session that the code that caused the AT&T network outage was old legacy code. [39]

AT&T was able to quickly isolate the faulty switch, and by 11:00 P.M., the faulty switch was isolated from the network. The remaining tasks were simply to rebuild the entire network, one piece at a time. By 2:30 P.M. on April 14, 1998, 99.9 percent of the frame-relay network was again operational. However, it took AT&T about a week before it was able to determine the cause of this outage, and on April 22, 1998, AT&T issued a report outlining the cause of the network failure.

The Lesson: 1998 Outage

Even though software defects were involved in the 1998 network outage, there were a multitude of culprits that contributed to this outage. This outage differed from the 1990 outage in that a procedural error in the upgrade process triggered the latent software defects. However, the similarities are many.

---

[38] "AT&T Announces Cause of Frame-Relay Network Outage," AT&T Press Release, April 22, 1998.
   McCartney, Laton. "One Year Later: A Behind-the-Scenes Look at the Causes of and Fallout from AT&T's Devastating Frame-Relay Outage," *Network World*, March 22, 1999.
[39] Bernstein, L., and Yuhas, C. M. "Chinks in the Armor: Will a Hybrid IP/ATM Architecture Protect the Network from Node Failures?" *America's Network Magazine*, July 1, 1998.

♦ Installation of new software was a triggering cause. The software, old and new, had numerous latent defects that were not uncovered during the normal software testing process. It took a change in the operating environment to trigger the defect that caused the network outage.

♦ The faulty code was not properly inspected. In the 1990 outage, it was the new code from AT&T. In the 1998 outage, the faulty code was old legacy code from Cisco Systems.

♦ The software defect in both cases had problems with obscure boundary conditions that were difficult to test and, in all likelihood, were probably never tested.

The 1998 AT&T network outage also highlighted numerous flaws in the procedures and processes of AT&T's network operation and demonstrated the difficulty in designing and maintaining a survivable network. Apparently, AT&T has learned from its mistakes and has corrected numerous procedural and process flaws and instituted a number of disaster recovery plans to mitigate the risk of another total network failure.[40]

Buffer Overflow

On July 18, 2000, a detailed description of the security vulnerability in Microsoft Outlook and Outlook Express was made public in the BugTraq mailing list. BugTraq is an electronic mailing list devoted to the discussion of computer security and vulnerability. This vulnerability essentially involves a bug in the software industry commonly known as buffer overflow. In its simplest form, when a program tries to put data into a memory holding area that is too small to hold the data, a buffer overflow condition occurs. The following code snippet shows an example written in C.

```
1.   char Array[10];
2.   strcpy( Array, "This will cause a buffer overflow" );
```

The size of the array is 10, and the message "This will cause a buffer overflow" has 33 characters. Strcpy() attempts to copy 33 characters into a space large enough to hold only 10 characters, so part of the message is written outside of the valid area. When this happens, the program sometimes crashes. At other times, the program might continue for a period of time with no side effects. But if the message is properly constructed, it can cause the program to execute the "virus" embedded in the message, which can cause the machine to be infiltrated by the offending message.

Up to this point in time, most security concerns for PCs include virus varieties, where users are required to perform some action to aid the intrusion, such as with the "ILOVEYOU" virus of 1999 or the "Melissa" virus of 1998. In both cases, in order to activate the virus, users were tricked into opening a file or executing a program. However, the buffer overflow

---

Bernstein, L., and Yuhas, C. M. "Chinks in the Armor: Will a Hybrid IP/ATM Architecture Protect the Network from Node Failures?" *America's Network Magazine*, July 1, 1998.

bug in Outlook requires no end user intervention. To be affected, you merely have to receive an email, which makes the attack that much harder to defend against.

Unlike other bug scenarios in this chapter, this bug is not limited to Microsoft Outlook. As a bug, buffer overflow has existed for the last 10 years, and it is a well-known security vulnerability. Outside of the network security focus, buffer overflow is also a very common bug—it seems like everyone has created one at some point in their career. Whenever you use a fixed size storage variable, such as an array, you run the risk of creating a buffer overflow defect. Because this problem is so prevalent, instead of describing the details of the Microsoft Outlook bug in the next section, we will talk about the buffer overflow bug in general—how the mistakes are made, what kind of security risks they pose, and what we can do to avoid them.

The Story

The cause of buffer overflow is simple to understand. It occurs when we attempt to put more data into a fixed storage area (the buffer) than it is meant to hold. To understand how buffer overflow can crash a program or become a security vulnerability, we need to delve into the inner workings of the computer.

When you write a program in a high-level language, like C, the compiler translates the program into assembly codes. Assembly code is essentially a sequence of primitive instructions and data. For example, consider the following main program:

```
1. main() {
2.   printf( "Hello World" );
3. }
```

The famous "Hello World" program produces 300294 bytes of binary executable using Gnu 'C' Compiler (GCC) on Windows NT, and it looks like this:

```
0x401000 55 89 e5 83 ec 10 83 3d 00 20 40 00 00 74 01 cc
0x401010 d9 7d fe 66 8b 45 fe 25 c0 f0 ff ff 66 89 45 fe
...
0x401040 48 65 6c 6c 6f 20 57 6f 72 6c 64 00 55 89 55 89
0x401050 e5 e8 94 01 00 00 68 40 10 40 00 e8 92 01 00 00
0x401060 83 c4 ...
```

Pretty incomprehensible stuff, huh? Those numbers are what computers use to execute the program that you have written. The numbers shown in the preceding code are represented in hexadecimals. The first column shows the memory address where the program will reside, and the remaining columns show the content of the memory at that address. Each column increments the memory address by one. So in memory location 0x401000, a value of 55 is stored. In memory location 0x401001, the value of 89 is stored, and so on. Some of these numbers are commands that tell the computer what to do; some of these are data that is used by the computer. In this case, the computer picks up the first value, 55, and interprets it as a command to perform a certain task. It then goes to the next value, 89. The computer knows that command 89 requires a parameter, which is stored in the adjacent memory address and has a value of e5. So, the computer executes the 89 e5 command, and then proceeds to pick up the value that comes after e5. In this way, the computer executes these values one at a time. In the Hello World program, the string Hello World is the data. If you can read hexadecimal and know the ASCII representations, you would be able to see that the string Hello World is placed at memory location 0x401040.

```
0x401040 48(H) 65(e) 6c(l) 6c(l) 6f(o) 20( ) 57(W) 6f(o) 72(r) 6c(l) 64(d) 00
```

This set of numbers looks totally indistinguishable from another set of numbers. What's preventing the computer from executing these values as a sequence of commands? Nothing except for the flow that's implemented in the program, which is the crux of the buffer overflow bug and vulnerability. If you make a mistake, the computer thinks these data values are commands and proceeds to execute the data as such. It has no way of knowing that they are data values. In this case, the command is nonsensical, and the program would most likely crash. So the task for the would-be intruder is to use the bug to trick the computer into executing the data they provide. Therefore, intruders who want to compromise your machine using your software need to do two things:

1. Insert their codes into the memory

2. Trick your computer into executing their codes

A buffer overflow bug provides the hacker a means to do both of these things. Because the program does not check for the size of the buffer when writing to it, the intruder can place arbitrary content into a memory location that is adjacent to the buffer—and that's half the battle. The other half of the battle for the would-be hackers is to figure out how to trick the computer into executing the codes they have introduced to your program. [41]

The Lesson

Out of all the case studies in this chapter, buffer overflow is probably the simplest bug to understand and present. It has been around forever, and yet it is still so prevalent. Do we ever learn anything as an industry? Why do we keep making the same mistakes?

♦ *The languages aren't helping.* Buffer overflow bugs are an epidemic in programming languages that do not have any built-in bounds checking mechanisms, such as C and C++. These languages provide programmers with the power that allows them to manipulate the computer at will. Programmers are entrusted with this power and are expected to program safely and correctly. They are also expected to perform explicit bounds checks when needed. In contrast, a language like Java performs explicit bounds checking, and

---

[41] "Aleph One", Smashing the Stack for Fun and Profit, *Phrack*, 7(49), November 1996.

the likelihood of a buffer overflow bug that can be exploited is rare. However, Java limits what programmers can do. It takes away the ability that allows a programmer to directly manipulate the memory space of the machine. This is not to say that it is impossible to buffer overflow a Java program. It just means that a programmer has to go through some serious contortions in order to overflow a buffer in Java. But when it does happen, it is usually very difficult to determine the cause. Furthermore, because most of the time a Java Virtual Machine is written in C or C++, there is always the potential of a buffer overflow bug in the Java Virtual Machine.

◆ *Programmers cannot be trusted.* Programmers are people, and people make mistakes. I have inadvertently created numerous buffer overflow bugs in my lifetime. Many times, these bugs occurred because I was prototyping a software module, so bounds checking was the last thing on my mind. But prototypes have a habit of finding their way into production. Other times, the bugs occurred because I made assumptions about the code and the usage, and I determined that it was impossible for a buffer to overflow. As is usually the case, as soon as I assumed something, someone would prove me wrong. Often, bugs appeared because I was lazy. Writing the code to check for buffer overflow is easy most of the time, but handling the conditions when the bounds checking fails can be difficult and annoying. Can I just cause the program to terminate when bounds checking fails? Or do I need to report the failure to the calling function? How does the calling function handle this failure? And do I terminate the program at the calling function ad infinitum? It's just easier to not deal with it and assume that it can't possibly happen. I'll deal with it when the testers prove me wrong.

◆ *Language constructs make it difficult.* Performing bounds checking with certain language constructs can also be difficult—using sprintf( ) comes to mind. Because sprintf( ) accepts a variable number of arguments, it requires the programmer to compute the size of the buffer using these arguments. It also is easy to overflow the buffer because you don't understand the nuances of the language. In C and C++, the string "Hello World" requires a storage space of 12 characters because the language defines the string to be null terminated. In other words, there is a null character appended after the "d" in the string. If you allocate a buffer size of 11, thinking that it will hold the entire string, and use any of the string functions, such as strcpy( ), you have a buffer overflow defect on your hands that's ready to bite you when you least expect it.

It is easy to talk about ways to prevent buffer overflow bugs from ever happening again. For example, stop using "unsafe" languages like C and C++ and have the discipline to program defensively. We know this is easier said than done. If we assume that a buffer overflow bug is inevitable and we need to use an "unsafe" language, then the only solution is bug detection. The earlier we can detect and find the bug, the lesser the chance of it causing us grief in the future.

From a security perspective, we don't care if the program crashes, but we do care if the bug can be exploited. The emphasis then focuses on how to prevent buffer overflow from being exploited. There are numerous research projects and commercial products that are designed to deal with these issues, and readers are encouraged to consult those documents for additional information. [42]

Summary

The bugs discussed in this chapter are but a few examples of bugs that have existed or that currently exist. At this time, there are thousands of software engineers working overtime to fix bugs. Some of the bugs are humorous and amusing, whereas others are mean-spirited or tragic. Regardless, it's no fun when you are the one working weekends to fix them. But the costs that software engineers have endured to fix these bugs are miniscule in comparison with the effects of these bugs. In this chapter, we have learned that the cost of bugs can be astronomical. Millions of dollars worth of equipment and labor disappear without a trace. Human pain and suffering, even death, can be caused by a simple mistake in the software.

We learned that despite all the testing and processes and procedures, bugs are inevitable. And bugs that manifest themselves in a production environment tend to be the result of a series of errors. There is usually not a single cause. Instead, there are a collection of contributing causes that prevent the bugs from been detected and eliminated prior to the fateful outcome. For example, a simple programming mistake was made in the AT&T 1990 outage. However, if a test had been run to check the execution of the code path through the faulty section of the code, the defect would have been exposed a lot earlier and would have saved AT&T the embarrassment of a nationwide long distance telephone outage. Is the root cause of the bug the programmer who wrote the incorrect code or the testing department that allowed the defect to escape into the production environment?

We learned that the ability to detect bugs is as important as the ability to prevent bugs. The earlier we can find the bug, the cheaper it is to fix it. We learned that the software can perform exactly as specified, and yet, we consider it defective when it's doing exactly as it was told. We learned that we need to be cognizant of the clues that are provided by the system and always question, evaluate, and understand the reason behind the clues. But most of all, we learned that we need to be humble in the face of bugs. The inability to admit that mistakes are possible and the unquestioning faith in our creations can blind us to the potential faults in the software. There is a reason that pride is one of the deadly sins.

We have identified many contributing causes to the bugs presented in this chapter. These contributing causes are recapped and summarized as follows:

- Lack of understanding of the tools and language constructs:

  - *Cases*—AT&T 1990 Outage, Buffer Overflow

  - *Description*—When the programmer does not understand the language constructs correctly, defects are introduced. In the AT&T 1990 outage, the mistake was an erroneously

---

[42] Cowan, C., et al. "Buffer Overflows: Attacks and Defenses for the Vulnerability of the Decade," *Proceedings of DARPA Information Survivability Conference and Expo.* Available from **www.wirex.com/~Crispin**.

placed break statement. A typical buffer overflow bug can be caused by not understanding the string manipulation package in the standard C and C++ functions.

- Reuse without understanding:

  - *Case—Ariane 5*

  - *Description*—The software module was reused, but there was a lack of understanding of the requirement of the reused software module. There was no attempt to evaluate the appropriateness of reuse.

- Software changes and upgrades:

  - *Cases*—AT&T 1990 Outage, AT&T 1998 Outage

  - *Description*—The bug manifested itself during and following software upgrades that were meant to make the system more efficient.

- Ignoring unexpected results:

  - *Cases—Mars Climate Orbiter*, Therac-25

  - *Description*—There were plenty of warnings and clues from various sources that something might be wrong in both cases. The warnings manifested themselves as unexpected results and behaviors. But the clues were routinely ignored and proper investigations were not performed. In the *Mars Climate Orbiter*, the problem was the inconsistency between computed models from the spacecraft and the ground station. In Therac-25, the problem was the continuing malfunction of the Therac-20 and the Therac-25.

- Not understanding the clues:

  - *Cases—Mars Climate Orbiter*, Therac-25, Company X, Company Y

  - *Description*—The clues that pointed to potential bugs were not interpreted correctly, which lead to all of the ultimate failures. With both Company X and Company Y, the clues perfectly described the cause of the symptoms, but were initially discounted.

- Lack of appropriate monitoring tools:

  - *Cases—Mars Climate Orbiter*, Therac-25, Company X, Company Y

  - *Description*—Good monitoring tools can help operational staff detect and solve problems before they become a big issue. It might be unfair to lump the *Mars Climate Orbiter* into this category because scientists were limited by the technology and the law of physics of what they could observe. But the fact that they could not observe the actual trajectory of the spacecraft limited their ability to determine the correctness of their model. In Therac-25, the malfunctioning messages were not descriptive enough to warn the operators of potential problems with the machine, and there was clearly a lack of feedback to let the operator know exactly what the machine was doing. Both problems at Company X and Company Y could have been mitigated if the operational staff could have detected the performance degradation of the database before the failure.

♦ Incorrect or poor specifications:

  ♦ *Case—Ariane 5*

  ♦ *Description*—The error handling of the *Ariane 5* software specified that the erroneous value be placed into the memory content used by the navigation computer. The software, as implemented, adhered to this specification. The navigation computer used the erroneous value to perform thruster maneuvers, which caused the crash. In this case, the error specification was incorrect and caused the crash.

♦ Not following specifications:

  ♦ *Case—Mars Climate Orbiter*

  ♦ *Description*—The specification for the *Mars Climate Orbiter* was very clear: The unit of exchange should have been in metric, not English.

♦ Reuse bugs:

  ♦ *Cases*—Therac-25, AT&T 1998 Outage

  ♦ *Description*—Software modules that were reused contained bugs that were not detected in their original incarnations.

♦ Proper procedure not followed:

  ♦ *Cases*—AT&T 1998 Outage, Company X

  ♦ *Description*—Procedures were designed to prevent us from making mistakes, and when the procedures were not followed and shortcuts were taken, undesirable effects resulted.

♦ Unsafe tools:

  ♦ *Case*—Buffer Overflow

  ♦ *Description*—One of the main causes of buffer overflow is due to the "unsafeness" of the C and C++ programming languages, where the software depends on the programmer to explicitly perform bounds checking to prevent buffer overflow.

♦ Human factor:

  ♦ *Case*—Buffer Overflow

  ♦ *Description*—We all know how to prevent buffer overflow, and yet, we keep on making the same mistakes.

♦ Ego and complacency:

  ♦ *Cases*—Therac-25, *Mars Climate Orbiter*

  ♦ *Description*—Ego can get in the way of objective evaluations of systems. Complacency can cause us to not question our assumptions. The result of these traits is that we do not pay attention to the clues presented and the potential for software defects.

♦ Incomplete testing:

  ♦ *Cases*—*Ariane 5*, *Mars Climate Orbiter*, Pentium, AT&T 1990 Outage

  ♦ *Description*—Hindsight is 20/20, but most of these bugs could have been detected with "correct" testing. In *Ariane 5*, the incomplete requirements and the lack of ability to simulate the operating environment meant that the engineering team had to forego the test that would have uncovered the *Ariane 5* bug. It is not clear whether testing was done on the *Mars Climate Orbiter* bug because the engineers were still fixing the software well into the space flight of the *Orbiter*. For the Pentium bug and the AT&T 1990 outage, the tests performed did not consider the nature of the algorithms, so some code was not tested. In the case of the Pentium bug, the random testing was not sufficient to test the validity of all the table lookup entries. In the AT&T 1990 outage, the test case did not cover the scenario for switch recovery.

Bug Puzzle

You were testing a set of web pages on your company's web site. You clicked on the link to web page A, and everything looked great. You continued testing other pages in the site, and by accident, you came back to web page A again. But this time, the content appeared to be out of date? You looked at it quizzically, and reloaded the page. It now looked okay again. Not really believing what you are seeing, you reloaded the page and the page appeared to be correct. Believing three time's the charm, you thought to yourself, if the page comes back correctly, maybe what I saw was just a fluke. You reloaded the page, and the content was out of date again. You butted your head against the monitor. After spending 10 minutes reloading the same page over and over, you determined that the page is loaded correctly 34 times, and incorrectly 12 times. What could be the cause of this bug?

Here are some clues to help you reason about the cause of this bug. Architecturally, there are five web servers handling browser requests. Each web server can communicate with one of four application servers. The application server gets its data from the database and implements business rules. To make things go faster, each application server stores data in a local cache.

Chapter 3
What Are Bugs?

Yuan Hsieh

In *Jacobellis versus Ohio* (1964), the late Supreme Court Justice Potter Stewart wrote in his concurring opinion:

"I shall not today attempt further to define the kinds of material I understand to be embraced within that short-hand description, and perhaps I could never succeed in intelligibly doing so. But I know it when I see it, and the motion picture involved in this case is not that."

Justice Stewart was writing about hard-core pornography, but as far as we are concerned, he could very well be writing about bugs. Bugs have similar illusive qualities; we all know one when we see it, but it is difficult to clearly define it. And in some cases, we disagree whether a bug is even a bug.

What Is a Bug?

When we were writing this book, we used instant messenger to communicate with each other on ideas for the book. (Okay, okay, we mainly used instant messenger to goof off so we didn't have to do any work.) One day, we were having an online conversation about the meaning of life...

> Matt: [snip] so you would have <a>,,<c>
>
> [Yuan is sufficiently confused, but just assumes that Matt can't type.]
>
> Matt: Note to self, don't use HTML tags.
>
> [Yuan goes aha!]

Yuan: you typed <a>, < b >, <c> and it parsed < b >!

(There are white spaces between '<', 'b' and '>')

[5 minutes passed by before a light bulb lit up in Yuan's feeble brain.]

Yuan: Is this a bug?

Matt: I don't think so. I think it is supposed to parse HTML tags.

Yuan: But it doesn't let me write < b > anymore.

Matt: <pre>**</pre>**

Matt: hmm, I thought <pre> is supposed to preserve the enclosed text. I wrote <pre> < b > </pre>. Maybe I am wrong about the tag.

[Yuan fumbled through an online HTML documentation site.]

Yuan: <pre> is the correct tag, I guess this IM doesn't parse all the HTML tags, just a subset. I think that this is a bug.

Matt: I am not so sure. I would have to see their specs.

Is this a bug? When a program crashes, it is easy to say that it has a bug. However, when software doesn't do what you expect it to do, does it have a bug? What is a bug?

As a word, *bug* is used daily in a software development organization to describe problems that need to be fixed. However, in most academic and industrial research literature, there seems to be a general avoidance of the word bug. The reason might be that the word has been used colloquially for a long time and has different connotations for different people. But this book is about bugs and debugging, not about software defects (nor faults, nor errors, nor failures), so we will take a stab at defining bug as commonly used in the daily life of software professionals.

A Simplistic Definition of Bugs

Bugs are undesirable behaviors of the system.

The problem with this simplistic definition is that one man's bug can be another man's feature. To continue with another cliché, a bug is in the eye of the beholder. In the instant messenger example, we thought the inability of the end user to transmit unparsed HTML tags was undesirable. (We can't even agree among ourselves whether it is a bug or not.) The specification the developers were working with probably only defined the requirement to parse HTML tags, but not a way to transmit unparsed HTML tags. Therefore, the developers of the tools probably consider it a minor annoyance. After all, the program is implemented according to the specification, and it behaves as it should (i.e., as implemented). Until the project management is notified, this undesirable behavior would not find its way into the system as a bug. Even if the project management is aware of this *feature*, it will no doubt be assigned a low priority; the management team will most likely agree with the developers that it is but a minor annoyance.

At this time, users of instant messenger have learned to adapt to these *minor annoyances* and have learned to work around them. (We placed a space character between characters of a potential HTML tag, so that it could be transmitted as is.) The undesirable behavior that we once considered a bug has somehow vanished. However, the equation changes when the user complaining to the vendor of the instant messenger is the president of an important customer. Then this *feature* will somehow find its way into the bugs' database and be assigned top priority, which brings us to our second definition of bugs.

A Cynical Definition of Bugs

Bugs are behaviors of the system that the powers-that-be find undesirable.

This is a somewhat depressing and fatalistic view of bugs and the software industry because it implies that bugs are arbitrarily defined, and that there is no standard. As described in Chapter 2 in the Pentium Bug fiasco, Intel, as a corporation, would like us to consider the floating point defect in its chips to be a minor inconvenience. In all likelihood, the chip designers at Intel probably deemed the defect a bug because it did not perform as designed. The user communities definitely considered the defect a bug and raised enough of a ruckus to force Intel to address the floating point defect as a bug. In this case, the engineers at Intel already knew about the defect and had a fix in place. Debugging was nothing more for Intel than setting up an exchange policy so that the user communities could receive replacement chips.

It is true that there are other instances where bugs are forced down our throat, or a bug is defined out of existence by some fancy semantic manipulation. For example, you work for a company that writes software for another company, let's call it Company A. After you deliver your initial release, Company A does not like a specific feature in your release and calls it a bug. Do you have a choice? It hardly matters if the specification is clear in the matter, or that the particular feature is ill-defined in the original requirement. Somehow, you will eventually end up fixing this "bug." At least that is the reality in the commercial software industry. In most cases, however, it is rather clear to all parties involved that a bug is actually a bug. As users of software products and services, we typically know what bugs are. There are behaviors in the system that we, as users, deem unacceptable. We have also worked as developers and testers. In those roles, we also intuitively recognize a bug when we see it because the system doesn't do what we, as developers and testers, expect it to do. Therefore, when the two sides can agree on the undesirability of a behavior, then the undesirable behavior is most likely a bug. Our new, improved definition of bugs may read as follows.

What if the parties involved cannot agree whether a feature is desirable or not? In that case, it all depends on which party has the most influence—which means we then revert to the cynical definition. Fortunately, in most cases, the parties involved can agree on the delineation of features and bugs. Disagreements usually center around unintuitive interfaces, desired features, usability, and mismatched expectations.

Does this definition of bugs get us anywhere? Absolutely! This definition is helpful even if it only states that bugs are something that people have agreed to call bugs. It indicates the importance of having a set of well-designed requirements, because a requirement document should list the agreed-upon desirable and undesirable behaviors of a system. It confirms the importance of a software development team to understand the business need and process of its customers. It verifies that the software development team needs to be able to communicate its vision of the system to the customer. It also validates the need to share our concepts and ideas with each other!

What Is a Software Defect?

Traditionally, in the software industry, the terms bugs and software defects are typically used interchangeably. However, we recognize a small yet subtle difference between software defects and bugs: Bugs are the physical manifestation of software defects.

The Intel Pentium bug illustrated this perspective clearly. Intel Corporation agreed with the user communities that there was a defect in its chips. The difference was that Intel did not consider the defect to be a bug. The company felt that the chance that a normal spreadsheet user would encounter it was once in every 27,000 years; therefore, the defect was inconsequential and there was no compelling reason for the average user to have it fixed. However, user communities disagreed. Eventually, Intel capitulated and changed how it viewed the defect. The defect became a bug, and Intel set up appropriate methods to deal with the bug and the user communities. We define software defects as follows.

Our definition of software defects is considerably broader than the industry norm. We argue that software defects can be introduced throughout the software development process and are not always associated with mistakes made in the implementation process. If a system is implemented and designed according to a set of conflicting requirements, eventually, it will manifest undesirable behaviors that will need to be corrected. In this case, the software defect resides within the requirements because in order to correct the misbehavior, the conflicting requirements must first be resolved. If a system is required to handle 1,000 concurrent requests, but is built to handle only 500 concurrent requests and is not scalable, we say the system architecture contains a defect. If the implementation of a system component does not check for the validity of a memory allocation statement and assumes that the allocation will always succeed, this implementation contains a defect that could eventually cause the system to crash or misbehave. Regardless of where the defect lies, it has the potential of causing developers and customers undue hardship.

Software defects have a potential to become bugs, but not all software defects will produce a bug. On average, 25 software defects exist for every 1,000 lines of code. For a program of 500,000 lines, it means that potentially there may be 12,500 defects. It is a wonder that we still rely on computers as much as we do! The reality is that software defects are simply that, defects in the software. Most defects never see the light of day. Why? Because they are part of the logic that is rarely executed; because the program is never run long enough; because of the way the program is used; and because we are lucky. Unfortunately, we were not able to find studies that attempted to determine the relationships between the number of defects and the number of bugs, so we do not know the exact relationship between defect level and bug level. However, it is safe to assume that the defect level and the number of bugs are proportionally related (i.e., the number of bugs increases with the number of defects).

Consider the following example:

```
int main( int argc, char **argv ) {
}
```

This little do-nothing main program has an implementation defect. It does not return an integer when leaving the main function. In most instances, this defect will not manifest itself as a bug. However, in a system where this program is a component and the exit condition of the program is captured and used (such as in a Unix shell script), this oversight can eventually promote itself into a bug. A bug that some poor debugger would have to track down and fix.

Now that we know what a bug is, what do we do with it? We debug it, of course!

What Debugging Isn't

I had a friend who worked for a major telecommunications company and was in charge of a client in a standard three-tier client/server system. His component used Application Programmer Interfaces (APIs) developed by the server team. One day, his component started to crash, although he had made no changes other than to link in the new API distribution from the server team. After verifying that the inputs to the client system were reasonable, he started poking his nose into the code. He soon found the location of the crash, and to his amazement, it was an explicit abort statement placed there by the server team (an assert(false) call), which did not exist in the previous release. Of course, there were no comments around the code to inform him of its rationale. A few minutes on the telephone soon resolved the mystery. Apparently, the server team had a bug report related to that piece of code. Unable to figure out the real cause of the problem, the server team decided to just terminate the program right when the code had reached an unacceptable state, because the server team felt that any "correct" usage of the API should not ever have reached that state.

This was not a case where the server team placed an assert() to trap the error in the debugging mode, and then released the debugging version by accident. This was a conscious decision. The team's rationale was if this assert was triggered, it was a programmer error and the program should terminate. Hopefully you will agree that the server team did not debug; it simply masked one bug and in the process introduced another.

In effect, the server team fixed the symptom of the original bug, which satisfied complaints from one client. However, the team failed to understand the reason behind the original bug and failed to understand the consequence of its changes. After this "fix," the original bug still existed and had the potential to manifest itself given another opportunity. But the "fixed" system still had one additional bug that the server team introduced. Believe it or not, this is a rather benign consequence of fixing the symptom; the system aborted automatically and informed other users and developers where the masking took place. Fixing the symptom becomes diabolical when no one knows the "fix" is there.

Consider an example of a memory corruption bug. You think it is a memory corruption bug because when you add an assignment statement (such as $x = 0$) in the right place, the program stops crashing. Relieved, you submit the change. What just happened? In all likelihood, you have just made the bug harder to find. The assignment statement that you added does not change the fact that the cause of the memory corruption is still there. You have merely delayed or moved its incarnation. A few months later, the program may crash somewhere else and you will have already forgotten the changes you had made. By that time, who knows what other complexity has been added on top of the application? The bug is buried deeper and deeper with every change made to the code.

However, there is some value in treating the symptom in a debugging process. In Chapter 9, we will introduce a technique that involves commenting out codes to help you observe and understand the behavior of the code. This technique is done in a controlled environment, where changes are never meant to be checked back into the repository nor masqueraded as a fix.

Fixing the symptom on an architectural or design level is an even worse sin. The main consequence of fixing the symptom at this level is that it leads to an unstable, nonextensible, and nonreusable system and components. The Blob and Swiss Army Knife anti-patterns are examples of problems that can result from fixing symptoms instead of fixing causes in the architecture or design.[1]

The Blob anti-pattern occurs when a single class monopolizes all the processes in the module. The Swiss Army Knife anti-pattern can be characterized as an excessively complex class interface in a single class. When a functionality is required that was not accounted for in the original design, instead of stepping back and rethinking the design, developers have a tendency to just find the easiest place to factor in the new functionality. Often, a convenient class is used to become the holder of the new attributes or methods. A few iterations later, this class takes on the similarities of a blob or a Swiss Army Knife; it ends up doing everything!

A popular misconception is that a lack of certain features in an application must be a bug. Some people treat adding new features as an equivalent to debugging. Missing features are typically due to oversights in the requirement and should be fixed at the requirement level. However, if we accept our definition of bugs, missing features are definitely not an "undesirable behavior of the system." They are a "desired but nonexisting behavior of the system." Furthermore, adding features does not involve fixing anything; we are not removing bugs and defects.

To be sure, adding a new feature to existing production quality software is not a trivial task, especially if it involves modifications at the architectural or design level. We have reserved a chapter on software maintenance that deals exclusively with this topic. This misconception might have arisen because we like to use the task of adding new features as an excuse to perform major overhauls to our architecture and design. It is an opportunity to fix design and architectural bugs. Another cause for this misconception is that in some cases, it is faster to slip a feature request through the bug tracking system rather than from the top down through the normal channel. The developer looks at the bug that is missing features XYZ and implements XYZ. Everyone is happy except that the new feature is never properly documented in the requirement or the design document. Soon, we have an unmanageable mess on our hands.

What Is Debugging?

We have argued that fixing the symptom and adding new features are not debugging. Obviously, adding new features adds codes to the code base and does not involve removal of undesirable system behaviors. Fixing the symptom is mainly a result of the lack of understanding of the system and does nothing to remove the underlying software defects. With this in mind, we can define the debugging process.

---

[1] Brown, William H., et al. *AntiPatterns*. John Wiley & Sons, Inc. New York, New York, 1998.

Debugging

Debugging is the process of understanding the behavior of a system to facilitate the removal of bugs.

When we debug, we seek to remove the root causes of the undesirable behaviors in the system. In order to understand the root causes of the behaviors, we need to understand the system as it is implemented. The keywords here are "understanding" and "as implemented." We need to understand what the system does—not what we think the system should be doing and not what someone else says the system is doing—what the system is actually doing. Furthermore, if we do not understand the system, we cannot hope to modify the system to do what we want it to do. Anything we do to change the behavior of the system runs the risk of breaking something, treating just the symptoms, or introducing more defects.

Debugging is more than a simple process of discovering and correcting software defects in the system. Some bugs are not caused by software defects. Software developers have a tendency to think that every bug can be traced to their codes. In most cases, this is probably true. However, the systems and applications that we build must run in an environment where they coexist with other systems and applications. When something goes wrong, we must put on our problem-solving hats and consider all facets of the problem. A cable could be unplugged and could be causing the system to be unresponsive. Someone could have installed a new and incompatible operating system patch that is causing a stable application to go berserk for no apparent reason. A standard procedure and process could be ignored and be causing a dramatic downtime in an Internet service. In a distributed computing environment, a minor glitch in one component can cause bugs to show up in another seemingly unrelated component. In the distributed computing example from Chapter 2, you saw that an unexpected slow response of the database caused the entire system to become erratic. There were many hidden defects in that system, and it was almost impossible to attempt to fix the bug by simply focusing on one component.

The art and science of debugging that we want to convey in this book addresses all of these aspects. We cover software and implementation related bugs, and we also touch on bugs that result from causes other than software defects. Our aim is to help you understand the causes of bugs so that they can prevent them. In addition, we want to provide you with an arsenal of tips, techniques, and processes to help make your debugging processes more efficient and painless.

Why Worry about Bugs?

We worry about bugs because they are expensive. Bugs cost us money, frustrate and demoralize the people involved, and damage our image and reputation. Of course, we also care about bugs because we are proud; we want to create the best software possible.

I was heading to the post office the other day attempting to buy a money order. When I got there, I noticed that the lights were out. On the door, there was a sign that simply read, "Due to electric outage, we cannot accept cash or credit card transactions." Cash? Credit cards I can understand, but an electric outage that can affect cash transactions is hard to believe. I give them the greenbacks, they give me stamps, what can be simpler? Our society has evolved to become increasingly dependent on technology, especially computer systems. Communications, digital photography and video, financial transactions, computer-based flight control, traffic lights, built-in diagnostics of automobiles, microwaves, and soda machines—everywhere you look, there is a computer (no matter how small) working on your behalf. The cost of the most inopportune bug, at the wrong time and in the wrong place, can have dire consequences. The Y2K bug was but an example of things to come.

In the short history of software, many bugs have directly or indirectly affected our lives.[2] Why worry about bugs? Well, in the extreme case, your life or at least your lifestyle might be at stake. But enough with these scare tactics, let's look at three major reasons why a company might worry about bugs.

Morale Cost of Bugs

One of the most often overlooked costs of bugs relates to the morale of the people involved with the project. Nobody likes to be associated with a shoddy product. We want to be proud of our creations. Perpetual bugs in a software product are an affront to our self-worth. Unchecked, buggy software can and will reduce the morale of the software development team, from project managers to developers and testers to customer service personnel.

Everyone involved in the software industry expects some amount of bugs in their products. In the current environment, a software development team can and does expect to spend the majority of its time dealing with bugs until the second release of its software. However, bugs start to become a demoralizing force when they are unrelenting, especially when you think you have already fixed the bug once, only to see it resurrect itself later. It can get to the point where a single change, even to fix a bug, can cause another bug to appear. When that happens, fatalism sets in, and you start to think there is no escape.

People get tired of dealing with the same problem repeatedly. Developers want to work on something new, something exciting. They want to design the latest cool products using the latest technologies and tools. Customer service personnel get tired of being yelled at for the same product failures over and over. Project managers get tired of harassing the development teams to fix bugs and meet deadlines. Like developers, they want to move on to new and interesting projects. Testers, poor souls, get to watch the bug list grow by the hour. Frustration sets in and running away to another company or to another project becomes a

---

[2] Neumann, Peter G. *Computer Related Risks*. Addison-Wesley Publishing, New York, New York, 1995.
Peterson, Ivars. *Fatal Defect: Chasing Killer Computer Bugs*. Vintage Press, New York, New York, 1995.

very attractive alternative. Fingers start pointing and meetings get longer and longer. None of this makes for a conducive work environment.

The result of a demoralized software development team is low productivity and a high turn-over rate. As any management book can tell you, a demoralized team can end up costing an organization quite a bit of money. Instead of trying to do the job to the best of their abilities, members of a demoralized team will start taking shortcuts so that they won't have to face any problems. Although shortcuts might appear to work in the short term, they tend to be more costly in the long run; new problems are introduced and the symptoms of the existing problems become hidden. Alternatively, a simple problem can drag on for days because no one is interested in working on it. Turnover means that new people must be brought on board, and recruitment costs are rather substantial. New employees need to be trained, and they have lower initial productivity, which also leads to more unnecessary expenses.

Cost of Reputation and Image

The software industry is unique among consumer goods industries—we have trained our customers to accept problems with our products as normal operating procedure. In addition, when we produce defective products, we get to charge customers for patches and fixes. But best of all, we force our customers to sign a license agreement where we don't promise to deliver anything useful, and they can't sue us for damages and liabilities. Is there any incentive for us to worry about how bugs can damage our reputation and image? Of course, thank heavens for competition.

Although consumers have been brainwashed to accept buggy software, it doesn't mean they like it. In January 1999, *PCWorld* reported its survey of users on the subject of buggy software. Among other things, the results showed that "64 percent of users who responded to our survey said they'd buy a software program with few features if it were bug free."[3] This implies that unless consumers are locked into purchasing from a particular vendor, they will search for a competing product that has fewer bugs.

Similar to other organizations, the success of a software organization is influenced by many factors. One of the key forces in a marketing campaign is brand-name reputation. When we think of software packages that manipulate digital images, we think of Adobe PhotoShop. Office products are synonymous with Microsoft Office suites. Quicken is the dominant personal accounting software package. These associations do not come cheaply, and a major gaffe in the product during the early phases of brand-name building can cause irreparable damage. Another key force in the software market is *lock-in*, whereby a customer is locked in to purchasing a product from a particular vendor due to dependencies on data format and familiar interfaces. Achieving lock-in allows a software company some freedom from the consequences of having a poor image.

---

[3] Spanbauer, Scott. "Software Bugs Run Rampant". *PCWorld*, January 1999. **www.pcworld.com/resource/article/asp?aid=8844**.

However, the Internet might be a major force in changing consumers' willingness to accept poor software products and services. If you have an e-commerce site, people are not going to tolerate downtime, poor performance, or missing orders; they'll try another site that sells exactly the same product, but has better services. The barrier to entry in the Internet/e-commerce arena is low and a brand name can only get you so far. There is virtually no concept of lock-in and no reason for consumers to remain loyal to inferior products and services. Once customers leave, the chance of getting them back is slim because they consider your site untrustworthy. The cost to acquire a customer is always more expensive than to retain one. If your business sells e-commerce software to Internet companies, these companies will not tolerate poor quality because it will affect their bottom line.

Prior to the Internet, network security was mainly a concern for giant corporations or military and industrial complexes. Now every mom and pop store has an e-commerce site, and network security has become a critical issue. Potential intruders usually exploit some bugs in the system or codes to gain access to restricted areas. As discussed in Chapter 2, the biggest threat to Internet security is the buffer overflow bug. However, hackers are not the only cause for concern. Internal bugs that may cause the release of private financial information to the wrong people are also of public concern. Additionally, if customers are overcharged or their orders are not accurate, business is lost. For example, if customers want to buy product ABC, and you ship them product XYZ and charge them 10 times as much as you should have, they won't come back again.

Monetary Cost of Bugs

Ultimately, everything leads to money. High employee turnover costs money. Poor image means that a company has to spend more to acquire customers. But even without all these indirect costs, a project with buggy software has a direct impact on an organization's bottom line. It is expensive to run a software project and produce a working system. When the system is buggy, it runs the risk of taking longer than expected. Taking more time than necessary means the product launch is delayed, and more resources are required to complete it. The return on investment of the software project diminishes every day it is delayed. Ultimately, the return on investment approaches zero, and the project is cancelled. However, a bug that escapes the development process and makes it into the real world can make the cost of a cancelled project look like a bargain by comparison.

In 1994, Capers Jones conducted a survey of approximately 4,000 software projects. The survey asked the participants for reasons for schedule overruns. One of the most common reasons reported was poor quality. Furthermore, he also reported that poor quality was implicated in nearly half of all the cancelled projects.[4]

Buggy software is also expensive to maintain. An analysis of 63 development projects and 25 evolution-of-maintenance projects shows that developing reliable software is almost twice

---

[4] Jones, Capers. *Assessment and Control of Software Risks* (*Yourdon Press Computing*). Prentice Hall. Upper Saddle River, NJ, 1994.

as expensive as the minimally reliable software. However, low reliability software was considerably more expensive to maintain than high reliability software.[5]

The cost of bugs in the real world can be astronomical. In order to pacify its customers after the wake of the Pentium bug, Intel agreed to replace all defective chips at a cost of more than $400 million. Development of the automatic baggage handling system for the Denver International Airport has had its share of problems and bugs as well. Originally scheduled to be operational by the end of 1993, the airport did not open until February 1995 because of the bugs in the baggage handling system. Every day the opening was delayed, it cost the airport and the city approximately $1.1 million. Because someone forgot to check the unit conversion in a module, NASA's Mars Climate Orbiter ended up creating another crater on Mars's surface. Couple that with the loss of the Mars Polar Lander, and the return on investment for this project was essentially zero. How much was the investment? Only about $327.6 million. The ultimate cost of software bugs is loss of life, human or otherwise. Therac-25 is the most often cited example—software that was designed to treat patients caused a radiation overdose. Three patients died as a result of this bug.

The Nature of Bugs

Every bug is unique. But every bug is also the same. "Know thy enemy" extols the old adage. In our eternal struggle to keep our programs functional, operational, and useful, our enemies are bugs that keep us glued to our seats. Our enemies come in different clothes. Some bugs are like a nuclear bomb—one detonation leaves your computer useless. Other bugs are subtle; they slowly destroy your weak links, one at a time, until they have rendered your system useless. There are bugs that act like double agents; they present themselves as unexpected useful features that wait for the most opportune moment to betray your trust. Some bugs can easily be prevented with some precaution. Some are easy to produce, but hard to detect. But all bugs share some common characteristics, which we can use to our advantage. Why squash bugs one at a time when you can spray them with chemicals that will wipe out 99 percent in one fell swoop? It works for the exterminators, and it should work for us. How do we create these chemical agents? We start by studying and analyzing the common traits of bugs.

Bugs Happen for a Reason

Despite popular belief, bugs usually don't rear their ugly heads just to make your life difficult. Bugs are also not created by silicon gremlins, as urban legend would have us believe. And unless you are working on space-borne vehicles or ground stations handling satellite transmissions, bugs are usually not caused by random solar flares or by cosmic radiation. On the contrary, bugs are slaves to the system of logic.

---

[5] Boehm, B. W. and Papaccio, P. N. "Understanding and Controlling Software Cost," *IEEE Transactions on Software Engineering*, Vol. 14, No. 10, pp 1462-1477, October 1988.

Software bugs occur within the software. Software runs on computers that execute one instruction at a time (multiple-processor machines not withstanding). A computer makes no assumptions. It does not generalize. It does not hypothesize. It does not make observations. It surely does not deviate from the codes that you have written. It's your slave and your creation. It faithfully follows your instructions to the last letter. If you tell it to leap off a bridge, it will (assuming that you didn't program in a self-preservation module or have a bug in your code). Our problem is that we do not think and act like computers. So oftentimes, the causes of bugs can be mysterious. To be an effective debugger, it would help to have a Vulcan mind. I have always wanted to create an ESP module that would do what I think it should do and not what I have implemented it to do (for the over-40 crowd, this is known as the Do What I Mean [DWIM] command). But until I come up with my creation and make my billions, we will all just have to learn to live in this imperfect world. So let's leave the gremlins out of it.

Bugs Are Reproducible

If bugs happen for a reason, it means that there is a set of causes that are responsible for their manifestation. If we can reproduce the causes, we should be able to reproduce the bugs. Sounds simple, right? If you have been working in the industry for a while, you know it is not always that easy because bug reproduction is more than half of the battle.

Some bugs are definitely a lot harder to reproduce than others. Bugs that seem to be irreproducible only seem that way because we lack the tools to simulate the operating environment and capture the application's input history. Some of the reasons for not being able to reproduce bugs include:

♦ Your customers may be using your products in a way that you were not expecting. When they report a bug, they may fail to include a few important facts about which you didn't think to ask. So you follow their instructions to reproduce the bug, but you are unable to re-create the problem.

♦ Your software could be working in a real-time high volume environment using time-dependent data. You simply cannot afford to capture all the input data just to make sure there isn't a bug. So, if a bug crashes your software, without good diagnostic information, it will be very difficult to reproduce the bug in any convincing way.

♦ You could have a multithread system where timing is everything. If you don't get the exact sequence of input events down with the exact same timing, you can't reproduce the bug. But none of this means the bug is irreproducible. If you want to reproduce the bug, you had better build some scaffolding into your system.

Difficulties encountered trying to reproduce a bug does not mean that it is not reproducible. But sometimes the cost of the reproduction is prohibitive. Other times, we do not understand all the interrelating causes and effects of the system to be able to create a reproducible case. It is often easy to re-create the bug once you have found it and understand it. However, without reproducibility, you will not be able to demonstrate that you know the cause of the bug, and that you have removed it. Without reproducibility, this would be a very short book.

Bugs Usually Manifest Themselves When There Is a Change

There is a strong correlation between the number of changes and enhancements made to a module and the amount of defects in the module. An analysis of a software component consisting of 70,000 lines of code was performed to determine the relationship between several design metrics and the defect level of the software. This study was able to estimate that approximately 0.628 defects were introduced for every change and enhancement made to the software component. [6]

Another study of approximately 1 million lines of executable code from a large telecommunications system lends additional support to the destabilizing effects of code changes. In this study, the authors attempted to determine the effect of reusing software modules on faults. For their system, there are 1,980 functional modules. They found that if there were no changes, they could expect about 0.52 faults on average per module. However, if the reused modules were customized or changed, the fault expectation rose to 1.753. Finally, if a new module was introduced, it was expected to have an average of 2.294 faults. [7]

The basic implication of this study is easy to understand. Changing the code increases the chance of injecting defects, which means it increases the chance of bugs. This implies that bugs are usually in the code that you have written, not in the operating system, kernel, or standard libraries.

Changing requirements and feature creeps are also changes that can affect system stability and the introduction of bugs. Ideally, when a requirement has been changed, designers and developers should sit back and think about the system anew. However, we often only think about the module that the new features can affect and only perform modifications locally without a global perspective. This can break existing interfaces. Oftentimes, requirement changes are introduced without extending the schedule. This means that designers and developers must work under unrealistic time constraints, which forces them to take shortcuts.

Furthermore, software is not static and does not operate in isolation. Disk space could run out, a network cable could be pulled, or another application could compete for the same resources. If you did not program for these environmental changes, you may have a defect waiting to metamorphose into a bug.

Software also interacts with people. People make mistakes, and software systems that do not anticipate and prevent human error are destined to break. For example, people can forget to

---

[6] Kan, Stephen H. *Metrics and Models in Software Quality Engineering.* Addison-Wesley Publishing, Reading, Massachusetts, 1995.

[7] Khoshgoftaar, T. M., et al. "The Impact of Software Evolution and Reuse on Software Quality," *Empirical Software Engineering*, Vol. 1, No. 1, pp 31–44, 1996.

re-index a database after new data has been inserted, so the database queries might take 10 times as long to run. A system whose architecture relies on a speedy database would all of a sudden find itself in trouble. The root cause would be the unindexed database, and for all intents and purposes, it's not really the fault of the software (other than the fact that the architecture is not sufficiently fault tolerant). But that won't prevent you, as the software developer on the system, from been called at three in the morning to fix the "bug."

Bugs Beget Bugs

We often joke that when we upgrade our software or download a patch to fix an existing bug, we are really trading bugs that we know with bugs that we don't know. Jokes aside, there are compelling quantitative experiments and personal anecdotal evidence that suggest that when you change the code, you run the risk of introducing more bugs into the software. When you debug a system, you introduce changes to the system. Because bugs thrive in a changing environment, the chance that you have introduced or uncovered a bug when you try to fix the system is pretty darn good. Anecdotal evidence suggests that the probability of introducing one or more additional "errors" while attempting to fix an "error" is estimated to range from 15 to 50 percent, depending on the situation.[8]

This further suggests that in large programs, the chance of introducing a severe "error" during the correction of an original "error" is large enough so that only a small fraction of the original "errors" should be corrected.

Another way bugs beget bugs is through the tendency of problematic pieces of software to remain problematic. If you have ever worked on a piece of code or a module that just refused to be fixed despite the number of man-hours and extreme amount of effort that were poured into it, you know exactly what we mean. A study of a set of modules with 70,000 lines of code showed that the previous defect level of a module can be a good predictor for the current defect level of the same module.[9] In other words, there is a strong correlation between the previous defect level and the current defect level in the evolution of a software module.

Bugs Attract Bugs

If bugs have a tendency to produce other bugs, it stands to reason that when you fix a bug in a module, you may introduce another bug in the same module. After a while, these modules become known as fault-prone modules. It is sometimes easier and cheaper to employ scorched earth techniques to eliminate these bugs by simply eliminating their habitats (i.e., redesign and reimplement the entire module).

---

[8] Adams, Edward N. "Optimizing Preventing Service of Software Products," IBM *Journal of Research and Development*, Vol. 28, No. 1, pp 2-14, January 1984.

[9] Kan, Stephen H. *Metrics and Models in Software Quality Engineering*. Addison-Wesley Publishing, Reading, Massachusetts, 1995.

A study of a military command, control, and communications system written using Ada with 282 modules shows that 20 percent of the modules contain 80 percent of the faults in the entire system. Furthermore, 5 percent of the modules contain 42.5 percent of the faults, and 52 percent of the modules contain no faults.[10]

There is evidence that suggests that 20 percent of the problems and bugs account for 80 percent of the total cost of fixing bugs.[11] This might be like comparing apples to oranges, but let's work with the numbers from these two studies as a simple mental exercise to see what the monetary cost of fault-prone modules is. If 5 percent of the modules contain 42.5 percent of the problems and 20 percent of the problems account for 80 percent of the cost, then we can estimate that the cost of fixing these modules will be more than 80 percent of the total cost. Buggy software modules can be expensive.

Bugs Demonstrate a Lack of Understanding

Can you solve a problem that you don't understand? Can you write a program to solve a problem that you don't understand? No and no? Good, then we are in agreement. If you answered yes to either of these two questions, we won't dispute your answers. But the questions we would raise are *(1)* How complete and correct are your solutions? and *(2)* Are you sure you are solving the original problem, or are you solving the problem that you have rationalized and reformulated from the incomplete understanding?

A study of the open source software process (The Apache Group) suggested that one of the potential reasons that open source releases had fewer defects than comparable commercial products is that open source developers are also users of the software they write. Hence, they have the domain knowledge of the problem they are working to solve.[12]

Our common sense tells us that this is a reasonable hypothesis and matches our experiences. Knowing the problem that you are trying solve and actually using the products that you are creating help you produce better solutions.

As software developers, we are constantly being asked to program for something we don't fully comprehend, and the time for comprehension is never factored into the process. So the design is changed in the middle of the project, existing requirements are changed, and new requirements are introduced. Is there any wonder that software has bugs?

Can you recall the first program you ever wrote? We try not to remember ours because they are embarrassing. When we were novices, a simple program took 10 times as long to write as it should have. We also made the stupidest mistakes and took forever to track down the bugs, all because we were not familiar with the programming language. The 1990 AT&T

[10] Khoshgoftaar, T. M., and Allen, E. B. "A Comparative Study of Ordering and Classification of Fault Prone Software Modules," *Empirical Software Engineering*, Vol. 4, No. 2, pp 159–185, 1999.

[11] Boehm, B. W., and Papaccio, P. N. "Understanding and Controlling Software Cost," *IEEE Transactions on Software Engineering*, Vol. 14, No. 10, October 1988, pp 1462–1477.

[12] Mockus, A., Fielding, R. T., and Herbsleb, J. "A Case Study of Open Source Software Development: The Apache Server," *Proceedings of the 2000 International Conference on Software Engineering*, Limerick, Ireland, pp 263–272, June 4–11, 2000.

telephone system outage had its root cause in an incorrectly placed `break` statement because the programmer was not familiar with the language construct. The following code illustrates another classic beginner's mistake in a typical C++ class definition:

```
1.Class ABuggyClass {
2.    public:
3.ABuggyClass();
4.ABuggyClass( const ABuggyClass src );
5.       virtual ~ABuggyClass();
6.       private:
7.       int SomeIntMemberVariable;
8.       };
```

Do you see the problem? Can you predict how the bug will manifest itself and what the symptoms will be? There is a simple fix, but unless you really understand how C++ works, you won't see it or understand it. You'll just stare at all the clues and will probably blame the bug on the compiler anyway. Everything else you do, aside from implementing the correct fix, will just fix the symptoms, not the cause.

Note

The copy constructor needs to get the input argument by reference, not by source. Therefore, the correct fix is:

```
ABuggyClass( const ABuggyClass &src );
```

Otherwise, the bug manifests itself as a recursive call to the copy constructor until the stack overflows and you run out of memory. Why that happens is an exercise left for the reader.

But even if you are a 20-year veteran, when you walk blindfolded into a system with 10,000 lines of code, you will still have a problem making the correct modifications. It is hard to make changes to an existing system when you don't comprehend it. You would worry about introducing bugs because you have no idea how the modifications you make would impact the rest of the system. To remedy the situation and start becoming familiar with the code, you would look for documentation, look for people who wrote the original codes, and ask a lot of questions. You need to understand how the module that you are changing interacts with the rest of the system.

Hard Codes Are Hard to Write. No Matter What!

One technique for creating fault-tolerant software is the practice of N-Version Programming (NVP).[13]

---

[13] Chen, L., and Avizienis, A. "N-Version Programming: A Fault-Tolerance Approach to Reliability of Software Operation," *Proceedings of the Eighth Annual International Conference on Fault-Tolerant Computing*, Toulouse, France, pp 3–9, June 1978.

In NVP, multiple teams of programmers are created. Each team is given the same specification and is asked to create a system from the specification independent of each other. The hypothesis behind NVP is that if each team develops the system independently, mistakes and errors made by one team might not be made by the other teams. Another premise is that if the software created by independent teams can be combined, the results from combined software should be more robust than the independently created versions.

Many experiments evaluated the effectiveness of NVP. These experiments suggested that the assumption that errors are made independently is invalid. In one of the experiments, 27 independently prepared versions of the software from the same specification were subjected to one million test cases. Independently, each of these 27 versions of the software had a reliability of over 99 percent, with 26 versions having a reliability of over 99.77 percent. The result of the experiments showed that there were 1,255 test cases (out of one million) where more than one version of the software failed. At the worst end of the spectrum, there were 2 test cases in which 8 of the 27 failed. On the surface, 1,255 out of one million cases seems rather low; however, each version had a reliability of over 99 percent. This means that independently, each version had at most 10,000 errors. In reality, only 4 versions had more than 1,000 failures. With this in mind, 1,255 common errors appears to be rather significant. Modeling the probability of independent failures, the authors of the report were able to demonstrate that the hypothesis of independence of failures can be rejected at the 99 percent confidence level for the particular problem that was programmed in the experiment.[14]

In the mid-1980s, Boeing 777s were developed. For its flight control software, Boeing decided to use NVP in an effort to produce a more reliable system. Three independent groups of developers were asked to create software from the same requirements, and three different programming languages were used: Ada, C, and PL/M. It turned out that the independently written programs tended to have problems in the same area. What is difficult to write for one person is also difficult for another, even when using different programming languages. In the end, Boeing abandoned NVP and refocused its resources on the more difficult areas of the system.[15]

It also appears that certain programming languages do have some impact on faults. Highly structured and strongly typed languages, such as Ada, have fewer defects, whereas low-level assembly languages have more defects. But the choice of languages does not seem to affect the common defects that are specification or design related faults.[16]

Similar bugs are created regardless of the choice of languages.

---

[14] Knight, J.C., Leveson, N. G., and St. Jean, L. D. "A Large-Scale Experiment in N-Version Programming," *Proceedings of the Fifteenth Annual International Symposium on Fault Tolerant Computing*, Ann Arbor, Michigan, pp 135–139, June 19–21.

[15] Joch, Alan. "How Software Doesn't Work," *BYTE*, December 1995.

[16] Bishop, P. G. "Review of Software Diversity," *Software Fault Tolerance*, M. Lyu (ed.). John Wiley & Sons, Inc. 1995.

If different people solving the same problem using the same specifications produce the same kind of bugs, the implication is that:

◆ The specification itself is ambiguous and problematic.

◆ We all tend to make similar implementation or design errors in the same place.

Either way, the hard part of the code can be difficult because it is difficult to implement, or it can be hard because it is difficult to specify. No matter what the reason, it just means that we all tend to make the same mistakes.

Bugs Created in Different Stages of the Software Life Cycle Have Different Characteristics

A typical software development cycle follows four distinct stages: requirements, design, implementation, and test. Bugs can be introduced and created at every stage. In one study, it was found that the majority of defects (more than 65 percent) were introduced during the implementation stage, as shown in Table 3.1.[17] However, another study of a product that contained 1.5 million lines of code produced a significantly different result, as shown in Table 3.2.[18]

It isn't clear what the causes of the differences are. Our speculation is that this is a result of different fault detection and counting techniques as well as the differences in the problem domain. This discrepancy merely showed us the difficulty in producing universally meaningful statistics and metrics for empirical software engineering studies. However, these two studies do provide additional insights into bugs and their relationship with the software life cycle.

Table 3.1 shows that the average time required to fix a defect is significantly longer during the early stage of the development cycle than near the end. This implies that it is more expensive to fix a requirement bug than it is to fix an implementation bug. This result

Table 3.1   Defect Introduction and Cost of Fixing the Defects Introduced.

Phase Introduced	Project #1		Project #2	
	% Defects Introduced	Average Fix Time	% Defects Introduced	Average Fix Time
Requirements/Specifications	-	-	3	575 hours
Design	20	315 hours	15	235 hours
Implementation	75	80 hours	65	118 hours
Test	5	46 hours	17	74 hours

---

[17] Grady, R.B. *Practical Software Metrics for Project Management and Process Improvement*. Prentice Hall PTR, Englewood Cliffs, New Jersey, 1992.

[18] Gilb, T. *Principles of Software Engineering Management*. The Bath Press, Avon, Great Britain, 1988.

Table 3.2   Type of Errors Introduced at Different Phases of the Life Cycle.

Stage of the Development Cycle	Total Number of Defects	% Missing	% Wrong	% Extra
Requirements	203	63	34	3
Development Plans	451	61	33	6
Product Specifications	1627	56	40	4
Design Specifications	503	53	39	8
Alpha Test Plans	472	71	26	3
Beta Test Plans	290	51	39	10
Code Listings	228	26	45	29

confirms the earlier observations reported, where the cost of fixing or reworking software is about 50 to 200 times higher in the earlier stages of the software development cycle than in the later phase.[19]

The implication here is obvious. It pays to prevent requirement and design bugs. At the minimum, early detection and correction of requirement and design bugs will pay heavy dividends.

Table 3.2 suggests that the majority of errors introduced in the requirement and design stage are due to missing requirements, missing features, or missing specifications. The majority of errors introduced during the implementation stage can be categorized as wrong, so the problem is an incorrect implementation. Surprisingly (or not), 29 percent of errors in the implementation stage are categorized as extra, meaning that the implementers added extra features to the product. These extra features introduce additional complexity to the system for developers and users, and they have the potential to ruin the conceptual integrity of the product and require extra efforts. They can be potential problems for both the users and the maintainers. [20]

Causes of Bugs in a Stable System Can Be Harder to Identify than Those in a Buggy System

When you create a system from scratch, it tends to be buggy. As the software evolves, you fix bugs along the way, and the system becomes more stable. Eventually, the software is sent to the testers; they find more bugs, and you fix those bugs. The software then goes into production. Hallelujah. Two weeks after the initial release, you get a constant stream of bug reports, so you work diligently to remove the bugs. Slowly but surely, the number of bug reports dwindles, and the system becomes increasingly trustworthy. You think you can finally put this project behind you and move on. The system goes into production for six

---

[19] Boehm, B. W., and Papaccio, P. N. "Understanding and Controlling Software Cost," *IEEE Transactions on Software Engineering*, Vol. 14, No. 10, October 1988, pp 1462–1477.
[20] ibid.

months and everything goes well. All of a sudden, the whole system crashes, and you scramble to find the problem. Just another day in the life of a software engineer, right?

When you are creating the system, you typically use a debugger or built-in diagnostic information that can help you find your bugs. In the middle of development, you are intimately familiar with the codes and the system that you are developing, so bugs are easy to find.

Once you release the system to the testers, you lose some of those built-in help utilities. But the amount of your efforts should not increase too much during this time because you have access to the machine the testers are using to perform the tests, and you can talk to the testers to see exactly what they are doing, so that you can reproduce the bug. You might also still have some auxiliary debugging tools hooked up, so the system can continue to produce detailed logging, or the testers might be running the debugging version of the system, and the debuggers can still be used. The software should still be fresh in your mind at this point, so bugs should not be a big deal at this juncture.

When the software is released to the real world, you might still be uneasy about its stability, so you leave some debugging aids in the system to help you if the needed arises. But when users report a bug, you no longer have direct access to users to interview them and work with them to reproduce the bug. In addition, the system that the software is running on is probably different than your machine. You start losing touch with the software, and bugs become infrequent and harder to isolate.

Once you think everything is rosy, and you start to remove the aids that help you find the bugs and track the system, problems become much more difficult. Furthermore, at this point, you are not as familiar with the product as you once were. Comments in the code don't make as much sense as they used to, and you need to relearn the system again in order to figure out what the problems might be. Bugs at this stage are typically very obscure and hard to trigger. Bug reproduction becomes difficult. Most of the bugs described in Chapter 2 are bugs that were reported within a stable system. Table 3.3 summarizes the tools that are available and the efforts required to find a bug in software with different maturity levels.

We tend not to trust a buggy system, so we leave tools in those systems to help us find bugs. Furthermore, because we are usually working within the software fixing bugs, we become familiar with the system and can find causes of bugs faster. On the other hand, a stable

Table 3.3 Efforts to Debug Software at various maturity levels.

Bugs Reported During...	Amount of Effort to Identify Causes	Tools to Aid Identification
Development	Low	Debugger, tracing, logs familiarity with codes
Testing	Low-medium	Similar system? Debugger? Tracing? Logs? Familiarity with codes
Initial Release	Medium	Debugger? Tracing? Log?
Stable System	High	Logs?

system requires no intervention from developers, so we pay no attention to it. We turn off or remove debugging aids because they interfere with system performance. But when something does go wrong, it becomes very difficult to track down bugs. Ironic, isn't it? Stability has its price.

Summary

Our analysis of bugs thus far has provided us with some interesting findings:

♦ A software defect is produced when we make a mistake in specifying, building, designing, or implementing a system.

♦ When defects exist in the software system, the system can exhibit undesirable behaviors.

♦ Bugs are undesirable behaviors of the software that we agree should be removed.

♦ Debugging is the process of identifying and correcting root causes of bugs.

♦ Bugs are not random or mythical events. Bugs are reproducible, but some bugs may be almost impossible to reproduce.

♦ Bugs thrive and reproduce in a changing environment.

♦ People tend to create the same bugs given the same problem.

♦ Bugs created at different stages of the software development processes have different characteristics.

♦ Bugs are created because we don't understand the specifications or the language constructs.

♦ Bug-prone modules contain most of the bugs in the system, and consume most of the debugging efforts and resources. But it can be difficult to find bugs in a stable system.

A cursory examination of these observations suggests many potential methods for preventing and identifying bugs. These findings will serve as a basis for many of the techniques and processes that are presented in this book. However, there is still quite a bit we don't know about bugs. Why do we create bugs? How do we create bugs? And how do we let bugs slip through testing? In the next chapter, we continue with the analysis of bugs. Now that we have some understanding of bugs, we are ready to ask more revealing questions, which will help us formulate strategies so that we can write better software.

Bug Puzzle

The instant messenger that was described in the introduction of this chapter also has another peculiar behavior. The instant message lets you send universal resource locators (URLs) to your friend on the other end. Your friend is able to click on the URL, as it has appeared, and displays the web page defined by the URL that you have sent. This instant messenger runs on the Windows environment, and some times, when you click on the link, the browser is invoked to display the web page. Some other times, the instant messenger hangs, and become unresponsive. It is also possible to locking up the entire machine by clicking on the URL. Sometime, only the browser is confused and become unresponsive. Other times, the instant messenger disappears after you have selected the URL. What can be the problem?

Chapter 4

Life Cycle of a Bug

Yuan Hsieh

"How can I be so stupid?" My cubicle neighbor exploded one morning after a stressful 18-hour day and night and day of tracking down a bug in the production system. His nerves were wired with caffeinated drinks, his eyes bloodshot, and his desk covered with a fine layer of hair that he had pulled out of his already balding head. "What in the world was I thinking?" He groaned and furiously typed away to fix the bug and release the patch. Later in the morning, before collapsing out of sheer exhaustion, he reported the bug and the solution to the project manager. Upon hearing it, she shook her head and said, "How could this bug possibly pass through our test department?" Bewildered, she continued, "Do they actually test anything?"

Is this a familiar scene? I have uttered those exact words at one point or another in my career as a software engineer. The sentiment of the hapless developer and the bewildered manager are surely not unique. But the questions remain unanswered. Why are bugs created? How are bugs created? And how do bugs slip through testing?

Why Are Bugs Created?

Bugs are created every day by each and every one of us. It seems as though we spend most of our working days dealing with bugs in one form or another. "To err is human," the ancient proverb advised. As software professionals, we err far too often. Why?

Complexity

We err because human thought processes are inadequate for dealing with complex systems and temporal interactions. Studies of human planning and decision-making processes have demonstrated the difficulty people have in dealing with complex problems.[1]

But what is complexity? Complexity can be linked to the number of interdependent variables in a system. Many variables and more interdependency between these variables in a system imply a more complex system.

Are software programs complex? It is possible for a 59-line program to have up to 36,000 unique execution paths for all possible inputs. Most of us are unable to plan for and consider these kinds of combinations, and when was the last time our code was only 59 lines? A modern day program starts at 100,000 lines of code or more; Windows 2000 has about 36 million lines of codes. Try to imagine all the possible code paths such a program could take and anticipate all the things that could go wrong. This is a difficult task for any human being, and it doesn't get any easier with more people.

In software engineering, complexity exists at multiple levels. The problem itself can be complex, which makes it difficult for the problem solvers to understand and consider all the variables or factors involved. A complex problem also makes it difficult to communicate the requirements clearly. The solutions to the problem can be complex, which means that it might be difficult to choose and implement a robust solution and, once a solution has been implemented, difficult to maintain and support that solution. Tools that are used to implement the solution can be complex, and that makes it difficult to use the tools effectively and correctly. Communication among team members can also be complex. How do you disseminate information efficiently and correctly? How do you coordinate efforts and interfaces? How do you deal with diverse personalities and political agendas? Additionally, the software development process can be complex and become a source of bugs.

Problem Complexity

A few years ago, I was working for a contracting company doing work for a major corporation. I was assigned to a project to develop software that recommended product packages to customers. The idea behind the software project sounded really simple. The corporation sold numerous products and services. Some of these products and services could be combined into packages, and the salesperson could attempt to recommend the package to a customer who was only looking for individual products. The software was supposed to consider the customer profile, evaluate a list of packages, and inform the salesperson of which package was appropriate for up-sale. You run into this situation almost every day. For example, you go to a random fast food restaurant looking only for a hamburger and a soda. But once you walk into the store, you see that for only 99 cents more you can buy a combo-meal that includes not only a hamburger and a soda, but also some french fries.

---

[1] Dörner, Dietrich. *The Logic of Failure.* Addison-Wesley, Reading Massachusetts, 1997.

The concept sounded very simple; after all, this type of occurrence is part of our daily lives. It happens everyday, and it happens everywhere. But trying to codify all these marketing rules was simply a nightmare. There were just too many rules and too many exceptions to the rules, which made it difficult to create an agreeable requirement. Product A could be combined with product B only if the customer already had product C. A customer could not buy product D if he lived in a particular area except if he already was a premier club member of the company. I could go on and on with all the seemingly contradictory business rules. No one could agree on what the precedent of the rules were, and no one even seemed to be able to grasp all the existing rule sets, not to mention all the possible rule sets. A marketing person from one part of the country wanted things one way, another marketing person from a different part of the company wanted things a different way. No one understood the problem that we were hired to solve, not even the customers who wanted the software product. To make matters worse, this major corporation had three legacy systems that contained customer information, four other systems that stored various product and package information, and no one knew where we could retrieve all the required information. We spent months working out the requirements. Eventually, the customer saw the difficulty of the situation and killed the project out of mercy.

Note

The lesson that I learned from this project is, never try to solve a marketing problem with software. Human minds are simply too creative to be limited by a set of algorithms.

What makes a problem complex? A problem is complex when there are more variables or factors that can affect the problem than we can comfortably handle. In 1956, George A. Miller observed that the human mind is only capable of handling approximately seven concepts at one time.[2]

This suggests that we will have difficulty with a problem that requires us to deal with more than seven variables or factors simultaneously. How can we tell if a software project is too complex? The following partial list of symptoms might help you identify a complex problem.

♦ *A requirements document that has more than a few pages*—If we can only deal with seven pieces of information (in this case, seven requirements) at one time, and the requirement document has more than seven items, a few requirements will be dropped when we are pondering the solution. Dropping requirements either intentionally or unintentionally is not a good way to reduce the complexity because the requirements that were dropped always find their way back at a later time. If a requirement was dropped unintentionally, it meant that you have forgotten about it, and the dropped requirement will ultimately become a bug. But even if a requirement was intentionally dropped, you run the chance of not incorporating the requirement into the design. This can become a self-inflicted feature creep when the dropped requirement resurfaces again at a later time.

---

[2] Miller, George A. "The Magical Number Seven, Plus or Minus Two: Some Limits on our capacity for Processing Information," *Psychological Review*, Vol. 63, pp 81–97, 1956.

♦ *Ever-changing requirements*—If the requirement changes constantly, it becomes obvious that the customers themselves have no clear understanding of their needs, and the problem is too complex. If customers understand what they want, they should not have problems clearly stating their requirements. The fact that they have to come back to you to give you new requirements usually means that they have dropped a few desired features. Why? Because they too are limited by their mental capacity of seven pieces of information.

♦ *Nonstop question-and-answer sessions*—If developers are constantly going back to the project management or requirement analysts asking them what the developers should do if this or that scenario happened, the problem is too complex. This usually means the requirement is incomplete, and the major reason for incomplete requirements is the complexity of the problem.

These three criteria seem to fit the bill on every software development project that I have been associated with. Is there anything that we can do to reduce and manage complex problems? Of course! We do it all the time in our normal day-to-day problem solving endeavors. In cognitive psychology, the concept of "chunking" is used to explain how people break a complex problem down into manageable pieces. Also, complexity is a subjective measure. We learn from our experiences. Our experiences form a gestalt, where a number of variables can be compressed into one. When we reduce the number of variables we must consider, we reduce the complexity. For a professional figure skater, the task of skating is no more complicated than walking down a street. For a novice, balancing on two blades without falling is a nontrivial task. As we get better at a problem, it becomes less complex. We can find ways to reduce the perceived complexity of the problem. In Chapter 12, we present some ideas on how you can reduce the complexity of software engineering problems.

Solution Complexity

Unfortunately, complex solutions often accompany complex problems. Internet commerce systems pose complex problems. Not only does an Internet commerce system have to implement the business logic of selling and shipping products, it also has to deal with security, performance, and volume. The system has to handle a potentially tremendous number of transactions while maintaining some minimum performance criteria 24 hours a day, 7 days a week.

So what did we come up with to solve the problems posed by Internet commerce systems? The solution was a multithreaded distributed computer system, which is about as complex as you can get in traditional software engineering without involving embedded systems or parallel computers. Multithreaded applications are notoriously difficult to debug and implement due to timing and synchronization issues. They are also difficult because it is difficult for developers and debuggers to visualize all the possible states of the system in any given instance. Distributed computing brings forth the idea of having a large number of computers working in conjunction with one another and introduces the concept of "systems engineering" to the purely software world. Not only do software engineers have to worry about bugs in an application running on a single computer, we also have to worry about bugs that are potentially caused by interactions between computers. We have to learn to do the job of system engineers in the traditional sense without the training or the background. Issues like fail-over, redundancy, fault tolerance, scalability, and survivability all become problems that we have to contend with. There are simply a lot more interdependent variables (the number of computers, for example) that must be factored into our solutions.

If architectural decisions can introduce complexity into a solution, so can design solutions. A study of Ada program design showed that *context coupling* measure of a design strongly correlates to the number of defects.[3]

What is context coupling? Two software modules are contextually coupled when they need to interface with each other. For example, one software module calls the functions or methods within another software module, or one module uses resources in another module. If we can assume software modules are variables in a software system, increasing context coupling measure of the system implies an increasing number of interdependencies between system variables. From our definition of complexity, we can conclude that increasing design complexity is more likely to increase the number of defects and failures.

There have been many other attempts to measure the design complexity of a software system and show how these measures correlate to the number of defects in a software system. Line of code is the simplest metric. One complexity measure that has withstood the test of time thus far is McCabe's cyclomatic complexity measure.[4]

Originally proposed in 1976, the cyclomatic complexity metric measures the number of decision paths in a software system. Many other proposed complexity measures exist. However, regardless of how software complexity is measured, all these studies support a similar conclusion: Increasing complexity will increase the number of defects.[5]

Again, in Chapter 12, we discuss some techniques that will help you reduce and manage complexities that might arise from your solutions.

Tool Complexity

After devising a complex solution to deal with a complex problem, let's choose a tool that is difficult to use. All sarcasm aside, tools to aid software engineers have gotten better in one aspect, but worse in other aspects. Development of high-order languages, such as Ada, Java, Visual Basic, and C++, are significantly easier to use than the assembly languages of yore. Code generation tools, such as C++Builder, reduce the pain of creating tedious code by hand. Reuse of commercial off-the-shelf software products, such as database servers (Oracle,

[3] Agresti, W. W., and W. M. Evanco. "Projecting Software Defects From Analyzing Ada Designs," *IEEE Transactions on Software Engineering*, Vol. 18, No. 11, pp 988–997, November 1992.

[4] McCabe, T. J. "A Complexity Measure," *IEEE Transactions on Software Engineering*, Vol. 2, No. 4, pp 308–320, December 1976.

[5] Arthur, L. J. *Rapid Evolutionary Development: Requirements, Prototyping & Software Creation*. John Wiley & Sons, Inc., pp. 41–47, 1992.

Putnam, L. H., and W. Myers. *Measures for Excellence: Reliable Software on Time, within Budget*. Prentice-Hall Inc., Englewood Cliffs, New Jersey, pp. 6–25, 1992.

Informix), middleware (Enterprises Resource Planning Systems), and class libraries (Microsoft Foundation Classes, Rogue Wave's Tools classes, Java Foundation Classes, Java Swing Toolkit API), reduce the need to reinvent the wheel. Configuration management and bug tracking tools help us manage the evolution of our software products. Debuggers help us pinpoint source the of bugs. These tools are beneficial and have helped us become more productive.

But one detail that is not often discussed in the software industry is the trade-off of using these tools. We agree that if properly used, these tools can and do improve productivity, and they pay for themselves in the long run. However, we have found that there are rarely any serious discussions regarding the nonmonetary cost of these tools. At a minimum, with every tool that we have chosen, it costs us to learn it. Not only do we need to learn how to use it, but we also need to learn its strengths and weaknesses. In addition, we need to learn the right time and the right place for using these tools. Placing your blind faith on marketing brochures is a sure way to court disasters.

There are many training classes that teach you how to write C++ or Java code, or how to be a certified engineer of one vendor's tool or another. However, none of these classes ever bother to compare one tool to another, nor reveal the potential pitfalls of using a particular tool. These classes mainly concentrate on one thing, which is how to use the tool. We believe that understanding the benefits and risks of every tool would do wonders to help us with our daily tasks.

Debuggers are great for finding certain classes of bugs, but as we will illustrate in Chapter 7, they have their own quirks; they can change the behavior of the software that you are attempting to debug. As if your software is not complex enough, the use of a debugger adds another level of variables, which you must consider when evaluating the debugger's results. If you rely on debuggers to fix all your bugs, sooner or later you will encounter a bug that cannot be repaired by the debugger.

Off-the-shelf software products, such as database servers and enterprise resource planning (ERP) systems, provide a lot of prebuilt functionalities that would be expensive to develop from scratch. However, these products tend to be all things to all people, which forces them to sacrifice simplicity for flexibility. They are notoriously difficult to configure, fine tune, and maintain. Because these systems also tend to be proprietary and are used as a black box, when there is a bug, it can be difficult to isolate the root causes. If these systems are not complex, why do we pay the database administrators and ERP system consultants such high salaries? Other off-the-shelf products, such as class libraries, fare no better in terms of reducing complexities. Class libraries force you to subscribe to their framework and philosophy. They frequently force you to use their package entirely, or not at all. This is not a problem if you understand the framework and philosophy behind their design. However, if you don't agree with the vision of the class libraries, you will most likely be trying to force a square peg into a round hole. Graphical user interface (GUI) builders are very good at prototyping graphical interfaces in no time at all. A few clicks here, a drag and drop there, and voilà, you have yourself a dialog box. That's great—until you have a bug. Then you will have to analyze code that you did not write, try to decipher classes and functions that you never knew existed, and try to figure out exactly how the code works. Have you ever tried to create a COM component using Visual C++'s COM wizard? When you are trying to create a COM object with one interface, it's easy. But when you want to do more with COM, which is usually necessary, the wizard becomes totally useless. This is another problem with code builders. Sometimes they don't do everything for you, and as a result, you have to tweak autogenerated code here and add a class definition there to get it to work correctly. When you want to do something the manufacturer of the code builders didn't want you to do, the complexity of the job increases. Not only do you have to understand how to do the original task, you also have to understand what the code builder will and won't do for you and how to work around its limitations.

Discussion of comparative programming languages can be compared to an intense holy war. We will refrain from engaging in one, lest this book become a 2,000 page tome. But suffice it to say that each programming language has its benefits and drawbacks. Therefore, in your design, you should leverage the strengths of the language as much as possible and design the software to reduce exposure to the drawbacks of the language. For example, Java's garbage collection mechanism is a boon to developers. Garbage collection releases them from the worries of dangling pointers, corrupted memory spaces, and memory leaks. On the flip side, resource leaking in Java becomes harder to find, and of course, the garbage collection introduces some inefficiencies. Resource leaks in Java occur when you forget to descope an object. For example, if you create an object to hold an array of a set of elements and don't explicitly remove the elements from the array, the element might never be deallocated. Resource leaks in Java also occur in global static classes; therefore, care should be taken when designing and using a Singleton pattern.

Furthermore, Java's garbage collection algorithm is very efficient; however, it can also be executed at the most inopportune time, and using Java can pose a risk to real-time systems.

Note

This might be true as of this writing. Java is always evolving and changing, so it is hard to stay up-to-date on its performance specification and features. Although this always makes Java new and exciting, the constant evolution also makes the language more complex. Questions such as, which JDK am I using? which JAR is installed? and how can I tell? demonstrate additional complexity involved in using the language.

There are many other examples, and our goal is not to degrade software tools. Under the proper circumstances and processes, they can greatly enhance the quality of productivity and the quality of your work. We merely want to point out the potential trade-off when using these tools, so that you can think about these issues and decide which tools make sense for you to use on your project and determine the risks that you might encounter and mitigate if you choose a particular tool set.

People Complexity

People complexity is not a factor in software projects that are done by a single person. However, one-person projects are rare. A typical software project involves a project manager, a technical lead, a group of developers, and a few testers. All of these people must learn to communicate with each other and work with each other. The project manager needs to communicate the problem, the requirements, and the objectives of the project to the team. The testers need to understand the problem that the software is trying to solve, so they can test for the right behavior. The development team must communicate with each other so that all of their pieces can be integrated and function together as a unit.

Communication is a problem in any engineering discipline. However, the problem is exacerbated in the software world. Software engineering, as a discipline, does not have a standard "blueprint" language that we can share with each other to clearly communicate the tasks and design at hand. The advent of design patterns and unified modeling language (UML) have helped to alleviate some of the communication problems. However, they have not solved the problem, and they bring their own trappings as well. The most precise and accurate language that we have for communication, unfortunately, is the programming language itself. Can we use a programming language to help us communicate? The answer to that is yes, and we explore the possibilities in Chapter 12.

People might choose to make a project complex for a variety of reasons. Sometimes, the reason might even be "altruistic." The project manager might be too willing in his work and accept every requirement change or feature addition that is requested because he believes it is for the good of the company, and the entire team suffers for it. We have all heard at one time or another that a particular feature must be implemented immediately, or it's the end of civilization as we know it. Even though the feature might take 10 months to implement, the company still wants it done in 2 weeks.

Increased complexity can also come from opinionated and outspoken members of the technical team. These people might throw a monkey wrench into the project because they are egotistic, and any solution that doesn't meet their approval is considered wrong.

There are also people that want to make the problem and project complex just to meet their own personal political agendas. Unwitting software project members are usually just in the wrong place at the wrong time. What are the incentives for a department to make your job any easier if you are writing software that will replace half of them? Consequently, members of the team you are replacing make the project as difficult for you as possible. They change requirements on you all the time. They withhold resources and don't answer questions.

Everyone in the industry talks about the importance of documentation. But what's the incentive for the development team to write documentation? Why do they want to make themselves replaceable? What do they gain by spending time writing documentation that they know no one will read when the company doesn't give them a reasonable amount of time to write it?

Note

There are millions of reasons why someone might want to make your life difficult. Sometimes, these reasons are not personal, but other times they are. You might think these issues are somewhat tangential to a book on bugs and debugging. They may not directly help you fix your bugs; however, understanding these issues might help you understand why the system that you have inherited is the way it is and help you determine what your options might be. Occasionally, the root causes of the bug might not have anything to do with the codes that you are looking at. The cause of the bug might be your project manager, it might be your coworkers, or it might be the company culture itself. Are you willing to fix the bug (can you?), or are you content to just treat the symptoms? Early recognition of these facts can save you a lot of grief later on.

Process Complexity

One day, we were upgrading our Web servers in the production site when all hell broke loose. Everything started breaking, and even rolling back the changes didn't seem to help. After about two hours of frenetic head pounding, we were able to isolate the problem to a JAR file that was supposed to have been deleted. The roll back script didn't remove the JAR file because it didn't know it was supposed to be removed. The installation script also didn't know of the JAR file's existence, so it couldn't alert anyone to the fact that the system had been contaminated with a foreign library.

Shared libraries, dynamic-link libraries (DLLs), and JAR files are meant to make it easier to distribute new software. One advantage of these DLLs is smaller executable size. Because the libraries are not compiled into the executable itself, the executable is smaller. However, the presence of these libraries is still necessary; so, the overall size difference is not dramatic, if the DLLs are used only by a single executable. But by separating the libraries and the executables, it is now possible to share the library across multiple executables, so that two or more executables can use the same set of libraries and the overall size of the executables can be reduced. Another advantage of using DLLs is that upgrading and changing the software becomes upgrading and changing the libraries. Instead of replacing the entire program, you only need to replace a specific library module. Furthermore, if the update is a bug fix, all other programs that use the module will benefit from the fixes as well.

But the flip side is that if you don't have a good process for controlling software releases, you can break your software system with the same ease as updating DLLs. Configuration management of binaries is as important as configuration management of the source code and is not a simple task. Just the other day, I was attempting to use Java's XML parser. Every time I tried to compile my code, I ran into an error that told me that a method for the class that I was using did not exist. But the method was defined in the Javadoc, and when I disassembled the class object, the method was there. I pulled my hair out for a while, and then started to eliminate variables in the CLASSPATH until I was able to compile the code. It turned out that I had a different version of the package under the CLASSPATH setting, and this package did not have the method defined. If this had occurred in runtime, the program would surely have thrown an exception, and the operation personnel would be no wiser as to the cause of the exception.

Configuration management of the source codes is easy when there is one developer and one set of source codes. But oftentimes, a group of software developers producing multiple "one-offs" is working from the same source codes. This means that there is a need to maintain multiple versions of the same program that does similar but not exactly the same thing. This leads to the concept of branching and merging. When a source is changed in one branch, the chance of breaking the software in another branch increases because we usually don't validate the changes with respect to the software in another branch. But the complexity of the process increases exponentially when there are a group of people working on the same software system at the same time. How do you prevent other developers from overwriting your changes? How do you make sure your version is always the same as the "official" release so that when you check something back in, the change doesn't break the system? How do you synchronize all the changes that are occurring at the same time? How do you ensure that someone else is not changing a source that has a feature that you are depending on? There are software tools that help us mitigate the risks from configuration management; however, they are just tools. They are complex tools that perform complex tasks, and people will still get confused and make mistakes.

Reality

We err because reality is harsh. Cheaper, better, faster, time to market, now—these are words that conspire and force us to take shortcuts. The prototype we write as a proof of concept is ushered into production. Our tight deadlines make it easier to just treat the symptom and get the customer and management off our backs. In addition, we are usually making fixes in the wee hours of the morning; who can think straight at 3:00 A.M.? The marketing department continually adds more and more new features, up to and beyond the day of code freezes. So we give up protecting our elegant architecture and design and begin to feverishly pile on feature after feature without thought or control. Unit test be damned, full speed ahead. Documentation, what is that?

In "Big Ball of Mud," Foote and Yoder present a reality-driven software architecture called the *Big Ball of Mud* and a set of associated antipatterns derived from it. Big Ball of Mud architecture is characterized by haphazard structures and spaghetti codes; it brings to mind duct tape and bailing wire. The developed systems resemble shantytowns, where changes and software modules are piled on with little thought of the effect on the big picture. Big Ball of Mud architecture is unregulated and inelegant, and yet, it is popular and common.[6]

---

[6] Foote, B., and J. Yoder. "Big Ball of Mud," in *Pattern Languages of Program Design*, ed. N. Harrison, B. Foote, and H. Rohnert. Addison-Wesley, 1999.

It is unregulated and inelegant because Big Ball of Mud systems are the results of expedient changes. However, Big Ball of Mud systems are popular and common because they serve a purpose and a function, and they are inevitable. These systems are driven by the forces of reality: time, cost, experience, and change.

- *Not enough time*—A study of 40,800 lines of code in a business system showed that the number of defects decreased when the planned development time was extended.[7]

  In this study, extending the development time from 13 months to 15 months reduced the number of defects nearly in half. When there is more time, the team has more time to do the "right" thing, and the number of errors committed is reduced. Our experiences concur with this study. There is usually never enough time to do anything right. Even if the management is kind and wise and is willing to let the developers come up with their own schedule, the developers, as a whole, tend to underestimate the amount of effort involved. There are always unexpected speed bumps along the way: A larger than expected number of bugs, a bad design decision, a new requirement, or a tenacious bug that just can't be isolated. The next thing you know, you are three weeks behind schedule. When there is no time, all formality gets thrown out the window because management and marketing just can't wait. The software is rushed, and bugs are introduced.

- *Not enough money*—When you give developers more time to think, design, and implement, you increase the development cost of the project. When you impose more formal processes, such as review sessions, you take time away from the engineers, and the cost of development increases. Training costs money. Tools cost money. Testing properly costs money. The pressure in any organization to get things done on time and on budget is tremendous; the temptation is to take shortcuts in order to meet these limitations, in spite of potential higher long term costs. This temptation can be overwhelming.

- *Constant changes*—In Chapter 3, we noted that bugs tend to be associated with changes: changes to the system, changes to the environment, and changes to the people involved. Why? Software systems are designed with a single vision of the problem. The system makes the statement: "This is how the world behaves." But when a requirement change comes along, the world no longer behaves as expected. When the environment changes, the world changes, and when people change, the statement itself changes because the vision may not be shared by the new owner of the project. When these fundamental events occur, the right thing to do is to rethink and redesign the system. This rarely happens. In reality, the system tends to be tweaked and perturbed to meet the demands. The precise statement, "This is how the world behaves," is transformed to, "This is how the world behaves with the following exceptions…" The system becomes more and more complex and less and less comprehensible—and the bugs flourish.

---

[7] Putnam, L. H., and W. Myers. *Measures for Excellence: Reliable Software on Time, within Budget.* Prentice-Hall Inc., Englewood Cliffs, New Jersey, 1992, pp. 139–140.

♦ *Lack of experience*—It is hard to know what the best path is when you have never traveled it before. Lack of domain knowledge about a problem can be a factor; lack of experience in the proposed solution is another major contributing factor in creating complexity and bugs in the solution. During a software development and design process, there are numerous trade-off and design decisions to be made. If you have never gone through this process before, it is difficult to understand the consequences of your decisions until you meet them face to face. We can all agree that asking a group of C programmers to work on a Java project is a disaster waiting to happen. Likewise, a different disaster is waiting to happen when you force design patterns down the throat of a team that has no experience with them. You can give them all the training and classes that they need, but classes are no substitute for experience. Classes don't point out when it is appropriate to use a Design Pattern and what risks are exposed. This is learned by experience. People often need an experimentation or trial-and-error period in which to learn the pieces that are relevant to the problems and solutions. But due to time and cost constraints, this rarely happens. So instead of coming up with a single, elegant solution, we come upon a cow path that meanders from point to point seemingly without reason. Decisions become harder to make, solutions become contorted, and the bugs lay back waiting to spring to life.

During the development process, any shortcuts taken tend to increase the complexity of the solution and reduce the comprehensibility of the system. Maintainers, because they don't have the time to understand the software, tend to continually degrade the structural integrity of the software. This situation will continue until the time comes when management decides that the cost of maintaining the software far exceeds the cost of creating new programs. The end effect of reality-driven software development and the maintenance process is the reduced comprehensibility of the software system.

Does software produced by reality-driven architecture and design tend to have more bugs than software produced with well-defined processes and procedures that can deter the agents of reality? It is difficult to empirically demonstrate a concrete answer to this question either way, because most, if not all, software projects are driven by reality. The only exception might be in places like NASA and the military, where the cost of any mistake is so astronomical that developers cannot afford to make mistakes. Anecdotal evidence suggests that a typical software product has about 25 defects per 1,000 lines of code, and space shuttle software produced by and for NASA typically has less than 1 error per 10,000 lines of code. However, the cost of producing NASA software is many times the cost of producing a typical commercial software product. It was reported that space shuttle software cost about $1,000 per line of code, whereas commercial software costs about $5 per line of code.[8]

Reality bites, doesn't it?

---

[8] Binder, R.V. "Six sigma: Hardware si, software no!" **www.rbsc.com/pages/sixsig.html**, 1997. Jones, Capers. *Assessment & Control of Software Risks*, Prentice Hall, Inc. Englewood Cliffs, New Jersey, 1994, pp 333.

Human Weakness

We err because we are frail, forgetful, and get distracted easily. We turn "==" in to "=" without realizing our error. We forget a pointer that we have allocated. We are too lazy to type a few more lines of code to check the validity of the input to our functions. We let documentation become inconsistent with the implementation. We misunderstand documentation. We write useless documentation. We don't think about the side effects. We are also egotistic and self-centered. We don't think about problems we don't have yet. We think a problem is trivial, so we put no effort or attention into it. We think we know how to solve a problem, when we don't even understand what the problem really is. We err because we are human.

There are millions of reasons why people make mistakes. We don't have the right experience. We don't have the right skill set. The problem is too hard. We are sleepy. I could go on and on. The fact is that we all make mistakes, and these mistakes turn into bugs. How do we prevent stupid mistakes? The first step is to admit that we are fallible. Once we accept this simple fact, we will be willing to accept changes and new ideas that will help us prevent mistakes and make finding mistakes faster. Some mistakes can be easily prevented; other mistakes might be harder. There are steps and processes we can implement that can prevent stupid mistakes, and there are tools we can use to help us identify and find bugs. In Chapter 12, we will look at some of these tools and techniques in detail.

How Are Bugs Created?

Complexity, reality, and mental weakness are the three fundamental forces that encourage bugs. In software engineering, these forces combine and manifest themselves in specific ways to cause bugs. Every time we change a line of code, we risk adding bugs to the code. Bugs can be introduced because we don't have good requirements that tell us what to write. We try to be clever and come up with a solution that is too hard to implement. The development team could have a different mental model of the system and introduce integration errors between various components. Finally, we also have the propensity for stupid human tricks and stupid bugs.

Making Changes to the Software

When you change code, you create a chance to introduce defects and bugs to the code. It is that simple. In Chapter 3, we showed results from numerous experiments that demonstrated the relationship between changes and the number of software defects. There are typically three reasons software defects are introduced during modifications. The main reason is poor comprehension of the software system that is being modified. This can apply to both the development and maintenance stage of the software life cycle. Tunnel vision relates to the lack of consideration during the design and development process of one system component to relate to another system component. Finally, feature creep, or requirement changes, can also contribute to the software defect level.

Poor Comprehension

Poor comprehension affects bug introduction in two ways. The first is poor comprehension of the problem and solution domain during the initial design and development efforts. This can result in poor specification, which is covered in a later section. The other way poor comprehension of a software system can affect bug introduction occur mostly in the maintenance phase when changes need to be made to the system. It is hard to change the software correctly when you don't know how your change can affect the system. Poor comprehension can be caused by poor documentation or poor design and usage.

What is documentation? *Documentation* is written support that helps describe the usage, design, purpose, and specification of a software system. Code is the final arbiter about the software. When all other sources of documentation have failed us, we turn to code to understand the system. Therefore, we consider source codes to be part of the documentation.

Poor documentation has the following characteristics:

♦ *Missing documentation*—Many organizations do not have design documents requirements. Many programmers do not write comments that explain what the code is supposed to do. The theory is that the code should be self-documenting. We agree that every developer should be able read code to understand what it does. But what the code actually does can bear very little resemblance to what the code is supposed to do and how the user should be using it. This is where any description of the problem can be helpful.

♦ *Misleading documentation*—The process of changing comments in the code to reflect changes in the code itself is often skipped. Maintaining design and requirement documentation can require a tremendous amount of work and is rarely done well throughout the life of the software. When documentation and comments become out of date, it means that documentation and comments can become red herrings that can send us on a wild-goose chase. When we assume the comment in the code is correct and we make changes accordingly, we are counting on the correctness of the documentation. If it is wrong, we have introduced a potential bug.

♦ *Documentation that is written for the wrong audience*—Often, we write documentation for people who are already familiar with the software, but we don't write documentation for people who are not familiar with the system.

Javadoc is a great tool for producing application programming interface (API) documents directly from the source codes. It encourages developers to write documents because it makes it easier and it fits in with their process. As a reference tool, it is great. But these API documents do not help if you don't already know how to use Java. The Java Web site mitigates this problem by providing Java tutorials, which gives a beginner a fighting chance. When we write documentation, we tend to write for "experienced" programmers. These "experienced" programmers are already familiar with the software, and the documentation is merely a reference tool. It is rare for a software project to produce tutorials for new employees. But the usefulness of tutorials is not limited to training new employees. The examples and discussions provided in a tutorial also help developers communicate their design phi-losophy and the intended use of the software. Presumably, the intended use of the software is the one code path that has been extensively tested. Therefore, the chance of running into a defect using the extensively tested code path should be lower, which means that there might be fewer bugs in the final product. The number of defects might be the same, but fewer bugs could be the result.

Tunnel Vision

When we write software, we usually only think about the specific piece of the code that we are currently working on. But the functions that we implement and the software modules that we develop do not operate in isolation or in stasis. On the contrary, they are usually part of a system and evolve constantly, and when we don't consider these other variables, we increase the likelihood of bug introduction.

During the software design and construction stages, ease-of-maintainability is usually not a consideration. We usually don't think about how to make the program comprehensible and changeable to people who might need to maintain the software. Consider the following architecture of a Web server. The system is meant to provide a service to a number of clients. The core service for every client is the same and is composed of a series of back-end server API calls. However, each client has its own specific business needs that need to be incorporated into the service. In the architecture in Figure 4.1, each Java servlet page (JSP) implements the client-specific service by using the backend server API calls.

In this architecture, if the backend server API changes, the maintainer will need to track down all the JSP pages that use the changed API and change them. When there are three JSP pages, this is no big deal. But if the business is good and there are 20 to 30 JSP pages, the maintenance effort becomes somewhat more significant. Furthermore, every JSP page will need to be tested against any backend server API changes. One way to mitigate these risks is to introduce an additional layer that encapsulates the common service components, as shown in Figure 4.2.

In this architecture, the common service API hides the complexity of the backend server API from the JSP pages. Changes to the backend server API only need to be tested and modified in the common service API. Instead of changing and testing three JSP pages, only one component needs to be checked if the specification for the common service API has not changed. The maintainability of the system is improved.

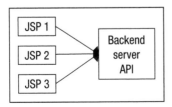

Figure 4.1
An example of a JSP Web server architecture.

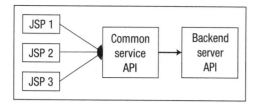

Figure 4.2
An example of a better JSP Web server architecture.

One day, we received a request that instead of accessing the service through JSP pages, one of the clients wanted to have an XML interface using Java servlet technology. The ease of incorporating this request depended on how generically the common service API had been designed. If the common service API was designed specifically for the JSP pages and HTML page flows, then it might be quite difficult to use the common service API as is for the XML servlet interface.

The lesson in this case is that by not considering the potential changes and uses of the system, we force upon ourselves risky implementation changes in the future. When the system cannot be easily extended, the number and difficulty of changes to the system will be significant, which in turn increases the odds of introducing software defects.

Feature Creep

Whenever feature creep is mentioned, we have this image of a slimy sales and marketing person. Even though this image might not be too far from the truth, we are not talking about the creep as a person. Instead, in this context, feature creep is the process of adding features to the software system during the design, implementation, and testing phases of the software development process.

The main driving force behind feature creep can indeed be the sales and marketing department. Through market studies, user interviews, and some domain knowledge, they conjure up all these features that the company must have in order to compete in the new industry. Other times, feature creep can originate from the upper executive management. For any number of reasons, someone decrees that the product must support X, Y, and Z; they become the company's new top priority. Feature creep can also be driven by the customers. The original requirement might have been poorly specified, so the features that were supposed to be in the requirement weren't. These features are then added, and as far as the development team is concerned, they are all unanticipated new features. Feature creep can be introduced by the development team as well when they feel that the product should also perform some tasks not called for in the requirements. The main reasons behind development driven feature creeps are the good intentions of reuse, flexibility, completeness, and other concepts of technological elegance. Halfway through the implementation, the developers may have had an epiphany and realized that if they just did things differently, everything would be easier and better. And so the design of the system is changed midway through the project.

But the path to hell is paved with "good intentions." By changing the software design, we increase the odds of introducing bugs. The impact of the changes is usually not fully analyzed because they have already been done (after all, we are in the implementation phase of the project, right?).

Poor Specifications

One of the main causes of the majority of bugs is poor specifications. There have been numerous studies performed on the relationship between requirements and bugs. These studies have shown that in some cases, more than 50 percent of bugs in a software system can be tracked to errors made during the requirement stage. Incorrect requirements and omissions are two of the most common requirement errors, followed by inconsistency and ambiguity.[9]

A specification should be complete, correct, and unambiguous. This is a worthwhile goal, but is difficult to achieve. The purpose of a specification is to provide developers and testers with a clear understanding of what needs to be implemented. Developers need to know what to write, and testers need to know what to test. As presented in Chapter 2, the destruction of Ariane 5 could be partially attributed to poor specifications.

Clearly, an incorrect specification will produce incorrect implementation, which will result in a bug.

An ambiguous specification could contain contradictory requirements, which will result in erroneous behaviors of the system. An ambiguous specification could also have requirements that do not have sufficient detail. An example of an ambiguous requirement with insufficient detail is subjective requirements. Requirement phrases such as "the system must be user-friendly" provide no objective description of the system goal that the designers can use. In such a case, developers would be forced to make assumptions and produce software using their subjective interpretation of the requirement. But most likely, a specification is ambiguous because it is written using "natural" languages, such as English. We all use the same word to mean different things, and we all use different words to mean the same thing. We are also prone to write in complex sentences, which might make the document more "readable," but difficult to extract the precise and unambiguous meaning.

However, the majority of errors found in a typical specification review are missing requirements; that is, the specification is incomplete. Incomplete specifications can result in missing features. Again, facing incomplete specifications, developers are forced to guess the proper behaviors of the system. A process, which more likely than not, will result in a software system not doing what it is expected to do.

One of the hardest items to describe in requirement specifications is error handling. Typically, requirements specify the handling of errors at the functional level. However, specification

---

[9] Gilb, T. *Principles of Software Engineering Management.* The Bath Press, Avon, Great Britain, 1988.

of error handling at the programmatic level becomes more difficult and is usually not defined in the specification. Questions and uncertainty arise, as in the following examples:

♦ How do I handle a memory allocation error?

♦ What if I run out of disk space?

♦ What happens if my stream gets cut off in the middle?

♦ Do I handle the error myself or do I trap it and report the failure to the caller?

♦ Which exceptions do I trap and which do I let go?

♦ Should I try to recover from this error or just report it?

Our experience is that incorrect error handling is a big part of latent errors that manifest themselves weeks and months into the production phase because they are rarely tested and difficult to trigger. Many times, developers just put something in because they have no clue how to deal with the error in a realistic fashion, or they never thought it could happen. Unfortunately, software engineering cannot escape Murphy's Law.

Complexity of the Solution

I used to work with a few people who believed that performance was everything in a program. This was in the glory days of C programming, and they did some of the funkiest pointer manipulations to speed up the program by a few milliseconds. They performed multiple operations on a single statement to save a few microseconds. They took pride in their ability to have the leanest and fastest program in the office. Unfortunately, their programs were also the hardest to maintain, painful to look at, impossible to debug, and fault-prone. I avoided their programs like the plague. Consider the following examples:

Example 1:

```
1.  #define SIZE 10
2.  int count;
3.  int sum = 0;
4.  int array[SIZE];
5.  … // array was filled
6.  for ( count = 0; count < SIZE; count++ )
7.    sum += array[count];
```

Example 2:

```
1.  #define SIZE 10
2.  int sum = 0;
3.  int array[SIZE];
4.  int *ptr0 = &array[0];
5.  int *ptr1 = &array[SIZE-1];
```

```
6.   … // array was filled.
7.   while ( ptr1 != ptr0 )
8.     sum += *ptr0++;
```

These two examples, although not terribly complex or difficult, can be used to illustrate the point. Both examples perform the same task—summing 10 values in an array. In our view, the **for** loop construct is a lot simpler to understand and less error-prone, whereas the **while** loop construct is more complex and has more opportunity for bugs. In Example 1, it is clear that the loop will execute 10 iterations before stopping by looking at line 6. In Example 2, the **while** loop only tells us that the loop will execute as long as ptr1 is not the same is ptr0. We need to look at lines 4, 5, and 8 to understand under which conditions ptr1 would be equal to ptr0. Termination of the loop will depend on the correctness of the initialization and increment of the pointer. Furthermore, it might be difficult for someone who is not familiar with the pointer arithmetic of the C language to understand the correctness of the statement. There are simply more opportunities for mistakes in Example 2 than in Example 1.

Poor design can also make a system difficult to comprehend, hence, difficult to implement and maintain. I remember looking for a bug in a proprietary middleware system. The designer was a big fan of design patterns, and these patterns were used throughout the system. There were Command patterns, Observer patterns, Façade patterns, Factory patterns, and Singleton patterns. These are not a big deal, if they are used properly. However, the system had seven Singleton patterns and two or three Command patterns. These seven singletons were spread out through the system and were initialized, modified, and used in multiple locations. It was very difficult to track through the code to understand the use and state of these singletons. Basically, the designer was using the Singleton pattern as a guise for global variables without realizing it. The Command patterns made the data flow complicated, and it was difficult to visualize how the data went from one class to the next. The fact that all these patterns occurred in approximately 20 different files didn't make my life any easier. It is great to talk about systems using pattern languages; you can almost treat each pattern as a black box and talk around them. However, in implementation and debugging, we cannot assume that these patterns are implemented correctly and are bug free. The elegance of pattern languages is shattered when we have to get into the code and to comprehend it. This is not an indictment that design patterns are evil and should be avoided. That is not our intention; nor do we wish to steer you away from design patterns. Design patterns is simply a tool. Like all other tools, it can be abused. When abused, it makes a solution more complex, which means more potential for bug introduction and more work for debugging.

Callback functions are popular because they are useful. They help us conceptualize the propagation of events within a program. When a software component is interested in an event from another component, it registers its interest to the source of the event. When the event occurs in the event source, the event source notifies all interested components of the occurrence. Once notified, the interested components can proceed to perform tasks that are dependent on the event. A very elegant abstraction that is not without its pitfalls and traps due to potential complexity can be introduced. Figure 4.3 shows an example. In the figure,

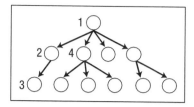

Figure 4.3
An example of a callback activation tree.

every circle represents a software component. The circle at the top represents the event source. From the event source (component 1), a set of arrows points to the software components that are interested in this particular event. After an event has occurred, the control of the program is handed to one of the components below it (component 2, for example). If component 2 has an event that component 3 is waiting for, then component 2 hands the control to component 3. This process continues until all the components have a chance to process the event, and the control of the program is returned to component 1.

The callback function mechanism tends to be single thread, which means that software components involved in the callback are processed sequentially. Figure 4.3 shows an example of a callback structure that looks like a tree. For this example, the program flow mimics a preorder traversal. The complexity that a callback mechanism introduces is precisely the direct consequence of its benefits. With callback, we no longer have to explicitly worry about the program flow when something happens. We merely have to write individual components that can perform a specific task, tell the module that this component is interested in this event, and let the program worry about the control flow at runtime. The downside to this is that we are no longer clear on all the components that are involved with any particular events. Instead of having a clean flow as shown in Figure 4.3, we might introduce strange dependencies between components. If component 1 is also dependent on component 3, we might create a circular dependency that can never be broken. The various components in the callback might share the same data, and the order in which this data is accessed and modified can be important. If component 4 should modify the data before component 3 can access it, the callback mechanism shown in Figure 4.3 would not function properly because component 3 would execute before component 4.

These are a few examples of popular design solutions and their potential exposure to bugs. In our research for this book, we noticed that different design solutions have different types of bugs. The kinds of bugs that result from callback functions are not likely to occur with programs not using them. In Chapter 12, we discuss different designs and the associated bug types in more detail.

In our experience, we have observed that people like to make things complicated. Instead of having a single class that does one simple thing well, people either have a single class that does multiple things, or they use multiple classes to do a single thing. Sometimes this is done in the name of flexibility, and other times, this is done in the name of reuse. Both are honorable intentions, but if done incorrectly, this can produce complexities. We argued earlier in the chapter that complexity is one of the major causes of bugs. "Keep it simple, stupid," is great advice in a presidential campaign. It is equally applicable in software engineering.

Lack of a Coherent Vision

When a software system is originally designed, the development team has the chance to get together to talk about problems and solutions at length. This process induces a kind of mind-meld, which ensures that the team members are all on the same page. Individual members might object or disagree with a particular interpretation or design that is adapted, but they understand the rationale for these design decisions and work with their disagreements. After this initial mind-meld process, the team tends to splinter into smaller groups to work on specific parts of a problem. The central vision slowly erodes from their minds and is replaced by their own particular vision. Any subsequent changes will not share the same design vision, and the integrity of a unified design is replaced by many competing design elements. This problem becomes worse in the maintenance phase of the project. Often, the people asked to make maintenance changes to the system are not privy to the original design choices and trade-offs, and changes are often made without concern for the original vision of the system.

How does the lack of a shared vision affect bug introduction? There hasn't been any direct study done on this effect; however, there is some circumstantial evidence that suggests this relationship. Joseph Dvorak introduced the term "conceptual entropy" to describe conceptual inconsistency among developers in a class hierarchy. In this study, Dvorak demonstrated that as programmers descend into the depths of class hierarchy, agreement among the programmers on the selection of the subclasses becomes rare. Instead of sharing a common view on the class representation, developers classify concepts and classes based on their individual viewpoint.[10]

Daly et al presented the result of an empirical study that demonstrated the effect of conceptual hierarchy when performing maintenance tasks. Their study showed that "object-oriented software with a hierarchy of three levels of inheritance depth has been shown to reduce the time taken to perform maintenance tasks in comparison to object-based software with no inheritance. In contrast, no such difference was found with object-oriented software with a hierarchy of five levels of inheritance depth. Subject's completion times, source code solutions, and debriefing questionnaires actually provide some evidence suggesting subject began to experience difficulties with this deeper hierarchy."[11]

Furthermore, it was suggested in another study that the "programmers were very susceptible to miscomprehending the meaning of objects, hierarchies, and important relations" and made mistakes in a study of software maintenance tasks.[12]

---

[10] Dvorak, Joseph. "Conceptual Entropy and Its Effect on Class Hierarchies," *IEEE Computer*, pp 59–63, June 1994.

[11] Daly, J., Brooks, A., Miller, J., Roper, M., and Wood, M. "Evaluating the effect of inheritance on the maintainability of object-oriented software," *Empirical Studies of Programmers, Sixth Workshop*, ed. W. Gray and D. Boehm-Davis, pp 39–57, Ablex Publishing Corporation, 1996.

[12] Douce, C. R., and Layzell, P. J. "Evolution and Errors: An Empirical Example," *Proceedings of IEEE International Conference on Software Maintenance*, 1999. Keble College, Oxford, England, August 30–September 3, 1999, pp 493–498.

Concept sharing and program comprehension are not just a problem in the object-oriented frameworks. The notion of conceptual entropy can be applied to the design and implementation of software systems as a whole. Sharing a common mind-set, in terms of both philosophy and style, can do wonders for productivity and reducing bugs. I had the wonderful experience of working with a few people who were almost an extension of myself. I didn't have to second-guess their code. I didn't have to look up a function name or function signature. I knew implicitly what their code looked like without even talking to them because we shared the same concept on how the problem should be solved and how the code should be written. Once, when I was working with a friend on a project, he wrote an API to a genetic programming algorithm, and I was supposed to use it. He was sitting right beside me as I was coding to his interface. There was no discussion on the design or implementation other than the understanding that he was to write the API for the algorithm. Without looking at a single line of his code, I wrote half of the program using code identical to his API. We were both astounded that I was able to anticipate his API. When there is this kind of mind-meld, there is not much of a chance of someone making a mistake because one person misunderstood the purpose and usage of the software.

A common vision comes in many flavors. It can be as simple as the implementation of a coding style or as complex as the choice of a software development process and methodology. It can be as concrete as the agreement on the component interfaces or as abstract as an agreement of the philosophy of design construct and understanding of the preferred trade-off choices. Typically, coherent vision within the software development team breaks down when there is a lack of communication among members of the team and a lack of training for the new members.

Because none of us has extrasensory perception, we can't just telepathically exchange thoughts and ideas with one another. Therefore, we must rely on verbal and written communication to enforce a unity of vision and purpose. When communication breaks down, disagreements between team members on how things should be done emerge and are never resolved. When there is a disagreement, people tend to solve the problem as they see it in their minds. With different people working on the same project trying to solve slightly different problems, the chance of integration-related bugs increases. The loss of the Mars Climate Orbiter, as described in Chapter 2, is a vivid example.

When new members join the team, they come with a new set of characteristics. These characteristics include their habits, their experience, their knowledge, and their style. We want to leverage their experience and their knowledge, but we also want to integrate them with the team. Without a training process, this is a slow and haphazard procedure. So, one new member does things one way, another developer does things a different way, and soon there are as many styles and methods as there are people. It is not easy to comprehend and learn the style of one person, not to mention the styles of 5 to 10 different people. The Java software development kit (SDK) API has a very specific design and interface philosophy. It is very consistent with how things are done and how things should be done using Java APIs. Imagine if this were not the case. Java would not be as popular as is it today because it would be too expensive to learn. When there are many styles within one project, the cost of program comprehension increases along with the chance of defects.

Programmer Errors

I saw the following bug on a poster from the C programming language newsgroup:

```
1.  while( I = 0; I < 10; ++I ) {
2.    printf("%d\n", I );
3.  }
```

The poster was complaining that this program does not compile. There were about five responses to this message, and only one respondent pointed out the fundamental problem with these three lines of codes. Apparently this is a construct for the **for** loop not the **while** loop. Some readers might be able to spot the problem right away, whereas it will take others some time to see the bug. This is the kind of senseless programming mistake that can take a veteran programmer a while to find. It took me two tries to see the mistake because I just glanced at it the first time and assumed the construct was correct. I didn't really read the code. How does this happen? Who knows? The programmer might be mulling over the choice between using a **for** loop versus a **while** loop and just confuse the two constructs.

In this case, the problem is syntactical, so the compiler will prevent the bug from escaping into the real world. However, similar mistakes can occur on a semantic level, which would make the bug hard to spot and identify. The following potential bug could escape visual inspection:

```
1.  std::vector<int>::iterator iter = alist.begin();
2.  while ( iter != alist.end() ) {
3.    cout << (*iter) << endl;
4.    if ( (*iter)== 5 )
5.      break;
6.  }
```

This is an example of another simple mistake. How early we can spot this bug depends on how early we can trigger the proper condition (iter needs to be incremented before line 6). If alist usually starts with the value of 5, then it might be a while before the bug appears. The problem is exacerbated a bit more if the expression for the **if** clause is:

```
4a.     if ( (*iter) = 5 )
5a.       break;
```

We might think we have fixed the original bug, only to miss the second bug in line 4a ("==" should be "="). You might think it is easy to spot this kind of bug. It can be easy in a book when you are reading it with a critical mind. But when you have written the code and have stared at it for a few hours, it is easy to miss these mistakes. The incorrectly placed "break" statement that caused the AT&T 1990 outage was a simple programming mistake that was never noticed, precisely because it was nonthreatening looking, and the software engineers saw what they wanted to see.[13]

Human mistakes are often made because we do not pay attention. On July 22, 1962, the *Mariner* probe to Venus was lost because DO 3 I = 1,3 was mistyped as DO 3 I = 1.3 in a FORTRAN program. As a result, instead of performing the **DO** command, the FORTRAN compiler interpreted the statement to mean "assigning 1.3 to the variable DO3I."[14]

Note

*However, this story is somewhat apocryphal. The official NASA Web site (**nssdc.gsfc.nasa.gov/cgi-bin/database/www-nmc?MARIN1**) described the cause to be "the omission of a hyphen in coded computer instructions". For additional information on this potential computer folklore, check out the articles posted to the Risk Digest on this topic, volume 5, issue 64, 65, 66, and 73(**catless.ncl.ac.uk/**).*

But there are other factors that can affect and contribute to foolish programming errors.

Lack of Understanding of the Tools

In Chapter 2, we described the causes of the AT&T 1990 long distance telephone service outage. The cause was due to an incorrectly placed "break" statement in the code. We don't know if the programmer made an honest mistake or did not understand the language construct. However, it would not be surprising if that particular programmer always used the break statement in this erroneous fashion. I have worked with self-proclaimed experts in many different languages and have found their lack of understanding in the usage of the language to be astounding. For example, I used to work with a C programmer who liked to dereference a function argument twice for no apparent reason. Instead of declaring:

```
1.   Function_Foo( int *a ) {
2.      ...
3.      *a = 10;
4.      ...
5.   }
```

he opted to declare it as:

```
1.   Function_Foo( int **a ) {
2.      ...
3.      *(*a) = 10;
4.      ...
5.   }
```

---

[13] Neumann, Peter. "Risks to the Public in Computers and Related Systems," ACM SIGSOFT *Software Engineering Notes,* Vol. 15, No. 2, pp 11ff, April 1990.

[14] Tropp, H.S. "Fortran Anecdotes," *Annals of the History of Computing.* 6(1), p. 61, 1984.

These two declarations and usage accomplish the same thing; argument a is assigned with the value of 10. However, in the second example, argument a is dereferenced one more time than necessary and can be a source of potential confusion and errors. To most C programmers, pointer-to-pointer-to-a-variable has different semantics than pointer-to-a-variable. I can picture cases where you might want to dereference an argument multiple times in this usage, and I had discussed this with him a number of times. However, he was never able to explain the rationale of his usage, and we eventually chalked it up to "stylistic differences." It would not have surprised me to know that he didn't have a good grasp of pointers, and his trial and error experiences showed that when he did things this way, his programs worked. So he always dereferenced a value twice without a real understanding of the underlying reason.

C++ did not make coding any easier. In fact, it probably made things a lot harder. Not only does it still have issues with memory management and pointers, but the introduction of object-oriented technology has also increased the complexity of the language. Confusion abounds regarding passing an object by value, by reference, or by pointers. Inheritance and polymorphism open up a whole new can of worms in regard to complexity. When I was a beginning C++ programmer, I used to make foolish mistakes with copy constructors and destructors because I did not understand all the intricacies and rules of C++. The thing was, I could pass any interview that you could throw at me, and I could recite all the rules from the programmer's manual. But at that time, I had not internalized the philosophy of the language, and I wasn't using C++ as it was meant to be used. I was using C++ the way I thought it should be used, which was incorrect.

I have heard many stories of bugs that have resulted from novices' mistakes. They returned and used data on the stack as if it were allocated. They nested loops 11 layers deep because they didn't comprehend the concept of evaluating multiple conditional expressions in an "if" statement. They forgot to allocate one extra space for the null-terminating characters using the string functions in C. Buffer overflow is another example where novices make mistakes. All of these situations were difficult for the novices to debug because they didn't know they were making bugs. They only knew the program didn't work, and often, the symptoms appeared hundreds of code lines away.

Using Inappropriate Tools

A side effect of using tools that you don't understand is that you run the risk of using the wrong tool. We could also use the wrong tool because we want to or for reasons unrelated to the project. We use the wrong tool because the tool is the latest silver bullet. We use the wrong tool because we want to learn about it and make ourselves more marketable. We use the wrong tool because we already know how to use it, and we don't want to spend the time to learn another. We use the wrong tool because we don't understand what the tool is for. What are these tools? Tools can be the debugger, the programming language, methodologies, commercial off-the-shelf components and applications, or class libraries and components.

In Chapter 2, we presented two incidents in which the bugs in the software can be partially attributed to using inappropriate tools—Ariane 5 and Therac 25. In both cases, the software components that caused the problem were reused inappropriately. In the case of Ariane 5, the specification of the component was reused from the Ariane 4 rocket, which had a different performance profile and specification than the Ariane 5.[15]

The differences were not taken into consideration. In the case of Therac 25, the software components that were reused were buggy; the same bug that caused overexposure existed in Therac 20. But Therac 20 had hardware protection that prevented the bug from causing accidents.[16]

Consider another example. Attempting to use the waterfall methodology in an Internet software development environment can be problematic. Waterfall methodology requires clear and definite specification of one stage of the development process before the next stage can commence. In Internet time, a more reactive methodology, such as a spiral or evolutionary approach, might be more appropriate.

Object-oriented design has become the de facto standard in software construction. The popularity of C++ and Java has made object orientation the design method of choice. However, does it make sense to use object orientation in every project? What's wrong with structural programming? What's wrong with top-down design? Inheritance and polymorphism, although powerful, make software harder to comprehend. Creating and designing a proper object class hierarchy and relationship can be difficult and can make a software project more complex than is necessary. But a well-designed, object-oriented system can also be very easy to use and understand. Top-down design may not be sexy, but it can be tremendously easy to follow.

Tip

Tools should be chosen based on the problem.

Laziness

Laziness is a virtue of a good software engineer. Good software engineers are lazy in that they do not like to reinvent the wheel. They are willing to reuse software components and modules. They find the simplest way and avoid unnecessary complexity because they don't want to go through any mental gymnastics. However, laziness can also be the mark of an inept software engineer. Inept software engineers cut and paste codes without attempting to verify the correctness and specification of the reused codes. They don't bother to check for error conditions, and they make solutions more complex than they need to be because they are too lazy to find a simpler way.

Laziness in a careless software engineer also manifests itself in the form of lazy codes. What are lazy codes? You have probably seen them and have even written them. I know I am

---

[15] Lions, J. L., et al. "ARIANE 5 Flight 501 Failure," Report by the Inquiry Board. Paris, July 19, 1996. Available at **www.esa.int/htdocs/tidc/Press/Press96/ariane5rep.html**.

[16] Leveson, Nancy, and Turner, Clark S. "An Investigation of the Therac-25 Accidents," *IEEE Computer*, Vol 26, No. 7, pp 18–41, July 1993.

guilty of writing lazy codes. Lazy codes are codes that can distract or mislead other developers, and they can take many forms. A lazy code could include a function that is defined but never used. It could be a variable that is never used. It could be a misleading or out-of-date comment. It could be a misleading variable name because you never bothered to change the name when you changed its usage. It could be a short but nonmeaningful variable name. Whatever it is, it clutters the code and reduces the signal-to-noise ratio. Comprehension becomes more difficult for other developers, and the chance of bug introduction is increased.

How Do Bugs Slip through Testing?

There are two kinds of bugs in the world, private bugs and public bugs. Private bugs are bugs that we discover in the course of the development process. These bugs are uncovered during reviews, development, and testing. Typically, only the people involved in the project know about the existence of these private bugs. Discovery of private bugs is good. It means that we get to fix our mistakes behind closed doors, and our stupidities are not subject to ridicule by others. On the other hand, public bugs are bad. Public bugs occur in a production environment and are typically reported by our customers, which can be a source of embarrassment.

We believe that creating bugs is an inevitable consequence of the software development process. Instead of attempting to create bug-free codes, we should strive to produce software with as few public bugs as possible. One way to accomplish this goal is to identify as many bugs as possible during the development process.

Bugs are introduced and created in the various stages of the software development process, in requirement analysis, system design, and implementation. We have many chances in the development process to identify and correct mistakes. But many bugs escape detection regularly. When this happens, we usually attribute the reason to improper or incomplete testing. In this book, we don't consider testing to be a separate or independent part of the development process. We believe testing is something that is done throughout the process by project managers, implementers, and testers. In the software industry, quality assurance (QA) is the term used to describe the process of eliminating bugs in the life cycle of software development. When a bug slips through testing, it has slipped through the QA process, not just through the testers. Obviously, when code is not tested, bugs will slip through. But the testing process and environment might contain some defects that allow bugs to escape.

Expensive to Follow Formal Procedures

Reviews, inspections, and testing are part of the QA process. However, performing these procedures can be a costly proposition. In order to properly review and inspect software documentation and products, qualified reviewers must be identified. Qualified reviewers tend to be senior-level analysts and engineers, and their time tends to be expensive and scarce. Documentation and codes need to be collected and provided to the reviewer ahead of time. This means more time and effort is required from the development team and the reviewers. Reviewing can take some time, and meetings are usually held to communicate the result of the reviews and inspections. Additional engineering time translates to additional cost.

Political/Marketing Decision

The release of bugs can be a conscious decision for reasons totally unrelated to the technical team. An organization could be diligently following the process. But at some point, the company may feel that the cost of fixing additional bugs does not justify delaying the release of the software. The software is good enough, and due to some perceived marketing advantage, the software needs to be released as is. So the software is released with known bugs.

In safety-critical industries, such as the medical or aerospace industries, it is not a good idea to release software with known bugs. But for other industries, it can be a judgment call. The decision to release software with known bugs needs to consider the severity of the bugs, the circumstances, and the potential consequences of the bugs from the perspective of the customers. In Chapter 2, we presented the Intel Pentium FDIV Bug. Using it as an example, even though the bug was not known to Intel at the time of the release, Intel did discover the bug later and withheld information from its users. The effect is the same. Intel evaluated the consequences of announcing the bug versus the consequences of hiding the bug from the public. It decided to withhold information because it determined that the risk of the bug was minor. It turned out to be a costly decision for Intel, but the decision to leave the bug out in the field was one that was evaluated and considered.

Not Enough Time

Testing takes time, the QA process takes time, and when the schedule slips, time that is allocated for QA is usually squeezed. Code review sessions are cancelled. Fewer test cases are run through. Testing is performed at the same time the codes are changed, so that the testing might be performed on the incorrect version. It is hard to do things right when there isn't enough time. When there isn't enough time, it is also difficult to prioritize the testing scenarios to figure out the functionalities and code paths that are critical to the users.

Optimistic and unrealistic schedules are the main culprits. Software developers could overestimate their own capabilities and underestimate the difficulty of the problem. Feature creep could contribute to the difficulty of the problem when the schedule remains constant. The schedule could be determined from a marketing perspective instead of from the technological feasibility. The development team could run into many snags and detours along the way. The software components that the team is planning to reuse could turn out to be buggy. Required hardware could come in late. People could get sick or have other personal emergencies. Your pet dog could eat your laptop, which contains the critical software. Hard disks could crash. Always keep in mind that anything that can go wrong will go wrong when there isn't enough available time.

Lack of Reproducibility

A tester's nightmare usually involves nonreproducible or semireproducible bugs. When a bug is not easily reproduced, it is difficult to find. The tester writes up the bug report and forwards it to the developer. The developer can't reproduce the bug and bounces the bug report back to the tester. The tester can't reproduce the bug, so the case is closed—until about a week later, when the tester runs into the same bug again. In such a scenario, the tester can easily spend days and weeks coming up with the reproducible case. In effect, the tester is debugging the software.

Reproducibility of a bug is intrinsically linked with the cause of the bug itself. Bugs that cannot be consistently reproduced can strike horror in a developer's heart. It means that you don't understand the system well enough, and it has taken on a life of its own. It means that you have failed to foresee a circumstance and possibility that the code can break. You then begin to fear that if you have one bug that you cannot find, there must be millions of other bugs that you don't even know exist.

There are many reasons why a bug can be hard to reproduce. It could be that the testers did not track and record their actions properly and correctly. It could be the physical limitation where software is to be used. It is hard to test aerospace software because there are many other hardware components that need to be simulated; the crash of Ariane 5 served as an example. It could be data and event driven. The AT&T outage of 1990 and Pentium FDIV bugs are bugs that slipped through testing because the triggering event was data-driven, and was rare and obscure. The system could be sensitive to environmental and configuration differences. The software could behave differently running on one machine than on a different machine. The bug could be in a sequence-dependent component, and the triggering of the bug could be dependent on executing the correct sequence with the exact timing.

Ego

The other day I watched *Titanic*, the movie about an unsinkable ship sinking; obviously the *Titanic* sunk because it ran into an iceberg. However, human pride and ego made the accident possible and made the disaster worse than it needed to be. Because of faith in the technology and human capabilities, the warning about potential iceberg danger was ignored. Because of human ego, not enough lifeboats were placed on the ship to evacuate all 2,200 people aboard. Why waste money on lifeboats when the *Titanic* couldn't possibly sink? *Titanic* was the worst maritime disaster of the century. Yet, we manage to produce software system disasters on the scale of the *Titanic* on a regular basis.

Developers are notoriously inefficient testers. How many times have you heard a programmer say, "But it works on my machine!" Of course it does. But the customers are not using your machine, so you need to put your ego aside and figure out what they are complaining about. Developers are not the only group with egos that need to be curtailed. Project managers can also be overconfident about their team and their product, and not pay attention to testing. The corporate culture can be too proud and not believe it is possible to release a buggy product. When you don't believe your software has bugs, you will not go looking for them. If you don't look for them, you probably won't find them. The case study of Therac 25 presented in Chapter 2 provides a grim example of this mind-set.

Complacency is an effect of ego and was cited as a contributing cause for the bugs in both the *Mars Climate Orbiter* and *Ariane 5*, described in Chapter 2. When we are complacent, we don't question all assumptions. We make incorrect assumptions. We assume all functions and all features work. We don't test diligently. We are not paranoid enough to question every little inconsistency, and defects slip through the cracks.

Poor Specification/Don't Know What to Test

Just as the developers need to know what to write, testers need to know what to test. A good specification can do both. A test plan can result straight from a good specification, and a tester can extract every requirement in the specification and test them. A good specification can also inform testers of the algorithm of the software module, so that the testers can devise the proper testing scenarios and cases.

While developing the Pentium chip, Intel was counting on random testing to test the FDIV algorithm in the Pentium chip. But the random testing approach was not capable of reaching all potential code paths in a uniform manner, so the result obtained was not representative of the FDIV algorithm that was implemented in the Pentium chip. If the tests used accounted for the FDIV algorithm, the likelihood of Intel finding the FDIV bug during the testing cycle could have been increased.[17]

Lack of Testing Environment

A good testing environment consists of three properties: testers with the right tools, the software being tested on a machine with the same system configuration as the customer's systems, and the usage of the user is understood and well modeled. When one of these properties is missing, it gives bugs a chance to slip through the testing process.

♦ *Lack of the right tool*—Sometimes, the tester simply does not have the tool with which to perform the test properly. When the test is not performed properly, we can draw incorrect conclusions about the reliability of the software. For example, in a high volume production Web site, the system's performance under load is important and should be understood as soon as possible. However, if the tester does not have the proper tools to do load testing or lacks the hardware resources, it will be difficult to simulate the load condition appropriately.

♦ *Lack of proper system configuration*—It is also difficult to create the environment in which the software will be used. In a standalone application, the testing environment consists

---

[17] Edelman, Alan. "The Mathematics of the Pentium Division Bug," 1995. Available from **www–math.mit.edu/~edelman/**. Also appears in *SIAM Review*, March 1997.

of the computer and the configuration of the software. It might appear trivial to construct a testing environment for the application until you start to realize the number of hardware and software configurations that your customer base might be using. In hardware and embedded systems, it might be difficult to simulate the hardware interface correctly.

♦ *Lack of usage model*—The ability to model and test the actual usage of the system can reduce the number of public bugs because most potential bugs can be ferreted out. A software system could have many defects; however, if the user never uses the code path that contains the defects, those defects would never become public bugs.

Summary

The reason for the existence of bugs can be summarized in one word: people. People are the creators and the destroyers. People make the mistakes, but people also find and fix the mistakes. If we want to make software more robust, we must start with people. We must understand why we make mistakes and how we make mistakes. Only then can we devise preventive actions and create tools to help us help ourselves. We also need to know how we can make it easier to find and correct mistakes. In this chapter, we identified many contributing causes of bugs, starting with the fundamental forces of complexity, reality, and human weaknesses. We then demonstrated how these forces interact to create specific bug-making circumstances. Finally, we discussed how we let bugs escape into the real world. We will revisit some of these understandings and findings in Chapter 12 to discuss preventive methods.

Bug Puzzle

Why do bugs happen? Sometimes for apparently no good reason at all, try out this real-life bug puzzle and groan.

You seem to have a problem getting away from working in an Internet company and you are facing with a performance problem on the company's new site providing some services to consumers. The nature of the service is unimportant, but the CEO is really annoyed with the poor response time of the system. Either you fix the problem, or you are gone.

You performed a series of performance experiments on the production site, and you observed a huge variant on the performance of the site, even loading the same page. So you set up a script to load the welcome page of the site once every minute for a day. The result shows that the load time for the welcome page range from 4.54 seconds to 34.31seconds, with average load time of 16.42 seconds and standard deviation of 9.43 seconds. You were very puzzled and you can't understand why there are such a variant in the loading of the welcome page. So you ran the same experiment on the development machine. However, the development machines have slightly different code and configurations (Because they are development machines after all.) You found that on the development machines, the load time for the welcome page range from 3.23 seconds to 4.76 seconds, with average load time of 3.56 seconds and standard deviation of 0.21 seconds.

The welcome page is written in Java Servlet Pages (JSP) and communicates with backend servers to construct the eventual HTML page that is displayed on the consumer's browser. You checked the performance of the backend servers for your tests, and the logs showed that both the production and development servers consistently responded to the JSP's requests within 3 seconds. What was the problem? Hint: Figure 4.4 shows the conceptual architectural/network layout of the system.

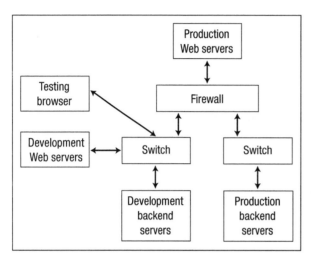

Figure 4.4
Conceptual, architectural, and network layout of the system described in the bug puzzle.

Chapter 5
A Bug Taxonomy

Matt Telles

W hen scientists talk about real bugs, the sort that sting and crawl and wiggle through your house late at night, they classify them into a taxonomy. A taxonomy is defined as follows:

> **taxonomy** \Tax*on"o*my\ (-m[y^]), n. [Gr. ta'xis an arrangement, order + no'mos a law.] That division of the natural sciences which treats the classification of animals and plants; the laws or principles of classification. [1]

What does this mean when we talk about the taxonomy of technical bugs? Bugs, after all, are not animals or plants. Because bugs are not either of these classes, we refer to the second definition—the laws or principles of classification.

Why is it important to consider the classification of bugs? The most important reason is that groups of bugs have important similarities. If you understand these similarities, you can quickly determine which type of bug you are most likely facing by examining its symptoms, and then looking them up in the taxonomy.

One of the most critical (and most overlooked) aspects of debugging is to understand why bugs occur and where they come from. If we can determine what kinds of bugs exist in a system and can somehow associate them with certain actions in the development process, we can improve that process to remove these bugs. In order to do this, we classify bugs into general categories to see if

---

[1] *Webster's New International Dictionary: Unabridged.* Merriam-Webster. Sprinfield, MA. 2000.

the relationships in those categories can lead us to better understand the root causes of bugs in our processes. So, by creating a taxonomy of bugs, we hope to create general classifications that lead to general observations about where bugs come from.

At present, two general bug taxonomies exist. The first was published by IEEE under the heading "ANSI/IEEE P1044-1994: Standard Classification for Software Anomalies." This taxonomy is mostly concerned with the root causes of bugs and concentrates on pinpointing the place in the software development process of the project in which the bug occurred. Although this is definitely a good place to start looking for problems, it isn't particularly useful to either software engineers doing debugging or testers trying to assign a bug to a category.

The second general taxonomy available was published in Boris Beizer's *Software Testing Techniques*, second edition.[2] Fortunately, Mr. Beizer released his taxonomy to the general public. It can be found in his book as well as in various places on the Web.

In our taxonomy, we want to consider a variety of sources and causes. Not only do we want to consider the kinds of bugs found in code, but also the kinds of bugs found in other parts of the software development process. In each phase of the development process, from project definition to final deployment, bugs can creep into the system. Finding and fixing those bugs is the purview of the software engineer in most cases, the operations staff in others, and the project architect in still other cases. By understanding where the bug came into the system and where it is best fixed, we can best assign bugs to the proper personnel and not waste the time of other people in the company.

What sort of information do we need to classify bugs? First, we need to know what stage in the development process the bug occurs. Second, we need to know who is responsible for creating (or not catching) the bug in the first place. Third, we need to consider who should ultimately be responsible for fixing the bug in the system. Although you as a debugger might think that all bugs in the final product are your problem, this is not always the case. If, for example, the problem can only be truly "solved" by redesigning the system, the solution lies with the project architect. If the problem is caused by a lack of understanding on the part of the user, the solution might lie with either the help writer or the trainer for the system. Don't always assume that just because a bug is reported in the bug database that it is the software engineer's problem. What this chapter does not cover is the last step of the process, finding and fixing the bug. You will find a discussion of the methodology to find bugs in Chapter 8 and a complete rundown of the kinds of techniques available to you for finding and fixing bugs in Chapter 9. Please refer to those chapters for any questions beyond classification.

Bugs tend to occur in specific areas of the development process. Let's first take a look at what those areas might be and what a "bug" means in each one.

---

[2] Beizer, Boris. *Software Testing Techniques*. International Thomson Computer Press, 2d, 1990. ISBN: 1850328803.

Classes of Bugs

Each class of bug consists of a stage of the development process and a set of problems associated with it. The different stages also have different types of resolutions associated with them and differing levels of risk. From previous studies, we know that a bug that passes beyond the level in which it was created is significantly more expensive to fix than one that is caught and "killed" at the level in which it was initially introduced.[3] Debugging often consists of more than fixing code. It can involve many other levels of work, as we will see in the following sections.

Requirement Bugs

The requirements segment of the software development process for a project is often considered the most crucial to the overall success of the system. If you want to learn more about this development phase, consult virtually any decent software engineering book. Many of these books are listed in the bibliography sections of this book. When we consider the requirements segment from a bug-centric perspective, however, we approach it from a very different angle. Requirements bugs are by far the nastiest to find and certainly the hardest to fix, as we'll see later in this section. That is why requirements bugs can be from 15 to 75 times more expensive to fix than coding bugs.

A requirements bug can occur for several reasons. First, a requirement could be omitted in the specification for the system. This leads to user dissatisfaction, and a program that is perceived as "buggy" by the end user. Requirements omissions are by far the most common problem among requirements bugs.

Second, a requirements bug type could contain conflicting requirements in the specification; for example, two requirements that must be satisfied yet have opposite meanings. We will consider the conflicting requirement problem as a specific bug type of its own.

Third, there is requirements vagueness. This is a condition whereby a requirement is stated, and even though it does not conflict with another requirement, its statement is not clear enough to lead to a single design decision. The end user often calls this a "bug," when in fact it is simply a design choice based on an incomplete or vague requirement.

Numerous studies have shown that requirements bugs are the most expensive to fix and the hardest to track down.[4] The reason for this is simple. If a bug is in the requirements, there is no "problem code" to detect. No test cases can show the problem because test cases are written from requirements specifications. Only the end user can point to a requirements issue, and then only indirectly point to a bug in the system.

---

[3] Boehm, Barry. *Software Engineering Economics*. Prentice Hall, 1981, ISBN: 0138221227.

[4] Daly, E. 'Management of Software Development,' *IEEE Transactions on Software Engineering*.
Boehm, B.W. 'Software Engineering,' *IEEE Transactions on Computers* Vol 25, No 12. pp 1126–1241, Dec 1976.
Fagan, M. 'Design & Code Inspections & Process Control in the Development of Programs,' IBM Report IBM-SDD-TR-21-572, December 1974.

Design Bugs

Design is the process of converting the vague and general statements made in requirements into the more concise technical descriptions of how the system will work internally. As with any system of translation, there are bound to be errors in the process. Design bugs are easier to catch than requirements bugs, but almost as expensive to fix in the long run. The main reason that design bugs are expensive to fix is that they tend to affect the system as a whole. Obviously, fixing an entire subsystem or the entire application system is harder and more prone to introducing errors than fixing a few broken lines of code or replacing a single module. To use an analogy, if requirements represent the entire automobile, then design represents the power train of that automobile. Even though the entire car might cost $20,000, the power train of that car might run $12,000 to replace. Obviously, this is also not a desirable situation. Kind of makes you wonder why there isn't insurance for requirements and design of applications, doesn't it?

Design bugs tend to fall into one of three categories: omission, conflict, and translation errors. Omission means the failure to incorporate one or more requirements into the final design of the application. To use another analogy, it is like talking to a potential home-owner about a house, and then forgetting to add the right number of bathrooms onto the final blueprint. Fortunately, similar to the house error, catching omissions isn't very hard if you do a specification review with the user. Of course, it implies that the specification will actually be both readable and be read, but you can only go so far in protecting people. Once the omission makes it into the final design, it will become a bug in the final product.

Conflict errors occur when two different design features have conflicting designs. This might be as simple as an outright conflict, where the design states that a file can be opened by two different people at the same time in the Open unit, whereas the underlying File unit is defined to only allow single user access. Bugs that result from conflicts at this level are often impossible to fix without completely rewriting the modules in the system. This is one reason that bugs at this level are so expensive to fix. There is rarely an "easy" way to fix them.

Translation errors are the most insidious of all of the design-level bugs. A translation error occurs when the requirements are interpreted incorrectly, at least from the perspective of the end user. If the designer either reads the requirement incorrectly or does not see the requirement in the same light as the user, an error will occur in the design process for that application. An example might be of some help in this case. Consider the case where the user wants the ability to "search for files in the application." This is a pretty vague requirement and certainly open to many interpretations. The designer might read this as the ability to "find" a file by name, author, or the date the file was created or last updated. When the specification for the design is complete, the user does not comment on the designer's interpretation. However, when the final application is delivered to the user, it is pointed out that the "search" feature is missing. The user was expecting a feature that allowed a full-text search of the files. Obviously, because the user did not get it, the design is flawed. You might think of this as an omission error because the feature was left out of the design. However, the feature was in the final design, it was just there in a different and incorrect format. Fixing a bug often requires visiting more than one "level" to correctly repair and eliminate the problem. Requirements documents are often reused for future software development projects.

Implementation Bugs

Implementation bugs are what most people think of when they talk about software "bugs" or software defects. Although a software defect is probably really a requirements or design bug, a software bug is usually an implementation problem. Implementation bugs are the most common, and in general, the easiest bugs to fix in the system. That doesn't make it any better or easier for the software engineer. You are still stuck with finding, fixing, and verifying all of the implementation bugs in your system.

The individual types of implementation bugs are mostly what we will consider in this chapter because they are the easiest to classify. Unlike design and requirements bugs, which tend to be application specific, programmers have been making the same kinds of mistakes in coding their applications since the very beginning of the computer age. Some kinds of implementation bugs, however, are unique to the environments in which they occur. For example, it is very difficult to run into firmware timing issues when working on a standard personal computer. However, these firmware bugs are quite common in the embedded world.

For our purposes, implementation bugs can be classified into one of five broad categories. We provide a quick overview of all five, which consist of:

♦ Error messages

♦ Graphical user interface errors

♦ Missing functionality at the implementation stage

♦ Program crashes and other serious defects

♦ Other implementation errors

Bugs that display error messages to the user when the process for a feature was followed properly constitute the first category. Although these messages can be legitimate, users might consider this a bug because they did things correctly and got an error display. Normally, when users obey the rules, they expect to get a legitimate result. An error message doesn't fit the mold of a legitimate response. Often, errors of this type are either caused by resource problems or specific data dependencies.

The second category contains bugs that consist of graphical user interface errors. These bugs can either be modifications to the application UI that are not standard and cause the user to do things incorrectly, or they can be standard components of the UI that are used in a different way than could normally be expected by the end user.

GUI bugs are often the easiest to fix, due to their ease in repetition and traceability, but are the most pervasive in an application. Consider, for example, the case where a screen consists of several inputs and two buttons, OK and Cancel. You might imagine that entering some data on the screen and pressing OK would take you to the next screen, whereas hitting Cancel would take you to the previous screen or out of the feature entirely. It would certainly be considered a bug if the program interpreted Cancel to commit all changes!

The third category consists of missing functionality at the implementation stage, which is always considered a bug. If the design specification states that you should be able to import formats x, y, and z, and your system can only import format x, this is most certainly a bug in the implementation. Likewise, if the specification states that your system should accept up to 10,000 entries into a spreadsheet and your spreadsheet only can handle 5,000, this is most certainly a bug. Missing functionality is usually caught early in the process by test cases written against the original requirements for the system.

Many testers and beta users will report bugs against the system that are really desirable enhancements. As a software engineer, it is not really your job to deal with these bugs, but they will be in the bug database, and they will exist. Your job, in the case of these bugs, is to screen out legitimate omissions from requests for things that were never in the specification. If you fail at this job, you will be subject to "feature creep" and all of the problems associated with that issue. We won't consider this as one of the possible bug categories, but you should be aware that many people do.

Program crashes, hang ups, and other serious defects are a category unto themselves in the lore of software bugs—our fourth category. There are very, very few people that will argue that when the program crashes or quits and corrupts the data file it uses, it isn't a serious bug. This whole section of bugs, however, comes under "undesirable behavior" problems. These problems consist of anything that the user or tester of the system finds less than perfect in manipulating the software.

Many people consider syntax errors, linking errors, and other such problems to be implementation bugs. They are not because the system would never have been released with such problems. Assuming that you can go through each and every feature in the system, the system must be complete to work. We will assume, at the implementation level, that the system is complete and that it builds correctly. Any other sort of problem in the build area is a build bug.

There is one form of the syntax error problem that is an implementation problem and bears mentioning. This is the case of a scripting language error that occurs only at runtime. Bugs like this are much akin to runtime problems caused by incorrect coding, such as division by zero errors or null pointer assignments. All of these things can, and should, be caught within the program source code, but are sometimes not. The program builds properly and deploys properly, but runs incorrectly.

Process Bugs

Process is that part of the software development cycle that involves configuration management, source code control, creating new projects, documentation, using scripts to automate tools, and the like, often repetitively. Process can also be part of large-scale client/server or Web-based systems, involving such things as backups, log file interpretation, communication between groups, and operational tasks.

You might not think that process bugs can get in the way of final development efforts, but you would be sadly mistaken. In fact, many bugs are caused by low-level process errors that propagate themselves into the final shipped product.

Let's look at two simple examples of process errors that cause bugs. The first involves a standalone shrink-wrapped product. The second involves a large-scale production Web site. In both cases, we will see how a process error caused a nightmare for the end user.

Case #1: The Case of the Improper DLL

A long time ago, I worked at a company that made products to help users browse, search, and read data on CD-ROMs. Okay, it was a *very* long time ago. But the concepts are still the same. This project was built in Windows 3.1 using Microsoft Visual C++. One of the odd things about working in the Windows environment is that the code you write makes calls to dynamic linked libraries (DLLs). These libraries exist as files on the user's hard drive. The notion behind DLLs is that you can "share" code between multiple programs that are using the same functions. As a result, only one copy of a DLL is loaded into memory, no matter how many programs are using it. This is a good strategy for working in a limited memory system, which Windows 3.1 most certainly was.

One of the biggest problems with DLLs, however, is the way they interact with the programs that load them. Windows provides the ability to use what is known as an "import library" to create stubs in the application, which the operating system then links to the loaded module at runtime. The DLL files themselves are loaded by finding the first file that matches the name of the library requested, using a path defined in the Windows environment. Now that you have this background information, let's move on to the actual issue.

While my coworkers and I were developing the application, we ran into a consistent problem. The program ran perfectly on the developer's machine, but would fail to run or would crash rather spectacularly when run on the tester's machine. Of course, the fact that the tester also happened to be my boss certainly didn't help the situation. The project developers had designed an installation script (this was before automated installation tools) that the manager/tester used to grab the most current copy of the program and put it onto his hard drive. The script then set up the various icons and such that were needed to launch the program.

Once the installation script finished, the manager/tester would simply click on the application icon, and the application was supposed to run. It ran on the development machines. It ran on the machines we used for clean testing the final product. It ran on the machines for the eventual customer of the product, who was trying it out to make sure that it did what he wanted it to do. The silly program, however, would simply refuse to run properly on the test machine.

When you install something, you try your hardest to make sure that all of the necessary components are installed with the system. In our case, we were well aware of the DLL problem, having been "bit" by it in earlier installation attempts. Therefore, our installation script carefully checked not only for the presence of the required DLLs, but also for their version numbers. If a version number (an embedded bit of information in the file itself) was not high enough, the script would copy the newer version of the DLL onto the machine. Therefore, everything should have been the same on all machines, which is the basis for process control. Note that you should make sure that all of the elements are the same before trying something new.

Because we knew that the library files had to be the same and that the manager was running the scripts properly, we frantically looked for anything else that might have been different on his machine. Finally, in a true moment of desperation, I decided to actually verify that everything was correct. For programmers, this is much like being reduced to reading the manual when you can't figure out how to do something, or perhaps like stopping to ask for directions.

While verifying each and every file, I discovered that the DLLs for the application were not being overwritten correctly. Older versions of the libraries were still present. This made no sense at all. After all, this is what our script did, wasn't it? Well, it turned out that we weren't quite aware of all of the factors in this situation. Windows, it seems, will not overwrite a DLL if that file is already in use. None of the other machines were using those DLL files, but the manager's machine was loading them via some startup program, which was loaded when he brought up the operating system. The script was not smart enough to determine that the function it was performing had failed, so the original DLL files were never updated. This is a perfect example of a process bug.

Case #2: The Case of the Broken Database

Back in the mid to late 1990s, I was working for an Internet startup, much like every other developer in the world at that point. My team was working on a product that was going to revolutionize the world, of course. As a part of that revolutionary spirit, we were using cutting edge technology on an Internet Web site. If there is a scarier, more bug-prone phrase than "cutting edge technology" when used with the word Internet, I'm not really sure what it might be. Boldly ignoring all of the typical little issues, we strode forward using an object-oriented database, a Distributed Component Object Model (DCOM) server, and an Active Server Page (ASP) front-end to implement most of our functionality. The remaining work was done primarily by using third-party tools integrated into our Web site. Ah, the folly of youth. Fortunately, those days are long past for all of us, right?

To get back to the problem at hand, we discovered one day that the login system on our backup Web site (yes, we had one, we were young, not stupid) wasn't working properly for internal users. Later analysis would show that it wasn't working for external users either. In fact, almost everyone was unable to log in—well, almost everyone. One small group of people was capable of logging in, but we had no idea why. The process used to log in was as follows:

1. Check to see if the user had already logged in. If so, deny access because we only allowed one person to log in from each account at one time.

2. If the user was not logged in, check the user's name and password. If they are valid and match, log the person in. Assign the time that the user logged into the system as the starting login time.

3. Check the user's customized properties to see which screens should be shown to the user first. At the top of each screen was a check to verify that the user had been logged into the system; otherwise a user could simply bookmark an internal page and then jump to it, bypassing the login system completely. This feature wasn't foolproof, but it worked.

4. Part of the login verification process determined how long a user had been idle. This was done by checking the user's last action time. Every time the user did something in the system, the last action time would be updated.

What my coworkers and I discovered, when digging into the ASP code for this site, was that the system was automatically logging a user off due to excessive idle time. This made no sense at all because the user would have just logged in and there was virtually no idle time at all.

Determining the cause of the problem took some time. There was considerable finger-pointing as to where the problem resided. Certainly, the most puzzling aspect of the whole situation was the fact that the components to the object database and its interface had not changed from the production system. In fact, the backup site was, quite literally, a mirror of the production site. This was the original intent, to simply get the backup running correctly with no changes.

It was with some trepidation, therefore, that I looked into the problem. Originally, my suspicion was that someone in the operations department had not set up one of the machines correctly. I made the mistake of voicing that suggestion and was immediately blamed for casting aspersions unfairly. So, as I should have done in the first place, I worked my way through the checklist of items involved in setting up the machine. Everything certainly did seem to be in place. The Web servers had all of the appropriate software installed. The back-end database system had all the correct settings for access and security. Everything seemed just fine. And yet, the database interface software was returning a huge number for the number of seconds that the user had been previously logged in.

There was really only one thing left to do. I stepped through the code line by line trying to actually understand where all the data came from and what information was being passed. The login time came from the Web server and was stored in the back-end database. The Web server then queried the back-end database for the last access time and the current server time. To compute the idle time, it simply subtracted the last access time from the current server time. That's when it hit me. The current server time. The current server, in this case, was the back-end database. The original login time came from the Web server. Normally, this wasn't an issue. The various servers were updated with the time when they started up, and we made sure that they were all synchronized from the master server on the network. The problem was, this was a backup system. It did not have a master server to synchronize with. In fact, part of the setup process was to verify that each machine had the same time on it. I asked the operations people about this and was assured that they had checked the time on each machine to verify that it was correct.

What was wrong with this process? Put simply, too much as assumed. The times on all of the machines did, in fact, match up correctly within a few seconds. However, the date on the database machine was one full day ahead of the rest of the machines. When it computed the "current time," it used the number of seconds since some arbitrary start date, as most computers do. In this case, however, it ended up with a time that was approximately 84,000 seconds ahead of the rest of the machines. When 84,000 seconds is divided by 24 hours, and then divided by 60 minutes in an hour, it turns out to be exactly one day. The date on the machine was reset and the problem was fixed.

Where was the problem in this case? Was it in the fact that the software reported an invalid number of seconds? Of course not. It was doing exactly what it was supposed to do, and it worked fine on other systems. Was it the fact that the Web server didn't check to see if it was running the same date and time as the database server? No, there is no way for this to happen. The process was supposed to ensure that the machines' clocks were synchronized. The process failed because it had a bug in it.

Build Bugs

A build bug is one that occurs because the build process contains an error, or the build engineer makes a mistake that causes the final product to fail. Build bugs can result from incorrect tags in source code control systems, incorrect settings in make files, and so on. Build bugs normally follow directly from process errors and are usually fixed by cleaning up the process so that such errors cannot happen again.

A build bug incident happened to me a few years ago. I was working for a company that shipped customized software to its clients. This customized software was built from a core product. In the core product, the customized sections were usually added via conditional compilation and internal make file flags. When a new version of the software was developed for a new or existing client, a new form was delivered to the build engineers that explained how to set up the new software for release builds, which were to be delivered to the client. The forms were stored on the computer and used the name of the client as a "key" into the system.

It just so happened that a new client of the company had the same beginning name as an existing customer. For example, call the original customer XYZ Corporation and the new client XYZ Ltd. Unfortunately, the build form given to the engineers often did not spell out the complete name of the company because this situation had never occurred before. You can pretty much guess the rest. The build engineer was told to cut a build for XYZ. He went to the computer and selected the first XYZ he saw. As fate would have it, the list of companies happened to scroll to the XYZ Corporation first and did not display the secondary name on the engineer's screen. As a result, he cut a build that was similar to, but different from, the build that should have been generated.

The day following the new build delivery, my teammates and I received a fax from the customer indicating its displeasure with the lack of several features we had agreed upon and had shown in a demo. In fact, the client stated, if this was the best we could do, the company could easily take its business elsewhere. We were, to say the least, dumbfounded. We had worked quite hard on the software, putting in long hours to get the requested features into the software. Fortunately, for all concerned, the error was found before too long and a new build was cut for the client. The customer ended up happy, the developers ended up happy, and the build engineers learned that even build processes can have bugs.

Deployment Bugs

Of all of the processes in the software development world, you would think that the deployment process would be the most bug-free. In most cases, you would be right. Thorough care goes into the software when it is a client deliverable or a shrink-wrapped product. When it comes to delivering internal applications or client/server server-side applications, however, the number of bugs increases dramatically. A deployment bug is one in which the software is correct, and the build process is correct, but the final software is not installed correctly.

In my career, I've run across numerous deployment bugs. Oddly, the more important the system and the more critical the install, the more likely it seems to be that there is a problem in the deployment. Probably, the most critical error that I've seen in the deployment process occurred while I was working for a company that sent out data via a satellite download system.

On one particular occasion, the system was supposed to send out a nightly download that contained an upgrade to the software of the satellite receiver box. This upgrade process had been followed dozens of times in the past with success. This time, however, the upgrade was done very quickly and rushed to the upload stage. Because the deployment process was rushed, the engineers doing the job cut corners to get the thing up and on the "bird" as quickly as possible due to upper management pressure. This caused them to bypass several critical checks for file integrity on the software. The download, which was in an encapsulated format specially designed for the satellite transmission, was corrupted in the copy process from the main office to the uplink facility.

The result of the corrupted download caused all of the satellite receiver boxes to have numerous problems, from being unable to view the satellite signal to losing all information on the box. Hundreds of people called the customer support line to complain about the problem, which could easily have been avoided had the process been followed properly. However, a process is only as good as the people that implement it. If you force them to cut corners, problems will ultimately occur.

What lessons did this experience teach? Unfortunately, very few. The next upload was done the same way, cutting corners to rush a fix to the user. It did not cause any problems, which in a way was unfortunate. I'm quite sure that the company involved continues to set themselves up for a disaster. They have bypassed the process that was established early on to ensure that a download was properly installed and would not cause the end user any problems. This is a typical deployment bug—avoiding the process when push comes to shove.

Future Planning Bugs

Future planning bugs are those bugs that could have easily been avoided had the designer or developer simply looked forward a bit in time. The single best example of a future planning bug is the so-called Millenium bug (the year 2000 bug). Programmers developed systems that used two-digit years in storage, which made it impossible to tell the difference between 1900 and 2000. This problem, which turned out to be a nonissue thanks to thousands of hours of overtime by developers, could have been avoided completely had someone simply pointed out the problem earlier and forced designers to consider it. The question, of course, is how to hold the designer responsible for going back and changing the design in response to such considerations. Without a give and take between designer and implementer, there will always be design bugs. For a sensible designer, therefore, it makes sense to take into account the knowledge and experience of others. As we will see in Chapter 15, this can be done quite well with the help of a professional debugger. Future planning bugs can be caused by cutting corners in memory, disk space, or user interface. A simple example of such a "corner cutting" would be the use of an in-memory sort because the designer never expects to have more than a few hundred items. When the total number of items exceeds a million, such a sort is unlikely to perform on the average user machine.

You might think that such bugs would be a thing of the past because the Year 2000 bug caused so much grief, overtime, and expensive rework on the part of so many developers across the world. Unfortunately, they are not. Several similar bugs lurk on the horizon, and you would do well to avoid adding them to your own systems. Some examples follow.

Consider, for example, the Social Security Number (SSN) problem. Social Security numbers, as you may or may not know, are of the form XXX-XX-XXXX, where all Xs are numbers. Counting the numbers, we see that there are 9 of them, allowing for a maximum of 999,999,999 numbers. The population of the United States is approximately 300,000,000 people. So, you would think that given our slow birthrate we would be safe for another 200 years or so. But, it's not quite that simple. SSNs are never reused. That means you can have a maximum of a billion SSNs. How many SSN holders have there been since the 1920s (when the SSN system was first created)? The problem is getting bigger, isn't it? It gets a bit worse. Each year, as people die, the numbers drop out of circulation. Because SSNs are not reused, the number of SSNs available will drop to zero in about 100 years at best. Throw in the fact that SSNs are allocated in "blocks" to each area, and you'll find that we could run out much quicker than anyone could imagine. What will happen when we run out of SSNs? How many systems use the SSN as a "unique" key and will need to be rewritten? A problem like this could make the Y2K problem pale in comparison.

What does this mean to you as a developer or designer? Imagine the number of applications that exist with hard-coded nine digit fields for the SSN field. Furthermore, imagine the amount of work that will be involved in making those fields bigger and fixing all existing data. Scared yet? You really should be. Learn something from the Y2K problem. Set up your SSN field to be variable length, and do not write code that requires the field to be nine digits. The easiest fix for this system, by the way, is to allow letters in the field. This would extend the life of the SSN for quite a while, but would break virtually all of the software that exists today.

If you aren't convinced that future planning issues are important, consider the lowly telephone number. With an area code, prefix, and number, the phone number is 10 digits long, which means there are 10 billion possible combinations. Given the population of approximately 300 million, this means that every man, woman, and child in the country can have up to 40 phone numbers. Hey, that doesn't sound so bad. Most people have nowhere near 33 numbers. Oh wait, that doesn't include businesses. It doesn't include cell phone numbers, or fax numbers, or pagers. Hmm, suddenly that 10 billion number doesn't sound so high after all. Worse, because many of those numbers are not available (the number of prefixes, for example, is limited), you reduce that number quite a bit. We are already seeing a shortage of phone numbers and splitting of area codes in many states. How long before these "bandage" approaches to the problem stop working?

The amount of code dedicated to phone numbers is astounding. We have code dedicated to pulling out the area code and determining the location (city, state) from it. We have specialized GUI elements dedicated to inputting phone numbers easily. We have directories and systems to find phone numbers for people. What is going to happen to all of this code when the number system changes?

Future planning mistakes that can be avoided just make you look inept if you don't recognize and consider them. How many programs written after the Y2K problem was public knowledge still had two digit years? How many arguments broke out in companies because they did not know if their third-party tools were Y2K compliant? When you can see something like this coming, as you should be able to in situations like SSNs, phone numbers, ISBNs (numbers for books), and UPCs (bar code numbers), you need to think about them for the future. Don't create bugs twenty years from now in systems you are designing today. Think about the future. Do not make the mistake of assuming that the artifacts and effects of what you're working on today won't be rattling around in applications code in twenty years.

Documentation Bugs

Documentation bugs are easy to define. The system does something one way, the documentation says it works a different way. Which one is "right"? In many cases, the documentation should be right because it was written from the original specifications for the system. Of course, that's really an ideal situation. In many cases the documentation was written by people after the fact, including assumptions about the way that they thought the system should work. In other cases, however, bugs are tracked down not to the code, but to the documentation. Documentation takes numerous forms: user guides for end users, internal documents defining the system, and even onscreen help files and prompts. Any of these areas can contain bugs.

Documentation bugs are grouped into three categories: vague, incomplete, and inaccurate. Vague bugs are those where the user is not given enough information to determine how to do something properly. For example, in a library routine, a vague document would contain information about how to call the function without specifying what needs to be called first or what side-effects (such as memory allocations) occur within the library function.

Incomplete documentation leaves the user without enough information to complete a task. For example, in a word processor document, a user might be led through four of the five tasks needed to adequately check his or her writing for grammar and spelling. This would leave the user to believe that the task was done properly when in fact there was more that the program offered. Bugs like this lead to user dissatisfaction with an application, even though the application is actually capable of doing everything that the user wants it to do.

Inaccurate documentation is the worst kind of documentation bug. In this case, the document is simply wrong and has no redeeming qualities. Document bugs like this often occur when late changes are made to the system or the specification, and those changes are not communicated to the person writing the documentation. Inaccurate bugs drive users nuts. There is nothing quite like being told exactly how to perform a specific function, only to find that two of the steps in the document do not exist in the final version of the application.

Finally, it is worth mentioning that documentation and requirements problems are often the result of ambiguous specifications and language. The computer world works in terms of ones and zeros. The human world, however, is shaded in the nuances of the language spoken by the people involved in the conversation. A simple misunderstanding in language, whether in the documentation or the original description of the problem, can easily lead to serious bugs in the final product.

Severity

No discussion of software bugs is complete without a discussion of the various severity levels of bugs. The actual levels of severity differ from company to company, but in general, we can classify bugs into one of three levels of severity, four if you include the ability to add enhancement requests to the system as a bug. Companies often have large numbers of severity levels, but I've found that restricting severity levels to three simple levels makes life easier. For the purposes of this taxonomy, we only consider the following three severity levels:

- *Minor Bugs*—Minor bugs are those that the average user will never notice and that many will never find. Minor bugs might include such things as misspellings on screens, missing help topics, tab order problems on screens, and other things that really are almost matters of opinion if they are bugs at all. One tester, for example, might consider it a bug when a time display appears on one screen but not on another. Many would simply chalk it up to a difference in user interface design and not think anything of it. Bugs of this nature will never impede a system from being released. On a scale of 1 through 10, a minor bug has a value of 1 or 2.

- *Annoying Bugs*—Annoying bugs are those that affect the end user, but have workarounds that allow the functionality of the application to be used. They are things like bad links in pages, misleading text on screens, or even crashes if those crashes are difficult to reproduce and will not affect a significant number of users. You have to be realistic when releasing software; as a result, some "bad" bugs will probably make it into the final release. Bugs that can be fixed in this area should be if there is sufficient time in the release schedule for them to be fixed. On a scale of 1 through 10, an annoying bug would have a value of anything from, say, 3 through 8.

- *Showstopper Bugs*—Showstopper bugs are those that stop the release of a product. A showstopper might consist of a bug that crashes the system or loses all data if the wrong key is pressed or if the wrong data is entered. Everyone understands showstoppers; they are the kinds of bugs with which you would never voluntarily allow a piece of software to ship. On a scale of 1 through 10, a showstopper bug has a value of 9 or 10.

Severity is most important when you are talking about triage of bugs in a system. There is always a limited amount of time and a limited number of resources (people) to fix the problems you find when testing a system. As a result, you need to classify the bugs into severity levels so that you can determine what can and what cannot be fixed. Once an agreed upon list of bugs that will be fixed can be determined, you can begin assigning them to resources and estimating the length of time it will take to release the software version.

The Bug Taxonomy

In our classification scheme, we have an entry for each type of bug that exists in the world. Note that these classifications are not the same as language definitions. You won't find, for example, "assigning a bad pointer to a variable" as you might have in C++. Instead, these bugs are all lumped together under the more encompassing title of "allocation of memory errors." For each bug classification, we consider the elements discussed in the following sections.

Name

Each bug classification is assigned a name, mostly so that we can refer to it later in a descriptive manner without having to type out the entire description again. We can simply refer to "memory bugs" and be able to come back to that section to see exactly what it is we were talking about.

Description

The description of the bug is simply a longer listing of what the bug is about. The description includes enough information to explain to anyone that has ever seen a bug in this class before what it is all about.

Most Common Environments

The most common environments are the environments in which you are most likely to find bugs of this class. An environment value may be *any*, which would mean that the bug can occur in any type of system. Alternate values are standalone, client/server, Web server, embedded, production systems, and thin client front-ends.

Symptoms

All bug classifications have a set of symptoms that are fairly unique to them. This doesn't mean, however, that the symptom set itself is unique. Although the classification always contains some of the set of symptoms, many different bug classifications may exhibit the same sorts of symptoms. The art of debugging is really the process of eliminating other bug classifications to determine what the problem might be. It is rarely a matter of saying, "Aha! That must be an <xyz> bug!" If you are expecting to be able to determine the classification of a bug uniquely by simply observing the symptoms, you are likely to be mistaken. It would be nice, but things simply aren't that different among the root causes of bug classifications, so the symptoms also tend to be quite similar.

Example

Each bug contains an example, so even if you can't figure out what I am talking about from the description, you can get an idea of the problem from the example cited. In most cases, the examples stem from real experience, so you can at least get a chuckle out of my misery over the years.

The Bug Classes

Bugs can be divided up into various discrete classes which can be uniquely identified by their symptoms and causes. In this section, we explore the various classes of bugs and look at the environments and symptoms that are best associated with each class.

Memory or Resource Leaks

A memory leak bug is one in which memory is somehow allocated from either the operating system or an internal memory "pool," but never deallocated when the memory is finished being used. Memory leaks need not be true "leaks," but instead can also be failures to reclaim resources. Memory, in this case, can be actual physical computer memory or other resources used by the system.

You might think that memory leaks can only occur in languages that support the allocation of memory and provide ways to deallocate that memory. For example, languages such as FORTRAN, Visual Basic, and Java would not appear to have memory or resource leaks because they either do not support memory allocation in the first place, or they have a garbage collection scheme that automatically frees up blocks of memory when they are no longer used. This is simply not the case. Resource leaks can occur in any language and are often due to simple programming errors.

Most Common Environments

A memory or resource leak can occur in any environment. It is most common in operating systems on personal or large-scale computers and in languages that support memory allocation and deallocation. For embedded systems, memory leaks can still occur, but are usually rare due to their dire circumstances.

Symptoms

Symptoms of a memory or resource leak include system slowdowns, crashes that occur "randomly" over a long period of time, and other "odd" symptoms. The most easily observable symptom in a memory or resource leak is that the total amount of system memory (or resources) decreases over time and does not recover. You can often test for this evidence using third-party monitoring tools to observe whether or not your program appears to be leaking memory.

More difficult symptoms are observed when working with embedded resources. Imagine, for example, that you have a pool of objects from which you can allocate an object, use it, and then return the object to the pool. If you fail to return an object to the pool, it quickly becomes "orphaned" and is not available to the next process that needs the object from the pool. Only by observing patterns of usage of the pool (logging entries to allocation and deallocation) are you able to see that the number of objects is steadily decreasing. If you are using a monitoring tool and have output logs to feed into it, you will observe a steady leak of resources.

Other symptoms of memory leaks include failure of "sure thing" allocations. For example, if you are allocating a block of 20 bytes of memory and it fails, you should suspect a memory leak of extreme severity in your system.

In the Windows environment, there is a limit on the number of system resources you can use. For example, you might have too many device contexts (DCs) open and you might fail to close them. Alternatively, in either a Windows or a Unix environment, you might have too many file handles open. In either case, an attempt to allocate a new resource will fail. If you notice that resource allocations are suddenly failing after succeeding for some time, suspect a memory leak.

Example

Let's take a look at a simple memory leak error that can occur trivially in a C program. This type of code is found in hundreds of programs across the programming spectrum. It illustrates the simplest possible case of a memory leak, which is when memory is allocated and not deallocated in all cases. This particular form of the bug is the most frustrating because the memory is usually deallocated, but not always.

```
char *buffer = new char[kMaxBufferSize+1];
memset( buffer, 0, kMaxBufferSize+1 );

// Do some stuff to fill and work with the character buffer

if ( IsError( nCondition ) ) // Did we get an error in the processing piece?
{
    Message( ("An error occurred. Skipping final stage") );
    return FailureCode;
}

// Final stage of code

// Free up allocated memory
delete buffer;
return OkCode;
```

Note that in many cases, this code works perfectly. If no error occurs in the processing stage (which is the norm) the memory is freed up properly. If, however, the processing stage encounters an error, the memory is not freed up and a leak occurs. In cases like this, you can fix the problem by using "smart pointers," which automatically free the memory they contain when they go out of scope. If the pointer is of global scope, however, it is up to you to make sure that you free up the memory when you are done with it.

The following code snippet from some old C++ code I once wrote contains a slightly more insidious bug. I'm rather ashamed of it, but it illustrates the point well, which makes it worth bringing up again.

```
class Foo
{
private:
    int nStringLength;
    char *sString;
```

```
public:
    Foo()
    {
        nStringLength = 20;  // Default
        sString = new char[ nStringLength + 1];
    }
    ~Foo()
    {
        delete sString;
    }
    void SetString( const char *inString )
    {
        sString = new char[ strlen( inString+1 ) ];
        if ( inString == NULL )
            return;
        strncpy( sString, inString, strlen(inString) );
        nStringLength = strlen(inString)+1;
    }
};
```

Let's discuss what happens. In most cases, the Foo object is created and nothing bad happens. If, however, you call the **SetString** method, all bets are off. The previously allocated string is overwritten by the new allocation, and the old allocated memory goes nowhere. We have an instant memory leak. Worse, we can do this multiple times if we accidentally call the method with a NULL string because it first allocates the block, and then checks to see if the input string was correct. My advice—don't do things like this. If you see an allocation in a class, check to see if the string can be allocated before it gets to that point.

Logic Errors

Logic errors are by far the most insidious of all programming problems. A logic error occurs when the code is syntactically correct but does not do what you expect it to do. Logic errors can occur due to programming typographical errors, or they can occur because you do not properly think things through. A logic error cannot be caught in a compiler, debugger, or code analyzer because the code is correct and proper and will run as written.

Most Common Environments

A logic error can, and will, occur in any environment using any operating system and any programming language.

Symptoms

The most obvious symptom of a logic error is when you see a programmer shaking his head and saying, "But that's not what I meant for it to do." Logic errors are caught because the code is misbehaving in a way that isn't easily explained. The program doesn't crash, but the flow of the program takes odd branches through the code. Results are the opposite of what is expected. Output looks strange, but has no obvious symptoms of corruption.

Example

A while ago, I came across the following code, along with the comment listed, in an application I was doing some maintenance work on. It would really be worth a lot to me to see the face of the programmer who wrote this code when he looks at it now.

```
// Make sure that the input is valid. For this value, valid ranges
// are 1-10 and 15-20
if ( ( input >= 1 && input <= 10) && ( input >= 15 && input <= 20 ) )
{
    // Do something for valid case
}
else
{
    // Do something for invalid case
}
```

If you don't understand C++, here's the equivalent code in VB.

```
IF ( (INPUT >= 1 and INPUT <= 10) AND (INPUT >= 15 and INPUT <= 20) )
BEGIN
    ; Do something for valid case.
END
ELSE
BEGIN
    ; Do something for invalid case
END
ENDIF
```

Looking at the code in any language, the problem remains the same. In order for the code to enter the valid case, the number must be between 1 and 10 *and* be between 15 and 20. If a number is between 1 and 10, how can it possibly be between 15 and 20 as well? Seems unlikely, doesn't it? This is a typical logic error.

Coding Errors

A coding error is a simple problem in writing the code. It can be a failure to check error returns, a failure to check for certain valid conditions, or a failure to take into account other parts of the system. Yet another form of a coding error is incorrect parameter passing and invalid return type coercion.

Most Common Environments

Some languages are naturally prone to coding errors. In addition, some coding techniques lend themselves more to coding errors than others. Strongly typed languages, for example, are less prone to parameter passing mistakes. Languages that do not allow easy coercion are less prone to mistakes of variable type conversion. Visual Basic, which is a weakly typed language, leads to more errors for type conversions. C programmers that use variable numbers of arguments for function prototypes are just asking for problems due to the wrong number or type of parameters being passed. Java programmers are exempt from not handling certain kinds of errors, specifically exceptions, but can easily cause problems by not handling those exceptions properly. Of course, if you program in FORTRAN and stick with common blocks, you are likely to run into problems if you do not follow standard conventions.

Symptoms

Unexplained errors in black box testing (which is testing the software with no understanding of the internal construction of the functions) are usually caused by coding errors. Other symptoms are compiler warnings, strange program crashes such as abnormal terminations, and failure to observe proper program flow.

When you think about it, coding errors are really at the root of all program problems. After all, if you had coded it "right," the problem wouldn't exist in the first place. The reason that we separate coding errors from other sorts of problems in the code is that we want to identify programming problems purely caused by the lack of attention to other problems that might be easy to create in the code.

Example

In the following example, a function accepts an input integer and converts it into a string that contains that integer in its word representation. Unfortunately, the programmer who wrote the function didn't take into account all possible cases. Let's see what happens when someone else (me) uses that function:

```
procedure ConvertToString(InInteger: Integer, OutString: String,
OutLength : Integer);
begin

case InInteger of
    1:
        OutString := "One";
        OutLength := 3;
    2:
        OutString := "Two";
        OutLength := 3;
    3:
        OutString := "Three";
        OutLength := 5;
    4:
        OutString := "Four";
        OutLength := 4;
```

```
5:
    OutString := "Five";
    OutLength := 4;
6:
    OutString := "Six";
    OutLength := 3;
7:
    OutString := "Seven";
    OutLength := 5;
8:
    OutString := "Eight";
    OutLength := 5;
9:
    OutString := "Nine";
    OutLength := 4;

end case;

end procedure;

{* My call of the function *}
var
    Length : Integer;
    Name   :   String;
begin
    Length := 22; {* Initialized for another use *}
    ConvertToString( 0, Name, Length );

    For I := 1 to Length
        Write( Name[I] );WriteLn

end;
```

There are a few things to notice in the preceding code. The **ConvertToString** function does not handle all cases of inputs, which becomes very obvious when I pass in a zero value. Worse, the function does not initialize the output variables, leaving them at whatever they happened to be when they came into the function. This isn't a problem for the output string, necessarily, but it will become a serious issue for the output length. When the function exits, the length is not reset, leaving it at whatever it was originally initialized to, in this case 22. The output string was never touched, so it remains blank. When the **for** loop executes, the program steps all over the memory that isn't part of the string and will likely terminate abnormally. Although the actual reason for the termination is a memory overrun, the underlying cause in this case is a set of coding errors that led to the symptom.

Memory Overruns

Ah yes, the joys of memory overruns. Put simply, a memory overrun occurs when you use memory that does not belong to you. This can be caused by overstepping an array boundary or by copying a string that is too big for the block of memory it is defined to hold. Memory overruns were once extremely common in the programming world because of the inability to tell what the actual size of something really was. With the advent of object-oriented programming and type safe languages, memory overruns are less common, but can still easily occur in code.

Note that simply accessing a block of memory outside of what you are permitted to will not always cause a problem. In fact, stepping through an array that is smaller than you believe it to be is often no problem whatsoever, although it will certainly return bogus values. The problem always occurs when you try to modify the data in the memory block that is invalid.

Most Common Environments

Memory overruns are seen in all environments, standalone, client/server, or Web-based systems. Several languages, such as FORTRAN, C, and C++, are most susceptible to these errors, although C++ mollifies the problem to some extent by providing classes, such as vector and string, that will catch such errors before they can propagate.

Symptoms

There are quite a few symptoms for a memory overrun. The most extreme is a program crash. If the program crashes quite regularly after a given routine is called, that routine should be examined for a possible overrun condition. If the routine in question does not appear to have any such problem, the most likely cause is that another routine, called in the prior sequence, has already trashed variables or memory blocks. Checking the trace log of called routines leading up to the one with the problem will often show up the error. Another much more indicative symptom of overruns occurs when values mysteriously change in the program. For example, if you are examining a value in the debugger and it mysteriously changes across two lines of code that do not appear to modify it, you might suspect a memory overrun. This happens because when you modify values beyond the end of an array, you have to change something. That something is quite often the next variable in memory. When you see a variable mysteriously change, check for the array defined most closely to it. You will often find that this array is the one being overwritten at some point in the program.

Many good debuggers can catch memory overruns. In addition, several third-party memory checking routines can catch overruns. If you suspect such a problem, you might try running one of these tools against your running program. If it shows a memory overrun, you will at least have someplace to start looking for the problem.

Example

I think I've been bitten by more memory overruns than any other type of error while maintaining software. Some of them have been in the code for years. The following code contains one of my favorites. I've abridged it considerably to fit it into this chapter, but the best aspect of it, to my way of thinking, is that the person that came in to fix it inserted a character buffer into the program to make it work properly. I've always gotten a kick out of that.

```
const kMaxEntries = 50;
int gArray[ kMaxEntries ];
char szDummyBuffer[ 256 ]; // This was inserted to fix a weird error
int nState = 10;

int ZeroArray ( int *pArray )
{
     for ( int i=0; i<100; ++i )
         pArray[i] = 0;
}


// Much later in the program

int Initialize()
{
    ZeroArray( gArray ); // Make sure that the array is cleared out to start.
    nState=10;  // We need to keep doing this because it keeps
            //  getting cleared someplace.
}
```

This particular example shows not only a memory overrun (and a serious one at that), but also how most programmers "fix" problems in an application. When I finally figured out what was going on, I almost laughed myself silly. If you look at the **Initialize** function, it first zeroes out the global array. I'm not really sure why this was necessary, but the original developer apparently felt that it was. The problem happens immediately. The **ZeroArray** function steps all over the array boundaries by initializing 100 separate entries. The problem is that that particular array only has 50 slots available in its allocation. What happens at that point is that the function goes past the end of the array and starts to walk on things beyond its control. The programmer obviously noticed that this was happening; he provided a comment that **nState** needed to be reset because it kept getting cleared. Of course it got cleared! The array overrun was wiping it out as well as any variables following it in the memory. It's amazing this program ever worked in the first place.

The curious thing is how it was "fixed." Somewhere along the line, the developer maintaining the software noticed that the **nState** variable was getting clobbered. Rather than figure out how it was happening, he or she inserted a large character buffer right above the declaration of the variable in the program. This made the clearing effect go away because it was now the buffer that got clobbered each time the **ZeroArray** function was called for the **gArray** variable. This didn't fix anything, of course. It simply moved the problem somewhere else. As we've mentioned before, fixes like this—ones that simply bury the problem further—aren't fixes at all. They are antifixes because they make it harder to determine what the real problem was.

Loop Errors

A loop error, not surprisingly, is an error that occurs around a loop construct in a program. Loop errors break down into several different subtypes. For example, we have infinite loops, nonprocessed loops, off-by-one loops, and improperly exited loops. Let's take a quick look at each type.

Infinite loops are loops that have exits. Infinite loops can be planned features, such as loops that process messages in a program forever. In this case, they are usually not bugs. In other cases, the programmer wanted the loop to be able to exit, but failed to provide a safe exit condition. Often, unintended infinite loops are so tight that the program appears to "lock up" the system it runs on, even though both the program and the system are working correctly.

Off-by-one loops are a strange breed of loop that only appear to occur in the programming world. The notion of "off-by-one" is caused by the fact that normal people think in terms of counting from 1 to an end value, such as 10. In a programming construct, however, it is more natural to count from zero to the value just before the terminating number, such as nine. The off-by-one condition occurs when you meant to count from 0 to 9, but instead counted from either 1 to 10 or 0 to 10. Problems like this are quite common in languages like C, where arrays start at the zero index value.

Improperly exited loops are loops where the program either exits too soon or too late. They can be a variant of the off-by-one loop in that the programmer may want to exit when the loop reaches 9, but the program exits when the loop counter reaches 10 instead.

Most Common Environments

Loop errors can occur in virtually any environment. Certain kinds of loop errors, specifically infinite loops, are less likely in embedded environments where "watchdog" applications normally terminate such applications after a given period of time has expired. Because of this termination, loop errors are much easier to detect and remove in embedded environments. Improper exit condition errors, off-by-one errors, and other kinds of loop errors are more complicated and quite often cannot be found except through extensive debugging efforts.

Symptoms

Different kinds of loop errors have different sorts of symptoms. If your program simply locks up, repeatedly displays the same data over and over, or infinitely displays the same message box, you should immediately suspect an infinite loop error.

Off-by-one loop errors are quite often seen in processes that perform calculations. If a hand calculation shows that the total or final sum is incorrect by the last data point, you can quickly surmise that an off-by-one loop error is to blame. Likewise, if you were using graphics software and saw all of the points on the screen, but the last two were unconnected, you would suspect an off-by-one error.

The improper exit condition loop can usually be noticed by watching for a process that terminates unexpectedly when it should have continued. You see these quite often in embedded loops, where one loop is nested within another. An improper exit condition in the secondary inside loop causes that loop to not be executed after the first pass through the process.

Example

Because these three cases of loop errors are really quite different from one another, let's look at a simple example of each one. The following is an example of an infinite loop coded in Visual Basic. It doesn't really look like it should be infinite, but it most certainly is:

```
Dim DoneFlag As Boolean
DoneFlag = false;
Do While Not DoneFlag
Get 1FileNum, , baChunk
If  baChunk = "EDN" THEN
        DoneFlag = True;
Loop.
```

The preceding code fragment is intended to read in lines from a file until it encounters a line that contains the string "END". This loop is infinite for two reasons. First, the string being compared is not "END", but is "EDN". The program will never find such a string, and so will continue. Second, the program does not check for an end of file condition. This eventually results in a file read error, which will abnormally terminate the program.

You might think that off-by-one errors are restricted to C and C++, but you are quite mistaken. The following is a simple example of an off-by-one error in Delphi.

```
var
anArray : Array[1..50] of Integer;
Index : Integer;
begin
Index := 50;
While ( Index >= 0 ) do
    Begin
        anArray[Index] := 0;
        Index := Index - 1;
    End;
end.
```

In this case, the programmer was trying to be smart. He worked his way backward through the array, assuming that this way there would be no chance of an error. Of course, if you examine the loop, you will find that it is performed 51 times. There are only 50 elements in the Array object. This will certainly lead to a problem later on in the program, if it doesn't first trigger an immediate exception from the Delphi system.

The final situation is an improper exit condition for a loop. This is most easily illustrated by using a set of nested loops. In the following example, we are trying to compute something within the inner loop for some number of iterations:

```
int nIndex = 0;
for ( int I=0; I<kMaxIterations; ++I )
{
        while ( nIndex < 20 )
        {
                ComputeSomething( I*20 + nIndex );
                nIndex ++;
        }
}
```

The code appears to do what we said it should do. It computes whatever it is we are computing in the inner loop for each iteration of the outer loop, 20 times. The problem, however, is that the exit condition simply says that **nIndex** should be less than 20. The first time through the outer loop, this variable will become 21, and the inner loop will exit. This is correct, and exactly the way you would expect this to happen. The problem, however, is that the next time through the loop, the inner loop will not be executed at all. Obviously, this is not what we intended to have happen. Why does it happen? Once the **nIndex** variable reaches 21, the inner loop terminates. However, the loop variable is never reset and thus, the exit condition is reached before the loop even starts. This causes problems and is a result of an improper exit loop condition.

Conditional Errors

A conditional error is one that occurs due to a poorly written or thought out conditional statement. In most languages, conditional statements are implemented via some form of the **if** statement or in conditional loops, such as while or do loops. Conditional errors can be simple misunderstandings of Boolean algebra, or they can be misplacements of nested conditionals.

Conditional errors can be quite similar to logic errors. They can also be similar to loop errors. In their own way, however, conditional errors are unique. For example, a program that uses nested **if** statements to accomplish a task might fail because the developer did not take into account the path through the conditionals correctly. Alternatively, the developer might handle a given special case through a conditional statement, but fail to consider the other possible conditions. This is known as a missing else statement case.

Tracking down conditional errors can be a royal pain for the debugger. Because you unconsciously assume that the logic of the program is correct and that the developer simply missed something, you can often overlook logic errors such as incorrect conditional usage.

Most Common Environments

Because conditionals can be in any operating system, any language, and any platform, you can expect to find conditional errors anywhere you find code.

Symptoms

The most obvious symptoms of conditional errors occur when the program flow does not reach the point it is expected to. Trace logs of the application will often show functions or methods that should have been reached but were not. Stepping through standalone applications using a debugger will show that the application logic skips over expected execution states. The easiest way to tell a conditional error from an unpredictable sort of error is to insert debugging logic into the code to show what branches are taken. If the error is conditional, it will always show the same set of steps, and those steps will always be different from what the predicted program logic should be given the requirements and design.

Example

Let's take a look at a conditional error that appears to be correct. In this case, the programmer checks for some various possible entries from the user. For each case, the program takes certain steps. In this example, we are using the C switch statement as the conditional operator:

```
int nOper = GetUserInput();
switch ( nOper )
{
        case kOpenFile:
            DoOpenFile();
            break;
        case kCloseFile:
            DoCloseFile();
        case kDeleteFile:
            DoDeleteFile();
            break;
}
```

There are two problems with the preceding code fragment. First, and most obvious, is that the default case is not handled. If **GetUserInput** returns something we don't expect it to, we need to handle this case. The code following this fragment could easily depend on the value of **nOpen**, and if that is something we don't know how to handle, we need to screen it out as soon as possible.

The second problem is a syntactical conditional error. Note that in the **kCloseFile** case, there is no "break" statement following the call to **DoCloseFile()**. This causes the program to drop through to the next statement, **kDeleteFile**. In other words, in all likelihood, whenever the user closes a file, that file will be deleted. Because of the order of the operations, this is likely to succeed, so it will become a bug the first time that someone tries it.

Conditional errors can occur in **if** statements, **switch** (or **case of**) statements, **while** loops, **do loops**, **for loops**, and the C ternary operator. Anything that must decide what to do based on a given condition can fall victim to the conditional error.

Pointer Errors

A pointer error is any case where something is being used as an indirect pointer to another item. Most programmers think of pointer errors as memory allocation problems. You allocate a block of memory, assign it to a pointer, something bad happens, and you have an invalid pointer. It doesn't have to be that way, however. Pointer errors can also occur when an index into an array gets corrupted or reassigned, and then that index is reused. The index is a "pointer" into the array, and when it is used to access an array element and the index is invalid, you will immediately have problems.

For memory pointers, pointer errors usually fall into one of three categories. First, there are uninitialized pointers. These are pointers that are used to point at something, but we fail to ever assign them something to point at. They are random things and usually cause odd results. Second, there are deleted pointers, which continue to be used. These occur when you allocate a block of memory, assign a pointer to it, and then delete the block of memory without clearing the pointer. The pointer is now pointing at a random location that might still contain what you expect it to if it has not yet been reused. Then again, it might contain total garbage because it has been reused.

The third pointer problem case is that of an invalid pointer. Unlike the deleted or uninitialized pointer case, an invalid pointer is something that is pointing to a valid block of memory, but that memory does not contain the data you expect it to. Invalid pointers are the hardest to track down because the language you use will generally coerce the data type you are pointing at into being what you want it to be. That coercion, however, cannot make the data type be a valid type; it just falls on the same boundaries. This is particularly bad, for example, if the data type you are pointing at contains its own pointers. Invalid pointer problems are, oddly, most prevalent in strongly typed languages.

Most Common Environments

Pointer errors are most common in languages that support dynamic memory allocation. In addition, they are most common in operating systems that support dynamic memory allocations. Most embedded systems and scripting environments do not have the pointer error problem.

Symptoms

Pointer errors have a number of unique symptoms. First, the program usually either crashes or behaves in an unpredictable and baffling way. Second, you will generally observe stack corruptions, failure to allocate memory, and odd changing of variable values.

If the problem is a pointer that is pointing off at some random value, changing a single line of code can change where the problem occurs. This should be an immediate clue that you are dealing with a pointer problem. If the problem "goes away" when you place a print statement or new variable into the code that you suspect contains the problem, you can be certain that you are dealing with a stray pointer.

Pointer problems that occur after deleting what the pointer is pointing at are a bit harder to detect. There are a variety of symptoms that occur when a deleted pointer is reused. One symptom is that, many times, allocations will fail because the heap pointer has been corrupted. Another is that the problem is usually reproducible, but doesn't appear to make sense. You will see that the program crashes while inside the method of an object (C++) or when the pointer variable is dereferenced (C, Pascal, Java). Some languages, such as Java, are "polite" enough to throw an exception when this occurs.

Example

Let's take a look at one of the most common forms of the pointer error, using a pointer after it has been deleted. As you can see by the following example, it is not always clear when you are doing this incorrectly:

```
void cleanup_function( char *ptr )
{
    // Save the pointer to disk
    SaveToDisk( ptr );
    // Now get rid of it so that we have room for others.
    delete ptr;
}
int func()
{
    char *s = new char[80];

    // Do some things with s

    // Cleanup s
    cleanup_function( s );

    // Do some more things

    // We want to make sure that there are no memory leaks, so we will clean up
    // after ourselves
    delete s;
}
```

It is not always clear when you might be reusing a pointer after it has been deleted. In this example, the programmer meant to be neat and tidy. He probably wrote the code originally to allocate the pointer at the top of his function, and then by habit put in a deallocation at the bottom of the function. This is, after all, good programming practice to avoid memory leaks.

The problem is introduced with the **cleanup_function** routine. This function was probably written at a later time by another developer and might have been used to ensure that all allocated pointers were stored to the permanent drive and then freed up to avoid any possible leaks. In fact, the code in question comes from a set of functions that was reused from a memory pool system that saved its data to disk before destroying the pointer, so that another pointer could be retrieved from the persistent pool. The problem is, the reuse did not take into account the existing system. This problem is common when reusing only parts of a system.

When the second delete occurs at the bottom of **func()**, the results are unpredictable. At best, the **delete** function recognizes that this pointer has been deleted already (unlikely) and doesn't do anything. At worst, memory is corrupted and you are left with a memory crash somewhat later in the program, which will be very difficult to find and fix.

Allocation/Deallocation Errors

Allocation/deallocation errors occur when the order in which the allocation and deallocation happen are incorrect. Obviously, the correct order is to first allocate something, and then deallocate it. However, there are three other possibilities:

♦ Deallocate something, and then allocate it. This happens, oddly enough, more often than you might think. It is usually a result of trying to avoid a memory leak by making sure that any previous allocation is cleared before reallocating a block of memory.

♦ Allocate something, allocate it again, and then deallocate it. This is a classic memory leak.

♦ Allocate something and fail to deallocate it. This is another classic memory leak.

In addition, for certain languages and operating systems, there is a fourth form of the error, which is to allocate something using one method of memory management, but then deallocate the memory using another form of memory management. Fortunately, this one seems to be diminishing as memory management becomes more standard.

How do errors of mixing and matching allocations happen? There are a variety of causes of this sort of error. One is when the programmer simply fails to initialize or check for an initial condition for a memory allocation. For example, if your object contains a pointer to a memory block and you initialize that pointer to be nothing (usually null or nil), you need to check to see whether that pointer has been initialized before deallocating it. Although this sounds obvious, it occurs in many applications.

Another serious problem that leads to memory allocation/deallocation problems is that of hidden side effects within library or utility functions. For example, a utility function might allocate a block of memory and return it to the calling routine. Without the source code for that utility routine or adequate documentation for the routine, you could easily create a memory leak by failing to deallocate the block of memory when you are finished with it in the calling routine. Likewise, if you assume that a utility function is allocating a block of memory and freeing it, you might create a serious problem if that utility function is simply returning a pointer to a static variable or to a global pool of objects that was never allocated.

Finally, one odd variant of this bug is the case where memory is not really allocated or deallocated, but instead kept in a pool of serviceable objects. Failure to return an object to the pool or returning an object to the pool twice will cause a similar problem.

Most Common Environments

Like pointer errors, allocation/deallocation errors occur most frequently in operating systems that support dynamic memory allocation. Errors resulting from failure to deallocate memory that has been allocated in your application occur most frequently in systems without built-in garbage collection. Memory pool errors, where you fail to return an object after using it or return the object twice, occur most frequently in embedded systems where memory allocation is not truly possible.

Symptoms

Failure to deallocate memory that has been allocated will display the same symptoms as a *memory leak* error. Deallocating a nonallocated block of memory will show up in the same way as a *pointer error*. Failure to return objects to a memory pool will generally show up internally as a leak, causing the program to run out of global objects eventually.

If you track allocations (whether dynamic or pooled) within your application, you will be able to see when an allocation is not matched by a deallocation. Tracing software to do this is available from third-party libraries, or it can be easily added to your own application in the case of pooling.

Example

The following code fragment contains a particularly annoying bug, which has two qualities that make it particularly difficult to find. Let's first look at the code:

```
class xString
{
 private:
     char *sString;
public:
     xString( void )
     {
     }
     xString( char *s )
     {
         sString = new char[ strlen(s)+1 ];
         strcpy ( sString, s );
     }
     ~xString( void )
```

```
    {
        if ( sString )
        delete sString;
    }
};
```

There are two distinct problems in this code, only one of which is apparent in the code itself. Note that if you use the void constructor (no arguments) of the class, the **sString** member variable is neither allocated nor assigned to be null. When the object is destroyed, the destructor (**~xString**) is called. Because we didn't initialize the **sString** member variables, it might not pass the **if** statement and will be deleted without being allocated.

The other problem is more insidious. If you were to write this code and test it on your own machine, chances are you wouldn't see any problems. This is because most developers compile and link code modules with debugging information built into them. One of the side effects of doing this is that all memory is initialized to zeros, which happens to be the same as the C++ null value. If you do not try the class in a release or production mode, you will never see this error, and it will only pop up the first time that it is used in a production environment.

Tip

Always test your software in a release or production environment.

Multithreaded Errors

Multithreaded errors occur because, in a program that implements multiple threads, two threads try to access or modify the same memory address at the same time. This is a major no-no in the computer world, and most environments will throw an exception or crash your application if this condition is detected.

Let's imagine, for example, that you have an array that you need to insert a number into. This array is modified by a certain function that changes the number of entries and the actual content of the array by moving data around. Functions like this are called nonreentrant functions because they rely on having total access to the array for the duration of the function. If the function was entered by another thread that wanted to modify the array while the first function was modifying the array, there is no telling what might go wrong in the system. There are numerous ways to prevent such modifications and include devices like semaphores, critical sections, and mutexes (MUTually Exclusive segments of code). All of these safety devices prevent one thread from modifying critical data while it is "locked" by another thread.

It's very difficult to detect and fix multithreaded problems. Some systems will fail and display an error message or exception to indicate that the problem has taken place. In other systems, you will see bizarre behavior because data is being changed from multiple places. Because there are few, if any, reliable multithreaded debuggers, it is difficult to track down a threading error. Most debugging of this sort is done by tracking the current thread ID in each function and either comparing it to the last known thread ID or printing it for the debugger to view. No matter how you go about finding a multithreaded error, you will be hard pressed to prove that it is a multithreaded error. Only by extracting the suspect code segment and running it in a test harness of multiple thread access will you even be able to detect it.

Most Common Environments

Obviously, to have a multithreaded error you need to have an environment and application that supports multiple threads. Client/server applications, Web servers, and some specialized standalone applications fall within this criteria. You can certainly expect to see this problem in a COM component used in a Web server. Other places where you would most likely find multithreaded errors would be in some sort of threaded application that performed background tasks, such as sorting or saving, or in an application that performed multiple socket connections to outside applications.

Symptoms

The most glaring symptom of a multithreaded bug is when the problem does not occur when the application is single threaded or has a single user. If, for example, you switch from a problem-free, single-user Web application to a multiple user application and see an immediate problem, you probably have a multithreaded bug.

Another revealing symptom of a multithreaded problem is a "hang" when two different threads try to access the same method or function. This is an excellent indicator that the function is not reentrant, and you should consider one of the signal protection devices (critical sections, mutexes, and the like) in order to prevent this from happening in the future.

Example

The following code fragment contains a particularly nasty version of a multithreaded error. In this case, we have two different "flags" that are used in an application. One is used to "lock" the database access for a program, the other is intended to "lock" an array that is used within the global space of the application across threads. This is what happens when the two collide:

```
int func1()
{
    WaitForLock( &arrayLock ); // Wait for the array to be free
    // Do something with the array
    WaitForLock( &dbLock );    // Wait until we have access to the database
    // Do some stuff with the database
    ReleaseLock( &dbLock);
    ReleaseLock(&arrayLock );
}
```

```
int func2()
{
    WaitForLock( &dbLock );
    // Do something with the db lock
    WaitForLock( &arrayLock );
    ReleaseLock( &dbLock );
    // Do something with the array
    ReleaseLock( &arrayLock);
}
```

You might think that there is nothing wrong with the preceding code. After all, each function waits for the appropriate lock (semaphore or mutex), does something, and then releases the lock. The problem is, what happens when **func1** and **func2** get called at the same time? In this case, **func1** gets the array lock, whereas **func2** gets the **dbLock** first. Then, each waits for the other to release a lock so that they can proceed. This condition, known as a *deadlock* condition, causes the two functions to wait forever for the other's lock. When you look at each function's code, however, all you see is that they get the appropriate locks and release them when they are finished. The error occurs because multiple threads are calling both functions at once.

Multithreaded errors generally occur because programmers cannot keep two simultaneous processes going in their heads at one time. If you need to write multithreaded code, you should be very careful to avoid a high degree of cohesion between modules or functions. To do otherwise risks hard-to-detect and debug problems.

Timing Errors

Have you ever tried to make a very tight connection between two planes when you land at one end of the airport and take off from the other end? If so, you have probably encountered a classic timing bug. What looks fine on paper when plotting out a connection doesn't work in practice because it is impossible to get from one gate to the other in the amount of time specified for the connection.

A timing error occurs when events are designed and implemented to occur at a certain rate or within a certain margin of error of another event. Timing errors can be seen most easily when you are writing an interrupt service routine and fail to finish the process you are running within the time allotted for the routine. In this case, another interrupt will be generated, and your routine will most likely crash.

Most Common Environments

Timing errors occur most frequently in interrupt functions or timer-based functionality. You will quite often see timer problems in operating system service routines or in embedded systems talking to hardware devices. Although it is possible to have a timing error in a multiuser or multithreaded environment, that bug is usually classified as a multithreaded bug. Timing errors are restricted to environments where the clock is of paramount importance.

Symptoms

Timing issues are best detected by observation. If an error only occurs when a certain amount of data is processed or when a certain other event occurs, you are most likely looking at a timing issue. For example, if your interrupt handler normally runs perfectly, but fails about once a day, you might examine what other contributing factors occur during that once-a-day process. You might find that the interrupt handler triggers a backup request in the application by adding too much data to a given buffer. If this is the case, the request will take too long, another interrupt will be triggered, and your program will crash.

Detecting timing issues requires that you have some built-in diagnostics and have given the matter some thought. Statistics, such as the number of interrupts or events processed in a given time period are useful, as they can indicate "spikes" in the processing curve that might lead to problems. In Chapter 9, we discuss how you can implement your own internal debugging tools. For timing issues, this is a must.

The most common symptoms of a timing problem include:

♦ Intermittent crashes that do not appear to be related to any of your code.

♦ Problems with input or output hanging and not resuming.

♦ Data flow that usually comes in smoothly, suddenly comes in drips, and then floods.

♦ Adding debugging code, such as output print statements, to a service routine suddenly crashes the application.

Example

A few years ago, I was working on a system that was embedded in a TV satellite box. This system was responsible for gathering input data from the satellite connection, buffering that data to disk, and then supplying the data to the output side of the box, which was connected to the TV. This system allowed us to do things such as record programs to a hard drive and pause "live" television. Nearly all of the time, the system worked perfectly. Once in a while, however, and always in the debug mode, the program would crash mysteriously. This never happened in the field, and my coworkers and I were at a loss to determine why it was happening.

The major difference between the debug mode of the box and the production mode of the box was that in debug mode, we would see diagnostic information be sent across a serial line to the computer attached to the box. Obviously, in the field, such messages shouldn't be sent because they would allow people to determine how the box worked and would also slow the system down. The problem was that sending such a message across a serial cable required something like 500 milliseconds. Each message sent would require that much time to format, prepare, and send to the serial port. With a large number of messages, the box would essentially shut itself down as it devoted all of its processing time to sending messages across the wire. One thing quickly learned when working on such a system was to keep messages to a minimum and to put as much information as possible into each message.

The question was, why was the box crashing at a given time for the debug mode builds only? The answer turned out to be the message handling system. At certain critical periods of time within the code, the interrupt service routine would dump data into the buffers as the data came into the system. On a regular basis, my teammates printed diagnostic information, such as the number of packets processed, the number of errors detected, and so forth, to the console via the serial port communication. The timing of the diagnostics was based on the amount of data processed, so that we could keep it from being too much of a drag on the system. This part worked fine and had no errors. However, when the satellite broadcaster changed the compression rate of the data being fed to the box to a higher rate, the system began to crash more often.

When we began looking into the problem, we quickly understood what was going on. Our interrupt service routine that gathered data was more than fast enough to process the new higher compression rate. However, the message system was still outputting messages based on the old compression rate. This caused the number of messages to increase dramatically, slowing down the entire system while the messages were output. Because we did not time-stamp each message, there was no way to tell that they were coming out faster in the newer version. As a result, it took hours of actually watching the output streaming across the console and comparing it with previous output to discover that there was considerably more output in the newer version. We changed the rate of the output to match the rate of the input, and the problem disappeared.

It is probably worth noting that what we did was not a true "fix." The problem is likely to recur should the data rate ever be increased again. For a variety of political reasons, however, the "right" fix was deemed too costly as well as too lengthy. Thus, we see how politics rears its ugly head in the debugging world.

Distributed Application Errors

Some errors can occur in any sort of environment: memory leaks, buffer overruns, coding problems, and the like. Some errors, however, are unique to the environment that spawns them. Distributed application errors are one such category. Although the root causes of such errors are the same in any environment—sloppy coding, poor design, or bad requirements—distributed applications have a whole new set of problems. Because they combine several different applications, potentially running on a host of different machines, there is no easy way to pinpoint an error that occurs in one link of the chain. Worse, because changes to one system can adversely affect other systems without a developer being aware of it, testing for such errors can be a nightmare.

A distributed application error, for our purposes, is defined as an error in the interface between any two applications in a distributed system. This could take the form of an unhandled message from one to the other or the failure to detect that a distributed application has crashed. Most distributed application errors are caused by either a failure to check for an error return code or a change in formatting in the messages passed from one application to another. Sometimes, the two applications do not "talk" directly to each other, but instead share data through some persistent medium such as a database. In cases like this, the problem can easily be caused by bad data being put into the persistent store or be caused by locking problems between the two applications.

One last type of distributed application error can be caused through the dynamic loading of components such as COM objects in the Windows world. Many problems occur due to changes in the interface or external forces acting on one of the components. If a COM component crashes, for example, the application using that component (especially in a DCOM environment) must check for this condition and handle it appropriately. The problem is not unique to COM, of course, but occurs in other systems such as print spoolers or communication handlers. In COM, however, the problem is readily apparent as your system stops running properly.

Most Common Environments

Distributed application errors obviously only occur in systems that have distributed architectures. True standalone systems will never show this error, nor will embedded systems. Only those that contain multiple applications running concurrently and sharing responsibility for the complete processing of the system will have this error. If you are writing a console application for Unix, don't bother thinking about a distributed application error unless you are using something like a database or pipe to connect to other applications.

Symptoms

Depending on the kind of error you are experiencing in a distributed environment, symptoms can range from a program crash to a hanging condition where nothing seems to be running. In addition, you may see very odd error messages from certain applications in the distributed chain due to a lack of connectivity between that application and others up or down the "stream" of systems. When working in a distributed environment, if you observe a program suddenly begin to act strangely, suspect a distributed problem. Look for connectivity or deadlock conditions between the applications in the program chain.

Example

Consider the following code, which comes from a COM object used by some ASP code in a Web server environment.

```
STDMETHODIMP IConnectObj::CreateUser(BSTR org, BSTR libCardID,
        BSTR name, BSTR passwd, VARIANT *vAccountID,
        VARIANT *vSessionID)
{
    Guard protect(mutex);
```

```
LOG_METHOD_START("IKnowObj::CreateUser")
long Acct = -1;
long SID = -1;

 HRESULT hr = GetAccountServer()->CreateUser(org, libCardID,
      name, passwd, &Acct, &SID );
if ( hr != S_OK )
{
    Logger::log(ERROR_LEVEL,"IConnectObj::CreateUser",
            "Unable to create user. Error: %ld", 1, hr);
    hr = E_FAIL;
}

if ( hr == S_OK )
{
    // Do some stuff.
}


   return hr;
}
```

In the preceding code, the COM object connects to a distant DCOM server via the **GetAccountServer()** function. This function will always return something, so it cannot simply crash. However, it can return an error message indicating that it could not connect to the remote DCOM application. In this case, we log an error message saying that the action requested couldn't be performed, and then return to the calling ASP script an error saying that the operation failed.

Normally, you would think that this is fairly error-proof code. It checks for errors, returns them to the caller, and handles the exceptional case properly. However, when you are on the ASP side of the equation, things change quite a bit. In fact, the code looks something like this:

```
ON ERROR GOTO HandleError
CreateUser organization,  libraryCard, name, password, accountID, sessionID
; Do something when we create the new user.


..
HandleError:
    PrintError "Unable to create user. Probably a duplicate user name"
```

Note that the preceding code assumes something quite different than the underlying COM code. If the user could not be created in the database, the assumption is that the user name already exists (an error in this system). If the connection to the remote database failed or the connection to the remote DCOM object failed, the error would appear to be a duplicate user name to the end user. This is a typical side effect of a distributed application error.

Storage Errors

A storage error occurs when a persistent storage device encounters an error and is unable to proceed. This can be a file system, a database, or some sort of backup device. In any case, if the error is not handled, the repercussions can spread throughout the entire system.

When a program interfaces with a database, there is a certain expectation that the database will safely contain the information stored in it. Under certain circumstances, such as a power failure or a disk corruption, that assumption might be invalid. In other cases, the connection to the database might fail, requiring a change to a backup device that does not contain the same information as the original. In either case, the application must deal with the fact that the expected data is not present.

Sometimes, you rely on storage for other things such as configuration files or backup files. Imagine, for example, if you are relying on data being available in a configuration file and that file is deleted. Would your application contain sufficient information to go on without the contents of the configuration file? Would the failure to load configuration information cause the program to crash? These are things you need to verify if your program uses external storage mechanisms. One of the easiest tests for a storage error is to simply delete the required configuration file, database table, or backup storage device and see whether it could cause a problem. If so, it could easily be the source of user errors.

Most Common Environments

Storage errors can only occur if the program in question uses a storage mechanism. In general, storage errors occur when you save your data into an output file, read your input from an input file, or use a backup mechanism to make sure your data is consistent and corruption free.

In systems that use a database for either retrieving or storing information, storage errors most often occur on back-end servers. It is unlikely that the local storage is the problem when the data is stored on a remote database server.

For configuration files and the like, the two most likely scenarios under which you will encounter a storage error are when the user deletes a file or the disk file system becomes filled or corrupted. If you do not have file monitoring systems in place, this is likely to occur in a client/server or production Web server environment. On a standalone system, of course, anything is possible if you do not first check for the existence of a configuration file.

Symptoms

There are numerous symptoms for a storage error. Most operating systems will warn you if you run out of disk space, so errors of this kind are easily detectable. This assumes, of course, that the machine running the application is monitored. If not, you will need to have some sort of remote monitoring system to ensure that the machine does not run out of memory and disk space.

For databases, a daily or weekly (depending on the load on the system) integrity check should be sufficient to verify that the database is in good shape and that there are no disk or corruption errors making it impossible to use. For configuration files, you will probably notice that the program is not responding correctly. A simple check is to embed a diagnostics screen in the system that can show you the current configuration settings at the press of a button. We will talk more about built-in diagnostics and their applicability toward debugging in Chapter 9.

If the system has been running correctly and suddenly loses its ability to find databases, backup machines, or other servers, you might suspect a configuration problem. If the code is open to you, you should probably inspect the source code to determine from where it is reading its configuration information on the disk. Verify that the configuration file is present, readable, and contains data. If any of these conditions is not true, you probably have a storage error.

Finally, if the same program, running on the same environment, with the same configuration fails on one machine and runs on another, check disk space requirements and accessibility requirements. One odd form of the storage problem occurs when there is plenty of disk space or the configuration file is present, but the program lacks permissions to get to the data in the files or on the disk.

Example

Let's look at the simplest possible case of a storage error, an unhandled error in opening a file. In this case, we want to simply open a file on the server, read some information from the file, and then do something with the data we read. Our example this time is in Java to show you how even handling exceptions isn't always best if you don't handle them correctly.

```java
import java.io.*;
import java.util.*;

public class StudyFileStream {
  public static void main(String args[]) {
    try {
      FileInputStream  theInput  = new FileInputStream( args[0] );
      System.out.println( "Copying from file: " + args[0] );
      theOutput.close();
    } catch (ArrayIndexOutOfBoundsException ie) {
      System.out.println("No filename is given");
    } catch (FileNotFoundException filenotfound ){
      System.out.println( "Could not open files." );
    } catch (Exception e) {
      System.out.println(e);
    }
    int valueRead;
    while ( (valueRead = theInput.read()) != -1 )
      System.out.println( valueRead );
```

```
        theInput.close();
    }
}
```

Note that in this case, we are opening a file and reading in a series of integers from it. Those integers are then displayed for the user reading the output on the console of the system. We properly handle the cases of the file not found or bad input for the file names. However, after properly handling the error, we then proceed to read the file anyway! In this case, the program simply crashes with an exception, which is really the best possible outcome in this scenario. However, if the program is not properly tested with bad input cases, the potential problem will not be known up front.

Storage errors are a way of life for the programmer. If test cases are not adequately created to deal with potential errors from the storage system, it is likely that such errors will occur in the production system. In these situations, you'll have no one to blame but yourself.

Integration Errors

Integration errors occur when two subsystems that have been individually unit tested and validated are combined and cause errors in the interface between them. One specialized form of the interface error is the storage error we just finished discussing, where the storage system is improperly handled. Most interface errors, however, occur because of assumptions made on the part of a developer on one end or the other of the interface.

One common form of the interface error is when one developer expects the input to his or her routine to be "clean," that is, free of any errors or invalid inputs. If a routine makes the assumption that a pointer passed in cannot be null and another routine passes in a null value, the first routine will crash. This is not an error on the part of the first developer, as he clearly specified that the routine would not properly handle null values. It is not truly an error on the part of the second developer, who might not have received sufficient information about the routine to know that a null pointer would cause the problem. Instead, the problem lies in between the two routines.

Most Common Environments

Integration errors occur most often in systems that have multiple, independent developers or in systems that use third-party software. They can occur in any kind of a system, from a standalone system to a multiuser client/server application. Integration errors usually stem from a lack of integration testing between subsystems, so any system that does extensive unit testing on each subsystem but lacks sufficient testing between subsystems will display this problem.

Symptoms

The most common symptoms of an integration error are when errors show up in production testing but do not appear in the unit testing for a given module. One good way to prove that you have an integration error is to compare the unit tests with the final production system.

If the production test plan shows test cases that are not handled in the unit test plan, chances are good that it wasn't thought through for integration testing.

Example

Imagine that you are writing a routine in Delphi to compute the average of a bunch of numbers. You might have an object called an **Array** that contains a list of numbers and a member function called **Count** that returns the count of the elements to you. You write the function:

```
Function Average ( anArray : ArrayObject ) : Integer;
Var
    I : Integer;
    Total : Integer;
Begin
   Total := 0;
   For I := 1 to anArray.Count() do
        Total := Total + anArray.GetAt(i);
   Average := Total / anArray.Count();
End;
```

Looks like it ought to work, doesn't it? You pass in an array, total all of the values in the array, and then return the average calculated from that total. You can even test the function by using negative numbers, positive numbers, and a combination of negative and positive numbers.

Now, imagine that along comes Charlie, another developer on the project. Charlie likes the function and uses it in his own code. There is just one problem. Charlie passes along whatever the user has entered into a dialog box to the function. So what is the problem? Well, Charlie doesn't bother to check whether the user has entered anything into the dialog. Therefore, the **ArrayObject** that is passed into the function can be empty. That doesn't seem so bad, does it?

The problem becomes clear at this point, doesn't it? If the **ArrayObject** is empty, the **Count** method is going to return zero. The division at the end of the function is going to return a division-by-zero error that never occurred in the testing process. Welcome to the world of integration errors. When you wrote the function, the assumption was that the array had something in it. When Charlie used the function, he didn't realize this assumption. Wham! Instant bug.

Conversion Errors

One of the most common problems in the computer world is that data is rarely in the format you want it to be in. Users enter data most often as text; that text must then be converted to numbers or other program input. Data in the program is in one format and usually needs to be converted to another. Data exchanged from one program to another must go from the "standard" format of the first application to the "standard" format of the other. Don't even get me started on the whole notion of "extensions" to standards.

A conversion error occurs when a piece of data in one format is converted to a different format incorrectly. This can occur for a variety of reasons. You could have a bad conversion process, or the data may contain information that cannot be converted correctly to another format. For example, what would "ABCD" be as an integer? I'm not sure what the right answer is, but I know there are a myriad of wrong ones. Other conversion errors come from implicit conversions from one data type to another. For instance, a function might expect a number in the form of a floating point value. When you pass in the value 123, the number is "implicitly" converted into 123.00. This is usually all fine and dandy, but sometimes the conversion is not simple. For example, suppose that I try to calculate the value of 12/24.

In most languages, when you divide 12 by 24, you get a half (0.5). Unfortunately, C and C++ are not "most" languages. If you divide 12 by 24 and assign the value to an integer, C will perform integer division. When you divide two integers, you get an integer result. That means that 12 divided by 24 results in zero, not a half. When looking at code that implements such statements, it is often quite difficult to realize while reading it that integer division is taking place. This is the root of most conversion problems—not realizing that the conversion ever takes place.

Most Common Environments

Conversion errors are most prevalent in operating systems and languages that do implicit conversions. Type-safe languages are less prone to this sort of thing, but as shown previously, it can happen in those languages as well. Embedded systems are not usually prone to this kind of problem, nor are scripting languages, although conversion errors can certainly happen in either environment given the right set of unique conditions.

Symptoms

The most common symptoms of conversion errors are bad outputs, bad formatting, and unexpected mathematical errors in the program. Division by zero is the most common problem, but problems involving NaN (Not a Number) values are also seen in many systems. For specific conversions, such as converting from a specified standard format to another specified format, the most common symptoms are poor formatting on the output due to unexpected values.

Example

Conversion errors are my all-time favorite bugs, and they are also the hardest to track down in code. In the following code, which was intended to screen invalid characters that a database could not store properly, the end result was the inability of the user to log in to the system from certain places. Take a look at the pseudocode for the problem, and then try to determine why that might be the case.

```
Loop
    If InputString.CharacterAt(Index) < "A" OR InputString.
    CharacterAt(Index) > "Z"
```

```
        SkipIt
    Else
        OutputString := OutputString + InputString.CharacterAt(Index)
While Index < Length(InputString)
```

The code in question was supposed to only allow characters for a login name and pass on the login name to the database so that it could be looked up for comparison of passwords and the like. On some systems, however, it didn't work. Why? The reason is really a conversion problem. On certain systems, using certain operating systems, the Spanish letters for n accent and m umlaut were not allowed into the system. The problem was, they were converted properly in some routines and not in others. Each character failed the test for "Is this a letter?" but passed in a different (lower-level) routine that used a different conversion method to test if it was a character or not.

Another problem with this code is that it assumes that the system it is working on has the property that "Z" is greater than "A". This is not always the case, nor is it always the case that the letters are in consecutive order from A to Z. Hard-coded conversion checks like this are often responsible for more errors than you might imagine.

Once the developers realized what was happening, they removed the offending code and replaced it with a single routine across all systems that worked the same way in all cases. Another conversion problem bit the dust.

Hard-Coded Lengths/Sizes

In my experience, one of the classic sources of bugs is the use of hard-coded numbers in applications. These so-called "magic" numbers are often placed into the code without a clue as to why they might be there or why they are important. In addition, rather than using a single constant across the application, magic numbers are sprinkled across the entire source tree. This makes it difficult to ensure that you change all of the occurrences when a given number needs to be changed.

Why do hard-coded lengths and sizes cause bugs? In general, it is because something changes that makes the length or size invalid. Because one part of the system, such as the piece that generates the data and thus specifies its length, can change independently of another piece, a bug occurs. Because communication between different groups is often an issue at many companies, changes aren't propagated to everyone that needs to know about them. Worse, if the source of the problem is an outside vendor or source, you might never realize that the change had occurred until it started causing problems in the application.

Most Common Environments
Hard-coded lengths and sizes occur most often in either client/server environments, where data comes from an outside source, or in standalone applications. Oddly, Web server environments and embedded systems rarely display this particular problem. This might be because

of the difficulty in updating embedded systems, which leads to the avoidance of change of input. Web servers don't show the problem as often, mostly because they tend to be scripting environments.

Symptoms

The classic symptom of a hard-coded length or size problem is when the input to a system changes and the system breaks. Another good symptom of the problem is when an inspection of the code reveals a large number of constant values strewn throughout the source code. Source code that contains numbers, embedded strings, and other such values should be treated with extreme suspicion in the best of times. When the program suddenly changes around you and the code stops working, you should seriously consider looking at the entire source tree to see where these values are being used.

Another symptom of the problem is when you run across variables with the same names that have different sizes. For example, you might have an array in one location that holds 20 elements. In another location in the source code, you might have an array of the same type and name that holds 22 elements. It is likely that the developer working on the code at the time changed one of the elements and not the other, leading to problems later on.

Example

The following shows a common error that you will see in quite a bit of code. This particular example is in C, but the underlying problem it exposes can occur quite easily in any language on any operating system. We examined this particular snippet a bit earlier, but let's take a look at it again to not make you flip back and forth through the book.

```
void ClearArray( int *Array )
{
     for ( int I=0; I<100; ++I )
          Array[I] = 0;
}
```

As you can see from this example, it is quite common to make assumptions about the size of arrays and other constructs in code. In this case, the programmer probably always used the "magic number" of 100 for the size of the arrays he used in his system. As a result, when wiping out the array for later use, he automatically used the constant 100 to step through all of the elements of the array. What is the problem in this code? Imagine that you are using this nice, safe-looking function in another part of code written by another developer. You might have some code that looks like this:

```
int anArray[ 50 ];
ClearArray( anArray );
```

When this code is executed, it is going to stomp all over the memory following the **anArray** variable in memory. *Stomping on memory* is a technical term meaning you wrote to places in the memory address space that you had no intention (and quite possibly no right) to write to. This happens because the developer made the invalid assumption that the size of the array was constant and that it could be safely used as a hard-coded number in the application.

It is worth mentioning that hard-coded numbers cause other problems. Imagine, for example, that you run into the following snippet of code in an application you are debugging.

```
mStartESCR = mFirstVideoPTS - 3*3003;
```

Would you have any clue what this code was meant to do? Assuming for the moment that you knew what **mStartESCR** and **mFirstVideoPTS** were and what they did, what do the 3 and 3003 values mean?

If the code were instead written as follows, you would certainly have a better idea of what the programmer meant to do:

```
mStartESCR = mFirstVideoPTS - kAudioFrames*FRAMESIZE;
```

In this case, the programmer is apparently backing up a number of frames in a buffer, perhaps. Given the constant names, you have a much better idea of what might be going on, and you would not have to try various permutations of the "magic numbers" to make changes in the behavior of the application.

Versioning Bugs

Versioning bugs occur when you change functionality or file storage format between two versions of the software and the results are not backward compatible or are not properly handled in future releases. The most obvious example of a versioning bug is when a file format changes for the persistent storage mechanism of a software application. If the previous file format is not properly handled or converted, you will end up with unusable data. Unusable data that used to be usable is a major source of irritation for users.

Versioning can also apply to user interface problems. For example, when many applications were moved from the text-based MS-DOS interface to the graphical user interface of MS Windows, there were many bugs reported because users could no longer find or use features that had existed and worked in previous versions. Some of these bugs were, of course, simply errors in documentation or misunderstandings about how the operating system worked. Other errors cropped up because the developers of the graphical versions neglected to look into how certain keystrokes or function keys were used in the original application.

Most Common Environments

Virtually any environment that changes can contain a versioning bug. The most common ones, however, are applications that contain user data that is saved in a proprietary format. Standalone applications seem most vulnerable to this problem. In client/server, Web server, or embedded systems, the problem of storage is too widespread to ignore during the testing process. In addition, it is normal for all data to be converted upon installation of the application in these environments. For these reasons, it is typical to find this problem most commonly in the standalone application realm.

Symptoms

Versioning problems are always shown by the usage of previous data or functionality. If you try to load a file that was created with a previous version of the software and it does not work or works inappropriately, you are looking at a versioning problem. Regression testing should be modified to test previous versions and functionality in order to detect versioning problems as quickly as possible.

There is another form of the versioning problem that is more insidious and in many respects worse than the proprietary format problem. This occurs when you are using a "standard format" that has multiple versions and fail to check for the proper version of the data. For example, you might have an HTML file that supports version 3.2 of the HTML standard, whereas your application can only load data from version 3.1. Failure to detect elements in future versions is just as bad as failing to load previous versions.

One immediate clue that you likely have a versioning problem in your software is when your files are not version-marked. If you can't tell what version of the software generated the file and the file format has changed, you will know immediately that you have a problem. Check all file formats for version information.

Example

One company where I worked had files that were binary in nature. That is, they consisted of binary data that could only be interpreted by the application that generated them. One application would write out a file and another would read it in and process it for further information and display. The file consisted of a header block and then a series of information blocks. Each information block contained a "tag," which indicated what sort of information was stored in the block, and was then followed by the information for the block itself. All of this worked well and had been working for some time.

One day, a new developer joined the project. He was an enthusiastic sort, and decided that he would add a few new tags, which would show other information that the team had discussed in a meeting. Unfortunately, he failed to talk to anyone else in the department about the new tags, preferring to "surprise" us with the work he had done. Normally, problems like this occur when someone that doesn't understand the system tries to make changes. This was certainly no exception, even though the process and file structure was well defined.

The developer in question added the new tags to the output file system and, in so doing, broke the entire system. Why? Actually, the reason was quite simple and led to some rather drastic changes in the way the department did things. Remember that developers at that company wrote out each tag followed by the data that it provided. There was no length shown for the tag, nor were there any delimiters to indicate where the tag data started and ended. As a result, if a program did not understand a given tag, it could not simply skip over it. Because the enthusistic developer failed to understand that there were other systems that read this data and failed to update the API used to read the files, anything that used the file did not get past the first instance of a tag it did not understand. All existing programs would simply display an error indicating that the file was corrupted and then exit. This was not exactly optimal behavior.

Once my teammates and I realized what it was that was causing the problem, we implemented a system whereby the file consisted of a main header block followed by mini-header blocks that contained a version information number, a tag indicating the type of data to follow, and then a length indicating how much data would follow the tag. That way, any application from that point on that did not understand a given tag could simply skip over it and move to the next data bit. Of course, this also required that developers provide a utility process (program, script, or instruction booklet) to update all existing files. Once you fail at some point in the versioning process, you will find that you have opened a huge can of worms that must be all be controlled or contained before you can go on.

Inappropriate Reuse Bugs

A good number of bugs are caused by inappropriate reuse of code or components in new systems. Reuse can be inappropriate when code or components are reused in a way that the original designers and developers didn't intend for them to be used. Examples abound, and one particularly devestating example was shown in Chapter 2. However, the basics of the problem are a bit more complicated.

If you reuse code, you run the risk of inheriting bugs from that code. This is a simple fact of life. The best case is when you reuse a discrete piece of code that performs a simple action. Compiler vendors have known this for a long time and distribute standard libraries with their systems, which perform standard actions. C/C++ has its Standard Template Library. Visual Basic has its built-in components and functions. Java has its Swing components and standard classes. We don't really think twice when we reuse these standard components because they have been tried, tested, and debugged over years of implementations. Yet there are certainly bugs remaining in some of this code as well. The best way to find these bugs is to use the components in a way that hasn't been done before. When you use a component in a way that it hasn't been used before, keep in mind that you are trying something the original designers never intended.

Most Common Environments

Inappropriate reuse occurs in languages that support reuse. Because you can, at worst, cut and paste code from one system to another, this means that inappropriate reuse can happen anywhere. Because the code itself is mostly independent on the environment in which it runs, reuse errors don't have a common environment.

Symptoms

The easiest detection of a reuse bug occurs when the code is called. If the response of the application reusing the code is not the same as the original application, chances are you are reusing code improperly. Detecting such a thing is best done as soon as the code is reused.

Another good way to tell if code is working properly is to reuse the test cases that came with the code that you "borrowed." If code does not have a test suite, you should create one for it and run it against both the original and copied versions.

The number one reason that reused code does not work as expected is due to side effects in the code itself. If, for example, the code relies on something else in the system performing a certain task and your application does not perform that task, the code is unlikely to work as specified. At a lower level, if your application defines a given constant as something other than what the reused code was expecting, you will find that you have created a suite of bugs by reusing that code in your application.

Example

One of the best examples of improper reuse occurs virtually every day in the Microsoft Windows operating system development world. I refer, of course, to the Microsoft Foundation Class (MFC) library, which ships with the Visual C++ programming environment. Although the MFC library is an excellent way to get a quick jump on developing a Windows program, it can just as easily get in the way if reused improperly.

One of the applications I was involved in earlier in my career was a system to allow people to browse and view documents. The system involved using a "multidocument window" system that allowed different groups of windows to be displayed on the screen at one time and allowed the user to maneuver between them. There is quite a bit of code in the MFC library that deals with multiple windows, and my coworkers felt that rather than develop the system from scratch, it would be better to use the existing framework. I certainly agreed, not wanting to reinvent the wheel yet one more time.

The problem came about as soon as the requirements became more concrete. Many of the requirements for the system, such as having multiple ways to view a given document (Table of Contents, Search view, and Document view) were simply not possible with that release of MFC. (Interestingly, they were later made a part of the system, but I digress.) When it came to making the system work within the framework, my coworkers and I found that we were forced to "hack around" many of the internal functions of the MFC system to get the results we wanted. Although this wasn't a major problem at the time, it would later turn out to be a horrible decision.

When the next release of MFC came out, supporting the new 32-bit operating system called Windows 95, my team immediately attempted to convert the software to the new framework to take advantage of the marketing possibilities of having a product out immediately. Of course, because we had reused the code improperly, we found that virtually everything we had done, which relied on the internal implementation of the system, no longer worked. All in all, it took longer to "port" the existing 16-bit application over to the new 32-bit system than it would have to write it in the first place. All because we wanted to reuse some code to save ourselves some time!

If you are going to reuse code and modify it extensively, you are probably better off simply "cloning" the software and then treating it as a separate product. Improper reuse will cost time, money, and the hair you pull out trying to fix the problems you introduce.

Boolean Bugs

Boolean bugs occur because the mathematical precision of Boolean algebra has virtually nothing to do with the equivalent English words. When we say "and," we really mean the Boolean "or" and vice versa. This leads to misunderstandings with users and misunderstandings with coders. In addition, Boolean errors are caused because of misunderstandings between what true and false mean in the code.

Let's imagine, for a moment, that we are reading a specification for some code. The specification says that the user must choose between A and B at the onset of the application. In Boolean algebra, A and B means that both the values A and B must be true for the equation to be true. But that doesn't make sense, does it? After all, what the requirements obviously mean are that you must choose either A or B to go on. You can't choose both. This is one inherent problem with using English to describe your project.

How can true or false cause problems? After all, true is true and false is false, and never the twain shall cross, right? The answer is, this is correct (or true, if you prefer), but that doesn't mean that one man's true is another man's true. Consider, for example, the return value from a function. If a function returns a Boolean value, does that mean that true means success and false means failure? Not always. Many developers prefer to return zero (or false in most languages) for success and a nonzero value (true in most languages) for failure. You might return –1 for an error, for example, or some specific error code that is always negative.

If your convention is always the same, you will probably not run into any problems among the members of the group that follow that convention. However, if the convention is not documented and someone new comes on board, you are going to have problems.

Most Common Environments

The two classes of bugs most associated with Boolean errors are requirements errors and logic errors. These can occur in any environment. This particular problem seems to be particularly horrible in an embedded system, where Boolean algebra is used more often than in any other environment.

Symptoms

Probably the most clear cut symptom of a Boolean error is when the program does exactly the opposite of what you expect it to. For example, you might have thought that you needed to select only one entry from a list in order to proceed. Instead, the program will not continue until you select more than one. Worse, it keeps telling you to select only one value!

For true/false problems, you will usually see some sort of debug output indicating an error in a function, only to see the calling function proceed as though the problem had not occurred. Alternatively, the caller might think the process failed when it succeeded. These are usually indications that you are misinterpreting the result of the function. Take a careful look at what is really being returned instead of assuming a success or failure value.

Example

The following code contains a simple example of a function that returns a counter-intuitive Boolean value and shows how that value leads to problems in the rest of the application code. This case performs an action and indicates to the user whether or not the action succeeded.

```
Function DoSomeAction( InputNum : Integer ) : Integer
Begin
    If ( InputNum < 1 or InputNum > 10 ) then
        DoSomeAction := 0;
    Else
    Begin
        PerformTheAction( InputNum );
        DoSomeAction := NumberOfActions + 1;
        NumberOfActions := NumberOfActions + 1;
    End;
End;
```

After looking at the function, ask yourself this—What is the return value in the case of success? What would it be in the case of failure? How would you know this by simply glancing at the function declaration?

Later on in the code, we might try to do something like this:

```
Var Value;
Var Ret;
Begin
    Value := 11;
    Ret := DoSomeAction( Value );
    If ( Ret )
        Println("Error in DoSomeAction");
End;
```

If you were debugging this application, you might start out by wondering why it didn't work. Further investigation would show that the error statement is never triggered in spite of the fact that the routine did, in fact, encounter an error. Why did this happen? It happened because the routine didn't return a nonzero value for failure, it returned nonzero for success. This Boolean value was not intuitive given the conditions of the function and led to a poor assumption by the programmer who wrote the code that used it. Which programmer was really at fault here? It's a good question, and one that you might want to think about.

Why Is Classification Important?

If you track the classification of bugs within your own organization, you will find that they usually fall into predictable patterns. Most of these bugs can be eliminated by eliminating the patterns and thought processes that caused the bug to become manifest in the first place. For example, if you find that the majority of your problems stem from memory allocation leaks, you should seriously consider a third-party library that provides so-called "smart pointers," which take the guesswork out of allocating and deallocating memory. If you find that the majority of your errors come from timing or multithreaded problems, you should seriously consider a management system that insulates you from such errors by making it appear that your code is all single-threaded (one such system would be Microsoft Transaction Server (MTS) from Microsoft for COM objects).

You can never completely eliminate bugs. You will rarely have a bug-free program because, as we have discussed, programs will always evolve into a state that contains bugs. However, you can reduce the number of bugs by careful coding. Your job is to figure out how to be more careful and learn from your mistakes. The only way that you can honestly evaluate your mistakes is to classify them as such. Your bug tracking system should contain entries for bug descriptions, bug types, and bug severities. This system should allow you to prioritize fixing the problems during the debugging process. More importantly, though, it should allow you to perform effective postmortems that do more than simply point fingers for blame.

Summary

In summation, we can say that bugs can be classified into several different areas. By understanding these classification, we can predict the sorts of problems that might arise from different sorts of bugs. By examining each of the stages of our development process for a given project, we can see what sorts of bugs arose from each particular stage.

The stages of the project are: requirements, design, implementation, process, build, deployment and future planning. Each falls at a particular time in the development process and each has a type of bug and a cost for fixing that bug associated with it.

By creating your own taxonomy of the kinds of bugs you encounter while developing and debugging software, you will have a better methodology for finding and predicting bugs in the future. If you can accurately predict the sorts of bugs to expect in a project in the future, you can easily cut down on the time necessary to do testing and debugging. Saving time saves money and results in a higher quality product in the end.

Bug Puzzle

When is a bug not a bug? When it is a design flaw, of course. This bug puzzle illustrates exactly that circumstance in a real-world application. In a project I was working on, we had a proprietary method of keeping information on a hard disk drive attached to the system. The data, in this case, was a set of recordings of video information. The hard drive was originally specified to be 8 gigabytes in size, later increased to 20 gigabytes.

The layout of the drive was as follows:

The drive was initially formatted and divided into partitions. The first partition, called the index partition, was five megabytes in size and was always the very first partition created. The remaining space on the drive was divided into four gigabyte partitions, called video partitions. These partitions held the raw video data that the hard-drive stored.

The first partition, the index partition, held pointers to each of the programs recorded in the raw video data. Each entry contained the program information, title, date shown, description, and so forth. In addition, each entry contained a list of the blocks used in the raw video area of the drive. The larger the recorded program, of course, the more blocks used for the program.

The system was a consumer electronics device, which meant that the user could not be expected to be particularly computer literate. Errors in the system had to be dealt with in a fashion that allowed the system to continue regardless of the severity of the problem.

Now, the bug description: Many of our users, having grown frustrated with the smaller disk drives put in the system, upgraded the drives by themselves to much larger ones. It was not unusual to have a forty, fifty, or even eighty gigabyte drive installed in the box. After a while, however, these boxes all seemed to experience the same problem. The box would stop, reboot itself, and after coming back up it would not have any of its recorded programs any more. This, obviously, was quite frustrating to the user.

Our initial hypothesis in this debugging effort was that the partitions containing the video information were somehow being corrupted. There was a single partition map for all of the partitions, and our suspicion was that this map was being somehow destroyed, resulting in the inability to find any of the partitions. The box, being a smart little device, would check for that map when it initially booted, and would create any partitions it could not find in the map. This seemed like a reasonable hypothesis.

Further observation of the problem, however, showed that the partition map was still valid after the box lost all recordings. Examination of the log files for the system suggested that the box knew what it was doing and had detected an error. This error, upon consulting the internal documentation, turned out to be a "Partition Full Error". When this error was encountered, the box would delete the partition in question and reboot itself to fix any problems.

The puzzle, of course, was why the partition was full. There was certainly sufficient space on the drive for additional recordings. In fact, this error normally occurred when a box with a sixty gigabyte drive was only about two-thirds full. You have all of the information we had at the time the problem was found and fixed. You even know a bit more than we did initially, in that this was not a true bug but a design flaw. The question is: what caused the case of the mysterious program loss?

Chapter 6
Detective Work

Matt Telles

Now that you understand the basic nature of bugs, how they are formed, and what symptoms they exhibit during the running of your application, it is time to begin the work of finding bugs during your development process. As mentioned previously, this involves a fair amount of detective work worthy of Sherlock Holmes. In this chapter, we begin to explore how you can utilize various methods to isolate the root cause of the symptoms you have observed in your application. Once the problem is isolated, we examine some techniques you can use to form your hypotheses and prove them one way or another, so that the problem can be fully solved.

By far, the biggest frustration in the debugging world is that of nonreproducible bugs. The customer calls in and says, "I do a, b, and c, and the program crashes." You go back to your desk, follow the instructions provided by the customer, in the same order, and discover that everything works fine. This is frustrating to customers because they are being told that what they saw and what they did is wrong. It is frustrating to the customer support people because they have to go back and tell the customer that the problem can't be duplicated, and thus can't be fixed. Finally, it is frustrating to the debugger because it is always difficult to make yourself believe that the customer didn't really see what they think they saw. All in all, this situation results in an unhappy customer experience and a nagging doubt in the back of your mind that the problem is really there and simply depends on what was done before a, b, and c, or is related to the customer's environment, or depends on the hardware configuration, or... well, you get the idea.

In order to really know if the customer is right or wrong, you have to understand whether or not the program is capable of doing what the report says it did. If the report says that the program crashed, well, you can certainly believe that to be true. All programs can crash given the right set of circumstances. The problem is in determining what those circumstances are. To fully understand the scope of the problem, however, you must fully understand the scope of your application. This brings us to our first topic in the detective work section—holistic debugging.

Holistic Debugging

The dictionary defines holistic as:

> **ho·lis·tic** (h-lstk) *adj.*
>
> 1. Of or relating to holism.
>
>   a. Emphasizing the importance of the whole and the interdependence of its parts.
>
>   b. Concerned with wholes rather than analysis or separation into parts: *holistic medicine; holistic ecology.* [1]

We focus on the fact that holistic emphasizes the whole and the interdependence of all of the parts of the whole. What this means is that a holistic approach focuses on the entire system rather than whatever piece appears to be broken. Holistic medicine, for example, concerns itself with the state of the body as a whole, not the disease that is currently attacking it. Similarly, programmers and debuggers must understand that you cannot treat the symptoms of a problem, you must focus on the application system as a whole.

Interestingly, the dictionary also has an entry for debugging. Let's take a quick look at this definition:

> **de·bug** (d-bg) *v. tr.* **de·bugged, de·bug·ging, de·bugs**.
>
> 1. To remove a hidden electronic device, such as a microphone, from: *debug a conference room.*
>
> 2. To make (a hidden microphone, for example) ineffective.
>
> 3. To search for and eliminate malfunctioning elements or errors in: *debug a spacecraft before launch; debug a computer program.*
>
> 4. To remove insects from, as with a pesticide.[2]

---

[1] *Webster's Third New International Dictionary: Unabridged.* Merriam-Webster. Springfield, MA. 2000.
[2] ibid.

Of course, in our case, it is the third definition that interests us. Notice that the dictionary focuses on the problems being removed. In this section, we explore why the dictionary (and most development people) is wrong about what the role of a debugger really is.

Now that you understand what holistic means, how do you apply holistic concepts to debugging software programs and procedures? Let's start by thinking about what emphasizing the whole over the individual pieces means in debugging. When you are debugging an application, you often simply look at the problem reported by the user and how you can make that problem go away. In the medical field, the analogy is treating the symptom without considering what that symptom means.

As a simple example, consider the case where the program mysteriously crashes at a particular point in the code each and every time the program is run. The point at which the code crashes makes no sense at all. For example, in C++, you might have a member function of a class that reads:

```
void SetX( int X)
{
     mX = X;
}
```

The program always crashes on the line that assigns X to the member variable mX (mX = X). Looking at this code snippet, we see very few valid ways in which the program could be encountering a problem at this point. Oddly, we might discover that inserting a message statement (**printf** in C lingo, **println** in Delphi or Pascal, and **PRINT** in Basic) makes the problem stop occurring when the indicated steps are followed for reproducing the problem. Is the problem fixed?

Most experienced programmers, managers, or debuggers would say that the problem is not fixed, although few could tell you exactly why that is the case. The fact is, in this case, we are directly treating the symptom (the program crashing) rather than looking into the actual problem. Although this is a rather extreme example of the issue, the problem of treating the symptom and ignoring the overall problem is endemic in our industry.

Copy and Paste Errors

Another aspect of looking at the entire system rather than just fixing the problem at hand is in the case of what we refer to as the "cut and paste" problem. In this case, the programmer has copied blocks of code (as a worst case) or the same basic kind of code (in the best case) into many areas of the application. When a problem is discovered in one area, it is often propagated throughout the rest of the application because of the copying of code.

Copy and paste errors, although rarely true copies, result in a different kind of problem. In the following BASIC program, we find a problem in a given routine that uses a specific kind of coding technique. The problem is fixed for that particular routine, but then turns up in a hundred other places in the code because the same technique was used everywhere:

```
ON ERROR GOTO 100
; This is a global array of 100 integers
DIM X(100)
; Before this point, we have put something somewhere in X, now we are looking
    for it.
FOR I=0 TO 100
    IF X(I) = myValue THEN
        DoSomething()
    END IF
NEXT I

100 PRINT "DONE"
```

Obviously, if you are a BASIC programmer, the problem in this code is that someone was most likely used to working in C or C++. BASIC begins its arrays at the 1 value rather than the 0 value. One thing that can make this problem even worse is when the developer uses named constants (such as **kStartLoopIdx** and **kEndLoopIdx**), since the debugger must then find or know the values at the time of execution and debugging. Because the programmer never tested this loop, it was never found to crash. Checking the 0 array element in most variants of BASIC causes a program exception. Because there is error handling above the loop, the program resumes at the PRINT statement. It will appear to the user as if the program is doing what it is supposed to do. However, the loop was never executed, and the user never found what they were looking for. This kind of "silent" error can be propagated throughout the program. If we simply treat the initial problem (Hey! It's never finding my value!), we ignore the fact that this problem exists all over the place.

This example, by the way, illustrates another aspect of the holistic approach to debugging and maintaining. Once you have discovered that the programmer who wrote this code was starting with a 0 index, you can then go through all of the code looking for such instances and correct them. Would you be finished, however? Well, no. You might just discover another more serious problem in the preceding code. The error handling in this case is not really handling errors at all! In fact, it is making the error worse by hiding it and making the code appear to work correctly. Two additional aspects of the "understand the whole system" approach, global variables and side effects, show you why this approach is necessary.

Global Variables

Most languages, with the exception of C and Java, support global variables. Global variables do not belong to a scope and cannot be found in a class or structure. They are the bane of a programmer's existence because there is no way to control how they are accessed or how they are changed. When you use global variables, you essentially offer the control of your program to any developer that chooses to use that variable in his or her code.

In order to fully understand a system that contains global variables that have an effect on your program, you need to determine everywhere the variable is modified. In addition, in each of those places, you need to understand the circumstances under which the variable or variables can be modified. This is a lot of work, and you can make your program vastly easier to understand and debug by not using global variables. Instead, provide access functions, methods, or objects to deal with these variables. Consider the following C code:

```c
int globalInt = 0;
int TestFunction()
{
    switch ( globalInt )
    {
        case 0:
            Initialize();
            break;
        case 1:
            GetInput();
            break;
        case 2:
            Finalize();
            break;
    }
}
```

Apparently, the programmer who wrote this was relying on the global variable **globalInt** to tell him what stage he was at in the process of performing a certain task. Why is this a problem? Well, if another programmer saw the **globalInt** variable and thought he could create a "shortcut" by setting it to 1 because there was nothing that needed to be initialized in a certain case, it could quickly create a bug. If a new member variable or other initialization data was added to the initialization functionality in the **Initialize()** function, you would immediately introduce a new bug into the system.

Tip

Maintain a function or method to dump useful statistics and global variables in your application.

Global variables can be useful. In general, however, they are bugs waiting to happen. When your program contains globals of any sort, a useful debugging technique is to maintain a function or method to print them out, so that you can check them easily at regular intervals. They are also an excellent place to start looking when what appears to be a localized change affects other areas of the program.

Tip

Check global variables when localized changes affect other parts of the program!

Side Effects

If global variables are the single greatest affliction working against the debugger, side effects are a close second. A side effect is any action, be it a statement or a function, that does something other than what it was supposed to do. As a simple example, a function that was supposed to count the number of blank spaces in a string might perform an additional job, such as incrementing the reference count for that string. This side effect, even if documented, can cause great problems in tracking down issues when reading through the code to find problems.

To understand just how devious side effects can be, consider the following Java code snippet. This class method is supposed to convert a string to uppercase and return it.

```
public string UpperCaseString( string InString ){string s = new string;
    for ( int I=0; I<InString.length(); ++I )
        if ( IsLower(InString.getAt(I) )
        s += ToUpper( InString.getAt(I);
    else
        s += InString.getAt(I);

    InternalReferenceCount ++;

    return s;
}
```

This function appears to do what you expect, for the most part. It converts an input string to an output string and returns a copy of that string. The original string doesn't appear to have been modified. However, notice the call to the **InternalReferenceCount** incrementing. Is it clear what this statement is doing? Not entirely clear, that is for certain. It could simply be incrementing the number of times this method is called, or it could be tracking the reference count for this object. Without documentation that reveals the state of mind of the programmer who wrote the code, it is difficult to say.

The work of discovering why this increment happens is the detective work of the debugger. It might be unimportant, perhaps it is a simple tracing variable used during the initial code writing for this object. It could be vitally important, maybe it's a reference count for an object that never goes out of scope and thus is a memory leak. Either way, it is a side effect that is completely surprising in the scope of the function it appears in. This type of side effect is most often benign. The following contains an even worse side effect, which is actually a part of the standard C library (this implementation is not that of the library, it is simply one way of doing it):

```
// strdup: make a copy of the input string and return it.
char *strdup( const char *instring )
{
```

```
        // Allow room for the trailing null
        char *temp = new char[ strlen(instring)+1];

        // Copy all including trailing null
        memcpy( temp, instring, strlen(instring)+1);

        return temp;
}
```

This function makes a copy of a string and returns it. It appears that there are no side effects in this code, just the actual implementation of what the function says it does. What could possibly go wrong with such a simple function? To understand this, you have to look at it from the usage point of view. A programmer calls this function to copy an input string in some fashion, such as this:

```
char *s = strdup("This is a test");
FunctionThatModifiesString(s);
PrintString(s);
return 0;
```

What just happened? The programmer used the function as it was intended to be used; didn't he? He made a copy of the input string to send to some function that modified the input string, and then printed out the result. He was all done, so he finished the function by returning a code to the caller, indicating that there was no error in the function. If you were to simply look at this function with a passing knowledge of the C standard library, you would not see anything amiss. There is, however, a rather serious problem here. The **strdup** function allocated a block of memory to use to copy the string. That returned pointer was then given back to the caller of **strdup**. From that point on, that allocated memory was the responsibility of the calling function. Nowhere in the calling function does that block of memory get freed. We have just created a memory leak that appears nowhere in the source code of the application. Functions like this are a nightmare to debug and fix.

Tip

Watch for and document unexpected or hidden side effects in your code.

Watch for Unexpected Messages or Results

One of the easiest tricks of the trade is to simply watch for the unexpected. When you are running the program, you should watch for odd messages being displayed. For example, you might become accustomed to a dialog box in your application that warns you not to overwrite a file when trying to save your work. If, on a given occasion, the dialog box failed to appear when you knew that the file existed, you might become immediately suspicious. Perhaps the box did appear, but didn't display the message correctly. Rather than asking if you want to overwrite file "XYZ," you might see a dialog that asks if you want to overwrite file "*&^(*&^." It is unlikely that you would use such a naming convention, so this could easily be an indication of a problem in the program. Keeping your eye open for occurrences like this can help you debug your program later.

Most problems in applications are never truly diagnosed by users. Instead, users observe something that doesn't look right to them, and they tell you about it. Often, by the time they observe the event and tell you, the details of what went wrong are lost in the exchange. It is important, therefore, to have a reproducible case in which you can observe the program feedback as you go along. In addition, it is important that you know how the program is supposed to work, so that you can quickly determine if the program is working correctly or not.

Consider this simple example of a program bug that is reported. The user writes, "When I try to record a program onto the disk, the program refuses to do so. I have been recording programs all day. Why does it suddenly not allow me to record?" In this case, the program in question is similar to a VCR. Investigation shows that the user repeatedly recorded programs from the television all day. Then, suddenly, the program refused to record anymore. Is this a bug? The answer, surprisingly, is "maybe." In this case, the program recorded events until it reached a predefined limit of 50 events. A simple inspection of the source code for the application revealed this to be a hard-coded limit on the number of events that could be recorded in advance. Is this a bug? No. The requirements did not specifically state that there was such a limit, but requirements are often vague on such matters. Informing the user that there was such a limit explained the problem, and he went away happy. So, why is the answer "maybe?" Because there was no feedback to the user indicating why the recording event was refused. If the user is unaware of this limitation, and you don't tell him about it, it is an unexplained observation. The user tried it, it didn't work, he complained.

Now, let's take a look at a similar example that shows the same basic problem, but illustrates a more serious bug. While observing the output logging information from a program that records events from the television to a hard disk, you notice a line that reads: "Error: Unable to allocate additional space for event."

The television event continues to play and appears to record to the hard drive. Yet, when you go to play it back, it stops playing after a fixed period of time into the event. Repeated attempts to play back the recording have the same result. No playback is shown after a certain point. Looking back at what you had observed, you can guess the actual cause of the problem: The disk ran out of space and therefore the movie stopped. Whether this is a real bug or not depends on the requirements definition for the application. In this case, the problem is not that the program ran out of space. It is the fact that the error is not handled correctly. To solve this problem, either other programs should be removed from the disk to free up space for the current recording, or the application should check to see if there is sufficient space for the recording in the first place. The user (and the programmer) should never be surprised by the behavior of a program, whether they are running it for the first time or the ten-thousandth time.

Keep Track of Diagnostic Displays

When you properly build in diagnostics for an application, it is important that you observe those diagnostics, whether manually or automatically. Diagnostic displays are not of much use if you don't pay any attention to them. They become like the oil light in older cars. People rationalize the fact that they are on. "Oh, that, it's always lit. I think it's the fuse." Gee, that seems a bit odd. Why would the manufacturer provide such a light if it wasn't supposed to indicate a problem? The same can be said about a dialog box that pops up in the middle of an application run indicating that there is a serious disk error. You could certainly ignore it. But why would you want to? If there is no serious disk error, the program contains a bug and should be fixed. If there is a serious disk error, you are probably treading on thin ice to keep your computer running, much less your program. In either case, it seems like a bad idea to ignore the diagnostic.

Diagnostics are not always visible to the user. Sometimes, they are only seen by a programmer. For example, system logs, debug output, and other logging information can be held "behind the scenes" for use in diagnosing a problem and finding out what caused it. Some information is used to track down a future problem, but isn't useful to the user at the time of the event. Such information is often found in diagnostic output and should be examined regularly. This can allow you to spot and diagnose problems before they become crises.

Debugging Methods

Now that you understand some of the techniques that you can use to debug your application, it's time to look at some of the generalized methods we use when debugging applications. Each method has its own strengths and weaknesses, and there are appropriate times to use each method and inappropriate times. It is often up to you to decide which method you are most comfortable with at any given point in your career or position.

Scientific Method

In true engineering fields, the scientific method is used to solve complex problems. The method states in its simplest terms: Make a hypothesis, offer evidence to prove or disprove the hypothesis, and iterate until you find a hypothesis that fits all known evidence and is not contradicted by any observations.

In the debugging world, the scientific method really shines in uses for which you can duplicate the problem. Observe the problem and note any and all symptoms you can find when the problem occurs, before the problem occurs, and after the problem occurs. In addition, gather any and all diagnostic displays around the period of time in which the problem occurs.

Once you have the evidence in hand, start out by making a hypothesis that might explain why the problem is happening. For example, you might hypothesize that running out of disk space during a search operation will crash the program. Look at the evidence you have.

What is the maximum size of the disk? How much data is being searched? What temporary files are created for a search of that size? Take into account the observations you made while the problem was occurring. Did you hear the disk drive churn repeatedly? Did the disk light come on and stay on? If your operating system supports such alerts, did a warning dialog box appear indicating you were low on disk space?

Take the observations you have made and see if they fit the hypothesis. In general, some will because you used them to generate the hypothesis in the first place. The evidence you did not use will be offered as a counterbalance to the hypothesis. Examine each piece of evidence you wrote down during the discovery phase. Do any of these symptoms directly contradict the problem? Using our search example, do you find as a piece of evidence that the program finished writing to the disk and then started sorting in memory? That would tend to contradict the out-of-disk-space argument. If you can find at least one definitive piece of evidence to contradict your hypothesis, you will need to go back to step one and create a new hypothesis. It's also possible that a hierarchy of hypotheses may be necessary to converge on a problem by beginning with a general hypothesis and then "drilling down" to a specific issue.

At some point, hopefully, you will discover a hypothesis that is not contradicted by any of the available evidence. This doesn't make the theory correct, of course. At this point, it is just a theory. If the theory is correct, you can solve the problem by creating a solution to your hypothetical problem. To do this, consider the problem from the point of view of your hypothesis. Offer a solution that would solve the problem if your theory were correct. From this point, you will need to actually write the code or implement the procedure that puts your solution into place. If, when the code or procedure is in place, the problem is no longer apparent, you've solved the problem, right? Well, no, you haven't—at least not necessarily. To understand whether the problem is really solved, you need to complete a few other tasks to verify your bug fixes. These tasks are discussed in Chapter 9.

Intuition

Intuition is probably the most commonly used debugging method by a debugger who is familiar with the code. Intuition is simply "knowing" where a problem probably lies from the symptoms observed. Although intuition is rarely anything other than a thorough knowledge of the code and the way the system works as a whole, it can appear to be magic to those who do not know the system as well.

Intuition is not a good indicator of generalized debugging techniques. In order to use it effectively, you must have a thorough holistic knowledge of the system. If you are an original developer of the system, this is not difficult. For anyone other than a long time developer of the system, intuition can only be based on knowledge of similar systems.

In a nutshell, intuition is the ability to look at the symptoms of a problem and be able to quickly narrow down the area of the code in which the problem is occurring. It also requires enough understanding of the algorithms used in the application to be able to narrow down the sort of error that could be causing the symptoms observed.

To understand the intuitive approach, let's look at a simple example. Suppose that you are working on a program that provides real-time values of a hardware device, such as a pump. The program runs smoothly for a while, and then begins to return bogus values to the application user. As an uninitiated developer, you might begin by digging into the code and looking at how the algorithm is structured and implemented. The original developer, on the other hand, would look at the output and realize that the connection to the hardware device was dropped and the condition was not detected. The numbers that were coming back were simply line noise on the listening port.

There is no way to teach intuition. It comes from a thorough understanding of the code and the ways in which the application works. It is mentioned solely for the purpose of understanding how people with such knowledge manage to do the things they do.

Leap of Faith

Leaps of faith are simply educated guesses as to the problem and are probably the second most common form of debugging today. Rather than going through the work of examining all of the symptoms, the developer selects a few symptoms and makes a quick guess as to what the problem might be. The developer then tests the theory by changing the code directly to impact whatever problem he has decided exists and observes whether the problem goes away.

Leaps of faith are often referred to as "stabs in the dark," for good reason. Although a leap of faith might find and fix the problem, it is more likely to lead you in the wrong direction and confuse the issue. The general quality of a leap of faith is directly proportional to the amount of information you know about the system. If you are fully knowledgeable about the system, a leap of faith approaches the intuition level. On the other hand, if you know very little about the system, leaps of faith are much closer to SWAG (Scientific Wild A** Guessing).

The worst possible kind of debugging luck is to have a leap of faith work on the very first try. When this happens, you tend to ignore the scientific approach and move forward with further leaps. The more you leap, the less chance you have of succeeding, although you might think you have succeeded. Scientific methods have a much better overall success ratio. So, in general, you should look before you leap.

Diagnostics

Pure diagnostics, which is sometimes called *advance strike debugging*, is an attempt to predict, in advance, the sorts of problems that will occur in the application and to log them, so that the programmer can find them and fix them at a later date. Although it is rare to use diagnostic debugging as the only form of debugging in your shop, it has been known to happen. Diagnostics are the best debugging evidence you have because they consist of statistics and events gathered at the time the problem occurred rather than observations and later reconstructions. Diagnostics are not the panacea of debugging, however. While a diagnostic display may tell you what the error was and where that error occurred, it will not tell you what happened to cause that error in the first place. Knowing, for example, that a low-level system routine received a NULL pointer is a good indication of what caused the system to crash, but it does nothing to help you understand why the pointer was NULL in the first place. Follow the hypothesis model at all times, even when you are given excellent diagnostic information.

If this is true, then why don't debuggers always use diagnostic debugging as their only form of debugging? The reason is quite simple. It is virtually impossible to identify every possible error condition that might arise or to print the values of every variable in the program. In Chapter 10, we look at several diagnostic data elements you will always want to monitor during a program run; but for now, accept the fact that you are somewhat limited. In addition, each diagnostic that is saved will occupy disk space from the user, and that disk space is a finite resource. If your system has no disk space, such as an embedded system might not, you are in even more trouble. Without knowing why your program is generating log files, the user might very well delete them in an attempt to reclaim these resources. Also, diagnostics take a definite amount of time to display and write to disk. This processing time can have a severe performance impact on your application. You do not want to consume the user's entire disk space and have them use a snail-paced program. Even if your application is bug free, nobody will want to use it.

Tricks of the Trade

For each type of debugging form and each debugging technique, there are certain tricks that you will learn as you go along to make your life easier. Let's examine a few of them at this point.

Built-In Debugger

It is possible, and often desirable, to build in a debugging system within your application. Such a system is not the same as using an external debugger; it has both advantages and disadvantages to such an external program. Your debugger can be left in and running while the system is deployed, allowing you to debug applications while they are running. Another huge advantage of an internal debugger over an external debugger, as you will see in the next chapter, is that internal debuggers do not change the conditions under which the application is running.

To implement an internal debugger, you need to create a specialized way to get to the internal code. This is usually implemented via some sort of a secret code mechanism, although it could easily be modified to use a login approach. In either case, it is preferable to not allow the casual user into the debugger as they would at best be confused and at worst might destroy data inadvertently.

Once the debugger interface is set, you need to decide what information you want to look at. Unlike conventional external debugging applications, internal debuggers can usually only perform tasks that are programmed into them. To make them more generalized requires more resources than the programmer would normally want to utilize in the user's computer. For this reason, internal debuggers normally track predefined variables. To specify particular variables, you can "register" variables you want to see or trace routes through the program you want to follow with the debugger at runtime. This allows you to decide what you want to see when you want to see it. This approach does have one drawback. If you later decide you need more information about other variables that were not predefined, it does not allow you to look at them. However, you can generally always go back, add them, and rerun the application.

Internal debuggers must be considered during the initial design period of the application. Adding a debugging system after a program is already up and running is a difficult task. Consider adding such a system only when doing a major overhaul of the system when you have the time to do it right. A badly written debugging system is actually more harmful than it is useful.

Logging Objects

By far the most useful debugging diagnostic is to understand what a program is doing at any given time. To do this, output logs are often used to trace through the information used by the application. Logging objects can easily be used in multiple applications, which more than justify their cost in design and development. A logging object is simply an object (a class in C++, Java, or Delphi, and a component in Visual Basic or ASP) that allows you to control the logging of certain information throughout a program run.

Important elements to consider when writing a logging object (or purchasing a prewritten one) are whether you can turn logging on and off at runtime, whether you can control what gets logged, and whether the object can be used in such components as interrupt handlers, where time spent writing data is often critical.

Warning

When creating logging objects, beware of their use in interrupt or time-critical routines.

Logging objects should not be confused with tracing objects, which we discuss next. Logging objects are general-purpose objects that write out only what you tell them to write out. They can be controlled at runtime or can be turned off by conditional code in your application to remove them from the production build.

Tracing Objects

Tracing objects are objects that allow you to trace through your program's flow at runtime. Unlike logging objects, tracing objects attempt to model the program flow through its run.

To best use tracing objects, you should be able to define the entry point into the system via a user command or process, and then pass that command or process name down through the lower-level objects that are called. When you use tracing objects, you can see at a glance each level that the calls were passed through and which branches were taken by matching the code back up to the object calls.

Tracing objects help the holistic approach to application debugging by allowing you to see what the system is doing without having to sit down and laboriously trace through the code for each command or process. Although it is best if they are implemented at the initial time of the program implementation, tracing objects can easily be added after the fact. All that is necessary is to put the proper objects into the code in each new function, method, or object. For example, you might have a tracing object implemented in C++ that does something like this:

```cpp
class Trace
{
private:
   std::string mFunctionName;
    Trace( const char *funcName)
    {
        mFunctionName = funcName;
        printf("Entering %s", funcName);
    };
   ~Trace(void)
    {
        printf("Exiting function %s", mFunctionName.c_str() );
     };
};
```

This very simple class could then be embedded in code in a manner such as this:

```cpp
int function1(void)
{
    Trace trace("Function1");
   // Do something
}
int Function2( void )
{
   Trace trace("Function2");
   function1():
}

int Function3(void)
{
   Trace trace("Function3");
```

```
    Function2();
}

int main(void)
{
    Function3();
}
```

The output from a single program run would be:

```
Entering function Function3
Entering function Function2
Entering function Function1
Exiting function Function1
Exiting function Function2
Exiting function Function3
```

By looking at the output and the function **main()**, you could easily trace through how the program works. Obviously, this simple and contrived example is trivial enough to just look at the code itself. When you are working in a language such as C++, Delphi, or even Java, however, you can quickly get lost in the layers of inheritance and overload virtual functions to the point where you have no idea what is being called. Tracing will help you discover this quickly.

Tip

Add tracing objects to your code while writing them.

Hidden Diagnostic Screens

Another useful technique for debugging programs at runtime, especially in a production environment, is to use hidden diagnostic screens. Hidden diagnostic screens are a lot like built-in debuggers, but are generally much simpler and provide a one or two page listing of all the important diagnostics that the programmer wants to keep track of during the program run. Some information in the list might include the environment under which the program is running, the amount of free memory, the amount of available disk space, and the version of the various components used by the application.

The advantage to diagnostic screens over built-in debuggers is their size and the ease with which they are added after the fact. If you want diagnostic information at runtime in a production environment, but have an existing code base that you loathe to modify at a low level, the next best thing is to figure out the pieces that you want to track, and then add hidden diagnostic screens to a single location. These screens are normally hidden from the user (hence their name) and accessible only by an odd keyboard combination or special login/password combination, which the average user is unlikely to use.

Tip

Add hidden diagnostic screens accessible only by special keyboard commands or specialized logins.

One last note on diagnostic screens: they can also be used for historical data on usage, which you might want to have when debugging. For example, you might track the number of new files that the user has created versus the number of existing files that he or she has opened. This can be useful in tracking down the cause of some bugs. If you observe, for example, that the user always opens an existing file, there is no point in looking for bugs for this user in the create file routine. In addition, by tracking usage patterns, you can determine where best to put your efforts in fixing and enhancing the application. Oh, and as a final note, if you notice that the user is accessing the help screens all the time, it might be worth looking into the usability of your program.

Saving Bug Data for Later Runs

Another trick of the trade is to keep track of data that causes bugs in your application. One of the oddest characteristics of programmers is that they have a tendency to make the same kinds of mistakes in a lot of places. Likewise, once they have made a mistake once, they are actually more prone to make those same mistakes again in later code. If you keep track of the kinds of data and processes that cause bugs the first time around, you can use this data later on for regression testing and for testing of new features.

Consider this example. Suppose that you have an input screen that accepts dates. The programmer implementing the screen has checked for "valid" dates, not allowing invalid months, invalid days (those outside the range of 1-31), and invalid years, such as negative values. However, the programmer failed to check for leap years. You might take note of this and add a test case for future work to look for leap year entries. It will save you a lot of grief and a lot of time tracking down problems.

It is probably worth mentioning that when you find a case, such as the leap year problem, you should consolidate the code that performs the verification of a date into a single location. That way, once the problem is fixed once, it will be fixed forever. In addition, it is that much less code you will need to slog through when trying to gain that all-important holistic view of your application domain.

Reproducible Cases

By far, the best way to gather evidence when trying to solve a bug is to have a reproducible case that illustrates the problem you are trying to fix. Let's take a look at some of the issues involved in creating and finding reproducible cases.

Test Cases

In order to actually be able to create a reproducible case, you must first have a test case that appears to illustrate the problem. Test cases are generally written by software testers, but can also be created by developers and debuggers. It is important that you be able to easily step through the process to create the bug's symptoms, so you should be sure that the test case is well documented and easy to follow.

As an example, a test case that reads "start the program and do stuff until the screen turns blue," would be very unlikely to produce any usable reproducible cases. What sort of "stuff" do you need to do? How long do you need to do the "stuff"? Will any kind of "stuff" work, or do you need to do specific "stuff"? All of these are valid questions.

Contrast the first example with the following test case: "Start the program. Go to File | Open, and select the file file001a.dat from the \ \ testcases share. Click on OK. Move to the thirty-third line of the file, and type the line 'Hello world'. Watch the program status bar carefully, and you should observe the column indicator moving with your typing." This instruction would go along with a bug report of "When exercising test case <xxx>, the column indicator does not correctly reflect which column you are in." This is obviously a much better description and will likely result in the debugger quickly and easily being able to reproduce and hopefully solve the problem.

It is very important that you keep track of your test cases so that the developers can see the sorts of events that cause problems. Like keeping track of bugs, keeping track of test cases will lead to better quality software because solutions are rolled back into the design and debugging processes.

Data Dependencies

The most frustrating bugs are those that are dependent on specific forms of input data. Because the bug cannot be duplicated unless a specific process is followed with a specific set of data, it is often very difficult to track these problems down. Data-dependent bugs can appear to be fixed because the right set of data isn't use to reproduce them. Like finding reproducible cases, finding reproducible data sets can often be a serious problem and an enormous help in debugging problems.

When finding and reporting bugs, it is important to keep track of the data you were using to create the bug in the first place. This is easy if you are responsible for creating the data for the application. It is more difficult if the data comes from an external source, such as a real-time data stream. In these cases, using a good deal of logging and tracing can help you determine exactly what types of data are causing the problems.

Generally, data-dependent problems are boundary conditions for the algorithms or limits that you use in your application. One of the best ways to find these boundary conditions is to fully understand the limits in the system. For example, a system might contain arbitrary limits on the number of entries that may be in a file. Knowing this limit, you can easily test and fix problems that occur when the file is empty or when it contains too many entries. Beware of hard-coded limitations in the application, such as "Maximum of 50 files" or "Only signals between 0.4 and 1.2 are allowed."

Separating Symptoms from Root Causes

When you are debugging an application, it is common to focus on the symptoms that you observe and to consider the problem fixed when that symptom goes away. Unfortunately, it is often the case that the real bug has little or nothing to do with the symptoms it exhibits. The most clear-cut example of this is the stray pointer problem that occurs in several languages.

A stray pointer problem occurs when you have an uninitialized pointer. A pointer, for those who do not use languages that have them, is a variable that points to a specific block of memory. In the languages that do use them, failing to actually point the variable at a given block of memory results in it pointing to a random area in memory. Such variables are called uninitialized. When such a pointer is aiming itself at a portion of memory that is critical, it can cause unexpected program results, such as crashes. Adding new code to the application (or even adding new variables) can change where the pointer is aimed and will appear to fix the problem. It does not fix anything, of course, it simply moves the problem to a new and so-far undiscovered location.

How then can you be sure that you have actually fixed the problem? Let's go back to the idea of hypotheses and solutions. If you have created a hypothesis that the problem is a bad piece of code and you fix that piece of code, then in theory the problem should go away. If, however, you put a few debug statements into your code to see what is going on (logging statements) and the problem goes away, it is unlikely that you have fixed anything. Only by being sure of what the problem is can you verify that you have found and fixed the root cause.

Gathering Observations

One of the best ways to determine when and where bugs are occurring is simply to observe the product in use. First, this is an excellent way to learn how the program works from the outside, which will allow you a better understanding of why it might work the way it does on the inside. Second, by observing the program when it is working properly, it is easier to trace the times when the program is working improperly.

When you gather observations about a program run, it is important to write down the steps you take as you go along. Think of gathering observations as following through test cases, but with a less problem oriented goal in mind. If possible, document not only what you were doing, but what data was entered into the program at each step. Then use these observations to trace through the code, using the data you entered to see what the result should be. If you see an anomalous display or the program does not proceed as it is supposed to, you will already have gathered much information about its usage before you ever look at the code.

Similarly, observations of areas that have been found to cause problems will allow you to see why the kinds of data that are causing the problems are getting through. It might be, for example, that the problem is deep within the algorithmic bowels of the application, but can be much more easily and efficiently fixed by not allowing data entries that cause the problem in the first place.

Keeping a project notebook of how the system is supposed to work from the outside can be a valuable tool in noting whether your observations are correct or not. You can take the project notebook and compare it to the requirements definition (if you have one) or the design of the system (if there is one) to see what was supposed to happen at each stage. As you saw earlier in the book, not everything that works in a way you didn't expect it to is a bug. Identifying bugs by observation is a powerful tool in the detective work stage of debugging.

Statistics/Metrics

Keeping statistics and metrics about your application is a double-edged sword. On one hand, you will be able to know if you are making headway against the problems in the application and be more able to identify the sections of the program that would be best reexamined or rewritten. On the other hand, metrics and statistics are often used for politically motivated campaigns to show one thing or the other depending on who holds the statistics. As the old saying goes, "Figures lie, and liars figure." This is not to say that there is a good reason not to maintain statistics and metrics for an application, but simply to note that it is not always the technical problems that get in the way of debugging.

So what sort of statistics and metrics are useful when debugging an application? It is often important to track which modules were last updated and the number of changes made to each module. When a bug suddenly appears, it is likely that the problem occurred in a recent change. At least, that change is suspect enough that it warrants a look. Although the bug itself might not be in that module, the change may have impacted another module and caused the problem there.

Another metric that is useful is to consider the complexity of the code in any given module. Although it is not universally true that complexity causes problems, there is a very definite correlation between complexity and the likelihood of a bug. Consider, for example, the following two pieces of Visual Basic code:

```
FOR I = 1 TO 100
    CALLPROC( I, I*I )
NEXT I
```

and

```
FOR I = 1 TO 100
    FOR J = 1 TO 100
```

```
        X = X + SQRT(Y) + I*X + X * (I*I)
        Z = Y + X
        DIF = Z - (X+R)
    NEXT J
NEXT I
```

Even if you did not understand what either snippet of code was doing, which one would you expect to be more likely to contain a bug? The second snippet is more likely to have bugs than the first, which comes as no real surprise. Measuring complexity is a fairly difficult job, but there are numerous measures that can be used. The McCabe Complexity Value is a good one to start with. The McCabe Complexity Value is an attempt to evaluate how complex a set of functionality might be in code. The number of paths in a function is used to compute the complexity measure of that function.[3]

Another area where metrics are useful is in tracking the number of problems in the code. If you measure the number of bugs fixed each day in the lifetime of a project following code complete, you will find that it resembles a bell curve. That is, there are fewer fixed at the beginning of the cycle because development is still going on and testing is just beginning. Then, there is a large upswing in the number of problems found and fixed as testing gets into full swing, and the debugging team takes full priority after the code is finally frozen. Finally, the number of bugs that are found and fixed begins to drop as the quality of the product increases. By studying several projects and the curves that represent them, you will have a better knowledge of how many bugs to expect in the code and how long it will take to fix them.

There is one final metric that is often worth keeping, but it is one that you must be very careful with. This metric is used to track the number of bugs per developer. By tracking the modules in which bugs occur and the types of bugs that occur in those modules, you can then assign each bug to the developer that created it. This is not a good measure for political reasons, but it is an excellent one for the debuggers. By knowing that developer A rarely causes a problem in his code, whereas developer B causes 10 percent more bugs, you can start testing and debugging in the right places. In addition, if you discover that 45 percent of developer A's bugs are in memory management, and the bug symptoms you observe are memory management related, you will have a better idea of where to look. Remember, though, that nobody likes to have his problems pointed out to him. This metric should only be used by debuggers, not by management.

This last point brings up an interesting observation about debugging versus application development. When you are debugging an application, you need to check your ego at the door. It is not important to note who created the problem or who fixed the problem. What is important is that the problem was found and fixed. Don't point fingers when you are debugging problems.

---

[3] McCabe, T. J. "A Complexity Measure." *IEEE Transactions on Software Engineering*, Vol 2, Number 4, December 1976, pp 308–320.

Summary

In summation, in this chapter we learned how to use detective skills in the debugging process. The scientific method is the paramount methodology used in debugging programs, regardless of the scale of the system. From tiny console applications to large scale distributed systems, the scientific method will permit you to reproducibly find and fix problems in your own projects.

You should have learned that there are several steps to finding a problem and creating a solution for that problem. First, you must observe the symptoms of the problem, taking careful note of what it is that is really going on in the system. Second, you must offer a hypothesis for the problem which takes into account all of the observable phenomena and is not contradicted by any observed symptoms. The third step is to test the hypothesis by checking it against not only the observable symptoms, but also by determining what other symptoms could be found if other input scenarios were used. If the hypothesis meets all of the available criteria necessary to prove it out, the fourth step is to offer a solution which will solve the specified hypothesis. The fifth step is to verify that the solution solves the problem and creates no new problems.

Hopefully, you have understood the importance of solving the actual problem, and not simply of treating the symptoms observed in the application. It cannot be stressed enough that simply putting bandages on a wounded application will only make your problems worse in the long run.

Bug Puzzle

In keeping with the theme of detective work in this chapter, let's look at an example that uses this detective work to determine exactly what is going on in an application to cause a problem for the end user.

While running through bug reports for the application that your company develops, you run across an oddity. A user reports that the program crashes once per day, every day, and at the same time each day. Furthermore, the user reports that the program did this some time before, then miraculously "fixed itself," and is now back to doing what it was doing before.

In tracking through the changes to the system between the time when the system "fixed itself" and the present time, you find only three differences. First, the program was fixed to use a new set of printer drivers to accommodate new printers that had been introduced into the world since the last release. Second, a bug was fixed whereby the automatic backup system, which had not been working correctly, was now working properly. Finally, there was a change to the memory management system to do a better job of garbage collection during its idle period.

Assume that the program contains logging information indicating what major events are occurring at certain times. Further assume that you have full access to the program source code and can examine any piece of it. Finally, assume that you cannot reproduce the problem with your "stock system" running in the lab. Decide what steps you would take to find the problem. Think about possible hypotheses for the problem and how you would go about fixing the problem.

Chapter 7

Debugging Tools and When to Use Them

Matt Telles

When you are debugging an application for the first time, it sometimes seems as though you are all alone. It also seems as though there are no tools that might work for your particular application, and no documentation exists to describe the bugs you are finding and trying to fix. There are, however, many existing tools that you can use depending on the problem you are facing and the conditions under which you are working. In this chapter, we examine many of the available debugging tools, determine when they can be used and, probably more importantly, advise you when not to use them.

Understanding the limitations of your tools is almost as important as understanding how they can be used to your benefit. Plenty of documentation exists on how the debugging tools we describe can be used. Very little of that documentation describes the problems you may encounter while using these tools or the ways in which these tools can at times make your job harder rather than easier.

Testing and Debugging Environments

The first debugging tool that we will consider is a *testing environment*. Testing environments include a suite of hardware, software, and test cases that can be used to model, investigate, and reproduce problems as the user sees them. Without a consistent way to determine what the real problem is, you are simply shooting in the dark trying to find the cause of a bug. With a consistent environment, you can easily test hypotheses and verify bug fixes. We will consider the debugging methods in order, from the highest level debugging techniques for paring down the sheer amount of code to look through for the bug to the lower level techniques for finding the actual problem.

Suite of Tests

Test suites are used to ensure that the program is doing what you expect it to do. In many cases, simply by examining the test cases, you can get a good idea of what areas of the code you should be looking at for problems and what areas you need not look at. If a bug directly contradicts a test case, then either the bug is a misunderstood part of the application, or the test case was never run successfully. In either situation, you can examine the way in which the code responds to the specified test case to see how it works. This will tell you quickly and easily if the test case is wrong or the bug is wrong. If the bug is wrong, you can explain the problem to the user and either reach an understanding on how the code should work (according to the user), or you can request an enhancement to the application. If the code is wrong and the test case is incorrect, you can modify the test case to be run according to the proper requirements, and then modify the code so that the test case runs properly. The test case is, therefore, the most easily reproduced case of the bug. To carry this thought just a bit further, you can utilize each bug report as a new test case. This allows you to verify that bug fixes really work and that any changes to the application do not re-create a known bug. Like the concepts we talked about in the previous chapter, you can use such test suites to verify that a bug is really fixed instead of simply examining the symptoms and assuming that it is fixed after you make a code change.

It is important to understand how test cases come to be and how they should be used in both the testing and debugging cycles. Test cases, ideally, should be written from the requirements and design specifications. Then, after coding, there are six possible result states for a test case test:

♦ The test case correctly tests the requirements-design item and the code correctly executes producing the output specified by the test case. This is the simplest case, and the most straightforward. We are saying in this case that the code was implemented correctly and the test verified this fact.

♦ The test case correctly tests the requirements-design item and the code incorrectly executes and does not produce the output specified by the test case. This is the simplest case of a "bug" in the system.

♦ The test case correctly tests the requirements-design item and the code correctly executes but does not produce the output specified by the test case. There are a variety of reasons for this one, but the most basic is an interface error in the coding system. It is also possible that the test case is incorrectly worded.

♦ The test case incorrectly tests the requirements-design item and the code correctly satisfies the test case and incorrectly executes the desired requirements-design item. This is a further way to verify the correctness of the code, the requirements, and the design.

- The test case incorrectly tests the requirements-design item and the code incorrectly satisfies the test case and incorrectly executes the desired requirements-design item. In this case, the test case needs to be checked.

- The test case incorrectly tests the requirements-design item and the code incorrectly satisfies the test case but correctly executes the desired requirements-design item. This is probably the most nightmarish of all scenarios. The coding was done properly from the system design, but the system design did not adequately reflect the requirements for the application.

Test Harnesses

One of the biggest problems with testing a hypothesis in a large-scale application is the sheer size of the code that makes up the application. In order to examine a core method, function, or process within the code, you might have to set up a dozen higher-level processes and enter a ton of information to drill down to the level you suspect contains the problem. There are, however, ways to avoid this problem. One of the easiest is the test harness, which is also called *scaffolding code* (or *application template*).

Tip
Build a scaffolding application to test each subsystem as it is written.

Scaffolding code is used to test small pieces of the code, such as utility functions or even core library routines. You can think of external scaffolding code as a benchmark test suite for the code you want to test. It is best, of course, if this code is written at the same time the actual functionality is written, so that it is easy to use as a test harness. If your company or department does not already require it, you should make it a rule to always provide a test harness, along with the source code and documentation, for any subsystem to be added to the application. If you cannot get the developers to do this, you should make it a point to use the initial investigation stage of the debugging phase of an application to write scaffolding code for each subsystem that you have the chance to work on.

Suite of Past Bugs

It might seem like a redundant observation to say that you should maintain a suite of existing and past bugs so that you can test your application. However, it might not be apparent that you can use other project's suites to test your own application as well. In addition, because programmers tend to create similar kinds of bugs, it is useful to keep bug suites from previous and current projects to compare to your own application. This allows you to compare features from other projects, which are often quite similar, to your own application and look for similar kinds of bugs. If your project reuses code from other projects, this is almost a necessity.

One of the nicest benefits of reusing code, libraries, and even requirements between projects is that you get a lot of work done without much effort; being able to reuse the code is only the tip of the iceberg. When you reuse a component at the requirement level between two projects, you not only get the requirement and (hopefully) the code that implements that requirement for your own project, but you also get the test cases that go to that subsystem and any test harnesses that were written for that subsystem. In short, you get a complete piece of the system that you can add to your own project. You might also get some documentation for the subsystem as well.

Tip

If you reuse requirements between applications, you can also reuse test cases, code, and debugging utilities.

Logging

We talked briefly in the last chapter about logging and its possible uses in your application. Now, let's take a look at how you can use logging to debug your application as well as when it is a bad idea.

Logging is an excellent idea when you are trying to learn how an application works and how the various pieces of the application fit together. Logging can show you the input to each method and the conditions under which various methods were called by enabling you to look back through a log of the branches selected. This is the good news about logging. Now, let's take a look at the bad news.

One of the biggest advantages of logging is also its biggest disadvantage when trying to debug a specific problem. The amount of information presented is staggering when you try to sift through it to figure out what really happened in the code. You can easily miss individual problems within the morass of output that your program can generate. One way to mitigate this problem is to use logging only in the scaffolding code to test a specific piece of the application. This works fine if you have already identified the logical subsystem that contains the problem. If you are looking at the application as a whole, however, you will find yourself overwhelmed with information.

How, then, can you use logging to help you when the program as a whole needs to be searched? The easiest way is to build smart logging objects. For example, you might have a function in C that looks like this:

```c
void LogMessage( int lvl, char *fmt, … )
{// Only log information above a certain priority level
        if ( lvl > gLoggingLevel )
        {
            vfprintf(fOutFile, fmt);
        }
}
```

This simple function uses two global variables (remember what we said about global variables) to track the "level" at which to output logging information and to track the file pointer to output the data into. In this way, you can better control the information that is logged so that it isn't as overwhelming. You can also use logging regions to further restrict the output data. Logging regions simply define the area of the program from which the data is coming. For example, you might define a logging region for each major subsystem of the application. This would allow you to turn the various logging regions on and off at runtime, giving you the information you want to see when you want to see it.

Note

There are times when you might need to write log analysis programs to summarize and display the logging data in order to determine where an error might have occurred. Writing such analysis applications is a lot of work, but is often an indispensible tool in your debugging arsenal.

In summation, logging is a good way to obtain a rough estimate of where the problem might be, and once you know where it is, to get the information about what is going on at that point. To use logging efficiently, however, you need to be able to whittle down the data coming into you at any given time.

Tracing

Like logging, we discussed tracing in the previous chapter from the viewpoint of using it in a positive way. Now, let's take a look at the work you need to do to make tracing work for you as a pure debugging tool. Tracing, like logging, has a tendency to output a large amount of debugging information, most of which has nothing to do with the area you want to trace. Also, like logging, tracing often outputs a lot of information that you don't need when you are trying to figure out what is going wrong. Once you have located the path taken by the code to get to the area you suspect is causing the bug, or at least have limited the scope of the program affected to a given area, you should probably turn off the tracing of program events or stop looking at the log.

One of the reasons that you don't want to continue examining tracing information once you have selected the area of the program to look at is simply because it can be confusing. You will find yourself bouncing from function to function, program area to program area, or object to object in an attempt to establish what might be causing the problem. This is rarely productive. Instead, you should pursue some of the other scientific methods for determining what the actual cause of the problem might be. It is difficult to formulate a valid hypothesis when you are juggling numerous parts of the code in your mind simultaneously.

Tip

Remove tracing code from your debugging application when you have found the likely subsystem causing the problem.

Tracing is a valuable holistic tool for determining how the program gets from state to state via the code. It is extremely useful for figuring out what path the code follows to accomplish a functional task. It is, however, normally far too high a level of debugging method to determine what the actual problem might be for a given debugging session. Tracing is also the last of the high level debugging techniques we will consider when looking at ways to find out what is going on in an application.

Middle Level Debugging Techniques

Once you have taken the ripsaw to your application to find the area of the program that is most likely causing the problem, you then need to use the smaller tools to examine the problem more closely. Most middle level debugging techniques assume that you have examined the symptoms of the problem, found the likely subsystem that is causing the problem (if possible), and limited the possible causes of the problem to a few possibilities. At this point, it is time to start looking for what might be causing the symptoms you have observed in the code itself. There are a lot of possible causes for any given set of symptoms. The more symptoms you can observe, the better chance you have of finding the actual code that causes the problem. Let's take a look at the middle level tools you can use to find the problems more accurately.

Memory Leak Detection Tools

If you are working in a language that allows the allocation of memory, you will likely run into memory leaks. A more general form of this problem is the case of resource leaks, which are really the same thing. Finding memory leaks in your application is usually a matter of matching the allocation of memory blocks with the deallocation of memory blocks. We examine some of the ways that you can look for these matching pairs in this subsection.

If you are working with a debugging environment that automatically tracks memory allocation and deallocation, you are ahead of the game. You will be able to use the built-in tools of your environment to find and fix allocation problems. If your environment does not track these functions, you will need to either use a third-party memory allocation tracker or write your own. There are many third-party tools to do this on the market, but if you choose to write your own (perhaps because you use a proprietary operating system or an unusual language), you should keep track of the following bits of information:

♦ What file and/or function performed the allocation

♦ What the allocation was done for

♦ What file/function performed the deallocation

♦ The amount of memory allocated or deallocated

If you are using a language such as Visual Basic, which has no true memory allocation, or Java, which has built-in garbage collection that would appear to eliminate the need for allocation/deallocation functions, you might be very surprised to find that memory leaks can still occur.

As a simple example, consider the following code from a Visual Basic application:

```
Private Type NCB
; Private members deleted for space
End Type
Private Type NAME_BUFFER
End Type
Private Type ASTAT
End Type
Private Declare Function HeapAlloc Lib "kernel32" _
        (ByVal hHeap As Long, ByVal dwFlags As Long, _
        ByVal dwBytes As Long) As Long
Private Declare Function HeapFree Lib "kernel32" (ByVal hHeap As Long, _
        ByVal dwFlags As Long, lpMem As Any) As Long

Private Function EthAddr(LanaNumber As Long) As String
; Setup code removed
lngASTAT = HeapAlloc(GetProcessHeap(), HEAP_GENERATE_EXCEPTIONS _
        Or HEAP_ZERO_MEMORY, udtNCB.ncb_length)
; Modification code removed.
HeapFree GetProcessHeap(), 0, lngASTAT
End If
EthAddr = strOut
End Function
```

As you can see, Visual Basic is quite capable of calling the Windows API functions HeapAlloc and HeapFree, which allocate and deallocate memory, respectively. The language does not automatically free up the memory you get using these functions. Worse, the leak that is created is very difficult to track down. If you wrap these functions in a "helper" routine, you will be able to track them more easily.

> **Note**
> *Helper routines are wrappers around a function or set of functions that allow you to track such things as the number of times a paired set of functions such as alloc/free are called. An odd number stored in a global variable invariably means a leak. A negative number means you are freeing something twice.*

Likewise, you can have a memory leak in Java. It doesn't seem possible, but in fact it can easily happen. Let's take a look at one of the more classic examples. The following code contains a listener object that loses its referenced object:

```
public class PrinterObject
{
      static PrintService single;
      PrintTarget target;

      public PrintService getPrintService()
      {
            return single;
      }
      public void setTarget(PrintTarget p)
      {
            target = p;
      }

      public void doPrint()
      {
            // Intialize
            // Print the object
      }
}
```

Why this object causes a memory leak is not readily apparent. It become obvious, however, when you understand what goes on when the **doPrint** routine is called after setting a target. Because the **PrinterObject** class contains a singleton (a type which may have only a single active variable at any given time), the **PrinterObject** object will contain a reference to the object in the target member variable. Once the **doPrint** method is called and the target is reassigned to a new object to print, there is a dangling reference to the object that can never be garbage collected. Memory leaks are, in fact, rarer in Java than in C, C++, or Pascal, but they are just as deadly. Errors such as these are harder to track down as well. You might want to have an Assign method for any object that is set to a member variable such as this, and then Assign could track what the variable is remembering.

Memory leaks and resource leaks are among the oldest problems in the software development world. Never use resources indiscriminately in your application; instead, track them very carefully, and you will have a much easier time tracking resource leaks.

Cross-Indexing and Usage Tools

Another very useful third-party tool that you should have in your debugging arsenal is the cross-indexer. This tool allows you to see where various symbols (global variables, methods, or functions) are used within the application. If you have such a tool and you have tracked down a given bug within a given function, you can then determine everyone that calls that function from within the application. The big advantage to this is that you can quickly and easily trace through the application from the bottom up rather than the top down.

There are numerous cross-indexing editors available on the market today. I would highly recommend that you use a cross-indexer for those times when you are trying to determine how a given problem got to the point where it caused a bug. Another really useful feature of this kind of a tool is that it will be able to easily show you "dead code," which is not being called from anywhere in the application. Some language development environments have this built-in capability.

If your code contains global variables, the cross-indexer is a necessity for when you are writing code or debugging applications. Without knowing exactly where a global variable is modified, you can waste valuable time trying to determine why it suddenly changed in the middle of a debugging run.

The final use of the cross-indexer is in the optimization process. If you know which functions are being called in a large number of places, you can start with those functions for optimization. This ensures that the work you do to make a given function faster or more efficient is not wasted due to the fact that it is never used in the application.

Debugger

It was inevitable, in a book about debugging, that we would eventually get around to talking about the debugger. One of the reasons we've avoided it to this point is that virtually every book on debugging is really a discussion on how best to use the debugger to detect bugs. Using the debugger is not really an appropriate topic for this book. Individual debuggers include directions for using them, and you will certainly find a plethora of books that discuss how to use various debuggers on various platforms to do your job.

In one respect, debuggers are the single greatest tool you can use when trying to find and fix problems in your applications. They provide ways to look at what is really going on. Debuggers allow you to stop your program at any given point, inspect the variables in your code, and even (for some debuggers) step backward over code lines to see what occurred before you executed the code. Debuggers have made the life of people tracking down problems just a little sunnier and a little easier.

The dark side of the debugger, however, is also part of a programmer's and debugger's life. Rather than concern ourselves with how you use a debugger and under what circumstances, let's take a look at why you might not want to use one. In addition, we will explore some of the cases in which a debugger is not only not wanted, it can actually not be used.

Hesienberg's Uncertainty Principle

Heisenberg said that observing the test can change the outcome. Nowhere is this more true than in debugging using debuggers. One of the most frustrating things that can happen for someone debugging an application is when the problem does not occur within the run of a debugger application. This can happen for a variety of reasons. Many debugging applications modify the memory that the program being debugged runs in. Many zero out memory before loading the application, which can hide stray pointer problems and uninitialized variable problems. Worse, a debugger can insert code into an application only in debug mode, which causes a problem to show up differently than it would in the release version of the application. This is one reason that so many testers hesitate to even try to adequately test a nonrelease version of the software.

Another problem with debuggers is that they give a false sense of confidence to the developer debugging the application. Developers use debuggers to examine what the program is doing at development runtime so they can find problems that they observe while they are creating the application. Debuggers can rarely use a debugger because the versions of the software they must use must match the conditions used by the user of the application. You can never use a debugger in a production environment, for example, because it would prevent users from accessing the application. Likewise, you cannot always load a debugger on a "clean" system to find a problem because the environment for that machine is unique. Loading any other software on the machine could cause the problem to change forms or move its location.

As you can see, the debugger is quite often not a professional bug fixer's friend. If you learn the tricks and techniques that do not require outside intervention, you will find that you can more easily find and fix problems in production quality code. Additionally, you will avoid the frustration of having a bug in the production release not show up in the debugged version of the code. This is not to say that debuggers do not have their place in application debugging; they most certainly do. However, they should be restricted to single-user products where the environment the program is running under is not the cause of the problem.

Built-In Diagnostics

In the last chapter, we talked briefly about building in diagnostic code for your application in the form of built-in debugging, hidden diagnostic screens, logging code, and the like. In this section, we talk a bit about how to use your knowledge of how the program works to build in diagnostic information that you can use to find bugs. The actual form of the diagnostic display can be log messages, diagnostic displays, log files, or other forms of output.

What is important is detecting the sorts of conditions that are worthy of being detected. In this case, you should consider the benefits of the preconditions, input, postconditions, and error handling (PIPE) approach. Let's examine each one of these elements and see what it means.

Preconditions are the assumption that you make before a method, function, or process is called. Any initialization that needs to be done, any other methods or functions that need to be called, and anything that cannot be done first is a precondition for the method or function you are dealing with. Preconditions can generally be found by looking at test drivers or scaffolding code for the function or method you are interested in.

Input deals with the input to a given function or method. Input can be parameters passed into the function, global variables that are set, or external resources that are used by the method or function.

Postconditions are the states, output parameters, global variables, and other settings that occur when the method or function is finished normally. Postconditions are also states of the object that are modified by a given method or function in the case of objects. Postconditions can be used to describe the conditions in the case of expected (or at least dealt with) errors in the method or function.

Error handling refers to either error statuses that are returned by the function or method or error conditions that can exist after the method or function is called. For example, if you were using a process that was implemented by a shell script in a Unix operating system, you might document an error condition that was the error log file generated by the process during its run. Checking for a simple error condition on a return is often not enough. Minimally, you must verify that all documented exit conditions for the process are completed. This should be part of the process documentation.

Side effects can also be considered either a postcondition or an error condition. Side effects might include setting a global variable or modifying an input variable to indicate a state. Perhaps your method or function takes in an object to perform an operation such as a save. Once this object has been serialized to disk in the save operation, it is marked via a "dirty" flag to indicate that it no longer needs to be written again. This flag is internal to the object being saved and is only used (apparently) by the save method. For this reason, you must be careful to document and note that the flag is set upon successful exit of the function, as this is the surest indicator that the method or function to save the object was successful. Checking this flag on exit from the method or function is a safe postconditional response to be sure that the method really worked. The side effect, in this case, is the dirty flag. When an object is serialized to disk (that is, written to persistent storage), it is normally left unchanged. This side-effect object modification could cause problems if the object were in a cache and the manager unaware of the change.

Using the save method as a good example, suppose that you had a method or function that saved a list of objects. The error return from the function might indicate that an error had taken place because any one of the objects being saved could not be written out. If you simply observed the error condition, you would think the save had not worked. And, in fact, it had not. Instead, one of the objects might be in the wrong state, which could lead to data loss later in the program. Now, suppose that a misinterpretation in the function writer's implementation of the function returned an error condition only if all of the objects could not be written. In this case, you would look at the postconditions, realize that you need to check the list to see if all of the flags were set, and report an error in the log indicating that one or more of the objects was not saved.

Using built-in diagnostics by checking preconditions and postconditions to a function, method, or process is one of the most important ways you have of verifying that your program is working properly. Tracking down problems where the code does not match the set of preconditions or postconditions is much easier than starting from scratch. Likewise, if you check all input to the function and error returns from the function, you will know in advance if there is a problem. Finding the location of the problem and knowing the result often constitutes the majority of the work in debugging. When all of this information is at your fingertips in an error log for the program run, you are far ahead of the game.

The Evils of Asserts

Although it has been mentioned elsewhere in the book, it is worth using the C assert statement as an example of the sort of diagnostic you do not want to use in your application as a replacement for other types of diagnostics. This is because a debug-only diagnostic will not help you track down problems in the production code. Worse, by using such a diagnostic in your development, you get a false sense of security because the data you provide to the application does not trigger the assert. If the problem is important enough to assert that it cannot be true, it is worth putting in some extra code checking to handle the problem if it occurs.

We discuss more about how you can keep errors from showing up unexpectedly in your code in Chapter 12. For now, accept that debug-only checking is a bad idea.

Working with Users

One of the most powerful tools that you have when debugging an application is to sit down and work with "real" users to view what it is they are doing, and how they are producing the problems you are assigned to fix. Too few debuggers actually work with real people, preferring instead to receive reports on the problems and test cases, which they can use to re-create the problem to fix it.

One of the benefits of working with users is that you can find out what it was they were trying to accomplish when they were using the application. Often, you may find that it isn't really necessary to fix the so-called "bug." Instead, it would be perfectly satisfactory to the user to make it easier to accomplish the task at hand and eliminate the method that caused the bug.

A good example of this might be a bug related to file corruption during a save. Imagine, for example, that the bug reads, "When I save an existing project in a new format, the file is corrupted, and the resulting project cannot be loaded." It might appear that the problem is the way in which the new file is written. Perhaps what is really happening is that the file is not cleared before the new format is written to the same area, creating a mess in the data. However, it might not be necessary to fix this problem at all. Consider the problem from the user's viewpoint. What the user really wants to do is update the format of the file to a newer set. To do this, the user saves the file in the new format with the old name. However, this can lead to several problems, not the least of which is that the user will not have an existing backup of the project if he or she needs to revert to it at a later time.

It is possible, in the case of the file update, that the "right" solution to the problem is to first rename the existing project file to a ".old" extension, and then create a brand new file that contains the project only in the new format. This will have the effect of fixing the bug, because the new file contains no old data, and making the user happy by creating both a new version and preserving the old version as well. You could easily have reached this conclusion by simply observing the user and asking the user what it was he or she was trying to accomplish. The user will be happy because you fixed the bug. The user will be happier, in fact, because you've not only fixed the bug but have also provided a new feature that was not in the previous version.

Never overlook the power of working with users when debugging applications. They can also have considerable knowledge of what might really be the problem. For example, a user might observe that a program crash only happens when a specific feature is used during a particular run of the application. It doesn't matter when the feature is used, nor does the program crash always happen immediately following the use of the feature. However, by listening to the user, you might start out with the hypothesis that something in that particular feature is corrupting memory or causing some other internal problem that only shows up later when that block of memory is used. Had you relied on a bug report, you might never have known about this critical bit of information.

Tip
Never overlook the power of working with users.

Bug Tracking

It might seem a bit odd to consider the tracking of other bugs as a tool you can use for fixing existing bugs. However, the tracking results of past problems and bugs are often very good tools to utilize in fixing present bugs. Furthermore, by determining how something was previously "fixed," you can quite often determine what steps you can skip in fixing the bug the second time around.

Statistics tell us that over half of all bug "fixes" don't work the first time. That is to say, the first time you think you have fixed a bug, the fix is either incomplete or incorrect. Additional cases where there are multiple symptoms that are treated and only one is fixed can cause more problems. In all of these cases, knowing the steps that were tried first can help you to see what the previous debugger was thinking when he thought the problem was fixed. This can prevent you from making the same mistakes in determining where the bug truly lies.

There is another reason for keeping track of the previous bugs in the system. Bugs tend to cluster, which means that a module that contained a large number of bugs in the past is automatically suspect when a new bug that is similar to previous ones is found. In addition, you can look at symptoms that were described in the bug database and see how the problems were fixed. Finally, by examining all of the open bugs and comparing them with closed or partially closed bugs, you can often find a simple solution that will work across the board to fix them all. This is by far the best of all possible worlds for a debugger.

Code Coverage Analysis

In general, code coverage analysis tools are used to examine whether all test cases are handled and whether there is "dead" code in the system. However, for the debugger, code coverage analysis can show you problems you might not have considered in the past. For example, consider the following snippet of Java code:

```
If ( x == 1 )
{
}

    if ( x == 2 )
{
}

    if ( x != 1 && x != 2 )
{

    return;
}

    // Do some stuff
    if ( x == 3 ) // 1
{
}
```

It might not be readily apparent from the preceding code, but no matter what you try, the case containing x as 3 will never be executed (marked as // 1 in the code). Let's take a quick look at the code to clarify this statement. If x is 1, the first if statement will be executed. If x is 2, the second if statement will be executed. If x is 3, what happens? The third if statement is executed because x is neither 1 nor 2. A good code coverage tool will detect this situation. Because the code below this if statement will never be executed, this event will appear in the log.

Tip

Watch for unused code in the application!

Even though cleaning up the code is not technically the purview of the debugger, it is usually a whole lot easier to debug code when the extraneous code is removed and only the parts that are really being used remain. Finally, if you remove dead code, you can quite often free up some memory, which can also be very useful in fixing memory constraint problems. Be alert, however, for dead code that is present on purpose. Hopefully it is annotated, such as: //.

This code will be re-activated in version 3.3. Dead code can often show up when features are temporarily scrapped or disabled to meet delivery schedule deadlines.

Compilers

Wait! The compiler isn't a tool of the debugger, is it? Actually, yes, it is quite often your most valuable tool in finding symptoms that can lead to bugs you need to fix. Let's take a look at some of the ways a compiler can be used to help debug an application.

> **Note**
>
> *For noncompiled languages, such as Visual Basic and Java, there are often equivalent settings in the interpreter to emulate the sorts of events we talk about in this section.*

Using Highest Warning Levels

The best chance you have of finding a problem is to check for all possible code that might not be completely correct. The best tool you have for checking code that might not completely conform to the standard of the language you are working in or might contain surprise side effects is to use the highest warning level on the compiler you are working with. This feature will often warn you about problems you might not even consider looking at otherwise. For example, in one shop that I know of, the debuggers use a special compiler setting that treats all warnings as errors. This forces the code writer to check all of the statements before checking in the code, because an error is considered an unforgivable breach of rules when checking code into the master source code control tree.

The other great advantage to using high warning levels is that compiler writers can check for situations that are quite hard to verify by simply reading the code. Consider the following code from C++:

```
int x;
call_func( x );
```

It might appear that this code calls a function, which then returns a value. And, in fact, that might very well be what this function does. However, consider the case where the function encounters an error and never sets the value of x to anything at all. What will x be when it returns from the function? Good question, and one you really shouldn't have to check the language rules to know. The answer, in general, is it is undefined. You do not want undefined values running around in your application. Had you used the highest warning level on the C++ compiler, you would have gotten a warning such as, "Warning: Variable x is possibly used before it is assigned." This would keep you from having to track down what could be a very hairy problem in the code when x is used later on.

Verifying All Messages

When compiling the code, you should also check all of the diagnostic messages that result from the compiler. The compiler is often capable of diagnosing problems you might not suspect. Furthermore, the compiler is capable of identifying variables that are never used (dead code) and variables that are assigned a value but never used. Check all the messages and make sure that you understand them. For example, if you are coercing (modifying the type of) a variable in one line of code, it's important to understand whether or not the coercion makes any sense. Check each message you receive from the compiler and verify that you know what the code is doing at that point.

Looking at Generated Code

Looking at generated code is not a "normal" debugging technique, but is a good idea in cases where you simply cannot understand why a piece of code is doing what it is doing. Most compilers generate either an assembler code representation or a p-code (pseudocode) implementation of the high level code you are writing. In rare instances, you may run across a problem in the compiler itself, which causes the actual generated program to run incorrectly. Problems like this are very, very hard to diagnose because we generally assume that the program works the way it is supposed to when it is compiled.

The easiest way to verify code output from the compiler is to extract the suspect piece of code and put it into a small test driver. *Test drivers* are simply framework applications that are hard-coded to exercise a specific set of functionality, such as a single class method or function. If the test driver does not work as expected, you can then begin to suspect the compiler. Use the compiler options to view the actual generated code to see what it looks like. If it does not look the way you expect it to, you have found an honest to goodness compiler bug.

Note

Compiler bugs are relatively rare. Check for such things only when you have exhausted all other possibilities.

If you find a compiler bug, you should first try rewriting the simple example so that it works, and then move the converted code into the main application. If this works, notify the compiler vendor and put a strong comment above the changed code to indicate why you made the change. Be prepared to put up with a lot of questioning from your coworkers. Finding compiler bugs is more of a "hitting the lottery" sort of event than a "fixing a bug" kind of event. But it does happen.

Language Features

The final consideration when using a compiler is the compiler-specific language features that can either help your debugging efforts or hinder them. Certain compiler vendors put in extensions to the language to aid developers in making their programs more robust and to make them easier to code. Sometimes, these language features can cause you serious problems.

A concrete example of such a language extension is the pragma statement in the C compiler. The statement itself is not an extension; it exists in most C compilers. However, its usage can vary greatly from compiler to compiler. For example, one particular compiler allows the use of the pragma statement to suppress certain warning messages within your code. The same thing can be accomplished through a command-line interface to the compiler through a series of flags. In either case, however, the compiler can mask certain symptoms from you when you are watching the output from the program. If you were unaware of these pragma statement extensions, you would be unable to determine why you were not seeing the diagnostic statements you expected to see in the compiler output. This can be frustrating.

Whenever possible, try to strip out all compiler-specific extensions in either the code or the compiler when you are trying to see what is going on in the application. You will end up with more portable code, which is good for debugging, and you will end up with a complete set of diagnostics.

Summary

In this chapter, we looked at the possible debugging tools that you can use in your own debugging efforts. From commerical tools like debuggers and code profilers, to home grown tools like logging objects and built-in diagnostic tools, you should have gotten a feeling for the kinds of approaches you can take toward debugging different kinds of applications in different kinds of environments.

Obviously, debugging a simple stand-alone application on a developer system is quite different than debugging a production system that runs on a variety of heterogeneous operating systems. Likewise, the tools that you would use to debug these systems are as different as the languages that implement the systems in the first place. Your job as a debugger is to determine the best possible tool that has the least possible effect on your users when debugging.

A carpenter would never use a hammer to drive a screw into a wood board. A debugger must take similar care in making sure that the tools used are appropriate for the scale of the project and the level of the application. You simply cannot use a stand-alone debugger which stops the application flow if that application is running on a production web server. Use the right tool for the job and you will find that the debugging effort is more smooth and the users happier.

Bug Puzzle

Let's take a look at a sample problem that can be found by using the tools we have talked about in this chapter. Consider the case of debugging a production program that is deployed on servers to which you have no access. The program crashes on a regular basis following the introduction of a new user interface in the Web pages, which call your application. You are unable to load any software onto the production machines to detect the problem. Identify what steps you would take to find the problem and which tools you can and cannot use during this investigation. Which tools are most likely to help in this case? Which are least likely to help?

Chapter 8
The General Process of Debugging

Matt Telles

Although we have spent the majority of the book discussing what debugging is, what it is not, and what tools you can use in debugging, we have not spent much time talking about the actual process of debugging a problem. This chapter is devoted to discussing the generalized steps you should take to find, fix, and verify problems in an application or process. Although not all of the steps will apply in each case, you can pick and choose from the list as long as you do what needs to be done. The goal is to fix a problem and make sure that it does not recur. The process of finding the problem consists of a set of possible techniques. The aim is to make it as easy as possible for you to debug an application like a professional debugger. The rest, of course, is up to you.

To some extent, we have discussed the general process of debugging earlier in the book. It is made up of four simple steps. First, you identify the problem. Second, you gather information about the problem. Third, you offer a hypothesis for what might be causing the problem and how it could be fixed. Fourth, you test the hypothesis, matching it against available observations to see if it fits all evidence. If the hypothesis is indeed correct, you put in the fix for the problem and move on with your life. In this chapter, we begin to examine what is meant by each of the four steps and how you can perform them easily and most efficiently.

Identify the Problem

The first step in any process is to see whether the problem can be reproduced and what the problem really is. This is not an attempt to diagnose what might be causing the problem in the underlying code. Rather, this is an attempt to see the problem from the user's perspective and understand how you can make it occur repeatedly, so that you can examine what is going on.

In the first stage of the debugging process, you will not need to look at the code at all. All you should need is the written statement of what the problem is reported to be and the set of requirements that apply to that section of the program. To determine what the problem really is, you need to play detective. Detectives ask a lot of questions, and a debugging detective is no different. So put on your Sherlock Holmes cap, stuff a pipe in your mouth, and start asking the questions.

Is It a Bug?

The first question to ask yourself when confronted by the user's problem statement is, "Does this really constitute a bug?" If you are a typical developer, you will quite often find yourself reaching a snap decision of "no" if you interpret these problem statements to mean people are saying nasty things about your code (even if you didn't write the code). You should reject that immediate reaction. What is important is whether the problem is a bug at all.

There are three basic cases where a *problem* is not a *bug*. First, the requirements specification for the program says that the program should work that way. In this case, the problem is, by definition, not a bug. Second, if the program was modeled after another application and works in the same manner as that application by design, the problem is not a bug. Third, if the bug report is prefaced with, "It would be really nice if," you can end the request with a period at that point. Requests for changes, enhancements, new features, and the like are not bugs. They might still require work, but they are not bugs. If none of these cases apply, it is extremely likely that the problem is a bug and needs to be fixed.

Why Is It a Bug?

To understand what is going on in the program, you need to know why the bug is a bug. This is often not as simple as it might appear. The simplest case is when the specification says that the application should work one way, and the code says it should work another. Another simple case is when the program does something that all parties agree is undesirable, such as rebooting the system and reformatting the hard drive. Unless the program was specifically designed and intended to destroy your machine, it is safe to assume that this might be a bug.

The gray area of the "why" question is when you aren't sure quite what the program is doing, you just know that it isn't doing what you want it to do. An example of such a bug is when you ask the program to print something and nothing prints. It is possible that the program is encountering an error condition that prevents it from printing to the printer. For example, there might not be a printer attached to the machine. This would certainly make it difficult for the program to print. However, the lack of feedback to the user would indicate that the action (printing) succeeded, and the user would be confused when nothing was found on the printer. In this case, the problem is a bug because it doesn't do what the user wants it to do.

Warning

It is important at this stage that you do not start digging into the code to determine what the program should be doing. You should be working solely from observation at this point, so you don't need to know what the code says. If rationality says that the program should print and the program doesn't print, it's a bug because it's not rational.

Let's look at an example of something that appears to be a bug and why that diagnosis is incorrect. A good example is a program that crashes. Assume that the user gives us a complete list of steps to reproduce the problem. Step one is to open a file that already exists on the machine. Step two is to modify the file by adding a new entry to it. Step three is to save the file back to the machine in a new format. At this point, on the user's machine, the program crashes each and every time.

Given this scenario, you might initially hypothesize that the problem is in the save routine. Observing the problem on the user's machine, you see that the problem does, in fact, exist exactly as he said it would. Does this hypothesis make sense? Yes, because it covers all of the available observations. Should you now dig into the code and see if there is something wrong with the save routine for this format? Before you do, consider the problem for a moment. Is there a test case that handles this particular save variant? If so, wouldn't the program have had to have passed the test case? Try the problem on another machine. Does it happen there? Let's assume, in this case, that there is an existing test case that the program passed in testing, and that the problem does not occur on another machine. Does your hypothesis still make sense? In this case, the answer is no. There are at least two conditions that should not exist if your hypothesis is correct, the program passed the test case and the problem did not exist on a second machine. There could be other reasons for the failure of the hypothesis, such as a bad tester or a different version of the software, but it is likely that your hypothesis is wrong.

This example illustrates why you should not start digging into the code at the outset. After observing that the problem does not occur on another machine, it is time to go back to the observation stage. What is different between the two machines? Further observation might show that the first user's machine was critically low on disk space. So low, in fact, that there was no room to save the backup version of the file before saving it in the new format. The program, discovering it could not save the file in a backup format, was unable to continue and posted an error to itself. It might later turn out that the "bug" is an error that is simply not handled. Is this a bug? Absolutely. The program should not crash when a bad condition is encountered. Why is it a bug? Well, that's more complex. It is a bug because the program should have exited more gracefully, not because it crashed. Termination was the only possible thing the program could do under these circumstances.

What Should the Program Be Doing?

Once you have accepted the fact that the problem reported is a bug, and you have determined why it is a bug, the next step is to determine what the program really should be doing at the point at which the problem occurs. This is not to say you need to know what the code is doing, but rather what the application should logically do at that point. Only by understanding what it should be doing can you figure out why it isn't doing what it should and how to make it do what you want it to do.

If the bug is the result of a requirement that is not being processed correctly, the logical conclusion is that what it should be doing is what the requirements say it should be doing. Unfortunately, these kinds of problems are rarely what you are trying to figure out; requirement bugs usually lead to other, more complicated, coding problems.

Let's relate this issue to the previous example, the case of the disappearing disk space. If disappearing disk space was the bug, the question would be what should it do in this case? There are several possible answers. First, the program could simply display an error message and exit. Second, the program could refuse to save the file and continue. Third, the program could delete space until it had enough room to save the backup and new format files. In all likelihood, the right thing to do would be to show the user an error message and exit. The program shouldn't really continue because changes would not be saved. Another possibility would be to inform the user that the file cannot be saved and allow the user the option of freeing up disk space.

Whether or not you look at the code at this point is dependent on the nature of the bug. For example, you might need to look at what internal data was being created and passed around to understand what should be happening. Until you know what the right answer is, you really can't fix the bug. All you can do is hack in something that appears to work. Hacking in solutions when you don't understand the problem is almost certain to come back and bite you each and every time.

Let's look at one more example—a problem that has external symptoms, but cannot really be understood without at least knowing how the code works. In this case, we are working with a system that takes in MPEG video, buffers it to disk allowing it to be rewound and replayed, and then outputs it to an output device, such as a television set. Normally, the data flows in, is buffered, and flows out so that the picture viewed on the receiver is perfect. In certain odd cases, however, the receiver "blanks" the screen because it finds no input from the system.

Is this a bug? Certainly. The system is supposed to provide a consistent flow of television video to the output device, but it is not doing so. Why is it a bug? Because the "user experience" is interrupted, and the video does not display as expected. What should it be doing? Well, at this point, we really need to understand a little bit of the technical details. The underlying technical problem, from the perspective of the receiver, is that the video data is not ready for processing when the system needs it. As a result, it resets itself, resulting in a temporarily blank screen. More technically, what it is supposed to be doing is providing data whenever it is needed. Yet, for some reason, the data is not always available when it is needed. The problem isn't that the data isn't present; it most certainly is. We can verify this by "playing back" the buffer that contains the data and showing that everything that came in is stored in the playback buffer (the hard disk in this case). So why isn't the data always available when it needs to be? That brings us to the final question: We know what the code is supposed to be doing, but what is the code really doing?

What Is the Program Really Doing?

You now need to investigate why the program is not doing what it is supposed to be doing. We can only determine the answer by examining the code, so it is at this point that you need to pause your observational work and begin your detective work on the code itself. In this case, we will continue using the television display example to see what is going on and why the code does not work as expected.

Because the example we are citing is a real-world example, we are unable to provide the proprietary code. However, it is certainly possible to examine the algorithm that is implemented by the code. In this particular case, code analysis has shown that the algorithm appears to be coded correctly. Therefore, you can assume that the problem is somewhere within the algorithm and implementation itself and not a simple coding error.

A general overview of what is going on in the system follows. There are three basic "threads" that run within the system. First, the input thread runs to gather data from the input side of the system. Second, the disk thread runs to buffer the data to disk and recall it from disk as needed. Third, the last thread takes data from the buffers maintained by the disk thread and puts them into the output side of the system, allowing them to be played back for the user to view.

Examining the problem further shows us that we can even understand the process just a bit better. The input thread fills buffers, which the disk thread writes to disk. Likewise, the output thread reads buffers, which the disk thread reads from disk. There is a pool of buffers that is constant in number. The number of buffers being used to read or write varies. The disk thread will not write a buffer to disk that is not full, nor will it deliver a buffer to the output thread until that buffer is full and no longer being written to.

The problem turns out to be that the output thread is always waiting for data in spite of the fact that the input thread is constantly delivering data to the disk thread to be buffered for output. Can you see the problem? It took quite a while to figure out all of the facts that were provided. Once those facts were apparent, however, the problem became clear very quickly. Don't feel bad if you didn't see the problem right away, we had to dig into the code for two months to figure it out.

Let's look at the steps that were taken to discover this problem so that you can get a better understanding of the debugging process in action. First, we came up with a hypothesis for the problem. Our initial hypothesis was that the disk simply could not keep up with the flow of data into the application and that caused input data to be wrong. When this was tested, however, by "recording" the data to disk and then playing it back in a separate event (rather than recording and playing at the same time), no data loss was observed. This allowed us to eliminate the possibility that the input side of the process was at fault. Likewise, by simply playing back the data from the file at a normal rate, we could discount the possibility that the output side was at fault. If the data played back correctly, the output side was working correctly. That left only two other real possibilities. First, we could have something interfering with the process, such as another thread or something else happening within the thread that "starved" the output process for time and ran it out of data. Secondly, we could have the interface between the input and output threads be at fault. Experimentation by "shutting off" the other events going on in the box eliminated the first hypothesis. Testing of the second hypothesis by measuring the input and output flow rates showed this to be the area of concern.

Remember that the disk thread will not give data to the output thread until a buffer is full. The input thread gets buffers to fill all the time. However, the rate of flow of data is not constant. At some points, there is a lot of data coming in, and at some points, the flow is quite low. At the point at which a low flow rate occurs, you will see an input buffer fill very slowly, as you can imagine. However, the output flow rate is constant. It requires data to be available each time an interrupt occurs. This leads to the problem where a buffer is not ready to deliver from the disk thread to the output thread because the flow rate is slow, and the input thread has not finished filling a buffer to deliver.

The bug results because the user experience is interrupted when the screen goes black. Is this a bug? Certainly. Why is it a bug? It is a bug because the requirements say that the user experience should be seamless. What is the program doing? Well, in this case, the program output is starving because the threading mechanisms were not well designed initially. Because the system is not delivering data to the output system, the user experience is not seamless. The last question, what is it really doing, is the puzzle. The system is performing exactly as it was designed to perform. There is no "bug" in the code that can be fixed. There are no "tweaks" that can easily be performed to modify the system so that it does what it is supposed to do.

As we discussed earlier in the book, bugs can occur at any level. The earlier in the process a bug enters the system and is not removed from the system, the more expensive it is to fix the problem. In this case, there were two choices for fixing the "black screen" bug. In the first case, we could have redesigned and reimplemented the system knowing what we know now about the data rate. This certainly would have been the better choice, as it would have allowed us to proceed with a stable, well-documented, and well-implemented system. Unfortunately, as you will discover in the process of real-world debugging, this was not feasible because it would take too long. Management required a solution faster than we could undertake a redesign and reimplementation. As a result, we were forced into what could only be described as a "hack" of the system.

The solution to the problem was to buffer more data during the initial contact with the input device. In this case, that meant delaying the start of displaying input data until there was sufficient data to ensure that there would always be one full buffer of data for the output thread to read. This was hardly a perfect solution. It was a compromise between making the user experience better and delivering a product within an acceptable amount of time. Compromise is often necessary in the debugging world.

The point to this whole example is that even though what the code is doing is not incorrect, it can lead to a bug. You need to be aware that sometimes design choices will influence the final product enough to cause bugs that the user will report. These bugs will often need to be fixed without modifying the basic design of the system. However, when these kinds of bugs occur, it is important to document them as well as the reasons they occurred so that when you get a chance to redesign the component of the system that caused the problem, you can do it correctly.

Tip

Always document design flaws so that components can be redesigned when there is time.

At this stage, we have identified the problem and have discovered what might potentially be causing it. We aren't really sure if we know the exact cause or not, but we do know what the problem is and what the program should be doing. We also know what the program is doing so that we can quickly discover why it is not doing what it is supposed to be doing. The next step is to gather information about the system and the application run so that we can start to identify where the actual flaw might lie.

Gather Information

Gathering information about the problem is quite often the most difficult part of the process. The goal of the information-gathering step is to produce a reproducible case that can be used to determine why the bug is happening in your application. There are quite a few techniques that can be used to gather information. Let's take a look at them and see which ones can help you at certain times in the process.

User Descriptions of the Problem

In normal circumstances, you will have a user description of the problem. This description might have been given to you directly by the user, or it might have been gathered by a customer support person or other nontechnical person. In any event, this data has to be considered suspiciously until you can get a firsthand description of what really happened. Firsthand accounts of the problem are always useful, so be sure to write down exactly what you are told. That way, you can compare several accounts of the same problem and look for similarities. Consider, for example, the following accounts of a reported bug in a system:

◆ "I started by trying to set up a Favorites list. I first went to the home page. Then, I selected Favorites from the menu on the right. I scrolled down to the third entry and pressed Enter on the keyboard. Then I moved to the fourth entry on the submenu and clicked it with the mouse. Finally, I entered my name as Irving, clicked on OK, and the program crashed."

◆ "I went to the programming menu and selected the New menu option. I then clicked on the Create Object menu entry and entered the name HouseObject for the object name field. Then I clicked OK, and the program crashed."

◆ "I selected the New Project menu option, and then clicked on the icon that looks like a Gear. I entered the name Rudolph for the project name, and then clicked OK. The program crashed."

These certainly don't appear to be the symptoms of a single bug, now, do they? After all, they appear to relate to three different sections of the program and describe three different situations. Yet, the underlying problem is present in each case if you just stop and actually examine what each of the users reported. You will have to perform a little interpretation, but that is fairly normal in the real world. People often skip steps or gloss over what it was they were doing at the time. Most people, when reporting bugs, focus on what they think was the important step in the process. It is quite often up to you to filter out the unimportant information and see what each case really has in common.

In the examples given, there are a few commonalities. First, each user clicked on the OK button to finalize the process, and the program crashed. It might seem likely, therefore, that the program OK handler contains a fatal flaw. A bit of experimentation will show whether this is the case or not. In this case, let's simply assume that this is not the problem and that, in fact, the program does not share any code either in common or copied and pasted to handle OK buttons.

Second, when we examine the statements of the witnesses, we notice that each was working with a menu. Because most programs contain a fair number of menus when they offer any sort of choices, this code is likely to be shared among the various pieces of the system. Furthermore, by careful examination of the statements, we can see that each person used both the keyboard and the mouse to select from the menus before clicking the OK button and having the program crash. Let's take a quick look at what each witness said about menus:

◆ "I selected Favorites from the menu on the right. I scrolled down to the third entry and pressed Enter on the keyboard. Then I moved to the fourth entry on the submenu and clicked it with the mouse."

◆ "…selected the New menu option. I then clicked on the Create Object menu entry…"

◆ "I selected the New Project menu option, and then clicked on the icon that looks…"

Notice that in the first and third cases, the user definitely used the keyboard to select an item from the menu. In the second case, the user mentions selecting a menu option and then clicking on a menu entry. We can infer, therefore, that the user in this case used both the keyboard and the mouse. As a result, the next logical place to look is in the menu handler to see whether it deals with mouse and keyboard entries differently. The final clue is in the third entry, where the user did not select anything from the menu with the mouse, but instead clicked on an icon. While looking at the code, I would try to see what happens when the program deals with a combination of keyboard and menu entries. Simple test cases would be to first use the keyboard and then the mouse to select something, and then reverse the process. It is likely, given the user discussion, that you will find the root of the problem in this area. Of course, after finding such a common bug, it is likely that the fix will repair a whole lot of problems at once. This is a debugger's dream.

We offer a word of warning when dealing with user descriptions. This warning especially applies to input from testers who log bugs in bug tracking databases. Because users are never really sure what is important to you, they will either try to bury you with information, or they will only provide a small segment of the information they remember in an effort to make your job easier. It is important that you don't make reporters guess at the problem. If they guess, they tend to slant their information in the direction that they feel most obviously shows what they think the area of the problem might be. Because the problem often lies in a completely different region of the code, make sure people describe everything they did from as far back as they can remember.

There is one last problem with user reports of bug problems. Quite often, a user will report a problem as "after playing around with the <x> system for a while, the system crashes." This kind of user report is worthless. It often masks the problem, and it provides no information at all. What were you doing before you played around with <x>? What does "playing around" entail? Did you use one particular function a lot? Was there an order to what you were doing? In cases like this, it is usually best if you actually sit behind the user and observe what they are doing or try the problem yourself. If you can duplicate the problem by "playing around," keep track of what you do. Perhaps the problem surfaces because of the order of the steps you take. Perhaps the problem lies in the number of times you perform a specific action. Watch carefully when either the original user performs the actions or when you copy the user's actions on your own. Write down each step as it occurs. After the problem occurs once, determine whether the same set of commands or actions produces the same result again. If so, you have a reproducible case, which you can then use to find the root of the problem.

Log Files

Log files can be an excellent source of observation material. Log files can contain information that can pinpoint problems as they occur in the code itself. The problem, of course, is first making sure that the log files contain the information you need to identify the problem, and second, determining what information in the log is the part that shows you where the problem really is.

Let's take a look at a hypothetical log file that was generated from an application containing a problem. Note that it is highly improbable that anyone would really write a program that generated log files like this.

```
Starting up…
Running first command…
Running second command
Second command failed!!
Problem with file
Error in function call parameters.
Bad script file.
Error! Danger Will Robinson!
GrepMe: I'm here.
```

At first glance, this program appears to be in serious trouble. All sorts of things are failing including invalid script files and function call errors. Chances are, however, that after looking at the code, it will show you that the so-called "errors" are in fact simply things that the program handles just fine. After all, if the program was generating the sort of errors that appear to be shown here, it would never run. Because the program is, in general, running fine, it seems unlikely that this level of error is being generated. So what is going on in this code?

The problem with most log files is illustrated (if somewhat exaggerated) in this file. Most log files contain information that the programmer considered to be important when trying to track down a problem. Unfortunately, these files often lack several critical criteria that you need when looking through the logs. At an absolute minimum, a log file entry must contain the following information to be useful:

◆ Date and time the event occurred

◆ Function, method, and process name of the system generating the event

◆ Severity level of the event

◆ A description of the problem being logged

◆ Any pertinent variable values present at the time of the event

Let's take a look at each piece of information and determine what it means and why it is important. The date and time of the event is important for a number of reasons. One reason is that if you know approximately when the event happened, you can quickly scan through the data to find out what was going on at that moment in the application. This saves you a lot of time and misinterpretation in discovering which errors match up to which program runs. More importantly it provides the actual execution sequence of the application and resulting errors!

The name of the component that created the event is important for two reasons. One, it saves you from having to search through all of the code in the project. This can be a life-saver, especially if the description contains several concatenated strings. If you can pinpoint the generating process quickly, you can find the problem quickly. The second reason to include the function or method name is that there can be multiple entries with the same description in the code. Imagine, for example, that the description is "Unable to open file." In an average program, this string could be found in the application source code many times in all likelihood. However, if the output is "Someobject::OpenFile – Unable to open file", you'd quickly and easily be able to pinpoint the problem in the code. It would be even better if the message told you the filename of the file that couldn't be opened! With a generalized object oriented open file handler routine you might be loooking at a long list of totally ambiguous "…Unable to open file." messages.

There are a few reasons why you would want to output the severity level in a log file. For example, if you properly assign severity levels to each log file entry, you can quickly and easily find serious errors while ignoring informational messages. It is most important that you properly assign the levels when you are outputting the log entries at the outset. My suggestion is that you work with four levels of informational statements: fatal, serious, warning, and informational. Obviously, they vary from most important to least important. Informational messages might tell you, for example, what user function a person was trying to execute. That would help you trace through the user's actions from the problems the user encountered. Fatal errors, on the other hand, might indicate when an exceptional event took place, such as running out of disk space or memory.

The reason for including the description of the event in the log file should be fairly evident. You want to provide enough information for the debugger to find out what happened, but not so much information that the debugger has to slog through the data to see what went wrong. Consider the following two log entries (only the descriptions are shown):

Entry 1:

```
Entering OpenFile
Checking FileName .. Ok
Checking Filestatus.. Ok
Checking File Exists .. Not Ok
Creating File.. Ok
File Created.. assigning pointer
Loading file contents..
Done with Open File
```

Entry 2:

```
OpenFile : Creating File
OpenFile: Blank New File
```

Both entries illustrate the same thing. In both cases, the **OpenFile** function was called. It tried to open an existing file and couldn't, so it created it. There were no extraordinary problems with the function and when it finished, the program continued normally. Why then, do we need to output eight lines to tell us this, as is the case in Entry 1? Imagine if this function is called numerous times. You'd flood your log file with extraneous data.

Tip

A simple rule of thumb for log entries: Be verbose for errors and terse for normal events.

Personal Observations

The best possible way to know what is going on when a problem occurs is to observe it personally. In this way, you avoid the problem of personal bias on the part of the observer. As a debugger, your observations should be as unbiased as possible. This means you shouldn't be thinking through the code, nor should you be pondering what subsystem the error might occur in. In order to properly observe something, you should watch it happen, taking careful note of what you did and what you saw. These notes will prove invaluable later when you are trying to form a hypothesis for the actual problem.

The best way to conduct personal observations is to start with a list of what you know at the outset. The list might include the system environment, the hardware installed, and the options selected for the application at runtime. In addition, you should note any actions you've taken, such as opening files, closing files, or performing actions within the program. You never really know what will prove a useful clue when you are trying to find the problem, so document everything. When in doubt, record the observation; err on the side of too much data rather than too little.

You should always have a pen and paper available when you are debugging. This will permit you to jot down notes about what you did and what the result was. For example, you might open a file and note that the file name was longer than the allotted area on the display for your application. This simple note might mean nothing to you at the time except perhaps that you need to increase the size of the display title area. You might find, however, that later on this observation leads to the discovery that not only was the title display area too short, but also the internal buffer space allocated for storing the title in the application. The resultant buffer overrun might cause problems that you observe later on in the program run.

Personal observations should always be tempered with the fact that you know what is going on behind the scenes. Because you do know what the code is doing (or at least think you know what it's doing), you will have a tendency to overlook potential problems. It is difficult to simply throw away your knowledge of the underlying code, but you should make sure that you actually see what is going on and don't simply assume it is working properly because it is doing what you expect it to do as you perform certain actions. Observe the whole program, check the memory usage of the application, and watch the amount of disk space being consumed. Finally, check any resultant output files. You might find that a problem that appears to be in the load function of the application is instead in the save function, which is writing out bad information that the load function cannot handle. Because you do know what the code is doing in the background, you should have a better understanding of what potential resources and output are being used or created. Check each link in the chain before making assumptions about what the problem really is.

Symptoms

When debugging an application, most developers and debuggers tend to overlook and not keep track of the symptoms that are observed. Sometimes the symptom is the actual bug that is reported. Other times, the symptom is indicative of what is going on behind the scenes. Let's look at a real-world example.

On a project that implements a satellite television recording system, the program was behaving oddly. Programs that were recorded to an internal hard drive would disappear on occasion. Other times, the system would not record properly, displaying a blank screen rather than the program it was recording. Additionally, recording events, which were scheduled times in the future to record programs, were either not occurring or were disappearing from the display of the box.

It might appear, and was in fact reported, that all of these events were separate problems. In this case, however, all of the reported "bugs" were simply symptoms of a more basic underlying issue. The code that was implemented to maintain the directory of the hard drive files was flawed. This flaw allowed the directory structure to be corrupted. When the system detected that the directory was corrupted through an internal validation mechanism, the program responded by removing the directory nodes that represented the corrupted entries.

Directory nodes in the satellite system were the same as file entries in a "normal" disk operating system. As a result, when a node was removed from the directory tree, the file it represented would "disappear" and could no longer be accessed by the system. To the rest of the program, it was as if the file never existed. Depending on which file was deleted, the results varied. If the deleted file contained the list of recorded programs, the result was that all of the programs recorded on the box were gone as far as the user was concerned. Likewise, if the deleted file was the file containing future scheduled events, these events would disappear from the box display. If the corruption was severe, the directory would be unable to properly create new files. In a roundabout manner, this caused the recording mechanism to fail, which prevented anything from being displayed on the screen for the user. In short, all of the "bugs" reported for the system were simply symptoms. The real bug was undetectable from outside observation.

Quite often, the best thing to do when tracking symptoms is to build a tree of the related subsystems that are affected by the observed behavior. If you have several bugs and they overlap at a given point, it is worth taking the time to understand how that particular subsystem could be causing the observed symptoms. If it is possible that the single subsystem caused all of the symptoms observed in a given set of bugs reported and a single problem can be identified that could cause that particular set of problems, then fixing a single problem will often result in the elimination of an entire collection of bugs.

Test Cases That Fail

Although it might seem obvious, failed test cases in your testing suite are often good indications of problems. What might not be so obvious is that a test case that fails is often an indication of a more low-level issue. Simply determining why the test case fails is often a good way to discover more about how a given section of the application is working, as opposed to how you think it might be working.

Test cases are written for a few reasons. In general, they are either written directly from the requirements of the application, or they are written from observations of how the program should be used by the user in real life. As a result, they will often show events that users experience when running the application much better than simple ad hoc program usage. In addition, test cases are generally much simpler than bug report directions. They usually contain only a few steps. Bug reports can contain dozens of steps, many of which can be redundant or unnecessary. As a result, finding a problem via a test case will often be easier and quicker to reproduce and, therefore, to find and fix in the source code.

We talk more about testing and how it fits in with the debugging realm in Chapter 13. For now, however, it is important that you remember to look at the results of all test cases, especially automated test cases. Regression test cases, for example, will show whether a recent change has caused a new problem. If you keep track of the test cases and their results and compare one run to another, you will often determine quickly what has changed and when it likely occurred in the change history of the program. Once you know what change caused the problem, fixing it is usually a pretty easy task.

Similar Problems

Examining similar problems is another area that really should be obvious, but one that many developers miss in their single-minded approach to fixing the bug at hand. By reviewing the bug listings, both current and historical, you can often find similar kinds of bugs. Because the same developers often develop many of the parts of an application, by seeing what sort of problem caused the previous bug, they can get an idea about what might be causing another problem.

In addition to historical bug lists, you can also get a good handle on similar bugs by simply running down a list of the current bugs for an application. In many cases, you will find that they are quite similar. In a project I once worked on, the following were reported as system bugs. Honest!

◆ Bug #1—On the data entry screen, there is a field that indicates I should enter a number from 1 to 10. I enter the value 11 and the program crashes.

- Bug #2—On the data entry screen, there is a field that indicates I should enter a number from 1 to 10. I enter the value 12 and the program crashes.

- Bug #3—On the data entry screen, there is a field that indicates I should enter a number from 1 to 10. I enter the value 13 and the program crashes.

This list continued until the value reached 99 (the field only allowed two digit entries). Obviously, this is a combination of an extreme case and a very naïve tester. However, I'm sure you will find similar kinds of entries scattered through the bug lists in your own application. In addition, if you have multiple testers for a given application, which most companies do, you will find similar bugs reported by different testers. This is an ideal situation because in many cases one tester will report different symptoms or steps to reproduce than another. This allows you to "triangulate" on the problem by using the different information supplied by two different testers. For example, consider the following two bugs reported by two different testers:

- Bug #1—When I change the ratings lock on the application and unplug the machine, the ratings lock is lost when the machine comes back up. If, however, the machine is allowed to stay on, the ratings lock works properly on the current channel.

- Bug #2—When I change the ratings lock on the application, shut the machine off, and then turn it back on, the ratings lock remains intact. However, the program that was showing will continue to show even if the lock is correct. Changing the channel makes the problem disappear.

Once again, this problem is from a satellite box software system. The "ratings lock" mentioned prevents little ones from seeing programs they are not quite ready for. Each show has a rating, and any show that has a rating "greater than" the allowed rating (such as G, PG, R, etc.) will not be shown until the unit is unlocked. In this case, turning the box off appears to save the ratings lock, but rebooting the unit does not. Of course, it helps quite a bit when you know that the box is normally always "on," even if the power light is off and the screen is dark. Only by removing power from the box does it actually reboot. This much we can easily glean from the two different bug reports. In addition, we can determine that the ratings lock works fine on the current channel when the box is left on, but doesn't work when the box is turned off normally and then back on. This last point is interesting because it shows that the problem is not in the channel side of the box, but rather in something that controls when the ratings lock is applied.

In the preceding example, it quickly became apparent that the box was only saving certain information when the unit was properly turned off. If it lost power or was unplugged, it would lose the settings that were only in memory. Looking back through the list of bugs, I found that there were numerous bugs of the same type. Data would be kept correctly if the unit was either running or turned off normally. The data would be incorrect or missing if the box lost power. Further checking revealed that the fix for the previous incarnations of the bug for different data was to save the data to disk immediately when it was changed. Putting a similar fix in for the ratings lock information fixed that problem as well. So, as you can see, going back through previous bug reports and corresponding code changes certainly paid off in this case.

Recent Changes

One of the most trite cliches in the software engineering world is the comment "but I didn't change anything!" whenever a problem suddenly pops up in an application following a new build or compile. Although it is certainly possible that a new problem can occur because of an external change or a new set of input data, the most likely explanation is that there was a change in the code that caused the problem. Even more likely, the most recent change to the software is probably the cause of the problem.

When you think about it, most recent changes are by definition the least well-tested changes. Changes made early on or those made in a previous build cycle are more likely to have been through a round of testing by the programmer or possibly the QA department in a subsequent test build. Only those changes made very recently are likely to have gotten into the code with little testing. In addition, last minute changes are often those that are inserted to add some additional feature that was not originally going to be in that release or to fix a problem discovered just before the release was frozen. These are the kinds of changes that will cause problems in new software releases. It is these changes, therefore, that you should begin looking at when a previously bug free part of the code suddenly exhibits bugs.

In order to determine which changes are most recent, you need to be able to look at the files or modules in the system that have changed. Because virtually every company in existence these days uses some form of source code control, this is usually just a matter of calling up a report of the most recent changes. If your source code control system cannot do this, you should seriously consider changing to a new system. One of the most useful forms of source code control is to be able to control changes on an individual check-in level. Your system should be able to identify a set of changes that applies to a given feature or bug fix. This will allow you to view only those changes that might have caused the problem.

There are several ways to use the change information to identify the problem. One way is to examine each change and see whether or not it could be causing the problem. Examining a set of changes is a difficult process because the actual "bug" caused by the changes may be caused by a combination of things modified in several different changes. Removing each change may show the problem modifications, but it might also simply move the problem to another location. You need to understand each change and why it was done, not to mention how it was done, before you can really know how the problem was caused.

A much better way to find and fix problems is to slowly back out changes until you run across the one that causes the problem to go away. Then, slowly put the changes back in, one at a time (or at least in the smallest increment feasible given the code) until the problem recurs. By simple elimination, you will be able to find out which change broke the code.

At this point, you have several choices. You can proceed with the remainder of the debugging process with the change in place, or you can stop the process with the knowledge of where the problem is and start the fixing steps. Which you choose to do is usually dependent on whether or not you can understand why the code change caused the specific problem. If you can immediately see what the problem was caused by and how to fix it, you can simply amend the change and continue with your standard testing. If, on the other hand, the change doesn't seem to explain the problem at all, you might want to simply mark that area of code for investigation and continue as if you did not understand the problem at all.

One last thought about recent changes. It is important to realize that if you cannot understand why a problem is caused by the change that appears to cause it, that change might not be the problem at all. Consider, for example, a function that uses a global buffer to maintain its data. A recent change to that function appears to break the software, causing it to crash. However, examining the code for the changes to the function does not reveal any possible problems. In this case, the bug could very easily be somewhere else in the code and is simply being revealed by the usage in this function. In the early days of programming, it was quite common to add a "printf" statement (a message output to the console) and have a bug disappear. Even worse, "solutions" like this were often left in the production code. Hopefully, we are past that particular era. Naturally, you would never do something like that; it is always the other programmer who is responsible.

Environment Information of the Run

After you have worked as a professional for some time, you begin to learn some of the tricks of the trade. One such trick is to keep track of the environment and other external elements of the machine your program is running on. If those elements change, you will find that they have an impact on your program. One bad assumption that many developers make is that their program is an island. Memory changes, disk space changes, operating system version changes, and other running programs can easily cause new problems in your application.

As an example of an environmental problem encountered in a real-world situation, consider this depressing story. On a project I once worked on, the system had been up and running solidly in a real-time environment for over a year. Nothing had been added to the program, nor had any modifications been made. One day, the program simply stopped working. My team had been working on modifications to it, so we were surprised that the system would fail before those modifications were put in place. What could possibly have gone wrong? Restarting the application led to the same problem. The program would run for a few minutes, then mysteriously die. There were no error messages, no log file entries, and no fatal errors detected by the internal debugger of the application. In short, it was a true mystery.

Once we verified that the program itself had not been touched, we started looking for external causes. We verified that the amount of memory on the box was still adequate for the program to run. We made sure the box was not running out of disk space (normally, you would check this first, but the program did an internal check for this and would have displayed an error message). We finally determined that the data operations group had made three changes to the machine in the time period that the program started failing. First, they had upgraded the operating system to a newer patch version. Second, they had installed some antivirus software that was intended to catch evil programs running on the box. Finally, they had installed a new watchdog program on the box that simply kept track of the amount of available memory and disk space. This last program was mostly passive, but did communicate with another server on the network to keep it apprised of the situation on the machine.

If you are like me, your first inclination on seeing a list of changes is to scream. Once that urge passed, you would probably suspect the operating system patch to be the problem. In fact, that's exactly what my team suspected. We went to another machine running the same software and installed the operating system patch on it as well. In this way, we were eliminating suspects one at a time without knowing what really went wrong. The program continued to run just fine with the operating system patch, confusing the developers and earning us a smirk from the data operations people.

We then checked the internally written watchdog program. Although we couldn't figure out how it could be causing the problem, we did determine that it was new and therefore was suspect. Unfortunately, all that got us was more wasted time and another smirk. That left the antivirus software, which everyone agreed would be very unlikely to be causing our program any grief. After all, all it did was watch for virus-like activity and pop up a warning banner to tell the user that a virus was suspected in a given program. Well, that's what we thought it would do, anyway. These machines, however, were generally unattended. So there was nobody around to check the banners. As a result, the person installing the antivirus software had told it during the install process that it was running in unattended mode. Some later checking of the software manual (always read the manual last, like a good programmer) turned up the salient point that in unattended mode, the antivirus software would terminate the program causing the problem and log the information to an internal log.

The antivirus software rationale for killing our application was simple. We were creating a log file in the system directory. Because we were modifying what appeared to be a system file within our application, the antivirus software assumed that our application was a virus and terminated it. Why did the program run for a few minutes before being killed? Because something had to happen within the software for a log message to be generated, and log entries were buffered and written out in blocks. As a result, it could take upwards of five minutes for enough data to be generated to modify the log file.

Once we determined what was going on, the antivirus software was changed so that it "knew" about our application and everything worked fine from that point on. However, it is important to note that no changes were made to the application with the "bug" in it. This was purely an external problem.

The kind of information you will want to keep track of varies depending on what sort of application you are creating. For example, if you are building a client/server application that runs on a server in your corporate headquarters, you will want to constantly monitor available disk space, memory used by your application and memory available, other applications running on the box, and the amount of CPU time used by your application to name just a few. In addition, you should have a utility that can, at any time, display the operating system version including any patches, any third-party programs used and their versions (such as databases, communications systems, Web servers, and the like), and the version of your software that is running.

On the other hand, if you are writing a standalone shrink-wrapped product, your approach has to be different. You should include within the program (or as an added utility application that ships with the product) a tool that keeps track of the minimum and maximum memory used by the program, the amount of available disk space when the program is running, the other applications running at the same time as your application, and any peripherals you are aware of attached to the system. This utility screen or application should be easily available to the user so that when a user calls your customer support people with problems, all of the information can be either read to the support person over the phone or attached to an email that the support person can view.

Ideally, your bug report form should contain spaces for all of the information that can be gathered while the application is running. In addition, if the program crashes for a known internal reason (such as lack of disk space), it would be nice if the application could print out diagnostic information that could be sent to you, the debugger, when you are trying to figure out what the user was doing when the program crashed.

Form a Hypothesis

At this point in the debugging process, you have identified that you really do have a problem and the nature of that problem from the user's perspective. You have gathered any and all information that you can obtain from the various sources we discussed in order to have all that you can at hand when looking at the code. Now it is time to figure out what is really going on in the application source code.

How you go about forming a hypothesis of the possible cause of the bug depends a great deal on your experience level with debugging as a whole and your experience level with the application source code specifically. If you have never worked with the application source code before, being a new developer on an existing project, you will take quite a different approach to the problem of guessing what the bug is caused by than if you were one of the original developers working on the system.

If you worked on the system from the very beginning or have at least spent substantial time on the actual development of the system, you will usually have a clue as to what piece of the source code relates to the problem area. For example, if you are given a bug that appears on the "FooBar Screen" of the application, chances are good that you will know what forms, code, or processes are called from that screen. This gives you a starting point to dig into the source code and see whether or not the problem is simply an error in coding. To do this, you will likely use the observations you acquired in the previous step of the debugging process and apply them to the code at hand.

If you are new to the project, finding the source of a problem by looking at the code can be difficult. There are a few steps you can use to find the proper place in the code to start working from in order to form a hypothesis as to which section of the source tree is the problem. One of the steps is to use tracing techniques to watch the output of the program. By placing a trace entry at the top of each function, method, or process, you can watch each one go by and see what is happening when the error occurs. Of course, if the error is actually something else that happens to be occurring on the machine at the same time, you will not see the correct trace entries in the correct order. This is a clue to what might be going on in the application.

Another technique you can use to form a hypothesis is code elimination. In this case, which we discuss in depth in Chapter 9, comment out or remove sections of code until you find the smallest possible set of code that reproduces the problem. This is quite similar to writing test drivers for the subsection you believe contains the problem.

Finally, if you have never worked on debugging large-scale applications before, you might consider paring down the code until you find a small enough area to begin working with. This is usually the top level of the code, where things occur at a macro level. You can view the "big picture" of the code, and then "drill down" into the section that contains the error at the highest level. For example, if your code contains menu choices, you might find the menu handler for all of the program screens. Then drill down into the specific menu handler for the item that is the starting point of the bug report. From that point, you are likely to see a list of events that take place in the form of functions, methods, or objects. Step through each one (either in the debugger or via logging) until you find the one that starts the problem. At this point, start the process over at this new level.

Debugging is quite often a laborious and recursive effort. You will find yourself digging down deep into the code to find out where the problem occurs, and then slowly backing up the source tree to find out what caused that problem to occur. In any event, you need to create a hypothesis for why the problem is happening, so that you can dig down to the lower level.

Once you have been working with debugging applications for some time, you will discover that problems usually fall into one of a few broad categories. Hypotheses are often gleaned from starting with this list of categories and eliminating ones that you do not believe can be causing the problem. In general, you will find that bugs fall into one of the following categories:

♦ Memory errors

♦ Coding errors

♦ Logic errors

◆ Requirements errors

◆ Failure to check for error conditions

◆ Timing/Multithreaded errors

◆ Externally generated errors

Not all bugs, of course, will fit perfectly into one of these categories. Some will fit into more than one, and some will not fit neatly into any of them. However, starting with the idea that the bug is likely to be in one of these categories will help you work out what is going on. Let's take a look at how you can best classify your problem into at least one category so that you have a starting point.

Memory errors are caused by one of a few conditions. You might be running out of memory due to excessive allocations, you might be failing to deallocate memory that you have allocated within your program, or you might have a pointer to a block of memory that was once allocated and then deallocated without the pointer being cleared. Another, more common, problem is that a pointer is simply not initialized correctly, or is initialized to the wrong value. The usual symptoms of memory errors are semirandom crashes within the application. Normally, when you add code to an application, the bad pointer or spot of allocation or erroneous or corrupted data appearing in the process or output will move in computer memory. If you add a few statements to a program and find the location of the problem has moved, you are likely looking at a memory error. Tracking these down is usually a matter of checking for memory leaks by using a third-party tool or looking for all deallocations within the program and making sure that the pointers to those allocated blocks are cleared. Two sure signs that you are dealing with a memory error is when you watch the amount of memory you use in your application continually increase and when (in C++) you see the object you are working on (the *this* pointer) become NULL.

Coding errors are by far the most prevalent software bugs you are likely to encounter. Coding errors simply indicate that you didn't do something correctly in the code. This could be calling a function, method, or process with an invalid argument or sending the wrong sort of data to an external file to be loaded at a later time. Coding errors are usually annoying to track down, but can be fixed with very little effort. To find a coding error, you need to understand what it is the code is doing at each step and determine whether or not the code is doing what you expect it to. The simplest form of coding errors are uninitalized variables, failing to check for NULL pointers, sending invalid arguments to a function, and failing to check for mathematical errors, such as divide by zero. These are usually quite simple to find, especially if you have a stack trace for the application crash. When in doubt, assume a coding error in your bug tracking.

Let's take a look at a very simple (and very dumb) error that can occur in coding a C function. We've been asked to code a function that initializes all of the entries in an array to a given value.

The code in the program is as follows:

```
void InitializeArray( int *array, int size, int value )
{
    for ( int i=0; i<size; ++i) ;
     array[i] = value;
}
```

This code certainly appears, at first glance, to do what it is supposed to do. There is no "off-by-one" error in the loop, nor is the array overrun by too many values. Because we have an integer array and are passing in integer values, we can't overflow the data type. Yet, after calling this function from an external program, we find that the array is not initialized at all! What could possibly go wrong with such a simple program?

Look again at the **for** loop. In C, a semicolon (;) terminates a statement. The **for** loop operates on the statement or block that follows it. In this case, the semicolon following the **for** loop makes this code a loop and simply runs through the loop size number of times. The statement following the **for** loop to execute is empty, not the array assignment we wanted it to be. Silly, isn't it? Yet this sort of thing happens all the time in code.

Logic errors are a specialized form of error that require a great deal of understanding of the program to find and fix. A logic error is simply a mistake in the actual program logic rather than a mistake in the code itself. For example, if the algorithm for a method was to find the odd number greater than the input number, you might write the following Pascal function:

```
FindNextOdd( inputNumber: integer ) integer
{
    if ( odd(inputNumber) ) then
        FindNextOdd := inputNumber + 2;
    Else
        FindNextOdd = inputNumber + 1;
}
```

You can guess, if you don't already know, that the **odd()** function returns true if the number given to it is odd and false if it is not odd. This function appears to work nearly all of the time, but contains a logic error. Can you guess what that error is? Note that the error is not at all in the code, but rather in the logic used to implement the code. Take a minute and look through the algorithm presented and see if you can come up with a hypothesis of your own as to why this function might fail under certain conditions.

Did you see the problem? If not, let's take a look at some simple inputs and outputs of the function in Table 8.1 and see if you can see the error.

Now can you see the problem? The program was designed for positive or unsigned input only. There is nothing in the code, however, to check for a negative input. The next odd integer "after" −1 should either be 1 or 3 for an overall monotonically increasing result

Table 8.1 Function outputs.

Input	Output
1	3
2	3
3	5
−1	0
−2	−1

depending on the requirements of the application. Normally, you would assume that the next odd number following −1 would be −3 for a monotonically decreasing negative result. You can make this mistake easily enough by not doing some background work to understand how the function is really supposed to work.

Requirements errors are probably the worst errors a software engineer can face while debugging. In the case of a requirements error, the problem is not in the code or the logic behind the code. Instead, it is a basic error in the system requirements document. This can be an oversight, a misunderstanding, or even a basic lack of understanding of the problem. It's not really possible to "debug" a requirements error. Instead, you are faced with either rewriting the core sections of the code that are wrong or making whatever adjustments you can to the code so that the program works as the user wants it to work.

Consider this simple example of a requirements error. When writing an application to process real-time data, the requirement was entered into the system that it be able to deal with 1,000 concurrent requests per second. The programming staff dutifully examined various possible implementations to satisfy this requirement and settled on one that appeared to satisfy 2,500 concurrent requests per second. Knowing that lab results and real-world results were often quite different, the team settled for this algorithm, figuring that the real-world difference would unlikely be two-and-a-half times greater than the requirement. In fact, the real-world performance of the algorithm was excellent, satisfying 2,250 requests per second, well above the stated need. So where is the problem?

The system breaks down when it is inundated with requests. Due to a misunderstanding between the requirements analyst and the hardware purchasing department, only a fraction of the machines were meant to be used in the system. Because of this, each machine started receiving 5 to 10 times as many requests as it was intended to. The software was working properly, but it could not keep up with 10,000 requests per second. Is this a bug? From the user and management points of view, it most certainly is. The onus falls on the software engineering department to "fix" the bug. The problem is that it cannot be fixed without either purchasing more equipment (an expensive solution) or rewriting the algorithm to deal with five times as many requests per second as anticipated. Either way, the blame is going to fall on the wrong people, and the solution is going to be ugly.

One of the more common problems in software development is not checking for error conditions and return values. This problem is rarely local to where the error happens. Instead, it bubbles up to the surface of the program where it is usually unexpected and causes bugs. There are good reasons why certain functions and methods return an error code. Failing to check those return codes can only result in problems that are hard to track down and even harder to reproduce.

Probably the most common problem that used to occur in C programs was in the failure of a file to open. Because C returns either a pointer to a file object or a handle that can be used by various file manipulation routines, it is dangerous to work with file manipulations without being sure the file is open in the first place. You can easily call this a bug in the underlying manipulation functions, but you can't really fix the runtime library. As a result, the end bug belongs to the software engineer working on the program.

Let's take a look at a simple BASIC program that contains a fatal flaw. This flaw will not always occur, but it can happen at virtually anytime. Read the source code, and then try to understand why the problem happens.

```
Function GetValue() As Long
If GLOBAL_X < 100 Then
 GetValue = GLOBAL_X
Else
GetValue = -1
End If
End Function
Sub Recurse(FileNumber As Long)
    If FileNumber <> 0 Then
        Recurse (FileNumber - 1)
    Else
        Print "File Number is Now: " + FileNumber
    End If
End Sub
Sub CalcRecurse(FileNumber As Long)
    Recurse (GetValue())
End Sub
```

Obviously, this example is a bit contrived, but it attempts to show how not looking for error returns can cause problems. The **recurse** function takes a number and uses recursion to count up to the number by calling itself until the number reaches zero. The **GetValue** function is intended to return a global variable unless that global variable reaches 100, in which case it returns the error code −1. Once the global variable does reach 100, the return code of −1 is passed down to the **recurse** function. This function checks to see if the value is zero; if not, it subtracts one from it and calls itself. Because the value is already less than zero, the function will recurse itself until either the stack blows or the system crashes. Neither result is a particularly appealing way to terminate the application.

Developers normally return error codes when something goes wrong. More important to the user of the functions or methods, however, is the fact that the expected results of the process no longer apply. Consider, for example, a function that is supposed to allocate a block of memory to represent a matrix. The function accepts a single argument, which is to be the pointer to the returned block of memory allocated. It returns an error code indicating whether or not the allocation was successful. If the function fails, the error code is set to a nonzero value, and the input pointer is not modified. When this happens, the caller must check the error code. If the caller does not check the error code, it is possible that the matrix memory pointer never initializes to point at anything at all. In this case, you get a typical memory error. So, you can see that return codes and the checking of those codes can lead to a number of different kinds of difficult to trace errors. Always remember to check return codes.

A corollary of the return code problem is the exception handling problem. Some languages, such as C++ and Java, solve the problem of return codes not being checked by throwing "exceptions." These exceptions are error objects that are propagated up through the stack until something handles them. The typical pseudocode for handling an exception is as follows:

```
try
{
     call_a_function_that_throws_exceptions()
}
catch ( an exception )
{
   do_something_with_error();
}
catch ( another exception )
{
   do_something_else()
}
```

How the language actually implements exception handling and throwing is really unimportant to us, as is the actual syntax for dealing with exception throwing and handling. What is important is that this problem is just like the return code problem and in some respects worse.

Exceptions are better than return codes in one respect; they must be handled or they will crash the application and display the exception. However, to the end user, they are just as bad. The program terminates abnormally, and users are left to deal with the consequences. Likewise, the programmer can see what the exception was, but cannot always see what it was that caused the exception. Additionally, you can "catch" exceptions in a generic fashion, which makes the problem that much harder to track down. The exception might occur, but the code simply ignores it. This is exactly the same problem as ignoring return codes.

The last type of error you might consider as your base hypothesis is that of a timing or multithreaded error. Symptoms of this error type were described in Chapter 5, but are worth mentioning again. If your program crashes in odd places while accessing global variables or shared memory, you might very well have a multithreaded problem. Likewise, if the program only crashes after adding a number of output statements to a real-time system, you might have a timing issue. Both of these problems are extremely hard to track down, so you might want to eliminate all other possibilities before you decide that the problem is a threading or timing issue.

In any event, once you have actually classified your hypothesis, it is time to determine where the problem lies. Given the category of your hypothesis, you should be able to limit the problem to a specific body of code. If you cannot limit the problem to that degree, you aren't really hypothesizing, you are taking wild stabs in the dark. Such stabs rarely work out and often end up treating the symptom rather than the underlying problem.

Let's walk through an example of making a hypothesis for a problem at this point. For this example, we will use the "black screen" problem we talked about earlier in the chapter. As you might recall, the problem occurs in a real-time television display, where the screen momentarily goes black as data fails to flow from the input side of the system to the output side of the system.

We gather information about the problem and find that although data is flowing into the system, it is not flowing out of the system. There are several ways that this could happen. One possible hypothesis is that we are losing the data in the transfer from the input side of the system to the storage side of the system and thus cannot transfer it to the output side. A second hypothesis is that we are somehow failing to keep up with the demands of the output side of the system or perhaps with the input side of the system. Our third hypothesis is that we are transferring data into the system fine, storing it fine, but not recalling it in time to deliver it to the output side of the system.

At this point, we have several possible hypotheses for what could be happening. The issue now becomes which of these hypotheses can be tested, which explain all of the symptoms and observations we have gathered, and which is the most likely culprit. One important note: When making a hypothesis, do not discard it because you have another that might be more likely. As long as evidence exists to support your theory, it remains a valid option. Put it on the list of things to check, prioritizing the list to the degree that you believe each theory is likely.

Tip
Never throw away a hypothesis because another seems more likely.

Test Your Hypothesis

The final step of your identification of the problem is to actually test your hypothesis for what is causing the problem. To adequately test the problem, you need to do three things. First, verify that what you think is happening is happening. Second, prove to yourself that the basis of your hypothesis is the root cause of the problem. Third, predict what should happen given your hypothesis and a different set of data. A hypothesis is nothing less than a mathematical proof of the problem and follows the standard rules for proofs. Prove it for the first case, assume it for a secondary case, and prove it for the third case.

> **Note**
> *As an aside, one of the great problems in the software engineering world is that we are called an engineering discipline, but rarely follow engineering precepts. Engineers do not simply assume things will work. They do not assume that the symptom of a problem is the root cause. Engineers never, ever fix something by treating symptoms or failing to understand the real problem cause. Until we follow the engineering discipline, we have no right to call ourselves software engineers. Perhaps software artisans would be a better term.*

The easiest way to illustrate how to create and test hypotheses is to use examples. This is primarily due to the fact that each hypothesis will vary based on the project and the problem. Although the general processes of debugging works for any industry and any problem, the specifics of solving problems does vary greatly from issue to issue.

The Case of the Crashing Web Server

All truly memorable bugs are more like mystery novels than dry engineering texts. Let's look at an example from real life that had all of the elements of a good mystery: a crime, a puzzle, intrigue, and arguments. Sorry, no murder in this one, perhaps next time. These debugging sessions can get rather heated, you know.

The problem occurred a few years ago when I was working for a small Internet startup. The company was attempting to put together an interactive Web site for users, which allowed them to search, browse, and view documents on the Web. The schedule for development was quite aggressive, and we were coming down to the wire trying to get the site up and running. Just two weeks before we were scheduled to go into final testing of the code for the site, a serious problem developed. The Web site would mysteriously and randomly crash. Because Web sites are, by their very nature, multiuser systems, it was very difficult to track down who and what was causing the problems. Accusations were flying between the internal components group that had developed all of the COM objects used in the site and the Web developers who had written all of the scripts and HTML pages for the site. Naturally, each blamed the other for the problem and each was convinced the error was not in its code. Naturally, because the sides had taken to blaming each other rather than looking for the cause of the problem, nothing was being fixed.

In the waning days before the final release of the code for beta testing, cooler heads began to prevail. The problem was put on the front burner of development, and people began to look into the issue more seriously. Observations were gathered, hypotheses were offered, and serious debugging began.

The initial step toward finding the problem was to identify what it was that was crashing. For this purpose, we chose to implement a logging object within the ASP code that made up the Web pages. Because the Web server was crashing, the reasoning went, perhaps we could determine where it was crashing first. This would allow us to eliminate parts of the system until we could get a better handle on where the real problem was. Using observations from the users and the programmers, we added logging statements to the scripts in areas that people reported to be using before they saw the crash. This allowed us to ignore large chunks of the system, using the assumption that if nobody was in those areas when the crash occurred, that code was unlikely to be causing the problem. This is a valid assumption in any linear or linear-like system, which a Web server usually is. We studied the Web server logs (created by the server itself rather than our internal logging efforts) to see what pages were being served up during the time period of the crash.

Within a day, we had tracked the problem down to a specific page in the server. With cooperation from testing, Web development, and server development groups, we had a reproducible test case, which would cause the problem to occur on command. At this point, we knew exactly what components were in use within that page so that reasonable hypotheses could be developed and tested.

The page that was causing the problem contained three distinct elements. First, there was ASP scripting code that was used to generate the HTML text, which the user saw for the page. Second, there were COM components developed by the internal server components group, which provided interfaces to our database system (an object-oriented database rather than an SQL database). Third, there were a few lines of Perl code to verify the existence of a local file on the Web server. Both the Web team and the server component team were assigned the task of verifying their individual components with valid test cases and determining if the crash could be caused through those means.

The first hypothesis offered by the Web team was that the COM components were returning an error code that the VBScript of the ASP pages did not understand. Therefore, the COM components were "bubbling up" the error to the server itself, which was crashing the server. As we had had a problem similar to this in the past, this hypothesis seemed reasonable. We looked at all of the COM component method calls on the page, and then checked the code in the COM components themselves to see what errors could possibly be returned. A test component was created, which returned each one of the possible errors to an ASP script to see what would happen when each occurred. In each case, no problems were detected.

The second hypothesis offered by the server component team was that there was a problem in the Perl script. The argument made was that the COM component didn't seem to work differently than in any other script, there were no odd problems reported in any of the test cases, and this was the only page that contained the Perl script segment. To test the theory, the Perl script segment was removed from the original script and placed in its own script file. Test cases were written for files that did and did not exist. The script appeared to work perfectly; no problems were detected.

At this point, we had two possible hypotheses, neither of which appeared to be correct. No other theories were forthcoming from the various developers. The developers decided that we needed to take a step back and observe the problem a bit more to see what was really causing the problem. Rather than trying to understand what might be causing the problem, we would simply observe the issue for a little while to see what symptoms and observations we could gather.

In order to track down the problem, we decided to limit the investigation to a single user on the system using only that page in a variety of ways. We added logging to the script on every line to see what piece of code the page was failing at. We tried various different inputs to see whether they would cause the problem. After a full day of observations, we reached the following conclusions. The server group was correct. The problem was most certainly in the small snippet of Perl. This was determined by several runs of the page with a single user and a few different inputs. We also determined that the problem was quite definitely in the routine that verified the existence of the file. This was actually a single line of code in Perl and usually worked fine. We had such code in other places in the system. So what was different about this code?

This brings us to the most interesting stage of debugging. Once the problem has been located but not identified, the next stage is to generate a new set of hypotheses that use what you have learned so far to find the actual root cause of the problem.

Once again, we looked into the mysterious Perl script problem and offered some hypotheses that tried to explain what we were seeing and what might be the root cause of the problem. Because the function in question checked for the existence of a file, we decided to try to determine if some component of the file was wrong. We hypothesized that the issue might be file attributes. A read-only file, for example, might cause the problem. We tested this hypothesis by creating a series of files that had all of the combinations of file attributes set. This involved setting various attribute bits in each of the file directory entries. Each was tested in the Perl function. Each worked fine.

We then tested the hypothesis that the problem might be caused by a function of long file names. This bug occurred shortly after the introduction of long file names in the operating system we were using, so this hypothesis appeared to make sense. Because not all of the files we were using had long file names, it could explain the intermittent nature of the problem. In addition, because a long file name could cause something akin to a buffer overrun in an internal storage mechanism, this explanation made a lot of sense. Tests were set up to try the function on various length file names ranging from blank file names (no characters) to very long file names. In each and every case, the function passed with flying colors. Another hypothesis was eliminated for lack of corroboration.

At this point, you should begin to see the process we were following. Given the set of observations that were gathered, we attempted to put together what we knew into a reasonable explanation for why the program was crashing. As each set of observations was bundled into a hypothesis, a set of test cases was created that would verify if the hypothesis could be valid or not. If the test cases indicated that the problem did not occur with that hypothesis, that idea was discarded and another was tried. Two important points at this stage are not to get frustrated by failure and not to allow finger pointing to start. Either one will derail the process and leave you with no clue as to how to continue.

Rather than spend a lot more time discussing all of the possible hypotheses that we ran through trying to find the problem, I'll explain what the problem really was and how we fixed it. It's important to understand, however, that no matter how simple the problem is, the process is often long and frustrating. Once you find the root cause, you usually end up wondering why you didn't see it right off the bat. This is perfectly normal and nothing to be frustrated about. It takes time to understand the problem. It takes time to dig into the problem and find the observations you need to get to the root of the problem. It also takes time to see how the observations you gathered are relevant to the problem you've discovered.

The solution to our mystery—the butler did it in the pantry with the knife, of course. The butler always does it. Actually, the problem was caused by the fact that our file names came from a database and that the path to the files was not always valid. Older entries in the database contained an invalid drive or invalid path on a drive. The Perl function in the version of the Perl interpreter we were using wouldn't handle an invalid drive or path error correctly and would cause an exception in the operating system. This crashed the process that was running the interpreter, which in this case was the Web server.

How did we discover this problem? One hypothesis offered involved the database fields that were passed to the Perl function. This forced us to actually look at the data being passed to the function. We did notice that the paths and drive letters were invalid, but simply assumed that the documentation for the function was correct, and that the problem would be handled properly. Mistake number one: Never assume the function works as specified. Always verify that it does. After all, if everything worked as advertised, there wouldn't be any bugs, would there? Once we tested the actual function with the invalid file paths, the program immediately crashed. The solution, therefore, was quite simple in this case. We rewrote the function in another language and verified that it worked fine with all of the test cases we had created in the hunt for the problem—mystery solved.

Testing the hypothesis is a matter of first matching the hypothesis with the set of observations that you acquired in the first round of debugging, and then seeing whether or not the hypothesis explains all of the observations. If it does, you must try to formulate additional data points generated from your understanding of what is causing the problem. If these data points match the observed data for the hypothesis, you have a starting point from which to begin fixing the bug.

Iterate until a Proven Hypothesis Is Found

Once you have proposed a hypothesis and have tested it, you may find that you need to discard it. This can easily happen several times in the debugging process. I've often found that I "knew" what the problem was upon seeing the bug report, only to find that the actual cause was something completely different. The important issue is to not become so wed to an idea that you ignore important observations that show your hypothesis to be incorrect. In addition, you must understand that there is no timetable for determining the correct answer. Consider this important tip for manager types: Never ask debuggers how long it will take to fix a problem until they have determined the root cause of the bug and have verified their hypotheses. Until this stage is reached, any schedule you are given to fix the bug will be, at best, overly optimistic and at worse, wrong.

Tip

You cannot accurately estimate the time it takes to fix a bug until you have a verified a hypothesis for its cause!

Note that there is another issue in the example we just discussed—even within a given hypothesis, iteration is often needed to target the real problem. Although we knew that the problem was caused by a given page on the Web server, we needed to find out what it was about that page that was causing the problem. This process of narrowing the focus down to find the underlying problem is iteration. Once you find the macro level of the bug, you need to strip away the extraneous code to find the line (or lines) that are causing the problem. In our example, we did this by logging the processing of each line until we stopped getting logging messages. By definition, in this sort of a problem, the line just after the last logging message should be the one causing the problem. Although this technique cannot always be used, it's often a valuable way to find problems when you aren't exactly sure what line of code could be causing the problem. Once you understand which line it is, the hypothesis process comes into play again, and you start trying to "guess" why the problem is occurring on that line. Once you have tracked down a problem to a given line of code, you can usually log the information that is being processed by the statement and bench-test the code with that information to see what the problem might be. As you can see from the example, however, if you do not have the source code for a given function or method and that method contains a bug, you will often have to do more detective work to see what is causing the problem.

At some point, you will find that you have extreme confidence in the source of the problem and that all of the observations support your conclusion. Once this occurs, it is time to actually fix the bug!

Propose a Solution

So you have finally solved the mystery and have discovered what is causing the problem. At this point, you usually offer a deep sigh of relief and relax a bit. The problem is, you haven't solved the bug at all. All you've done is identify it. The powers-that-be aren't going to be satisfied with a simple explanation of why the problem exists; they want it fixed. The next logical step in the debugging process is to propose a way to solve the problem.

The actual act of proposing a solution, of course, depends on what the bug is and how the code is structured. To discuss the "right" solution for your particular problem requires that we know a lot about your application and the bug in question. It would be difficult for us to propose a specific solution for each kind of problem you encounter. What we can do, however, is examine some of the factors that should go into your solution proposal.

In an ideal world, you would simply fix the problem that you identified in the hypothesis proving stage. Unfortunately, the real world often demands that we do things in a less than ideal manner. You will often have to find the smallest level change that can be made to fix the problem. That can often mean going back to your hypothesis stage and looking at it more carefully. As an example, let's consider the mystery of the crashing Web server case. Suppose that our final hypothesis was that the problem was caused by the inclusion of Perl functions within the Web pages. Although this is a valid case and is supported by the observations that we made while running the code, it isn't a very good final answer because the complete Web site might contain hundreds of files that use Perl functions. The resulting changes could easily cause more problems than they solve. In addition, the sheer amount of time needed to change all of those files might be so great that it would make it impossible to launch the product on time. In these cases, management would certainly balk at such a simplistic answer as removing all Perl code from the Web pages. They would, understandably, want a better answer. In a case like this, you would be forced to go back and further refine your hypothesis to determine exactly which function was causing the problem.

One of the first rules you will learn as a professional debugger is to make the most minimal change to effect the result you want. If the problem is caused by bad data coming into a specific function, it is usually easier and safer if you simply check for the data on entry to the function and return a reasonable error code to the caller. If the problem is caused by someone clicking a button multiple times on a dialog box, the solution is usually to disable the button after the first time it is clicked, and then enable it again when it is safe to do so.

Another good rule to learn early is that before you propose a solution to a problem, see what the solution entails. You might be promising something you can't deliver. Not only will this result in unhappy people, but it will also affect your credibility within your organization. Both results can cause you great grief in later stages of the project.

Before you propose a solution, especially if you did not work on the original implementation of the system, you should talk to a developer that worked on that section of the code. This will stop you from proposing a solution that has already been tried or suggesting a solution that will cause other problems. You should also check the bug tracking system to see if a similar solution was tried before and removed because it caused problems. Once again, trying solutions that have already been attempted and have failed is a good way to look very bad in front of your coworkers and management.

Your proposed solution should cover three areas. First, it should explain why the change will fix the problem. Second, it should show the affected areas of the application source code if they lie outside of the original source of the problem. Third, it should offer some assurance that the cure will not be worse than the disease, meaning that it won't cause additional problems.

Test the Solution

Once you have proposed your solution and have implemented it, the next step is to test your solution in the final product. There are really two steps to this process. The first is to verify that the steps you discovered to reproduce the problem be followed to see if the bug still exists. The second is to try other methods of causing the same problem, which you believe would cause the same problem and see if it recurs.

The only true way to validate a problem fix is to know exactly how to cause it. If you cannot produce a specific set of steps that causes the problem, you don't really understand the problem, and you can never be sure that you have fixed it. In effect, what you are doing is circumventing the problem, which at a future time might show up in some possibly mutated form. My advice is not do this; you will drive yourself crazy in the long run. Create a reproducible test case and verify that your solution fixes the problem.

Coming up with other ways to cause the problem can be harder, but it is definitely worth the effort. If you know several ways to get the problem to surface, you can easily verify that your solution wasn't simply a surface patch that only fixed the initial test case. If your solution solves all of the possible ways to produce the problem, it is a valid fix, and you can consider the problem fixed.

Iterate until Solution Is Proven

Quite often, you will find that your hypothesis is correct, but the solution you have selected does not work. In this case, you need to look at the problem again, find another possible solution, and test it. You need to continue this process until the solution works and solves the problem adequately. At this point, you can call the bug fixed and turn it over to the QA department for regression testing.

Another key task to perform at this point is to look for similar pieces of code that might suffer from the same problem. Running the equivalent test cases that reproduce the problem in one area can often turn up problems in other areas of related code. This is particularly important for code that has been cut and pasted from one area of the system to another.

One very important point worth mentioning is that if a solution does not solve the problem, it should be removed completely before moving on to the next possible solution. If you do not do this, you will suffer from two problems. One is that you might cause a new problem that masks the old one and makes a valid solution appear to fail. The second problem is that you might end up with orphan code that makes no sense in the broader scheme of the system. You will also not be testing the real problem anymore. Be smart and remove all of the code first. It is important to understand the integrated nature of all of the fixes that were applied to the code in the first place. You need to understand how to restore the code to its original intended state before you start hunting for a bug.

Regression Test

The final step in any debugging session is to do a full regression test of the system to verify that in fixing one problem you didn't cause another problem. It is extremely important that you do this immediately after fixing a problem. Ideally, you should have an automated regression test script if your software supports such things. That way, you can immediately verify that you didn't cause any other problems.

By far, the most frustrating result for developers and users alike is a software release that fixes one or more problems but causes a group of new ones. Even if the new bugs are less severe than the bug that was fixed, new bugs in a bug release version can affect the credibility of the software. Users who were willing to put up with existing bugs that they knew and understood are less likely to be happy about new bugs they have no idea how to encounter or avoid.

Regression tests should take two forms. First, there should be an automated script that tests the most common issues. Second, the full system should be tested to verify that there are no new problems caused by the change made to the system for the bug fix. One good way to perform accurate testing is to group your test cases into areas of the application that have either been identified or discovered to be interrelated. If you can determine in advance what areas of the application are likely to be impacted by a change, you can do a quick and dirty test by running the test cases that apply to only that area. This is not a substitute for a complete regression test, but it should give you a warm fuzzy feeling that your change didn't break anything new.

Once you have run a complete regression test and have satisfied yourself and the QA department that the problem is fixed and you haven't introduced any new problems into the system, you can mark the bug as fixed.

Summary

In summation, let's take a quick look at the steps you should take to solve a problem in your system. This process should work for software bugs, process bugs, or even requirements bugs. The actual internal procedure of each step might vary for the different kinds of bugs, but the process will remain the following:

◆ Identify the problem. Determine what it is you are trying to fix and whether or not the problem is really a bug that needs to be fixed, an enhancement that needs to be added, a documentation error that needs to be modified, or a simple misunderstanding on the part of the user.

◆ Once you have established that the problem really does exist and that the system needs to be modified, gather information about the problem. Determine how the problem is occurring, what the symptoms of the problem are, and what users expect to have happen when they follow the prescribed steps.

♦ After you understand the problem and have gathered enough information to make an educated guess as to what the root cause of the problem might be, you can form your hypothesis. The root cause might be related to the symptoms or might be completely separate. Your hypothesis should explain the symptoms and observations made in the application.

♦ If you have a hypothesis, you need to test it to make sure that it explains all of the possible observations and symptoms. You should take the next logical step at this point, and see what other information you can predict, given your hypothesis. The testing stage verifies that the predictions match the actual behavior of the application.

♦ The next stage is to iterate through the hypothesis and proof stage until you come up with a solution that passes the tests and explains all of the problems observed. At this point, you have a working hypothesis that seems to be accurate.

♦ Assuming that the hypothesis you find eventually passes all tests, the next stage is to offer a possible solution to the problem given the observations and the hypothesis. Obviously, the proposed solution needs to fix the problem and must take into account reasonable compromises, such as time and resource availability.

♦ At this point, you implement your solution and test it. If the problem is solved, your process is complete and ready for testing. If the problem continues to persist, your solution is invalid and needs to be removed. A new solution should then be proposed and implemented. This process is repeated until the solution is valid and removes the problem.

♦ The final stage of the debugging process is to subject the system to a complete regression test to verify that no other new problems have been introduced into the system as a result of the changes you made to the system.

Bug Puzzle

While designing a database for a Web site, you create three tables. One table models the user information, name, address, phone number, and so forth. The second table models tax rates by ZIP code. The third table contains the tax return information needed by ZIP code so that your e-commerce system can pay taxes to the government properly. The designs for the three tables, stripped down to their essentials, look like this:

Table: Customer Data

```
Name : String
Address : String
City : String
State : String
Zip Code : Long Integer
```

Table: Tax By ZIP Code

```
Zip Code: Long Integer
Tax Rate: Float
ExemptFlag : Boolean
```

Table: Tax Paid

```
Zip Code: Long Integer
Total Taxable Amount: Long Integer
```

When the system is implemented, two serious bugs are reported. The totals in the tax paid tables are not matching the totals reported from the actual sales in the e-commerce section, and some of the ZIP codes are not reporting correctly in some parts of the system.

Looking only at the table layouts, can you envision reasons why these problems might be occurring? How would you track them down? How would you fix them?

Chapter 9
Debugging Techniques

Matt Telles

We've talked a lot about theory, situations, and examples, but at some point you actually have to consider how you are going to go about looking at the code and the problem and fixing the bug. There are numerous techniques that you can use to perform your job. In this chapter, we look at some of these techniques and explain how they can be applied to real-world situations.

One of the most annoying aspects of books on computer science is that they restrict themselves to the "perfect case." You get to start with a clean slate. You get to work from a perfect set of requirements. You have an infinite amount of time to come up with all of the possible scenarios. This just doesn't happen in the real world. Compromise is the name of the game. Insufficient resources, poorly defined requirements, and corner cutting in the code are often the reality. It would certainly be nice if this wasn't true, but when you are trying to fix problems, you need to take these factors into account. For this reason, we look at techniques that work outside of the "perfect" world and more in the "real" world.

In an attempt to make this chapter most useful to the professional debugger, we divide the techniques into three sections. The first section discusses techniques that will help you in the long run—techniques you should apply on a day-to-day basis. You can use them at any time with or without bugs to track down. The second section discusses techniques that work well on products that you can test and debug at your desk. You can consider "at your desk" techniques to be "dirty" machine techniques, that is, techniques on machines where you cannot be absolutely sure of the environment. The third section provides techniques you can only use when you are working in a production environment on "clean" machines.

Before we start discussing the actual techniques and their descriptions, let's take a look at some of the attributes of debugging techniques. In order to know when you should or should not use a given technique, you really need to understand it. You need to weigh certain considerations, such as what it involves, what it modifies, and what the risks to using the technique are when choosing a technique to solve a given problem in your system.

One last word about debugging techniques—some will work for you and some will not. It is important to try the ones that are best suited for a given type of debugging first. If they work for you and fit with your debugging style, great. If not, by all means try out different techniques until you find one that works correctly for you. The important thing is to find and fix the bug, and using a well-defined process is an important part of achieving your goals. Using a specific technique is not nearly as important as knowing that there are available techniques to use and finding the right one for your work. Consider this chapter to be more of a recipe book approach. Find the recipes (techniques) that you like and that work well for your organization. Look at techniques that you haven't tried before in an effort to see if they might be added to your "menu" of techniques that you use whenever you run across a bug. Mostly, don't be afraid to try something new. Keep in mind that you can always go back to what worked in the past.

Intrusive vs. Non-intrusive Debugging

Intrusive debugging techniques are generally those that involve modifications to the system or the environment for the application at runtime. An non-intrusive debugging technique is one that requires no modification to the source code or the environment that the system runs in. In general, you should not consider intrusive debugging techniques for production systems unless the intrusion is such that it will not affect the running of the program on a nondebugging system or there is no other viable alternative. As we implied earlier, sometimes the "real" world dictates that we have to do things in ways we would rather not if there were better alternatives.

A simple example of an intrusive debugging technique is using a debugger on your application. The debugger requires that you modify your source code by including debugging information in the form of symbol tables and the like when linking it into the final application. In addition, the debugger modifies the conditions under which the application is running. The program running within the debugger cannot be considered to be running "normally" due to items like breakpoints and conditional modifications to variables.

Non-intrusive debugging techniques are those that are completely external to the system at runtime, such as observations and monitor applications. Frequently, these programs can provide you with insight into the runtime behavior of the application without modifying the system or the application.

Although it might seem obvious that your preference would be to use non-intrusive debugging techniques for most applications, the truth is that you will need to weigh the urgency of the problem, the severity of the bug, and the amount of time you can have with the system for debugging before deciding which technique to use. If the problem is so severe that users cannot use a client/server application, it might be worth the cost to use a severely intrusive technique to find the problem quickly, even though the effort might prevent even more people from using the system.

To determine if a technique is intrusive or non-intrusive, ask yourself the following three questions:

♦ Does the technique require modifications to the source code that would not otherwise be present?

♦ Does the technique modify the environment under which the program would normally be running?

♦ Does the technique introduce logging, special diagnostic screens, or abnormal terminations, which would not happen during normal operation of the system?

If the answer is yes to any of the three questions, the technique you are examining is intrusive. If the answer is no to all three questions, the technique is non-intrusive. Both intrusive and non-intrusive debugging techniques involve what is commonly called "instrumentation." The term is borrowed from scientific experiments and hardware systems testing. Hardware systems experiments and tests are *instrumented* with instrumentation hardware to monitor operations and collect data that can be analyzed into information that will identify and quantify what is being tested. Software debugging experiments and tests are no different. They require instrumentation to monitor and collect data relevant to the problem being debugged. Hardware debugging can require software instrumentation tools as well as hardware instruments. Likewise, software debugging can sometimes also require hardware tools as well as *software instrumentation* to identify problems bugs.

Short-Term vs. Long-Term Debugging Techniques

When working with a technique, you should also consider whether it is a long-term technique or a short-term technique. Long-term techniques are intended to find problems while the system is running normally over a fairly significant amount of time. Short-term techniques, on the other hand, are "quick fix" kinds of approaches. If you are running the program to track down a problem and that is the sole reason for the types of processes you attempt, you are trying a short-term technique. If, on the other hand, you trap for a specific error and log special information or go to a specific diagnostic screen when that error or change occurs in the application at any time, you are using a long-term (intrusive) technique.

In general, short-term techniques are more intrusive than long-term techniques. Suppose, for example, that you suspect that a given process causes a memory leak, but only with a certain form of input, which you have not determined. You might put in code to notify you via email or via a special pop-up screen when your hypothesis is confirmed. This notice might include information that is useful to the programmer so that he or she can fix the problem once the hypothesis is confirmed. If the message is never received but the problem recurs, you might consider the hypothesis as incorrect.

Running a program in a debugger is quite definitely a short-term technique. You can't really run the program in the debugger in a production environment, nor can you release software that only runs in the debugger as a shrink-wrapped product. Using the debugger is a fundamental case of the short-term technique, however. Consider the case of adding logging after each line of a Web server script. The logging would not only slow down the process to an unacceptable rate, it would also either fill up your log file or bury the screen in data in short order. Obviously, this is not a good long-term solution for your end user unless one makes provisions for those considerations in the system's design. Such logging would normally be a short-term technique.

To determine if something is a long-term or short-term technique, ask yourself the following question: Can the system run "normally" with the technique in place?

If the answer is yes, the technique is long-term. If the answer is no, the technique is short-term. Short-term techniques are normally only used when you can debug the application in a developer environment rather than a production environment. Alternatively, a short-term technique might be used in the case where the problem stops the application or service from being used by the end user. In these cases, it is normally acceptable to use a short-term technique even in a production environment.

Compromises for Production Environments

Production environments, whether in a client/server model or a standalone application model, present a unique problem for the debugger. For example, you will find that the quality assurance (QA) department will often not allow you to install monitoring software or specialty debugging software on a production or QA system. The reason for this is simple. If the system in question does not accurately reflect how the system will look when the product or service is released, you are not really testing it at all. You are testing a modified environment that has nothing to do with how the software will work when it is released.

There are many compromises that can be made when dealing with a production environment. Obviously, installing a debugger is out of the question. However, running a specialized copy of the software that contains additional logging or diagnostic screens is not unreasonable. Although both of these techniques could be considered moderately intrusive, they might be acceptable if the problem severity is high. Actually, if the problem is so serious that you cannot run the software for the users, management and QA will often waive all restrictions. However, it is not a good idea, from a political point of view, to do this very often. You end up like the boy who cried wolf, and eventually nobody listens to you when a real problem arises.

The following is a partial list of the sort of compromises you can expect to make when working in a production environment:

♦ You will likely be unable to install your software directly; instead, you will have to rely on operations people to do the job for you.

♦ You will have to rely on operations people to monitor and deliver logging files for you.

♦ If you are working in a client/server environment, you will be unable to segregate yourself from the rest of the populace. You will be forced to perform debugging with multiple users online.

♦ If you are shipping a standalone product, a possible compromise is to ship a specialized debugging version to only a small, fixed set of "beta" users. This can result in better feedback and not annoy the marketing and customer support departments.

The Techniques

As we discuss techniques in the following sections, we will list a few attributes for each one. Each entry will consist of the following:

♦ Technique name.

♦ Description of the technique.

♦ Whether the technique is intrusive or non-intrusive.

♦ Whether the technique is short term or long term.

♦ What categories (standalone, client/server, or production) the technique is best suited for. Note that some levels do not apply to the install level. These categories are marked as internal only or external only.

♦ If applicable, a step-by-step approach for applying the technique.

Having Real Users

One of the most frustrating factors in the early phases of a project is to try to guess how the product will be used. With only developers using the system, you get a very warped idea of what problems exist and how they might appear. Developers, especially those that are writing the system, have a tendency to use the application in a way they think it is "supposed to" work rather than the way in which a real user might use it. For this reason, one of the best ways to find problems and reproduce them is to utilize real users. In the software development industry, we often have a group of "beta testers" who use the product and help us determine if it is ready to be shipped or not. Unfortunately, we rarely have a group of people that is most likely to be using the product on a daily basis available to test new features as we implement them. Debugging is done on a daily basis during development, so why not do testing at the same rate?

Modification type: Non-intrusive

Modification length: Long term

Appropriate levels: Any

Note Observations

One of the best ways to keep track of events that you observe in an application is to maintain a program journal. Not only will this allow you to collect all of the information you see, read, and discover about an application into one place, but it is also a valuable document that can be passed on to future developers. Observations about the code consist of where events take place, what the various subsystems do, and what assumptions are made throughout the system. Observations about the running of the application might include such things as odd things that rarely happen or changes you might want to make in certain areas of the application. Each time you run the application, you should note what you did and what the results were, especially if they are not exactly what you expected. Recording correct operations and results (implementing a process) is just as important, if not more so, than recording incorrect operations and results. Later, when a bug is reported in the system, you can often check back through your journal to see if you observed something that might be a clue. If so, you will have a list of things you can try to reproduce it immediately. Noting your observations is an easy, cheap way to maintain your thought processes about the application and a great way to transfer knowledge from one group of developers to the next "generation" on the project.

If correct operations and results have been recorded in your project/program notebook you have a history of cases that do not have to be (re)developed and tested to begin converging on the problem area. Those correct operation notes will also provide a quick execution sequence path for regression testing and problem redefinition confirmation testing. One of the more annoying circumstances in debugging is the bug that "disappears" during the debugging process, even when you "didn't change anything." Having the execution sequence path for correct prior operations is invaluable for verifying such occurrences.

Modification category: Non-intrusive

Modification length: Long term

Appropriate levels: Any

Document the Code and the Process

Probably the best long-term technique available to you as a professional developer or debugger is to document the code you are writing as well as the problem it is intended to solve and the process the system uses. Although most developers do document their code internally, there is usually little documentation on the system from an external point of view. Developers are so close to the system design and development that they gloss over the assumptions that they make while writing the code. If you are coming in after the initial development is complete, you should make an effort to document observations from your own perspective as you learn about the system. Over the years, I've found that most of the bugs that entered the system were caused by a breakdown of the development process. The developer either failed to test a segment of code or change adequately, or he did not follow proper procedure in making sure that a change did not affect other segments of the code. If you properly document the processes needed to complete projects within your company, you will remove these problems. If you document how the system works and the assumptions that are made within the code, you will prevent problems that might occur by someone who didn't realize that certain assumptions were made.

What should be documented? In my humble opinion, each developer should be handed a manual upon starting at a company. This manual should contain detailed instructions on what software needs to be installed along with the versions of that software. It should contain details on the source code tree and which files do what. It should contain process documents that explain how to build, install, and debug the system. Change management processes should also be covered in any document. Testing processes should be covered in the manual as well.

Modification type: Non-intrusive

Modification length: Long term

Appropriate levels: Internal only

Similarity to Other Code and Problems

Using this technique, you search for other problems that had the same symptoms in the past or share code that had problems in the past. This technique makes certain assumptions about your development processes. For example, it assumes you keep a historical record of the problems that have occurred in the system and their current state. Furthermore, it assumes that there is a documented relationship between the change to the code and the bug that it fixed. If your company does not maintain such records, you are going to be hard-pressed to use this technique. An alternative mechanism might be to use comments in the code, such as "Fixed a problem with <xxx>." Searching for such comments will often accomplish the same thing as a bug-tracking database, although in a less efficient manner. Of course, you work with what you have.

The basic reasoning behind this technique is that similar kinds of problems have similar causes, and that similar code produces similar problems. It's difficult to actually prove this assertion, but in general it seems to pan out pretty well.

Modification category: Non-intrusive/Intrusive (using comments)

Modification length: Long term (for tracking)/Short term (for finding problems)

Appropriate levels: Internal only

Applying the technique: Assuming that you have a bug database, use the keywords from the bug description to search for similar bugs. A word about keywords. It is important to have keywords that adequately reflect what the bug is all about. If a given sub-system is involved in, say, MPEG decompression, it is worth putting the keyword MPEG into the bug description. Make it easy for people to find what they are looking for, and they will find the information and use it appropriately. Alternatively, if your bug database supports the subsystem of the application in which the problem occurred, look in that subsystem for similar items.

Another way to apply this technique is to look for similar code in the location where the problem is found and determine if any of the code has been modified. This will find and fix "cut and paste" code that was only fixed in one place in the code.

In addition, if you can find out who wrote the piece of code you are finding the problem in, you can look for bugs that were reported on other pieces of code written by the same developer. People tend to make the same kinds of mistakes regularly. If you can determine the developer's general approach, you can often find similar bugs and code segments. This will allow you to "share" bug fixes with those other reported problems.

Simplify Reproducibility

When a particularly complex problem comes to your attention, you will often be given a list of actions to take to reproduce the problem. In general, these steps will be the first attempts that were tried to reproduce the problem for a given user or even a set of users. It is important to reduce the reproducible case to the smallest possible set of steps needed to solve the problem. You simplify these steps for two good reasons. First, it is much easier to retry the test each time using less steps, and there is much less chance of an error in reproducing the problem. Second, and more importantly, each step in the process requires that you look into a certain number of features in the system to see if they could be causing the problem. The more features you have to look at and the more interactions there are between the features, the longer it will take to fix the problem. You want the process to take less time, not more time. So, pare it down to the simplest set of steps needed.

Modification type: Non-intrusive

Modification length: Short term

Appropriate levels: Any

Applying the technique: Given a set of steps to reproduce a bug, begin by eliminating the steps individually. If a given step does not seem to make a difference in producing the bug, remove it from the list. If it does make a difference, add it to the permanent list. In fact, you will need two lists, one of "items to test" and a list containing "required to reproduce". For steps that are required to get to other steps that do make a difference, keep the related step as a note to the process once the step that causes the problem is identified. Continue until you have run through the entire list enough times to remove all the steps that are unimportant. At this point, you should have the minimal number of steps needed to reproduce the problem.

Pare the Problem Down to Its Simplest Elements

Given any software bug, eliminate all extraneous information to get to the source of what the problem really is. Normally, when a software bug is presented to the software engineer for debugging, the problem is stated in simple terms and related to an example of what happened. Often, the actual problem is unrelated or at best superficially related to the actual bug. For simplicity's sake, consider this example. "I was using the <x> feature of the system, and I entered 02/30/00 for the start date. The resulting display was completely messed up. I tried to click Continue and the system crashed." There are several symptoms that are related in this situation. First, the display was "messed up" (a technical term meaning it didn't look quite right). Second, the program crashed (a nontechnical term meaning the program crashed). After reading the description again, the actual problem is neither of these two occurrences. The date entered was 02/30/00, which is the 30th of February, and, of course, February never has 30 days. Pared down to its simplest form, the problem is that the date check routine is not called or is incorrect.

Modification type: Non-intrusive

Modification length: Short term

Best suited levels: Any

Applying the technique: The easiest method for performing problem-paring is to break down the bug report into individual sentences. Take each statement in the bug report and write it on a different card or on a separate line of a sheet of paper. Then take a look at each statement or card and attach the problems that can be explained by other problems to each other. Using the example, this would mean attaching the messed up display to the system crash. In all likelihood, the system crash was inevitable when the display messed up because the internals of the application were already corrupted. The "using <x> feature of the system" statement does not rely on any other statement, so it stands alone. The entering of the 02/30/00 date is dependent on the selected feature. The attempt to click Continue is dependent on entering a date and selecting a feature. As a result, we have two possible trees to check. Look at each one and determine the simplest explanation for getting to that point. Scanning through the list, we see the invalid date. Entering an invalid date is independent of any other problems in the system and is likely the contributing factor. If entering a valid date does not cause the same problem, you can pare the problem down to the invalid date as a starting point.

Of course, you must be willing to go back and reassess your base assumptions if they prove incorrect. For example, if we pared the problem down to the invalid date, fixed the date check routine, and still had the problem, it would not be reasonable to say that the date was the root cause of the bug. You can either select another branch of the tree (pressing Continue, say), or you can assume that you don't have enough information to reduce the problem any further. If more information is needed, you must return to the investigation stage.

Code Elimination

Code elimination is a good technique for finding a problem in code that you understand reasonably well. In this technique, pieces of code are removed from the system until the problem is isolated and the specific line of code (or specific function or method call) can be identified. Although best suited for linear coding styles, code elimination can be used in any system. It requires that you understand enough about the code to determine what can be removed from the flow and what cannot. For example, if you remove an initialization step, you will find that the program doesn't produce the problem, but it does crash! Obviously, this is not the desired result of the debugging effort.

Code elimination cannot be performed on a production system without severely compromising the usability of the system for end users. You would normally do this when you have full access to the code and rebuilding the entire system is not an all-day affair. The technique works well in cases where you know how to reproduce the problem, but cannot understand what in the code can be causing the result. In these cases, you are doing fundamental detective work, solving the crime by logic, eliminating each potential suspect. The only problem is that in the typical software development effort, the suspects could be thousands or even millions of lines of code. This technique is often best combined with the simplify reproducibility technique in order to first find a good starting point for elimination.

There are a few important details to note about the code elimination technique. First, it is quite definitely a brute force approach to problem solving. This technique is best used in small applications, such as command-line utilities. Second, it is often important to have an absolutely valid reproducible case before you use the technique. If you do not, you might incorrectly identify the line causing the problem, leading you down a false path and wasting a lot of time. Third, it is important that you keep the functional equivalent of the original program that produced the bug intact. For example, if you remove an entire subsystem that was essential for getting to the problem originally, you might find that the problem disappears. The problem may not disappear at all, but its disappearance might be caused by the fact that a new path through the system is taken when this subsystem call is removed. Path analysis is crucial to verify that the program gets through the same series of choices during each run. If you find that a given path is causing the problem, you can usually use this particular method on that path's code and possibly find the cause of the problem.

You should also understand that by using code elimination, you are admitting that you haven't a clue as to what is going on. If you choose to use this technique, you should discover what the problem is, then go back and use more normal detective techniques to see whether it makes sense for the problem to be caused by the discovered line or not.

Modification type: Intrusive

Modification length: Short term

Best suited levels: Standalone, client/server nonproduction

Applying this technique: To use this technique on your own code, you need access to the source code for the system. If you don't have access to the source code, this technique will not work. Determine a good starting point by using simplify reproducibility and pare the problem down techniques. At this point, you need to consider the application in two different halves. First, you have the front half of the system, which consists of the user interface and business logic. Second, you have the back half, which consists of the functionality you are actually using in the application. Once you have a starting point, begin by removing code from the front half of the system in functional chunks until you have discovered the line that is causing the problem. Once the problem line is identified, slowly replace the code in the system, verifying that the same line continues to cause the problem. Note that if the problem line moves when additional code or data is added or replaced in the system, it is likely that you are looking at a *stray pointer problem* and should reconsider your technique choice with that bug type in mind.

Reductionism

By far, the most difficult job in a software engineer's life is starting from scratch and finding a problem in a given subsystem when that subsystem is buried deep within the application code. For example, if you suspect that the problem lies in a low-level disk routine and that routine is only called at the end of a very long source tree of code, you will be annoyed and frustrated each time you need to restart the debugging process to return to that point. In cases like these, the best technique to use is reductionism. When we suspect that a given problem lies in a low-level subsystem, we remove that particular subsystem from the main program, replacing any routines we need to provide outside input. We then write a simple test driver to test the particular problem that we suspect is happening within the subsystem.

There are certain assumptions built into this technique. It will not work with a system that is so tightly coupled that you cannot remove the suspected system to create a test driver for it. It also assumes that you can provide the same level of input to the lower levels of the code as the original system did. If you miss something, such as a global variable or side effect of a function, you will not be duplicating the initial code, and your test will be meaningless.

Put simply, reductionism can be summed up with the following statement: If you have a theory on the cause of the problem, write the simplest possible example that proves it. Reductionism works best when you have a good idea what is wrong with the code. It works poorly when you have no clue as to where to find the problem. You can easily use this technique in a standalone application or in a QA system for a client/server application. It is very difficult to use in a production environment, although if you can specify the test case well enough, it can be used there too. The best thing about reductionism is that it can often reduce what is considered a horrible problem, such as debugging a multiuser system, into a simpler problem, which might be debugging a simple console application. The art to reductionism is finding the smallest possible set of functionality that causes the problem with the smallest possible set of inputs.

Modification type: Intrusive

Modification length: Short term

Best suited levels: Standalone, client/server nonproduction

Applying the technique: The best approach to reductionism is to write a test driver for the suspected problem system. If this can be accomplished, you will need to simulate the remainder of the system that accesses the problem area. Put together a simple test driver that contains the subsystem, the problem input, and the replaced external links and see whether the problem occurs. If the problem does occur, you can often debug it using more standard techniques within the test driver rather than trying to debug a production level, multiuser, multithreaded application.

If you cannot reproduce the problem within a test driver, the next best choice is to reproduce the problem with a small data set that emulates the problem. This can be accomplished by stripping off the user interface layer of the code and "feeding" in the inputs you want to use for the lower levels. Of course, this assumes that the user interface layer of the code can easily be removed from your application logic code. If it cannot, you might consider making this possible.

Tip

Always maintain the ability to remove the user interface segment of the code in order to test lower level functionality.

Let's suppose, for example, that you are writing a client/server application, which has a thin client-side Graphical User Interface (GUI) that passes along information to a back-end server application. The back-end server crashes on an infrequent, but annoying, basis. You have been given the task of determining why the program might be crashing. To use reductionism, you need to first have an idea of what might be causing the problem. So, you use a first-tier debugging technique, such as inspecting the logs of the server, to see what might be causing the program to terminate abnormally. While looking through the logs, you discover what might be an invalid input being passed in from the thin client. However, the invalid input never appears to be quite the same each time. It strikes you as odd, however, that the invalid input only seems to occur when another thin client passes in a certain data value in the previous transaction. Your hypothesis is that the initial data value causes some corruption in the buffers that carry the data to the back-end server.

In order to test this hypothesis, you could either set up two different thin clients, figure out how to get them to send the requested data, and then try them, or you could strip off the thin client and write a simple test driver that sends specific messages to the back-end. If you had such a test driver, you could easily test the hypothesis by sending the message, checking the state of the system, and then sending the second message. If your hypothesis was correct, this simple test driver would prove it easily.

Using the Debugger

Although it seems intuitive to use the debugger to do debugging, it is actually a fairly limited scope technique. The cases where you can use the debugger are quite often more restricted than the cases where you cannot use the debugger. Let's take a look at each set of situations.

You can use the debugger for:

♦ Standalone applications that are single user

♦ Console applications, such as Common Gateway Interface (CGI)scripts or other applications that are really multiuser but can be run via a test driver

♦ A select group of multiuser applications where the bug occurs with only a single user

These are really the only suitable situations for using an integrated debugger application. Specialized debuggers, such as hardware debuggers, can also be used for situations such as device drivers, system services, and other components that run in the background of an operating system. If you are willing to stretch the meaning of "debugger," you can also use one when trying to debug scripts or other interpreted systems.

You cannot use the debugger for:

♦ Any multiuser system that requires multiple users to create the problem

♦ Any production system running on a clean machine

♦ Any timing-related system (such as a real-time data collector)

♦ Any system where you change the speed or flow of the data through the system. Using a debugger is impossible here, because it will prevent the application from proceeding and will likely cause its own system crash.

Using the debugger causes problems when certain classes of bugs are actually made more difficult to find if you choose to use a debugger. The most obvious two choices are stray pointer (or other memory pointer) problems and uninitialized variable problems. The reason for this is that the debugger normally initializes the entire block of memory it uses to load the program to a known (usually 0) value. This, of course, wipes out the uninitialized variable problem because all variables are then initialized. Likewise, a pointer that is not really pointing anywhere will be assigned the value of 0 or null in many programming systems.

Because this removes the problem, you will be unable to find it. For situations that contain these types of bugs, do not use a debugger; instead choose another technique.

Modification type: Intrusive

Note that it might not be apparent why this method is intrusive. Because you must normally compile an application with different options to create a debuggable application, you are changing the conditions under which the program runs.

Modification length: Short term

Appropriate levels: Standalone

Leaps of Faith

As we mentioned previously in the book, a leap of faith is a technique that is normally combined with another technique, such as code inspection or code elimination. Leaps of faith assume that you know a lot about the code behind the system. It is probably best suited for original developers of systems who know the code like the backs of their hands. In cases like this, seeing a symptom will often trigger a subconscious process that analyzes the parts of the code that you understand and allows you to select the regions that might be responsible for the behavior you are observing. A leap of faith is really more of a system elimination technique. If you know that a given subsystem cannot cause a particular error, you can eliminate it from your thinking. By eliminating a large number of subsystems, you are left with a small number of areas to consider. In your mind, you will most often rank these systems based on the complexity of the code (more complex subsystems are always more suspect), the number of problems that you have encountered and their symptoms for each subsystem, and the kinds of things that the subsystem does.

For example, if the symptom is a corrupted data file, you might immediately eliminate such subsystems as the modem control software, the GUI software, and the memory allocation software subsystems. This might leave the file-handling subsystem and the object cache subsystems as suspects for the corruption. By subconsciously realizing that you have seen the output of the object cache system and it was not incorrect (meaning you didn't see anything out of the ordinary, but you didn't verify it for correctness either), you will have a leap of faith that will take you to the file-handling subsystem.

The number of caveats that apply to the leap-of-faith technique is astounding. It is even more surprising that this is the technique that most software engineers use when searching for a bug. First, the leap-of-faith technique almost never works if you don't have a really good grasp of how the code works and what it is capable of. Second, if you choose the leap-of-faith method and are incorrect in your assumption, you have completely wasted the time spent proving your hypothesis. Unlike other debugging techniques, the leap of faith generally adds nothing to your store of knowledge of the problem. Third, the leap of faith can be wrong, but appear to be right. This is because this technique does not follow the "normal" flow of debugging, and you can easily treat the symptom without finding the underlying cause. It is highly recommended that if you try this technique, you go back and make sure that the problem you are solving is the real problem in the system. Don't treat the symptom; treat the underlying "disease."

Modification type: Non-intrusive

Modification length: Short term

Appropriate levels: Any

Because this technique either works or it doesn't, it really doesn't matter what sorts of systems you are working on. Also, because you are making semi-educated guesses as to the problem, this technique will work on a production system as well as a development system.

Divide and Conquer

The divide-and-conquer technique can be used in several ways. You can divide the application into subsystems and slowly remove the ones that seem to have no effect on the problem. Similarly, you can divide the problem itself into symptoms and allow multiple developers to look into each potential symptom. Once each developer has a possible cause for the symptom, you can check the various causes against each other and see which one (if any) can be used to account for all of the problems. Divide and conquer is an extremely powerful technique when done properly. It can easily be combined with other similar techniques, such as code elimination, reductionism, using the debugger, and paring down the problem to find individual symptom causes.

Although the goal of debugging a system is to find the root cause of all of the observed symptoms for a problem, it is often easier to find the apparent cause of each symptom. Once you know what might be causing each problem, you can often trace back through the program logic or even the requirements for the system and discover what they have in common. This allows you to formulate a hypothesis more easily, as there are less variables to control. When you think about it, debugging is like solving a mathematical set of equations. Unfortunately, we usually have n equations and $n+1$ variables. This makes it rather difficult to solve. In fact, the mathematicians in the crowd will tell you that you cannot "solve" such a system, you can only come up with a possible set of answers. Deciding which answer is correct is the hard part.

Divide and conquer is best implemented as a binary search. Start with the group of possible areas that might contain the problem. Arrange these areas into groups of related functionality. Eliminate everything above a certain range, and then repeat the process. As an example, you might start by grouping all of the possible subsystems into the GUI arena and the low-level logic arena. Remove all GUI elements from the system and provide the same input to the low-level arena subsystems. If the problem persists, you can eliminate all GUI elements. If the problem disappears, you can proceed with the assumption that the low-level logic is correct, and the problem lies in the GUI elements. Of course, you must be willing to go back and rethink your logic if the GUI elements do not show the problem either. Remember that even when divided along these lines, a system has three parts, not two. There is the GUI section, the logic section, and the interface between the GUI and the logic. The problem could be in any of the three sections. If the GUI works and the logic works, it might be worth looking at the interface section.

> **Note**
>
> *Divide and conquer differs from the Code Elimination technique in that it can be used without removing code at all. By partitioning the system into its component pieces and slowly identifying the relationships you can use the binary search approach to determine which components might be involved in the bug at hand. This approach usually requires some level of code scaffolding to be effective.*

Modification type: Non-intrusive

Modification length: Short term

Appropriate levels: In general, this technique can be used in any level of the application. However, if you suspect the problem is in the internal logic of the application and not in the requirements or GUI logic, it will not work well at the production level because you really can't see what is going on at that level.

Error Seeding

The technique of *error seeding* actually comes from the QA world. The idea is to liberally "sprinkle" a set of known errors into the code so that you can get an idea of your testing effectiveness. It might not appear to be relevant as a debugging technique, however. After all, the notion is to remove bugs, not add them to the system, right? Consider, however, that you might not always catch an error condition properly in the code. This error could propagate itself upward throughout the system to cause a completely different sort of problem with hard to detect symptoms. Error seeding allows you to intentionally trigger such a problem and then observe the results. It is quite similar to reductionism in that you are already starting with the idea that there might be a problem. However, error seeding will permit you to see what a lower level problem might cause.

Suppose, for example, that in your fruitless attempts to track down a particularly nasty and hard-to-reproduce bug you notice a low-level function that is not handling an error condition correctly. You might wonder what that error condition could be caused by and what sorts of symptoms that error condition might cause in the overall application at runtime. By selectively causing the error to occur in the code, you can see what the overall effects of that error might be. Of course, this requires that you actually introduce the error specifically into the code, which renders this technique useless for production-level systems.

At this point, you can almost hear the purists in the crowd screaming, "But if you find an unhandled error condition, you need to *fix* it!" Although it is true that you should fix such errors when you find them, it is also true that you should know what problems you are fixing before making any changes. One of the most frustrating things for a developer is to be given a bug from the bug database and not be able to reproduce it, nor find a fix checked into the source tree for it. Your first step in this case is to determine what it is you might be fixing. Then make the change and test to see whether it fixes the problem. Finally, see what else you might have fixed along the way. This last step, by the way, is always the most difficult. Imagine scanning through thousands of bugs to see if the memory leak you detected might be a cause. This is what regression testing is all about.

Modification type: Intrusive

Modification length: Short term/Long term

Appropriate levels: Standalone, development servers, QA servers

Applying the technique: Error seeding is usually done when you already have a suspicion that a problem exists. You can also use it during the discovery phase of a debugging session, just to verify your assumptions about what the program will do when a low-level error is encountered. Normally a testing technique, error seeding is also a valuable detective technique.

The easiest way to implement error seeding in your application is to provide an internal method that you can call, which will directly call the chain of functions you want to test. Provide this method with the data values you want to test. For example, if you have a method that opens a file and reads in a data value, you might provide a higher level routine with such elements as a NULL file name, an invalid file name, or perhaps a read-only file name. Because the higher level functions are still called before reaching the lowest level function, you can be assured that if the error was caught by something else on the way up (or down) through the trace, you will still reach that error checking. On the other hand, if your code relies on checking the GUI to verify input from the user, but then calls the low-level function within the body of the code, there will be no error validation, and the error you suspect is happening might appear.

Compiler Check

One of the most powerful techniques you can use in your everyday debugging is to simply compile the program with the maximum warning levels set. You'll be surprised at how many problems you can find this way. Some of the simpler problems that you can find this way are coercion-of-data types, missing or bad parameters to functions or methods, uninitialized variables, and unused variables in functions. A study by Brocklehurst[1] has shown that

---

[1] Brocklehurst, S., P. Y. Chan, Bev Littlewood, and John Snell, "Recalibrating Software Reliability Models," *IEEE Transactions on Software Engineering*, Vol. 16, No. 4, 1990.

functions and methods with unused variables tend to have a much higher level of problems than a function in which all of the variables are used. In addition, you can free up some space in memory if your compiler does not optimize unused variables. Either way, if you eliminate unused variables, your code is cleaner and easier to read. Consider the following little snippet of Visual Basic code. If you were to run this code and not read it very carefully first, you'd be surprised at the result:

```
START_MONTH = 1  ; Default to January
IF START__MONTH < 3 THEN
    DO_FIRST_TWO
ELSE

    DO_LAST_TEN
END IF
```

Admittedly, the font in this book probably makes it more difficult to spot the problem than it might in a normal programmer's editor, but normally, it is tough to detect anyway. The problem in this code is that there are two underscores (_) in the second variable name and only one in the first. You might not immediately understand why the **if** statement is behaving incorrectly. A decent basic compiler, however, would force you to declare all of your variables up front, which would immediately flag the second incident (as long as you didn't have a variable also called START__MONTH in the program).

Using the compiler as an error checker is a cheap, easy way to verify simple correctness in the syntax of your application source code. It doesn't really hurt anything in any case and can save you hours of tracing through source code looking for problems that could have been caught right away in the program build step.

Modification type: Non-intrusive

Modification length: Long term

Appropriate levels: Standalone

Applying the technique: Set your compiler for maximum error checking. Treat all warnings as errors. Make sure that all files compile "cleanly," and then verify all output from the compiler. If possible, use a "lint-like" tool to check the source code to watch for any automatically detectable errors or mistakes.

Holistic Thinking

Holistic thinking, as we discussed in a previous chapter, is the concept of looking at the program as a whole rather than as a set of lines of code or of individual subsystems. Holistic thinking allows you to consider bugs in the source code to be complete system defects rather than individual problems in modules or lines of code. One of the advantages of holistic thinking is that it allows you to envision what a change to a given module will affect in the system as a whole rather than finding out when your change breaks something.

Although holistic thinking really isn't a specific technique to use when debugging your application, we include it because it is useful when combined with other techniques. For example, while using code elimination to track down a particularly strange problem, you might consider what the eliminated code does to the rest of the system. That way, you are not surprised when something completely different happens in the code. Holistic thinking will permit you to see the "big picture" and realize why this is happening without catching you off guard. Being aware of what may happen in a given situation is always useful when you are trying to figure something out.

It is difficult to set specific procedures for holistic thinking. Understanding all of the components of the system is a must. Understanding the interfaces between those various components is also essential. One of the things that holistic thinking will do that "standard" debugging techniques will not is catch problems that lie between two subsystems. These problems, called interface errors, often occur because two different people with two different ideas developed two different subsystems. Interface errors are often the hardest to track down because they don't really happen on either side of the interface. Instead, the problem is an assumption made on one side of the interface that is not carried through to the other side of the interface.

A simple example of an interface problem is a memory leak. Suppose that in module A, we have a process that allocates a block of memory and puts it into a list that is then returned to module B. Unfortunately, module B assumes that the memory in the list is either static (not allocated) or that it will be taken care of in the destruction process for the list. Module A, on the other hand, assumes that once the memory is allocated for the list, it belongs to the caller of the function that allocated the list. The result is a memory leak in the system. Is the "bug" in the fact that module A allocated the memory but didn't deallocate it? Not really because it was in the contract for module A that the memory belonged to the caller. Is the "bug" in the fact that module B failed to deallocate the memory in the list? Not really because that module made the assumption that destroying the list would destroy the memory allocated in that list. The only other explanation would be that the "bug" is in the list routine itself, which should be deallocating all memory in its contents. This, however, is contrary to the philosophy of the list, which is to simply act as a container for the items put into it.

Implementing a holistic approach to the problem, we would track the input into each module, the output from each module, and what happens to the system as a whole as the result of calling the modules. In this case, we would observe that system memory decreases by a certain amount after the call to allocate the list in module A. We would then observe that the total system memory does not return by the same amount when the list is deallocated in module B. By observing the system as a whole, we can track down the problem to the memory allocated within the list. The fix could then be to simply identify the problem to the writers of modules A and B and allow them to negotiate the responsibility for freeing the memory.

Modification type: Non-intrusive

Modification length: Long term

Appropriate levels: Any

It really doesn't matter at what level you choose to understand the system as long as you fully understand the system at that level.

Use Another Compiler on a Different Operating System

There are times when you will find that the errors that should have been caught by the compiler were not. The reasons for this vary, but the inability to catch errors is mostly caused by either a deficiency in the compiler or a compiler-specific flag you might be using during the compilation phase. For code that is portable between operating systems, you can often try another compiler to see if it picks up errors that your compiler did not. This assumes, of course, that you are not using compiler-specific code in your system, and that the make files (or other configuration scripts) that you are using are easy enough to port from one system to another.

Why would you want to use another compiler? There are a variety of reasons you might consider this option. First, and probably the most unlikely reason, is that you suspect a problem in the compiler or code generator for the system you are using. In cases like this, checking the problem against another compiler can turn up errors you might otherwise never be able to track down. Because very few bugs can be tracked down to compiler errors, this should really be a last resort. Second, you might be looking for portability issues between two different operating systems. In the case where the system works fine on one system but does not on another, using a different compiler might turn up differences in how certain constructs are handled. Perhaps you are making assumptions about the way code or data is aligned in memory. Perhaps you are making assumptions about the side effects of certain code. In these situations, you will more often than not find the problem by using a different compiler.

Another operating system can display problems differently as well. Some operating systems, for example, will tolerate memory corruption errors. This was particularly apparent in older operating systems like CP/M and MS-DOS. A program that appeared to work perfectly (with odd errors that were often explained by strange hardware configurations) on an MS-DOS system often crashed immediately on a Unix system. Simply moving the code over to the other operating system would instantly show where the problem was and save you weeks of debugging time trying to track down bugs that didn't happen in the same place each time.

When should you consider using a different operating system or compiler? If you are writing "portable" code, you should already be working on multiple operating systems. In this case, using a second compiler to verify warnings and errors is almost a no-brainer. Not only will this allow you to find additional information, it will also allow you to keep yourself free from compiler-specific problems and additions. If you are not writing for multiple operating systems, you should consider this technique when the following conditions are true:

- You have reduced the problem to a single line or function.

- You have inspected the code causing the problem and can see no issues with it.

- You suspect that someone is not using proper coding techniques and want to flush it out with a different compiler.

- You need to test the portability of a given function or method.

If none of these conditions apply to you, this technique is unlikely to be useful to you in your debugging endeavors.

Modification type: Non-intrusive

Modification length: Long term

Appropriate levels: Internal only

Change One Variable at a Time

In the rush to try to find and fix bugs, we often get so caught up in the excitement of finding what we think might be the problem that we forget to follow simple engineering principles. One of these principles is to only change a single element at a time. This technique, although basic common sense, is often overlooked when the heat is on to find a solution to an important problem.

Why is it important to only change one element at a time? The most basic reason is that you might not know which change fixed the problem. A more important reason is that you might create a new problem or reinforce the existing problem with a given change and fix it with another change. This causes you to overlook the fact that you fixed the problem in your change and forces you to continue looking into the problem when it is already fixed. Therefore, try one revision at a time before making additional changes.

Another important factor when changing variables is to make sure that you change them back before moving on to the next possibility. This is important for the same reason that changing only one variable at a time is important. If you have previous changes in the code, you might create a new problem that hides the original bug. In addition, you could easily have a lot of junk code in the system when you check in the fixes to the ultimate source code repository. Take out the previous change and return the code to a pristine state before making a new change. If your source code control system supports it, you can do this most easily by reverting the checkout of the file, and then checking it out anew to get the original copy back.

Changing one variable at a time allows you to focus only on the hypothesis you are testing at a given time. You don't have to worry about other factors entering into the problem, nor do you have to worry about figuring out which change fixed the problem or created a new problem. The most important thing to consider, however, is that once you make a change, test it, and throw it away, you must also throw away the reasoning behind it. It is far too common a mistake to make a second change to the program using the same reasoning as the first change without realizing that the second change has a completely different set of hypotheses behind it.

Modification type: Intrusive

Modification length: Short term

Appropriate levels: Nonproduction

Numerology and Boundary Conditions

Although numerology sounds like a strange religious belief, it is in fact the study of numbers. One of the more interesting facts about the study of numbers is that certain numbers don't work well together. This leads us to the concept of "boundary conditions" of numbers. It is much easier to simply show an example of what we are talking about rather than try to delve into the low-level math.

Consider the case of computing the area of a square. The formula, as most beginning math students could tell you, is:

```
Area = length x width
```

This means that to compute the area for a given rectangle (of which a square is simply a special case), you would take the length of one side and multiple it by the length of the side that is perpendicular to that side. Area has certain special properties; it must be a positive number. It doesn't make sense to have the area be negative. What would that mean, anyway? That the square takes up less room than the sides it contains? Of course not. The problem occurs, however, when we try to apply the real world to math. For example, consider a graph that contains the x, y pairs of points listed in Table 9.1.

Table 9.1 contains points on the negative side of the normal axes. If you were to compute the length of the sides, you would find that the "normal" calculation leaves you with a negative result for at least one side. This causes you to have an area that could be negative. We've already discussed the fact that this doesn't make any sense. What would you do with

Table 9.1   Sample x, y pairs.

X	Y
−1	−1
−3	−1
−1	−4
−3	−4

a negative area? Obviously, the "real" formula for the area of a rectangle when calculated by a computer program should be:

```
Area = abs(length) x abs(width)
```

In this case, the abs in the equation stands for the absolute value function, which always returns a positive (or zero) result. This will ensure that because you are multiplying two positive numbers, you will return a positive result.

How does something like this apply to debugging? Well, in several ways, actually. You need to understand the domains of the data you are working with. If you have a simple variable in a program that represents a traffic light, you would expect that the domain of that variable be the set of colors { red, yellow, green } for all normal traffic lights. If the value was, say, pink, what would that mean to the program logic? It would probably result in an error. When you are reading through program source code, make sure you understand the mathematical and logical domains of the data variables you are working with.

Boundary conditions are another important consideration when you are debugging an application. A boundary condition is one in which an "edge case" exists that causes the program not to work properly with a certain set of input. In a previous chapter, I discussed a project I once worked on, a satellite television receiver that stored program data on a hard drive. The process was as follows: The data came in from the satellite, was buffered into a memory cache of fixed size buffers, and then was written to disk. On the other side of the process, data was read from the disk, put into the cache of fixed sized buffers, and fed to the output device, normally a television set. Nearly all of the time, the system worked perfectly. Data would flow in, be stored on disk, and then be sent to the output. The television experience was uninterrupted. On some occasions, however, the experience would be interrupted by the blanking of the screen for a short period of time. Research showed that this blanking was caused by a lack of data flowing to the output side. The rate of data coming into the system was always nonzero, so data should have always been available to send to the output. What was happening?

After digging into the problem, I discovered that the boundary condition in this process was that the buffers on the input side were not committed to disk until such time as they were filled. The original designer had not considered the case where the output buffers would not be filled because of a lull in the input side. The specific condition was that a high rate of input would be followed by a very slow period of input. This would cause the output buffers to be full, but the input buffers would not be quite as full. The output process would empty the output buffers, but the input buffers would not be ready for writing out. This caused a momentary outage of the output process, which caused the short blank out.

The problem with both numerical issues and boundary conditions are that they are hard to detect in the code. To find them, you need to go back to the original requirements and algorithms to find out where the conditions might exist. Armed with the knowledge of what might cause a boundary condition in the code, you can then examine the actual source code in the system to see if that condition was handled properly. If not, you can then test for that particular condition in the source code and verify the hypothesis to see if the condition is being met. What you do from that point depends on the system and the level of severity of the problem. Quite often, the only true "solution" for a numerical error or boundary condition is to rearchitect and rewrite the system. However, this is not usually feasible due to budgeting and scheduling constraints. The optimal solution being eliminated, you will often find that you are forced to "hack" the code to handle the exceptional case. This certainly isn't the best way to repair problems, and you should be careful to document your "hack" so that eventually it can be resolved. With most boundary conditions, documenting the problem is the best first step toward solving it in the long run.

Modification type: Non-intrusive

Modification length: Long term

Appropriate levels: Any

Check Recent Changes

Imagine that you are working on an existing system. The system, which had been working perfectly in a regression test the day before, suddenly develops a problem in an area that is tested. Would you:

♦ Assume that the problem was there all along and see what might have caused the problem to occur?

♦ Assume that the test case is invalid and ignore the issue?

♦ Assume that something recently changed and broke the code so that the bug suddenly appeared?

If you chose the first answer, you are probably on the right track, but it will take a long time to get to the root of the issue. If you chose the second answer, chances are you should seek out a new profession as you are not long for the programming world. If you chose the third answer, you understand the root of this debugging technique. Changes, especially recent changes, are usually the root of problems that suddenly crop up in code that used to work fine. This probability approaches 100 percent when you ask the programmer about the change and receive an answer such as "But all I changed was...<x>, and that shouldn't have any effect."

Assuming that you have a change control system in place, it should not be difficult to track down the change that might have suddenly broken your system. If you do not have such a system in place, your job will be considerably harder. In that case, you might try the following:

♦ Look at time and date stamps for all files in the source tree, isolating the most recent ones for comparison.

♦ Run "diff" comparisons using a file comparison tool that shows you all of the differences between two versions of files you suspect to have problems.

♦ Ask all of the developers on the project which files they have recently changed.

As you can see, a system that automatically keeps track of the most recent changes and allows you to view some sort of report of those changes is much more useful than the manual version. If you do not already have such a system in place, seriously consider adding it to your processes.

One other consideration should be regarded for changes. Changes are not always made only to the source code for the system. If nothing in your source tree has changed and a problem suddenly occurs in the code, you might consider looking at environmental changes to the system that the application is running on. For this to work, you need to know what has changed in the environment. I seriously recommend that you track the current system environment (including the operating system version and all installed versions of applications) when you do an install of the system. If you have a tool to do this, you can then use the same tool to do a current measurement of the environment to see if anything has changed. Common causes of problems include network changes, operating system patches, new application versions of third-party tools, and changes to the hardware attached to the machine in question. By tracking all of this information in a log for the test machine, you can verify that it was a change to the system that caused your program to fail and thus get a head start on what might be affected.

If the problem occurs in something external to your system, this does not mean that the bug is not in the source code. It does mean, however, that the problem most likely has always been in the source code. In cases like this, you should return to the original steps of debugging the problem with the added knowledge of the variable change that caused the bug to surface.

Modification type: Non-intrusive

Modification length: Long term

Appropriate levels: Any

Clean Up "Dead Code" in the System

One of the most frustrating things when trying to debug a system is to be looking at a block of code trying to understand why it isn't working the way it should, only to find out that the code is never really called in the system at all. Consider the following block of C programming source code:

```c
for ( i = 0; i<10; ++i )
{
    DoSomething();
    if ( i == 8 )
```

```
#ifdef DEBUG
        DoDebugSomething();
#endif
#ifdef MIPS_CHIP
        DoMipsStuff();
#endif
#ifdef INTEL_CHIP
        DoIntelChipStuff();
#endif
}
```

Ignoring the fact that this is just plain ugly code, can you tell which block is executed at runtime? Probably not, especially if you aren't quite clear on what MIPS_CHIP, DEBUG, and INTEL_CHIP mean. They might be the processor type and the debugging mode, or perhaps they have nothing to do with those things at all. This code could contain a bug, or it might not contain a bug. It is very hard to tell, even if you know that the DoMipsStuff function contains several errors. Perhaps it is never called.

If you don't think the preceding code is confusing enough, take a look at this code (which is from a real system):

```
if ( theCell != nil ) {
long row = theCell->GetRow();
long col = theCell->GetColumn();

#if !defined(UPDATECHECKMARKUSESCRIPT)
ulong bitNum = (col * kTVChannelTableRowCount) + row;

if ( fMultiSelect )
{
if (fIsCheckedBits & (1U << bitNum))
fIsCheckedBits &= ~(1U << bitNum);
else
fIsCheckedBits |= (1U << bitNum);
}
else
{
if (fIsCheckedBits & (1U << bitNum))
fIsCheckedBits = 0;
else
fIsCheckedBits = (1U << bitNum);
}
#endif

theCell->SetDisabled( false );
theView->ExecuteSelectable( theCell );
theCell->SetDisabled( true );
```

```
#ifdef UPDATECHECKMARKUSESCRIPT
long channel = fChannelTable[row][col];
UpdateIsChecked(channel, col, row);
#endif
```

The code in question is trying to either set or clear a flag. You wouldn't know that from all the copious comments, but that's the basic intent. Note that there are two different blocks of code. One of them does all of the work inline. The other one calls a function that does the same thing. While trying to debug the code, I first spent a *lot* of time checking into the function case because I could not find the UPDATECHECKMARKUSESCRIPT symbol defined anywhere. It would later turn out to be included in a define file, which was included in the make file for the project. After saying the things you can imagine I would say under such circumstances, I fixed the problem in the inline code.

How do you fix a problem like this? The easiest way is to use a system such as the C preprocessor to produce a version of the code that shows only the code that really goes into the final system. This is also a case where walking through the code with a debugger on your workstation will show what is in the build version. This allows you to find and fix problems more easily. If the language you are using does not have an equivalent to the preprocessor, you will likely have to hand pre-process the code or write an application to solve the problem. Reduce the amount of code that you have to look at, and you will increase your chances of finding problems in the code.

Some of you might be thinking, "Yes, but I don't work in languages that have precompilers, so I don't have that problem." Sorry, but the same problem exists in many languages, whether or not it is enforced by the compiler. Consider the following Visual Basic snippet:

```
; Uncomment the correct value for your machine
const Machine=1         ; Intel
REM const Machine=2  ; MIPS
REM ;const Machine=3; // Alpha
If ( Machine = 1 ) THEN
BEGIN
   Do_Something
END IF
If ( Machine = 2 ) THEN
BEGIN
    Do_Something_For_Mips
END IF
IF ( Machine = 3 ) THEN
BEGIN
    Do_Something_For_Alpha
END IF
```

The same basic problem can occur with any language on any operating system. It simply happens more often with C and C++. This is due to the fact that the compiler allows direct conditional compilation and the fact that C programmers often use the #ifdef mechanism in place of commenting out a section of code. That is:

```
#if 0
// Some code to comment out
#endif
```

is functionally equivalent to:

```
// Some code to comment out
/* Code */
```

Modification type: Non-intrusive

Modification length: Long term

Appropriate levels: Any

Question Assumptions

One of the reasons that programmers find such difficulty in testing their own code is that they have a tendency to stick with the basic assumptions made during the development phase. When you are debugging code, especially code that you have written, you need to discard those assumptions in order to make sure that you find the real problem. Assumptions can be simple things, such as "this block of code is called in response to that if statement." Assumptions can also be complex things, such as "the highest rate of data input into the system will be <x> bytes per hour." If your assumptions are incorrect, all of the code based on those assumptions will be incorrect. This leads to bugs in the system.

How can we avoid making assumptions when debugging existing code? The answer is that you must employ ego-less programming. Even if you think you know exactly how a given subsystem, module, or function works, you must verify that it does what you think it does. Never simply take for granted any piece of the code. Consider, for example, the following piece of Delphi code:

```
X := 1;
Y := 2;
PrintOutXAndY();
X := X + 3;
Y := Y + 4;
```

If you are a Delphi programmer, you will likely look at this block of code and assume that following the last line of the displayed code the result for X will be 4, and the result for Y will be 6. After all, the **PrintOutXAndY** function is unlikely to change those values, isn't it? This is an assumption, and quite possibly a bad one. Imagine, for example, if the **PrintOutXAndY** function looked like this:

```
Function PrintOutXAndY() : Integer
Begin
    X := X + 1; (* Adjust for offset in file *)
    Y := Y - 1; (* Adjust for line count *)
    PrintLn X;
    PrintLn Y;
End;
```

In this case, it is quite obvious that X and Y will not remain the same following the function. They are somehow adjusted in the function for some extraneous reason. It's hard to say why a programmer would change the values of systemwide variables in a function, but such side effects aren't as uncommon as you might think. Never assume anything while you are debugging until you have proven it to yourself conclusively first. Once you have stepped through a routine and have verified in your mind that the function or method does not have an effect on the data you are looking at, you can then safely ignore it.

Another case where an assumption can get you in trouble is when you use the "that can't be causing the problem" assumption. Consider, for example, the following snippet of C code:

```
int vars[MaxVars];
char theString[20];
GetFormTitle( FormID, theString );
for ( int I=0; I<MaxVars+1; ++I )
    vars[I] = 2 << I;
Form.Title = theString;
```

The bug we are searching for in this code is why the form title is always blank. The **GetFormTitle** method appears to set the variable correctly, but it never displays on the screen. If you were making assumptions, you might first assume that the form title is not stored properly in whatever database it comes from. Alternatively, you might assume that if the form title is loaded properly, something later in the code is wiping it out. After all, there is nothing in this portion of the code that could be doing it, is there?

These are assumptions in action. In fact, the GetFormTitle routine is returning the right value. The assumption is that because we do not modify the string in the code following that retrieval, it must be correct. If this were a standalone application and you were in the debugger, you could test this assumption easily enough. Add the variable **theString** to the watch list for your program. Step through the code. I'm pretty sure you will see the variable change at some point. Why? Well, that's a bit more complicated. But the code shown really does contain all of the information you need to solve the problem.

Still lost? Okay, it does take a little bit of explanation and a bit of C programming knowledge. Notice that the **vars** array is defined to be a constant size (**MaxVars**). Also notice that the loop goes through **MaxVars** times. In C, an array runs from the index of 0 to the index of the array size −1. This means that the last time through, the loop is pointing at a memory location after the array size. In the case of the 'C' language, that would be the next defined variable (normally, your compiler may vary), which is **theString**. That means that once we step on the memory address of **theString**, we wipe out what is in that address. As a result, when you assign **theString** to the form title, it is already messed up. The only way you are going to find a problem like this is to step through the code line by line, examining all of the variables in question. If you assume that a block of code cannot change a particular variable, you will be lost before you start.

Modification type: Non-intrusive

Modification length: Short term/Long term

Appropriate levels: Any

Look at Untested Code

In any large-scale codebase, there will be areas of the code that were never tested. These areas might not have test drivers, or perhaps the code itself is simply never exercised in a test case within the overall test plan. Sections of untested code are usually the ones that cause the most problems because nobody has really beaten on them to determine if there are any problems. Good examples of untested code are features that are not exposed to the end user by the layers above that code.

Imagine, for example, that you are looking at a library of functions that were used to implement a given feature in your application. The developer of the library, wanting to provide as complete a package as possible, adds a bunch of functionality that will not be used in the first release. This code is then used in the next release to implement the features the original developer had wisely anticipated. When the next release is tested, however, the new features have several bugs that cannot easily be traced to the new code added to the system.

In cases like this, where the problem appears to be in a new function in the system, you might normally assume that you had introduced the problem in the new code that you added. This correlates to the "look at recent changes" technique. However, this is not always the case. In this example, the problem was already in the code and had been for a long time. Nevertheless, that particular bit of code had never been tested. If you could simply "know" that the code had never been tested, you would be able to pinpoint the place to start looking for the problem. The question is, of course, how you know what has been tested and what has not.

There are a variety of ways to accomplish this. The first, and hardest, way is to look at all of the test cases and determine by hand which branches of code, which functions, and which subsystems have been tested and which have not. This is certainly a worthwhile endeavor, but I wouldn't be tempted to do it myself. I would prefer if someone else did all of that grunt work. As a result, I would take the test drivers for the system and apply a code coverage tool to see what is and what is not used. If you do not have test drivers for your subsystem, another tool that can be applied is a cross-index tool. This sort of tool shows you what functions are called by what areas of the code. If you see a section in the previous release that is not used, but is used in this release, you can start your detective work from that point upward.

Use code coverage and cross-index tools to determine what is being used.

One of the issues that this particular technique brings up is how little we usually understand about what is being used in our code. Although the tools to determine this information have been around for a long time, they are rarely used for detective work. Instead, code-analyzing tools, such as cross-indexers, are used to determine "dead code" that can be safely removed from a system. Another way that such tools are used is to determine the most heavily used areas of our systems so that we can better optimize them. Although both of these are worthy goals, these tools are rarely used for true debugging, which is what occupies the majority of our time. If you are more proactive in your debugging efforts, you will find that your reward is a better system that requires less time to fix problems.

Modification type: Non-intrusive

Modification length: Short term/Long term

Appropriate levels: Any

Invariants

An invariant is a state of the system that must be true at all times. Put simply, the invariants are laws under which an application runs. Error conditions result when problems that can be handled by the application code are not handled properly. Crashes and corruption occur when invariants are violated.

Examples of invariants in all systems include available memory to load the program, available disk space to save the program state, and working hardware to enter values into the system and modify them. Such things simply must be working in order for your program to work at the outset. However, other invariants might exist within a given type of system. A good example of this is an accounting system. In accounting, it is absolutely required that the total system balance at all times. That is, the total number of debits plus the total number of credits must equal the balance of the account at all times. Another way of saying this is that, for an accountant, assets must be equal to liabilities. If this condition is violated, the system is no longer valid, and a serious error will occur.

Invariants can be technical requirements of the system, such as the availability of a hardware device such as a "dongle" attached to the computer. Invariants can also be business rules, such as the fact that to get to a given feature a user must be logged into the system. Additionally, invariants can be things that the program relies on to continue, so they must be present and true. Consider, for example, the case of an interactive television listing system. This system permits you to search the channels for actors, actresses, titles, and the like. This system requires, of course, that you have some sort of data for the listings so that you can do the searching. The availability of the listing information, therefore, is an invariant of the system.

Now that you understand what an invariant is, how can you take advantage of this knowledge to use it in your debugging effort? Once we recognize that the failure of an invariant to remain true results in a serious problem in the application, the best thing to do is to become proactive and make sure that the invariants remain invariant. To do this, you should collect all of the data points you know must be true in the system and put them in a single diagnostic routine. This routine can be called from a "safe" place in the code. *Safe places* are areas of the code that are called regularly, but will not impact any production level operations. Note that if you place such a function into a production level system, it is imperative that you handle the errors gracefully and not simply exit the application.

One possibility for handling the error is to notify the administrator (in the case of a client/server application) or the user (for standalone applications) that something very bad has happened and that they should shut down the application or fix the problem immediately. How the problem should be handled is dependent on whether the invariant can be fixed or not. If a file was supposed to be on the system and it is not, this can be fixed. If a "magic cookie" in a structure is supposed to contain a specific value (such as a checksum) and it does not, it probably cannot be fixed by the user. Your mileage may vary, but you should err on the side of caution.

In the debugging process, invariants are a good way to detect a serious problem in the system. If you can discover that an invariant is being changed, you can then backtrack through the system and discover what is making that change. Knowing what the underlying cause of the problem is can be the first step toward finding the root cause of the change and fixing the problem correctly.

Modification type: Non-intrusive

Modification length: Short term/Long term

Appropriate levels: Any

Memory Usage

When you are debugging a system that fails in odd and inconsistent ways, the two most likely causes of the problem are stray pointers and memory leaks. Of the two, memory leaks are much easier to detect because the total amount of memory available to the system will continuously drop with no corresponding bounce when the memory should be freed. Although detecting a stray pointer is a rather difficult job, detecting a memory leak is fairly easy and straightforward.

If you keep track of the total memory used in the system, you can easily identify a memory leak. From that point on, finding the location of the actual leak is sometimes more difficult. To do that, you need to know when memory is allocated and deallocated. There are several ways to do this, depending on the language, compiler, and operating system you are working with. In most cases, it is not necessary for you to do any extra work. The allocation/ deallocation routines in the standard libraries of either the language or the operating system can be changed to "point at" debug versions of these routines.

One last "trick" to debugging with memory is to keep a hidden way to monitor the total amount of memory allocated (or alternately the total amount of system memory free) while your program is running. A special diagnostic key combination might display a special window with the value while the system is running. Perhaps you could write the amount of free memory into a program log at predetermined intervals to make sure it is remaining where you expect it to.

Remember, however, that a program that "eats" memory does not always contain a memory leak. Sometimes, the loss of memory in a system is caused by a design flaw. Imagine, for example, that you allocate a small bit of memory to keep track of each keystroke that the user enters in the system to be able to log it or undo those commands. Without putting an upper cap on the number of items you keep in the user list, you might eventually run out of memory in the system. There is no memory leak in this instance; you are never intending on freeing the memory in the first place. In cases like these, a memory snapshot with a dump of what routine allocated each memory block is the best way to find and fix design flaws such as these.

As mentioned previously in the book, do not think that simply because you use a language that does not directly allocate memory, such as Visual Basic, or a language that does its own garbage collection, such as Java, you are free from memory allocation concerns. Even these languages have methods whereby you can "leak" memory. In addition, any language that allows any sort of memory allocation can fall victim to the infinite memory allocation design problem.

Modification type: Non-intrusive

Modification length: Short term/Long term

Appropriate levels: Any

Mutex

The word *mutex* is an abbreviated form of "Mutually Exclusive." It represents an object that is a turnkey in a system. Although one entity owns a mutex, all others waiting for the right to access the mutex must wait until the owning entity is finished. Mutexes are extremely useful programming constructs, especially in a multithreaded environment. So what does this have to do with software debugging?

When you are debugging a multiuser or multithreaded environment, you will often find that the problem is not easily reproducible due to the fact that some code will work fine unless it is accessed at the same time by two different places. For example, consider the following piece of code written in C:

```c
int func()
{
    static int index = 0;
    extern char gGlobalArray[ 100 ];

    for ( int i=index; i<100; ++i )
    {
        call_a_function( gGlobalArray[i] );
    }
    index ++;
}
```

This particular function suffers from a number of problems. Let's look at two of the more egregious ones. First, it uses an external global array. Second, it contains a static variable. If you don't program in C, a *static variable* is one that retains its value from call to call within the function. Normally, however, these are not horrible errors. If the function is called multiple times from multiple places, the internal static counter is incremented. There are times, however, when the function might suffer from multiple reentrancy issues. *Reentrancy* is the condition whereby another thread or routine calls into a function before the last call to that function has finished processing. This generally isn't a problem because a copy of the local variables will be made for the second calling thread on its own heap space. A static variable exists in the global heap and cannot be copied. Likewise, the global array in this function lives outside of the program space of this function. So, when the second call to the function occurs, bad things can happen because two pieces of code in two different threads of the program are accessing the same piece of memory at the same time. At best, you will occasionally end up with incorrect values. At worse, you might get a program crash due to a memory error. If you are curious, this particular snippet, while modified, comes from a real production system.

A mutex can help identify these types of situations. Depending on your programming language and operating system, mutexes may be implemented at the system level. In other environments, they may be programmed within the compiler library. In any case, consider what would happen if we suspected that the problem in the preceding function was due to multiple threads accessing the function at the same time. We could add a mutex object to the function. This mutex would then screen out any calls that came in while the first call was still operant. As a result, the program would run ever so slightly slower, but would never run into crash conditions.

Mutexes can be fixes to problems, or they can identify that a problem exists. The actual solution is often up to you, the software engineer. If you can live with a function being single-threaded in a multithreaded environment, then a mutex is the right debugging technique to use to find locations that have this problem as well as the right solution to the problem.

Modification type: Intrusive

Modification length: Short term/Long term

Appropriate levels: Multithreaded production systems

Visualize the System Running

One very good technique for tying together the source code for a system with the bug reports you are given is to visualize how the system will be running while looking through the source code. Conversely, you can also visualize what the source code is doing while you are watching the system run. In either case, you will be able envision the "big picture" of how the system works. As we have emphasized throughout this book, you cannot adequately debug a system without having firsthand knowledge of what it is doing and what it is supposed to be doing.

How do you go about visualizing a running system from the source code? To do this, you need to be able to first map the high-level subsystems of the source code to the feature level functionality of the running application. This mapping allows you to "see" the individual components that are called when each feature is invoked by the user. Let's consider two simple examples to show you how it might be done in your own application.

Let's first look at a standalone application that runs on the user's box. When the user selects File | Open from the main menu, the program calls the menu handler to find the proper function to call in response to this menu item. That menu handler then displays a File | Open dialog, which allows the user to select a file to be loaded. The routine that actually does the physical opening of the file and loading of the information in the file is then called. For argument's sake, let's say that the routine performs the following steps:

1. Physically open the file.

2. Load the header block from the file and verify that it is correct for this version of the program.

3. If the header block is not correct, display an error and stop.

4. If the header block is correct, load the individual components from the file into memory and create a new display for them.

This is the sort of sequence you need to be thinking about when you are watching the system "open a file." It is important that you do so for a number of reasons. First, you will have a good idea where the problem might be when the system does not work properly for a given case. Second, you will know what is supposed to happen next, so that you can be aware of problems before they culminate in a symptom, such as a program crash. Third, by knowing what the system is trying to do, you can get a good idea of what sorts of things it might encounter and have problems doing. In the preceding example, to name but one, we might see the program crash when we tried to open a file that was not of the correct format. In all likelihood, knowing the stages the system goes through, that problem might occur in either step 2 or potentially in step 3 if step 2 incorrectly identified the file as valid.

The alternative approach is to visualize what the program is displaying when you are stepping through the source code. For example, you might notice that in the source code, after physically opening a file, the status bar is supposed to be updated with a message telling the user that the file is being loaded. Next, you can recall the system displaying a "wait cursor," and then the file contents being displayed on the screen. Knowing this sequence of events, you could then look to see what was going on between the time the contents of the file was displayed and the time the wait cursor was put up for the user. This permits you to identify all of the steps in the code that are being executed. If, for example, you notice that the program crashes at a given point, you can associate that with the code you observed at each step.

Understanding the relationship between the state of the running system and the internal state of the source code is critical in finding and fixing problems in the code. You can't fix an error, even if you know exactly what is happening, unless you can track down where in the code it is happening. Likewise, you cannot verify that a change to the source code will fix a problem unless you know exactly how to get to the source line that you changed.

Modification type: Non-intrusive

Modification length: Long term

Appropriate levels: Any

Compare the Code with a System That Is Known to Work

One of the most common problems when making changes to source code is to have the program mysteriously stop working or suddenly develop odd behavior. If you have just added or modified source code in the system, that code is the most likely target for your investigation (see the "Check Recent Changes" section). However, sometimes it is completely unclear as to why the changes you made might have affected the program as a whole. In cases like this, it is often beneficial to compare the code to a system that is similar and is working properly. This might mean comparing the system to a previous stable version of the code, or it might mean comparing the source code for a function to another implementation of the same algorithm that is working properly.

Imagine, for example, that you have decided to reimplement a given subsystem in the code to optimize it and clean up the overall source tree for that subsystem. When you have finished implementing the code, you discover that it appears to work properly except in certain cases. In this case, you already have a version of the source code that works, and you know that the case in question worked fine before you started modifying that subsystem.

Given that the previous version worked, you could step through the code that implements that version and see what it is doing in that previous version. You might discover, for example, that there was a "special case" handler for that particular situation. Perhaps you might find an edge case that doesn't work with the algorithm you have selected to implement or that your implementation was done incorrectly for the type of input that can occur. In either case, you should reexamine your source code to see how it should be fixed, so that it works in the same manner as it did previously.

Another possibility is that the existing source code implementation has certain side effects that you did not take into account. This can often happen in code that has been around for some time, as the "spaghetti effect" finds its way into what had been clearly delineated modules. Software debuggers find that the "clean" edges between modules may require some "tweaks" to handle certain events that the original developer either did not take into account or couldn't design because the other features weren't present at the time. A system that had been originally designed with extremely low coupling between modules becomes a rat's nest of interlinked modules. This effect, known as *software entropy*, is often the leading reason why systems are rewritten. [2]

If you have an existing implementation of an algorithm or subsystem to compare your code to, you can usually determine what the problem is. Fixing the problem, on the other hand, requires that you not only understand the algorithm you are implementing, but how that piece of code fits into the system as a whole. Consider the following factors when a new algorithm does not work:

◆ Edge cases caught in the existing code

◆ Coupling between the existing code and other modules

◆ Differing input or output variable types

◆ Differing return types for functions

◆ Static variables or other state holders in the existing code

Modification type: Non-intrusive

Modification length: Long term

Appropriate levels: Any

Understand the Algorithms

Most software systems implement some sort of algorithms in the source code for the system. Often, these are "industry standard" algorithms for the industry that the software is written

---

[2] Cunningham, Ward, Andrew Hunt, and David Thomas. *The Pragmatic Programmer: From Journeyman to Master.* AddisonWesley, Reading, MA, 1999. ISBN: 020161622X

for. If you do not understand the algorithm that the software is implementing, it is rather difficult to debug that code.

Let's consider, for example, the algorithm that is used to calculate real sales tax for applications in the point-of-sale industry. If you are like me, the first time you run across it, you are hopelessly confused. Sales tax, you see, isn't a rate at all. It's a series of "buckets" that need to be filled. Each bucket has a lower bound (the starting number of pennies for that bucket) and an upper bound (the ending number of pennies for that bucket). Basically, it works like this:

1. Compute the number of whole dollars for the sale, and apply the total rate for a dollar to that value.

2. For a partial dollar, add each amount in the bucket that has a starting value less than the number of remaining pennies and an ending value greater than the number of remaining pennies in the total.

3. Add the totals. This is the sales tax.

I suppose this could be more confusing, but I'm really not sure how. This is how it works in the real world: The people in the county that assign sales tax rates establish "levels" of the tax rate for each number of pennies they choose. This means that you can have a sales tax rate of 8 percent and charge 5 cents for amounts of 50 cents and above. This certainly isn't very clear, but it is the way it works in many counties. In other counties, the rate is flat, meaning that you simply take the amount of the sale, multiply it by the rate, and then either round up or down to get a whole number of pennies.

If you understand the algorithm that is applied in this example, the numbers that result when you calculate sales tax for a county make sense. If you do not understand it, you will think a bug exists when in fact there is no problem. Worse, you might think that no problem exists when there is a serious problem involved. Algorithms usually implement some form of the business logic for the application. Although the source code might be right or wrong, the business logic must be right for the application to succeed. Imagine, for example, if you found out that all of the point-of-sale devices that you programmed, which were being used in the world, were charging too much tax! You would not be popular in the retail world. Furthermore, you'd likely be liable for a rather serious tax penalty when the governing agencies found out about your software.

When you encounter an algorithm in your system, it is in your best interest to document it and verify it with an outside source (such as the business analyst at the company). Additionally, if you put an algorithm into your application from an outside source (such as a sorting or searching algorithm from a book), it is best to not only document how the algorithm works, but also provide a "link" to the source of the technique. This allows someone coming into the project from the outside world to be able to read the original documentation and discover whether there are any known problems with it outside of the company.

Modification type: Non-intrusive

Modification length: Long term

Appropriate levels: Any

Check Connectivity

Although connectivity might seem like the most obvious of problems, many client/server type bugs are caused by a drop in connectivity between either the client and server or between the server and a back-end service, such as a database. Obviously, this is something that ought to be tested before the system ships, but it is also something that often breaks and is not verified. Programmers quite often have the attitude that programs will work properly, and that there is no reason to check for something like the availability of a database. Connectivity errors are quite common and should be on your checklist to verify before you attempt to dig into the code.

Think about the following scenario and, in your mind, try to decide what might be causing the symptoms displayed. In a Web server, one of a group of such servers, users will at times be denied access and given the error message "User Name or Password is Incorrect, Please Try Again." No matter what user name or password is entered, the result is the same. This is your bug report. Oddly, when the machine is rebooted, the error disappears. This is your symptom.

This information doesn't seem like a lot to go on, now does it? Looking at the code for the Web server, we see that it follows the following pseudocode (the actual code is not used because the Web server code is simply too ugly and complex):

```
On Error GOTO HandleUserError
Extract User Name from HTML edit box
Extract Password from HTML edit box
Connect to UserDatabase
Check User Name in UserDatabase; Note that error will go to HandleUserError for
record not found
    Check Password in Record returned
    If Password <> Record.Password goto Bad User
    Go to Login Successful Page
HandleUserError:
    Display "User Name or Password is Incorrect, Please Try Again"
    End
Bad User:
    Display "Password does not match, please try again"
    End
```

In the preceding pseudocode, we can see that the reason the user sees the displayed message appears (from the comments) to be because the user name was not found in the database. This generates some sort of "Record Not Found" error and jumps to the error handler. The record is obviously not found, right? There could be a lot of reasons for this. For example, perhaps we store the user name in uppercase. Or maybe we strip out blanks in the INSERT statement. We could be working in some other language set, or there could be a trailing space at the end of the record. There are hundreds of possibilities.

If I was debugging this error, I'd first move the error handling, and I'd print out exactly what the error was. For example, in the step where the program connects to the database, I'd jump to a different error handler. And, lo and behold, I bet the problem would be the fact that the machine has lost its connection to the database. This is certainly just as serious an error as any of the others mentioned, but it's quite different from them as well. At this point in the debugging process, I would start looking into permission problems, network errors, and the like instead of areas such as case conversion errors or padding problems.

Connectivity errors are probably responsible for more client/server bugs than all other errors combined. Checking them at the point at which they occur will save you huge amounts of time and grief in tracking down odd problems that are hard to reproduce.

Modification type: Non-intrusive

Modification length: Long term

Appropriate levels: Client/server, Production

Core Files

In most modern operating systems, a program that crashes leaves behind a "dump file" that contains state information about the program at the point it crashed. In the Unix operating system, these files are called "core dumps." In Windows, they are usually in some form of a Dr. Watson file. In any case, they contain information that can aid you in tracing down the cause of the program crash. When you get a core dump or a Dr. Watson crash, you should hold onto these files for later examination.

One nice feature that I found in my days of working with an embedded system was that core files could be produced within the system via the internal debugger, and then uploaded to the main site of the company for inspection. Information in these core files would include items such as the function that caused the crash, what sort of crash it was (bad stack frame, null pointer assignment, and the like), and what the program state was at the time of the crash. Although these files could be a bit much to dig through and examine, they could be crucial for tracking down certain of the more "odd" problems that the system would encounter.

In your own applications, you can create the equivalent of core files. Consider the following piece of simple C code:

```c
char *x = (char *)malloc( someSize );
if ( x == null )
    assert( "Memory Allocation Error!");
```

Leaving aside my feeling toward asserts, which should be well known by this point, this code really doesn't do any good at all. If a memory allocation error happens, all you get is a simple diagnostic display telling you that fact and a program termination. What you will not get is the state of the function that was being called, nor will you know what sort of memory size the program was trying to allocate. Imagine, instead, if the program displayed something like the following:

```
Memory Allocation Error in function foo File: Bar.c Line: 200
Input: FileName="fred.dat" someSize=-3
Global Variables:
<gX=1>
<gY=2>
…
```

and so forth.

I'm sure you can see how much more useful such a display would be instead of something like "Memory Allocation Error in bar.c Line 200. Program Terminated." In the first case, you might think that your program is running out of memory and start looking for memory leaks. In fact, looking at the secondary output, we can see that the program wasn't running out of memory at all. Instead, we were trying to allocate a negative amount of memory. The standard library function **malloc** returns NULL if you try to do this. Thus, the result is a memory allocation error.

To implement a diagnostic like this, you need to maintain a "debug" object that resides in each function. This debug object should contain the state of that function. It should also contain the inputs to the function, the calling context for the function, and what might have gone wrong from the program's perspective. These global objects are pushed onto the global "debug stack" when the function starts and popped off the stack when the function ends. This allows you to pinpoint exactly what went wrong. The whole function can be triggered by a call similar to an assert, but that prints out the stack, much as a Java application would in the case of an unhandled exception.

Seriously consider implementing something like this in your own application. Generating your own core files can be an extremely useful sister function to using the core dump files generated by the operating system.

Modification type: Intrusive/Non-intrusive (depending on whether you implement your own)

Modification length: Long term

Appropriate levels: Any

Add Tracing

We have discussed tracing extensively throughout the book, but if you are only reading the techniques section or are referring back to this section, it is worth repeating the concept. Tracing gives you the ability to track through the flow of a program from the program source code point of view. As each function is called, a trace is generated designating the function called and, potentially, the input to the function at that point. A trace display might look something like this:

Start User Feature x

Function 1 (Input x=1, y =2, z=3)

Function 2 (Input z=4, a=5, b=6)

Function 3 (No input)

End User Feature x

By seeing the trace display, you would know that when you tried to invoke the user feature <x> from the user's perspective, the internals of the system called Functions 1, 2, and 3. This allows you to learn a lot about how the system works internally. Combined with the visualization of the system running technique, you can learn a lot about how a system works, especially if you have not worked on the project previously. Tracing is also valuable for people that have worked on the system from its infancy. It allows you to see what is really going on rather than what you think is going on. This allows you to capture bad program flows and see why things happen the way they do when you believe that the outcome should be different.

Because tracing is discussed extensively in other chapters, we will not belabor the point in this chapter. The only point worth making is that tracing works poorly in real-time systems without extensive work. In addition, in embedded systems, tracing is often problematic as it requires somewhere to put the data.

Modification type: Intrusive

Modification length: Long term

Appropriate levels: Any

Data Dependency Checking

There are three cases where your program can be considered data dependent. First, there is the case where the code requires that some data exist to work properly. Examples of this include needed configuration files and data relationships that need to exist in a database, such as category information loaded by the program. Second, there is the case of data dependency where certain types of data break the system. This would be the type of data that is not expected by the program or data and is outside the legal boundaries for a given input.

For example, your program might expect the user to enter a value between 1 and 5. If the user enters a number, such as 8, or enters a nonnumeric entry, such as A, the program might break. In this case, the problem is dependent on the data being incorrect. The third case of data dependency is where you expect a specific rate of data or amount of data. In the example from the previous chapter where there was a lull in data to a satellite television system, we expected a certain rate of data input.

How do you determine whether or not your program is data dependent and in what way? You should first study all of the configuration files that ship with the system. You can consider a configuration file to be anything that isn't a form of executable file in the installation system. Make a careful list of these files, and look through the source tree to see where they are referenced. You will often find that the programmers who wrote the original system rely on the existence of these files and do not provide adequate defaults for anything that was read from the files. One easy way to test this is to rename one of the files and try running the program. If the program crashes in the spot you suspect the bug to be, you can then trace it back to the configuration file data dependency.

The second form of data dependency, which is really finding exceptions to the algorithm you are using, is best found by studying the algorithm and looking at the types of input allowed for it. This might be documented in the algorithm itself, or it might be something you need to discover. Consider the following equation:

Ratio = (Total – Used) / Total

This formula is fairly simple. It has two factors: Total and Used. They are used to compute the ratio. Given this simple formula, what sorts of data will cause a problem? Obviously, if Total is 0, the formula breaks and divides by 0. Are there other cases that could cause a problem? There are no obvious ones, although the case where Used = Total could be a problem. This would result in a ratio of 0. Although this might be fine, and acceptable in the general program, we don't know how this ratio is used. Perhaps it is used in a calculation of its own, such as:

Calc = Cost / Ratio

Obviously, if Ratio in this case is 0, you get the same division by 0 problem. Now, consider the following equation:

Calc = Cost / (Total – Ratio)*100

If Total = Ratio, the problem is obvious and will break the system. However, remember that Total is a factor in computing Ratio to begin with. You might think, therefore, that there is no way that Total could ever be equal to Ratio. Mathematically, there are an infinite number of ways this could happen, but the easiest is the case where Total = 1 and Used = 0. In this case, we get:

Ratio = (1 – 0)/ 1

The result of this computation is 1. Because Total and Ratio are the same, the Calc computation crashes with a division-by-0 error. Any computation that contains a potential data dependency needs to be checked for in your code. If you have a division, for example, you need to check for the divisor being 0. If you have a multiplication that needs to result in a whole integer, you need to check for negative results. Going through the code and looking for problems like this will save you a lot of time in the long run.

Modification type: Non-intrusive

Modification length: Long term

Appropriate levels: Any

Playback Capability (Recording Actions)

Adding the ability to record actions and play them back is a technique that will help you immensely in tracking down problems and reproducing them. If your system does not already have macro capability (the ability to save and replay keystrokes and actions), you should seriously consider adding it for your own sanity.

What does macro capability buy you from the perspective of debugging? It allows you to keep track of what you are doing. It also allows you to turn it on for a tester, keep track of what they do, and then examine the log of actions in the macro to see what they were doing when the system broke. This is a huge boon for the developer. It no longer requires that you, as the debugger, watch over someone's shoulder to see what they are doing, or that the tester write down each and every step he takes to see what might have caused the problem. Testers should be screaming for macro capability in all systems, but they generally don't. Show them what they are missing, and they will be your friends for life.

Once you have a solidly reproducible case, the macro recording also allows you to define a set of keystrokes that will generate that test case. You can then ignore the actual workings of the program and concentrate on the hypothesis you are trying to find or verify. This assumes, of course, that you already have the reproducible case. If you do not, you still need to go through all the work of figuring out what set of commands causes the problem. In addition, if you have an editable macro, you can modify the parameters to each of the commands. Imagine, for example, if you have a macro that opened a file and searched for a string. You could change only the macro itself to search for different strings and observe what happens internally within the program. All of the other steps in the process would remain the same.

For all of these reasons, you should consider adding macro capability to the system. Even if you do not allow the external user access to it, it will aid you in your debugging efforts. How complicated does the system need to be? In actuality, it doesn't need to be complex at all. You can accomplish similar functionality with many testing programs that "send" keystrokes to a program. Beginning with the simple ability to turn on recording, you will at least reap the benefit of seeing what the user is doing at each step of the program. For client/server or Web-based applications, this simple ability can be crucial in finding out why problems occur.

How can you even begin to track down what could be wrong with a user's system remotely if you can't see what he or she is doing?

Modification type: Intrusive

Modification length: Long term

Appropriate levels: Any

Production System Mirrors

An ideal software development system for client/server applications consists of four separate complete systems. First, you have the development system that allows debugging of applications using the tools that developers are accustomed to using. Second, you have the standard QA system that allows testers to test new development efforts in a controlled, clean environment. The third system is, of course, your production system, which allows end users access to the system. This is the system that has to be available, no matter what. The fourth system, however, is a mirror of the production system, which allows the developer to debug the system with real data and real software. It does not contain the debugging tools or other changes that a development system contains. Instead, it has a copy of the production system that can be played with. You can put new software on this system without the blessing of QA. You can modify the software to print out variables or other trace information at runtime without worrying about the user experience. In addition, you can take the system down at any time without worrying about affecting anyone except the other developers debugging the system.

If your company does not already have a production system mirror that is dedicated to developer use, you should seriously consider having one. It is not essential that this system exactly mirror the production system. If money is tight, you could go with a stripped down version of the system. For example, if your production system contains 20 servers and 5 back-end databases, you could get away with having, say, 4 servers and 3 back-end database machines, as long as the proportions are reasonable. What you cannot do is to have a single server or back-end database machine. This would not duplicate the flow of the real system.

One advantage you can promote for creating such a system in your own company if management is averse to the idea is to note that such a system can also serve as an emergency backup system in case the actual production system crashes. In addition, it can be used to test new concepts during slack times in development. You might completely change the look and feel of the application using such a system. You could also test new theories on how to improve system performance. Keep in mind that debugging tools aren't always just for debugging. Sometimes they can be used for long-term improvements to the system as a whole.

Modification type: Non-intrusive

Modification length: Long term

Appropriate levels: Client/server or Web applications

Summary

Debuggers have developed numerous techniques over several decades. By reading through the techniques that others have used and understanding how those techniques work, you can become a better debugger. That being said, keep in mind that there is no case in the debugging world where one size fits all, and no single technique works all of the time. Depending on the circumstances and the environment, different techniques will have different outcomes. By understanding the situations that others have encountered the techniques that they have used and why those techniques fit their respective environments, you can better prepare yourself to different bug types.

Bug Puzzle

A Web server login page has three requirements. First, verify the user name and the password of the person trying to log in to the system. Second, make sure that the user is only logged in from one place. Third, make sure that the total number of people logged into the system never exceeds a maximum count. The pseudocode for the system looks something like this:

```
Increment Number of Users by One
See if Too Many Users
If Too Many Users
    Exit Login
End If
Check User Name in Database
If User Name Not Found
    Tell User Bad User Name
    Exit Login
End If
Check Password in Database for User Name
If Password Doesn't Match
    Tell User Bad Password
    Exit Login
End If
See if User is already logging in
If User Already Logged in
    Tell User Only One Login Per Account
    Exit Login
End If
Add User To Login List
Exit Login
```

The pseudocode shown has one fatal flaw and two security risks that could easily turn into bugs later on. What are they?

Chapter 10

Debugging Different Application Types

Matt Telles

I f there is one fact that experienced software engineers know about debugging, it is that one size definitely does not fit all. The approach you might take to a 10-line console application is quite different than the approach you take to a 10,000,000-line system that runs the space shuttle. Not only is the approach different, but the techniques that you use to approach problems are different as well. With the space shuttle application, you would likely spend the vast majority of your time simply figuring out where the program starts and what the general flow of the application is. With the console application, on the other hand, you can almost determine the entire scope of the project, including everything that it does, in one quick glance.

When you debug large-scale applications on a production server, you need to take a very different approach than if you were debugging small-scale standalone applications on your development workstation. In this chapter, we examine the kinds of things you can do to make your life easier when tackling problems of varying size, including the ability to scale down a problem until you can use the technique of your choice. You'll learn what not to do on a production Web server as well as what you shouldn't do with a simple utility application. It is quite often the first steps we take that determine whether or not we successfully solve a debugging problem. With different application types, that first step can make the difference between a disaster and a hero's welcome.

In this chapter, we start by debugging small-scale standalone applications, which are entirely self-contained, and advance to debugging large-scale client/server applications, which might not only use third-party libraries and components, but also middleware, heterogeneous environments and operating systems, and real-time systems. In addition, we take a look at debugging embedded systems, Web-based systems, and simulated systems running on another operating system.

Up to this point, we have treated debugging as a general science. We've stepped through famous cases of bugs. We've looked at all kinds of bugs and techniques used across the debugging spectrum. At this point, however, it is important to not only look at how these techniques apply to different scales of applications, but also to look at some of the tips garnered from years of doing debugging work.

Small-Scale Standalone Applications

When we say something is a "small" scale application, we aren't referring to the number of lines of code or the amount of memory required to run it. Instead, we mean applications that are created by small teams of between one and six developers working on a project of fairly short duration (say, under one year). Applications such as these tend to have small enough codebases to be completely understood by a single developer. In addition, small-scale standalone applications have the benefit of running in a self-contained unit. This doesn't mean that they don't interface with external systems, such as the Internet or a database system, it means that the application itself is a single program.

The majority of developers debug this type of program in the first few years of their careers. Standalone applications are used for such varied purposes as shrink-wrapped software and internal applications for corporations. In general, a standalone application is one that can run on a single machine, even if it accesses information on other machines. There is no client/server relationship and no interprocess communication in such applications.

Be a User of the System

If you really want to understand and be able to debug a system, you need to use that system as a "regular" user. This means using the system as it was intended to be used by the end user, not as a debugger or software engineer. Using a system is the best way to understand how to get from one area to another, as well as to understand what should happen when the system is running correctly.

There are really two reasons why you should consider using your system regularly. First, you will have a much better idea of how things are supposed to work normally and will catch problems long before they get past testing and into the user community. Second, by using the system regularly, you will have a much better idea of what might be a useful enhancement and what bugs are most important to fix. Users appreciate people that understand the systems they work on.

Some time ago, I worked for a company that used the Internet as a library device. Electronic books were displayed for the user to read. A "check out" mechanism was in place so that publishers could be sure that the books were only in use by a single person at one time. While working at this company, I discovered that the books weren't always formatted correctly. Tables would appear jumbled, and pages would be missing from the texts. Rather than wait for users to complain about the system, I went directly to the people responsible for the book editing and formatting.

The people in the editing department were surprised by the problems we were encountering. It turned out that they never viewed the books on the Web site. They had internal tools that they used to view the final results of their editing work. Because they never saw the actual Web site, they had no idea that the internal tools did not match well to the final product. In fact, they were off by quite a bit. These editors were not users of the system; they were simply workers in a corporate assembly line. They could not prevent problems from occurring in the Web system because they never tried using it.

Duplicate the Environment

Another important issue when working in a standalone environment is the ability to duplicate the end user system you are working toward. Many problems in standalone systems occur because developers did not check the system against the final expected deployment machine. Consider the following simple rules.

If you are developing a system intended for use on an "average" client machine, don't develop and test it on a high-end loaded machine. I can't tell you the number of complaints I've seen from users claiming that a system was too slow while running it on a 133 MHz Pentium machine, when in fact, it had been developed on a 700 MHz Pentium III. It hardly seems reasonable to test the system on anything other than what the user is most likely to be using. Of course, developers do need higher-end equipment than the average user. But you should make absolutely sure you regularly test your software against the standard setup.

Beware of developer boxes for debugging. Quite often, the developer box is loaded with components that change the environment under which a program runs. Debug dynamic link libraries (DLLs), built-in debuggers that pop up when an error occurs, and third-party tools that monitor memory are almost standard on a software developer's box. Unfortunately, the presence of many of these tools can cause problems that might occur on a user box not to appear on the developer box. This results in the "but it works on my machine" problem that you hear so often in testing and debugging labs.

You must be sure you are running the same versions of software that are running in the field. For example, if you expect your system to be run on a Windows 98 machine, it is best to debug and test it on a Windows 98 machine and not one running Windows 2000. Certainly, it makes a great deal of sense to test on a more stable operating system, but you are not getting the same results that your users are. There are definitely issues that occur only on some operating system versions (Linux, Mac, Windows, etc.) and not others. Without duplicating the environment of the problem, you cannot be sure that you have fixed the problem. That said, of course, you will want to test your fix on all other versions of the operating system for which the program runs to be sure that your fix did not break anything on those systems. We discuss this topic in more detail in Chapter 13.

Professional debugging engineers are often running systems that have had additional changes made to them for future features or other bug fixes that have not yet made it into the field. One of the hardest lessons to learn in the debugging field is to always start with a "clean" version of the source code when debugging a new problem. If you do not do this, you will often be unable to reproduce a problem because it has been further masked by changes you have already made. This is a hard lesson to learn because it means that you need to start with two complete copies of the source code on your machine. This means two sets of code to debug and the likelihood that you might run into bugs that you have already fixed while debugging another problem. If you do not take this approach, I assure you that you will regret it in the end. It might be a hassle, but it's a hassle that will save you a lot of grief. Version control and source code branching are just as important, and need to be a part of your arsenal.

Tip

Always start with a clean copy of the source code when debugging.

Beware of DLL Hell

Although the origins of the term *DLL Hell* are somewhat lost in the mists of computer development history, the term itself is most closely associated with the Microsoft Windows operating system. I first ran into the term in an article by Rick Anderson of Microsoft Corporation. Put simply, DLL Hell is when a group of external components used by an application have differing and contentious versions.[1]

Although the term really only applies to the Windows operating system, the underlying problem can occur on virtually any operating system. When you rely on shared code from any sort of system library, such as core library functions, database functionality, or communications routines built into the operating system, you are at the mercy of the versions of the libraries installed.

One very important tip for working with external components, such as DLLs, is to take regular "snapshots" of each version of the components you are working with. If you do this and two versions do not match, you can easily warn the user as well as yourself of this fact. This will save you enormous amounts of time and energy in tracking down problems that occur because another "rogue" application has installed an older or otherwise incompatible version of a library that you depend on to run your application.

Tip

Take regular snapshots of all external component versions!

---

[1] Anderson, Rick. "The End of DLL Hell." Microsoft Corporation, MSDN online **http://msdn.microsoft.com/library/ techart/dlldanger1.htm**, January 2000.

Input and Output Errors

Nearly all errors in small-scale standalone applications are of the input and output variety. Programs that allow invalid input cause problems in the processing stage. Programs that mangle the output can cause errors in display or errors in processing.

One simple tip for most standalone applications is to define and restrict the domain of each input type your application can handle. Then use input controls or filtering components to be sure that the input that reaches your application is only within the bounds you expect it to be. If you add this layer to your design and implementation, you will immediately discover numerous benefits. It will no longer be necessary to check the values at each level of the functionality. If you clean up the data coming in, your processing becomes faster and more efficient because you know that it is correct. Of course, this assumption should be well documented in your code in case someone else chooses to reuse the code in a less clean environment. Output errors occur for several reasons. For example, you simply might not properly deal with certain cases of output process computations. Obvious cases of this occur when you have a list of values that an output value may be chosen from and fail to handle the exceptional case of "Other." Bugs like this occur when a select-type statement fails to have a default case. Mappings of this sort require that you deal with cases where the mapping fails. This might be an error in your application, or it might be a simple oversight in the requirements.

Tip

Always assume mappings can and will fail in your application.

Another cause of output errors is that of formatting. Formatting errors consist of output that does not "look right," output that is of the wrong type, and output that doesn't show the user what they want or are expecting to see. Formatting errors can be the result of poor requirements or design. They can also be the result of programming or logic errors. In either case, you are faced with an unhappy user because the results they are looking for do not appear.

In order to properly debug a formatting error, such as a bad display, you need to know how the screen for that display was generated. I highly recommend that you maintain a "photo book" with screenshots of each input and output screen in the system, along with a log of how that screen is created and the code that will be impacted by changes. Not only is this a godsend when you are trying to debug an unfamiliar application, but it is also valuable for the designer and architect who are trying to make changes and need to estimate the level of code change involved.

Tip

Maintain a "photo log" of all screens in your system with the code that creates them.

Mid-Size Standalone Applications

For the purposes of this discussion, the difference between small standalone applications and mid-size ones is that mid-size applications generally accept data and other input from sources other than itself. That is, although a standalone application might have to deal with versioning issues of its own data or perhaps importing static data from other applications, a mid-size application needs to deal with constantly changing data from other applications or devices.

As soon as you lose control of the format and content of data coming into your application, you immediately create an entire suite of bugs waiting to happen if you do not properly plan and code for them. Most applications that contain bugs due to outside data have these bugs because they assume that everything will go correctly and that the data will be in a proper format. Nothing is more unlikely in the programming world than a perfect input data stream. Even hardware devices that supply data often deliver missing or corrupted data due to the interface between the application and the hardware devices. If you do not plan for data corruption, you can be assured that data corruption will happen. Think of it as insurance for your program.

Tip

Never assume the data coming in contains no errors.

Because most errors are probably data related, it makes sense to do a few things when debugging applications that contain such data. First, you should log all errors when you find them. Second, you should verify in the code that the data input must be what you expect it to be. If not, the data should probably be completely rejected, and the errors logged to some external file device. Third, you need to make sure that the order in which events happen is correct. In many applications, for example, the data is read in, stored in some persistent (or internal) format, and then verified. Many times, the original data that is replaced by the newer data is discarded before the new data is verified. This is obviously error-prone and will lead to bugs when there is no data present.

As a simple example, consider a point-of-sale device (commonly called a cash register). Data containing price and taxation information is often cached at the register to prevent lookups from taking place each time a common item is purchased. If the input data for an item is corrupted, the price and taxation information can, and does, get mixed up in the machine. In a system I once worked on, a horrible bug was caused by a corrupted database entry in one of the item lookup databases. The corrupted data would be sent to the register, which cleared out its cache entry to update itself with the new data. When the corrupted data was added to the cache, it not only messed up that item entry, it also caused all other items in the cache to be incorrect. Of course, the original developer did not check the validity of the data when it came from the master database. That data was considered sacred and was only to be looked at in a read-only fashion.

Because this error occurred frequently, I eventually tracked it down to a corruption of the data coming into the box. I was astounded to find that the application did no sanity checking for prices. A negative price for an item is extremely unlikely. After all, what store could make money paying you to take its merchandise? (Well, besides Internet startups, I mean.) Likewise, the taxation information was a coded field that represented which levels of tax (local, state, federal, excise, etc.) were to be applied to a given item. Only a simple sanity check was present in this area; the excise tax flag could never be set if the local tax flag was on (this was a rule of this particular store). If the data was corrupted, the two flags were often on at the same time. This caused other logic in the application to fail, resulting in improper receipts and improper collections. The store was not pleased when it discovered it was losing money due to a computer error!

Our solution was to do basic sanity checking on each item when it came in. If the item was invalid, it was discarded and another request made. If two sequential requests were invalid, the item was flagged and the manager notified by a code displayed on the register. This showed the manager which item was invalid, and he or she was then told to check the master database (a system out of our control). Likewise, if an item sold for $10.00 on our first request, and then sold for $99.99 on the next, the item would be flagged and rejected. By using simple sanity checks, we eliminated thousands of dollars of merchandise pricing errors each year. Needless to say, we were popular programmers at that store.

Mid-Size Client/Server Applications

What, exactly, is a mid-size client/server application? In the past, mid-size client/server applications were generally intranet kinds of applications for corporate servers. Such applications were used by the employees of the companies. A hundred or two hundred employees might use an application like this simultaneously. Such concurrent usage implies a certain load on the system, but is generally within a predefined limit. When designing for corporate applications, you usually had a very good idea of the number of people that would be using the system from year to year because you knew what the current employee base was and what the projected hiring numbers looked like. In a nutshell, you weren't going to be surprised by load in a mid-size client/server application.

Most client/server applications in today's world have a few things in common with past applications. They tend to be thin-client applications, and they tend to use a form of persistent storage. That storage is normally some kind of a database. Most applications have some form of login process, whereby the user identifies himself in a certain way and provides a password for access. In addition, many such applications allow some form of customization for the user, so that the user can make certain tasks easier and more efficient. For the debugger, this immediately brings to mind certain classes of bugs.

Login problems come about when the user either types in an invalid character while creating a password or somehow modifies his or her user name so that it cannot be easily entered in order to log the user into the system. One of the most common problems occurs when creating a new user in the system. The system often prompts you to enter your password, and then asks you to verify this entry by typing the password again. Unfortunately, the system normally allows you to simply copy the password from one field and paste it into the verification field. Obviously, if an invalid character was present in the first field, that invalid character would appear in the verification field as well. By simply screening invalid characters (or at least warning the user that there is an invalid character present), you eliminate a host of debugging problems.

As a debugger, you should periodically sweep the database to check for odd characters or invalid entries in fields. This process, often called *prebugging*, permits you to catch such problems before they manifest themselves in the production system and cause errors. Another tip is to look for combinations of uppercase and lowercase letters. In many cases, users do not mean to use such combinations and end up with the correct letters for their password, but the wrong cases. While using such a combination is often encouraged in many systems, it is important to notice that the user enters one combination of cases when signing up, but another when trying to log into the system. Once again, this leads to users not being able to log into the system, and these odd problems will certainly be reported as bugs.

Tip

Watch for uppercase and lowercase combinations, trailing spaces, and invalid characters in user names and passwords.

How can you make your life easier when debugging mid-size client/server applications? Two good techniques that you should use when debugging problems in such application types are described in the following sections.

Create a Snapshot of the Back-End Database for Testing

When you are trying to debug a client/server application, a common need is for a test bed of information to work from. Although you could simply create a test database by entering random values into the tables, it makes a lot more sense to use a snapshot of the production database for testing your hypotheses and fixes.

Using a production snapshot has several advantages. First, you know that you are working with real-world data including all of its problems and inconsistencies. Second, if the problem is actually being caused by a specific user in the database and his or her settings or values, the debugging process will be considerably easier if you have the real data to work from. Because the alternative for a specific user problem is to debug on the production system itself, using a snapshot is a considerably safer idea, too.

In order to adequately test your hypotheses or changes, you need a system that is a complete copy of the production system, down to the database level. You need not have the same level of system, however. For example, if your production system consists of a dozen servers and database machines, you could "model" this system with perhaps two or three of each. The closer to reality, of course, the better for the purposes of finding and fixing bugs in the system. Of course, this assumes that the system is deployed and in active use.

Keep Usage Data so that You Can See what Features Are More Commonly Used

Usage data basically includes the tasks each user performed in the system and what the parameters for each function they invoked might have been. For an accounting system, for example, you might have a log that showed that the user first posted a deposit, then a withdrawal, and then some tax expenses. Knowing what a user was trying to do can make it much easier to figure out what went wrong. For a problem that involves multiple users working on the same account, for example, simply asking one person who experienced the problem would not give you sufficient information to track down the bug. You would need to know that a second user was changing the data at the same time to really understand the problem.

Usage data must, at a minimum, include the user identifier (perhaps the user name), the time and date of the action, the action itself, and any pertinent information about the action. At its best, usage data can be used to completely reconstruct any action by the user. In fact, at one company I worked for, when the database was accidentally destroyed through an error on the part of the operations department, we were able to completely reconstruct the database using only the usage data logs.

Large-Scale Applications

Of all of the types of systems that programmers work on, large-scale systems are by far the most difficult to envision solutions for and to debug. A large-scale system is one that has an open model; that is, there are no limits on the number of people that could use the system, in theory. Good examples of large-scale systems are Internet Web sites and Internet Service Provider systems. In both cases, you might have an idea how many people are likely to use the system at one time, but that number is, at best, a guess. In addition, usage is variable, subject to surges in use based on marketing events, product roll outs, or posting on Internet discussion sites.

The difficulties in a large-scale system are obvious. There is no predicting at any given time how many people will be using the system. Because the system is open to anyone, there is no way to predict which features will be most commonly used. Problems in a large-scale system are usually very difficult to fix. Time constraints become more important than anything else. Systems are expected to run 24 hours a day, 7 days a week. That doesn't leave a lot of time for debugging or maintenance. When a large-scale system such as an e-commerce Web site goes down, the powers-that-be want it back up yesterday. Trying to explain to a senior vice president of the company that you need a few days to study the problem is not very likely to succeed.

Some techniques that you can use to debug large-scale systems more easily and effectively are discussed in the following sections.

Build in a Back Door for Testing

Although it is a good idea to keep a backup system mirror of the production system, some errors simply cannot be viewed in such an environment. Obvious choices are load problems and multiuser interactions. In these cases, you need to view the real system under the real load to see what is going on. A "back door" into the system is always a good idea in these situations.

A back door provides you with a special login name and password, which allows you to view debug output while the real system is running. Of course, this presupposes that you have built some sort of diagnostics into your system as we discussed in Chapter 9. If you haven't, this is good time to read about these diagnostics and determine how they might apply in your case.

One of the best things you can do is provide tracing information to such back door logins. A trace log shows you exactly what was going on in the system, and what path it took through the code. In addition, if the problem turns out to be a deadlock condition, you can see exactly what statements caused the problem and who the users were at that point.

In one production Web server system that I worked on, there was a problem with several user accounts not being able to view their customized displays. My team could not understand why this was happening, as we regularly viewed such data on our own backup system with no problems. In order to see what was going on, we built in a specialized login that would allow us to "pretend" to be any other user on the system. This provided two benefits. First, it allowed us to view the system in the same way as a real user. Second, the system protected the confidentiality of the user by simply showing us what the user saw without allowing us access to the user's password. Third, the special login only allowed read access to the user's accounts; we could not change any settings or parameters. This special login also provided us with the ability to view debug information within the code, using a specialized debug object that could toggle the data display on or off based on the user's privileges.

In the Web site, we quickly found the problem by simply viewing what the user was seeing and understanding why the code was not displaying what it was supposed to. In this case, it was a simple logic problem that was causing the user to be sent to the wrong page due to the user's affiliation within the system. However, tracking down such a problem without the special login would have taken considerably longer.

Watch for External Content Changes

Most large-scale systems do not provide all of the content for the users. For example, most Web servers rely on content that is provided from external sources. Sometimes the external source is simply another division of the company, outside of development. Sometimes the external source is another company or Web site from which data is gathered.

One of the most amusing comments you hear in our industry is, "We are standardizing on the <x> interchange format to avoid any more problems." When you are debugging a system, you will discover just how nonstandard a standardized interchange format can be. Consider eXtended Markup Language (XML), the new "savior" of data interchange. XML is basically a tagged data format, which includes a tag name and a tag value. You wouldn't think that much could go wrong with such a system, especially when the format is standard and can be validated.

However, XML relies on getting the tag names right. If you are given an XML file and told to parse that information into your system, you can validate that the file is in proper format, and you can parse all of the tags and their values. What you cannot ensure, however, is that the tag names match what you expect them to be. There is no standard for this, only agreements between the content publisher and the content receiver. If the publisher suddenly decides to change one or more aspects of the content he is sending to you, you may suddenly find that your application is failing or providing incorrect results.

Real-Time Systems

A real-time system is one that must respond to input and provide output within a very short time period. An example of a real-time system is a stock trading firm, which must make a purchase or sale decision based on stock prices that come in every second. Another example is a satellite television system, which must process the input signal and provide output to the television set instantly.

Obviously, real-time systems have a set of problems all their own. Debugging them is quite often a serious challenge because you cannot simply stop the system to see what is going on. In most cases, debugging real-time systems is a matter of analyzing previous data to see what happened before you encountered the problem, and then guessing what the cause of that problem might be based on the debug information you have gathered.

There are quite a few caveats in debugging real-time systems and a few techniques that work particularly well. Let's take a look at some of the factors you might want to consider when dealing with a real-time system.

Beware Adding Debugging Statements

In general, it is difficult to add a lot of debugging statements that display information for a real-time system. This is due to the fact that events need to happen in a very short period of time, and each additional statement overhead can cause the system to change the frequency with which statements are executed.

In particular, it is generally almost impossible to output any meaningful information in an interrupt service routine of any sort. Formatting data, in fact, can be nightmarish due to the amount of computer cycles required to execute a simple formatting command. For this reason, you should seriously consider a buffered logging approach to debugging interrupt routines. In such a system, you output data in its "pure" format, usually in a tagged data and value approach. The data is buffered in memory and written out when time permits, usually in a separate thread. This allows the interrupt routine to proceed unimpeded and still gives you the kind of information you might need to debug the interrupt routine.

Watch for Hardware or Software Contention

One of the real perils of a real-time system occurs when two separate parts of the application want to use a given resource, whether that resource be a hardware device or a software subsystem. Such problems are usually extremely difficult to track down, simply because they are so dependent on timing and data.

In one system I worked on, real-time data came in through a single input device, but was split into three different threads of information. On rare occasions, the system would crash for no apparent reason. There were no data dependencies that my coworkers and I could see in the incoming data stream. There was no diagnostic information displayed for a detected error in the system. In short, there was nothing to go on when trying to track down the problem. Because this was a real-time system, tracing and logging the entire system was not a possibility. Instead, we were left doing hand traces through the code to see what might have been causing the problem.

We used the only method left open to us in debugging this system—divide and conquer. Essentially, we stubbed out individual pieces of the system until the problem vanished. Then, they were slowly added back in until we could see what was going on. It turned out that a particular buffering scheme was used for two separate parts of the system. This wasn't really a problem, as separate buffers were allocated for each input stream. However, a single routine was used to track the total number of buffers available to the system as a whole. This routine was not safely reentrant and was sometimes called from two different threads at the same time. This caused an internal access violation, which would crash the program and cause the bug we were observing.

When debugging real-time systems, watch for overlaps in hardware or software used between two or more independent subsystems in the application. If you find such an overlap, be sure that synchronization problems have been taken into account in the design and implementation of such a subsystem.

Timing Issues

Timing issues are the bane of the real-time system's programmer and debugger. Problems that only happen during certain key time periods in the application life span are harder to track down than any other form of bug. Imagine, for example, if you have an application that has a nightly download of system information at 3:00 A.M. If you want to track down the problem, you need to be present at 3:00 A.M. to see what is going on. Of course, if you miss the first download event, you need to stay up the next night as well. It's not a desirable way to debug an application.

Other sorts of timing issues abound as well. For example, if an event needs to take place within a few milliseconds (or less) of another event, such as an acknowledgement (ACK) response for a message, and something else happens to monopolize the CPU resources once in a while, the result is a timing error. Determining what might be taking up the time you so desperately need is more than an act of detective work, it more closely resembles a treasure hunt.

One of the most important factors to determine when you are debugging a real-time system is what the timing-critical areas of the application might be. Depending on your system, you might have threads of different priority that fire in order to accomplish different kinds of tasks. It is certainly annoying when a low-priority monitoring thread interferes with a high-priority data retrieval thread due to a silly oversight on the part of the original developer. If you know that a task is going to require near instantaneous response time, you know that that task is the one to give the highest priority and least amount of code.

Embedded Systems

An embedded system runs on a specialized chip or platform running within another device. Embedded systems run on things as small as digital watches and as complex as space shuttles. The trick to dealing with embedded systems is generally to realize that you are at the mercy of the environment around you. It is normally impossible to strictly "debug" an embedded system in place unless you have been provided with an interface to the internal system. Most embedded systems are debugged in simulators rather than in place.

Simulator Problems

Because most of the work of unit testing, debugging, and implementing code in an embedded system takes place in the simulator, it is not surprising that most of the problems occur in that location as well. The very thing that simulators are best at—emulating the environment in which the application will run—is the very thing that makes them so hard to work with. Because simulators tend to emulate the environments they run on well, they do not tend to have the odd problems that an embedded environment will have in the real world.

Voltage spikes, odd messages caused by line garbling, and failures of key components are rarely implemented in simulators. As a common theme in the software development world, we focus on what goes right and how to take advantage of it without worrying about what might go wrong in the system. You can certainly catch logic errors, buffer overruns, and other programming mistakes in a simulator. What you cannot catch are the problems that occur because things do not happen the way you expect them to. If you could, of course, you would have coded for them in the first place, right?

Interrupt Suppression

Previously, we talked a bit about interrupt routines and how you have to be aware of interrupt timing issues when working in real-time critical systems. These same problems exist in the embedded world as well, as it is often a variant of the real-time system. Another interrupt-related problem, however, is the suppression of interrupts. Interrupt suppression occurs when a subsystem shuts down the interrupt routine, presumably to do something that would not be safe while interrupts are taking place. One obvious place that this occurs is in an interrupt handler itself.

In interrupt handlers, there exists the danger that you will not finish what you are doing before another interrupt is generated and your routine is called again. For this reason, it is common to shut down the interrupt system during the processing of an interrupt and restart it when the routine has finished. Most of the time, this works well, and the program continues to process interrupts properly. There are two times, however, when this process breaks down.

First, you might shut down all interrupts in a given interrupt handler without giving proper thought to how this might affect other parts of the system. There is usually more than one interrupt handler in a mid- to large-scale embedded system. There might, for example, be both an input and output handler for data. If you shut down the entire system, the output handler might fail to fire, starving whatever other system is serviced by the output data. This causes problems in that system, but the bug can ultimately be traced to your own code.

A second reason that interrupt suppression can be bad is when you fail to restart the system. This can happen in the case of an error in the interrupt handler, where the routine is abnormally exited. If you fail to restart the interrupts, the system grinds to a horrible halt.

Protocol Errors

Protocol errors occur when a piece of hardware that you are talking to is changed without correspondingly having the software that talks to it changed. This can happen easily in firmware environments where the protocol is implemented via downloadable software. When the firmware that is used to implement the protocol is changed by download, the software on the other side needs to be changed as well.

The most common protocol errors occur because the application programming interface (API) used by the software to talk to the firmware does not keep pace with changes to the firmware. In many cases, there are no true changes to the API, but simply side effects that are not communicated to the software developer. In cases like this, the software blithely assumes that all is well, even though the firmware is well aware of a problem. Many times, an acknowledgment message is sent from the firmware to the software, but is ignored because the message identifier is not understood by the software.

Watchdog Timers

A watchdog timer is an independent process that runs on most embedded systems. It watches for some sort of heartbeat mechanism indicating that the software is still running. In the event of a catastrophic error in the software in which the system freezes up, the watchdog timer restarts the entire system.

Watchdog timer resets are usually not bugs in and of themselves. Instead, they tend to be symptoms of other problems. If your watchdog does not log the reason it reset the system, you should make sure that this functionality is added as soon as possible. Of course, this assumes that you also add the ability for the watchdog timer to understand the reason that it failed. It is very difficult to track down a problem with an embedded system when the system simply resets itself for no apparent reason.

Debugging Embedded Systems

There are numerous ways to debug embedded systems. If the problem is suspected in the hardware, you can use line analyzers to check the input and output to the system. Voltage meters can be used if you suspect a bad connection or wrong electrical settings. For software in an embedded system, however, there are really only two ways to debug the system.

Logic analyzers are used when software controlling the hardware is not providing the proper output to the hardware system. A logic analyzer is a hardware device that sits on the line between one piece of hardware and another and decodes packets going from one to the other. If you know what the protocol for talking to a piece of hardware is supposed to look like, and the logic analyzer shows that the protocol is being implemented incorrectly or is out of time synchronization, you have a huge head start on finding and fixing the problem.

Emulators are another great way to debug embedded systems. Using an emulator, you can track down problems in the software itself. Of course, you need to beware of the problems of working with emulation and simulation devices mentioned a bit earlier in this section.

Distributed Systems

Distributed systems are systems that run with separate components, possibly running on separate machines. Obviously, besides the usual problems in debugging systems, a distributed system adds a new level of complexity to the matter. Distributed systems are nondeterministic due to the high number of possible ways to enter and exit the systems. In addition, distributed systems often have multiple languages, hosts, and operating systems on which they run, using middleware to connect all the pieces. This makes debugging even more difficult because you must become an expert in many different technologies in order to find the problem.

In addition, most distributed systems are built using commercial off the shelf (COTS) components. These components are rarely shipped with source code, leaving you in even more muddied waters to try and find the problem.

Middleware Errors

Of all of the distributed system debugging problems, middleware errors are by far the most frustrating. A middleware error occurs when there is a bug in the actual code for the middleware that you expose in your own system or when you call a middleware component incorrectly. Tracking down the latter is usually a matter of using the divide and conquer debugging technique to find the component causing the problem, and then reviewing the instructions and specifications for the component until you find out what you are doing wrong.

A true bug in a middleware component is usually a nightmare. Because you rarely have the source code for such components, you are left with two choices for debugging the problem. First, you can discard the component and replace it with something that does the same job. This usually involves rewriting tons of code and changing the architecture of your system. Second, you can try to work around the problem by not using whatever method of the component you are having problems with. In this case, you will often find yourself taking extreme measures by hacking into the code to make it work the way it was originally specified. Obviously, neither of these solutions is optimal.

The best way to avoid middleware component bugs is to strongly test the methods of the component before you ever drop it into your design or implementation.

Deterministic Errors

Determinism is the ability to say, in advance, what is going to happen in a given situation. In a distributed system, however, it is often quite difficult to know what is going on at any given moment. Changes in routing, machine unavailability, and differences in loading time for components can all change the order in which events occur in your total application.

Deterministic errors occur when the developer decides, ahead of time, what the order in loading and running given parts of the system will be and writes code that relies on that order. If the order changes or fails to happen as expected, errors that are hard to detect and even harder to fix will occur. One common error to watch for in a distributed environment is the failure to load a component before using it. Another possible problem can occur when updating components. Verify, via a logging mechanism, that all servers running the component have been updated. Further verify that the component version was tested with the remainder of the system before it was updated. If either of these items is not verified, this is a good place to start your debugging efforts.

Connection Errors

One of the most common problems in distributed systems is a connection error. *Connection errors* occur when one component in the distributed system loses its ability to talk to one or more of the other components in the system. This can happen due to mechanical failure, protocol failures, or security errors.

Communication errors are simply a fact of life in the distributed world. The fact that they are going to happen should be taken for granted when designing the components that use other distributed components. Bugs crop up in distributed systems when connection errors are not detected or handled. In cases like this, the error normally propagates itself throughout the system and is very difficult to track down. If a connection error is not detected at the point of its occurrence, debugging the system is quite difficult. In many cases, however, connection errors can occur during any function call that is used from any component. Most programmers do not check for such errors, assuming that a simple **get** or **set** method cannot return such an error.

Consider the following code, which might be found in a VBScript page on a typical Web server application:

```
Dim X as DBObj
X.SetName myName
X.SetAddress myAddress
On Error Go to HandleError
REM  Do some lookups using the information stored.
```

In the preceding code snippet, the programmer was expecting an error in the lookup or search routine after he or she had set some data values to search with. What wasn't considered, however, was that the **SetName** or **SetAddress** methods of the DbObj object could easily return a form of a connection error. If DbObj is a Common Object Model (COM) component running on another machine, and the Web server loses its connection to that remote machine, there will be an error returned from the **SetName** method. This error will not be handled and will bubble its way up until it eventually is displayed for the end user to see. Sooner or later, this will come to the attention of an operations person, who will turn it over to you as the debugger on the project. Finding this problem could take days.

Security Errors

Security errors occur when either a security policy is broken or a component attempts to use resources that it does not have legitimate access to. In many cases, security errors occur due to mistakes on the part of operations, which deny access to legitimate systems that need those resources.

One of the most common security errors occurs when a database user system is changed. For example, the user name and password that might be used by a Web page could be denied write access because the database administrator did not realize it was necessary. In a Web site project I once worked on, a new database administrator was brought on board. One of his first actions upon taking his position was to "clean up" the user access to the database. He felt that there was a serious security risk in allowing users full access to the database. The only problem was that several of those "user accounts" were actually used by system level utilities that loaded data and cleaned up data in the tables used by the Web server. The immediate result was that these utilities failed and did not update the database tables properly. Eventually, the problem propagated itself to the end user, who saw invalid data in the display. As you might imagine, tracking down this problem took quite some time.

Security problems can involve directory and file permissions as well. For example, under the Unix operating system, permissions problems can cause certain applications to not run at all unless they are under a privileged account. If you find that a previously working program suddenly stops working, you might want to start your debugging process by checking security issues for that application.

Information Repositories

When you run components on multiple machines over potentially disparate networks, you can run into information repository problems. One of the most common forms of this is the Windows Registry problem. In these cases, different machines have different machine or software settings that cause components to behave differently on different systems.

External registry problems are among the hardest problems to track down for the professional debugger. Because we are accustomed to seeing the problems found within the code of the application, an external problem presents an entirely new set of challenges. Worse, because the settings can be external even to the application configuration information, you might have to track through the entire system to determine which settings are causing the problems in your code.

A simple example of this occurs in the distributed environment known as Distributed Common Object Model (DCOM) in the Windows world. If your system uses DCOM components, you will find that system settings for the DCOM world have a serious effect on your application whether or not you are aware of them. This reliance on external systems can cause your application to fail on some machines and work on others.

The best approach for working with information repositories is to have the ability to display the relevant information from those repositories in your own program log. This allows you to compare the logs from machines that work with those that do not in order to determine what settings might be different. Similar to DLL problems, settings problems are usually a matter of detective work to determine what is different between machines. If you make the process as palatable as possible, you will find that the process goes much smoother.

Postmortem Analysis of Logs

When you are working in a distributed system, it is often impossible to predict exactly what was happening when the system failed. This is due to the nondeterministic nature of distributed systems. In many cases, because of problems with timing, security, or simple interference, what fails one time will not be the component that fails the second time.

As a simple example, consider two components that are trying to lock the same record in a database. In some cases, the first component reaches the record first and manages to acquire the lock. In this case, the second component fails. In other cases, the reverse happens, and the first component fails. Determining what might be going wrong is always a complicated matter due to the timing of the system.

How, then, can you determine that the problem is a matter of record locking and not a security or timing issue? The answer lies in the postmortem analysis of the system following a crash or other problem. The best source you will find for such an analysis is the logs of the system. For distributed systems, having an adequate logging system and log collection facility is an absolute must. If your system does not contain such a logging subsystem, you are going to find yourself spending very long hours in the computer room watching scrolling text go by at 3:00 A.M.

Simulated Systems

In many cases, particularly when the hardware or operating system is not yet complete or available, developers turn to simulators in order to develop and test their systems. Simulated systems have their own problems and their own unique debugging concerns. For instance, you always have to wonder whether the problem you are encountering only happens in the simulator or whether it will show up in the "real" product as well. In addition, the opposite problem exists. Does the bug that occurs in the real product also occur in the simulator so that it can be debugged?

If you are working with a simulated system, there are a few tactics that you can take to make your life easier. Let's take a look at the problems you are likely to run into and the approaches you can choose to make debugging less of a headache.

Encapsulate Hardware Interface

When you are working with any sort of hardware interface within your application, it is important that the interface be encapsulated into a single area of the code. In a simulated environment, chances are good that the simulator will respond exactly like the real application except for one important deviation. The simulator is unlikely to return errors when the hardware fails because a simulated piece of hardware rarely fails.

If you build an encapsulation for the interface to the hardware, you can replace the "pure" simulator hardware API with your own functions, which can randomly return error values when either a global flag or some fixed number of iterations occurs. Let's consider, for example, the case of a serial port input that comes into a simulator. There are a variety of ways to implement this, but the most common way is to "play back" an existing file from a disk to the application. In this case, it would be quite difficult to introduce errors such as dropped characters, line errors, or checksum errors. How can you validate your handling of such errors if they don't appear in the simulator? The simple answer is to add them on your own.

Encapsulate Simulated Calls to Provide Error Returns

Similar to a hardware simulator, the idea of simulating an operating system call and returning errors has a lot of merit in debugging a system. If something is working perfectly in the simulator, but fails on the real system, chances are that some of the software or hardware interface functions aren't working properly in the real system. This could simply be due to a bad simulator implementation, or it could mean that there is an unhandled error coming from the real system to your software.

A while ago, I was working on a point-of-sale system. The hardware for the system and the final interface API code were not ready at the time we were developing the system software. As a result, we worked by creating a simulator for the system, and then built our code inside of that simulator. We tried to imagine every possible scenario under which the hardware or software could fail and built this into the simulator under a random occurrence setup. The hardware would randomly fail during a given run and would display that error for the user. Likewise, the software would randomly return the error codes we could find in the system documentation and inform the user of the simulator that an error had occurred.

When the final system was ready and installed on the hardware, the system worked nearly perfectly from the very start. Our simulator had taken into account possible problems and allowed us to work through the problems ahead of time, using prebugging techniques. Better yet, because we had already dealt with all of these problems, we could debug using the simulator by simply forcing it to generate a given error, and then tracing through the code to see what the result was in our system.

Strip Problem Down to Simplest Form on Real System and Simulator

A particularly ugly problem when dealing with complex systems is how to test changes and problems with small sections of lower-level code that can only be reached by doing an extremely large number of actions in the complete system. With a simulator, this job can be done considerably easier.

Given a small framework that exercises the particular subsystems that you want to work on, you can use a simulator to test the simplest example of the problem you suspect. You can then take the framework and move it to the "real" system for further testing if the simulator does not show the problem you are trying to find. For this reason, simulators are an invaluable part of the debugging experience for embedded and non-native systems.

Summary

The techniques we use in different debugging environments are often a result of the factors in those environments. In this chapter, we explored many of the most common types of systems and looked at how the various debugging problems and techniques could be applied when working with them.

As with all other elements in the debugging world, there is no "right" way to debug a specific application type. Your results will vary, and your experience will determine the best and easiest way for you to find and fix problems. By examining the environment and the problem domain, however, you can better determine the best way to debug your particular project.

Bug Puzzle

Some problems are incredibly complex and require a great deal of knowledge of the application, the problem domain, and the programming source language. Other problems, such as the one described in this example, simply require that you think and examine the code. The problem is presented in the C programming language, but the particular language really doesn't matter. That's your clue.

The following two small utility programs were written to keep track of what was going on in a production Web site. The first program accepts a few input arguments and prints out some status information to a file. The second program reads that file and displays the information for the operations person on a regular basis. When the program runs, however, it doesn't seem to print out useful status information. Why?

Program 1 Source Code:

```c
#include <stdio.h>
#include <string.h>
#include <stdlib.h>
int main(int argc, char **argv )
{
    if ( argc < 3 )
        return -1;
    int numVisitors = atoi(argv[1]);
    int numDownSeconds = atoi(argv[2]);
    // Open the file for append.
    FILE *fp = fopen("TODAYSDATA.DAT", "a");
    if ( fp != NULL )
        fprintf("%d %d", numVisitors, numDownSeconds );
    fclose(fp);
    return 0;
}
```

Program 2 Source Code:

```c
#include <stdio.h>
#include <string.h>
#include <stdlib.h>
int main(int argc, char **argv )
{
    int numVisitors, numDownSeconds;
```

```
// Open the file for input.
FILE *fp = fopen("TODAYSDATA.DAT", "r");
if ( fp != NULL )
    fscanf(fp, "%d %d", &numVisitors, &numDownSeconds );
fclose(fp);
printf("Number of Visitors: %d, Number of Downtime Seconds: %d",
  numVisitors, numDownSeconds );
return 0;
}
```

Chapter 11

Post Debugging

Yuan Hsieh

W hat do you do after you think you have fixed a bug? You install the changes and test the fix. You then check the changes into the configuration management system, and notify your testers so that they can test your changes. Some time later, they come back and tell you the changes look good, and they are posting the changes to the production environment. You pat yourself on the back. Smiling to yourself, you put your feet up, break out a cigar, and pour yourself a glass of cognac. As you watch the wisp of smoke swirling all around you, you lean back in your chair to savor the tranquility of bug-free software. This moment lasts about half a second; then the "You've Got Mail!" alert pops up on your screen. Once again, it is an email from the bug tracking system informing you of your next bug assignment. Chewing on your cigar and squinting, you peer through the haze to read the screen. After reading the email, a smirk forms on your face. You think to yourself, "This bug sounds interesting!" So you push aside what remains of your cognac and you take the stub of a cigar out of your mouth. Still staring at the screen, your mind races to formulate a strategy and a plan of attack. Not thinking, you jam the burning stub on your mouse pad, extinguishing it. You are ready to take on the challenge.

We all go through a debugging process that is similar to the steps described in the previous paragraph. We fix a bug, we test the fix, and we go on to the next bug. We spend very little time in between bugs.

Submitting the changes and passing the regression test is not the end of the debugging process. Most of us would never think twice about going on to the next bug or the next project as soon as we have submitted the changes into the configuration management system. After all, you have fixed the bug, why worry? However, a good debugger anticipates rather than reacts to potential bugs. Why wait for the bug to show up, when you can find the defects and fix them? Why go through fixing the same bug again at a later time in a different file? Why reintroduce dynamic tracing "print" statements a few weeks later when fixing another bug? The end of one debugging process is the perfect time to lay the foundation for the next debugging process. It is also a good time for some introspection and learn from your mistakes.

You should ask yourself five questions while you are getting ready for the next bug:

♦ *Did I make the same mistake somewhere else?* If you made a mistake because you misunderstood a particular language construct and usage, it is likely that you made the same mistake somewhere else in the same code. This knowledge might allow you to do some preventive maintenance.

♦ *What's hiding behind this bug?* Often, one bug might mask the symptom for another bug. You peel away a layer of an onion, only to find another layer underneath it. Care should be taken to inspect the effect of your changes.

♦ *How can I make this kind of bug easier to find?* Consider what you can do to make bugs easier to find the next time around.

♦ *How can I prevent this kind of bug?* Consider preventive measures that you can take to help you prevent making the same kinds of mistakes in the future. It is infinitely easier to debug a program when you don't introduce defects to the program in the first place.

♦ *Am I getting better?* Attempt to measure your own growth as a software developer.

In this chapter, these questions are addressed in more detail and some answers are provided for them.

Did I Make the Same Mistake Elsewhere?

When mistakes are caused by a lack of understanding in some aspects of the problem or the tools used, we tend to make the same mistake elsewhere. And if we can fix several similar types of bugs for every one that we find and fix, we can be much more productive as debuggers. The trick is to understand the potential causes and the pattern of the bug.

For example, a bug is caused because the original developer forgot to count the null characters in considering the length of a string (for C or C++). What is the potential cause for this defect? It is possible that the original developer simply made a typo. It is also possible that the original developer did not understand the definition of the C string and did not know that a C string is null terminated. It is also probable that the original developer was doing some kind of fancy pointer manipulation and just made a mistake.

If you suspect that the developer was not familiar with the language specification, then it would be prudent to inspect the codes written by the same developer and look for the same kind of mistakes. If the developer was not familiar with the C string, we can probably anticipate other problems with the usage of string functions, such as **strcpy()**. In fact, it is highly likely that the same developer would have problems with other memory and pointer manipulations. For errors due to a misunderstanding of the language construct, it is useful to extract the concept that is misunderstood by the developer. Then extend the misunderstood concept with other related concepts and see if mistakes were also made relating to the other concepts. For example, if the developer did not understand the concept of null terminated strings in C, then it is likely that they will make mistakes in using **strcpy()**, and allocating memory for C-strings.

On the other hand, if you hypothesize that the cause of the defect is a typo or a simple mistake, then it might not be necessary to check for similar mistakes elsewhere. But a good debugger is paranoid and would double-check anyway.

These lines of thinking assume that you know the skills of the developer who introduced the bug. However, as a debugger, you probably have no way of knowing what the developer knows and doesn't know. So how do you go about finding out if the mistake is due to a misconception or not? You start by finding the bug. By looking at the bug, you can attempt to determine if the bug is related to a particular misconception. In order to do this, you need to know a fair bit about the language and the concepts behind the programming language. You also need to draw on your past experiences and domain knowledge. In other words, you usually need to have more experience than the developer who made the mistake. Once you have identified a potential misconception, you can then look for other manifestations of this misconception in other parts of the code.

Using the C string bug as an example, let's assume that the defective code looks like the following:

```
1. char *string;
2. string = (char *) malloc( sizeof(char)*11 );
3. if ( string != 0 )
4.   strcpy( string, "Hello World" );
```

As a debugger, you can spot the defect right away and know that the correct fix is to change the constant in line 2 from 11 to 12. The original developer forgot to account for the null character at the end of the string. This is an easy fix. But the more important question at hand is, is this kind of defect prevalent in other parts of the code? From our experience, we know that the null-terminated string concept in C is not an intuitive one. We had the same misconception when we were novice C programmers and made similar defects. Being paranoid, we then do a "grep" on other parts of the code to see if the same mistakes were made. If all other usage of the C string appears to be correct, we can then hypothesize that the mistake might have been a simple typo. However, if the same mistakes consistently show up in other parts of the code, it is safe to assume that the developer had this misconception. It would then be necessary to check for related misconceptions. An example of a related misconception to a null terminating C string would be the incorrect use of the **strlen()** function. A developer who made the preceding mistake could have easily made the following mistake:

```
1. char *string1;
2. char *string2 = "Test String";
3. string1 = (char *) malloc( sizeof(char)*strlen(string2) );
4. if ( string1 != 0 )
5.   strcpy( string1, string2 );
```

In this mistake, the developer wasn't aware that **strlen()** does not account for the null character at the end of the string, so string1 is allocated as one character too small.

Obviously, looking for similar errors is not limited to looking for mistakes in using the standard system functions or APIs. It also applies to the usage of in-house libraries and codes. If a common misconception about a particular API is evident, it could suggest that the API is difficult to use. For in-house APIs, it might be useful to revisit the APIs to see if it is possible to make them less likely to induce faults and become safer to use.

What's Hiding Behind This Bug?

Once you have fixed a bug, you might unveil other bugs that were previously hidden. The fixed bug could have been hiding some other defects. The bug might take the program down into one code-path, and the fix might take the program down into another section of code that was never tested or executed. The bug might set some variables with a certain value, and the fix might have changed the value of the variables and caused a bad interaction with other parts of the code. Good debuggers don't just fix the bug at hand. They also try to prevent introducing bugs by understanding how the bug they are fixing can affect the software. Good debuggers will also ask themselves the following questions:

♦ *Which variables does this change impact?* Whether you have changed the assignment of a variable or the control path of the program, you will have impacted some variables in the code. In software, the content of the variables determines the state of the system. When the content of the variable is changed, you can potentially change the state of the system, which could affect the correctness of the software.

♦ *How are the impacted variables used?* If the content of a variable changed due to your fix, you might have broken some previously untested assumptions on the valid range of the variable. For example, if the variable changed is the denominator of a division operation, and the code did not check for division by 0, you might want to evaluate your changes to ensure that the assumption is still valid.

♦ *Would the potential new values for the variable change the control path?* Often, variable values are used to determine the branching condition or the number of times software should iterate in a loop. By changing the variable values, you could change the way the program behaves. Sometimes, the change is desirable (a bug fix), but be aware of unanticipated changes.

These questions assume that your change does not affect the preconditions and post conditions related to the software module that contains the change. If it does, you should also evaluate how the changed module is used throughout the system.

How Can I Prevent this Bug?

The end of a debugging cycle is a great time to think about how you can go about preventing the bug from recurring. After spending hours looking for the cause of the bug and hours making and testing the changes, the bug is still fresh in your mind. Use this time to figure out if you can prevent this bug from happening again.

Understand the Causes

If you are the developer who introduced the bug, you can try to think back to the time when you were working on this particular piece of code. What were you doing? What were you thinking? If you forgot to check for an error condition, what can you do to prevent yourself from forgetting? Would it be helpful to have it better defined in the design? Would it help to check the requirement document if the handling of the error condition is specified in the requirements? Could someone else inspecting the code help remind you of your mistakes? Would it help to turn on some compiler settings that would warn you of a problem? Would it help to change the design of the software so the bug is not even possible?

If you were not the developer who introduced the bug, you would not be able to be as introspective. Nevertheless, you can still try to look at the bug and speculate on the reason for it. Is it because the developer didn't understand the language construct? Is it because the developer didn't understand the problem domain? Is the design too complicated? Even if you can't come up with a reasonable speculation, you can still try to identify ways to prevent someone else from making the same mistake. Design reviews and code reviews can help provide some form of mitigation. Better training can help prevent other problems. Maybe tools can be changed. Maybe the problem is with the communication between customers and developers. There are a lot of options, but the right choice is specific to the people and process at your organization.

Keep Test Cases for Future Releases

One way of preventing the bug from escaping into the production environment is to catch it during test time. To accomplish this, there is nothing better than to go looking for the specific bug. This can be done by keeping the reproducible case for the bug as a test case. The test case can become part of the regression test suite that can be used for future releases.

Use Bugs for Future Design

Some bugs can be prevented at design time. In Chapter 2, we talked about the buffer over-flow bug. Buffer overflow bugs can easily be prevented if we design our systems to avoid static buffers. We can avoid buffer overflow bugs if we move away from unsafe languages like C and C++. These two options might not be feasible in the real world. However, the danger of buffer overflow bugs can still be mitigated if we can provide a convenient mechanism to check for the length of the buffer and the content prior to any execution that can poten-tially cause buffer overflow. How? This can be done by providing a safer wrapper over the unsafe function calls. For example, one of the more confounding features of the C program-ming language is the null-terminating string. Numerous bugs are created because developers forget about it. But has it ever occurred to anyone that it is trivial to wrap the standard functions in the *string.h* with a safer version? The following **CopyString()** function is an example of wrapping **strcpy()**.

```
1. BOOLEAN CopyString( char *buffer, /* The buffer to set the content to */
2.                     int size, /* The size of the buffer */
3.                     char *from ) {
4.   if ( (strlen( from ) + 1) > size ) /* Don't forget the null */
5.     return FALSE;
6.   if ( buffer == NULL )
7.     return FALSE;
8.   strcpy( buffer, from );
9.   return TRUE;
10.}
```

Obviously, there is still some risk with the **CopyString()** function as written. The **CopyString()** function is merely an example of what can be done to make the code a little safer. If the programmer is lazy, they might not check the return of the **CopyString()** func-tion call, and would still use the buffer as if it has been allocated correctly, even when the **CopyString()** returns a FALSE. Furthermore, the possibility exists that the developer might pass in a value for the size argument that is not the size of the buffer array. But the function prevents a novice from making a mistake and an expert from making errors due to a tempo-rary mental lapse.

Consider another quick example: In e-commerce, money is used a lot. After all, money repre-sents the price and value of the goods that are sold over the Internet. But how many systems have you found that simply represent money in the design using either a floating point value or a double precision floating point value? Is there a problem with using floating point values to represent money? Well, not exactly, except that money, as a concept, has more constraints and rules than the floating point type defined by the language that is used to implement the system. Why not just define a money data type in your system and use the money data type instead of the generic floating point value? We can prevent many bugs by making the soft-ware more strongly typed. This concept is explored in more detail in Chapter 12.

How Can I Make this Kind of Bug Easier to Find?

If we can't prevent all the bugs, then we want to at least make the bugs easier to find. We can create tools to help us in our testing and development processes. We can document the bug as a lesson for other developers and debuggers. And, we can leverage the tools and codes that we have created to find the bug, so that they can be reused.

Creating Tools

Creating tools to help you visualize and test the code can help you become more efficient. In many development environments, editors will show you the available methods for a class and the signatures for these methods. Editors in these environments can help prevent foolish defects and bugs. Things like makefiles, configuration management systems, and debuggers are some of the standard suite of tools that we all use to make our life a little easier.

But tools are more than just the development environments. There are application-specific tools that you can develop that will help you debug. For example, if you are working on a class library that deals with three-dimensional geometry, it might be useful to write a simple application that can help you visualize and manipulate the three-dimensional geometric figures. An added advantage of creating debugging and diagnostic tools is that these tools can be given to operational staff and customer service to become your first tier of technical support. For example, I developed an Extended Markup Language (XML) interface to a product and service that were part of the company's offerings. Prior to the XML interface, the company hosted solutions and designed Web sites for our customers. It was easy for our customer service department to go to the Web site to determine if the system was still running and to validate customer complaints. But with the XML interface, there was no longer a graphical representation of the solutions. When there was a problem, it was not easy for customer service to address the complaints. It was quickly decided to create a Web page that used the XML interface to mimic the customer's usage, to provide a tool for customer service to use, and to make it easier for me to test the XML interface.

Designing, creating, developing, and testing these tools might take some time away sometime from the normal debugging and development schedule, but they are worth the efforts.

Document the Bug

Documentation is the bane of software development. We all dread it. But documentation can be very valuable. If we hope to learn from our mistakes, we need to document the causes and solutions to these mistakes. Documentation also allows other people to learn from our mistakes and to understand our changes and rationales. Documenting information about a bug can give a debugger some clues as to the interrelation within the system and make it a little easier for a debugger to find the bug. Documentation can be done inline, as comments in the code. It can also be done in an external document or as part of a comprehensive bug-tracking system.

Update Existing Documents

Design and API documents are usually out-of-date because they were created without regard to how these artifacts could be maintained. When we fix a bug, if the fix is implementation related, few external documents need to be changed. However, if the change relates to the design or changes the precondition or post-condition of a module, or introduces side effects, these design-related changes need to be documented and propagated into existing documentation. This is why inline comments are the preferred documentation strategy; it is easier to change the comments along with the code rather than having to hunt down and change another document. Javadoc is a great example of a tool that makes the life of the debugger and developer easier by giving them an easy way to document their codes and make the document look good without extra work.

External documentation is usually difficult and time-consuming to change, therefore, the less it needs to be changed during the debugging process, the more likely that we'll do it instead of leaving out-of-date documentation around. We prefer to use external documentation to document domain level knowledge. Domain-level knowledge, once understood, should not be changed often. This means that external documentation that contains only domain-level knowledge should be stable and does not need to be changed often.

Documenting Why the Bug Occurred

In the previous few sections, we talked about understanding the cause of the bugs. We argue that this understanding can help us find and prevent similar bugs. If we document the causes, we can help others learn the same lessons.

Documenting How the Bug Was Found

Debugging often seems like a magical process. "How did you find this bug?" "Oh, I was looking through the shopping cart class, and then I remembered that the catalog class stores the price of the product in floating point value, so I thought I would check to see how the shopping cart calculated the total price. And I found that the shopping cart was using it as a double." Is this kind of documentation useful? Sure, because without even looking at the design or the code, we are aware of many aspects of the software. For example, (1) the shopping cart and the catalog class are somewhat related, and (2) the price for the products in the catalog is stored in one format, and the price for the same product in the shopping cart class is stored in another format. Listening to and reading about the debugging process can provide information into the software without requiring us to actually look at any of it. This kind of information provides us with small clues that might be hard to gather if we were to inspect and read the code. We might read that the shopping cart class stores the price as a double precision value. We might also read that the catalog class stores the price as a floating point value. But it is easy to forget these small details, and we might miss the relationship between them. The process of debugging draws out the correct relationships, and the story provides an entertaining way to relate the dependencies of the classes. In addition, the stories might provide us with new ideas about tools and techniques to find other related bugs.

There are very few people who actually document how bugs are found. But we discovered that everyone loves to talk about it. So it can be very educational to interview debuggers about particularly difficult bugs to see what you can learn from their efforts.

Leave Debugging Scaffolding

When we were novice programmers, we introduced debugging aids by putting explicit print statements in the code. In the following C example, we are checking to see if the function to calculate the sales price of a purchase is correct, so we introduce the print statement in line 8 and 13.

```
1. float calculateTotal( int numberOfItems, float *itemPrices,
2.                     StateCode state )
3. {
4.    int count;
5.    float total = 0.0;
6.    float tax = 0.0;
7.    for ( count = 0; count < numberOfItems; count++ ) {
8.      printf( "Count:%d, price:%f, total:%f\n",
9.              count, itemPrices[count], total );
10.     total += itemPrices[count];
11.   }
12.   tax += StateTax[state]*total; /* StateTax is some static global array. */
13.   printf( "Tax for %s = %f%% = %f", /* StateCodeString also. */
14.           StateCodeString[state], StateTax[state], tax );
15.   total += tax;
16.   return total;
17. }
```

After we have uncovered the bug, we usually just delete the print statement because the print statements make the code look unsightly. Generally, removing the print statement is not a problem until we find another bug and need to see what the same function is doing again. We then have to add the print statement back in, probably in a slightly different format with different content. But this time we learn our lesson. After the bug has been fixed, we decide not to delete the print statements because we might need to do a trace at a later time. Instead, we just comment it out. However, if we are using a language like C or C++, we might leverage the capabilities of the preprocessor to comment out the print statements, as in the following code:

```
1. float calculateTotal( int numberOfItems, float *itemPrices,
2.                     StateCode state )
3. {
4.    int count;
5.    float total = 0.0;
6.    float tax = 0.0;
```

```
7.     for ( count = 0; count < numberOfItems; count++ ) {
8. #ifdef DEBUG
9.       printf( "Count:%d, price:%f, total:%f\n",
10.               count, itemPrices[count], total );
11.#endif
12.     total += itemPrices[count];
13.    }
14.    tax += StateTax[state]*total; /* StateTax is some static global array.*/
15.#ifdef DEBUG
16.    printf( "Tax for %s = %f%% = %f", /* StateCodeString also.*/
17.            StateCodeString[state], StateTax[state], tax );
18.#endif
19.    total += tax;
20.    return total;
21. }
```

The advantage of using the *#ifdef* and *#endif* mechanisms over commenting out code is that we can change the behavior of the code without changing the code. To get the function to print out debugging information, we merely have to change the compiler options at compile time. This technique works out great for shrink-wrapped software. Commenting out debugging statements makes the code a little easier to read, and it runs a little faster. Furthermore, our debugging statements are invisible to the customer.

But sometimes using the preprocessor directives or commenting out debugging code is not an ideal solution. The difficulty stems from the fact that the debugging information is only available if the code is recompiled. Switching from production and debugging versions of the code is annoying and prone to configuration management errors. The solution then is to turn debugging on and off using command-line options or configuration files. So we can change our code to look something like this:

```
1. float calculateTotal( int numberOfItems, float *itemPrices,
2.                        StateCode state )
3. {
4.     int count;
5.     float total = 0.0;
6.     float tax = 0.0;
7.     for ( count = 0; count < numberOfItems; count++ ) {
8.       if ( debug ) { /* debug is some global variable */
9.         printf( "Count:%d, price:%f, total:%f\n",
10.                count, itemPrices[count], total );
11.      }
12.     total += itemPrices[count];
13.    }
14.    tax += StateTax[state]*total; /* StateTax is some static global array.*/
15.    if ( debug ) { /* debug is some global variable */
16.      printf( "Tax for %s = %f%% = %f", /* StateCodeString is */
```

```
17.                                     /* also some static global array.*/
18.                StateCodeString[state], StateTax[state], tax );
19.   }
20.   total += tax;
21.   return total;
22. }
```

With this approach, we don't have to compile two versions of the same code. To turn debugging on, we just restart the program. But in a 24 x 7 environment, you might not have the ability to turn the software off at will. So we thought about this and came up with a solution. Why even shut the program down at all? Why not build in the ability to control debugging information while the program is running? And, as long as we are going to spend all this extra effort to build in a debugging support infrastructure, we should make it reusable and put in some useful features. An example of a debugging feature is the ability to control the amount of detail in the debugging output. This can be done by using a numeric value, so that only the debugging statement designated below the specific value is produced. Another feature might be the ability to print debugging information for only certain blocks of codes, such as a function.

The following code shows the **calculateTotal()** function using such a debugging infrastructure and the function declaration for the debugging infrastructure in C:

```
1. extern void debugEnterFunction( char *functionName );
2. extern void debugExitFunction( char *functionName );
3. extern void debugSetLevel( int maximumDebuggingLevel );
4. extern void debugLogging( int level, char *format, … );
5.
6. float calculateTotal( int numberOfItems, float *itemPrices,
7.                     StateCode state )
8. {
9.    int count;
10.   float total = 0.0;
11.   float tax = 0.0;
12.   debugEnterFunction( "calculateTotal" );
13.   for ( count = 0; count < numberOfItems; count++ ) {
14.     debugLogging( 3, "Count:%d, price:%f, total:%f\n",
15.                 count, itemPrices[count], total );
16.     total += itemPrices[count];
17.   }
18.   tax += StateTax[state]*total; /* StateTax is some static global array. */
19.   debugLogging( 3, "Tax for %s = %f%% = %f", /* StateCodeString also. */
20.                 StateCodeString[state], StateTax[state], tax );
21.   total += tax;
22.   debugExitFunction( "calculateTotal" );
23.   return total;
24. }
```

The idea of leaving debugging scaffolding brings us back to a debugging technique called Trace Debugging, which was mentioned in Chapter 9. There are many ways to implement debugging scaffolding, and we have shown several in this section. Having a standard and consistent way of building in debugging support is an important technique for finding bugs. We will revisit this idea again in Chapter 12.

Am I Getting Better?

How do we measure our personal improvements? Physically, we gauge our growth with measurements of height and weight. In school, our performance is measured by tests. In athletic competition, we measure the time to run a 100-yard dash or the distance that we can jump. However, in software engineering, there does not seem to be a universally defined measurement of professional growth. This problem is reflected in our interviewing process. In an interview, we seek to identify the performers from the nonperformers. We want to hire engineers with high productivity. Sometimes, we confuse years of experience with productivity; other times, it's the number of programming languages known. Often, we equate expertise in a particular programming language by the fact that the potential candidate can answer esoteric language questions with some competency.

However, these measures only tangentially relate to productivity. From a business perspective, a productive software engineer is one who can maximize lines of code written per day while minimizing the number of bugs and defects introduced. These are all measurable quantities. We can easily measure the amount of time it takes to implement a particular feature and determine the number of bugs uncovered during subsequent unit and acceptance testing. Obviously, there are other measures of productivities, such as creating scalable and extensible design, that are also important qualities of a software engineer. For debuggers, such a measure might be misleading. Because a debugger's job does not involve writing code, it is not a part of their job description. For debuggers, a measure such as the over-under measure might be more appropriate. An over-under value measures the number of bugs introduced over the number of bugs fixed. A skilled debugger should have a small over-under ratio.

The personal software process proposed that individual software developers could improve their productivity and reduce their defect rate by analyzing and understanding their own processes.[1] By writing down their processes and getting feedback about their mistakes, developers can correct processes that contribute to their mistakes. This requires tracking bugs and defects that were made and fixed by individual developers. Furthermore, developers can look at the historical values of their defect rates as a measure of their own improvements.

Bug Metrics

Measurement implies quantitative measurements. Physically, we measure our height using units of length. In school, we are measured by either a letter grade or a numeric value. In

---

[1] Humphrey, W. S. "Introducing the Personal Software Process," *Annals of Software Engineering*, Vol. 1, pp 311–325, 1995.

athletic performance, unit of time, length, weight, and number of points are often used to differentiate winners and losers. In software engineers, we can look at their defect rates. Typically, a defect rate is measured by counting the number of defects or bugs over a number of lines of codes. This is by far the easiest measure. By looking at our defect rate over time, we can get a measure of our improvement in productivity.

But looking at defect rates alone does not help us improve. At best, it can only tell us if we have improved. We need other information to point out our bad habits and errors. Therefore, a bug metric needs more information. The following are items that you might want to consider tracking in your bug metrics.

♦ Description of the symptoms

♦ Root causes of the bug

♦ Remedial measures; steps taken to fix the bug

♦ Location of the bug; name of the document, function, module, feature, screen, class, or method where the defect is located

♦ Lessons learned from finding or fixing the bug

Bug Tracking

From management's perspective, a bug-tracking system can help control bugs, understand the stability of the system, and keep track of outstanding issues. They also may need additional information associated with bugs. The following list is an example of the types of information that may be required. However, because every environment is different, you may need more or less of the items in this list:

♦ *Bug identifier*—Some identifier that can be used to refer to this bug. The identifier can be used to track code or files that have been changed in relation to this bug.

♦ *Report date*—The date the bug was reported and entered into the system.

♦ *Bug status*—Identifies the status of the bug as it works itself through the system. A bug that is reported has a "New" status. A bug that was assigned to a debugger may have an "Assigned" status. Likewise, a "Testing" status may refer to the fact that a bug is currently undergoing verification testing. A "Fixed" status may refer to bugs that were fixed and validated.

♦ *Bug assignment*—Identifies the developer to whom the bug was assigned.

♦ *Start date*—Identifies the date the debugging process was started by the assigned debugger.

♦ *Severity*—Identifies the severity of the bug as described in Chapter 5.

♦ *Project/application name*—Identifies the name of the project in which the bug was discovered.

- *Report by*—Identifies the person that reported the bug.

- *System name*—Identifies the software or hardware system that contains the run-time application relevant to the bug.

- *Component name*—Identifies the software or hardware component of the project in which the bug was discovered.

- *Files modified*—Identifies a list of files modified in order to fix the bug.

- *Reproduction*—Identifies the steps necessary for reproduction if the bug is reproducible. The steps will become the test case that can be part of a regression test suite.

- *Environment*—Identifies the hardware platform, operating system, and other relevant environmental related attributes where the bug was identified.

- *Description of fix*—Identifies the fix that were used to fix the problem. This should be written in comprehensible English.

- *Date of fix*—The date the fix is put into place.

- *Tester*—Identifies the tester responsible for validating the fixes.

- *Test date*—Identifies the date the tester ran the test to validate the fix.

- *Test results*—Identifies the result of the validating fix.

- *Regression testing requirements*—Identifies a set of requirements necessary to conduct the regression test.

- *Tester responsible for regression tests*—Identifies the person responsible for performing the regression test.

- *Regression testing results*—Identifies the regression test results.

What to Do with the Data?

The goal of bug metrics is not assigning blame, nor is it to rate the performance of a developer. Instead, the goal of bug metrics is to empower a developer to learn from his mistakes and to evolve and improve as an engineer. Bug metrics also helps management determine the risks of the project and the state of the software system by monitoring the bug introduction and bug fix rates.

Currently, debuggers and developers learn about causes and effects of bugs one bug at a time. When a bug is assigned to them, they look at the symptoms of the bug and work their way through the code to find the root cause and then fix the bug. This particular bug then becomes a nugget of knowledge that is tucked away and becomes part of their repertoire. Over time, with experience, their knowledge increases, and they become more efficient debuggers. This is a slow process, and it works on an individual basis. Experiences learned by one debugger cannot easily be transferred to another. However, the collection of the symptoms and causes written in the bug metrics can help mitigate this inefficiency. Developers and debuggers can look at past bugs and learn from them. They can absorb someone else's experience and incorporate it as their own.

Developers can look at all the bugs with similar causes and determine if there are ways to prevent the same kinds of bugs and defects from occurring. This is different from the bug-prevention ideas presented in the earlier section "How Can I Prevent This Bug?" In that section, we discussed ways to identify bug prevention techniques local to a particular bug. However, with bug metrics, developers can look at all the bugs and come up with a generalized approach to perform bug prevention. This is a technique that looks for systematic errors, and it is part of the bug prevention concept called defect causal analysis as described in Chapter 12.

Often, bugs can be a result of an inappropriate process. Project management can use the bug metrics to determine if any process changes can help with bug prevention or make the debugging effort more efficient and productive. In addition, the bug metrics described previously allow project management to determine the historical cost of debugging efforts and the rate of bug introduction and bug removal. These numbers can also help project management determine the cost associated with maintaining the software. The concept of software maintenance related to debugging is further explored in Chapter 14.

Summary

In this chapter, we looked at the activities that could and should be performed after a bug is fixed. The purpose of these activities is to transform debugging from a reactive process to a proactive process. Instead of waiting for bugs to occur, we ask ourselves the following five questions to anticipate and prevent bugs.

♦ *Did I make the same mistake elsewhere?* We ask this question so that we can seek to fix the same kind of mistakes in other parts of the code that we have written.

♦ *What's hiding behind this bug?* We ask this question to prevent introduction of bugs that result from our changes.

♦ *How can I prevent this bug?* We ask this question to learn from our mistakes so that we don't make the same mistake again.

♦ *How can I make this kind of bug easier to find?* We ask this question to make our debugging efforts easier next time. We try to understand our process for finding a bug, and attempt to find a way to help make the process better and more efficient.

♦ *Am I getting better?* We ask this question to measure our improvements, in our skills and the software that we have produced.

Your answers to these questions can help you prevent bugs and make bugs easier to find. In Chapter 12 we will discuss some of our answers to these questions.

Bug Puzzle

In this chapter, we used the C string functions for many of our examples. Therefore, we thought it might be useful to have the bug puzzle be related to the misuse of C string functions. Consider the following code:

```
1.  #include <string.h>
2.  int main(int argc, char *argv[])
3.  {
4.    char firstname[20];
5.    char *lastname;
6.    char *ptr;
7.    char *username = NULL;
8.    if ( argc != 2 ) {
9.        printf("Usage: %s username\n", argv[0]);
10.       exit(1);
11.   }
12.   username = argv[1];
13.   printf( "username:<%s>\n", username );
14.   /* Find the space character */
15.   ptr = index( username, ' ' );
16.   *ptr = NULL;
17.   /* copy the first part of the user name */
18.   strncpy( firstname, username, strlen(username) );
19.   ptr++;
20.   /* copy the last name of the user name */
21.   lastname = (char *) malloc( sizeof(char)*strlen(ptr) );
22.   strcpy( lastname, ptr );
23.   /* See what it looks like */
24.   printf( "first name:<%s>\n", firstname );
25.   printf( "last name:<%s>\n", lastname );
26.   return 0;
27. }
```

The purpose of the program is to find the first name and last name of the name of a user. The user name is passed in through the command line argument. We will assume that the first name and last name of the user is separated by a white space. Can you identify all the defects in the code?

Chapter 12
Prebugging

Yuan Hsieh

Certainly, many of you are veterans of numerous battles of cyber-infestations. You can share the various battle scars with your colleagues including the number of continuous allnighters, pyramids of soft drinks, and wall-to-wall empty pizza boxes (or Chinese food cartons, depending on your personal preference). In many cases, your efforts were probably well rewarded: You found the bug and came up with a fix. Management was ecstatic. The product shipped the next day, and you were hailed as a hero right before you passed out from physical and mental exhaustion. We have all lived it. When we were fresh out of school working our first job as software developers, we were proud of our abilities to stay up all night and find bugs that were deemed too important and too difficult. We viewed bugs as a challenge that needed to be conquered. We lived for the praises and incredulous comments from our colleagues and peers. Comments like "You stayed up how many nights?" "Wow, you *fixed* it!" and "How *did* you figure it out?" do wonders for the ego of a twenty-something.

Years later, although these kinds of comments are still desired, we no longer share the same enthusiasm over the prospect of debugging. We saw firsthand the costs of bugs. We observed the same mistakes made repeatedly. The same types of bug haunted us regardless of computer language, operating system, industry, or environment. It got old. We were tired of fixing the same bugs no matter where we went. We also have matured and developed a sense of professionalism where we pride ourselves in our abilities to only need to work 40 hours a week and receive no panic calls from the network operations at 3:00 A.M. We like it when things run so smoothly that no one in the company seems to be aware of our existence. This is our idea of software Valhalla; our reward for fighting and surviving the countless battles. How can we achieve this software bliss? We make our codes safe. We try to understand the problem that we are trying to solve by asking the right questions. We learn to work within the real-life constraints that we have; we learn to make trade-offs. We learn from our mistakes. We make it possible to quickly and easily detect, identify, and corrects bugs. In effect, we practice the process that we call prebugging.

What Is Prebugging?

Prebugging is the process of bug reduction. The goal of prebugging is to reduce the odds of making mistakes, and when we do make mistakes, to have the infrastructure in place to detect, identify, and eliminate these mistakes quickly and painlessly. Chapters 2, 3, and 4, attempted to describe the causes and nature of bugs. We leverage the understanding gained in these chapters to eliminate and prevent bugs in our software.

In this chapter, we outline and discuss some prebugging techniques. Some of these techniques are applicable in every phase of the software development life cycle, whereas others are more focused on a specific stage. Some of these techniques should be considered at the organizational level, whereas others are more applicable for individual developers. We present some techniques in detail, but we also present techniques that are more conceptually based. For these conceptually based techniques, you need to understand the concepts and figure out how to apply them to your own specific circumstance. Where appropriate, we have provided some examples. However, these examples are necessarily simple in order to illustrate our point.

Mind-Set of Prebugging

The first and foremost criterion for producing quality software is the desire by an organization to shoot for the moon: bug-free software. With this desire, you must then learn humility. You are only human, and you will make mistakes. With humility, you can open your mind, seek to find answers, and be willing to do tasks that you might find difficult and annoying. If it sounds like we are preaching, it is probably because we are. Quality is a conscientious decision, and quality does not happen by accident.

Presumably, you are reading this book because you are looking for answers. You have already taken the first step. If you want to produce quality software and you already understand your own limitations, there are two more fundamental psychologies of prebugging that can help you achieve the goal of producing quality software: always be paranoid and be egoless.

Be Paranoid

In our view, the most important mind-set for prebugging is the acknowledgment that we will make mistakes. We need to work with the assumption that the software that we are working on contains millions of bugs. We need to be paranoid. It doesn't hurt to imagine a global conspiracy that is out to get you with bugs.

Designing, and implementing software systems under the assumption that things will go wrong requires a totally different way of thinking. It forces you to ask a lot of questions, for example, "How do you want me to handle X if Y happens?" "Can Y ever happen?" "What would happen if Y happens?" and "How can I tell if Y happens?" If you are paranoid, you will realize the need to check variable values and design for fail-over, fault-tolerance, and redundancy. But you just don't stop at that. You then think about how other developers could use your interfaces incorrectly and cause your code to fail or their codes to fail. So you define very narrowly focused ways to use your interfaces. You write sample programs to show them how to use the interfaces. And you write documentation that explains what the side effects and the expected inputs and outputs are. You help them prevent bugs in their programs by making it impossible for them to use your codes incorrectly.

Being paranoid also means that you double-check the input and the output to the interfaces that you are using and make no assumptions, especially if you are not familiar with the interfaces. Ask yourself questions, such as "Do I have the arguments in the correct order?" "Does this method allocate the memory of the object that I am supposed to free, or does this method only pass me the pointer to the object that it manages?"

If you are paranoid about bugs in the software, you will also start to question every little inconsistency that appears in the output of the application and the behavior of the software. When you observe unexplained behavior, your task is to understand why the system is behaving in such a fashion. Even if there is no bug, you will gain much insight into the software. These understandings will help you find bugs and explain other behaviors at a later time.

Being paranoid means that every time someone mentions a peculiar software behavior, you jump out of your chair and grill them to find out all the details. You then work through the codes and the system to understand if it is possible for the system to behave in such a way, and why it does. You don't dismiss bug reports, even if the problem is truly a user error. A user error can signify a bad or confusing user interface, which can result in the misuse of the system and software. These misuses can cause problems in the system environment or even trigger bugs in some obscure code paths in your software. You should assume that users cannot make mistakes. A user mistake that can crash your system means that your system is too fragile and should be fixed.

However, being paranoid does not mean you must analyze everything to the last detail. Paralysis by analysis does not help anyone solve problems or prevent bugs.

Be Egoless

Not too long ago, I was in a design meeting where one of the senior developers was presenting his ideas on a design. The majority of the other developers disagreed with his design. There was a philosophical difference, and neither group was willing to consider compromise or an alternative. It became a religious war. The two groups butted heads, and nothing much was accomplished in the meeting.

When your ego becomes attached to your work, you lose your objectivity. When that happens, you will not be able to take criticisms, you will not believe in bug reports, and you will become defensive. None of these traits is conducive for creating bug-free software. Keep in mind that when people point out mistakes in your design or implementation, they are pointing out mistakes on a piece of paper. They are not talking about a personality flaw or making an accusation. It is just work, try to keep it professional.

General Techniques

The idea behind quality software is that software of "quality" has few bugs. But bug prevention can start before even a single line of code has been written. In Chapters 3 and 4, we argued that software modifications can contribute to bugs. This implies that whenever possible, we want to reuse existing technology as a method for bug prevention by reducing the amount of software changes. We discussed human errors, misinterpretation of requirements and design, lack of communication, and improper testing as sources of bugs. Techniques that can help us detect and trap bugs can be invaluable in reducing the odds of leaving bugs in a production environment. Complexity is a main cause of bugs and defects. Therefore, if we can find ways to reduce and manage the complexity, we can hope to reduce the number of bugs.

The general techniques presented in this section, if implemented correctly, should give you the most bang for the buck. These are global preventive measures that can be performed at both the individual and organizational level.

People in Prebugging

People make the software. People make bugs in the software. People fix bugs in the software. People are the first line of defense against bugs, and people typically are a management issue. As software developers, the problem is that we usually have to work with other people. Sometimes, we have the opportunity to interview and select the people that we want to work with. And sometimes, we have a chance to influence management's approach and decisions.

Hire Good People

Interviewing is not a scientific process. It is difficult to determine the proficient engineers from the inefficient engineers by just looking at their resumes and having a few hours of conversations. It doesn't matter what kinds of tools they know or how many year's experience they have, inefficient software engineers will make more bugs than proficient software engineers. Numerous studies have shown that hiring good people is a bargain.[1] There are many articles written about questions and techniques that you can use to interview candidates

---

[1] Boehm, B., and Papaccio, P. N. "Understanding and Controlling Software Costs," *IEEE Transactions on Software Engineering*, Vol. 14, No. 10, pp. 1462–1477, October 1988.

that we will not repeat in this book. However, we prefer to hire problem solvers. We have found that good engineers are good problem solvers. They can solve a problem regardless of the language, tools, and problem domains. Good problem solvers also tend to be good debuggers as well.

For a senior-level software engineer, we like to look for the following traits, and we ask questions that can help us identify these traits:

♦ Do they tell us something that we don't already know? Do they have any new insights into a problem or a solution? Even if we disagree with them philosophically, we tend to prefer candidates who have some opinions that can be backed by rational thinking.

♦ Have they internalized the concepts? Good senior-level engineers should have internalized the problems and the solutions of their expertise. Good C++ engineers should have internalized the concept of abstract classes and methods and should be able to talk about it in their own words and provide analogies, not just regurgitate the syntax of abstract classes and methods.

♦ Can they give us trade-offs? Software engineering is nothing more than making trade-offs. Good software engineers understand the risk and benefits of one design solution compared to another. They make trade-offs based on the information at hand; sometimes they make the right one and sometimes the wrong one. But at least they know the risks they are taking.

♦ Given an incomplete and ambiguous problem statement to solve, good software engineers tend to avoid assumptions and ask questions to help them understand the problem that we have presented. Bad engineers will give you an answer based on their perception of the problem.

Maintain Continuity

Because most organizations are plagued with poor documentation, it is essential that there is some continuity in a project. Ideally, the continuity should be provided by technical personnel, but in a pinch, the role can be filled by anyone. The role of such a person is to provide background information about the project and serve as a resource for new members. Furthermore, a person who is familiar with the software should be more efficient at fixing bugs and preventing bugs.

The best way to maintain continuity is to keep the original team on the project as long as the project lives on. This obviously is not tractable because people get bored if there are no new challenges. And bored people leave the company. Therefore, you must allow team members to move on to different projects with the understanding that they will provide some form of technology transfer, either via documentation or hands-on mentoring. Regardless, the knowledge must be passed on.

Hire Backup

One way to maintain continuity is to hire backups. Each person on the team should have a backup that can do the job as effectively as the original person can. This is to prevent the "been hit by the bus" syndrome. For those of you not familiar with this syndrome, this is a description of a worse case scenario. Imagine that a critical piece of the software is known and understood only by one senior software engineer. One day, said engineer got hit by a bus on their way into work. Now you have a piece of critical software understood by no one within the company and there is no documentation. What's the cost of not having a backup in this case? A way to create instant backup is to utilize the paired programming technique proposed by the Extreme Programming methodology.[2] When you have two people working on the same project, they have to communicate and learn about each other's tasks. As a result, the knowledge is disseminated.

Hire the Right People for the Environment

Capability Maturity Model (CMM) is defined by the Software Engineering Institute (SEI) to measure the maturity of a software development organization. SEI defines five CMM levels. A CMM level 1 organization is chaotic, with no processes. CMM level 2 can be characterized by repeatable processes. If your company works in Internet time and can't afford to implement CMM level 2 processes, then don't kid yourself and hire people who are dogmatic about the software engineering process. No matter how good your intentions are, you will never have the time to implement and devise these processes. How many of us have the backbone to say "no" to senior management? Hire "hackers" instead; they will be happy, they don't care, and they will get the job done. A good hacker has the knack of figuring out what the system does with minimum documentation. They love to get down and dirty, and they have no problem taking shortcuts to meet your daily requirement changes. On the other hand, if you hire process-oriented engineers, they will gripe and complain about the lack of process and documentation. If you give them a requirement change half way through a project, they will want to spend three weeks analyzing it. As a result, everyone will get annoyed at everyone else, and there's no fun in that.

If your company is CMM level 3 and you hire a hacker, the hacker will quit in a matter of a few weeks. If you are managing a group of "Dirty-Dozen" workers (employees just as individualistic, unruly and opinionated as the soldiers in the 1967 film, possibly who even consider themselves to be on a similar suicide mission), then any attempt to introduce formal processes will be doomed to fail; to formalize your procedures you would have to replace them with people who can deal with processes. You can save yourself a lot of grief if you can be honest about your environment and the people that you have on staff.

Change the Play Book or Change the Players

If you work in a hacker-oriented environment, you are not doomed to stay in a CMM level 1 environment. Hackers have a process too, and hacking can be a documented and repeatable

---

[2] Beck, Kent. *Extreme Programming Explained*. Addison-Wesley, Upper Saddle River, New Jersey, 2000.

process. Hacking does not have to be senseless. This is where you earn your keep as a project manager or CTO; you need to figure out how to utilize your personnel to their fullest potential and how to find ways to fit them into a repeatable process. A good analogy can be taken from the world of sports. As a football coach, do you ask your quarterback, who is known for accuracy within 20 yards but lacks a strong arm, to throw 40 yard passes all the time? The fans will be screaming to have your head. If you have a weak offensive line, do you call in plays to have the quarterback sit in the pocket for more than three seconds? The defensive linemen will have your quarterback's head. In basketball, if you have a team with tall and big center and forwards, do you take three-point shots all the time? Of course not. As a coach, you would devise game plans to use your strength against the weakness of your opponent according to the circumstances. Managing a software development team is no different. The software development process is not exactly an assembly line, and the members of a software development team are not shaped from a cookie cutter. You must figure out a game plan for the talents that you have. This can be done by understanding the goal and purpose of each step in the idea process and find a way to achieve that goal within your environment.

The other option, of course, is to change the players. You can simply impose a process and remove any developer that does not come on board. It's as simple as that. But first, you better have a strategy to replace the knowledge locked into those players.

Evolution Not Revolution

A point to consider is that it is not necessary to change the world in one day. Evolution works for biological systems, it can also work for a software development process. In an evolutionary approach, you don't make a wholesale change in the way a team works. Instead, you introduce one change at a time. The change you introduce depends on the circumstance and the team that you have to work with. The following list contains a collection of techniques for you to consider:

◆ *Isolate the chaotic element.* In the majority of software development environments, the chaotic element is the development team. But that doesn't mean the testing process has to be chaotic as well. Testing teams can do bug tracking, create test plans, and document test results. These can all be accomplished independently from whatever the developers are doing. The development team might never check the bugs database, but the existence of one can allow the management to assign bugs to hackers. It allows testers to track what got fixed and what didn't. It is not as powerful as if it is integrated into the entire development process, but it is a first step. Furthermore, by isolating the chaotic elements, you can create structure and organization and processes around these elements, and will be ready to replace and change the chaotic elements whenever appropriate.

◆ *Introduce process elements one at a time.* This can be a process element that your development team is willing to implement because they believe it is important, or you can have one person whose job is to bridge the gap between the chaotic environment of today and the process environment of the future. For example, most developers and hackers acknowledge the usefulness of a configuration management environment, and are willing to suffer the inconvenience of using one. They believe that the cost of having no configuration management process is more costly than been forced to use one, and this brings up the next point.

♦ *Provide incentives.* There are two kinds of incentives; positive and negative incentives, and you can use both to your advantage. Positive incentives should be familiar to most, so let's focus on the negative incentives. A process can be a series of tedious tasks that no sensible hackers are willing to do, even out of boredom. But the pain of not following a process can be even worse. For example, no one likes to be woken at 4:00 A.M., and no one likes to sacrifice a weekend. So when a disaster strikes and developers are suffering the agony of the disaster, you can introduce the notion of documentation and training. For example, you can remind them that "If you would just write a training guide, then the operational folks could handle the problem that they are suppose to handle anyway" or "If you have a backup, then that person can be called instead of you." Of course, there is the risk that the developer might just walk away. In that case, it might be necessary to introduce another person to do the job.

♦ *Plan for replacement.* If your developer is dead set against any sort of process, then it might be necessary to replace him or her. It is typically very difficult to smoothly replace a developer in a chaotic environment because there is so much knowledge locked in the developer's head. Therefore, you can't just fire the person out of the blue; you must plan a way to disseminate the knowledge. This is obviously the last resort. In the current software industry, planning for replacement is a necessary strategy regardless of your company culture. Because developers come and go at will, the last thing you want is to be held hostage by a disgruntled employee. There are numerous techniques that you can implement to plan for replacements. Documentation, mentoring, and training are just a few examples.

Defect Causal Analysis

A wise man once said that we should learn from our mistakes. Bugs certainly are mistakes, but it doesn't appear that we are learning from them, even after we have fixed them. During the development stage, we write our code, we test it, we find a bug, we fix it, and then we move on to the next bug or the next code. We never document and analyze these bugs. When we are in the testing stage, bugs might be reported and recorded, but these bugs are rarely collected and analyzed to find a fault-prone module and determine systematic errors that could be learned from and prevented. There are some reported successes of defect prevention using some form of defect analysis. NEC implemented one form of defect causal analysis in 1981, and they were able to track and monitor the defect introduction rate and observe a decreasing trend in the 10 years of the implementation.[3] IBM and Computer Science Corporation also implemented some form of defect causal analysis in their software development processes. Over a span of two years, they reported a 50 percent decrease in defect rate.[4]

---

[3] Kajihara, J., Amamiya, G., and Saya, T. "Learning from Bugs," *IEEE Software*, pp 46–54, September, 1993.
[4] Card, D. N. "Learning From Our Mistakes with Defect Causal Analysis," *IEEE Software*, pp 56–63, January–February, 1998.

Analyzing the cause of defects can be accomplished at the organizational level and at the personal level. At the organization level, the causal analysis needs to be integrated as part of the software development process with teams, meetings, and forms.[5] At the personal level, the process can be less formal and opportunistic. Regardless of the formality of the defect analysis, the goal is the same: Identify the cause of defects and seek methods to prevent these defects from recurring. Some of the ideas that we have presented in this chapter are the result of analyzing our own mistakes and mistakes that we have seen others make, although some other ideas are culled from available empirical studies.

Systematic Errors

The main contribution of defect causal analysis to bug prevention is the identification of systematic errors. These systematic errors account for a large percentage of defects found in a typical software development project.[6] If we can prevent these systematic errors, we can proportionally increase the quality of the software and reduce the defect level.

An error is systematic if it occurs frequently due to the same reason. Errors are also systematic if they frequently occur at a particular time and place. In Chapter 3, we identified changes to the software to be a main reason for introducing bugs. Therefore, errors due to software changes are systematic errors that can be reduced by implementing techniques to reduce the amount of changes or reduce the effects of changes on software quality. Lack of system and program comprehension is a reason that changes tend to be bug prone, so we need to find a variety of techniques to help the maintainer and developers understand the programs and systems. If the bugs in your system tend to occur in the interfaces, you should evaluate the way you design your interfaces in order to make them less fault prone.

The key to identifying systematic errors is to observe patterns. Individually, the error might be intriguing and educational, but it may not help us remove a large class of errors in one fell swoop. We need a way to help us see these errors from 20,000 feet.

Identifying Systematic Errors

In order to see a pattern of the errors that we are prone to make, we need to have a record and history of the errors that we make. What should be recorded about the defect and bugs that have been found and fixed? At the minimum, a defect record should answer the following questions:

- *What was the defect?* This is a description of the defect. We can use the description to help us categorize and collect similar defects for pattern analysis.

- *Where was the defect located?* We are interested in the location of the defect at different levels. We like to know which software module contained the defect. We like to know where the defect occurred in the module. Was it in the interface or in the initialization?

---

[5] Card, D. N. "Learning From Our Mistakes with Defect Causal Analysis," *IEEE Software*, pp 56–63, January–February, 1998.
   Jones, C. L. "A Process-Integrated Approach To Defect Prevention," *IBM Systems Journal*, Vol. 24, No. 2, pp 150–167, 1985.
[6] Card, D. N. "Learning From Our Mistakes with Defect Causal Analysis," *IEEE Software*, pp 56–63, January–February, 1998.

Was it in the data structure definition or in the computational process? Did it occur in the data transformation process or in the conditional logic?

♦ *When was the defect introduced?* We want to know at which stage of the process the defect was introduced. Did the defect originate at the requirement, the design, or the implementation phase? What were we doing when we introduced the defect? The answers to these questions can help us understand which part of the process we need to improve.

♦ *Why was the defect introduced?* The person that introduced the defect might remember the exact circumstance. The reason given might be speculation or an educated guess. Whatever the case, these reasons can help us devise a way to prevent the defect from recurring.

Once we have a history of defects, we can cluster these defects according to where and when they occur. With these clusters, we can attempt to identify the principle causes of the defects in these clusters and devise methods and processes to remove the causes.

Personal Defect Causal Analysis

You can still perform defect causal analysis even without organizational support to help you better understand the kinds of mistakes you tend to make and why. Keeping an engineering notebook where you write down your thoughts and bugs that you have fixed is always a good idea. Another way to track your own mistakes is to document them directly in the codes after you have fixed it. Later, when an opportunity presents itself, you can collect these comments to review your errors. The following example shows a way to comment your code while keeping a record of defects that can be easily retrieved and analyzed.

```
1. //some codes
2. /* ## 12/25/2000 orderEntry.cc getOrderItems() ych
3.    ##   I read the design incorrectly.  I was supposed to
4.    ##   return a list even if there was no item in the order,
5.    ##   but I returned a null when there was no item in the order,
6.    ##   and that broke the orderManager.
7.  */
8. // code with defect that was fixed.
```

The ## symbols in the comments make it easy to extract the comments relating to the defect. The time, the file name, and the function name give you an idea of where and when the defect was found and located. The description tells you why you made the mistake, and what you did to fix the mistake. With a tool like grep, you can easily collect all the errors that were made and provide an overview of your mistakes.

Another advantage of having defect comments in the code is that it allows the maintainer to read the code and understand the rationale for the changes that were made to it. It gives the maintainer a chance to understand why things were done the way they were.

Another place where you could record defect information is in the commenting feature of most version control systems. Most version control systems allow you to write about the changes to the files when you are checking the file into the repository. The same kind of information should go into these comments so that they can be analyzed at a later time.

Detecting Defects

Because bugs are manifestations of software defects (as defined in Chapter 3), it stands to reason that one way to prevent bugs is to detect and correct defects before they transform themselves into bugs in runtime, especially in the production environment. There are two approaches to detect software defects. The first approach is inspection, and the second approach is the transformation of defects into bugs under our control; otherwise known as testing. Inspection is a static technique, whereas testing is considered to be a dynamic technique and is covered in Chapter 13.

Inspection

The idea behind inspection is to have another pair of eyes look at requirements, design, and implementation in order to identify any mistakes that might have been overlooked. In formal software development methodologies, inspections tend to occur during reviews: requirement review, design review, and code review. There are numerous studies on the effectiveness of inspection and the process of inspections.[7] For our bug-centric view of the software development universe, the claims of inspection is that inspection could produce software with 10 to 100 times fewer defects and reduce testing time by up to 85 percent.[8]

How Not to Do Inspection

I have been involved in a few formal design and code review sessions at various companies. Typically, the project manager or the chief engineer would call for a review session. The reviewers would receive a package of materials, sometimes a week in advance, but most often a day or two before the review meeting. When the designated time had come, my fellow reviewers and I would converge in a conference room, and the designer or developer would present their materials to critique. Was the inspection useful? To be honest, not the way we were doing it. The problems were the same as everywhere else: The company wanted to develop an inspection process, but no one in the company really had any clue about inspection. Requirements were never reviewed, which meant that although the design and implementation might be great, they would need to be changed due to defects that were found later in the requirements. The majority of comments in code reviews were on coding style violations. Relationships of codes to design were rarely discussed or mentioned, mainly because the reviewers never had a chance to understand the designs of the system under review. Design reviews became the soapbox for designers to discuss their grand vision. It was difficult to comment on the design because none of the reviewers really had a chance to digest and understand the requirements that the design was supposed to satisfy.

---

[7] Gilb, T. *Principles of Software Engineering Management*. The Bath Press, Avon, Great Britain, 1988.
 Porter, A., and Votta, L. "Comparing Detection Methods for Software Requirements Inspections: A Replication Using Professional Subjects," *Empirical Software Engineering*, Vol. 3, No. 4, pp 335–379, December 1998.
[8] Gilb, T. *Principles of Software Engineering Management*. The Bath Press, Avon, Great Britain, 1988.

How to Do Inspection

The key to a good inspection process is to have quality inspectors. These are people who are familiar with the problem and the solution. We can help create a knowledgeable inspection team by preparing them with materials and time to learn the materials. We can increase the knowledge level of the inspection team by having more than a few inspectors. The following four items are the keys to a successful inspection:

♦ *Familiarity*—The inspector is expected to be familiar with the problem, the product, the solution, and the implementation to be inspected. In a code review, the inspector should understand what the software is supposed to do and how the software fits in with the rest of the system. Inspectors should be proficient with the language used in coding, and they should understand the risk of different implementation choices. In a design review, the inspector should be familiar with the functional and performance requirements of the system. The inspector should also understand the trade-offs for different design elements. The more familiar the inspectors are with the problem and the solution, the more effective they will be in the inspection process.

♦ *Preparation*—One way to help inspectors to understand the problem is to prepare them for the inspection. Preparation means that the developers should present documents and artifacts to inspectors as soon as possible. It means that the inspectors need to be given sufficient amounts of time to understand the problems and the solutions that are presented.

♦ *A lot of eyes*—Having more than one inspector inspecting the same artifact will help improve the effectiveness of defect detection. After all, one person can only have so much knowledge about the problem and the solution. He or she can grow fatigued and distracted. A second inspector helps increase the overall product knowledge in the inspection team. The second inspector can also cover other inspector's weakness. Likewise, adding a third and fourth inspector can also benefit the effectiveness of the inspection process. However, we suspect that at some point, it is counterproductive to have too many inspectors. There could be too many voices. One way to find the optimum number of inspectors is to use the scenario inspection technique as described in the "Inspection Techniques" section.

♦ *Track inspection data*—Feeding the results of the inspection data back to the inspection team can help the team and the organization perform defect causal analysis of their processes and defects. This information will assist them in modifying their processes to make them more efficient. Furthermore, tracking inspection data can also help the management team visualize the progress of the development process and make hard decisions.

What Should Be Inspected?

Everything should be inspected, but at the minimum, we feel that the following items should be inspected:

♦ Requirement specifications

♦ Design specifications

◆ Codes

◆ Test plans

These items should be inspected for internal correctness and completeness. In addition, the relationship of one item to another should also be inspected. If the design does not meet the specification of the requirements, the design is defective and should be fixed.

Inspection Techniques

In general, there are three inspection techniques: ad hoc, checklist, and scenario based. In an ad hoc technique, all the reviewers are given the same responsibility, which is to look for errors in the documentation or the codes. In a checklist approach, the reviewers are given a list of things to look for, but it is similar to the ad hoc technique in all other aspects: All the reviewers are responsible for errors in the entire documentation and codes. In the scenario-based approach, each reviewer is asked to focus on a set of specific scenarios. The scenarios can be a set of features in the requirement, a set of use cases, or a set of functionalities. In one study, it was determined that the overall requirement inspection performance could be improved using the scenario-based approach.[9] Surprisingly (or unsurprisingly), the same study also found that review meetings do not contribute to the overall defect detection rate.

In the scenario-based approach, individual reviewers use systematic procedures to address a small number of specific issues. This approach can be applied to requirement, design, code, and test plan reviews. Instead of having every reviewer doing the same design review on the entire system, individual reviewers might be responsible for different modules. For example, in an e-commerce system, one reviewer might be responsible for the shopping cart module and another reviewer be responsible for the order-entry module, whereas a third reviewer might be responsible for the interfaces between all the modules.

One advantage of scenario-based inspection is that the reviewer of a specific scenario in the requirement review can then be asked to participate in the design, implementation, and test plan for the given scenario. Because the reviewer has already reviewed the requirements of the scenario, we can assume that he or she is familiar with the requirements. Therefore, the reviewer is well qualified to judge the correctness of the products produced during the latter stages of the software development cycle.

However, the disadvantage of a scenario-based inspection is that more resources are required, which can be costly. Because a reviewer is only responsible for a single scenario, a large number of reviewers might be required to inspect the entire project.

Alternatives to Formal Inspection

Inspection can be a very cost-effective way to prevent bugs, if you can afford the formalism. Inspection is a strategy that needs to be mandated by the management and is driven by the

---

[9] Porter, A., and Votta, L. "Comparing Detection Methods for Software Requirements Inspections: A Replication Using Professional Subjects," *Empirical Software Engineering*, Vol. 3, No. 4, pp 335–379, December 1998.

constraints of reality. However, if you don't have the time and resources available, how can you achieve the goal of inspection without a formal inspection process? Before we answer this question, let's first understand exactly how inspection helps us prevent bugs.

Inspection is not a new idea originating from the software industry. During our school years, our homework was inspected by our teachers. When we double-check our math, we inspect our own work. An inspector is a proofreader. The whole point of inspection is simply to have one person (the inspector) check another person's work. If the inspector is familiar with the problem and solution domain, the theory is that the inspector should be able to evaluate the correctness of the work and point out flaws.

Inspecting Your Own Work

In high school and university, my English teacher always told me to proofread my own writing when I was done with it. In fact, he said it was better to put the writing away for a while, and then come back and read it again. With a fresh set of eyes, it is always easier to find your errors.

The same advice can be applied to the products of software development processes. When you are focused on producing a requirement document or writing a program, you try the best you can to avoid mistakes. But mistakes do happen, and you hope to catch them by simply walking through the document or program. The main problem with inspecting your own work is that when you attempt to inspect it shortly after you have finished your work, you might still be so wrapped up with your own thoughts and assumptions that you might not recognize apparent defects when you see them.

The most effective way to inspect your own work is to put it away and come back to it later. At a later time, you might be able to look at your work objectively. If time is not on your side, you might need to do some creative time management to make this work. For example, if you are a developer working on a project, you tend to be responsible for multiple features. You can finish one feature, test it as well as you can, and then move on to another feature. When you are done with your second or third feature, you can come back to the implementation of your first feature and do a walk-through of your first feature.

Consider another idea for inspecting your own work: Most developers tend to write documentation after the implementation is done and is being tested by the testing team. This is a perfect time to perform inspection. When you are documenting your interfaces, you can use this time to revisit and review your code. You will be able to write better documentation, and you will also have a chance to beat the testing team in finding bugs in your own code.

Putting your work away for a later time might be difficult to do if time is very short. You may not have the chance to come back to your product at a later date. Another risk of inspecting your own work is that if you don't understand the problem, the process, the tools, or the solutions in the first place, you may not recognize your mistakes the second time around.

Homogeneous and Heterogeneous Paired Inspection

If your time is short, it might be necessary to do the work and inspect it at the same time. This can be accomplished by adapting the idea of paired programming. In Extreme Programming methodology, paired programming promotes the idea of having two people work on the same problem at the same time.[10]

The practice of paired programming can be applied to inspection and to other stages of the software development life cycle, including the requirement specification stage, the development of the test plan, and the design process. There is no reason why anyone has to work in isolation. On the other hand, it is not strictly necessary to have two requirement analysts working together on the requirements or two testers working on the test plan. It might be more useful use a *heterogeneous* paired inspection team.

In a heterogeneous paired inspection team, people with two different roles are put together to work on the same tasks. There are many advantages to this approach in addition to accomplishing inspection. First, people with two different roles can learn about each other's tasks and responsibilities, and they can learn how to make each other's job a lot easier by anticipating the needs of one another. Second, the core competency of the organization is increased because some employees are learning aspects of different jobs. Third, it is possible for the people with different roles to get a jump start on their own tasks and be able to think ahead to their own tasks.

For example, a requirement analyst and a chief designer can work together on requirements. The advantage in this situation is that the designer can question requirements that do not make sense or are not technically feasible. But the designer also gets a preview of the tasks ahead. The drawback of having a technical person work on the requirements is the risk of making technical decisions too early.

Consider another example: Having a requirement analyst work with a tester to craft the test plan has the advantage of combining the skills of both positions to create a test plan that not only tests the software according to the letter of the requirement, but also tests the spirit of the requirements. After all, who else is most qualified to answer questions about requirements than the requirement analyst? Furthermore, after seeing how the tester creates the test plan using the requirements, the requirement analyst can learn to create requirements that are more testable.

The main difficulty of a heterogeneous pair inspection approach is in choosing the right people. Some skill sets are a natural fit, and some are not. It might be difficult and unreasonable to have a requirement analyst work with an implementer on codes. In addition, some people are not interested in learning or understanding a different job, and some people are not capable of learning a different job. Some people are easily intimidated in an unfamiliar role and would not benefit the inspection process. These types of people would not be appropriate as part of a heterogeneous paired inspection team.

---

[10] Beck, Kent. *Extreme Programming Explained.* Addison-Wesley, Upper Saddle River, New Jersey, 2000.

Producer-Consumer Relationship

An alternative to the paired inspection is to establish a producer-consumer relationship between team members, and let the consumer inspect the work of the producer. Because the consumer has to use the work completed by the producer, both members of the team have a self-interest in evaluating and inspecting the work as part of the delivery and acceptance criteria. The delivery and acceptance criteria can be formal or informal, depending on the culture of your organization.

There is a natural producer-consumer relationship that occurs between different stages of the software development process. Designers consume requirements produced by requirement analysts. Developers use design documents produced by designers. Testers consume requirements and implementations. In all these cases, the consumers must use the results of the producers in order to perform their task, and it is natural for the consumers to want to ensure that the quality of the product they are using is first-rate.

However, even within the same stage of the software development cycle, it is possible to establish a producer-consumer relationship. For example, one developer could be producing a module in the business layer, and another developer could be working on the graphical user interface (GUI) in the presentation layer. Because the GUI developer needs the application programming interfaces (APIs) from the business layer, he plays the role of the consumer. As part of his job, it is advantageous for the GUI developer to review the implementation of the business layer, ensure the correctness of the business layer product, and understand the usage and design of the business layer.

Risk of Inspection

Good inspection results can create false confidence. In one reported instance, even though the development was proceeding well, the inspection process revealed many errors. However, the project was ultimately cancelled because a basic flaw in the requirement was never detected. The basic flaw in this case was that the business need for the project was never properly defined and rationalized. In another case study, the project's inspection data showed that the project was doing well in the implementation stage. However, the project was ultimately unsuccessful due to continually changing requirements. In this case, the requirement and design was never inspected, and code inspection alone was not capable of ensuring the success of the project.[11]

The lesson is simple: Inspection can help prevent bugs, but by itself, it cannot ensure the success of a project.

Reuse

Conventional wisdom about software reuse states that there is an advantage to building a system using reusable components. The advantages that are commonly cited are enhanced

---

[11] Weller, E. F. "Lessons from Three Years of Inspection Data," *IEEE Software*, pp 38–45, September, 1993.
  Gilb, T. *Principles of Software Engineering Management*. The Bath Press. Avon, Great Britain. 1988.

efficiency and productivity of the software development process, reduced maintenance requirements, and an increase in the reliability of the software. Empirical studies of reuse have demonstrated some of these claims. For example, in one study, it was shown that reusing implementation without modification on average resulted in 0.02 faults per module in contrast with the average rate of 1.28 faults per module for a new module.[12]

Resistance to Reuse

If reuse provides such advantages, why do we not all practice reuse as much as we can? Actually, we do reuse more than most people think. We do not write operating systems from scratch. We reuse existing text and code editors. We buy and use existing database servers and Web servers. We don't write compilers from scratch. C++ programmers reuse STL. Java programmers reuse a large collection of Java APIs. We call these components tools, and we have no problem reusing them. Yet, when it comes to building our software, we still tend to build code from scratch. Lynex and Layzell performed a survey and interviewed 19 organizations to identify reasons for the resistance to reuse.[13] They identified nine inhibitors spanning management, process, economic, and technological reasons.

From a technological perspective, it is difficult to create reusable components and software modules. Reusable components require simple interfaces, and reusable components need to be documented. Furthermore, it is more fun to engineer new solutions than to work as component integrators. Also, when there is a bug, it is not easy to go through someone else's code to find the bug.

Economically, developing reusable components and modules requires additional investments. Categorizing, publishing, publicizing, and documenting reusable components cost money and resources. Maintaining collections of reusable components is not necessarily cheap in the short run.

Existing processes are difficult to change, and working in Internet time means that the current fire is always the top priority. Why change something that works? Inertia makes it difficult for companies to change to a more promising course.

Fundamentally, reuse is not a technological problem. The difficulty in reuse is how to integrate it into the business. The business will not see an immediate return on investment from implementing reuse, and it requires organizational and management commitment to make it work. This means that the organizational structure of the company might need to be reworked. This also means that management needs to be educated on the benefits of reuse. Reuse needs to be mandated from the top down.

---

[12] Selby, R. W. "Empirically based analysis of failures in software systems," *IEEE Transactions on Reliability*, Vol. 39, No. 4, pp 444–454, 1990.

[13] Lynex, A., and Layzell, P. J. "Understanding Resistance to Software Reuse," *Proceedings of the Eighth IEEE International Workshop on Software Technology and Engineering Practices*, pp 339–349, London, United Kingdom, July 14–18, 1997.

However, Java programming might prove to be an exception to the top-down reuse mandate. From the very beginning, Java programmers are trained to access the Java Web site to download the available SDKs and APIs, and they have also been trained to look for prebuilt APIs. When I have to write Java programs, the first thing I do is go to Java's Web site to see if there is an API for it. I'll try a keyword search to identify the category for the solutions that I need. I'll then go through the archives in the appropriate newsgroups and search the Web for software that I can reuse. Java also provides tools to ease documentation efforts in the form of Javadoc. Given the right environment and the right tools, developers can be encouraged to think about reuse from the start.

Reuse with No Modification

How do we utilize reuse as a strategy to prevent and reduce bugs? In a study of software module reuse using a sample of modules that contained approximately 1.3 million lines of code from a large telecommunication system, the study revealed that:

♦ When the software module is reused with no change, the expected error rate in the software is about 0.52 faults per module.

♦ When the reused modules are modified, the expected error rate in the software module is 1.75 errors per module.

♦ Developing equivalent new software modules from scratch is expected to have 2.29 errors per module.[14]

Another study of software faults demonstrated a similar result.[15] However, this study of 30K to 100K lines of code also measured the amount of effort required to find the fault as a function of reuse. The result of this study showed that:

♦ In a new software component, the average number of faults is 1.28 per component, with each fault taking an average of 2.1 hours to isolate.

♦ If the software components are reused with major modification, the average number of faults per component is about 1.18, and each requires about 2.3 hours to find. In this study, major modification implies greater than 25 percent of changes in the software.

♦ If the software components are reused with minor modification, the average number of faults per component is 0.58, and each requires about 1.1 hour to isolate. In this study, minor modification indicates that the change is less than 25 percent in the reused codes.

♦ If the software components are reused with no modification, the average number of faults per component is 0.02, and each required about 0.02 hour of effort to isolate.

---

[14] Khoshgoftaar, T. M., et al. "The Impact of Software Evolution and Reuse on Software Quality," *Empirical Software Engineering*, Vol. 1, No. 1, pp 31–44, 1996.

[15] Selby, R. W. "Empirically based analysis of failures in software systems," *IEEE Transactions on Reliability*, Vol. 39, No. 4, pp 444–454, 1990.

These studies did not reveal any surprising results, but instead confirmed what our experience and common sense would indicate. Reused modules have had more testing and operational use than new modules, hence, fewer bugs. Modifying the reused software module will negate some of the benefits and increase the odds of bugs occurring. The interesting result from the second study is the observation that it is most difficult to find bugs in a software module that is derived by substantially modifying an existing software module. The conclusion is simple: When we reuse software, we should reuse each module as is with no modifications and no customization. It doesn't pay to change codes. Plug-and-play software components are a key to bug prevention.

Reusable Components

One way to achieve reuse of software without modification is to reuse commercial off-the-shelf components (COTS), such as database servers, Web servers, enterprise resource planning systems, and so on. Another way is to build your own reusable binary components. Enterprise Java Beans (EJB), COM, and Common Object Request Broker Architecture (CORBA) include some recent attempts in defining an interface for the implementation of reusable components. However, the best implementation of reusable executables belongs to an idea that originated in the Unix operating system. Unlike COM and CORBA, which require complicated interfaces and setup, Unix components are small programs that can communicate via pipes or files. These programs can be linked together using pipes to perform complex but sequential series of tasks. To perform nonsequential tasks, you can write shell scripts that use simple looping and conditional commands. These Unix programs and ideas have since migrated to other operating systems and greatly simplify certain tasks.

For example, I like to run my production servers in logging mode, so that when something goes wrong, I can immediately see that (a) the server is still running, and (b) exactly what the server is doing at the time. The log file tends to contain a lot of text that may not be relevant to the answer I was seeking. But it is too much work to write a program to parse and present the data because I don't often know what I should be looking for until a problem has occurred. The solution is to use a combination of "grep," "sed," "awk," "tail," and "more" commands to automatically reduce the data into exactly the form that I am looking for. In less than a minute, I can be looking at the information that can help me solve my immediate problem. The only bug that I have to worry about is issuing the wrong command to these programs. But because I don't have to compile anything, I will know if I make a mistake right away. It is easy and fast.

While I was working on a research project in the university, my team and I liked the idea of reusable programs so much that we even wrote an entire system using simple components that were controlled by "make." The "make" program executes the content of the "Makefile." Typically, Makefile is used for compiling binary libraries and executables. In its simplest form, Makefile is a rule-based system that is composed using the following rule:

```
if ( A is older than B  ) then execute Some Command(s)
```

A and B are some files on the machine and can be data files or executables. B can be a single file, or B can be a set of files. Representing the same rule in the Makefile syntax, the rule would look like this:

```
A: B
    Some Command
```

Using Makefile for more than compilation is not a new or novel concept. Makefile has been used in other applications, such as regression-testing and self-testing of applications. But, how can you use Makefile and reusable programs to build a system? Imagine a system that is comprised of a series of tasks. Each task can be performed by one program, and the output of one program is fed as the input to another program. The outputs of the programs are saved on the disk as part of a baseline or as archived results. So a simple Makefile could look like this:

```
output_of_A: A
    run A
output_of_B: B, output_of_A
    run B with output_of_A
output_of_C: C, output_of_A
    run C with output_of_A
output_of_D: output_of_C, output_of_B
    run D with output_of_B and output_of_C
```

If the Makefile is run for the first time, outputs of A, B, C, and D will be produced, because none of them existed previously. If no changes were made, running the Makefile again would have no effect. But if C is updated with a bug fix or feature enhancement, running the Makefile will automatically rerun C (because output_of_C is now older than C.) This will then invoke the command to rerun D. There is no inefficiency; only the data that needs to be recomputed is recomputed. You can see the output of every stage of the task, which might help you debug the system. But the best thing is that you don't have to write a program to manage all the complexity that the Makefile provides. This means that you can concentrate on solving the problems of A, B, C, and D and not have to focus on the periphery components of these four tasks. Consequently, you don't have to worry about bugs that glue the tasks together, and if you need to add a task F, all it takes is half a minute to add it to the system.

Reuse in Earlier Stages of the Software Development Process

Reuse should not be restricted to the implementation stage. In fact, reuse should start as early as possible in the software development cycle. There are many advantages of early reuse. In our opinion, the most compelling reason for reusing early stage products is easier reuse of the subsequent life-cycle products that were derived from these early stage products. In one study, nearly 100 types of artifacts produced during the conception, analysis, specification, architectural, and detail design stage of a software development cycle were identified and analyzed.[16] This analysis found that:

- Artifacts that define the scope of the problem and methods used in the problem solution are regarded as having the highest reuse value. These artifacts are typically produced during the system analysis, specification, and project conception stages.

- Artifacts having the highest potential for reuse tend to be textual. This means that it is harder to automatically categorize and analyze the content of these artifacts.

- Artifacts in the early stage of the software development life cycle are produced by business managers, project managers, and system analysts.

This analysis showed that requirements produced by the management and system analysts during the initial stage of the software development cycle have the greatest reuse value. In practice, we have seen attempts of requirement reuse in the form of requirement templates. However, these reuses tend to stop at the level of cutting and pasting existing requirement documents for a different client. It makes the job of the project manager somewhat easier in creating new client specific requirements; however, it does nothing to help the developers reuse the software modules or create bug free software.

The value of requirement reuse diminishes if we cannot tie design elements and the software modules to the requirement. Ideally, when the project management reuses a set of requirements, the software module that implements the requirement module can be reused in the final implementation. This introduces the concept of requirement modules. After all, it is difficult to relate one single requirement statement to any software module. Typically, a software module is comprised of a set of related requirements, which define a specific functionality or feature of the software module. Therefore, we can say that a requirement module defines a feature. This implies that the way to design reusable requirements and software components is to create feature-based software modules.

Cost of Reuse

Reuse can be expensive. Typically, developing a reusable component requires three to four times more resources than developing a nonreusable component.[17] In a case study of the implementation of a component-based architecture in an industrial setting, it was demonstrated that the cost of reuse could be substantial.[18] It was observed that significant and complex development, maintenance, and design processes are required from the organization in order to realize the advantage of the component reuse.

---

[16] Cynulski, J. L., Neal, R. D., Kram, A., and Allen, J. C. "Reuse of early life-cycle artifacts: workproducts, methods, and tools," *Annals of Software Engineering*, Vol. 5, pp 227–251, 1998.

[17] Szyperski, C. *Component Software*. Addison-Wesley, 1999.

[18] Crnkovic, I., and Larsson, M. "A Case Study: Demands on Component-based Development", *Proceedings of the 2000 International Conference on Software Engineering*, pp 23–31, Limerick, Ireland, June 4–11, 2000.

From a maintenance point of view, reusing software can produce a maintenance nightmare. When you receive a software patch from a COTS component vendor, do you apply the patch, even if your system is running fine? How do you evaluate the stability of the patch with respect to your usage? Ideally, any changes to the system should be performed in the quality assurance (QA) system, where the changes can be regression tested and simulated usage of the system can be applied to observe the effect of the changes. If the COTS component has a bug and causes a crash, it is not a trivial process to narrow the bug to the COTS component and convince the vendor that a bug exists in its product.

If the reusable component is developed in house, there is the advantage of easier maintenance and easier bug tracking. However, if a component is successful, it would have many clients. Over time, all these clients would place demands on the component. If the clients all have new functional requirements, should the component evolve and change its requirements to meet the needs of the clients? If so, how do you make sure the changes that you make for one client do not adversely affect another client? How do you resist feature creep in your components?

Designing Reusable Components

One way to approach reuse for bug prevention is to produce simple components and resist the urge to make "do everything" components. When a component is simple, it is easier for users to understand the use and effect of the component. It is also easier for the creator and maintainer of the component to design the code, write safe code, and understand how the code works. When the component is simple, it is easier to achieve a bug-free component.

We'll illustrate our point with an analogy from another industry, where the use of components is more prevalent. In the electronics industry, electrical engineers use resistors to regulate voltage and currents in their system. In most circuitry that we have seen, most of the resistors that are used offer only one level of resistance. A resistor that is rated at 50 ohms provides 50 ohms of resistance within some specified tolerance. There is no knob that one can turn to change the resistance of such a fixed value resistor. To achieve different resistance values, electrical engineers have an arsenal of fixed value resistors that they can use. These fixed value resistors have various discrete resistance values. When electrical engineers desire a resistance that is in between the discrete resistance values of the resistors they have available, they can construct a small resistor circuit to achieve the desired resistance value. This is done by hooking up the resistors in parallel or in series.

Adjustable resistors, where you can change the resistance with a turn of a knob, do exist. However, you tend to find these adjustable resistors used in circuits where the end user is expected to adjust the resistance. Such adjustable resistors are not used everywhere throughout the circuit. The reasons they are not used are as follows:

♦ Fixed-value resistors tend to be cheaper.

♦ Adjustable resistors have more moving parts and are more fault prone.

- Using adjustable resistors in the part of the circuit that does not expect changes of resistance introduces risk of failure due to environmental changes. (For example, when the product containing the circuit is dropped on the floor.)

- Not using adjustable resistors reduces user errors. If users cannot adjust the resistance, they can never adjust it incorrectly.

Make Reusable Components Simple

In our view, a reusable software component should be like a fixed value resistor. It does only one thing and does it well. If you want something else, create another component. A reusable software component should be simple and have the same characteristics as a fixed value resistor. They should be cheaper to build and be less complex, which makes them less bug prone. Current software engineering thinking tends to prefer components like adjustable resistors; we want components to do as many things as possible. We erroneously believe that if a component can do everything, it is more "reusable." In fact, we would probably modify the adjustable resistors to be able to act as a capacitor with a flip of a switch. Sure, such a component would be more "reusable" in the sense that more software could use it, and it could be used in more places. But this is accomplished at the cost of higher complexity for the designer and the user as well as the cost of ever-changing functional requirements of the component.

A reusable software component is easier to specify if it only has few functions or features. This makes the requirement simple and clear. It is easier to write an unambiguous requirement if the system only does a few things. A simple requirement encourages reuse of the requirement because it is simple. When the requirement can be reused without modification, the design and implementation derived from the requirement can also be reused without modification. The simplicity of the description of the component makes it easier to store, to archive, and to search. The simplicity makes it easy for others to comprehend as well. And if we don't like the way the component is written, it is relatively inexpensive to just throw it away and write a new one.

Some might argue that it is easy to write simple components for fundamental data structures, such as a tree or link list, but business level components are going to be complex. True, business logic tends to be complex, but we also tend to make business level components complex because we want to develop software modules to solve all of the business problems in one module or in one system. This is not necessary. Business logic typically can be divided into a series or sets of workflow. Using this approach, a simple component would implement a solution for one workflow. A set of components that implement a set of workflows could then be combined to solve the entire business problem.

When we speak of simple components, we do not mean that the functionality or the features of the component are simple. The simplicity in this context means that the component is easy to use, simple to understand, and has a simple interface. A component could perform a function as complex as solving the speech recognition problem. But if we could just pass a

WAV file to your component and retrieve a text representation of the speech, we would call the component simple. On the other hand, if the component requires that we set up a configuration file, tweak 15 parameters, and call a specific sequence of APIs in order to initialize and use the component, then the component is too complex.

Consider this basic guide for use as a simplicity check: Create a process or procedure for the use of a component, and give this procedure to an unsuspecting victim. When said victim can use your component without faults, count the number of steps in your procedure. If there is only one step, congratulations, you have a simple component!

Encourage Reuse

Consider this simple thought experiment that contrasts "reuse" of a flexible do-everything component with reuse of a set of small simple components, which can be combined to perform the same desired functions. The documentation for the flexible generic component might be 50 pages long, whereas the documentation for each individual simple component is only a few pages. Which one is easier to understand? Would you be willing to reuse a component that you do not fully comprehend?

It is useless to create reusable components if no one will reuse them. In order to achieve reuse, team members must know the existence of the reusable components and artifacts. They must also be able to find the appropriate components and artifacts and be able to retrieve them. Additionally, team members must trust the quality of these reusable products so that they will commit to using them.

Achieving reuse in a large enterprise-wide organization is a technically daunting task. Creating tractable and effective processes and tools for the classification, storage, and retrieval of reusable products is nontrivial. A survey of storage and retrieval techniques can be found in "A Survey of Software Reuse Libraries".[19] However, in a small to medium-size development group, the best way to encourage reuse is to make the members of the team aware of these software components and foster ownership of these software components. The following list contains some ideas for inducing reuse in a small to medium-size development group:

♦ *Create a component repository.* A component repository can be located in either the standard configuration management repository or in a separate configuration management environment.

♦ *Publicize new features.* Oftentimes, we have observed that when a developer has created a new functionality, the new file is quietly checked into the configuration management, and no one else is informed of these additions or changes. In order to reuse components, people must be made aware of the new functions. Even if other developers do not need this functionality, at least they would know about its existence and might recall a particular component at a later date. There are many ways to publicize new components or

[19] Mili, A., Mili, R., and Mittermeir, R. T. "A Survey of Software Reuse Libraries," *Annals of Software Engineering,* Vol. 5, pp 349–414, 1998.

features. You can use email or local newsgroups, which are the easiest and the most obvious methods.

♦ *Establish group ownership.* People will look for reuse if they think they have had a hand in the development of the reusable software. People are more likely to reuse what they are familiar with. So how do you establish group ownership? Require people to add to the component repository, and require them to maintain a part of the component repository. This is best done when you have hired a new developer. In one of my previous jobs, all new developers must spend some time contributing to a software module, by either adding new features, or fixing some bugs. This process served as an introduction to shared code-base, but also foster group ownership. Once developers get in the habit of looking into a component repository, they will likely go back for more.

Risk of Reuse

Reuse is not a silver bullet for bug prevention. In Chapter 2, we studied a number of famous bugs that could have been directly attributed to reused software modules. Therac-25 reused buggy software modules, and *Ariane 5* reused software that was not appropriate for the new system. An important point to remember is that when you reuse a software module, not only do you reuse features and functions supported by the module, but you also reuse defects and bugs contained in the module.

The safest way to reuse code is to reuse requirement modules along with their associated design and implementation modules. In order to reuse code safely, it is important to have documentation associated with the components and artifacts that are being considered for reuse. However, it is rare in most organizations to have this kind of infrastructure and documentation in place. The section called "Documentation in the Real World" will provide some ideas for alternative documentation techniques that can help you disseminate knowledge. But because code reading might be required, it is important to have a clear and simple design and implementation to ease the task of software comprehension as much as possible.

Reduce Complexity and Manage Complexity

We have argued that complexity is one of the major contributors to bugs and defects in a system. When systems are complex, we lose track of issues, we fail to consider a path, and we are helpless in the face of all the interdependent variables. Reducing complexity is one way to reduce bugs and defects, but we run the risk of not meeting customer needs while trying to solve a slightly different problem. It is better to manage the complexities, but it's not always possible.

Have a Process

In the movie *Apollo 13*, we saw Hollywood's depiction of a series of crises conquered by the ingenuity of NASA engineers. Launching a manned spacecraft safely is not a simple task. There are millions of moving parts and billions of ways things can go wrong. It is a complex problem, and NASA manages the complexities with processes. There is a specific process for determining whether the vehicle should be launched. There are processes to determine when the mission should be aborted. There are processes for dealing with most conceivable failures. In the face of these complexities, there is no time to put together a solution in an ad hoc manner.

We were struck by the way NASA engineers solved the air filter problem on *Apollo 13*. It was not that they were able to piece together a working system using only items available on the spacecraft. That's impressive, but not striking. What was striking for us was that they created a process for the astronauts to follow, so that the astronauts could build their own air filter, 10,000 miles away. The NASA engineers made a complex problem and a complex solution solvable by the astronauts. If NASA engineers were software engineers, they would have sent the *Apollo 13* astronauts a description of a set of items (objects) and instructions on how these items could be attached (interfaces), and then would have expected the astronauts to figure out how to put all the pieces together. It's no wonder we have so many problems in the software industry.

Processes and methods reduce the complexity to manageable steps. It allows us to reduce the number of interdependent variables because other developers have already figured out the interaction among these variables. They have already distilled these interdependencies into a series of steps that we could follow. Although ideally process is an organizational concern, implementing personal processes can still be of benefit. The Software Engineering Institute introduced the Personal Software Process in 1995 with the same belief.[20]

Which processes and methods should you choose? Frankly, we don't think it really matters. What is important is to have a process or a method, and evolve it to meet your needs. Every job has a process. This process might be informal and might not be written down, but people doing a job have a way of doing it, even in a CMM level 1 environment. The first step might simply be to formalize these informal steps, and then proceed from there.

However, processes and procedures do have their own drawbacks. One of the risks is that creativity might be limited. We have all heard those inane stories about people mired in the processes of a huge corporate bureaucracy. In addition, with a method in place, we might be prone to knee-jerk reactions. When we encounter a problem, we might tend to just choose a process and go with it without fully understanding the problem that we are facing. But as an industry, software engineers have swung too far to the side of ad hoc, chaotic environments, so it doesn't hurt to err on the side of processes every once in a while.

Don't Make a Problem Too Complicated

We have observed that a lot of complexities in software engineering are self-inflicted. We have a propensity to shoot for technical elegance to provide a generic solution, and in the process, we make the problem and solution as complex as we possibly can.

---

[20] Humphrey, W. S. "Introducing the Personal Software Process," *Annals of Software Engineering*, No. 1, pp 311–325, 1995.

Why do we have to solve the generic problem? Why do we have to have the most elegant solution? Usually, when we raise these questions, the reasons that we get are the holy grails of software engineering: extensibility and maintainability. But do we understand the problem domain well enough to create a generic solution that can withstand the test of time? If not, we will be bound to making changes to an almost generic solution. We will have to attempt to factor in the new requirements to our existing abstraction. Sometimes this is easy, but more often than not, it is almost impossible without coming up with a new abstraction that would require us to throw away most of our existing solutions. So we usually hack some code in instead. Our elegant solution is ruined, and our general solution is mostly general except in one or two places. As a result, we make it harder for ourselves in the short run because it is harder to come up with a good general solution. And, we make it harder for ourselves in the long run because we hack changes in and make the solution harder to comprehend. When was the last time you heard of a complex system that was easy to maintain?

The software industry is marked by constant changes: changes in technology, changes in the market, and changes in customer demand. This means that our problems and solutions will also change constantly. Creating a stable, generic, and elegant solution may not be the most cost-effective path to take in the short term, nor in the long term.

Chunk Correctly

Software development and debugging is problem solving. When we debug, we observe a symptom, and it is our job to understand the underlying model of the system and posit a cause for the symptom. When we develop software, we attempt to formulate a model that is capable of representing the problem that we are trying to solve. This involves understanding the variables that can affect the problem. We can learn a lot from psychological studies of human problem-solving processes and apply them to the art and science of prebugging.

In cognitive psychology, it is hypothesized that we solve complex problems by *chunking*. In effect, we reduce a complex problem to a more manageable size by breaking it into pieces. We also chunk when we solve software engineering problems. In object-oriented methodology, the problem is decomposed into a set of objects and interactions between these objects. To create an application to handle student enrollment in a university, we create classes, such as student, course, and schedule. These classes decompose the problem into constituents. Instead of solving the original problem of student enrollment, we can now solve a problem for a student, a course, and a schedule. The combined interaction between these three classes solves the original problem.

However, object-oriented decomposition might not necessarily be the right mechanism for breaking down a complex problem. A problem is complex because it has many interdependent variables. Figure 12.1 illustrates this complexity. The figure shows a representation of the complexity in the form of a graph. The nodes represent the variables, and the link between the nodes represents interdependency between connected variables.

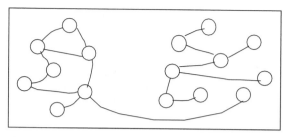

Figure 12.1
A graph denoting the complexity of a problem.

In the graph, there are 16 circles representing 16 variables in the problem. The line between two circles represents an interdependency between those two variables, that is, changing the value of one variable (circle) affects the value of the variable that's connected to it. When we chunk, we can visualize the result as combining a number of variables into one, as shown in Figure 12.2.

In Figure 12.2, the dark outline represents the result of arbitrary chunking of variables. The problem is now somewhat easier because we can concentrate on the variables within each chunk first, and then worry about the interaction between chunks. Between chunk 1 and 2, there are four lines connecting the two chunks, which represent four different ways that chunk 1 and 2 can affect each other. Likewise, there are five ways chunk 2 and 3 can affect each other. But if we are to partition the variables, we might as well partition them based on our understanding of how these variables interact and reduce the interactions between chunks. The number of variables that need to handle inter-chunk interactions is 12, which is more than half of our original number of interdependent variables.

Figure 12.3 shows the results of chunking, which partitions the variables using our understanding of the interdependent variables. We still have three chunks. The size of each chunk varies, but there are fewer interactions between chunks. This means that after we solve the problem of chunk 1, we only have to worry about one interaction from other chunks that

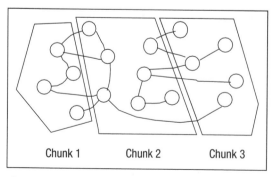

Chunk 1   Chunk 2   Chunk 3

Figure 12.2
Result of arbitrary chunking.

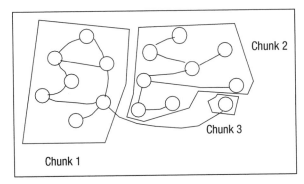

Figure 12.3
A better chunking solution.

can affect chunk 1, and they are isolated in two variables. In all, only two variables are involved in inter-chunk interactions.

In software engineering, we can map each variable to a requirement, a class, a variable, or a software module. We can also map a chunk to a requirement, a class, a variable, or a software module. The level of detail and the mapping is purely arbitrary. The key point is that the problem can be partitioned in many ways, structural, functional, or object-oriented. Some decomposition might be more appropriate for one problem domain than another. Selecting the right decomposition for the right problem can mean the difference between an easy problem and a hard problem.

Saying No to Feature Creep

"Of course! Why didn't I think of that?" You are muttering to yourself, sarcastically. Just saying no without attempting to understand the reason for the creep or an alternative is a losing proposition. As a software engineer, you are not going to win the feature creep battle with your project manager. And, as a project manager, it would be political suicide in most cases to say no to your senior level executives.

One way to resist feature creep is to get the requirements right at the outset. To get the requirements right means that we have to try to understand the problem domain and avoid defects in the requirements. However, many times, we have found that our customers have grand visions and concepts. Because customers are not technically inclined, it is difficult for them to articulate what they want and need. Therefore, it is usually beneficial for a technical member of the team to work with customers to gather the requirements. Some of the issues and tips for problem understanding are covered in the section titled "Prebugging in Requirements." Another tip is to inspect requirement documents, which we discussed earlier.

However, even if the requirements are done correctly, feature creep still happens. As technical professionals, we usually attempt to minimize the effect of feature creep by using technical solutions. We try to make our solution generic and extensible to accommodate as much feature creep as possible. But reality has a way of playing tricks; features usually creep in from unanticipated directions and make our generic solution useless. There are many ways to minimize and mitigate the effects of feature creep. Consider the following examples:

♦ *Experiences*—If you have solved a particular problem once before, you tend to have a pretty good idea of what customers might want, but have not articulated. How can you do this? Well, because there are very few original problems out there. Most business and technical problems have been solved at one time or another by somebody. The trick is to find the people who might have solved a similar problem previously, have them identify the potential direction of feature creep, and then devise safeguards against the creep.

♦ *Market analysis*—Market analysis might not be something that technical or project management personnel are inclined to do. But by looking at what your competitors are doing and what your customers are demanding, you will have some idea of what your senior management will want in the future. This means reading trade journals, watching the market, talking to your customers, and studying your competitors.

♦ *Prioritize*—A process-related suggestion is simply to prioritize the features and set schedules for them. If you can establish a schedule for an existing set of features, you might be able to show how the additional features could adversely affect the schedule, and you might be able to get the management to prioritize these features.

♦ *Provide alternative solutions and features*—Sometimes, the requested feature is simply not possible given the time allotted. However, the feature that was requested might simply be a solution to a business problem. If you can understand the original business problem, you might be able to propose an alternative solution that might be more feasible.

No Hand Waving

When we see someone hand-wave during the presentation of a solution, we know that that person hasn't thought it through. It tells us that there might be hidden complexity in the portion of the solution that was hand-waved away. If a solution is clear, it can be easily and clearly communicated, and no hand waving is necessary.

The main problem with hand waving is that the difficulty that was originally hand-waved away always reappears. Consequently, the hard part of the problem gets delayed until there is no time to think about it, and then decisions are made regarding the complexity without due consideration. Who wins? Bugs win.

Documentation in the Real World

Every book on software development talks about the importance of documentation. Everyone in the software industry agrees on the importance of documentation, and yet no one ever seems to do it. Why? We believe the reasons are that not only is it tedious, it is also perceived to be a useless endeavor. Does a wall full of class diagrams in 9 point font with 100 classes help anyone other than the original designer understand the system that it implements?

Does a 500 page description of the system APIs help someone you have just hired use the API for his or her project? Our answers are no to both questions. In addition, studies on maintenance tasks showed that maintainers only spend time looking at documentation when they are not familiar with the software. Once they become familiar with it, they rarely refer back to the documentation; they much prefer to go straight to code.[21]

Documentation helps us prevent bugs by helping us understand the systems. The goal of documentation is not to produce a dusty tome or to kill acres of tree. The purpose of documentation is simply to promote comprehension of the system from the problem, the solution, and implementation perspectives. What should be documented? Anything that can help us understand all aspects of the system should be documented. The key is to foster understanding. Instead of pushing for documentation, we should push for ways that will make the system more comprehensible.

Separate Roles of Designers and Implementers

One way to induce documentation is to separate the responsibility of the designer and the implementer onto two different people. If designers are not allowed to write code, then they have to figure out how to communicate their design to implementers. This communication will usually end up as some form of design document.

This approach works better with junior implementers because designers have to be more explicit in their designs. Designers have to create detailed documents and processes that a junior implementer can understand and follow. Senior implementers have the ability to take an idea and run with it. Senior implementers can fill in the gaps and overlook poor documentation, which results in less useful documentation.

When we are designing an object-oriented application, we specify the classes and the methods for each class. We specify the interaction between classes. We define the precondition and post-condition of methods. We can see the code behind these specifications in our mind. The only thing missing is the code to make the design a reality. As far as we are concerned, writing code and drawing class and sequence diagrams are the same. For a senior developer, there shouldn't be any difference between writing design documentation and writing code. The only difference should be the medium and the tools used in creating the product. But with a junior implementer as the audience, the designer needs to take complexity of the design into consideration. If the design is too complex, then it might be difficult for the junior implementer to implement the design, which puts the timeliness of the project in jeopardy.

We have had a few chances to implement this technique with mixed results. In all cases, we produced detailed documentation, which included requirements, architectural, design, and test plans. We wrote the documentation and watched others attempt to use it. It quickly

---

[21] Corritore, C. L., and Wiedenbeck, S. "Direction and Scope of Comprehension-Related Activities by Procedural and Object-Oriented Programmers: An Empirical Study," *Proceedings of the 8th International Workshop on Program Comprehension*, pp 139–148, Limerick, Ireland, June 1–11, 2000.

became clear what needed to be documented and what didn't as well as what helps and what doesn't. Many of the lessons learned are presented in the following sections.

Provide Overviews

At the minimum, documentation should provide its reader with an overview of the problem and a solution to the problem. As professional software developers, we all assume that our fellow developers are capable of reading codes and understanding what they do. But source codes cannot describe the context of the source code within a software system. Reading a 100-line software module isn't going to tell us how this module fits in a program or what the underlying architectural model of the system is. We could read the few thousand lines of code if it is the size of the entire application. But when a software system approaches hundreds of thousands of lines, the task becomes more daunting. Worse, the source code cannot tell us what problem the software was designed to solve. If we don't know what problem the software was solving, it is difficult to know if the software is solving the right problem.

One of the most important pieces of documentation for a software project is an overview of the problem and the solution. This overview helps a new developer, tester, or project manager figure out where to start. There should be an overview in the requirement document that tells the reader what the problem is and provides a set of high-level categorizations of the requirements. The document should be able to answer fundamental architectural questions about the system and provide basic descriptions of all the major software modules and interactions among these modules.

Use Pictures

"A picture is worth a thousand words." Graphical documentation has been shown to help maintainers understand the system better than purely textual documentation.[22] Pictures tend to reduce the complexity of the written word and help generalize the concepts in a document by representing these concepts with shapes and spatial relationships. We have found that for high-level documentation, graphical representation of the problem or the solution is an invaluable tool to aid understanding.

What should you use to document your system graphically? If your graphical documentation is meant to aid an understanding of high-level concepts, any tool that you and your reader agree upon should work well. However, if this graphical documentation is intended to be part of a design specification, then a more formal modeling language, such as the Unified Modeling Language (UML) or Entity-Relation Diagram would be more suitable for the task.[23]

FAQ Style Documentation

Frequently Asked Questions (FAQs) originated in the Usenet newsgroups in the mid-1980s. The purpose of an FAQ is to document a standard list of questions and answers to prevent

---

[22] Kemerer, C. F. "Software complexity and software maintenance: A survey of empirical research," *Annals of Software Engineering*, No. 1, pp 1–22, 1995.

[23] Fowler, M., with Scott, K. *UML Distilled: A Brief Guide to the Standard Object Modeling Language*, 2d ed., Addison-Wesley, Upper Saddle River, New Jersey, 2000.

the rehashing of the same old questions by every new reader to the newsgroup. We have found FAQ to be concise summaries of topics that it addresses. Recently, we have found more and more FAQ-style documentation associated with products and APIs and have found these FAQs to be equally helpful in providing a high-level overview of a software product.

The question and answer format of a FAQ makes it easy for readers to find what they are looking for. When we consult documents, we usually have a set of questions in mind. "What does the program do?" "How do I do XYZ?" "How does this object relate to this other object?" The questions that FAQs pose fit this approach perfectly. The answers in a FAQ can be detailed, or they can serve as a pointer to another document.

This question and answer format also makes it easier for developers to write documentation. Given a blank sheet of paper, it can be difficult for developers to know where to start, what level of detail is appropriate, what to write about, and how to address the content to the right audience. But given a question, it is typically easier for developers to answer the question as posed because it doesn't feel like writing. Most of the documentation you need could probably be completed by sending off questions to developers one at a time. Their answers to these questions would more or less be the documentation you are looking for.

Questions in a FAQ can come from anyone who might have a question about the software or the system. Questions and answers can be saved to create a knowledge base.

Project History

How many times have you wandered into a seemingly inexplicable set of codes? These are lines of codes that do not appear to do anything remotely useful, and yet, when they are removed, the application fails to operate correctly. Better yet, in every system, there are usually some weird design artifacts that defy explanation and seem moronic. But you know the original developers were experienced and proficient. Wouldn't it be nice to know why they did the things they did?

Understanding the evolution of the software is useful for maintainers because they won't be tempted to reverse changes that were made for performance or bug fixes. Project history is useful for designers and developers to understand the issues as well. When it comes time for the system to be redesigned, it won't be necessary for them to travel down the same path again. Project history also enables the project management to qualitatively evaluate the software development processes by looking at the changes, the problems, and the discussions that have occurred.

The following list contains some suggestions on how to capture project history information:

♦ *Meeting notes*—Questions, answers, and discussions that occur in a meeting can bring invaluable insights to the design of the software. Capturing these discussions can help us understand the evolution of the software.

♦ *Local private newsgroups*—Set up some kind of intranet newsgroup to host project discussions. The postings to the newsgroup can be archived for future project historians.

- *Saving email exchanges*—Set up project-specific folders in your email application, and save every email that you get regarding a project. Also, save every email message that you wrote regarding a project. These old emails can come in handy. When someone wants to know why something was done, you can produce an outline of decision processes that led to the final implementation with references. You can recycle answers to questions that are asked more than once. You can also revisit bad decisions that you made, and these emails can serve as a learning experience and a reminder of your past mistakes.

- *Version Control History Logs*—The comments and history logs contained in a version control or configuration management system can be a valuable source of information. These logs contain all the changes made to the software and can be reviewed.

- *Comments in the codes*—When a change has been made to the code, it is useful to comment directly in the code as to why the change was made, not what the change is. We can all read code, and with any configuration management tool, it is easy to see what was changed. It is harder is to see why the code was changed.

Self-Documenting Codes

Because programming languages are the most precise languages that we have, it makes sense to leverage them in our documentation and communication. Furthermore, many empirical studies indicate that as developers, we tend to read most of the codes in order to fully understand the software that we are looking at.[24] These insights behoove us to make our code as comprehensible as possible.

Self-documenting code is more than just having explicit function and variable names. It is also the result of system and interface designs. We discuss these design issues in the "Prebugging in Design" section.

Test Programs

One of the best ways to learn about an API is in a tutorial. Tutorials are full of examples, and examples of the API usage can help a novice of the API understand how the API will be used.

When we create an API, we need a way to test the API. This often involves creating test programs. These test programs help us test the functionalities and features of the software.

Therefore, it seems natural to us to save the test programs as part of the design documentation. On one hand, we need examples for our documentation. On the other hand, we have programs that test the software as it is meant to be used. Is there any reason why we shouldn't use these test programs as examples in part of our documentation? These test programs can serve as part of a regression test suite, so that if the specification of the API changes, the test programs will also need to change. When the test program is changed, the example used in

---

[24] Corritore, C. L., and Wiedenbeck, S. "Direction and Scope of Comprehension-Related Activities by Procedural and Object-Oriented Programmers: An Empirical Study," *Proceedings of the 8th International Workshop on Program Comprehension*, pp 139–148, Limerick, Ireland, June 1–11, 2000.

the documentation is automatically changed as well. Talk about an easy way to keep a document up-to-date.

Organizationally, an intranet, HTML-based documentation system is appropriate for code examples. The HTML page provides links to code examples. When the link is accessed, the latest test programs are displayed. Regardless of how or where the example is kept, its availability still needs to be publicized by all the developers.

Built-In Infrastructure Support

Software bugs are like cockroaches. No matter how well we test our software, there is always a chance that undetected defects are waiting to appear. In a production environment, bugs can appear anytime, and when they do, it is to our advantage to identify them as soon as possible. Therefore, we need to provide tools to help us observe causes and effects. Infrastructures to enable detection and reproduction of bugs should be in place before we need them.

Snapshots

In most operating systems, there is a way to produce a state of the software by dumping the content of the stack and memory to a file that can be visually inspected. In Windows, there is Dr. Watson. In Unix, there are the core files (or core dumps). These files give us a snapshot of the application when something bad happens. In a Dr. Watson's dump file, we can see the function where the fault occurred. In a core file, we also have the content of the variables and the call stack, which is a list of functions leading to the location of the crash.

The usefulness of the snapshot is limited. One disadvantage of using snapshots as a bug detection and debugging aid is that it is usually only available when the application crashes. But crashing is not the only way for bugs to manifest themselves. The other disadvantage is that if the cause of the bug is not in the call stack, it can be very difficult to fix the bug. For example, if the cause of a bug was a memory corruption that occurred in a branch of the code 100 instructions prior to the current code path, you might be able to see that the content of a variable is erroneous, but there would be no clue as to why the content was corrupted. Without understanding why the memory was corrupted, you would not be able to fix the bug.

Typically, when we have a snapshot of the application, we backtrack from the point of failure to form reasons for the cause. When the cause does not present itself in the snapshot, we can only hypothesize, and then test our hypothesis.

Tracing Log Files

The main difficulty with using the snapshot of the system is that it is a static technique. It presents the symptoms at a particular point in time. However, computer applications tend to be dynamic in nature. The program goes from one state to the next, and the clue for the root cause of the application may not be contained in the state where the symptoms occur. One way to assist us in visualizing the execution of the program is to produce a snapshot of the application at different times. This can be accomplished by producing a tracing log file. The tracing log file can be as simple as producing a statement when the program enters or exits a function, or a major program functional block. It can be as complicated as dumping out the content of some of the more critical variables.

The main advantage of a tracing log is that it helps us visualize the dynamic behavior of the program prior to a failure. We can see what the program is doing before it has a problem. Most debugging books talk about using tracing information during debugging. But these books also tell us to comment out the tracing information in a production environment. The main reason cited is usually performance. Logging tracing information can degrade performance. We don't deny that this is true, but in most environments, the performance degradation due to logging doesn't justify not being able to see what's going on. Also, usage in the production environment is usually hard to reproduce, and when something goes wrong, we want as many clues as possible when it happens. Additionally, by commenting out the code, it means that if we want to turn on logging in the production environment, we must recompile the program and run the risk of introducing a problem due to configuration management.

Ideally, we prefer a trace logger to have the following features:

♦ The logger should be controllable at runtime, so that we can turn it on or off at runtime.

♦ The logger should record error information and capture data that can assist us in debugging.

♦ The logger should be able to write error and debug information to a file.

♦ The logger should be capable of producing information at different levels of detail. When things are going smoothly, only the high-level information is necessary, and when things are going wrong, we can see everything that the application is doing.

What kind of information do we need in our tracing log file?

♦ *Date and time*—This gives us a history of the program execution. In a distributed computing environment, it also helps us match events from one machine to another machine.

♦ *Thread/Process identifier*—This is useful in a multithreaded application to track the messages from different threads.

♦ *Location where the log entry is written*—This can be the name of the function, the file, or the line number.

♦ *Debugging information*—This can be anything that we think can help you debug.

There are many benefits to the implementation of a trace logging package. A good trace logging package allows others in the organization to use it, which means a consistent usage of the trace logging facility. Everyone in the organization should know how to read and interpret the information presented in the logs. As a result, individual programmers no longer have to come up with their own ways of producing logs in a haphazard fashion.

Have a Bug Reproduction Environment

When your system configuration is different than the production configuration, how do you truly verify that you are fixing the right bug? How do you reproduce the bug? In most circumstances, it is probably not necessary to reproduce the bug because it is typically not related to your system configuration. However, when it is, your ability to isolate the bug will be relative to your ability to reproduce the production environment.

About two years ago, I was working in an Internet company. The company was an application service provider (ASP) and hosted services for clients. It had a series of Web servers, database servers, and a host of machines for the company's services. My coworkers and I were working on a project for a client. We had passed the alpha and beta tests, and we were able to sustain all the loads that our client and we could muster. We went live, and the system ran for about 15 minutes. It then crashed, restarted, and crashed again. This kept happening for about five hours. We decided to pull the plug and investigate.

Like all the difficult problems, we were not able to reproduce the problem on our development machine. The problem seemed to be load related, but we were able to subject our development system to more load than what the production environment was experiencing. To make a long story short, it turned out that one of the patches for the operating system, which was recently applied to our production machine, had an unexpected side effect on our software. In order to verify this hypothesis, we had to pull a production machine out of production so that we could perform the proper experiments. We could not change the development system because it had a completely different set of systems and software on it.

Ideally, you want to have an environment that duplicates the production environment down to the last patch. This environment is the *bug reproduction environment*. The purpose of a bug reproduction environment is to set up machines where you can experiment in a production-like environment to reproduce bugs, to isolate bugs, and then verify bug fixes. It is dangerous to perform experiments on a production system for obvious reasons. But the development or QA environment might have additional configurations and software that are not available in the production environment, which could invalidate the results of your experiments.

Ideally, a bug reproduction environment should have the following capabilities:

♦ The ability to reproduce the inputs. This allows us to play back the inputs that the production environment experienced during the time of failure and feed them to the bug reproduction system in order to reproduce the bug.

♦ The same system configuration and software version as the production environment.

♦ The ability to make changes one at a time and to roll back changes.

Prebugging in Requirement

Catching defects and bugs as early as possible is essential because the cost of fixing bugs increases in an exponential manner as a function of time. Fixing a bug that was introduced in the requirement stage in the acceptance testing stage can be 500 times as expensive as fixing the same bug during the requirement stage. This concept is well known and has been confirmed by numerous studies. The most cited study is presented in Barry Boehm's *Software Engineering Economics*.[25]

What is a requirement and how does it affect bug introduction? There are many definitions of requirements, but they can all be stated simply as testable behaviors of a software system.

A requirements document is primarily a document between the customer and the development team about the software product. It helps the parties to agree on the proper behavior of the software. If the software produces a behavior that is contrary to a requirement statement, the behavior is a bug because both the customer and the development team have agreed on the desired behavior of the software. This bug is most likely a design or implementation-related bug. On the other hand, if the software produces a behavior that was not confirmed nor negated by the requirement, then there might be a bug in the requirement because the requirement is incomplete. If the software produces a behavior according to the requirement, but the behavior is not desired by the customer, then the requirement might be ambiguous or incorrect.

The key to a good requirement is that it is testable, and in many ways, a good requirement document is also a good test plan. A requirement that is not testable is prone to misinterpretation due to imprecision of the natural languages that are used to create the requirements. A nontestable requirement can become a cause for disagreement between a customer and the development team because neither side can agree on whether a behavior is a bug or not.

There are two key prebugging concepts regarding requirements: understand the problem that you are attempting to solve and get it right in the first place.

Understand the Problem

One main cause of bugs is the lack of understanding about the problem. A typical software development process includes requirements gathering, design, development, and testing stages. So when do developers and testers get to understand what the problem is? Apparently, developers and testers don't need to understand the problem. They only need to follow the requirements as laid out by the requirement analyst. If they can code and test according to the specification, the assumption is that everyone is happy, and there are no bugs. However, it is rare to have a good requirement. Without a good requirement, software developers are forced to discover the deficiencies in the requirements as they work on the project. This prompts software and requirements changes in the middle of the project.

---

[25] Boehm, B. *Software Engineering Economics*, Prentice-Hall, Englewood Cliffs, New Jersey, 1981.

Conceptually, a good requirement is complete, correct, and unambiguous; therefore, it contains everything developers and testers need to know about the problem. Even if a theoretically perfect requirement is possible, we argue that a requirement document is not the place where developers should learn about the problem.

If the designer and the architect involved in the project do not understand the problem, it will be difficult for them to come up with the right abstractions. The requirement document defines what the system should do, but not necessarily what problem the system is solving. Furthermore, it is difficult to piece together individual requirement statements to form the big picture. For example, consider the following simplified requirements:

```
R1.0 The vehicle shall have 4 rubber wheels.
R1.1 The vehicle shall have an internal combustion engine.
R1.2 The vehicle shall have a steering wheel.
```

What are we being asked to build? Most of you would say a car. But the requirement could also specify a driving lawnmower. Aha! So the requirement is incomplete! Of course it is incomplete. A complete set of requirements for a car could have thousands of individual requirement statements. Do you think you can read all these requirements and still come up with a simple statement indicating what the vehicle should look like and what problem we are trying to solve?

Present Problems, Not Solutions

To us, the real crux is that software engineers are more than just programmers; they are also often architects, designers, implementers, and problem solvers all rolled into one. It is difficult to propose a good solution without understanding the problem. It is also difficult to test the real usage of the software if testers don't understand what problems the software is solving, who will be using the software, and in which environment it will be used.

How often has the following scenario happened to you as a developer or project manager?

Project Manager: "Can you add feature XYZ to the system and finish in two weeks?"

Developer: "No. It's not possible."

Project Manager: "But you must. The future of the company depends on it!"

[The developer goes on a sleep deprivation experiment and fails at the task.]

What's the problem with this exchange? From the developer's perspective, the project manager's question "Can you do XYZ in two weeks?" is like asking a developer, "Can you run a mile in three minutes?" The project manager is not willing to take no for an answer, and it is physically impossible for the developer to do either. They are at an impasse; it's a no-win situation. However, if the project manager had asked, "I need you to get to point B in three minutes. Point B is a mile from here. Can you do it?" The answer might be, "No problem," as the developer hops into a car and races to point B. In the first case, the project manager's question constrains the developer's solution domain (he has to run). In the second case, the project manager's question clearly defines the problem (get from point A to point B in three minutes) and allows the developer to come up with an appropriate solution (he can drive a car).

To be honest, we have never been involved in any project where we relied on the requirements alone. In every project that we have worked on, there is always a kick-off meeting of some kind, where the project manager attempts to describe the conceptual system and problem to the designers in addition to the requirements. Furthermore, there are always continual discussions with customers and project management about the problem itself.

Involve Architects and Designers in the Early Phase of the Requirement Analysis

In our experiences, we have found that problem understanding is usually informally accomplished throughout the life cycle of the project. We have found that we spent a lot of time in meetings attempting to understand the problem that we were trying to solve. The project manager or requirement analyst presented the requirements, and we asked questions. A day later, we came back and asked more questions. But instead of asking the project manager or the requirement analysts after the requirement gathering phase of the development process, why not just have the designers ask questions of the customers directly during the requirement gathering stage? Why have middlemen?

One way to involve technical personnel in the early phase of the development process is to implement the heterogeneous paired inspection technique as described in the inspection section "Detecting Defects" of this chapter. On-site customer techniques proposed by the Extreme Programming methodology is another way to have experts be involved and help the development team understand the problem.[26]

Iterative Methodologies

Another way to achieve problem understanding is by implementing some form of iterative software development methodology, such as Boehm's spiral methodology. In some iterative methodologies, the project teams cycle through all phases of the project more than once. The project team performs the analysis, design, implementation, and testing in the first iteration. At the conclusion of the first iteration, another iteration of the analysis, design, implementation, and testing process is performed again, leveraging the lessons learned and the products of the first iteration. This process continues until a goal has been met.

The iterative methodology helps the project team understand the problem and solutions by actually doing the project more than once. It allows the team to learn by trial and error. However, if you do not believe iterative methodology is right for you, you can still attempt to learn the problem and the solution by actually doing it. You build a prototype, or a proof of concept system, during the requirement stage.

Prototyping

The best way to understand a problem is to actually try to solve it, once, twice, or as many time as it takes. In the software industry, we are blessed and cursed with tools that are

---

[26] Beck, Kent. *Extreme Programming Explained.*, Addison-Wesley, Upper Saddle River, New Jersey, 2000.

completely flexible. With our tools, we have the ability to make changes quickly. We are able to put together a prototype to demonstrate our solutions. If our solution is incorrect, we can change it and present another solution. We can change it as often as we like until we have found a solution that we like. But there are dangers to this power. When abused, we end up with unstable and buggy software.

There is always a danger of prototyping. The danger is that the management or the customer wants to use the prototype as if it is a finished product. When we prototype a solution, our goal should be to gain understanding about the problem domain and the potential solutions. This goal should be communicated clearly to the management and the customer. We should not confuse a prototype with a final product. If time is an issue, it is usually possible to cordon off modules in which we have gained sufficient understanding. These modules can be designed and implemented for a production environment.

Options in Requirements

Sometimes, it might be difficult to come up with a correct requirement because the customer is not exactly clear on how the software should behave. When this kind of situation occurs, it is useless to keep pressuring the customer because until they have a chance to try it, the customer does not know if the solution is good or not. The risk of writing down any final requirement when it is not clear how the system should work is that it is likely that it will change. The risk of having no requirements is that there is no clear agreement between the customer and the development team, and it will be impossible to create an criteria in which the customer can use to accept the software as complete.

Some solutions for this dilemma are to use an iterative methodology or a prototyping approach. If these two approaches are not a feasible in your organization, another approach is to have multiple "optional" requirements that are aimed at addressing a particular feature. By using this approach, all options can be implemented, and the customer is required to choose one solution after they have had a chance to look at and evaluate all of the options. This approach works well when both sides can agree on a set of potential solutions, but neither side can agree on which one is the most appropriate. The advantage to the development team using this approach is that it mitigates the risk of changing the requirements. The team also has a chance to design a solution that can accommodate more than one way of doing things.

Getting the Requirements Right

Producing a good requirement is difficult. A good requirement is complete, unambiguous, and correct. In order to create a good requirement, it is essential that the problem domain be understood. The problem domain is the environment, people, and processes in which the problems reside, and the solution must address the problem in the context of the environment, people, and processes. The software might encompass the entire solution, or it might only be a part of the solution. The interactions between the software solution and the problem domain define the desired behaviors of the software and can be documented as requirements. Capturing and documenting these desired behaviors is normally considered to be the requirement gathering phase of the software development cycle. Some members of the development team, typically project managers and requirement analysts, interview the customer in order to understand the project and document the requirements. Their job is to produce a good requirement. Because it is so difficult to create a good requirement, the following sections provide some ideas that might be helpful.

Standard Tips

There are numerous tips on how to write and gather requirements presented in a number of books and articles.[27] These books cover topics ranging from how to gather requirements and how to write requirements to how to spot ambiguous requirements. We outline some of the major ideas in the following list.

♦ Avoid ambiguous, subjective, comparative, and vague terms. These terms are typically qualitative in nature, like, for example, the word fast. Well, how fast? Does a robust system mean 24/7? What is a user-friendly system? Quantify these terms if possible. Otherwise, interview the customer to determine their expectations and document them as literally as possible.

♦ Keep the requirement as simple and straightforward as possible. Avoid using "and" or "or" to combine requirements, and keep each requirement as atomic as possible.

♦ Perform requirement inspection and reviews. Requirement inspection and reviews can be utilized to fix requirement errors as early as possible. Requirement reviews with customers can be especially useful.

♦ Use iterative methodologies and prototyping to assist the development team in creating a good requirement.

Involve Testers

Earlier, we defined a requirement to be a testable behavior of the software. And we have observed that a good requirement is no different from a test plan. Therefore, it stands to reason that a tester is a perfect fit for assisting and evaluating requirement documents. This suggestion combines the heterogeneous paired inspection technique and the producer-consumer technique adapted from the inspection section.

Testers are trained to find bugs and test unexpected interactions. For example, if you have an interface that allows users to enter a date, a good tester would enter a valid date and a list of invalid dates, such as 13/0/2000, −1/−1/−1, or 12/43/1900. The tester would also need to know the expected response of the system given an invalid input. If requirements for invalid inputs were not specified, the testers should be able to help make the requirement more

---

[27] Robertson, Suzanne, and James Robertson. *Mastering the Requirement Process*. Addison-Wesley, Reading, MA, 2000.
Weigers, K. E. *Software Requirements*. Microsoft Press, Redmond, Washington, 1999.
Hunt, L. B. "Getting the Requirements Right—A Professional Approach," *Proceedings of IEEE International Workshop on Software Technology and Engineering Practice*, pp 464–472, London, United Kingdom, July 14–18, 1997.

complete by fleshing out error scenarios. In this case, testers would act in the role of an inspector and provide their experiences and knowledge to assist requirement specification efforts.

Work on Test Plan at the Same Time

Writing the test plan at the same time as the requirement gathering has added benefits of avoiding ambiguity because testers cannot create a test plan with ambiguous requirements. If the requirements stated:

The system shall be very fast

a good tester would come back, throw up her hands, and say, "I don't know how to test for that!" The word "fast" is a subjective term and is not testable. The requirement would need to be restated to something like this:

The system shall return a response within 500 milliseconds of receiving a request when the system has up to an average of 20 requests per second.

This requirement is testable, and the tester would be able to work with this requirement. Using this requirement, she can run the system with a number of trials and measure the average response time. If the average response time is greater than 500 milliseconds when there are 20 requests per second, the tester can say the system has failed to meet the requirement.

In fact, a good tester would immediately flag any requirements that are not testable and give them to the requirement analysts to review and redefine.

Prebugging in Design

The design of a software system presents a solution to a problem. The solution must satisfy the requirements. If this is not the case, the design has bugs, and we say the design is incomplete or incorrect. With this kind of design bug, it is sometimes trivial to spot the deficiency of the design early on. Testable features, such as GUI interaction and functional features of the requirements, are some examples. However, design bugs related to performance requirements are harder to determine in the early stages. Sometimes it is impossible to know for sure that there is a design bug until you have an implementation handy to try it. General techniques presented in previous sections, such as prototyping and inspection, are useful in preventing these types of design bugs.

However, when we talk about bad design in the software engineering industry, we are usually not talking about designs that do not meet the requirements. Instead, we normally equate bad designs to inflexible design. These kinds of designs are hard to reuse, hard to modify, and hard to extend. Object-oriented design principles are presented as a solution to these issues.[28] Design pattern is another potential solution to this problem.[29]

---

[28] Gamma, E., Helm R., Johnson, R., and Vlissides, J. *Design Patterns*. Addison-Wesley, Reading, Massachusetts, 1995.
[29] Meyer, Bertrand. *Object-Oriented Software Construction*, 2d ed.. Prentice-Hall PTR, Upper Saddle River, New Jersey, 1997.

In addition, a design could increase the chance for formation of bugs. These kinds of design issues are rarely discussed and are our focus in this section.

Different Design Choices Have Different Bug Types

Typically, in design sessions, the discussions about the merit of a design revolve around extensibility, maintainability, technical elegance, and performance. Very rarely does anyone raise the issue of bugs in a design discussion. However, our experience shows that the design choices that we make have a direct impact on the kinds of bugs we can expect.

In Chapter 4, we presented some design trade-offs involving the use of callbacks. You can probably come up with other design elements and examples from your personal experience. In this section, we present a few more examples of design issues and the type of bugs that are prevalent. The four examples presented in this section are only meant to help you understand what you will be exposed to with these design concepts. We hope the examples help you think about what the risks are in the design choices that you might be making right now. By understanding the risk and benefits of different design elements, you can make rational trade-off decisions and watch out for likely bugs in the designs and implementations associated with these design elements.

Risk in Sorting

Back in the days of Computer Science 101, different sorting algorithms were discussed: bubble sort, insertion sort, binary sort, and quick sort. You name it, we covered it and implemented it. However, I don't ever remember implementing a sorting algorithm since leaving the university. Because **quicksort()** was available in standard C libraries, and C was a popular language at the time, I stuck with **quicksort()**.

Sorting is a well-known problem and has a set of well-known solutions, so what can be the problem with it?

When we consider using sorting algorithms, we hardly ever consider the case when the number of elements that are required to be sorted is beyond the memory capacity of the hardware, or that the performance requirements makes any sorting algorithm impractical. Can your machine handle the sorting of one million records? If your system has a certain performance requirement, can your machine sort ten thousand records within that performance requirement? Do you need to design the system differently so that size and performance does not become an issue?

In many ways, this is a requirement issue. But as designers, we often don't question size and performance requirements when it comes to sorting or other well-understood algorithms, and we often don't notice when these requirements are missing because sorting is considered a solved problem. When a customer says he needs the data to be sorted, we say no problem. We know how to sort, so we don't think twice about it.

Risk in Parsing

Another example of a design with similar risks is the design of parsing algorithms. Because XML is a popular message format today, we will use XML parsing as an example. XML has become the fad du jour; people want to use it as a standard message format for Internet communication and everything else. There are many standards in many different industries that are attempting to define XML specifications for the problem that they are solving. One such standard is a product catalog. In this standard, XML is defined to hold information about a product: a name, a description, a picture, a price, and any other attributes that are appropriate.

In one of my jobs, the company was using this XML standard as a message definition to its catalog server. One day, a client wanted us to batch-load its products into our database. We said no problem, and we proceeded to convert the client's data to XML format, so we could load it using our XML interface. However, when we were loading the XML data into our system, the system came to a screeching halt, and eventually crashed the servers. The reason this happened was that the XML data that was generated was too large to be safely handled by the machine. Internally, the interface parsed and stored the entire XML message and content into the system before it did any processing. The design of the application never considered the size of the message as a potential risk.

Risk of Recursion

Recursion is a powerful and conceptually elegant mathematical model for solving a certain class of problems. Computation of Fibanocci series is a popular example used by nearly all textbooks. A function is recursive if it can call itself, as shown in the following example:

```
1. void func_A( int some_argument ) {
2.   if ( some_argument <= 0 ) return;
3.   func_A( some_argument-1 );
4. }
```

func_A() is not very exciting, and it does not provide any useful computation. But it is recursive. If you call **func_A()** with an argument of 3, **func_A()** will be executed three consecutive times with arguments of 2, 1, and 0 before returning the control of the execution back to you. The conditional statement in line 2 is the only item that will prevent **func_A()** from calling itself forever. Without line 2, **func_A()** will call **func_A()** and will call **func_A()** until you get a stack overflow error.

What is a stack overflow error? When a function is called, the arguments and local variables of the function are placed into a stack. These arguments and variables are removed from the stack when the function exits. The memory size of the stack is typically limited. When the stack is full, a stack overflow error occurs because there is no place to store local variables.

The obvious risk with recursion is getting a stack overflow error because the program will most likely crash when it occurs. One way to incur a stack overflow is to design and implement the termination condition incorrectly. For example, if line 2 was missing from the previous example, **func_A()** would not terminate, and a stack overflow error would occur. The other way to incur a stack overflow is to incorrectly implement the recursive call in line 3. **func_A()** might get a stack overflow error if instead of calling **func_A()** with *some_argument–1*, we call it with *some_argument+1*.

But even if the recursion is implemented correctly, there is still a risk of a stack overflow error if the design of the recursion is faulty. For example, calling **func_A()** with argument of largest valid integer value on the machine might be enough to cause a stack overflow error because the stack size simply cannot store all the variables. This could happen because the algorithm requires a deep recursion.

Risk of Object-Oriented Design

Due to the popularity of object-oriented design and language in the software industry, there have been many empirical studies of software defects and errors relating to the object-oriented design principles. The benefits of object-oriented design, such as inheritance and polymorphism, are well publicized.[30] Although concepts of inheritance and polymorphism can provide many benefits that the object-oriented proponents claim, these studies show that the application of these concepts can cause many difficulties.

In an industrial case study of fault proneness of object-oriented design, it was found that coupling between classes and methods can affect the fault proneness of a software module.[31] In particular, the authors suggest that method invocation, import coupling appears to be a strong, stable indicator of fault proneness. In this study, method invocation measures the number of occurrences where one method invokes another method at least once. In a study of the effect of polymorphism, it was determined that polymorphism can increase probability of fault in object-oriented software.[32] However, this study also found that polymorphism tends to occur in software with a large number of methods and a deeper inheritance class hierarchy, which implies a more complex system. The results of these studies should not come as a surprise. A large percentage of bugs occurred between interfaces of software modules or classes due to misunderstanding, ambiguity, or faulty interface design. It hardly matters if object-oriented design is used or not. Polymorphism, with its dynamic nature, makes it difficult to understand and is simply more prone to cause errors.

Object-oriented design provides a nice conceptual way of envisioning and partitioning the problem; however, difficulties set in during maintenance of the software system. We explore how object-oriented design affects maintainability of the software in Chapter 14. The main

---

[30] Meyer, Bertrand. *Object-Oriented Software Construction*, 2d ed. Prentice-Hall PTR, Upper Saddle River, New Jersey, 1997. Rumbaugh, J., et al. *Object-Oriented Modeling and Design*. Prentice-Hall, Englewood Cliffs, New Jersey, 1991.

[31] Briand, L. C., Wüst, J., Ikonomovski, S. V., and Lounis, H. "Investigating Quality Factors in Object-Oriented Designs: An Industrial Case Study," *Proceedings of the 1999 International Conference on Software Engineering*, pp 345–354, Los Angeles, California, May 16–22, 1999.

[32] Benlarbi, S., and Melo, W. L. "Polymorphism Measures for Early Risk Prediction," *Proceedings of the 1999 International Conference on Software Engineering*, pp 334–344, May 16–22, Los Angeles, California, 1999.

risk of object-oriented design is that people unfamiliar with trade-offs tend to view object-oriented design as a silver bullet. It can help you achieve your software ideals, but only if you use it correctly.

Designing Interfaces

Most empirical research has shown that a majority of bugs can be correlated with the amount of couplings between software modules. Simplistically, coupling between software modules is related to the interfaces of the modules. Two modules are coupled if one module uses another module via its interfaces. Obviously, design of the module can affect the design of the interfaces and can contribute to bugs that occur at the interface level. However, the flexibility and ambiguity of the interfaces can also contribute to the bug-proneness of the interfaces.

Designing Modules

As we do with most problem-solving endeavors, we tend to break down a software engineering problem into a collection of smaller problems. We then create solutions to solve these smaller problems. In effect, solutions to these smaller problems are what we call software modules. In structural programming, a software module can be considered a collection of related functions. In object-oriented programming, a module is simply a collection of related classes.

Conventional wisdom tells us that large monolithic modules are harder to maintain and debug. Nevertheless, modules that are too small also present a problem.[33] In a large monolithic module, the complexity resides in the internal logic of the module. Because a large monolithic module is unlikely to be devoted to a single task, the functions and classes in a module are required to handle the entire myriad tasks that the module is supposed to handle. The complexity shifts from intramodule complexity to intermodule complexity when the large monolithic module is partitioned into smaller modules. When the module becomes too small, the complexity of the system resides predominantly in the interfaces between modules, because a large number of modules need to communicate with each other in order to perform a task.

This presents a difficulty in determining the correct size of the modules in an application. The general rule of thumb appears to be "whatever feels right." Our experience in this matter is that it is not necessarily the size of the module that is the problem, it's the conceptual responsibilities of the modules that determine the over- and under-modularization. When a module is designed to do too many things, it tends to be large and suffers from the problem of undermodularization. But when the responsibility of a module is too limited and too fine-grain, the module suffers from overmodularization, and the size of the module tends to be too small. Our approach in defining the software module tends to be in the direction of feature-based modularization, where the features are created in a hierarchical fashion using a top-down approach.

---

[33] Kemerer, C. F. "Software complexity and software maintenance: A survey of empirical research," *Annals of Software Engineering*, No. 1, pp 1–22, 1995.

We will use an e-commerce problem as an example. In this example, we are responsible for creating an e-commerce system. The system should present a Web page that allows customers to browse the catalog, select products for purchase, and purchase the product. In this example, there are three features necessary to the system: catalog browsing, shopping cart support, and product ordering. We can then drill down to determine the features that are necessary to support these three main features. Using the product ordering feature as an example, we find that we need to support credit card verification and validation, delivery selection, and invoicing. We can continue to decompose these features down to the finest level of detail. But at every level, we will evaluate the complexity of each feature and estimate how each feature will interface with other features in order to determine which feature needs to be further decomposed.

Furthermore, feature-based decomposition of software also tends to produce modules that are more cohesive. This is because all the tasks that support the feature tend to fall within the module and nowhere else. This limits interactions between modules and makes them more independent, which helps reduce the errors in the system.[34]

Like everything in software engineering, modularization can be an iterative process. During the design, if you don't like the way a problem has been decomposed, you can always do it again. You can always combine overmodularized software modules or break down an undermodularized module at a later date.

Limit Flexibility

In designing a GUI, a developer typically has a choice of components that a user can use to enter information. The choice of the components can affect the complexity of the software and the risk of bugs.

For example, suppose you want to create a Web page where a user can enter his state of residency. As a GUI designer, you have two choices. You can give users a text field where they can type in the name of their state of residency, or you can provide them with a list of states to choose from. What is the trade-off between these two choices? In the first case, using the text field entry provide users and designers with flexibility. Because the entry is an open text field, users can type anything they want into the field. If you need to make the page international, codes do not need to be changed at the presentation level. On the other hand, the solution using a list of choices means that you will need to provide additional entries for the value of states of a different country.

But an open text field can potentially mean that you will need to do a lot more error checking on the back-end. Users could type in a standard abbreviation or a nonstandard one. Users could choose to enter the full name of the state, or they could also make spelling errors. You will need to check and anticipate all these potential errors, and if you miss one, well, you could potentially have a bug in your software. Using a list of choices mitigates this problem because the flexibility of the users is limited; they can only enter the values in the list.

---

[34] ibid.

The same concept applies to the design of an API. When you give a user of an API a lot of flexibility, you make your job a lot harder. There are more conditions that you have to check, more code paths to consider, and more potential for bugs and defects. Consider the following four method declarations:

```
1. void doSomething_A();
2. void doSomething_B( boolean a );
3. void doSomething_C( boolean a, boolean b );
4. void doSomething_D( int c );
```

Method *doSomething_A()* accepts no parameters. Conceivably, the implementation of *doSomething_A()* flows in a top-down manner. There is no branch and no condition to check, it can't be any easier. Method *doSomething_B()* accepts a Boolean value argument. This implies that *doSomething_B()* must check the value of the argument and potentially creates two code paths. Method *doSomething_C()* requires two Boolean arguments and potentially four code paths in the method. Method *doSomething_D()* takes an integer argument, which means that potentially you will need to consider all possible integer values that can be represented on your specific operating system, and also handle overflow and underflow conditions, which creates the potential for more things to go wrong.

The same concept can be applied to other design tasks. For example, XML is emerging as a standard message format for the Internet. An XML message has a data specification component called the Document Type Definition (DTD), which defines the valid format and content of the message. Given the DTD, an XML validating parse can be used to validate the content of an XML message itself. If the message does not validate, the parser usually returns an error. Therefore, why not specify the DTD so that as much validation work can be done by the parser instead of your application code? Using this approach, the code can be implemented to handle as little error checking as possible, and you will have reused as much "code" from the XML validating parser as you can.

Tip

Don't think you are doing users a favor by giving them a lot of unnecessary flexibility and ways to do things. They only want to get things done, they may not care about flexibility, and they certainly don't appreciate bugs.

Minimize Interface Ambiguities

There are many ways an interface can be ambiguous, for example, using *varargs* in the C and C++ programming languages. In Java, an example of an ambiguous interface is one that accepts the base class *java.lang.Object* as an argument. By doing so, you run the risk of runtime class cast exception errors when you try to access it incorrectly. In object-oriented design, you can create an ambiguous interface when you use multiple inheritance in your class hierarchy and create confusion about which member functions are used in the derived classes. Basically, an interface is ambiguous when the user of the interface cannot easily determine how the interface should be used, and the interface provides no clues on how it should be used.

The following code snippet illustrates a seldom-discussed example of an ambiguous interface:

```
101. // Some codes.
102. UnsafeAddress addr = new UnsafeAddress( "100 Main Street",
103.                                          "AnyCity",
104.                                          "AnyState",
105.                                          "00001",
106.                                          "USA",
107.                                          "555-555-5555",
108.                                          "test@test.com" );
109. // some other codes.
```

If we tell you there is a bug in these three lines of code, can you find it? Our guess is no, not without looking at the class definition of the UnsafeAddress class. The class definition of UnsafeAddress is:

```
1. public class UnsafeAddress {
2.    private String street;
3.    private String city;
4.    private String state;
5.    private String zipcode;
6.    private String country;
7.    private String phoneNumber;
8.    private String email;
9.
10.    public UnsafeAddress( String _street, String _city,
11.                          String _zipcode, String _state,
12.                          String _phoneNumber, String _email,
13.                          String _country ) {
14.       street = _street;
15.       city = _city;
16.       state = _state;
17.       zipcode = _zipcode;
18.       country = _country;
19.       phoneNumber = _phoneNumber;
20.       email = _email;
21.    }
22.    // other accessors and methods.
23. }
```

Can you see the bug now?

If not, the solution follows. The arguments for the constructor of the UnsafeAddress in lines 102–108 do not match the signature of the constructor. Table 12.1 demonstrates the errors in lines 102–108 by listing the expected signature of the constructor and the parameters passed in by the usage in lines 102–108.

Table 12.1 Expected signatures and signatures in line 102.

Expected signature	Signature in line 102
street	100 Main Street
city	AnyCity
zipcode	AnyState
state	00001
phoneNumber	USA
email	555-555-5555
country	test@test.com

There is no way that anyone can look at those seven lines of code alone and find the bug. The difficulty of this defect is that it appears to be reasonable, and there is no reason for anyone to suspect that it might be a problem. Even with the class definition handy, it would not surprise us if someone missed the defect the first time because the creator of the constructor chose to accept the arguments to the constructor in an unconventional way. As you learned in Chapter 4, people tend to see what they want to see. The constructor interface is ambiguous and presents two risks:

♦ The signature of the constructor is different from the way it is listed in the variables. In addition, the order of the parameters in the signature is not listed in a conventional order. This can easily cause another developer to write the code as shown in line 102–108. Instead of writing to adhere to the definition, the developer writes the code to fit how he thinks the constructor should be defined.

♦ The fact that the constructor interface accepts seven strings means it has an ambiguous interface. The compiler cannot assist in error detection because the arguments are all of the same type. The developers and code inspectors cannot perform any semantic validation by looking at the statement alone. Other files must be considered.

However, if we only provide the default constructor that accepts no arguments and force the developers to set the content of the object explicitly using the "set" methods as shown in the following code snippet, the defect is immediately obvious:

```
101a.   // some codes
102a.   SafeAddress addr = new SafeAddress();
103a.   addr.setStreet( "100 Main Street" );
104a.   addr.setCity( "AnyCity" );
105a.   addr.setZipcode( "AnyState" );  // an error
106a.   …
107a.   // some other code.

1a. public class SafeAddress {
2a.    private String street;
3a.    private String city;
4a.    private String state;
```

```
5a.    private String zipcode;
6a.    private String country;
7a.    private String phoneNumber;
8a.    private String email;
9a.
10a.   public SafeAddress() {
11a.      street = null;
12a.      city = null;
13a.      state = null;
14a.      zipcode = null;
15a.      country = null;
16a.      phoneNumber = null;
17a.      email = null;
18a.   }
19a.   // other accessors and methods.
20a. }
```

Without even looking at the class definition, a red flag should be raised simply because of the look of line 105a. This is what we mean by minimizing interface ambiguities. The design makes it nearly impossible for a developer to make foolish mistakes. The design also makes it easy for others to look at the code and question its correctness without having any knowledge about the **SafeAddress** class itself. In a way, this is self-documenting code because the code itself provides clues on potential defects.

However, using the default constructor is no guarantee that you will minimize the ambiguity of the interface. Imagine that you have a **Circle** class, which defines a geometric figure that looks like a circle. In a two-dimensional world, a circle is defined by a center position (x and y) and a radius. Does it make sense to define your **Circle** class in the following way?

```
1. public class Circle {
2.     private double x;
3.     private double y;
4.     private double radius;
5.     public Circle() {
6.        x = 0.0;
7.        y = 0.0;
8.        radius = 0.0;
9.     }
10.    public void setX( double _x ) { x = _x; }
11.    public void setY( double _y ) { y = _y; }
12.    public void setRadius( double r ) { radius = r; }
13     …
14. }
```

The risk with the design of this **Circle** class is that you can potentially have an ill-defined circle. If this is not an issue in your system, then this design might not cause any problems.

However, if your system expects only "valid" circles, this design provides someone with an opportunity to introduce a bug by forgetting to set one of the properties of the circle. A safer design of the **Circle** class might be:

```
1. public class BetterCircle {
2.    private double x;
3.    private double y;
4.    private double radius;
5.    public BetterCircle( double _x, double _y, double _r ) {
6.      x = _x;
7.      y = _y;
8.      radius = _r;
9.    }
10.  …
11. }
```

This design prevents you from having an ill-defined circle because you cannot produce a circle without specifying all the arguments. But the user of the class can still pass in 0 for the radius, which might be undefined and undesirable for your system. In this design, you also have the same problem as the **UnsafeAddress** class; that is, it is easy to mix up the arguments to the constructor, for example, confusing the x argument with the y argument. What's the solution?

```
1. public class SafeCircle {
2.    private double x;
3.    private double y;
4.    private double radius;
5.    public SafeCircle( TwoDLocation loc, PositiveDouble r ) {
6.      x = loc.getX();
7.      y = loc.getY();
8.      radius = r.getDouble();
9.    }
10.  …
11. }
```

TwoDLocation and **PositiveDouble** are two new classes that we have created and will let the compiler do as much "semantic" checking for you as it can. **TwoDLocation** defines a two-dimensional location class that stores the 2-D Cartesian coordinate. **PositiveDouble** is an object that only contains a value greater than 0.

The trade-off of this approach is obvious. By using these two additional classes, we have increased the complexity of the system, but we have also made the class a little safer to use and easier to read. We've also made the interface explicit. As with any other suggestion that we have presented in this book, you must take your system and your environment into account before deciding which approach you will use.

A Minor Tirade About Exceptions

For those languages that support the concept of exceptions, the alternative here is to deal with undefined circles or bad parameters by throwing exceptions. However, the danger of using exceptions is that it decreases happiness for the users of your APIs. We have discussed in Chapter 4 that handling error conditions tends to be the hardest task that a software developers can do. To us, the usage of exceptions is a mark of lazy developers. Instead of trying to make the module safe and easy to use, these developers opt to pass the buck to the user of the APIs, and let them worry about how to deal with these errors and exceptions. Why not design the software to make it nearly impossible to have error conditions? Why not design the software so that it is nearly impossible for the user of the software to make any mistakes? Why give the users a rope to hang themselves?

Design Self-Documenting Code

In most books, self-documenting code refers to having meaningful variable names and having meaningful function or method names. But that's only one aspect of self-documentation. The other aspect of self-documentation is to have all the information for people reading the code in one place. If possible, we want the code to tell us what it does and what it expects, all in one location. In self-documenting code, we also want the compiler to do as much checking for us as possible. The design of **SafeAddress** and **SafeCircle** described in the previous section presents an illustration of what we mean by self-documentation.

In **SafeAddress**, the **setStreet()** method is self-documenting because most of us can agree on the semantic meaning of the street, and it is possible to inspect the content of the value and see if we have made a mistake in passing a nonstreet value to the method. In **SafeCircle**, class **PositiveDouble** prevents the user from creating a circle with a negative or zero length radius. The class name is intuitive, and the **SafeCircle** class does not have to handle many extra error checks because we have eliminated the possibility of creating invalid circles.

Prebugging in Implementation

Implementation is where the rubber meets the road. This is where the concepts laid out in the requirement specification and design documents are realized. By and large, we create bugs during implementation because we don't understand the tools that we are using to create the software, or we are too lazy, write buggy codes, and use unsafe constructs.

Understand the Tools

There are many developers who simply lack the appropriate training to be good and safe programmers. There are holes in their knowledge about design principles, language features and usage, and software development processes. They lack problem-solving skills. They also make more bugs than more efficient programmers.

Why should you care about other people's mistakes? Software developers do not work in isolation anymore. The days of lone hackers hiding away in basements cranking out code are long gone. Nowadays, we work together as a team, and we rely on each other's software modules to produce a working system. If you are working with someone who is not well trained, his or her bug is your bug. We don't like to find and fix our own bugs, and we particularly don't like to find and fix other people's bugs. One way to prevent having to find other people's bugs is to make sure they are as good a programmer as we are. It makes my job a lot easier.

On the other hand, if we are the weak link in the system, then it is in our own best interest to improve ourselves. It's difficult being a scapegoat.

Understand the Language and the Principles behind It

In the early days of assembly programming, there weren't many principles behind the language design. The program proceeded from one instruction to the next, and you were just shuffling bits around. To write assembly programs meant that you had to be able to think sequentially and keep track of registry and memory values. With Pascal and C, the notions of abstract data types and procedural decomposition were required. Although the program still ran in a sequential fashion, the problem was solved at a more abstract level. The program organization and structure of Pascal and C reflected these abstractions. C++ and Java brought object-oriented principles to the mainstream and required a whole new way of thinking. Object-oriented programming languages bring forth the concept of inheritance, polymorphism, and abstract interfaces. Although these concepts are powerful when used correctly, they are also very destructive when abused. We can compare the use of object-oriented programming to the use of nuclear energy. When we harness nuclear power properly, we can provide electricity for millions of people. If we make a mistake with it, we can destroy the same millions of people just as easily.

How many times have you seen language features being abused? There is usually only one reason why people abuse language features and that is because they don't know they are abusing them. (The other reason is that a person abusing them knows the language so well, that he or she feels comfortable doing so. The abuse is usually used as a shortcut and introduces a whole set of its own problems—mainly, because it confuses everyone else.) When the language is abused in a program, the program becomes harder to comprehend, harder to maintain, and is more prone to mistakes. If you don't understand how pointers work, you are going to have a hard time programming in C and C++. Using the Swing toolkit from Java means that you need to understand how Model-View-Controller architecture works. If you want to use Microsoft Foundation Class (MFC), you should understand that it is nothing more than a thin wrapper around the Win32 API. Understanding how templates work is the key to understanding STL. Unfortunately, these kinds of understandings are difficult to achieve in a class or training setting. Classes can provide you with an overview of the features, but not explain what the features mean or how they relate to the problem or the solution space.

Mentoring

There are many things that we simply cannot learn from a class. Recently, I had a chance to work with a few recent graduates on a project. I was acting as the mentor, they were the apprentices, and together we released a software system under real-life pressures and constraints. During the project, I could see them evolve and getting better. They became faster at writing code. They understood why things should be done a certain way. They became more proficient with the language and the tools available to them. But the project also benefited me as well. The graduates helped me learn about the difficulty of software engineering and inspired me to make the problem easier to solve. They taught me communication; how to relate technical ideas to another person regardless of their skill level.

Mentoring can be a formal process or an informal one. Formally, the company can assign a mentor to an apprentice, either permanently or on a project-by-project basis. Informally, mentoring is nothing more than identifying an expert on your team who knows more about a subject area and learning from him or her. This is done by listening to the expert in meetings, looking at his or her code and design, and asking questions. These are good ways to improve your skills.

Defensive Coding

Techniques for defensive coding practices abound in the literature.[35] Techniques such as avoid deeply nested loops, use proper indentation styles, use Hungarian notations,[36] use good layout techniques, use meaningful variable and function names, avoid global variables, and avoid gotos are well known and frequently discussed.

The Evils of Asserts

When we were surveying books and articles written about debugging and bug prevention, one technique that stood out in all of these books and articles was the encouragement to use asserts. Frankly, we do not see the value of asserts in producing quality software. In fact, we believe that usage of asserts is the mark of a lazy programmer as we discussed in Chapter 4. We believe that asserts can increase the odds of bug formation and introduction, and that usage of asserts should be avoided.

Let's review exactly what **assert()** does. Typically, an assert statement looks like this:

```
assert( condition, message );
```

When the program execution reaches the assert statement, the condition is evaluated. If the condition is false, the optional message can be printed to the screen, and the program terminates. In addition, asserts tend to be active only in the debugging mode. The compiler

---

[35] Binkley, D. W. "C++ in safety critical systems," *Annals of Software Engineering*, No. 4, pp 223–234, 1997.
Kernighan, Brian W., and Pike, Rob. *The Practice of Programming*. Addison-Wesley, Reading, Massachusetts, 1999.
Maguire, S. *Writing Solid Code*. Microsoft Press, Redmond, Washington, 1993.
McConnell, Steve. *Code Complete*. Microsoft Press, Redmond, Washington, 1993.
Meyers, S. *Effective C++: 50 Specific Ways to Improve Your Programs and Designs*. Addison-Wesley, Reading, Massachusetts, 1998.
[36] Simonyi, C., and Heller, M. "The Hungarian Revolution," *BYTE*, August, pp 131–139, 1991.

has the option of compiling asserts out of existence in the production mode. As a result, **assert()** is part of the code in the debugging mode. In the production mode, **assert()** does not exist and is not executed. The rationale for removing asserts in the production mode is to increase performance. After all, if you have ensured that a condition cannot occur in the debugging mode, it should never occur in the production mode, right?

Why would you use **assert()** at all? In most usage situations, it is typically used to ensure that a prerequisite condition is valid, and that the code will not continue with an invalid precondition. The following code snippets show a typical usage of **assert()** using C:

```
1.   void ABadFunction( int parameter )
2.   {
3.     int *array = NULL;
4.     assert( parameter > 5 );
5.     ...
6.     array = (int *) malloc( sizeof(int) * parameter );
7.     assert( array );
8.     ...
9.     assert( Foo( array, parameter, 5 ) );
10.    ...
11. }
```

In line 4, **assert()** is used to ensure that the input parameter is greater than 5. In line 7, **assert()** ensures that the allocation of the array is successful. In line 9, **assert()** is used to make sure the result of the function call **Foo()** is true. In debug mode, if any of these asserts fail, the program will exit and provide the appropriate error messages. Presumably, the programmer can use these error messages to debug the program. However, in production mode, when these assert statements are compiled out of existence, what happens?

In production mode, you lose all error checking capability provided by the assert. Now, the function can be called with a parameter of less than or equal to 5, which might trigger some bugs that the function is not prepared to handle. The memory allocation in line 6 can fail, which will result in a null array. The usage of the assert in line 9 is even more problematic in production mode because function **Foo()** will not be invoked at all. If **Foo** is merely a validate function, that is, it does not change the state of the program execution, then we lose the validation capability of line 9. However, if **Foo()** is an active function and its computation can be used in the latter part of the program, we will lose the computation, and the program will execute erroneously.

In this example, we identified two major risks of using asserts:

♦ Just because the **assert()** did not fail in the debugging mode, doesn't mean it can't fail in the production mode. An **assert()** is used because there is a chance that a false condition can occur. If you think this condition can be false in a development or debugging environment, is there any reason to believe that it cannot be false in a production environment?

The common belief is that during the unit, integration, and system testing, assert can be used to detect *all* invalid uses of the interface. In the preceding example, **ABadFunction()** requires the value of the parameter to be greater than 5. But we have no way of knowing if the caller of the function will enforce the constraint, or that the testing process had tested all possible ways that the parameter to **ABadFunction()** can be generated, and thus, ensuring the parameter will satisfy the precondition of the function. Just because it didn't happen in testing and debugging, doesn't mean it can't happen in production.

♦ Running different version of the code in debugging and production environment. Because the assert can be compiled out of existence, using asserts means that what you use in a production environment can be different than what you use in a debugging environment. Using the preceding example in a production environment, if the missing line 9 caused a bug, and we attempted to debug the code in the debugging environment, the bug would disappear because line 9 would no longer be missing; it would exist in debugging mode. But, how long would it take you to realize this?

For argument's sake, let's say you decide to still use **assert()** but leave it running in the debugging mode under the production environment. When an **assert()** fails, what happens? For instance, line 7 failed because the program ran out of memory, so the program terminated and produced an error message. The end user sees the message, but has no idea what it means. That is the least of your worries. The bigger danger is that if the program has any unsaved data, that data will be lost because the program terminated ungracefully. Does the user care why his or her data is lost? Is it important to the user that the programmer decided that nothing can be done because the machine ran out of memory? Or that somewhere in the application, a programmer decided to call **ABadFunction()** with a parameter of 0? If you don't think this can happen, think again. Users have a knack for doing unexpected things.

In many books that preach the use of **assert()**, authors recognize the danger of using **asserts** incorrectly and encourage their readers to redefine the **assert** function to prevent them from using asserts in a harmful manner. Paragraphs of warnings are written about when not to use **assert()** and when to use it. But these warnings are too complicated and too unsafe. Unless we can guarantee that the asserted condition can never be invalid, compiling asserts out of existence in the production environment is always a risk. It is easier and safer to use explicit error checking where you would use an assertion. This makes the codebase larger but safer. This also forces you to understand different error conditions and have specific strategies to handle errors caused by different reasons. In most circumstances, you would want to handle an invalid parameter differently from an out-of-memory error. Any error-handling mechanism for a condition that is not well specified should be propagated back to the requirement level, which will help refine the requirements and make them more complete and unambiguous.

The following code snippet is a better reimplementation of the previous example. There is some added complexity to the code with all the additional error handling. But in our view, the trade-off is worth it.

```
1.  int ABetterFunction( int parameter )
2.  {
3.     int *array = NULL;
4.     int FooResult = 0;
5.     if ( parameter <= 5 ) return ERROR_CODE_1;
6.     ...
7.     array = (int *) malloc( sizeof(int) * parameter );
8.     if ( array == NULL ) {
9.       graceful_exit(0);   /* might save the data...etc */
10   }
11.    ...
12.    FooResult = Foo( array, parameter, 5 );
13.    if ( FooResult == 0 )
14.      return ERROR_CODE_FOO;
15.    ...
16. }
```

Combining Explicit Error Checking with Log Tracing

In **ABetterFunction()**, we have removed the use of asserts and returned all possible error conditions. But as we noted in Chapter 4, handling error conditions is one of the hardest tasks in writing software. It is hard to specify error handling correctly, and it is easy to forget about checking for error conditions. In **ABadFunction()**, if the caller had a bug in his code and called the function with an invalid parameter, the **assert()** in the function would force the program to terminate and notify the developers of the problem. However, in **ABetterFunction()**, the developers receive no such explicit notification. Developers must check for the error returned by **ABetterFunction()** in order to realize their mistakes. If they forget to do so, they could be in for a long night of debugging because their bug is hidden in the design.

A solution to this problem is to combine log tracing with explicit error checking as shown in **ABetterFunction2()**:

```
1.  int ABetterFunction2( int parameter )
2.  {
3.     int *array = NULL;
4.     int FooResult = 0;
5.     if ( parameter <= 5 ) {
6.       logger( ERROR_MESSAGE, "AbetterFunction2",
7.               "Parameter must be greater than 5" );
8.       return ERROR_CODE_1;
9.     }
10.      ...
11.    array = (int *) malloc( sizeof(int) * parameter );
12.    if ( array == NULL ) {
13.      logger( ERROR_MESSAGE, "AbetterFunction2", "Cannot allocate array" );
```

```
14.      graceful_exit(0);  /* might save the data…etc */
15.    }
16.    …
17.    FooResult = Foo( array, parameter, 5 );
18.    if ( FooResult == 0 ) {
19.      logger( ERROR_MESSAGE, "AbetterFunction2", "FOO Failed" );
20.      return ERROR_CODE_FOO;
21.    }
22.    …
23. }
```

Logger is a function that accepts an error severity code, the name of the function, and a message. The logger is designed with the characteristics described in the "Tracing Log File" section. It can aid the developer during the development of the software, and it can also aid debuggers and maintainers.

To summarize, there are three fundamental risks associated with the use of **assert()**. The first risk is that using asserts will result in two slightly different versions of the program—one in the debug mode with asserts active, and the other in the production mode with asserts inactive. The second risk is that **assert()** gives the developer a false sense of security. There is no guarantee that if the **assert()** did not fail in testing then it would not fail in production. The third risk is related to having **assert()** active in the production environment. By leaving asserts in the production environment, you risk terminating the program unexpectedly, when an assert failed.

Let Compiler Help As Much As It Can

When we compile our codes, we usually turn on every warning that the compiler supports. Our goal is to produce an error-free and warning-free compilation output. It is usually difficult to ignore error messages because the compiler would not produce an executable program. However, it is extremely easy to ignore warnings, especially if you think they are senseless. But these warnings can help you avoid stupid mistakes and force you to be disciplined in making your code explicit. Some C++ compilers warn you about casting from one object type to another. Some compilers also warn you about potentially ambiguous evaluations. It might be prudent to follow a compiler's advice. For example, the following code line:

```
if ( a == b && c != 0 || d > 5 )
```

may cause the compiler to complain, and we might want to rewrite it as:

```
if ( (a == b) && ((c != 0) || (d > 5)) )
```

in order to pacify the compiler. Another advantage of this construction is that we no longer have to guess at and evaluate the precedent rules. We have made the code explicit and easy to understand.

Sometimes, we'll turn off some warnings because we know they will not provide any useful insight and instead only clutter other potentially useful information. The best example of warnings that we usually turn off is the warning that is produced by Microsoft Visual C++ when it needs to truncate names to fewer than 255 characters. This usually occurs during template instantiation and can clutter the output screen which makes it impossible to find useful warnings.

But we can do more than just turn on warnings. We can design and implement codes to let the compiler do as much validation as possible. One thing that we can do to empower the compiler is to make our code as strongly typed as possible. A programming language is strongly typed if it can guarantee that no typing violation will ever occur. Java is not a strongly typed language because it is possible to get a class casting exception error during runtime. C and C++ are similar in that they allow a programmer to cast a pointer of one type to another type at will.

In the section "Minimizing Interface Ambiguity," we discussed the idea of using specific structure and classes to implement functional interfaces in order to make the semantics of the interface arguments explicit and minimize the need for error checking. Instead of using a "double" for passing in the radius of a circle, we suggested creating a class that allows only positive double values. That way, the circle class does not have to worry about the validity of the radius. By making the interface argument unambiguous, we also make it possible for the compiler to help us because we have made the type for passing in a radius "stronger."

Implementation Choices

How you choose to implement a design can also affect the kind of bugs that you are likely to make. If you use **strcpy()** and static memory, be prepared for buffer overflow errors. If you allocate memory, be prepared to deal with memory leaks and handle out-of-memory errors. The simple rule of thumb when choosing an implementation is to keep it as simple and as clear as possible.

Avoid Obscure Language Features

I remember interviewing a candidate for a C++ programming position a few years ago. Near the end of the interview, I asked him what questions he would ask himself to assess his own C++ competency. Immediately, he started to go into some obscure C++ features dealing with global variables. To be honest, I had no idea what he was talking about, and I don't remember a single thing he said. It was a C++ usage that I had never heard anyone talk about. I remember asking him how he ever encountered this feature, and his response was that it was related to some problem that he was tracking down. Apparently, it took him a few weeks to track the problem down, and my immediate thought was, why? What was he doing that would require such an obscure language feature? Couldn't he have found another way to design his software so it didn't depend on this feature?

The problem with obscure language features is that they are just that—obscure. Not many people know about them. Not many people even care about them, other than language lawyers. And most likely, not all compilers support them either.

Issues with Pointers

Issues with pointers are obviously not a problem with languages that don't use pointers and explicit memory allocation and deallocation. Pointers are not a problem in Java because of garbage collection, and the fact that every object in Java is essentially a pointer. This is not an issue in C because all memory allocation and deallocation must be handled explicitly. However, in C++, pointers are one of the thorniest issues. The basic issue comes down to who is responsible for allocating and deallocating pointers in a class member variable?

We will start with an example to illustrate the difficulty with this problem:

```
1.   class B {
2.      ...
3.   };
4.   class C : public B {
5.      ...
6.   };
7.   class A {
8.      public:
9.        A();
10.       A( const A& src );
11.       virtual ~A();
12.     private:
13.       B *pointer;
14.  }
```

In this example, when class A is instantiated, presumably, the pointer variable is also allocated and created. When an object of class A goes out of scope, the destructor should be responsible for deallocating the pointer member variable. This implies that the copy constructor must also explicitly allocate the pointer member variable and copy the content of the pointer member variable from the source object.

However, one reason that we might want to use a pointer is because we want the code to be more efficient, so we don't have to copy and create objects all the time. The other reason is that we want to leverage the concepts of inheritance and polymorphism in our code. For instance, in class A, we want the pointer variable to be able to store both an object of class B and class C. We need to create a set method for the caller of the class to set an object, as shown in the following code snippet:

```
7a.  class A {
8a.     public:
9a.       A();
```

```
10a.     A( const A& src );
11a.     virtual ~A();
12a.     void setPointer( B *data );
13a.   private:
14a.     B *pointer;
15a.   };
```

With **setPointer()**, we can call the method with a pointer to an object of class B or class C and meet our requirement. But we have introduced a dilemma. The dilemma is, who owns the pointer member variable? If class A owns the pointer member variable, it means that every time the copy constructor is called, pointer variable will need to be copied. The destructor will also need to delete the pointer member variable. If class A does not own the pointer member variable, then the user of the class will need to keep track of the memory allocated for the pointer variable. Furthermore, **setPointer()** is naturally ambiguous. It is unclear to the user of the class who owns the data without reading the documentation.

We can make class **A** less ambiguous by removing the **setPointer()** method as follows:

```
7b.  class A {
8b.    public:
9b.      A();
10b.     A( const A& src );
11b.     virtual ~A();
12b.     void setB( const B &b_src );
13b.     void setC( const C &c_src );
14b.   private:
15b.     B *pointer;
16b.   };
```

The setB() and setC() interfaces make it clear to the caller that the caller doesn't have to worry about tracking memory at all because class **A** will handle the memory of the pointer variable. In fact, the caller doesn't even have to know what the underlying representation is. The obvious drawback is that if you create a class **D** that also inherits from B and you want to pass **D** to class A, you need to modify A in order to fulfill this need.

Test as You Go

We have a personal process in the implementation stage. It is a simple two-step process, implement and test. When we have a coding project, we mentally decompose the project into small functional sections. The project can be the size of a software module or a set of class libraries in which the functional sections might be individual classes. The project can be a class, and the functional sections may be the major methods and interfaces within the class. Or the project can be a single method or a function. For a project of this size, the functional sections are the steps within the method.

Once we have finished implementing a functional section. we test it. When the functional section has been tested, we move on to the next section. At the conclusion of the implementation of the second section, we test the combination of the first and the second section. We repeat this process until we have completed the project.

This process is time-consuming if the functional section is very small. But the major benefit of a test-as-you-go process is that you always have a working set of codes. If you made a mistake when you are developing a new section, it is most likely in the code that you have just written, and not the code that you have tested. The cause of the bug might be in a tested section, but it is the usage in the new code that triggers the bug. Working this way will help you narrow down the trigger and causes of bugs in fewer lines of codes.

Bottom-Up/Top-Down Test-as-You-Go Approach

There are many ways to implement a test-as-you-go process. One way is to implement the functional sections in a bottom-up approach. In a bottom-up approach, the functions and classes at the bottom of a dependency hierarchy are implemented first. So when you implement a functional section, all the classes and functions that you need are implemented and available to you. Because you will be implementing and testing for the desired behaviors and features in a bottom-up approach, it ensures that the desired behaviors are implemented correctly.

In a top-down approach, you implement the top-level function first. When you need another class or function, instead of implementing it, you can implement a shell and have the shell return error conditions, if appropriate. So your top-level function first implements the codes to handle error conditions. You can then flesh out the desired behavior of the lower-level classes and functions.

In practice, we use a combination of bottom-up and top-down test-as-you-go approaches, depending on the situation, the time available, and what we think is the hardest part of the project. If wethink the hardest part is to get the feature right, we'll follow the bottom-up approach. On the other hand, if we think the hardest part is to get the error handling right, we'll follow the top-down approach.

Don't Ignore Bugs

Let's say that you are implementing some code, using any process or methodology. Everything is going great, but when you test your implementation, the program crashes. You look high and low. You scratch your head until you determine that the reason the program crashed was because it couldn't find a file that it needed or an entry in an external file that it needed was corrupted. So what do you do?

You fix the file and continue testing, or you fix the program so it doesn't crash with bad files, and then fix the file.

We have seen many programmers just fix the file and continue testing. For some reason, they don't consider their program's misbehavior due to bad environmental dependencies a bug. In this case, we used bad files as an example. But the problem could very well be a corrupted database entry, a bad network connection, or a hard disk failure. Regardless, these events are rare, and when you encounter one, you should take advantage of the situation to implement codes to handle these rare events correctly. Consider it a chance to test these codes under a real usage situation. It can be very difficult to replicate these kind of conditions in testing and maintenance.

You should, in fact, fix the program so it doesn't crash with bad files, and then fix the file. Fixing the file and continuing your testing merely masks the symptom and leaves the defect in the program. If you don't know what the correct behavior of the program should be when it encounters a bad file, consult the requirements or ask the requirement analysts. Don't just leave a defect in the program for someone else to run into at a later time.

Summary

We all know the steps and procedures that can produce quality software. It is easy to say that if we have solid, complete, clear, attainable, and testable requirements that are agreed to by all the stakeholders, we can produce quality software. It is easy to see that if we have realistic schedules, so we have time to think about design, time to gather requirements, and time to test, we can produce great software. It is understood that we need to communicate and use the right tools. Usually, reality has a way of derailing us from our grand visions.

What we have tried to do in this chapter is offer some suggestions that may help you implement some of these steps and procedures in a realistic environment. We have also attempted to outline some issues that do not get a lot of airtime and provide solutions to these issues. Engineering is marked by evaluating risks and making trade-off decisions. Some of our prebugging tips are meant to help you think about your problem and outline trade-offs that you might want to consider during your decision-making process. We have also tried to present techniques that can address reasons and causes for bugs in software systems that were presented in Chapter 4.

In Chapter 4, we talked about complexity as a main cause of bugs, and we offered many suggestions for handling and managing complexities. Overall, having a process can assist us in dealing with complexity. We can manage the complexity if we can understand the problem correctly and get the requirement correct from the start. We can make solutions easier by decomposing the problem domain correctly, by creating the right modules, and by making the interfaces simple and unambiguous. We can also make our solutions simpler if we don't always try to create the most elegant solutions.

Reality is another major contributing factor to bug formation. Lack of time and resources are the main culprits, and short of making time and hiring more people, we need to learn to make do with what we have. Many suggestions presented in this chapter have many alternatives that account for time and resource constraints. Constant change is a force that will not soon disappear. We have suggested ways to capture requirements and reuse techniques to mitigate the risk of change. In addition, we offered ways to create documentation in the real world and use defect causal analysis techniques to pool corporate knowledge and experience to fight against inexperience as a source of defects.

Human weakness was another main cause of bugs described in Chapter 4. We all make mistakes for one reason or another. Inspection and various defensive coding techniques can be implemented to help reduce bugs that are the result of simple human error.

One final point: Ideas and techniques presented in this chapter are meant to be a starting point. They are biased toward our experiences and our habits. We are all different, and we all work in different environments. What worked for us may not work for you. But it is worthwhile to think about these ideas and try them. If they help you, great! If not, try to determine where the idea failed, and maybe you can come up with something better. For more ideas, we suggest that you read some of the articles and books presented in Appendix B. It is important to read what other people are saying and thinking and see how it applies to you and your environment. Creating bug-free code requires a lot of discipline, commitment, and introspection. It's not something that will happen overnight, and it won't be easy.

Bug Puzzle

Earlier in this chapter, we talked about the risk of reuse. This puzzle relates to another way that reuse without thinking can cause problems.

In this case, we have a client and server environment. The client side can be anything, but basically, it is a GUI that displays some information. For simplicity, let us assume that the GUI displays the catalog of widgets that the company makes. On the left side of the display, there is a list of categories of widgets, you can click on each category and the GUI will display the widgets in that category on the right side of the GUI. In addition, there is a pull-down menu that also contains the list of categories on the GUI. The GUI uses a set of standard APIs to communicate with the server, which serves up the contents needed by the client.

The customer is not happy with the performance of the GUI client, and you are in charge of making the system go faster. As you dig through the code and log files, you discover that the server seems to be requested by the client to perform the same task twice, one after another. The task is to retrieve a list of categories from the database. Why is the log showing this behavior? How would you go about finding out the problem?

We can start by listing a set of potential problems and questions that we might have about this behavior:

♦ Is there a bug in the way the server is reporting the usage?

♦ Is there a bug in the server software?

♦ Is there a bug in the API?

♦ Is there a bug in the client software?

Let us assume that every piece of code is written properly and that there is no bug in the software. (Hint: think about what must be in the API and how a lazy programmer would use the API.)

Chapter 13
Testing

Matt Telles

N o book on debugging would be complete without a chapter on testing. Testing and debugging go together hand in glove. Without testing, there would be very few bugs to fix. Without debugging, testers would never see any improvement in the product or have new things to test. Testing is simply the process of finding bugs, whereas debugging is the process of removing them. You can't have one without the other.

Because this is not a book about testing, refer to the book list at the end of this chapter for the many excellent books on testing. This is a book about debugging, so when we talk about testing, we do so from the perspective of the debugger and, more importantly, from the perspective of the bug. This is, after all, a bug-centric book.

From the perspective of the professional debugger, there are three unique kinds of testing: unit testing, verification testing, and quality assurance (QA) testing. The first two are included in the realm of the debugger; the third is really an external sort of testing. Let's take a look at each type and see what they involve.

Unit Testing

Unit testing is done on individual modules by the developers that originally wrote them. Basically, a unit test is used to prove to the developer that the unit works as designed. In general, a unit test will not tie in any other modules except the one being tested. The only other required modules for a unit test are those included in the actual module being tested.

What Is Tested?

Unit testing tests, at a minimum, all of the paths through the module. It should test the interface of the module completely. In order to accurately ensure that the module is fully unit tested, the interface should be tested with all valid forms of the types of data passed to it. In addition, as many invalid forms of the data should be tried as possible to ensure that the module adequately validates input correctly. Output from the module should be hand calculated and printed out in addition to the output actually generated from the module. Only in this way can you guarantee that the module really does what you think it is going to do.

One of the most common problems for developers writing unit tests is to forget that there might be a variety of ways to get to the data type they are using. For example, if you are using a scripting language, such as Javascript, you might get automatic conversions of various data types to the data type you are expecting. In cases like this, it is important to verify that the data you get is correct.

Why Is Unit Testing Important?

From the perspective of the debugger, unit testing is important because it allows you to concentrate on other aspects of the functionality of the unit rather than worrying about whether the "standard" uses of a module work properly. In addition, you can use unit tests to verify that changes to a given module do not break existing functionality or change the behavior of the module.

There is another reason that unit testing is important, and is one that might not be obvious at first glance. Unit tests provide a sanity check for documentation for a given module. For example, your unit test can be used as a simple example of how to use a given module. Quite often, other developers will use a unit test as the basis for their own development because they know from the test results what does and what does not work for the module interface.

How Does This Apply to Debugging?

Unit testing applies to debugging in several ways. As mentioned previously, you can use unit tests to verify that at least your proposed fixes do not break any existing expected behavior of the code. In addition, you can use test cases to look for problems that might have cropped up in the last set of changes to a given module. If you can find the problem quickly and simply through a unit test, you don't have to go through the pain and annoyance of tracing through the entire codebase for the application, but can instead restrict your debugging efforts to a single module.

What Are the Important Issues in Unit Testing?

There are really three issues you should strive for when writing unit tests, especially for code you have not written yourself. This is the norm for the class of debugger that comes in after the project has been released for the first time and is now in an enhancement and maintenance mode.

Unit tests are important for understanding how to use the code. From documentation, existing source code usage, and internal studying, you should be able to discover what functions or methods need to be called before other functions and methods. Unit tests should be written not only to verify that the code does properly report the error when the proper calling order is not followed, but also as a kind of documentation example to show later developers how to use the code properly.

Another important feature of a unit test is to study the interface of the function or method that you are testing and verify that you have selected not only valid input types, but also distinctly invalid ones. For example, if the code expects a pointer to an object, as many C and C++ functions do, you might try passing it a NULL pointer, a pointer to a local variable, and a pointer to a global variable as some of the possible values. Likewise, if the code is expecting an integer value, you might try passing in a floating point value, a negative value, and a zero value. These are simple test cases that can easily reveal problems in the underlying functionality you are testing.

The most important function of unit testing is to verify that you have examined each and every branch within the code. By forcing the code to go through all of the branches in the routines you are testing, you ensure that the complete coverage of the code is examined. This is important because many bugs only show up when a specific piece of the code is executed for the very first time. In many cases, these branches disclose exceptional cases or serious errors that the original developer never expected to happen and did not really think through properly. You will find that code coverage analysis tools are available to see how much code in the subject module the unit tests actually exercise.

Verification Testing

Verification testing is the most basic form of testing and should be done by all developers regardless of whether they do any other testing with the code they write. Put simply, verification testing indicates whether the code does everything it is supposed to do. Note that this does not mean it verifies that the code does everything the requirements say it should do. Given an interface to a module, verification testing simply shows that using the correct set of inputs, the module will produce the correct set of outputs.

In most cases, verification tests are the first wave of unit tests. By testing the module with correct values, you can easily see what invalid values might be. In addition, by only testing the modules in the order they are supposed to be called in, you can also see sequences that might result in problems. Verification testing is not sufficient to consider whether a module is of release quality, but it is a good way to see if the implementation you have selected and written is done properly.

Once again, like unit testing, verification testing is a good documentation tool for the debugger, maintenance person, or person reusing the module in another application. From the perspective of the debugger, verification tests allow you to pull together just the modules that you want to test and try out various scenarios with them. It is quite possible that a perfectly valid input will result in an error in the final version if certain other criteria are present (or omitted). By rendering the system down to a smaller version, you can concentrate on only the modules you suspect of having the problem and can feed data you suspect is causing the problem directly into the module in question.

Quality Assurance Testing

Normally, when we talk about testing in the software world, we are referring to the QA (Quality Assurance) type of testing. QA is structured testing performed by trained QA personnel. QA testing goes well beyond the scale of seeing whether something works or not. It ensures that the software doesn't do what it is not supposed to do. This is a strange way of putting it, but it is nothing short of the truth. Programmers worry about software performing as specified, whereas QA people worry more about using the software in ways that it was never intended to be used.

Let's consider, for an instant, a function that is supposed to calculate the square of a number. The square of a number, of course, is simply the number multiplied by itself. Normally, this is a rather trivial function that you might implement like this:

```
double square( double in )
{
    return in * in;
}
```

This function certainly seems simple enough. You might test it by trying it with various inputs, such as 1, 2, and perhaps even 0. If you were particularly thorough, you might even try a value like –1. All of these inputs are perfectly valid ways to test the function. For a language such as C, these are also about the only reasonable numbers with which to test the function. You could try fractional numbers, such as 0.5, and you could try very large numbers, such as 1,000,000. In any case, you will almost certainly find that the function works as specified.

Now, let's consider a more complex example. Imagine that you have a screen that allows you to input a number from 1 to 10. This number is then used to take you to another screen, depending on the number entered. The function that handles this decision might look something like this:

```
void choose( const char *input )
{
    switch ( atoi( input ) )
    {
        case 0:
            DoScreen();
          Break;
```

```
case 1:
        DoScreen0();
        Break;
    // Remainder of cases to 10
    }
}
```

Once again, this function seems simple enough. As a developer, you would certainly test it by calling it with inputs such as:

```
choose("1");
choose("2");
choose("3");
choose("9");
```

A QA engineer, however, might try a considerably different set of inputs to the function. Assuming that the function simply takes whatever is input on the screen, the QA engineer might try entries such as "ABC", "–11", " ", and "J". All of these are certainly valid keyboard inputs, and inputs that you might never have thought about when you were designing the function. In fact, simply not entering anything and then telling the screen to select is a case most programmers would never consider.

Testing, Maintainability, and Complexity

The relationship between testing and maintainability is a complex one; however, there are certain easy criteria you can use to determine parts of that relationship. For example, the number of test cases for a given feature, module, or function are a good indication of the complexity level of that item. Because complexity is a good indicator of maintainability, you can see that the number of test cases for a given feature or module is also a good indicator of how maintainable that module or feature will be in the future.

Complexity is important because, as we have shown, the number of bugs in a module is directly proportional to the complexity of that module. Because the number of initial test cases is a good indicator of complexity, it is also a good predictor of the number of bugs a given feature is going to have. It is important, therefore, to break your features down to the lowest possible level to accurately predict the number of bugs you are going to find. Because the act of finding bugs is primarily the purview of the tester, you can see that debugging and testing go hand in hand.

How can you estimate the number of test cases (and hence the complexity) of a given module? One good way is to look at the interface for that feature or module. Open bounded types, such as pure integers or floating point numbers, are obviously more error-prone than user-defined types, which restrict input to valid values. Likewise, enumerated types, such as month values, are going to be less dangerous than the simple numbers 1 through 12 (or worse, 0 through 11).

Testing Methods

In many ways, testing is a lot like trash on city streets. Everyone likes to talk about it, but few people like to do anything about it. The problem, really, is that few developers and debuggers really understand how to do testing. As with debugging, the best way to understand testing is to understand the techniques available to you and decide which technique is the best for you.

Unlike debugging, testing has no single answer to a question. With debugging, you find the solution that fixes the reported problem (the bug). But with testing, you don't decide that something works by running a single test against it and verifying that the test works. Instead, testing is more a matter of convincing yourself that you have verified, to the best of your ability, the possible ways in which something could break and deciding that you have covered them adequately. The real problem with trying to test a system is that as the complexity of the system grows, the number of test cases that can be written for that system approach infinity. Because it is impossible to run an infinite number of test cases, no matter how reasonable your schedule and management, you need to use the most efficient and effective techniques.

In the following sections, we examine these available testing techniques. We describe each technique, the environments and systems in which it is best used, and an example of how to use the technique with either real code or program pseudocode.

Flow (Path) Testing

Flow testing is the art of making sure that every path through the system is exercised by the minimum number of test cases needed to be sure that the path is working properly. This means that each conditional, each loop, and each branch within the code must be run through by as many test cases as needed to make sure that they are correct.

Let's look at a simple example of this testing approach using a chunk of code written in Visual Basic.

```
Sub Foo(X As Integer)
    If X < 1 Or X > 10 Then
        Exit Function
    End If

    Dim Flag as Boolean

    Flag = False
    For I = 1 to X
        Select CaseI
            Case 1
                Do_Something
```

```
        Case Else
            Flag = True
            Do_Something_Else

    End Select
End For
GnotFound = False
If ( Flag = False ) Then
    GNotFound = True
End Sub
```

How many test cases are needed to assure that all of the possible paths through this subroutine are executed? To answer this question, let's first look at the conditional statements within the code. There are three conditional statements: two **If** statements and one **Select** statement. The **Select** statement has two conditions to it, adding a minimum of two test cases to execute to go through all of the paths for it. In addition, there is a single loop, which executes within the subroutine.

Let's look, for example, at the first conditional statement in the subroutine. This is the line that reads:

```
If X < 1 Or X > 10 Then
```

Above this line, note that X is an integer value passed into the routine. Because we do not calculate it, we can test this statement by simply passing in values of X for the subroutine from a harness routine. In order to minimally test this statement, how many values of X would you imagine you would need? The answer turns out to be an absolute minimum of five. We have the upper bound (10), the lower bound (1), a middle value (say, 5), and values to either extreme (0 and 11 in this case). If you want to be complete, you would also note that high and low values for the data type (–32,767 and 32,768) should be passed as well to be sure that we are not seeing some sort of coercion problem. That is seven test cases for this statement alone!

Likewise, consider the **Select** statement in the code example. Statements such as this have one test case for each option within the select statement plus one additional test case if there is no default case. In this example, there are only two possible select options, as the second one already takes into account all default values.

This brings us to the final conditional **If** statement in the code, which is based on a Boolean value set elsewhere in the function. To adequately test this condition, we need to worry about how that value is set. Looking at the code, we can see that the condition that sets the Boolean value is also the one that is dealt with in one of the select options.

If you follow the procedure outlined in this section for designing your unit test cases for each module, you will ensure that you have a good flow test set for that module. Path coverage, or flow testing, is an important consideration when you think about the fact that many bugs in code are not found until a new branch of that code is executed.

Transactional Testing

A transaction is a series of events that must either all succeed or not happen at all. In a transaction, the important thing is that when an event fails, the system be restored to its state prior to the execution of the transaction. In addition, a transaction is considered to be an atomic event. That is, no matter how many transactions are occurring in a system at the same time, the ones that affect given entities will all finish before another transaction is given access to those entities.

Testing transactions is one of the most difficult parts of system testing. If there are three ways that each event in a transaction can fail, and there are five events in the transaction, you will find that the number of test cases becomes extraordinarily high in no time at all. Not only must you test each possible failure method, but you must also test it against each possible success of the other events. This leads to a geometric progression of possible test cases. It is no wonder, therefore, that transactional testing is the one area most likely to end up with missing test cases and therefore bugs in the final system.

To best examine a transactional test suite, let's take a look at the pseudocode for a simple bank transaction. In this case, person A writes a check to person B, and the check is cashed.

```
Person A writes Check
Person B presents check to bank
Check is debited from the account of Person A
Check is credited to the account of Person B
Person B receives confirmation of the deposit
Person A receives confirmation of the check clearing
```

It is reasonable to assume that writing the check and presenting it to the bank are events that can have no bugs associated with them. In fact, any process can have a bug in it as we have discussed previously, but we will not worry about them in this example.

Let's just consider what can go wrong from the point at which the check is deposited for payment at the bank of Person A. First, the check could be deposited to the account of Person B, but not debited from the account of Person A. Second, the check could be debited from the account of Person A, but not credited to the account of Person B. Any or all of the confirmations could fail to go through. In any of these cases, the only solution is to abort the transaction and revert the state to the way it was before the check was written. Failure to do this will result in an accounting nightmare.

How can we test this process to see where the transactional problems might be? The obvious cases would be to have the debit fail or the credit fail. The test case might involve locking the account so that posting to or from it will not work; however, the credit or debit to the other account would. When the transaction fails, the test would be to see if the final result was the same as the starting values.

What if the confirmation stages were to fail? Would the system revert to the previous balances in both accounts A and B? Would the proper accounting posts be found in the logs of each account? These are important considerations when dealing with transactional systems. The system must either completely succeed, or it must act as though nothing ever happened in the first place. If the transaction fails, of course, it is expected that there be a log of the error and an audit of the money or other information moving back and forth in the accounts. Failure to do this would result in a system that did not balance or could not be audited.

Input Verification

If programs received no input, the number of bugs in systems would not only be vastly reduced, they would be much easier to find and fix. Because there is an infinite number of different inputs and there is no real way to predict what a user might enter, input is the single largest source of problems in program execution. Verifying input consists of two phases. First, input that is correct should produce the correct output or process. This is simple verification testing and should be a part of every developer's unit test for the application or module. Second, input that is not valid must not cause problems. Bad input should be detected and reported as soon as possible.

Input comes from a variety of sources. Input can be entered directly from the user, in the form of command-line arguments, program entries, or file selections. Input can come indirectly into the application from containers, such as files or other programs. In addition, input can come from mechanical devices, such as scanners, hardware attachments, or other peripherals attached to the system. In order to understand how to adequately test the input for your application or module, you need to understand the input coming into that system.

Let's look at a very simple module to understand the kinds of input that can occur:

```c
int main( int argc, char **argv)
{
    if ( argc < 2 )
    {
        printf("Usage: filter <filename>\n");
        exit(1);
    }
    FILE *fp = fopen(argv[1], "r");
    while ( !feof(fp) )
    {
        if ( !fgets(szBuffer, kBufferSize, fp) )
            break;
        FilterLine( szBuffer );
        printf("Filtered line: <%s>\n", szBuffer );
    }
```

```
        fclose(fp);
        printf("Completed. Hit any key to continue");
        getch();
        return (0);
}
```

If you happen to understand the C language, you will find not one, not two, but three different inputs to this module. Each needs to be verified to ensure that it works properly. First, there are the command-line arguments to the program. These come in the form of the **argc** and **argv** inputs to the main function. The **argc** variable is the count of arguments that come into the function (starting at 1, the 0th element is the program name in C), whereas the **argv** array contains the actual elements as strings. Because we are obviously using the array and assuming that it contains data, the program verifies this by checking to see if the count is high enough to contain a file name to process.

Once the file name is read in from the command-line arguments, the name is then used to open a file of that name. The file is then read in, line by line, and the input from that file processed. Finally, the file is closed, and the user is prompted to press any key to continue and exit the program. This is probably done to avoid having the file just disappear if it is run as part of a batch file.

At this point, we have examined the application from the perspective of a developer. Now, let's switch hats and take a look at the input possibilities from the perspective of a tester.

The first, most obvious test would be to pass the program no arguments. In this case, the **argc** value would be 1 (the program name), and the **argv** array would not contain any valid file names to process. This condition is caught by the first conditional statement in the application, and the program exits after printing a diagnostic error message. So far, so good. The second test would be to pass more than one file name to the application. As it is written, the application would ignore any additional file names passed in. This might be a bug, or it might be fine, depending on the requirements of the application. As a tester, you might feel inclined to write up a bug stating that the program should either print out that it only processes a single file or it should process all the files in the list.

Once the file name is processed, the next step is to open the file. What happens if you pass in an invalid file name? As written, the program would crash. Obviously, this has to be considered a bug. As a result, we discover the first tip in input processing—all file names need to be checked for validity and access. Why access? If you simply check to see if a file exists, and you want to read or write from it but do not have permission, the program will encounter problems. Make sure you can open the file for the mode you need to use that file in.

Tip

Check all files you are opening for validity and access.

Because there are different kinds of files, there can also be problems in processing a file. There are text files, binary files, and mixtures of the two. In order to adequately test our system, we would need to try all of the kinds of files we might be given during a real run of the system. On some systems, these files might be raw database files, text files, and binary files. Remember to try all of the possibilities, not simply the ones that the developer thought about when he or she was designing the application.

So far, we have discussed three different sections of the code. At least one of the sections (open failure) would result in the program crashing. Another section (processing) might cause serious problems if the wrong kind of file is used. There are only two sections left, closing the file and getting the user to press a key to continue. Let's examine these last two possibilities.

Closing the file can only lead to problems if the file is not open in the first place. Because we have already dealt with that problem, we can simply attach that issue to the first bug report to the developer and not worry about closing the file problems. Pressing a key to continue could also be a problem. Does any key really work? There are a lot of possible keystrokes on the keyboard. In addition to the standard alphanumeric keys, there are also the shifted versions of the keys, the function keys, and the Ctrl and Alt keys, as well as all of the permutations they bring. In this case, however, it really isn't that big of a problem. The most likely test cases are to check whether the enter key (return on some keyboards) and any letter key work. If not, the "bug" is that the output line from the program should be changed to specify which key the user should press. We aren't checking for the key press or what is valid, so any further tests are unnecessary in this case.

The other kind of input that many programs receive is from graphical forms, which collect entries from the user. In cases like this, the best thing that you can do is restrict entries from the programming side to only the valid data you know to work. As a tester, you should try things you know will not work, such as entering letters for numeric fields or invalid dates (such as 02/30/2000). A complete listing of all possible bad data for a given input type is nearly infinite, so you are best suited by testing the gross combinations of letters where numbers are indicated, and vice versa. In addition, you should try pressing the various modifier keys such as Shift, Alt, and Ctrl. Function keys are good choices also, as they often expose functionality you did not intend a user to find.

As you can see, input programs can cause a lot of issues in software development. By working with testing people to determine what valid input might be, you as the developer can screen out all input that is not valid. Although not always the best possible way to code applications, this method will lead to bulletproof data entry screens, which is really what the user wants in the first place.

Algorithmic Testing

Nearly every program implements an algorithm in some way. Some algorithms are very simple—collect some data and plug it into an equation. Other algorithms are very complex, such as decoding video streams. In all cases, however, the algorithm that is implemented has a process to complete. If that process is identified in the documentation for the system, as it should be, testing the algorithm should be considered a major part of testing the system. You aren't testing the actual underlying algorithm, of course, you are testing the implementation of that algorithm in the code.

Sometimes, as a tester, you will find that examining the algorithm selected for the implementation of the system leads you to specific test cases. For example, if the algorithm was one that implemented a binary search, you would be sure to test the cases where there were no items to search. If the algorithm was a sort of some kind, you would be sure to test the case where all the items were the same.

In order to understand algorithmic testing, let's take a look at a simple algorithm, and then look at the code implementation of that algorithm. We will design test cases based not on the code but on the algorithm itself.

The algorithm we are going to select is a simple one, but one that is most often used in computer science classes. This algorithm is the factorial calculation. The factorial is defined as the sum of all of the numbers leading up to a given number, multiplied by each other. In other words, the factorial of a number is:

```
1 * 2 * 3 * … * (n-1) * (n)
```

for any given value of n.

As a simple example, the factorial of 4 is: 1*2*3*4 or 24.

One of the reasons we selected factorials is that they are one of the best examples of recursion in computer science. To implement a factorial, you use the following algorithm:

```
If Number = 1
    Return 1
Else
    Return Number * Factorial(Number-1)
```

Because this algorithm is recursive (that is, it calls itself), it will simply go backward through the numbers until it finds the starting point (1), and then multiply each number by the sum of itself until it reaches the start again.

```
Function Factorial ( Number : Real ) : Real
Begin
If Number <> 1 Then
    Return Number * Factorial ( Number-1 );
Else
    Return 1;
End;
```

Note

Both of these algorithms are presented in pseudo-code form only. This is not intended to be valid Pascal.

As a developer, you can look at this code and think that it implements the algorithm perfectly. After all, there are only two decision points in the whole code. First, we determine whether the number is 1 or not. Second, we multiply that number by the factorial of the next number less than this one. What could possibly go wrong?

As a tester, we recognize that there are a lot of problems with this code and algorithm. For example, there is no error checking. What happens if the number is negative? In this case, let's examine the algorithm. For a negative 4 (–4), for example, we would do the following:

$$-4 * -5 * -6 * -7 * \ldots$$

As you can see, the number will never approach 1 because it is going in the wrong direction! Obviously, this test case would fail, probably with a stack overflow. A zero value has the same problem. But what happens with really large numbers? For example, you might try a number like 10,000. You will find that the program crashes on most machines because each recursion forces the stack to push itself down one more level. As a result, sooner or later, you run out of stack space, and the program crashes.

As you can see, we don't have to look at the code for any of these test cases. Instead, we look at the algorithm itself for the underlying code. The algorithm, even if implemented absolutely faithfully in the code, contains all problems inherent in the equation itself. By understanding the algorithm implemented, we can understand how the code should work. This allows us to write test cases and expected results, and even allows us to predict program failures without seeing the code.

Decision Tables

A decision table is a simple cross-reference of rules and decisions, as shown in Table 13.1.

As you can see, the decision table is a matrix. When certain binary conditions are true or false, certain actions either will or will not be taken. The nice thing about decision tables is

Table 13.1 An example of a decision table.

	Rule 1	Rule 2	Rule 3	Rule 4
Decision 1	True	True	False	False
Decision 2	False	False	True	True
Decision 3	True	False	True	False
Decision 4	False	True	False	True
Action 1	Yes	Yes	No	No
Action 2	No	No	Yes	Yes

that they lead almost directly to both program code and test cases. Because you can write the code as a series of conditional statements, you can automatically generate the code from a decision table if you want to. Likewise, because test cases will have a binary true or false outcome, you could create complete test suites from the simple matrix shown in the preceding table.

Let's look at another simple example of a decision table, Table 13.2, and see how it translates into both program code and test cases. Imagine that you are programming a robot car. The car has to stop at red lights, go at green lights, and slow down at yellow lights. In addition, it needs to signal when turning right or left. We have a few conditions that lead to decisions, and a few rules that can be enforced.

As you can see, we can almost write the code directly from the preceding matrix. For example, the first column (stop at red light) would code itself as:

```
If ( LightIsRed() )
    StopCar();
```

Similarly, the test case for this condition would be: If the light is red, does the car stop? The expected result is that the car will stop.

State Machine Analysis

A state machine is one in which the machine moves from a specified state to another specified state given certain conditions in the machine. In most systems, either the entire system or individual features can be mapped easily to a state-based machine. As a simple example, consider the login prompt of a well-known national Internet Service Provider (ISP). It displays a dialog screen that shows you that it is dialing, then negotiating with the network, and then finally logging into the system. Each of these segments of the login process is a state. Within the application, each state can only move in one of two directions. If the requirements for success are met for the state, it moves to the next state in the process.

Table 13.2   Decision table for a robot car.

	Stop at red light	Go at green light	Slow for yellow light	Signal for turn
Questions				
Is light red?	True	False	False	False
Is light green?	False	True	False	False
Is light yellow?	False	False	True	False
Is car about to turn?	False	False	False	True
Actions				
Stop car	True	False	False	False
Make car go	False	True	True	True
Slow car	False	False	True	False
Turn car	False	False	False	True

If the failure conditions for the state are met, it either moves to the previous state or to some well-known error state.

How does understanding the states of the machine help us in testing and debugging? Much like logic tables, machine states can translate directly into test cases and, in some cases, program code. If you know the preconditions to enter a state and the postconditions to leave a state, you should know whether or not the program is behaving properly by simply setting some or all of these conditions and seeing whether the program properly transitions into the state it should be in given those conditions.

Let's look at an example of state transition to give you a better idea of how to test state transition information. Consider the case of a satellite television system. As a user, you change the channel by entering a new number via the remote. If the channel is authorized and valid, the television set magically tunes to that channel, and you watch it. Behind the scenes, however, there is a considerably more complex set of logic being processed.

1. State 1: Watching the initial channel. If something is waiting in input queue, go to state 2.

2. State 2: Is there input from the user? If so, go to state 3; otherwise return to current state 1.

3. State 3: Did the user request a channel change? If not, go to state 4; otherwise go to state 7.

4. State 4: Did the user request a volume increase? If so, go to state 5; otherwise go back to state 1.

5. State 5: Is the channel the user requested a valid channel number? If yes, go to state 6; otherwise return to state 1.

6. State 6: Is the channel the user requested authorized? If yes, go to state 7; otherwise return to state 1.

7. State 7: Attempt to tune to user-requested channel. If unable to comply, display error screen, return to initial channel, and go back to state 1.

8. State 8: Tuned to new channel. Return to state 1.

Each state has a reason for transitioning to another state. In this case, we really have seven discrete states and seven reasons to move from that state to another state. Furthermore, by reading the state transition list, we can come up with simple tests to verify that the system is working properly. For example, we can enter both valid and invalid channel numbers. We can enter both authorized and unauthorized channel numbers. We can press the volume control in the middle of entering a channel number to see what happens.

State machine analysis is a powerful technique for understanding how a program moves from one mode to another. It is particularly useful for programs that have specifically different states, such as different screens or different input modes. If your system has a series of screens that permit the user to accomplish a task, that set of screens is really a state machine. By understanding what information is required to move from screen to screen, you can easily design a test suite that either satisfies or fails to satisfy those conditions to verify that the code does what it is supposed to. More importantly, you can design test suites that verify that the code does not do what it is not supposed to. The idea of preventing errors is, after all, the basis for testing.

Integration Testing

As a developer, you usually think that your job ends when you have written a module, debugged it, unit tested it, documented it, and released it to configuration management. This idea could not be further from the truth. Integration testing starts when the unit testing for modules has been completed. As its name suggests, integration testing is the testing of the interfaces between modules and the gaps that might occur due to miscommunication or poor error testing.

How does integration testing work? Well, let's assume that you have two modules, A and B. These modules implement two pieces of functionality. Let's say that module A gets input from the user filling in a form. Module B is responsible for saving that input to a persistent storage device, such as a database. The programmers responsible for the two modules have tested each extensively. Module A gathers data properly, does not allow bad data, and makes sure that all fields are entered. Module B accepts an input object that contains data, and then writes it to the database. Module B has been tested to ensure that it properly writes the correct fields to the correct database columns, that no errors occur in the database write that are not captured and checked, and that all possible error returns are converted back into the accepted norms for that module.

It appears from the description that the two modules are done, correct? As soon as the modules are checked into the configuration management system and the build completed, we can think of this set of modules as complete, right? Of course not. The number of problems that might occur in the combination of the two modules is staggering. Suppose, for example, that module B made certain assumptions about the format of dates passed to it by module A. What if module A assumed that module B didn't return an error code, but instead threw an exception? All of these possibilities exist for problems in the interface between the two modules.

Rather than show you a code example, it's easier to explain integration testing by looking at a real-world example. One of the most classic examples of an integration problem occurred in the Mars Climate Orbiter crash in 1999.

The Mars Climate Orbiter left earth on December 11, 1998, and reached the Mars atmosphere (such as it is) nine months later. Unfortunately, it crashed on the Mars surface and was not heard from again. A postmortem analysis (discussed in Chapter 2) revealed the reason, which was not a software "glitch," but a simple misunderstanding between two pieces of the system. It seems that the interfaces between the probe software and the mission control software were perfectly in sync except for one little detail. The controller software was using English units to send measurements, such as speed and distance, whereas the probe software assumed it was receiving them in metric units. The interface problem caused the spacecraft to be too low and too fast when it approached the surface, which caused the final crash, according to NASA reports.

Would this be a bug? Most people would probably agree that a spacecraft crashing is a serious problem. Because the crash was caused by software, you might question why the unit tests of the software didn't indicate this possibility. The answer is simple. No unit test on earth could have detected this problem. The reason is that the problem wasn't in a specific module to be unit tested, but instead existed in the interface between two modules. Had proper integration testing been done, complete with unit printouts from both sides, this problem could have been detected and fixed, saving hundreds of millions of dollars. Needless to say, such interface testing was added as a result of the postmortem evaluation of the project.

Top-Down versus Bottom-Up Testing

Although it is not really a technique of testing, the question of top-down versus bottom-up testing often comes up during both the development and debugging/testing phases of the software life cycle. Bottom-up testing is simply the idea that you start with the lowest level modules in the system and test your way up until you are satisfied that each level works properly. Top-down testing, on the other hand, puts forth the idea that you can start from the highest level of the system and, through adequate test cases, work your way all the way down through to the lowest level of the system. Both have their advantages and disadvantages.

In bottom-up testing, you start by testing the foundation of the system and work your way up to the pieces that use that foundation. In this respect, you will find more bugs simply because you are testing the pieces that are doing all of the work first. That's the theory, anyway. The problem with bottom-up testing is that it does not approach the testing process from the viewpoint of the user. Thus, although you are likely to find more low-level problems using a bottom-up approach, you will miss some of the more glaring errors from the user's perspective. This is due to a finite amount of testing time. Starting from the bottom means less time at the top.

In top-down testing, you are more likely to find problems that the user is likely to encounter because you are working from the user's perspective. Top-down test cases are usually written directly from the specification and user guide, so they are easier for us to understand and predict outcomes. The problem with top-down testing is that it will not uncover the most insidious bugs in the system, which are the lowest level ones. These bugs are usually the ones that end up causing the maximum amount of grief over the lifetime of the product for the end user.

Ideally, of course, you would simply mix and match the two testing techniques in order to ensure maximum coverage of the product and make sure that the majority of problems most likely to be encountered by the user are found. Unfortunately, reality usually gets in the way of such solutions. There is a set amount of time that you can work on testing. That time shrinks as new features are added to the system and as bugs are uncovered. Because a change to the code to fix an existing bug causes the testing process to essentially restart, every bug you find reduces the number of new bugs you can test for, since it will require time to fix the bug found. For this reason, the best approach is not really a 50-50 split, but instead a more weighted approach.

The best recommendation for testing a system is to use an up-front, bottom-up testing system. Because unit test suites should be written for each module of the application, you can use the test harnesses to test the lower-level parts of the system before the entire User Interface (UI) is ever in place. This allows you to actually start testing the system long before it is "ready for testing." In addition, it gives testers a better understanding of the implementation and limits of the system.

Once the user interface layer of the system is complete enough to begin demonstrating what it is supposed to be doing, top-down testing can begin. Although the two testing techniques will never "meet in the middle," you will be assured that a reasonable amount of testing was done at both ends of the spectrum. This approach will catch the majority of large-scale problems the user is most likely to encounter. In the notion of "good enough software" proposed by Ed Yourdan, if we annoy the user only a small fraction of the time while keeping them happy the majority of the time, we will have a successful product.

Remember, testing will never find all of the bugs. It is both mathematically and physically impossible to do so. Instead, we try to find the bugs that are most likely to interfere with the user experience and fix them before they become full-blown bugs in the released product.

Configuration Testing

Differing configurations are the bane of both the developer and the tester. Different operating systems, different versions of DLLs, and different programs running make the job of configuring your system to look just like the user's impossible. The job of testing configurations most often falls on the tester during the development phase. For this reason, keeping track of the configuration you are using becomes paramount when you are trying to report bugs.

A few years ago, I worked for a company that developed software for the CD-ROM industry. The software itself ran on MS-DOS, Windows 3.1, Windows 95, and some variants of PC-Unix. When a bug was reported to us in development, it was often unclear as to which version of the operating system the program was being run on. This led to confusion and bad feelings as the developers would often report back that a bug was not reproducible, when in fact they were testing it on the wrong operating system.

Eventually, we created a simple form for bug reporting. It would later grow as we identified new and unique differences that might affect our application while it was running. For example, in the MS-DOS world, printers were a serious concern because there was no standard way to "talk" to a printer in the MS-DOS environment. Different printer drivers offered different capabilities and different problems.

When you are testing a system, you should first document the configuration under which it is running. This includes the operating system, the computer type (manufacturer and type, such as laptop or desktop), the versions of the system DLLs you are using, and any other applications that might be running at the time you are using the program. All of this information is critical to the debugger who is trying to figure out why things don't work on your system when they run fine on his. In addition, you should note what drives and directories the system is installed in and what other applications were installed besides the application program itself. Examples of other installation issues might include specific versions of DLLs, configuration files for the application, changes to registry or INI files, or privileges used by the account in a Unix environment.

You might think that obtaining this information and recording it would be almost impossible to do because it is difficult to know exactly what was changed when the system was installed. This is really untrue, however. The application, via its installation program or by itself, will know what it needs to run. This should be documented as part of the basic system documentation. In addition, system information can usually be retrieved by an automated process. In Unix, for example, you can check the time and date stamp of the system files used via a *where* command. In the Microsoft Windows world, you can find this out via the msconfig program that ships standard with the operating system. Your installation log should contain the information needed to re-create what was changed. In addition, as mentioned in Chapter 9, you should build into your application the ability to display the locations and versions of the various system files it uses.

One last issue concerning configuration testing is that of program settings. Unlike system settings, program settings are optional configuration information that is specific to the program itself. Like the system setting dump, your application should be capable of showing you all of the settings that are operable at any given time. A copy of this information should be appended to all bug reports, as this information might make it easier for the programmer to detect whether or not the system is malfunctioning or whether it is simply doing what you asked it to do in the settings arena.

Let's look at a simple example of a settings problem in the next section. In this case, we will be using an initialization file to store the information for our program.

Crash Recovery and Power Failure Testing

What usually happens to you when your power goes out? The VCR starts blinking 12:00. The alarm clock loses the time and resets the wake up time. Your lights go off and then come back on. But what happens to your program when the power goes out? If your program allows the user to create data, does that data get lost when the system shuts down unexpectedly? Are program settings saved if they have been changed while the system was running? These are questions that you need to know before you start testing an application.

Before you can test a crash recovery system, you need to know what it is designed to do. For example, if the system simply acknowledges that the data in memory will be lost when the power goes out, then testing the system becomes easy. Pull the plug and see what the application does. Unfortunately, very few systems keep the entire block of data they are working on in memory. Some keep the data cached on disk and may even maintain current state information on that disk. It is applications like this that need to be tested most extensively for power failure and crash recovery.

The other extreme is a program that is designed to survive and restart in the case of a power failure. Examples of this sort of application are embedded system software, operating system software, and monitoring software. In each case, you must know the various states of the application and how to test for a power failure. Let's take a look at the pseudocode for one such application and see what test cases we can envision to verify that it would work properly in the case of a power failure.

```
Startup: Check for power failure.
If failure detected (no shut down), reload
current state,
Initialization: Clear memory, load machine list
into memory from disk.
Monitor Phase: For each machine in machine list,
check current status. Write status to status
registers for that machine. Save state.
Error Phase: If a machine reports an error, print
out status message to console. Update current
machine state. Save state.
Save State: Write all machine registers to disk.
Add Machine: Add a new machine to the memory list.
Delete Machine: Remove a machine from the memory list
if it exists.
Shut Down: Save state.
```

For crash recovery and power failure testing, it is imperative that you understand the states the machine can be in. Each state will define a specific slice of the information that is stored for the application. You must know what information the application is maintaining and where that information is maintained, whether on disk or in memory. For our example, you can see the following test cases immediately.

♦ Create power failure condition immediately upon starting the system.

♦ Create power failure condition immediately after initialization.

- Create power failure condition at start of monitoring phase.

- Create power failure condition in middle of monitoring phase.

- Create power failure condition immediately following monitoring phase.

- Create power failure condition immediately before error condition is reported.

- Create power failure condition immediately after error condition is reported.

There are many more test cases, but this list should give you a good head start. In each test case, we create a power failure condition, and then restart the system. What do we look for when the system is restarted?

1. The system comes up properly.

2. The system is orderly and not in an unknown state.

3. Data is transactionally secure; that is, either all of the data for a given process is available or none of it is. There are no cases where the data is "somewhat" there.

4. Additions, deletions, and modifications are saved and restored when the system is restarted.

As you can see from our pseudocode, the system in question is likely to fail condition number four. When an addition or deletion is made, the data is not immediately written to disk. This is probably not a huge problem, as it still maintains condition three, transactional security; however, it might be a bug.

Tip
Always test your system for power failure to ensure that it starts properly.

Power failures are simply a way of life in the computer world. Even with Universal Power Supply (UPS) systems and battery backed up memory, you are going to see the computer crash unexpectedly from time to time. If your system is not tested with this in mind, you are likely to get some very hard-to-reproduce problems later on from real users.

Security Testing

Security testing ensures that the right people can get into the system when they need to, and the wrong people can't get into the system because they aren't allowed to. Although security might involve login names and passwords, it can also be achieved by using machine names, IP addresses, machine "dongles," and other features. The mechanism of security is important to the developer implementing the security features for the system. What, then, is important to the tester verifying that the security features work?

Testing security is one of the most important, and most overlooked, aspects of system testing. Security is often of paramount importance to the users of the system, yet the developers and designers generally give it short shrift. Although a system might have a "secure" login and password facility, what good is it if that information is stored in plain text on the hard drive? Is a program "lock" secure if you can reboot the system and get past it? All of these questions must be answered by security testing.

There are two forms of security testing. First, the tester tries to break into a "secure" system by either circumventing the security system or by using an automated tool to attempt to generate random names and passwords to login to the system. The second is in using backdoors or program errors (such as buffer overflows) to gain access to the system. Security flaws can be identified as successes in gaining access or in error messages that reveal too much information about the system. For example, consider the following transcript of a login attempt to a system:

```
System: Enter user name:
Tester: fred
System: User name "fred" not found in database. Oracle error 0x87654
```

What problems can we see from a security testing standpoint in this exchange? Let's ignore the grammatical problems in the sentence and focus in on the security issues. Why is the application telling us that "fred" is not a valid user name? By doing this, you eliminate about a zillion possibilities for hackers trying to get into the system. Rather than trying to guess the user name and the password, you've given them an easy way to determine that the user name is invalid, so they can simply skip over that user name and move on to the next logical one. If you asked for both the user name and password before indicating an error, and not have that error tell them which piece of information is incorrect, you would decrease the chance of someone hacking into the system by several orders of magnitude.

Okay, so the user name part is not right. What else is wrong? The next logical problem is that it tells me what the Oracle error is. This is bad for two reasons. First, by knowing what database you are using, you give hackers a better chance at finding a backdoor into that database system. Most database systems come with a default login and password for the system administrator. You would be surprised by the number of places that never remove that default. Because we can pass that information into the login prompt, we might very well have given hackers a cheap way into the system. The second reason is a bit less intuitive. By showing the user the particular error message you are using, you run the risk of exposing more information about the system than you might have wanted to. For example, if the error message displayed (which was made up) happened to be that the database was down, you might be giving hackers enough information to bypass your security system altogether and go to a page that didn't handle that error properly. At that point, hackers could gain complete entrance into your system.

Before finishing the topic of security testing, it is worth stressing that the largest number of security problems are caused by either overloading a system or by sending a buffer too big for the processor in the system to handle. You should experiment with any client/server application to see if these problems apply to your system. There are many standard testing tools available for sending inappropriate or invalid messages to a system to see if they are handled properly.

Third-Party Testing

Imagine trying to test a system that was completely undocumented and had no specifications for how it worked. In general, this situation describes trying to test systems that work with independent third-party tools. Not only are you looking for all of the bugs in your own system, but you are also looking for all of the bugs in someone else's system. It is like debugging an operating system without a user's guide. Testing third-party tools is by far the hardest job for any tester.

There are really two basic approaches to testing third-party tools. The first is to create a specific test suite for that tool, and test it outside the context of the system you are really creating and testing. In this case, you are verifying that the tool works the way you expect it to, and that it doesn't have any weird surprises waiting for you. The second method for testing is to simply treat the tool as an integral part of the system, and write the test cases so that they best exercise the way the tool is used within your system. In this case, for example, you would worry about how the tool is called by your own code, not how it handles issues in general. In the first case, we are treating the third-party tool as an independent process within the system. In the second case, we are treating the tool as just another subsystem within the main system.

It is difficult to provide decent advice about how to test third-party tools used in your application except to say that you need to do it. If you do not, developers will consistently blame the tool, whether or not the tool is the actual problem. Worse, management will eventually come to distrust the tool (because it is blamed for everything) and will replace one component with another without addressing the real problem.

It is worth mentioning that when debugging, if you suspect the problem exists in a third-party tool, you should write a simple test case that illustrates the issue. If the problem doesn't happen in the test case, you must assume that the problem is really in your own code after all. Third-party tools are no less susceptible to bugs than your own code, but you have to focus on the parts that can be fixed easily. If the problem is in your code, you can fix it. If it is in the third-party tool, the best you can hope for is a workaround until the next version of the tool is released. While some systems ship with software, allowing you to "fix" the problem in the third-party tool, this is to be discouraged. If you fix a problem in the tool, the fix may or may not ship in the next release of the tool. If the next version does not contain the fix, you will find yourself back in the same position all over again.

Multiuser Testing

If you are working on a system that supports multiple users at the same time, it is imperative that you test the system with multiple users at the same time. Although this might seem like an overly obvious observation, you would be surprised at how many systems are tested by a single person doing one task at a time.

When you consider multiuser testing, there are several important tests that need to be run. First, you need to consider the case of both users doing exactly the same thing at exactly the same time. Second, you need to consider the case of both users doing exactly opposite things at the same time. Third, you have the case of two users doing the same thing, but a few steps apart. You can, and should, try all of these situations with more than two users, of course. In fact, you should test the system with the expected load of users that might occur. When we talk about performance testing, you will see that in actuality, it's a good idea to test the system with more than the expected maximum load of users.

Certain classes of problems are more likely to occur in multiuser environments than in single or batch mode systems. Problems such as reentrancy issues, database locking issues, and resource sharing issues are vastly more likely in a multiuser environment. Test cases, therefore, should be structured to account for not only the "normal" set of problems in any system, but also the specific multiuser problems that might occur. Let's look at a simple example.

Imagine that you have a simple accounting system running on your corporate intranet. The accounting system uses a database to keep the accounts and a set of configuration files to keep track of what accounts you are entitled to view. Login and password information is also kept in the database. The accounting system has screens to input debits and credits for various accounts, and it allows multiple users access to the same account at the same time. Changes to the account are supposed to be propagated to every user that is using that account when they occur.

What kinds of tests can we come up with that test our various sets of requirements for multiuser systems? Let's list a few.

♦ User 1 posts a payment to Account 1. User 2 posts a payment to Account 1. The expected result is for the account to contain both payments.

♦ User 1 posts a payment to Account 1. User 2 posts a check written from Account 1. The expected result is for the account to contain the net of the payment less the check plus the initial balance.

♦ User 1 posts a payment to Account 1. User 1 posts a check written from Account 1. User 1 posts another payment to Account 1. User 2 posts a payment to Account 1. User 2 posts a check written to Account 1. User 2 posts another payment to Account 1. The expected result is the initial balance plus all payments minus all checks written.

♦ User 1 posts a payment to Account 1. User 2 posts a payment to Account 1. User 1 posts a check written from Account 1. In this case, the expected result is the two payments less the check plus the initial balance.

What we are looking at in these cases is transaction integrity. Because multiple people can post to the same account at the same time, we want to be sure that the accounts maintain the transactions properly. This isn't nearly enough, however. We also need to test for reentrancy problems. How do we do that? The easiest way is to have two people set up payments to a single account, and then press return at the same time to post the payments. If that works, you should try using three people, and then four people. How many is enough? You should try using as many people as you expect to have working on the system simultaneously. Of course, there is no real reason that the "users" need be people. If the tests to run are understood in advance, scripting systems can be used to automate the process.

Load and Performance Testing

When your manager tells you to test a production system, he or she usually means load and performance testing. These testing methods, although extremely useful in determining the future success of a system, are not the best methods available to verify that a system is working properly. Load testing simply determines how many people or processes the system can handle before it finally crashes. Performance testing shows how system performance degrades over time and usage.

When you are trying to load test a system, you need to identify the limiting factors for the system. For example, if you are trying to load test a single user application that sorts data, the limiting factors are probably the amount of memory available, the amount of disk space available, and the amount of data to sort. On the other hand, if you are load testing an Internet Web site application, the limiting factor is almost certainly the number of concurrent connections to the site. Without knowing what factors limit the system's ability to perform, you cannot do adequate load testing.

The basic approach to load testing is to start out with a reasonable number of whatever the limiting factor is, and then double it until the system dies. Then, decrease the limiting factor number until the system works again. The result is the top end of the system for that factor. Repeat this technique with each factor until you know all of the possible factor limits. Unfortunately, you aren't done at this point, you just know what the individual problems are. The next step is to start combining factors and see if the limits change. For limits that change, you can conclude that the two factors are related. All related factors can be treated as their own sets. Continue this approach until you have identified all single and related factors. Note that factors will be affected by things like disk space, memory size, and CPU speed. Once you have the entire spectrum mapped out, your next step is to start increasing system parameters (memory, disk space, etc.) and determine what the effect on the limiting factors might be. If there is no effect, there is no point in increasing that parameter.

The result of a load test should be a set of data that contains the following information: the minimal system configuration that can run the expected number of users and the maximal system that has any effect on the system performance. For example, if raising the memory size to 256MB speeds up the system, but raising it to 257MB does not, then there is no point increasing memory beyond 256MB. That is the maximal memory size for the system. You also need to find the optimal size for the system. This is the most acceptable speed and performance of the system with the most reasonable set of hardware and software configurations. You should determine what the maximum limit of the system is in terms of limiting factors as well. If you are working on an Internet Web system and the back-end database can only handle a maximum of 100 concurrent users, nothing you can do will increase that limit. The total number of concurrent users possible on the system will be 100 unless you add a second database system.

Performance testing is a bit different than load testing. With performance testing, you start with a fixed configuration for the system, and then do measurements to see how well the system is performing. The actual metrics you gather will vary from system to system, as it depends on what is important in your application. In general, however, you will concern yourself with the time to perform various actions, the memory used by the application during those actions, and the amount of storage space needed to perform the actions and possibly keep the results.

Let's look at a simple example of performance testing for a standalone application. In this case, we will consider a program that implements a word processor. What sorts of things would you consider to be "performance" measures for such a system? Obviously, the speed with which the system responds to keystrokes is important. If the word processor performs background spell checking, the time that this function takes away from the regular processing of the system matters. In addition, the amount of memory consumed by the application while it is running is important. Also, the size of the file containing the document being processed is important, as users do not appreciate their hard drives being consumed by overly large files.

Performance testing is something that is done in most projects at the end of the development cycle. This is unfortunate, as there is little that can be done by that point if the testing detects a problem in the software. It makes considerably more sense to do performance testing along with unit testing as the development proceeds. Likewise, load testing can easily be done for each of the modules in a system to determine what their limiting factors might be. Once you know what the lowest common denominator across the system is for a set of modules, you know what to change in order to increase the speed or number of concurrent users for that system.

Tip

Do performance and load testing during development, not at the end of the project.

As a final note, you should not consider performance or load testing to be any sort of substitute for testing and verification of the system. Performance testing is done to plan for changes to the system and make enhancements to critical areas. It does not in any way masquerade as any sort of functional testing for the system. Load testing is done to identify limits on the system functionality. Although load testing can produce true bugs when working from requirements that contain performance criteria, it is also not a substitute for "real" testing.

Measurement and Statistics

When we talk about bugs, testing, or other measurements of the quality of software, the question of using metrics and statistics is always likely to rear its ugly head. Metrics are simply the numbers that we acquire while testing the software. You can measure the number of bugs found in the software, the number of modules in the software, or even the number of lines within each module. You can measure the complexity of each module, the number of parameters to each function or method, and the number of lines of comments found in the source code. Not all of these numbers directly affect the bug rate of the software, but many hold interesting corollaries for the increase or decrease in the bug rate.

It has been a basic tenet of this book that the number of bugs in software has a direct correlation to the complexity of the software. Metrics and statistics are the best way possible to prove this conviction. The following list contains just a few of the metrics you should consider keeping track of in your own application development process.

- *Bugs*—Track the time and date found, the module in which the bug occurred, the name of the person who found the bug, the person responsible for fixing the bug, when it was fixed, and who fixed it

- *Modules*—Complexity, number of lines, when they were created, and who created them

- *Screens*—Number of bugs found on a screen, number of objects on the screen, and number of code modules written to support screens

- *Databases*—Number of columns, number of rows, rows added per day, and number of data defects found

- *Performance*—Number of users, average time to process each request, and number of requests

Obviously, this is a very short list of possible metrics to track in your own application. However, remember that metrics are only useful if you use them. If you track everything under the sun, but never use the information, you will find that those tracking the metrics for you quickly become discouraged and do a poor job of providing you with useful information.

Summary

In this chapter, you learned how important testing is to the development of systems in general and to the debugger specifically. By understanding the fundamentals of the techniques of testing, you will make yourself a better debugger and overall a better developer. In addition, by understanding the processes that testers go through when they are testing a system, you will have a better appreciation for how to go about finding problems when they are reported to you.

Like debugging, testing is really more of an art than a science today. By understanding the techniques available to you and by taking a more methodical and measurable approach to your testing, you can move testing into the realm of a science. By utilizing the testing techniques in your debugging efforts, you can help move debugging into a science as well.

Bug Puzzle

The C preprocessor is the bane of the C programmer and the C debugger. So many bugs have been created by using the preprocessor that it almost deserves a book of its own. Let's take a look at one of the more famous preprocessor bugs along with an explanation of how the preprocessor works.

Imagine that you are writing a simple macro to return a random number that is defined within a specific range. The C programming language library comes with a function called **random()** that returns a random number. The problem with the function is that it is not in the range you want it to be. So, being a smart programmer, you write a simple macro to solve the problem:

#define Random(n) random( ) % n

This macro simply forces the results of the random number generated by the function to be within the range of 0 to n–1. Now, you can simply use *Random* in place of *random* when you want a number in a predefined range. This all seems simple enough, doesn't it? So, you can write a simple statement that looks like this:

```
int ran = Random(j-i+1);
```

and it should generate a random number in the range from 0 to j-i+1 for whatever *j* and *i* happen to be. Most programmers, even C programmers, reading this line of code would understand what it was you were trying to do. For those that do not understand, allow us to explain. Assuming that you were in a loop and that *i* was equal to 10 and *j* was equal to 20, the statement would be the equivalent of finding a random number in the range 0 to 11.

Let's take a minute to review how the preprocessor actually works. When you compile C code, the preprocessor is used to expand predefined constants, included files, and macro expansions such as you just wrote, into code that appears in the final product. For example, when you write a constant definition, such as:

```
#define kMaxValues 10
```

and then use that constant definition in some code:

```
for ( int I=0; I<kMaxValues; ++I )
    do_something(i);
```

the preprocessor will run through the code and expand it as a series of tokens. In this case, the result will be:

```
for ( int I=0; I<10; ++I )
    do_something(i);
```

It is worth noting that the preprocessor really isn't very bright. It does a literal substitution for your tokens, character by character. Therefore, if you make a silly mistake, such as this:

```
#define kMaxValues '10'
for ( int I=0; I<kMaxValues; ++I )
    do_something(i);
```

the preprocessor is going to expand it to be a statement that is not legal, and the compiler (which runs after the preprocessor) will catch it and complain. Sometimes, the complaints are less than clear due to the token replacement process. Either way, however, the result is always a literal replacement of the requested token with the token passed in by the user. Therefore, when you write a statement using your new macro *Random*, you get the following replacement in the final code:

```
int ran = rand() % j-i+1;
```

Unfortunately, this macro doesn't work. Your job as a debugger is to figure out why and determine how to fix it.

Chapter 14
Maintenance

Yuan Hsieh

Maintenance is a loathsome word in the software development industry. Being assigned to maintenance duty is akin to being sent to Siberia or the Russian front during War World II. Most software developers dread it. Often, developers leave a company because the product that they were developing has entered the maintenance phase, and there is no new development work. And yet, maintenance can be the most costly phases in the life cycle of the software development process. It was estimated that 60 to 80 percent of software dollars that are spent in an organization are spent on maintenance,[1] and that maintenance activities accounted for the majority of effort in the software production process.[2]

How does maintenance affect bugs? In a survey of software maintenance processes in the financial industry, it was found that only 35.1 percent of changes due to maintenance tasks did not produce new errors. As a matter of fact, on average, 16.2 percent of maintenance tasks added more than 15 errors in this study.[3] This should not come as a surprise because maintenance can be characterized by changes to the system, and you learned in Chapter 3 that the majority of bugs are introduced when you attempt to make a modification.

---

[1] Pigoski, T. M. Practical Software Maintenance: *Best Practices for Managing Your Software Investment.* John Wiley & Sons, Inc., 1996.

[2] Sousa, M. J. C. and Moreira, H. M. "A Survey on the Software Maintenance Process," Proceedings of International Conference on Software Maintenance, pp 265-272, Bethesda, Maryland, November 16-20, 1998.

[3] ibid.

What Is Software Maintenance?

The International Electrical and Electronics Engineers, Inc.(IEEE) defines software maintenance as:

> The modification of a software product after its delivery (to the customer),to correct errors, to improve its performance or other attributes, or to adapt the product to a modified environment.[4]

Maintenance tasks are commonly classified into three categories: corrective, adaptive and perfective.

- *Corrective*—Fixing bugs, that's the name of the game in a corrective task. The maintainer's responsibility is to identify the cause of bugs and fix them.

- *Adaptive*—Otherwise known as porting, the goal of an adaptive task is to replicate the functionalities of the system for a different environment. The maintainer might need to port the software to a different hardware platform, different operating system, or different programming languages.

- *Perfective*—In a perfective task, the goal is to improve the system. The maintainer is responsible for adding new features, improving efficiency, improving functionality, improving system design, and performing other improvement related tasks.

Some classifications of maintenance tasks also include preventive maintenance. Preventive maintenance is characterized by tasks that are meant to prevent foreseeable errors and problems in the software system. However, we consider preventive maintenance to fall under the category of perfective or corrective maintenance. All the work that were done to prevent the Y2K bug are the most visible example of preventive maintenance.

Based on our observations, the predominant type of maintenance tasks in an organization appears to be related to the maturity of the systems that are in the maintenance phase. In the early stages of maintenance, corrective maintenance tasks dominate; the reason is that the software still has not been exposed to most of the likely usages. Slowly, the software matures, and perfective tasks start to assert themselves. During this stage, most of the bugs have been ferreted out, and the organization starts to accept requirements changes and becomes concerned about the improvement of the system, so that the system can evolve with time. In addition, if the system has matured and survived to become part of the core of an organization, it might be ported to another environment. Either an adaptive effort will take place to use the latest technology to implement the legacy system, or the adaptive task will port the system onto a more popular hardware platform running the latest operating systems.

---

[4] IEEE Standard 1219-1992, *Software Maintenance Standard*, Published by IEEE Standards Office, P. O. Box 1331, Piscataway, New Jersey, 08855-1331.

Maintenance Efforts

Typically, there are four steps involved to fulfill a maintenance task: the request, the understanding, the change, and the verification.

Step 1: The Request

A maintenance task typically starts with a request for modification. The request can come from anywhere, and in most cases, it doesn't really matter where it comes from. If the maintenance request is a bug report, we try to reproduce it. If it's a request for new features, we attempt to understand the nature of the request and then obtain requirements. The process of understanding the nature of the request can take anywhere from a matter of a few minutes (because the bug is easily reproduced), to a few days (getting and understanding the requirements), to a few weeks (when it's impossible to reproduce the bug.)

Step 2: The Understanding

Once we have some understanding of the request, we then need to determine how to fulfill the request. This means that we need to figure out where in the software we need to make the change and how the change might affect other parts of the software. We also need to understand the program. How much time this step takes depends on how large the program is, how easy it is to comprehend, and whether or not documentation or the original developers are available to answer questions. The majority of time spent in the maintenance effort is spent on this step. Estimates show that programmers spend between 47 to 62 percent of their time attempting to understand the documentation and logic of programs.[5]

Step 3: The Change

Assuming we can figure out how to make the change, we then physically change the software. This is often the easiest step because by this point, maintainers should have a pretty good idea about what it is they are doing because in step 2, did all the leg work deciding what the changes will be and how the changes will affect the software. If you are unsure as to the effect of the change, repeat step 2.

Step 4: The Verification

We then need to make sure the changes that we have made do whatever they are supposed to do. We also need to make sure that we haven't broken anything else by making the changes, which is the most important step in a maintenance task.

The Challenges of Maintenance

Based on our experience, maintenance is the hardest part of any software-related tasks. Maintainers are the unsung heroes of the software industry. On one hand, they are asked to

---

[5] Pigoski, T. M. *Practical Software Maintenance: Best Practices for Managing Your Software Investment.* John Wiley & Sons, Inc., 1996.

make modifications to the system. On the other hand, they are not allowed to break anything, because the system is usually in a production environment. Maintainers are usually not involved in the original development of the software; they are usually hired after the software is in production. They have had nothing at all to do with any of the existing defects, ill-considered interfaces, or inflexible and inextensible designs. Yet, maintainers receive the full brunt of the tirades from management and customers alike because the system has bugs. It is a thankless job.

Maintenance is difficult for primarily five reasons. First, personnel turnover is high in the software industry. This means that there are frequently new people being asked to work on software that they are not familiar with. Second, a software system of any size is going to be complex, which makes it difficult to understand, especially when documentation about the software is usually missing or out of date. Even when it does exist, documentation usually doesn't help because it doesn't answer relevant questions. In addition, because it is difficult to understand the software, maintainers generally have difficulty determining all the places that changes should be made and the effects of these changes. Furthermore, the software in production can make maintenance difficult, because it will be difficult to make incompatible changes. Obviously, poorly designed software can also contribute to the difficulty of software maintenance tasks.

Degradation of Software Due to Maintenance Efforts

The difficulty in maintenance means that maintainers tend to make mistakes when they implement their changes to the software. These mistakes can be classified into three types:

♦ Obvious mistakes

♦ Latent mistakes

♦ Conceptual mistakes

Some mistakes are obvious, and these mistakes usually show up as bugs during unit testing or regression testing. Other mistakes are more subtle; these are *latent defects*. Latent defects are defects as defined in Chapter 3. For example, an inproper handling of error condition in a program is a defect within the program. Although these types of defects do not contribute to program execution, they do have the potential to become bugs. An empirical study of the effects of maintenance showed that 34 percent of all modified programs contained an error, and five out of eight modifications of the same program contained at least a latent defect.[6]

The last type of mistake is more insidious. Conceptual mistakes do not break the software, and they are not defects. These mistakes degrade the design of the software a little at a time. The class hierarchy is slightly modified, and the classes are no longer reusable or extendable.

---

[6] Douce, C. R. and Layzell, P. J. "Evolution and Errors: An Empirical Example," *Proceedings of IEEE International Conference on Software Maintenance*, pp 493-498, Keble College, Oxford, England, August 30-September 3, 1999.

New dependencies are added to the structures and functions as the software becomes more rigid and fragile. As software ages, bit by bit, the original design of the system degrades and entropy sets in. All the original attributes of good design slowly erode and we end up with an unmaintainable mess.

Creating a Maintainable Software System

What is a maintainable software system? From our perspective, maintenance is simply the process of changing the software in a production environment to fix bugs, add new features, or make the software better. Maintenance is change. If maintenance is about change, a maintainable software system is one that is easy to change regardless of the motivation underlying the change. If a bug is found, it should be easy to identify and correct the mistake. If requirements have changed, it should be trivial to add or modify features in the existing system. But what attributes of a software system can affect ease of change?

Let's get back to basics. Recall the four steps of maintenance effort presented in the previous section. Step 1 requires the understanding of the change request and does not concern the software system. Step 2 involves understanding the software and coming up with the change. Therefore, the software needs to be easy to understand and easy to change. Step 3 implements the change and usually does not impact the maintainability of the software because compilers and source code editors are the primary tools used to implement the change. Step 4 verifies the changes and should involve regression tests. If regression tests are complete and efficient, there is more chance for iterations, which can make the verification of maintenance tasks a lot easier.

Creating Comprehensible Software

Because maintainers spend a majority of their maintenance effort attempting to understand the program, it is safe to say that if the software is easy to comprehend, it should help make the software more maintainable. But what makes software easy to comprehend? Clearly, documentation is part of the answer. Clean, easy to read source code is another. But before we address the subject of comprehensible software, let's look at how maintainers attempt to learn about the software they are maintaining.

Program Comprehension Strategy

Imagine that you are a new employee walking into a software development group. The first day on the job, the project manager tells you to go fix a bug. You are given a pointer to the configuration management repository. There is limited documentation, and no one from the original development team is available. How do you go about learning about the software that you are about to change?

One approach might be to simply start going through the codes one file at a time. This approach is known as the *systematic strategy*. The goal of the systematic strategy is to understand the design of the original developer. In order for the systematic strategy to work, you need to read and understand a majority of the code. If the software codebase is large, this approach might not be feasible. So instead of trying to understand the entire codebase, you try to find the module or sections of the code that you think you need to change. This is called the *as-needed approach*. In the as-needed approach, you try to minimize amount of the code that you have to read. You seek to understand only the codes that are necessary, so that you can fulfill the maintenance request.

Whether you decide to read the entire codebase or a limited subset of the codes, you must start somewhere. The question is, where? Most of us like to start at the top. We look at documentation if it exists. We look at class hierarchies in object-oriented software or function declarations in procedural software. Class hierarchies and function declarations help us gain a high-level understanding of all the pieces and how these pieces relate to each other. This is known as the *top-down comprehension approach*. But sometimes, when we think we are close to the codes that we want to know more about, we switch to what is known as the *bottom-up approach*. In the bottom-up approach, we read the source codes to understand the detailed programmatic flow of the software. We might also use the bottom-up approach when we have no knowledge of the problem that we are trying to solve. So instead of looking at header files to form a mental picture of all the interconnecting pieces of the software, we might opt to start with the main program and trace the flow one instruction at a time.

Documents versus Codes

Does anyone actually read the documentation that I wrote? Or is it just a checklist item for project managers? I have always wondered about this question, and you have probably wondered about it as well. In one study, the behaviors of the programmer attempting to learn about both procedural and object-oriented programs were recorded.[7] The behaviors were recorded for a study period and two maintenance tasks. This study produced the following observation: Programmers' access of documentation decreased as they gained knowledge about the program. By the time the second maintenance task was performed, the use of the documentation file was near zero. The implication is that as programmers begin to comprehend a program, their need for abstract documentation information is reduced. So instead of reading documentation, they read code instead.

But does documentation help? The answer might be related to the quality of the documentation, but empirical evidence suggests that documentation could help make the maintenance task go faster and be less error prone. An experiment conducted to measure the effect of documentation showed that the group with access to documentation required less time to comprehend the system and made higher quality changes.[8] The same study suggests that the performance of the maintenance tasks for the group with documentation was limited by the

---

[7] Corritore, C. L. and Wiedenbeck, S. "Direction and Scope of Comprehension-Related Activities by Procedural and Object-Oriented Programmers: An Empirical Study," *Proceedings of the Eighth International Workshop on Program Comprehension*, pp 139-148, Limerick, Ireland, June 1-11, 2000.

[8] Porter, A. "Fundamental Laws and Assumptions of Software Maintenance," *Empirical Software Engineering*, No. 2, pp 119-131, 1997.

programming skill of the group members, because the programmers didn't have to spend a lot of time comprehending the program. On the other hand, the group with no document must spend significant amount of time to understand the software; hence, the member of this group cannot benefit from their programming skill and make lower quality changes. The implication here is that the availability of documentation can positively affect the quality of maintenance tasks.

Searching Source Codes

Even with documentation, we eventually have to look at the code. It turns out that how we look at code depends on the underlying motivations.

During the program understanding phase, when we are trying to understand the structure of the system, we tend to look for function and variable definitions as well as how these functions and variables are used in the code. When we have formulated a model and an idea for changes, we tend to look at codes to determine the impact of making these changes. For impact analysis, we often look for all uses of a particular variable or function to make sure that we understand all the dependencies. When we look for bugs, we tend to identify the function that is misbehaving and track usage of variables in and out of the function.

A study of how maintainers search codes determined that when we search for information in the code, the predominate kinds of information that we are looking for include:[9]

♦ Function definitions

♦ All uses of a function

♦ All uses of a variable

♦ Variable definitions

Difficulties in Comprehension (Lessons from Object-Oriented Design)

Due to the popularity of object-oriented design in recent years, there have been numerous studies on the effect of object-oriented design on maintenance and program comprehension. The results of these studies show a few side effects of object-oriented design on program comprehension:

♦ *Problem decomposition*—It was observed that object-oriented design tends to make it difficult for a reader to understand the purpose of the software.[10] Object-oriented design provides the reader with a set of objects and a set of interfaces for those objects without any hints of how an object might be put together. This is similar to giving someone a box

---

[9] Sim, S. E., Clarke, C. L. A., and Holt, R. C. "Archetypal Source Code Searches: A Survey of Software Developers and Maintainers," *Proceedings of the Sixth International Workshop on Program Comprehension*, pp 180-187, Ischia, Italy, June 24-26, 1998.

[10] Rugaber, S. "The use of domain knowledge in program understanding," *Annals of Software Engineering*, No. 9, pp 143-192, 2000.

of jigsaw puzzle pieces without providing the picture showing the solution of the puzzle. We might understand what an individual object does, but it is hard to know what the program should do and how the pieces fit in the solution.

♦ *Delocalization*—When information that is needed for analysis is scattered in many different places, it is difficult for a maintainer to find and collect all the relevant pieces. In software engineering, delocalization occurs when codes that are conceptually related are not physically related. It was observed that inheritance creates opportunity for delocalization because in order to understand a line of code, the maintainer might need to traverse the inheritance hierarchy of the class.[11] It was also observed that a maintainer is likely to misinterpret the program and make incorrect modifications when information is scattered.[12]

♦ *Conceptual entropy*—In one study, it was proposed that when the class hierarchy becomes deeper, it becomes harder for developers and maintainers to agree on the inheritance hierarchy itself.[13] Another study, focussing on the effect of conceptual entropy as related to maintenance tasks, showed that the time to perform maintenance tasks on object-oriented software with a class hierarchy of three levels deep was faster than noninheritance-based software. However, when the class hierarchy was five levels deep, inheritance showed no such benefits. It was observed that the maintainers actually had difficulty comprehending the deeper hierarchy.[14]

♦ *Dynamic binding and polymorphism*—Dynamic binding and polymorphism cause problems because of their very nature. With polymorphism, it is not known until runtime which implementation of the polymorphic method will actually be called. This means that when we attempt to understand how the code works, we must look at all the classes that implement the polymorphic method. This is especially problematic for classes in a deep inheritance hierarchy.

♦ *Multiple inheritance*—The problem associated with multiple inheritance is well documented. The primary difficulty with multiple inheritance is the determination of which method of the base class will actually be invoked.

Even though these five causes of poor program comprehension are framed in terms of object-oriented design elements, none of the preceding identified causes are specific to object-oriented design. When maintainers don't understand how the problem is being decomposed, it doesn't matter if the code is designed using an object-oriented approach or a

---

[11] Soloway, E., Pinto, J., Letovsky, S., Littman, D., and Lampert, R. "Designing Documentation to Compensate for Delocalised Plans," *Communications of the* ACM, Vol. 13, No. 11, pp 1259-1267, 1988.

[12] Wilde, N., Matthews, P., and Huitt, R. "Maintaining object-oriented software," *IEEE Software*, Vol. 10, No. 1, pp 75-80, 1993.

[13] Dvorak, J. "Conceptual Entropy and Its Effect on Class Hierarchies," *IEEE Computer*, Vol. 27, No. 6, pp 59-63, 1994.

[14] Daly J. et al. "Evaluating Inheritance Depth on the Maintainability of Object-Oriented Software," *Empirical Software Engineering*, Vol. 1, No. 2, pp 109-129, 1996.

top-down structural approach. When maintainers have to look in many places just to understand what the code does—whether this is caused by bad package design, bad file placement, inheritance or polymorphism—they are going to have a harder time understanding the code. And when maintainers have conceptual differences with the developer of the code, maintainers are going to have to spend more time trying to understand the developer's design and intentions. The lesson is obvious: Keep it simple, and keep it accessible.

Characteristics of Comprehensible Software

Comprehensible software should assist maintainers in understanding the software in a top-down fashion by providing high-level knowledge about the problem and the solution. Comprehensible software should also assist maintainers in understanding the software using a bottom-up approach by helping them produce a programmatic model of the software and making it easy to find relevant information. Comprehensible software is more than just code, it is also all the artifacts and documentation surrounding the code that can be used to help maintainers understand the software.

Based on what we have presented, the following tips are provided to help you create software that is more comprehensible:

♦ *Provide domain knowledge*—Maintainers should have the same knowledge about the problem domain as the original designers and architects. Otherwise, it might be difficult for them to appreciate the solution that was developed. The domain knowledge should include the problem and decomposition of the problem. It should also define terms and vocabulary related to the domain. Additionally, business needs and user scenarios related to the problem are helpful to the maintainer to understand how the system is to be used.

♦ *Provide high-level solution documentation*—High-level documentation provides a road map for the maintainers. It helps them with their top-down comprehension strategy. High-level documentation outlines the relationship between software modules or components. Control and data flow of the software at the module level should also be documented. In addition, the documentation should provide relationships between classes or files for these modules and components.

♦ *Provide comments*—Numerous empirical studies have shown that comments in the code have a dramatic effect in increasing the comprehension of the maintainers.[15] Of course, we all know that comments that repeat the code is useless. Comments should provide information that is not apparent from the code, such as the purpose of the code snippet or high-level algorithmic descriptions.

♦ *Provide dynamic tracing mechanisms*—A dynamic tracing mechanism is a fancy name for a runtime debugging trace. This can be done within either a debugger or using the tracing log file. This mechanism helps maintainers visualize the control and data flow of the

---

[15] Kemerer, C. F. "Software complexity and software maintenance: A survey of empirical research," *Annals of Software Engineering*, Vol. 1, pp 1-22. 1995.

program, which is helpful in their bottom-up comprehension approach. A discussion of dynamic tracing mechanisms can be found in Chapter 12 under the section of Tracing Log Files.

◆ *Provide function definitions*—Providing function definitions might be the easiest tip to implement in this section. This means defining function prototypes in the *include* file for C. For C++, the function definitions are given within the class definition. For Java, Javadoc can be used to provide a collection of function definitions without all the codes in the source file. This will help maintainers perform top-down code searching.

◆ *Provide consistent naming convention*—A consistent naming convention is more than just coding convention or using Hungarian notation.[16] Hungarian notation defines a detailed guideline for naming variables and functions, and it is popular in Microsoft Windows programs. However, providing a consistent naming convention means that you should associate a consistent variable name to a concept. For example, if you have a system that uses a customer's name in many places, it might be helpful to use one variable name, such as *customerName*, to hold the name of the customer, so that it is easier for the maintainer to find all uses of the customer's name in the software.

◆ *Document feature entry points*—In software that supports hundreds of features with hundreds of thousands of lines of code, it can be difficult to know where to start looking for a feature. As an example, if someone came to you and asked you to fix a bug in the "undo" feature, would you even know where to start looking for this feature? Wouldn't it be nice if there was a document that could tell you which part of the code or which file you should start reading? The documentation for the entry point of a feature can assist a maintainer performing an as-needed approach of program comprehension. It can help maintainers narrow down the portion of codes that they would have to read.

◆ *Design linear code*—Polymorphism is difficult to comprehend because maintainers must consider all possible options. Options create complexity. To make things simple, we can reduce the number of available options. This means that comprehensible code should be linear and sequential.

◆ *Limit object-oriented features*—It can be easier for maintainers to comprehend an object-oriented system if inheritance is limited, and the class hierarchies are kept shallow. In addition, maintainers typically have a hard time tracing through dynamic invocations, and polymorphism should be avoided. "But, but," the object-oriented proponents would argue, "these are the features that make object-oriented designed software easier to maintain." True, if the maintainers happen to be the original developers. When you understand the class hierarchy and can move freely from one abstraction to the next, these constructs provide no barrier to program comprehension. However, when the maintainers are not the original developers, it takes a while for them to understand and embrace the

---

[16] Simonyi, C. and Heller, M. "The Hungarian Revolution," BYTE, August, pp. 131-139, 1991.

conceptual beauty of the design. They usually don't have the time to admire the technical elegance. They only want to know where they should make the change and what the change will affect; therefore, use object-oriented features judiciously and appropriately.

♦ *Limit global variables*—The risks of global variables are well publicized and understood. The effect of global variables on program comprehension is that it requires the maintainer to have to search for and understand all uses of the global variables within the software. Instead of dealing with a small local section of code that uses global variables, the maintainer has to understand the entire codebase.

♦ *Reduce delocalization*—Reducing delocalization means that we should try to keep all the relevant information together. Relevant information is all the information that affects a specific functionality or feature. For example, if a feature requires loading some parameters, the code that does the initialization of these parameters and the code that loads these parameters should be close to each other. This way, a hapless maintainer doesn't have to search all over the codebase for them. The relevant information for a global variable is the content of the variable. Hence, the use of a global variable increases delocalization because you need to look in many places to determine how it's being used and set in the code.

Design for Maintainability

It is futile and frustrating when you can understand the software within a few minutes, but you cannot safely make any changes without rewriting half the code. The software needs to be architected, designed, and written to be maintainable from the start. Software is maintainable if it is easy to change. But what makes a software system easy to change?

Characteristics of a Maintainable Design

A maintainable design makes it easier for the maintainer to make changes to the software. When a maintainer is fixing a bug, he or she needs to understand the nature of the bug and find the exact location in which to fix the bug. When a maintainer is attempting to add new features to the software, he or she also needs to determine the location where the changes should be made. In both cases, the ease of the change is affected by the number of changes that have to be made in order to support and make the desired change. Usually, the more changes you have to make, the harder it is.

In other words, a maintainable design is one with the fewest interdependencies between software modules. A software design is hard to change if there are many dependencies between software modules. A software module can be defined as a component, a class, or a function, depending on the scope of the change that you are considering. The problem with dependencies is that if you attempt to change one module, you must consider the effect of the change in relation to the dependent modules. And if you have to make a change to a dependent module, then further analysis is necessary to determine the effect of that change. The further the effect of the change extends, the harder it is to change the module.

In a survey of empirical research relating software complexity and software maintenance, the conclusion seems to be that software is hard to maintain if the software modules are heavily coupled and not cohesive.[17] However, the problem is not necessarily the existence of interdependencies between modules. The problem is also incorrect dependencies.

For example, let's say we are working on an e-commerce system. For simplicity, let's assume that the system has a model for two kinds of users: buyers and sellers. The sellers sell things to the buyers. Also, the original requirements have one seller in the system, which is the purchaser of the system. So in the design, you create a one-to-many relationship between a seller and buyers. One day, a potential customer walks in the door. This customer is interested in using your system, but has a slightly different business model. It turns out that the customer is a distributor and has more than one seller. Instead of a model of one seller to many buyers, you now need to change the design to account for the model of many sellers to many buyers. How easy it is to change the system depends on how much of the system depends on the one seller to many buyers model. For example, if your database schema has this assumption built in, it might be difficult to change the existing tables to work with the new model. If your accounting module hardcoded the relationship between a seller and buyers, then the accounting module might need to be redesigned as well.

Design a Framework instead of a Solution

One way to avoid incorrect dependencies is to create a framework for your problem and build the framework into a solution, brick by brick. When we are presented with a problem, we tend to want to jump in and quickly come up with a solution to solve the problem. Using a functional decomposition approach, we determine the top of the solution and proceed to decompose the solution into a series of functions. In an object-oriented design, we determine all the objects in the problem and their interactions. However, these approaches tend to be "problem-centric" in that we tend to devise the design specifically for the problem that we are facing. When the problem changes, we find that it is not easy to change the design to meet the new problem.

Instead of thinking about solving the problem in a problem-centric design, we should think about providing tools to solve the problem. And, instead of providing a solution, we should provide a framework. What is a framework? In this case, a framework is a collection of building blocks that you can use to construct a solution. Building blocks are simple and dumb. In electrical engineering, building blocks are resistors, capacitors, and wires. In the construction industry, building blocks are two by fours, nails, screws, and plywood. In software engineering, building blocks are simple objects and functions that represent one and only one abstraction. Standard template libraries in C++ are a collection of building blocks. The Java Swing toolkit is another set of building blocks. In object-oriented design, you can think of building blocks as a set of abstract interfaces that can be structured to solve a problem. When you try to solve a business problem, you can also create a set of building blocks for your problem domain.

---

[17] ibid.

For the e-commerce problem presented in the previous section, the framework might be a set of users and a set of relationships between users. The data structure representing the users, such as buyers and sellers, are just containers. They contain no relationships between these users. The relationship data structure maintains the relationships. And if a new business model breaks the relationship, it is easier to create a new relationship data structure than to change the user classes.

Maintainability through Processes

This might come across as a heresy, but there is nothing wrong with clone and go, or creating one-off solutions. Sometimes, having numerous one-off solutions is more maintainable than modifying a generic, do-everything solution to do one more thing. Consider an e-commerce system that implements a certain business model. Assume that the e-commerce system has been in production for a while and is running very smoothly. During the design phase, you tried to make the business model as extensible as possible in order to accommodate the needs of many industries and business processes. However, one day a customer comes in wanting to buy your e-commerce solution. You find out that your existing business model doesn't fully apply to the customer's requirements. You have to make some design changes in order to accommodate the new requirements. Of course, the customer wants the solution immediately. What are your options?

- *Option 1*—You determine how the new requirements can fit into the existing design, which is otherwise known as hacking. You then release the hack as part of the standard release to both the new and existing customers.

- *Option 2*—You take the new requirements back to the drawing board. You redesign the new business model component that incorporates the new requirements. The new implementation is incorporated back into the existing product, and the new and existing customers all receive the same upgrade.

- *Option 3*—You rip out the existing business model in the existing system. You design and create a specific business model for the new customer and give the new customer a system that is different from your existing solutions. The existing customer is unaware of this "one-off" version.

In our experience, everyone talks about doing option 2, but it is rarely done. The reason is that we usually don't have the time. But another reason is that it is truly difficult to create a solution that can accommodate all the possible ways that something can be done. So, we often resort to option 1. Option 1 is probably the most dangerous option because it ruins the conceptual integrity of the system and leads to spaghetti code. It also makes future changes and modifications to the system difficult. With both option 1 and 2, you are also making changes to an existing production system. We learned in Chapter 3 that bugs tend to manifest themselves when there are changes to the system. So by choosing option 1 and 2, you choose to destabilize the production system and run the risk of introducing bugs to an otherwise working system.

Option 3 seems to go against everything that we were taught as software engineers from day one. Existing literature is full of warnings about the unmaintainability of one-off systems. The conventional wisdom contends that one-off systems are unmaintainable because every time you make a change, you have to find all the places to make the same changes. And, if you don't, you will end up needing to maintain more than one system. But we create one-off systems all the time. A cardinal rule of a graphical user interface (GUI) design is to separate the presentation layer from the business layer. Why? Well, it makes it easier to change the presentation for different customers. Isn't that a one-off system? Don't we think it is totally acceptable to have a different GUI for different customers? And do we question the maintainability of such a design? Of course not, because we accept the fact that different customers require different interfaces, and the separation of the presentation layer from the business layer makes it easy to change both layers.

The unmaintainability of a one-off system is not inherently due to the one-offness of the system. It is unmaintainable because we don't design the maintenance process along with the design of the software. In the design stage, we don't ask the question, "If someone wants to have a different business model, how would I go about changing the business model?" It is unmaintainable because we don't design the system to be a one-off system. This requires the software to be designed in a modular fashion so you can replace the existing business model with a new business model. This also requires us to think about interfaces and other issues as presented in the previous section. But designing for maintainability is only half the battle. The other half is the design of the maintenance process to go with the software. The maintenance process needs to clearly define where the changes need to be made and which module needs to be swapped out. The maintenance process also needs to specify the steps for propagating changes from one system to another. Without a maintenance process, it would be difficult to maintain and manage all the different one-off systems, and the argument against one-off systems would have merit. With a maintenance process, even if your software is not modular, it is still possible to maintain one-off systems.

If done correctly, a one-off system has many advantages. For one thing, creating a new system does not have to impact the stability of existing systems. Also, a one-off system can potentially create many reusable components and bring us closer to the plug-and-play software construction. The new business model created for option 3 can easily be swapped out and replaced by a third business model. In effect, we now have three business models that we can reuse in other products, if need be. Finally, creating one-off solutions means that you don't have to worry about how your changes will impact an existing solution. It makes it easier to test and design a solution appropriate for the customer.

Provide A Regression Testing Environment

Most of all, the characteristic of a maintainable software system can be marked by the existence of a test environment in which changes can be readily evaluated. Having a regression testing environment makes it easier to iterate through the fix and test cycle. Ideally, the regression testing environment should be automated so that the maintainer can quickly test the changes without a lot of additional work. If the project is large, the number of test cases in a full regression test suite might be too large, and the amount of time to run through the test cases can become too long and impractical. Therefore, the regression testing environment needs the capability for the maintainer to extract a subset of test cases that can be tested in a feasible amount of time. Of course, a full regression test would need to be run through by the testers prior to the release of the changes.

Create a Maintenance Environment

Software developers are pampered with tools, methodologies, and development environments to make their jobs easier. Maintainers have the same needs as well. In fact, because maintenance is typically the longest and costliest phase of software, it is cost-effective to give maintainers a comfortable environment to make them more efficient. A comfortable maintenance environment includes a set of processes to support maintenance tasks, an environment that allows maintainers to learn about the system, a set of tools to facilitate program understanding and changes, and an environment that promotes immediate feedback of the correctness of the changes. The following five ideas can help an organization to create a maintenance environment to promote productivity.

♦ *Design an organizational maintenance process*—A maintenance process is more than just a formal bug report, bug tracking, and bug fixing process. A maintenance process also needs to have a process for requirement changes and new features. In an organization, these processes need to be defined, so that all the stakeholders (such as sales and marketing, customer service, and development groups) are aware of the impact and schedule of a maintenance request. The process should also allow the stakeholders the ability to prioritize different requests to meet the business needs.

♦ *Design a technical maintenance process*—A maintenance process of a specific software solution needs to be defined at the same time as the design of the software. This means that when the designers are designing the software system, they need to be cognizant of the maintenance requirements. This means that when they are designing the system, they need to ask the following questions: (1) How would a maintainer debug the system? (2) How does a maintainer add a new feature to the system? The answers to these questions should be documented and translated into a set of processes, and the corresponding technical solutions should be incorporated into the design.

♦ *Provide learning systems*—It is easier to learn a system when you can work with a running system. Ideally, every maintainer should be able to work with a system that mimics the production system, even when there are no active maintenance tasks to perform.

♦ *Provide a maintenance environment*—A maintenance environment includes tools that help a programmer search the code and visualize the software. On Unix machines, there are many tools available to aid code searching and reading (emacs, grep, find, gdb are the tools that I use most). On a Windows platform, the various commercial development environments provide many search and visualization capabilities. Beyond these tools, you may find that by opening many windows that contain a set of searchable source codes on your screen, you can see everything at once, and it may help combat the delocalization problem. Tools that can help you visualize the dependencies between software modules as well as programmatic flow of the system are also useful. Such tools can include a debug tracing component that allows you to easily trace the control and data flow of the software as well as visual development environments, which can help you visualize the usage of variables and functions throughout the system.

♦ *Create a regression test environment*—Coupled with a learning system, it is also helpful to have a regression test environment. When a maintainer makes a change, he can immediately run the test suites to determine if his change has any ill effect on the system.

Maintaining Existing Software

It would be ideal to have maintainable systems to work with all the time. But most of us must work with what we have, which is usually an undocumented software system in a semichaotic environment. So how do we maintain existing software? Very carefully! But even if we have the luxury of starting out with a maintainable system, we still want to change the software very carefully, or we run the risk of turning a maintainable software system into an unmaintainable nightmare.

Changing Existing Software Systems

We are not kidding when we answered, "Very carefully!" That is precisely our sentiment and approach when we have to modify existing software. We try the best we can to understand what the software is doing, and what we have been asked to do. We spend enormous amounts of time mulling over changes that we will make, making them, and then testing them. And when our changes don't work, we back everything out, leaving the code in its original state, and start over. Of course we also document the changes that we made and keep the existing documents up-to-date.

Seek to Understand the System

Prior to actually making any changes, we need to figure out where we should make the changes and the potential effects of our changes. This requires us to understand the software that we are about to modify, which is especially difficult if you have no prior knowledge about the software. The following ideas can help you get started.

♦ *Read the documentation*—Obviously, if documentation exists, you should read it. In many cases, it can give you a high-level understanding about the software. But don't trust it too much because it might be inaccurate. Use it more as a guide rather than the literal truth.

♦ *Read the code*—I usually prefer to start at the top, and work my way down. So I would start at the package level, trying to figure out what each package does, and how it relates to another package. I then continue to the module level and perhaps the class level, just to get a road map of where all the pieces are. I still would not be ready to make any modifications at this point, but I might have a clue as to where to start looking.

♦ *Turn on tracing*—If the software is equipped with a trace logging capability, turn it on, and watch it run. The trace log is a fast way to do bottom-up program comprehension without having to read the code.

♦ *Draw pictures*—If the program is complex and the codebase is large, it can be easy to lose track of all the dependencies and programmatic flow. When this happens, it can be useful to draw a visual flowchart to help you recall what's happening when. In your drawing, you can invent whatever graphical representation fits your purpose. You don't need to break out a drawing program and use Universal Modeling Language (UML) to represent the program. These tools would more than likely slow you down. But once you have an accurate picture in your head of how the system works, you might want to consider documenting that picture for someone else.

♦ *Run/trace test programs*—The original developers just might have a few test programs lying around. These test programs are useful to help you understand how the software is used, and they give you an entry point to perform the bottom-up code reading process.

♦ *Talk to testers*—Testers need to test the software, so they must have some idea of what it is supposed to do. Because they must use the software in order to test it, they would have tools, such as testing scripts, application usage and expected outputs that they use to run and verify the software. Their tools might be used to help you understand the usage and purpose of the software.

♦ *Talk to original developers*—Talking to the original developers is very helpful, but ensure that what they say is verified in the code. Sometimes, the code might have changed between the original design and the time you see it. Other times, the original developer might tell you what he thinks he developed, not what he actually developed. At the very least, they can provide clues as to where their minds were when they wrote the code. More often than not, it's better than nothing.

♦ *Treat the code as gospel*—If what you read in the documentation contradicts the code, then you know the documentation is wrong. If what someone told you about how the software works doesn't correspond to how the code works, that person is wrong. Your changes must be based on the existing code and nothing else. Of course, you might want to find out why the person is giving you what appeared to be incorrect information. Did the code changed? Did the requirements changed? You might also want to correct that person's misconception to prevent them from making a mistake somewhere else.

Leave Only Actual Changes

Maintainers have nasty habits of making "test" changes to the code, just to see what the effects are. If the "test" code doesn't appear to work, they tend to just comment out the code that does not work and add another test code. For a complicated bug or feature, this trial and error approach can take quite a few iterations, and the codebase can grow very large. This approach is fine to use when you remember remove all the extra codes that don't work before checking the fixes back into the configuration management repository. But when you check in all the trial and error codes as well as the actual fixes, it can confuse a future maintainer who then has to try to figure out what all the extraneous code does.

You should track every change you make to the system, so that you can reverse the changes if necessary. Most source control tools allow you to throw away modifications and revert the code back to the current version. These are great tools to use to trace the system changes.

Document the Changes

Unfortunately, there is no getting away from documentation tasks as a maintainer. You can document your changes in the following manner:

♦ *In the code*—Comments in the code have helped many maintainers; therefore, as maintainers, it behooves you to make the life of other maintainers easier as well. Put a note in the code to say why the change was made, who made the change, and when. This way, others will know who to ask if they have questions about the comment. In fact, every line that was changed should have a comment or a marker on it so that it is clear to anyone reading the code that the line has been changed.

♦ *In the change log*—The change log should maintain the changes done to software for every maintenance task. The change log can be used as a source of measurement metrics to help determine the maintainability of the software. More information about the content of the change log and its use is presented in the section titled "Keep Track of Changes."

♦ *In the existing documentation*—The biggest hurdle facing maintainers is the existence of out of date documentation. As a maintainer, you like to use the documentation because it typically reflects high-level information about the software. But if one piece of information in the documentation is out of date, it makes you question the entire document, and you will less likely be willing to read it.

♦ *Publicize the changes*—Let everyone know the changes that have been made. You can use comments in the code or the change log. In any event, publicize changes so that everyone is aware of them. In some cases, the original developer might notice the change and suggest potential side effects that you did not consider.

Working around Existing Requirements and Design Bugs

You can always work around existing requirements and design bugs. It is done all the time in this industry. The real question is not how to work around existing bugs, but how to minimize the degrading effect of the workaround to prevent software from rotting and becoming unmaintainable

The answer depends on your resources and priorities and in a lot of cases, luck. The nature of a design or requirement bug in the production system means that there is no simple workaround in the implementation. If you are lucky and the bug is very localized, you might be able to get away with a simple design change. However, we are usually not that lucky. Typically, a workaround involves hijacking an artifact and making it do something it is not meant to do. For example, the artifact can be a class; instead of coming up with a new abstraction, you graft a new method and add a few member variables to it to force it to do your bidding. (Even when you use inheritance to do this, you have still performed a workaround. If the inherited class is conceptually different from the class that you have hijacked, it will probably come back to haunt you at a later time.) The artifact could also be the programmatic flow. For example, you put in an extra branch or some delays, and the program then does what you want it to do, even though you have just introduced a side effect to the function that you have changed.

The best that you can do, short of a redesign, is to understand the trade-off of the workaround and document it. If the system was well designed from the start, workarounds are glaringly obvious. They are codes and artifacts that deviate from a unified vision. But if the software was not well designed or it had been in maintenance mode for a year or so, it might be difficult to spot workarounds. The software will lack a certain conceptual integrity, and everything will look like one big hack. Regardless, clear documentation of the incongruity will help other maintainers understand code and prevent them from undermining your workarounds.

Regression Test Thoroughly

As mentioned many times in this chapter, regression testing is perhaps the most important element in the maintenance process, especially if you have not achieved total comprehension of the system. Obviously, you have to test the maintenance work. But regression testing means that you have test cases from the time before the maintenance work, and you run these test cases through the new system. By definition, maintenance modification occurs when the system is already in production, and the last thing you want to do is to break something that was working. If a bug is serious enough, the entire release might need to be rolled back. Making changes upon changes upon changes can rapidly degrade the maintainability of the software.

Tip

When in doubt, test. When not in doubt, test again. When you finish testing, test some more.

Keep Track of Changes

Tracking changes is more than just writing comments when you commit the changes into the configuration management repository. You also want to track the nature of the change request, the originator of the request, the files modified, and the effort needed to fulfill the request as a function of each request. But it is useless to track changes and modifications if no one ever looks at them. These measurements can be collected and used to help you analyze the progress and maturity of the software. They can also be used to identify and predict bug-prone modules that might be due for an inspection or a redesign. They can help you convince your management that the system has become unmaintainable and needs to be redesigned. The following items are some of the more useful measurements that you can gather from your change tracking system to help you understand the evolution of your software.

♦ *Determine where the change requests are coming from*. If most of the change requests are coming from sales and marketing, find out exactly what they are selling. Maybe their concept of the product is different from the development group's idea of the product, and a discussion with sales and marketing might be in order. Instead of continuing to make changes to the existing system, it might make sense to develop a new product to meet the everchanging market needs.

♦ *Identify modules with an abnormally high number of changes*. There are a few reasons why a module might have more changes than average. (1) The module might be bug-prone. This can be determined by looking at the originators of the change requests that affected the module. If the module is indeed bug-prone, it would be prudent to reevaluate the design and implementation of the module. (2) The module is a do-everything module. Depending on your system, this might be a design and architectural weakness. (3) The module is the hub of the system. This means that a lot of modules depend on this module, and whenever someone needs to change another part of the system, they are forced to modified this change-prone module. This could imply a design weakness, and the design of the system related to this module might need to be reevaluated. At a minimum, this means that whenever you want to modify this change-prone module, you need to do so with caution because the change can affect a large part of the system.

♦ *Track the scope of changes*. A scope of changes can simply be defined as the number of files, functions, classes, or lines of codes modified per change request. If the scope is usually small, it means that either the change request is localized, or the software modules are still loosely coupled, and there aren't a lot of dependencies between software modules. However, if the scope is usually large, an alarm should go off in your mind. It means that either the system is not doing what it should be doing, or the system has become unmaintainable (i.e., it has a lot of intermodule dependencies.) Tracking the history of the scope of changes can provide a valuable clue into the evolution of the system's maintainability.

♦ *Track the effort of changes*. The effort of change measures the amount of time a maintainer spends understanding the change request, understanding the code, making the changes, testing the changes, and submitting the changes. By itself, the effort of changes helps track the cost of maintenance. But combined with the scope of change, it could tell us if the program or the module is approaching unmaintainability. For example, if the maintainer spends a significant amount of time making a single line change to the software, it could cast doubt on the comprehensibility of the software.

When Do You Give Up?

It is hard to give up on a software system. The old Cobol mainframe systems that were used to house corporate data developed 20 years ago are still in operation today. To transition into the PC era, C middleware was created to define a standard set of application programming interfaces (API) to hide the complexity of the original systems. The middleware sends a request to the mainframe using a particular type of messaging protocol. It can also use some form of API if it exists, or it could do screen scraping. Fast forward to the Internet era, and the data in the mainframe all of a sudden needs to be Web enabled. So a set of Java servlets were created using Enterprise Java Beans (EJB) to talk to the original C middleware, which talks to the COBOL mainframe system (or you can replace servlets and EJB with Active Server Page (ASP) and COM in the Windows environment, if you prefer.) Instead of phasing out old systems, we tend to pile wrappers (or middleware) on top of wrappers on top of wrappers to get the behavior that we want.

From the point of view of risk management, this makes perfect sense. We already know that the mainframe works, so when we put a wrapper on top of that, we only have to worry about the correctness of the wrapper. Whereas to create a new system, we have to worry about the correctness of the entire system. We also have to concern ourselves with migration of the existing data to the new architecture. Furthermore, we need to come up with a new set of operating procedures to handle errors in the new system. Dealing with a wrapper seems so simple in comparison to creating a new system. And the cost of creating a new system seems so astronomical in comparison to the incremental cost of maintenance.

It seems that we will only give up when there are some external influences to force our hand. What are some forces that could make us phase out old systems?

◆ *Running out of replacement parts*—Software runs on a computer, and computers become obsolete. When they do, and you can't find replacement parts, it might be time to think about porting the software system to another platform.

◆ *Running out of maintainers*—During the Y2K crisis, we heard stories of old Cobol programmers coming out of retirement and getting paid obscene amounts of money to help fix the Y2K bugs. This occurred because the new generation of software developers had no training in Cobol or mainframe environments. Within the next 10 years, the number of Cobol literate developers might be down to a few thousand. Then who will be around to maintain these systems?

◆ *Third-party vendor goes out of business*—If your system relies on third-party solutions, and the vendor that supplies the solution is no longer in business to support the software, it might be a perfect opportunity to change and redesign your system.

◆ *New personnel*—When there is a change in top-level management or technical expertise, there is often a chance for wholesale change to a system. The new person hired might have a completely different idea of how software should be constructed. He or she might see many unacceptable risks and defects with the existing design, or there might be other reasons that a change is made. Usually when there are changes at the top of an organization, there is a chance that an "unmaintainable" system might be discarded.

♦ *No possibility of teaching an old dog a new trick*—Over time, a software system might become so rigid that it becomes impossible to make any changes without breaking something. Or it is simply impossible to modify the software to meet the new requirements.

Ultimately, the decision between maintaining an existing system versus creating a new system needs to be made by the management. However, as technical professionals, we can provide managers with measurements that can help them understand the cost of maintaining an unmaintainable system. Decision makers are not going to commit to a new development project just because you are having nightmares about the existing system. But you can help persuade them to make changes by giving them numbers and metrics that are related to the cost of maintenance. Numbers such as bug introduction rates, bug fix rates, and debugging efforts can help the management see when maintenance is becoming a hopeless cause. These numbers are especially beneficial when the bug introduction rate is increasing faster than the bug fix rate, and the debugging effort is growing exponentially with time. The rate of introducing a new feature and the efforts required to implement a new feature might also be a convincing number that you can use to argue your cause.

Summary

As we have demonstrated in this chapter, creating maintainable software is not simply a technical issue. Due to the nature of the technology, design for maintainability can only carry you so far. Because software is "soft", it can be easily changed to suit our needs of the moment. This flexibility is our undoing. To us, creating maintainable software is to create a maintenance environment under which the software will be created and evolved. The maintenance environment is a combination of technology, process and a way of thinking. We have presented ideas that will help make your software more comprehensible. We have described ways to design and think about maintainable architecture and design. We have also proposed the creation of maintenance process in conjunction with software design and development. Ideas presented in this chapter can help you create more tractable maintenance tasks.

However, like debugging, maintenance is a poorly understood subject in software engineering. Like debugging, maintenance also does not receive a lot of airtime. Rarely do we consider maintenance when we create software, and none of the popular methodologies addresses software maintenance. We are creating the legacy systems of the future. It will not be surprising if our children and our children's children curse and mock our primitive tools and attempts to create and support software.

Bug Puzzle

You are working for an Application Service Provider (ASP) company. Basically, your company creates and hosts applications for your clients on the Internet. You have been working there for two years, and everything is going great. The company is growing in the midst of dot-com fallouts. You are getting more clients, you are adding new hardware to handle the increasing traffic on your applications. The development team grew from 10 people to about 30. By all accounts, your company is doing great! However, there is a nagging feeling in the back of your mind. What could be wrong? (A Hint: What is the reason that the development team grew from 10 to 30? i.e. what are they working on?)

Chapter 15
Debugging as a Profession

Matt Telles

Throughout this book, we have discussed debugging as it applies to development, testing, and the methodologies of software engineering. In this chapter, however, we explore the concept of debugging as a profession unto itself.

The notion of a professional debugger is one that is likely to be scoffed at by most "purist" software developers. Debugging is something that is done as a facet of the development process or in maintaining software after it has been released. Debugging, like debuggers, is a set of tools and techniques that are used to solve the problems encountered due to poor implementations of software.

As you have seen throughout this book, however, debugging is not an ad hoc art. Instead, it is a science; one that should be applied at all stages of the software development process, from initial requirements analysis to final deployment and maintenance. In this chapter, we explore the concept of debugging as a profession of its own. As with the architects, requirements analysts, software engineers, and testers, debugging could be a full-time position. We explore the requirements of such a position, the benefits to the company, and the skills and attributes that would best describe such a person.

Learning to Be a Debugger

Certainly, the first question that comes to mind when you discuss debugging as a profession is how you learn to be one. After all, there is no degree in debugging. There are no tests you can take that prove that you know how to debug or not. You rarely see the position advertised in newspapers. "Wanted: Debugger for large-scale software development company. Must understand basic principles of debugging and be able to find bugs in under a week." Although it would certainly be an interesting ad to run, it is doubtful that you would get a lot of applicants. So how do you learn to be a professional debugger?

Working on the Maintenance and Enhancement Team

One of the best and easiest ways to learn debugging of a system is to work in an environment that does more debugging than original coding. As you have seen throughout this book, the skills needed for debugging are rarely developed through writing code. This is unfortunate, but it's simply a fact of life. For this reason, the best recommendation for learning to be a debugger is to work on a project that has a lot of bugs.

It's certainly amusing to watch people's faces when you tell them you want to work on a project with lots of bugs. Finding and fixing bugs is usually considered "grunt work" belonging to the lowest paid and lowest tenured person in a company. New entry-level people are often sent to the "bug mines," as established software projects with some history behind them are known. The way this usually occurs is simple. First, the high-powered, long-tenured, developers of the company begin a new project. Often, because they have considerable authority and know their subject matter well, they will be given the task of developing something on the level of the *death march* scale.[1] These are projects that are given varying requirements, with compacted schedules, and little hope of success. A death march project can succeed, however. Usually though, the developer involved in it will often flee once it does. At this point, you have the worst of all possible scenarios in the development world. A project that was done with little or no forethought, little testing, and a schedule that allowed for no thinking about future expansion, maintainability, or the actual desires of the user.

Death march projects that succeed are the ideal breeding grounds for the professional debugger. It's not the way most of us would like to break into the industry, however. So how can we better prepare people to work as debuggers without driving them screaming out of the industry? The answer lies in the maintenance and enhancement team. Any successful project (that is, one that sells or is used) will require maintenance. Certainly by this point in the book, you realize it is simply impossible to turn out bug-free software. For this reason, any production-quality software will contain at least some percentage of bugs. This will happen in even the best of software. In these "best of show" projects, the best debuggers are born and bred. Because the software is in demand, and the projects were done well, the work of debugging is more of a scientific endeavor than a death march scene.

You might think that if you want to be a better debugger, you should begin by going back and fixing bugs within your own projects. This couldn't be further from the truth. Fixing your own code is a world apart from fixing someone else's code. For one thing, you know

---

[1] *Death March: The Complete Software Developer's Guide to Surviving 'Mission Impossible' Projects (Yourdon Computing Series)*, Ed Yourdon, Prentice Hall, Upper Saddle River New Jersey, 1999. ISBN: 0130146595.

where everything is in the system. For another, you understand what the system was designed to do and how it accomplishes that task. This eliminates the entire job of code and process understanding for the system. In fact, you will likely make the problem worse, as you have no way of seeing the system any other way than the one in which you originally implemented it. It is considerably better to start with someone else's codebase and work your way into the understanding phase from that point.

How do you get assigned to a maintenance and enhancement project at your own company? Unless you are working for a very unusual enterprise, it is more likely to happen to you than not. In fact, one of the best ways to move onto such a project is simply to express the desire to do so. Because nobody else is likely to volunteer for such a position, you will often be given your choice of maintenance jobs to take on. If you are a manager, assigning people to such tasks is often met with resistance and anger. This is because these positions are seen as dead-end jobs at many companies. People who do a good job of debugging a system are usually stuck with that system for the remainder of their careers at the company. It is your task to see that the people who do the best jobs move to other positions in the debugging arena. In this way, you can encourage the development of really good debuggers within your company. As you will see in the "Where can Professional Debuggers be Used" section later in this chapter, having a company that contains professional debuggers will make your job easier and produce better-quality software in the end.

Tip

Move your best debuggers from project to project to improve learning and avoid boredom.

Once you have become a part of the maintenance team, how do you hone your debugging skills? The best way, of course, is to debug code. Take the methodologies and techniques that we have discussed in this book and apply them to problems as they come up. Find the set of techniques and approaches that work best for you. Not everyone will select the same set of techniques, nor will any two debuggers approach a problem in exactly the same way. This doesn't make debugging any less of a science than, say, astronomy. Given any three astronomers, you will find that they use three slightly different approaches to show, for example, how the universe expands or contracts. Not one of them would be "wrong," as far as we know, but they would all be different. When you look at a mathematical proof, you do not examine it for the correct order of steps. Instead, you look at the steps themselves to be sure that they make sense and that they follow logically from step to step. Likewise, with debugging, it is not the order or the specific technique that is the issue; but rather, it is the logical way in which the techniques are applied to each other.

To be a true professional debugger, you need to debug many different applications. Applications for different environments, different industries, and applications written by different groups. The problem with debugging the same applications by the same groups in the same industries is that you only acquire a body of knowledge that cannot be applied to other systems. When you move to a new environment, you will find that the items you took for granted do not exist. Although it is true that most applications written by a single company tend to fall in the same industry, you will be amazed at the wide range of variation within that industry. Some systems will be written for the end user. Other systems will be written for customer service people. There is also an entire class of application that will only apply to the operations group within a company. All of these applications are likely to contain bugs. In addition, all of the bugs are likely to be different, because different kinds of applications spawn different kinds of problem types. By utilizing the knowledge you have gained in this book to understand what the most likely kinds of bugs are for each environment, you will have a head start on predicting what kinds of problems you will encounter.

A professional debugger can, in fact, predict in advance many of the sorts of problems that will occur given an application type and the developers who are creating it. In addition, by knowing what the scheduling for that application is, you can often predict how many problems of each severity level you are likely to encounter. This makes the professional debugger essential to the management of software development projects as well. Don't think that simply because you debug applications you are destined to be a grunt. In fact, we can easily see a time when debugging will be a natural path to project management.

Tip

Good debuggers can predict how many and what type of bugs they are likely to encounter.

A Good Way to Learn the Code

Suppose that you do not want to be a full-time professional debugger. Why then would you volunteer for a debugging assignment, where you are likely to just fix other people's problems? The role of the professional debugger can also be a transitional one. A role that leads you to bigger and better opportunities. Some people refer to this as "paying your dues." One of the biggest drawbacks to the lack of available development staff is that newer developers, fresh out of school, are often thrown into the fray of developing brand new code for brand new application areas. Because these new developers have not spent time in the industry, they lack the essential skills needed for the projects they work on to succeed.

The very best way to learn how to develop code properly is to learn from other people's mistakes. After all, if you see the kind of mistakes that other people make, you can try not to make them yourself. This applies not only to writing code, but also to the processes that you should adhere to while doing the development. Imagine, for example, that you find that a given method of an object doesn't work when you pass it a null pointer. Yet, nowhere in the documentation or requirements does it say that it should be passed a non-null pointer. When you are writing your own code, and your method accepts a pointer value, you will be certain to remember to make that check, right? Well, maybe not always, but once you see it a few times, you will remember it forever. For this reason, debuggers are also excellent at helping to design and implement systems, not to mention knowing how to test them. By seeing all the mistakes made in the past, you can ensure that your future work contains none of these mistakes. This will simply lead to new mistakes, of course, but at least you will be able to eliminate large classes of errors in your future work.

Where Can Professional Debuggers Be Used?

If you are a professional debugger, you need to earn your keep. Not all companies will have projects at the stage when debugging is needed, so why should they hire you? It seems like a rather expensive extra to have around in a time when cost-cutting might be in the works. For startups, companies that have no product at all but are developing one, would it make sense to hire a debugger at the same time that you hire the remainder of the project team? We will argue that not only does it make sense, but in addition, the use of a professional debugger should be considered essential in any project, new or old.

At Design Time

Why would anyone want to have a debugger around when designing a system? That's like having a handyman around when you are building a new apartment building. It doesn't appear to make any sense. If you think about it, however, there is nobody you'd really rather have around at that point. First, the debugger is used to seeing problems in the design of systems because he or she has had to track them down and fix them in the past. Second, debuggers understand what makes a system nonmaintainable. Do you want to start with a design that makes the system impossible to maintain and enhance in the future? Of course not.

There are a number of reasons that debuggers are useful at design time: They are accustomed to working their way through the system and discovering how things work. Given a design plan for a system, they can work their way from point A to point B and see what holes are encountered along the way. One of the biggest problems at implementation time is discovering elements that don't quite mesh in the design. This forces the implementation team to make their own design choices. There was a reason that you hired a designer in the first place, wasn't there? So, if you eliminate the possibility that they will encounter problems in making the design work, you eliminate an entire host of bugs.

Debuggers understand cause and effect. The impact of certain choices in the design stage not only impacts the implementation, but often the performance of the system as well. Performance problems are one area in which debuggers often have extensive experience. As with most problems, if you catch a performance issue before it becomes a programming problem, it's a lot easier to fix.

Software engineering pundits say that a bug caught at design time can be up to 500 times less expensive to fix than one caught after the product has been released. Because debuggers are good at catching these sorts of design bugs, due to their testing and debugging experience, doesn't it make sense to have them available at design time?

At Requirements Time

Bring up requirements to a typical software development shop, and you hear something along the lines of "We have requirements analysts to do that. We don't need any developers involved in requirements gathering." It is hard to see how anything could be farther from the truth. After all, if the requirements are incomplete, or incompatible, there is simply no way for the project to succeed. Lack of quality requirements is by far the most common reason for project failure. The question is, who should we have at the table to represent the development group at requirements gathering time? The answer we suggest is, of course, the debugger.

Requirements gathering is a two-fold process. First, you need to understand what it is the user is trying to accomplish so that you can implement a solution. This is the "big picture" problem that we have discussed as being important to debugging applications. Who better than a debugger to see the complete problem? The second part of the requirements gathering process is to make sure that your requirements are complete and compatible. Although it is difficult to see whether requirements are complete or not, the task is considerably easier when you try to put it all together. Once again, this is what debuggers do best. Debuggers inspect all of the various parts of the system and assemble them together into a flow. They can then look at these flows to see whether they run from one end to another. If the flow is incomplete, the requirements are incomplete. Like design problems, requirements problems are expensive. Why not have someone there that is used to dealing with such problems? Compatible requirements, on the other hand, are the perfect breeding grounds for bugs. If requirement A says to do one thing and requirement B says to do something completely contradictory, you will have problems with the final system. Here too, the debugger comes shining through.

In most cases, the debugger would be a consultant to the requirements phase. Debuggers are good at seeing and solving problems. It is less obvious, however, that debuggers are also good at interviewing people to understand problems. When you are given a bug to work on, you will find yourself going back to the original source of the problem report and questioning the source about what he or she was doing before the problem occurred. You might find yourself asking if there were other applications running, or if a particular hardware configuration was being used. All of this information is equally important in the gathering of requirements. The interviewing process is probably more important to the debugger than to any other role in the software development process. Why not put that skill to work in the environment where it is best suited? Make sure a debugger is available when you are in the requirements stage.

At Code Inspection Time

Do you do code inspections? If you don't, you really should consider doing them. Code inspections are one of the most efficient and cost-effective ways to find problems before they creep into the released product. A code inspection is simply a formal reading and review of the code by a group of unbiased individuals. The idea is to bring in as many people as you can deal with at one time to look over the code and point out potential problems they might see. The starting point of a code inspection is a body of source code for a project. The ending point for the inspection is a list of comments, critiques, and action items that the developer who wrote the original code should attend to. It's probably fairly obvious why you would want a debugger available at this stage of the development process, but let's take a look at some of the less obvious reasons.

One of the more serious problems with code inspections is that they tend to be done by people who write new code. For this reason, issues of maintainability rarely come up and when they do, it is usually a matter of "I wouldn't do it that way, I would do it this way," with no real supporting reasons. Debuggers are accustomed to dealing with completed code and know what makes it maintainable or not. They can give accurate, unbiased opinions on whether they could understand and easily modify a body of code at maintenance time. In addition, debuggers can spot problems that developers of new software are never going to see. For example, you might write a function that uses a database API function to get back some data from the database. A new developer would look at this function and not see a problem. A debugger, however, would realize that the company had changed database systems three times in the last five years and would insist on wrapping the API functions for the database in some generic way so that when the database system changed again, the system would require less work.

Another problem with code reviews is that of ego. When you write code for a living, you have a tendency to invest a lot of yourself in your work. It is painful to have someone else point out problems in the code, and you often accuse them of having their own agendas for their criticisms. In many cases, this is the truth. Because each developer is likely to come up with their own way of implementing something, they are unlikely to see your approach as the best possible one. After all, they didn't think of it. When a code inspection turns into a battle of egos, there will never be a winner. There will only be a set of losers. The ultimate loser, of course, is going to be the project, which is not going to have the best possible code implementing it. When you think about it, that's the only thing that really matters. Debuggers don't come into code inspections with an ego, because they don't work on new code. Instead, they look at the code from the personal perspective of someone who is going to have to fix it. All they care about is that the code be as clean and as bug-free as possible.

Another problem with code inspections is that of competition. When you have a group of developers together, they are always in some form of competition. The one that does the best work is the one most likely to be chosen for the hot new project that everyone wants to work on. For this reason, there is a tendency to put other people's work down, even if they don't mean to do it. This is really just another form of ego, but a less blatant one, and one that often is completely unconscious. Debuggers, however, don't compete with other developers. After all, if there is a hot new project, they are eventually going to work on it. So why worry about whether they are the stars of the project or not? By the time debuggers get around to debugging an application, it has lost a lot of its glitter and appeal anyway.

You can see why having debuggers at the code inspection meeting is a good idea. They can see problems that developers of new code won't, because they are accustomed to only debugging code to the point where it works sufficiently for the requirements specification, but before users actually try to use the system. They can act as mediators when issues of ego come up. In addition, they have been exposed to many, many coding styles and techniques and have learned which ones are most likely to cause harm in the long run and which ones are most likely to be the easiest to maintain.

At Code Turnover Time

Code turnover is a phase of a project that most development people, programmers, and managers never think about. At some point, the development staff has to pack up its editors and development logs and move on to another project. You can't expect developers to work on a single project for their entire lives; it's simply not realistic. You can either give them new work to do, or they will go to another company to find it. Whether code turnover is a clean, well-defined event or whether it is a chaotic disaster is often determined by the people on the project and whether they understand the process. The code turnover phase of a project occurs when the last of the original development team leaves the project and hands the reins over to someone else to either develop or maintain the product.

There are really two possible approaches to using a debugger at code turnover time. First, you can use a debugger as a bridge person to go from the original development team to the new maintenance or development team. Second, you can use a debugger to evaluate the "transition documents," the code and documentation for the system, to see whether the new group will understand the system. Let's take a quick look at each one of these scenarios to understand how each might fit into your corporate culture and project model.

Using the debugger as a bridge is an approach that many companies utilize to get from one phase to another in a project. Debuggers are the ideal for the transition because they have a tendency to be involved in all facets of the project, from development and documentation to testing and installation. Because debuggers know a little something about all of the pieces of the project's pie, they make good sources of information about each one. In addition, because debuggers are often required to dig into things to discover how they work, they make an ideal detective for a project by knowing where to start looking. When you think about it, the only other choices for a bridge person are developers and testers. Developers are not good choices, primarily because of the negative perception of being "left behind" when others go on to new projects and new teams. Testers are not really good choices simply because they do not have the breadth of experience necessary to understand the system internally. Testers have an excellent grasp on how the system works and how people use it, but they do not usually understand how the internals are put together and what impacts what other feature.

The debugger as an evaluator of transition documents is a newer concept, but one that has a lot of merit. One of the biggest problems that occurs in project teams is the lack of documentation that has any value to anyone else but the writer. Consider, for example, a document that shows you the methods of a C++ or Visual Basic class. Your typical document contains a listing of each method in the class along with a definition of the types of information that each one should be passed when it is called in the program. If you are the writer of the document, you see this as useful. It tells you what you need to know when you need to know it. But how does it help the person that really doesn't understand how to use the class or when it should be used? How does it help someone that is looking for a class to do something and has no idea what it might be called? As a debugger, these are the questions you are most accustomed to dealing with. As a result, you can point out the need for "User's Guides" to the code rather than reference material. After all, if you know how to use the class, you can always look at the code itself to see how it is supposed to be called. In this case, letting the code be its own documentation (for a technical manual) makes more sense than duplicating the information in two places. Also, because documents are often mostly static, whereas code is mostly dynamic, it is important that the document reflect reality as it is now rather than as it was when the document was written.

Very few companies take the transition period for software seriously. As a professional debugger, this is your best chance to shine at a company and show just how valuable you can be. Unfortunately, the life of a debugger is rarely a well-rewarded one, so any chance that you have to validate your existence is one that you should leap all over.

Summary of Project Phases

As you can see, the life of a debugger is considerably more than sitting in a dingy back office with no windows fixing bugs late into the night. The professional debugger of tomorrow will be involved in every phase of project development, from initial conception to final installation and beyond. Companies should seriously consider looking at the people that they have and examining them for the skills that make a good debugger. These skills can, as we have shown, be used in all phases of the company's work and can often replace the duties of two or three other people. This saves money, saves time, and allows for a better generalization of the company talent. All of these are good things.

Of course, the next natural question is: What exactly are the skills needed to be a good debugger? That, as it happens, is the next topic we cover in this chapter. Knowing what you need to be good at is a useful way to determine whether you are cut out for a particular job. In this case, we examine the traits of really good debuggers and see what is good and bad for the position.

Traits of a Good Professional Debugger

When you think about good debuggers, what are the traits you associate with them? The ability to make lightning-quick decisions as to what might be causing the problem? The ability to work long hours deep into the night the day before a project is to be released? The ability to subsist on "flat food" that can be slid under the door while the debugger is working on a particularly hairy problem? All of these are images that come to us when we think about horrible debugging jobs in the past. However, they are really the exceptions rather than the rules. Good debuggers need the ability to debug over the long haul, to keep the code maintainable, and to make sure that new problems are not introduced into the system when they are fixing existing problems. What are the personality traits that lead to these abilities? From years of observation and from watching those that could become professional debuggers, we have identified the traits that good professional debuggers possess in the following sections.

Tact

Debugging your own code requires that you admit to yourself that you have made a mistake or didn't understand the problem. Debugging someone else's code requires that you tell the other person (in one fashion or another) that he or she has made a mistake. It is against human nature to deal easily with the fact that we have made mistakes. We become defensive and tend to strike back when we feel we are being accused of any wrong doing. Dealing with the personality issues in debugging requires a degree of tact.

Tact, one of my former managers used to tell me, is the skill of being polite to someone when you really feel like choking the life out of him. It is the ability to not assign blame or make people self-conscious about their mistakes, and simply do the job and get the best possible product out the door. A debugger that has tact will fix problems as they are assigned without running to the person that created the bug and yelling at him or her. In addition, tact means not making a production out of finding and fixing bugs, because that is simply part of the job.

Although tact is a trait we should all maintain in the computer industry (and all others, for that matter), it is particularly important in the role of debuggers. If you keep people thinking on a professional level and treat all problems as problems in the code and not problems with the programmer, you will create a much more stress-free working environment. With woefully inadequate schedule times and constantly changing requirements, we are under more than enough stress in the work world. There is simply no reason to add to that stress. Strive to work with the utmost tact and respect, and you will find yourself solving problems at a more than acceptable rate.

Patience

If there is a single most important trait of a really good professional debugger, it is patience. Patience comes into play in so many different ways in the debugging process. You need patience to wait until you can see the symptoms of a bug and patience to wait until you are sure about the causes before leaping in with a solution. If you are patient, good things will usually come your way. Nowhere is this more true than in the debugging world.

One of the most common problems for developers is the need to rush on to the "next fun thing" without adequately testing and debugging their code. This is one of the reasons that code is often released before it is ready. The work of testing, debugging, documenting, and analyzing the performance of code isn't much fun, nor is it very glamorous. Human beings do not generally do dull work very well. This is especially true for intelligent human beings. Because most programmers are on the high end of the intelligence scale, they will most likely want to get away from the dullest work. If you are patient, and work your way through the process completely, you are much less likely to create problems that will haunt you down the road. In addition, if you are patient and do a good job, you will be rewarded by being allowed to move on to the new fun software application without being dragged back in to consult and fix the old application. Patience is a virtue that is often rewarded.

Patience is important in the debugging process itself. You need to make sure that you understand the problem before you can fix it. You need to make sure that your fix works before you release it. You need to make sure that your fix doesn't break anything else in the process. All of these steps require the patience to follow the process and not cut any corners. Debugging is *not* a good field for those that "think they know what they are doing." If you want to debug, you must follow the process to the letter, or you are certain to cause more problems than you solve. If you are patient, and follow the process each and every time, you will be rewarded by an easier time debugging and a happier group of people around you.

Patience is also important in the debugging interview process. It is quite common for people to omit critical details in describing a bug, simply because they do not see them as important. Little things like what they were doing before the bug happened, or the fact that they were trying to run an MS-Windows application on a Macintosh. Hey, it happens. It is often necessary to go back two or three times to talk to the observer of the bug. If you do not have the patience to sort through what the user is saying, and simply leap at the first conclusion you reach, you will often find yourself pursuing blind trails and wasting a lot of time and energy.

Detective Skills

After reading the preceding chapters in this book, you understand the importance of detective skills in the process of debugging. The question is, what are detective skills? Think of the great detectives in history: Sherlock Holmes, Charlie Chan, Scooby Doo, and others. What did they all have in common? They noticed details that other people overlooked. They stayed on the trail when other people saw dead ends. They ate really weird things (what *is* a Scooby Snack?). When you read through mystery novels, you are actually watching the truly elite debuggers at work.

When you are debugging, you should think of yourself as one of those great mystery detectives. Make sure that you follow each lead that you encounter while you are running through the symptoms of the bug because each is a clue to the mystery. Try to understand the motive of the person that committed the crime, that is, created the bug. Most bugs are caused because of a lack of patience or a lack of understanding of the problem. Make sure that you understand the problem. If you do, you can envision how it could be solved and, in so doing, understand why the programmer made the mistake. If you just focus on the surface behavior of the bug, you often destroy valuable clues to the mystery.

In all of the great murder mysteries, you always discover that evidence was planted. In all of the great bugs of the world, you will discover that the symptoms are quite often just a façade that covers up the real problem. Make sure that you dig down deep and preserve all of the evidence before you arrest the bug.

Another facet of detective work is knowing what has changed in a crime scene. Some of the most baffling crimes of history have been solved because someone noticed that something was out of the ordinary. The Sherlock Holmes case of the dog that didn't bark is a classic example of this. Likewise, if you have an output log from an application that suddenly develops a bug, you should examine that log to see if anything has changed. Even the most minor difference could be an important clue in solving the mystery of the new bug.

Ability to Deal with Stress

In today's "get it done yesterday" world, everchanging requirements and the emphasis on revenue figures ensures that stress is a natural part of the software engineer's day. For debuggers, this stress is often doubled or tripled because a bug needs to be fixed immediately before it causes any more harm. The trade journals and daily newspapers abound with stories of companies that have crashing Web sites or security leaks in their software. Someone is needed to fix those problems, and that someone is quite often the debugger for the project. It is one thing to debug a project that will be released in six months. It is quite another to debug a system that is expected to be up 24 hours a day, 7 days a week and is crashing on the hour. If you are on such a project, you don't need to be reminded of what stress is or what the effects can be on the development staff.

Stress has two effects on developers and debuggers that are worth mentioning. First, it makes them irritable and short-tempered. This combination is harmful because it tends to reduce their patience, which results in missing important clues. Second, stress makes them less interested in the project as a whole and more interested in simply removing the source of the stress. This causes problems because people who don't want to work on a project are unlikely to have the incentive and desire to do a good job. If you don't care about the outcome of the project, you are not going to do your very best.

How can you reduce stress when you are in a problem-solving mode under serious time constraints? One way is to simply walk away from the problem for a while. You can either work on another problem, or just remove yourself from the situation for a time. Go jogging; exercise is a great way to reduce stress. There are a number of different ways that you can get your mind to relax and allow your subconscious to take on the problem.

The more confidence you have in yourself and your abilities, the less stress is going to bother you. The more control you have over the schedules and requirements creep that goes on in a project, the less stress will be generated. If you are a manager, you should understand that motivation will only carry a project so far. Incentives, such as bonuses or extra vacation, are only minor motivators when the people on your project are under severe stress. It is natural for stress to come at the end of a project, but only because of the way development is done nowadays. In an ideal world, we would have wrapped up the project two weeks before the deadline and would be spending the extra time testing and planning for the next release. If you are scheduling your people to work 12-hour days, be very sure that you only do it for a few days or weeks at a time. People simply cannot maintain that level of effort for long periods of time without getting very stressed. Once stress exists, it is very difficult to eliminate.

Engineering/Scientific Methodology

The engineering methodology is important to the professional debugger. This methodology states that first you observe the phenomena you want to explain. Once you have observed the event, you should put together a theory that explains all of the symptoms you have seen and would not result in other end products. That theory should then be tested and the results verified. If the theory appears to test out, you then go a step further and predict the outcome given another set of input. If that outcome is also verified, you may assume that your theory adequately explains the event you are witnessing.

What does this mean for the professional debugger? As we have stated many times, when you are debugging an application, you need to follow the process. This process is nothing more than a scientific method. Observe first, form a hypothesis, test your hypothesis, offer a solution, implement the solution, and then test the solution. It doesn't seem like rocket science, but in fact it is the basis for rocket science. There is no way to short-circuit the system and come to a conclusion any faster. There is no way to avoid observation or making a hypothesis. Any professional debugger that tries to skip any of these steps should feel uneasy about his choice, and terrified by his conclusion.

One of the points we have tried to make in this book is that process is important. The better the process, and the more faithfully that process is followed, the better the results. Processes, of course, need to be refined to take into account new knowledge. The question that is always asked is, where do you come up with the process in the first place? For debugging, the answer is the scientific method. Start with this process, and add in the steps that you discover along the way. For example, you might start testing your hypothesis by feeding specialized input data into the system. This works well if you are working with a standard, user-oriented application. What happens if you are working with a real-time embedded system, however? You can bench-test the hypothesis in a simulator, but that is not an ideal solution. The scientific method requires that you observe the problem in its most realistic setting. For this reason, you might modify the process to include some kind of specialized hardware that can feed in real data, which you modify before it reaches the target system. At a later time, testing a new form of input data is a simple matter of modifying that data in a different way. As a result, you have created a process by which the hypothesis testing can go forward.

If you want to be a world-class professional debugger, you simply have to follow the rules. This is not to say that at some point in your career you will not follow some of them in your head without doing them formally. It is quite common for people to follow the rules to the letter, but appear to omit many steps along the way. All of these steps are being followed, of course, but only in the mental process of the person performing the work. For example, you might observe a bug that has been reported as you are working on something else, always keeping your eye out for symptoms that might apply to another problem. Hypotheses might be made mentally and tested by adding scaffolding code to the application to verify that what you think is happening is really happening. This is really the essence of what makes a good debugger and what makes for successful debugging. When the process of the scientific method becomes so ingrained that it becomes a habit, you will know you have become a true professional debugger.

Low Ego

If there is one negative feature that is most likely to interfere with getting any sort of productive work done, it is ego. Ego makes you unwilling to listen to what other people have to say. Ego makes communication difficult because you feel that you know better and do not need input from others. Worst of all, ego blinds us to the mistakes we make, forcing us to blame others for our problems. We dismiss bugs and errors in our code as "unimportant" or "something the user will never see." All bugs are serious, and someone, somewhere, is going to find the bug annoying and bad mouth the application because of it.

How can you avoid having a huge ego in your work? The best way to avoid having ego problems hinder your work is to keep your attitude strictly professional. This is quite difficult for many people to do. For some professionals, such as programmers, they are expected to put their heart and souls into their work. It is hard to give that level of effort and not get emotionally involved. Consider, however, that work is just that, work. It is not your life and should not be treated as such. If you fail to understand that, you are destined to be disappointed with your job.

How do you recognize when your ego is getting in the way? One good way to tell is to take a step back and see yourself as others see you. Are you making arguments that are built on logic and proceed to a natural conclusion? If not, perhaps you are simply arguing because you don't think that someone else's idea is as good as yours. This is a sure sign that ego is getting in the way. If you cannot refute someone's argument without using a personal attack or a flip comment, such as "that will never work," you are letting your ego get the best of you. It is natural to do so, of course, because ego is just part of your mind's defense system. The problem is that when you allow yourself to be consumed by your ego, the quality of your work suffers because you lose objectivity. Stop every now and again and look at what you are doing. Are you doing something to make yourself feel better? Are you doing something because it will undermine someone else? Are you doing something because you honestly believe that it is the right path, having reached a conclusion by logical thinking? Until you can answer yes to the last question and no to the first two, you are allowing your ego to run your thinking.

Perseverance

In many ways, perseverance is similar to patience. Both require that you stick to something and do it right. But perseverance means sticking to something after you either believe it cannot be fixed or someone tells you to just settle for a simpler fix than you know is necessary. Perseverance means wanting the best possible solution that is reasonable. Stubbornness, by the way, is wanting the best possible solution without considering all of the factors, such as cost or resource availability.

Sometimes, perseverance will get you into trouble. While I was working for a company that produced satellite television software for settop boxes, we ran across a bug. The bug was quite serious and affected the viewing experience of the user. For this particular project, there wasn't anything more serious than ruining the television viewing experience. I looked into the problem for almost a month and a half. During this time, I acquired a new project lead who was the liaison between our group and the upper management group. The project lead was anxious to "prove himself" to the management group and leaped in to the problem to "help" fix it. Unfortunately, he chose to accept a solution that was considerably less than optimal. I fought the decision as much as I could, but was forced to allow him to make the changes he wanted. In the end, the problem became worse, additional problems cropped up, and nobody was happy. Had I persevered with my opinion and removed my ego from the process, I would have made people understand that the solution offered was not the correct one.

Perseverance has a side benefit that might not be immediately apparent. If you persevere with something instead of allowing someone else to choose a bad solution or a wrong solution to a problem, you avoid the issue of the "I told you so" situation. This occurs when you are talked out of something and the alternative doesn't work. When the failure becomes apparent, the person who was forced to change his mind has little alternative but to respond with "I told you so." This is self-defeating, of course, because all it does is make the original person feel even worse about the decision and forces him into a defensive mode.

When you have the combined traits of patience, perseverance, and egoless work, you have respect for your actions. People will trust your actions, because they know that those actions come from reasoned thought and in-depth analysis rather than a desire to be important. Your work will become more polished because you will focus more on the good of the project as a whole instead of your advancement possibilities. Because the projects you work on will succeed, you will advance in spite of yourself. Sometimes, it's really true that goodness is its own reward.

A Day in the Life

It is fitting to finish this chapter with a look at a typical day in the life of a professional debugger. This isn't an ideal day, but instead, a fairly standard one. It's a day that you might encounter during any given week on the job. The life of a debugger is far from the glitzy, stylized life you might see on some television show. There are very rarely any great break-throughs, nor are there any horrific accidents that cause us to work late into the night to get something done. Not that those late night debugging sessions don't happen, it's simply that they aren't the norm. Instead, the day of a typical debugger goes something like this.

8:00 A.M. I arrive at work, check my email, and look for new problems or reports. There are two new bugs reported in my email. One is of moderate severity, the other of low severity. I decide to leave them for a bit while I read the remainder of my mail.

8:15 A.M. I finish the mail. I bring up the application that has been running all night and check the debug log to verify that there were no problems reported. I then scan through the log to see whether the events I programmed last night actually fired. All appear to have worked normally.

8:30 A.M. I get a glass of water, and then settle down to read the specification that was forwarded to me for the newest feature to be integrated into the system. I make a few notes in the margins about possible sources of errors, and then edit the electronic document to add the notes as annotations. I send the document back to the originator with a request for a specification review later on in the week.

8:45 A.M. I begin the real work of the day, looking into the bug I had started on yesterday. I have been tracing through the code to see why a certain error branch was being reached when the actions of the user are perfectly normal. Our application, a satellite receiver for the top of a television set, allows users to configure a list of television channels the way they want to see them. This feature, called a Favorites List, allows users to customize the display of the channels so that their favorites are at the top. Unfortunately, although the list seems to work, upon exiting the set up feature, an error is reported when trying to save the favorites list. I've looked at several debug logs, but don't understand why the program is getting into this state. I add a few new debug statements to the code and recompile the system.

9:15 A.M. I download the new software package to the settop box. This takes quite a few minutes, so I go off to talk to one of the Quality Assurance people about another problem I heard mentioned in the hallway the day before. Feeling that I should gather as much information about the problem as I can before it is actually written up as a bug, I discuss the steps taken to reproduce the problem and the outcome. I agree with the tester that this is a bug and encourage him to write it up with all of the detail he has given me.

9:45 A.M. Upon returning to the debugging session, I rerun the test to duplicate the Favorites List problem. In this case, I have added tracing code to see exactly what steps the application is going through, because I cannot see anything wrong with the way the code appears to be written. Reviewing the debug output, I discover that a variable I had assumed to be a Boolean value of true is in fact set to false. Looking back through the code, I further notice that the value is only set to false if a very strange error condition is true. Because I can't see why the error condition is set, I trace back up through the code to see what might be setting that flag.

10:15 A.M. Smiling broadly, I modify the code to fix the problem. The error turns out to be a misunderstanding about the way a C++ class was used. I had assumed that the class, which implemented a date and time wrapper, defaulted to today if no data was given to it during the initialization phase. It turns out this was an incorrect assumption. The class defaults to no value at all. This caused the routine that was checking for the date the event happened to assume that it had happened before and not now. The error flag was set, and the user was taken to the error screen instead of the success screen. I initialize the variable correctly, recompile the code, install the system, and run a series of regression tests to verify that the problem is fixed.

10:45 A.M.–11:30 A.M. I run a series of tests to verify that the problem is fixed and that my fix has not broken anything else in that part of the system. Satisfied that the code is working properly and that the specification has not been altered, I check in the code with an explanation of the change I made. I then update the bug database with the notation that the bug has been fixed, indicate the change that was made, and specify which release is expected to contain the bug fix (our next release). Happily, I settle down for a quick crossword puzzle on the Internet before continuing. Hey, even debuggers need a reward!

12:00 P.M. I attend a meeting to discuss the status of the application, the future of the project, and the issues we need to deal with this week. Generally, pretty boring stuff. We don't have any new crises, so the meeting is primarily a rehash of the previous week's meeting. Sometimes I feel that meeting simply because a meeting is scheduled is the biggest time waster in the business world.

1:00 P.M.–3:00 P.M. After reviewing the remaining bugs on my slate in the bug database, I select a new one that involves setting up back-to-back recording events and checking to see if there is overlap between them. I first set up two recordings, 30 minutes each, and see whether there is overlap. There does not appear to be. I then set up another two events back to back after the first two. There still does not appear to be any overlap. Sighing, I mark the bug as "Not Reproducible" and move on down the list. The next bug involves something that only happens on Fridays. Because today is Tuesday, this would be difficult to reproduce. Finally, I settle on a "simple" bug that is reported by usability. It seems they would like a clock display on one of the pages, similar to other pages in the system. How hard could that be?

4:00 P.M. Frustrated by the undocumented code and lack of examples, I give up trying to get the clock to work right. I take a few minutes to note in my journal what I got done today and what I am thinking about for tomorrow. After saving all of my work and backing it up to the server, I clean up the disaster that is my desk and pack my stuff to go home.

4:30 P.M. I leave the office.

So there it is, a day in the life of a typical debugger. It doesn't sound all that glamorous, now does it? Does it sound appealing? Does it sound like the kind of job you could see yourself doing for years and years? If you are like most "normal" developers, the answer is probably no. However, if you got the same rush that I did when you discovered the root cause of a bug and fixed it, then perhaps the life of a professional debugger is one you might consider for your own career.

This is a typical day, not an extraordinary one. Some days the professional debugger gets nothing but failures—new bugs, reports of old bugs that have not been fixed, and new disasters caused by fixes made in the past. Some days, the news is all good. The bug that has been in the code for months and months is fixed, the customer is so happy that they write you an email to congratulate you. These types of days, however, are few and fairly between. Most days for a debugger are similar to those for a regular developer, grinding out the problems, going to meetings, and drinking lots of coffee.

The most important thing that you can take from this chapter, and in fact this entire book, is that debugging is not a black art. Debugging is not something that is an innate skill, nor is it something that you can learn simply by doing. Debugging is a science, and as a science should be treated with equal parts of disbelief and awe when new techniques and discoveries are made in the field. Like biology or geology, there are simply no magic bullets that explain how to fix any and all bugs. There are no panacea methodologies that can eliminate all bugs from code before it is ever written. Debugging is a fairly young science, and as such, mistakes are likely to be made in determining what is the "best" way to fix bugs.

Summary

The life of a professional debugger is really no different than that of any other computer professional. If debugging were considered a true profession instead of simply a job that developers do only when they are forced to, we would have a better process for software development. Debuggers should be included at all levels of the software development process because they have valuable skills that can be contributed at each level. From initial project conception to final delivery date, a professional debugger can make a difference in the software development world.

Bug Puzzle

This chapter's puzzle concerns problems that can occur due to a lack of foresight in thinking through the problem. That's the only clue for this puzzle.

The Acme DotCom Works (ADW) Corporation runs a specialized service for people. People store important information in databases in the ADW servers and can retrieve that information from anywhere in the world by using the Internet. Basically, the company is a giant electronic FiloFax.

Rather than have patrons log in with a unique user name and password, the ADW programmers wanted to come up with a better idea. They reasoned that people could forget their weird login names, especially with the requirement that they be unique. After all, there could be thousands of John Smiths in the world, said the chief architect. An off-site meeting was scheduled in which various solutions were offered.

The lead programmer on the project suggested that the Social Security Number (SSN) be used for the unique identifier. This idea was shot down for several reasons, not the least of which was the fact that people were unlikely to share their SSN with a dot com. They went back into the conference room to hash the solution out further. After many hours of debate and numerous pots of coffee and tea, one of the developers suggested phone numbers. Nearly everyone has a phone, they reasoned. Phone numbers are unique, after all. So it was with great fanfare that the ADW site was launched with the idea of phone numbers as access codes. Clever little jingles were written about using your fingers to dial into the system.

For the first few months of the life of the system, everything seemed to be going great. People didn't forget their user names, and the few that forgot their passwords were easily reminded and emailed. Life seemed to be going wonderfully for the company. Then, one cold dark day, the problems began.

It started innocently enough. One of the customer service representatives (CSR) received a call from an employee of a major downtown bank. It seemed that the customer could not log in to the system to retrieve his information. Then another call came in from the same bank—then another, and another, and another. None of the users could access their data.

At first, the CSR thought that the problem was involved with the way in which that particular bank implemented its firewalls. This would not turn out to be the case. Another downtown company called, this one an insurance firm. Once again, multiple users from the company could not retrieve information they had stored on the site. The management was in a panic over the situation. The developers were also in a panic over the problem because they didn't have a clue why it was happening. The problem was conveniently handed over to you, the debugger.

To solve the mystery of the broken account access, you need to think through the problem starting from the very initial assumptions made by the corporate developers. Work it through in your head, ask yourself the same questions they did, and see if you come up with the same answers. This is mostly a test to see whether you can spot the flaw in the reasoning of the system design. There are no programming errors to find in this example.

Appendix A
Bug Puzzle Solutions

In the world of debugging, finding the solution to a problem is the entire goal of the process. Reaching that goal, however, can be a frustrating and sometimes impossible process. Sometimes you never really know exactly what caused a bug, you simply verify that whatever it was you did fixed it. Hopefully, by now, you realize that this is a bad thing and that you should always know what was causing the bug you set out to fix.

For each chapter, you will find the solution and any lesson you might want to take from that problem.

Chapter 1

The answer to the problem turned out to be the connection between the Web servers and the database that stored the stock information. As the programmers found each problem with the database connections, due to malformed requests or syntax errors, they encountered the problem that the operations people were rebooting the database to make it reconnect. It wasn't that the Web servers were losing their connection, it was simply that they were "hung up" trying to handle the error in the database queries themselves.

How would you have known this? By studying the two groups together, rather than in separate worlds, you would have observed that the programmers were finding syntax errors and the like. Operations people, meanwhile, were simply observing that given connections to Web servers from the database were timing out waiting for requests. By combining these two facts, you would have found the real problem.

The answer to the problem? Better communication between the two groups, and a process for telling each side what the other side was doing.

Chapter 2

The problem description of the bug and architectural description of the system provided plenty of clues to help you deduce the potential causes of this behavior.

The description "The page is loaded correctly 34 times and incorrectly 12 times" implies the following:

♦ The originating source of the data that is used to display the page is correct, because if the originating source was incorrect, the page would be loaded incorrectly all the time. This observation rules out the database as a culprit.

♦ If the database has the correct content, then it must be the application server that is serving the bad data. Are all application servers producing bad data? Unlikely, because our observation shows that only one in four pages is incorrect (three correct pages for every incorrect page). This observation implies that one of the application servers is at fault, since we have four application servers in the system.

How can we verify the hypothesis that one of the application servers is responsible for producing the incorrect Web page? If you have the appropriate infrastructure in place, this should pose no problem. You can simply send the request directly to the application server and see what the result of the request looks like. However, without the capability to directly interrogate the application servers, it might be difficult to verify the hypothesis directly. But let us assume that the hypothesis is correct, that we were able to determine the particular application server as faulty.

Following this train of thought, is the bug in the code of the application server? Checking the version of the program residing on the application revealed that they are all running exactly the same version. Therefore, it is unlikely that we have a versioning problem. So what could be the problem?

We will go back to the problem description and look for our second clue. The description "The content of the page is out of date" implies that the content is time-based. Furthermore, since the application server caches the data, it is possible that the content in the cache did not expire correctly. This can be easily verified by looking at the cache, if you have built in the capability to extract the cache from the application server. Assume that you can verify that the cache content is incorrect, you can fix the problem short-term by deleting the cache, and you can force the application server to reload its data from the database. But that's just fixing the symptom; what could be the real cause? Is there a bug in the code? Or is there a bug in the environment?

We always believe in looking for the simplest cause first, and in this case, we checked the system time of the computer. It turned out that the system time on the faulty application server is a few hours late. Since the cache is based on time, the application server with the erroneous time thought the content was still up–to–date, therefore, there is no need to upload the new data to replace the out–of–date content.

Chapter 3

The observation of the behavior of the instant messenger clearly points to some kind of memory corruption bug. The different symptoms are the result of memory content at the time that you click on the URL. The memory used by the system can be corrupted. The memory used by the browser can be overwritten. Depending on which application is affected, different behaviors are produced.

The cause of the memory corruption can be difficult to determine. But the most likely case here is the buffer overflow. This is based on the observation that there is no ill-effect to receiving the URL. It is not until you have clicked on the URL that something bad would happen. What happens when you click on the URL? Programmatically, the instant messenger must extract the URL from the screen and save the string that defines the URL. The instant messenger then submits this string to a browser. If the buffer used to save the URL string is too small, the URL will overwrite the memory outside of the buffer, and corrupt the memory of your machine. This would be our first hypothesis regarding the cause of the bug.

Chapter 4

The more astute reader will immediately think the problem might be related to the network because we provided the network layout for the system under discussion (repeated here at Figure A.1). However, another clue for the potential hardware problem can be found in the result of the experiments. The clue is the variation of the response time because software defects are usually consistent and predictable. However, you still have to rule out software as the potential cause of the problem and assist in identifying the specific hardware failure. How would you do it? The steps that we used to isolate the problem are as follows.

First, we could rule out any problem on the backend server because the timing on the backend servers was consistent on both the production and development environments. If the problem was in the software, it must be in the software that was running on the Web server.

Second, we needed to ensure that the performance was not related to the load on the system. Therefore, the timing experiments were run on an idle system.

Third, we needed to rule out the potential effect of the Web server and the servlet engines that executed the JSP. This meant that we needed to perform the same experiment using a simple Java application that executed the same requests as the JSP. To accomplish this, we

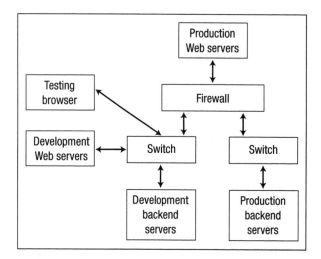

Figure A.1

The conceptual, architectural, and network layout of the system described in the Chapter 4 bug puzzle.

ran the Java application on the production Web server and the production backend server. We also ran the Java application on the development Web server and the development backend server. The results of the experiment have not changed; therefore, the problem was most likely a network issue.

Finally, we still needed to rule out the client–side API and Java virtual machine as potential culprits. This involved using the same Java application as described above. We ran the Java application on the production Web server to communicate with the development backend servers. The result of this experiment was consistent with the result of running the Java application on the development Web server communicating with the development backend servers (i.e. the performance was consistently fast). This showed us that the client–side API and the Java virtual machine could not be the culprit. Furthermore, this experiment showed clearly that there is a communication problem between the production Web server and the production backend server.

After some detective work by the network operation team, it was eventually found that the cable connecting the switch used by the production backend server to the firewall is faulty. The faulty cable was causing packets to be lost between the machines, and resulted in the prolonged and unpredictable response time. As soon as the cable is replaced, the performance of the production site is on par with the performance of the development site.

Chapter 5

The answer was actually given in the bug puzzle description. The problem was very simple, the box was filling the partition, which caused it to reboot and delete that partition. Why did this happen when the box had plenty of drive space left? Very simple. It was not the partitions containing the video data that were filling up. Instead, the problem was in the single index partition. When this partition filled up, the box tried to write more information for the next show, or tried to update an index for the current show, found no room, and caused the error.

The problem, in this case, was in not recognizing the potential for problems when choosing a fixed size for the index partition. Had each video partition had its own index, with a simple master index that kept track of what partition each video segment started on (this would be a very small file and would be unlikely to ever overflow a partition, but prudence would say to allow it to extend itself as well), the problem never would have happened in the first place.

This problem could have been fixed in numerous ways. The solution chosen—creating a new partition of double the size of the original index partition and then copying all data into it from the original—solving the problem but leaves the potential for it to happen again. The tradeoffs in selecting this solution were simple. We needed to get something into the customer's hands as quickly as possible, while maintaining existing boxes and their data. The solution was documented, along with the assumptions involved and the notation that this could happen again. Additional debugging messages were added to the code to validate this fact, and to warn the programmer if it were to recur. It was not a true "debugging," but it is more true to the real world than a perfect solution would have been.

Chapter 6

The problem is being caused by the backup change. The program locks a given resource when backing it up, and if the user is using that program and that resource at the time (and this user was), the program would crash the application because of a contention between the two processes.

Identifying this sort of a problem is usually a process of elimination. You find all of the items that are in common between the processes that are running, and then slowly work through each one to see what might be failing. Once you have identified the process that fails, you further eliminate each step of the process until you see which step fails. As soon as the problem step is identified, you use the standard debugging process to find the issue.

In this case, you would find the problem by looking at each of the steps and finding that the resource was in use from the logs of the various processes. By knowing that the resource was in use, you could then take steps to modify the process, or run it at a different time to fix the bug.

Chapter 7

It is impossible to load a debugger or a compiler onto the production machine, so these tools would be completely useless. Testing harnesses will only help if you can identify the source of the problem that is coming in. Is it a bad call from the Web pages? This would be easy to detect by simply doing PIPE analysis on the input and expected output. If that is the problem, you will find it quite quickly. If the problem is not in the calls themselves, it is likely to be a boundary condition on the input coming in. Examining the new Web pages to see what sorts of data are passed through, you could then examine diagnostic logging information to see what was going wrong. Finally, if none of these methods worked, you could turn on tracing in the application to see exactly where the program is crashing. Between the combination of tracing and logging of input data to the various functions, methods, and processes, it should not be difficult to track down the bug.

Another possibility is that the new load on the software has exposed a memory leak. It would be prudent to use a memory usage tracing system to see if you are exposing a new leak and if it is running the application out of memory. Finally, you might consider asking the Web developers (the users of your application) if they have seen anything that would help you in debugging the application.

Utilizing all of these methods, it is certain you will find the bug sooner rather than later. If you tried bench-testing the software on your own machine, you will likely be unable to find the bug if it is caused by a real-time set of data. Debugging production applications is something we talk about in Chapter 10.

Chapter 8

There are several possible problems at work here. First, because the ZIP code is repeated in two different tables, it is possible that a ZIP code was either added to the customer table or updated in it, and possibly did not make it into either the tax table or the tax paid table. Since there is no referential integrity implied by the design, it is impossible to determine if this is true or not. A simple scan of the database for things in one that are not in the other would find this.

The other problem here is probably more basic and more important. ZIP codes are really not numeric entities. They appear to be, because they contain only numbers at this point in time. The problem comes, when you actually look at the numbers. ZIP codes can, and do, start with 0. When a ZIP code is converted from a string into a numeric value, the 0 is stripped off. To go back to the original form of the ZIP code, you would need to be able to reformat the number back into the "string" version of the software. This is an often overlooked problem.

Finally, it is worth noting that the American-centric view of the programming world often causes bugs. In the ZIP code example, we considered only the US ZIP code, which contains only numbers. In other countries, such as Canada, ZIP codes contain both numbers and letters. A program that assumes purely numeric ZIP codes would certainly create problems when sold in another country.

Chapter 9

The fatal flaw is the fact that the number of users is incremented before any checks are done on the user login. If the login fails, there will still be one added and the total number of users who actually logged in could easily be 0.

Security Risk #1: If you tell the user that a user name is invalid or a password is invalid, you run the risk of letting a hacker know what is and what is not valid. It would be better and smarter to not tell them anything except invalid user/password combination.

Security Risk #2: By checking for multiple logins, but not checking to see if they are both from the same machine/location, you run the problem of having a user who logs in, somehow loses his settings, and then is automatically logged out. This will cause the same problem as Security Risk #1 eventually.

Chapter 10

The problem here is quite simple. The names of the files aren't the same in the writing application and the reading application. The file is therefore never read and the variables never set. Because of this, and the fact that the variables in the reading application are never initialized, the results are unpredictable.

Note that in the writer, the name is: T0DAYSDATA.DAT

In the reader application, the name is: TODAYSDATA.DAT

The first one has a zero in the name, while the second has an O.

Chapter 11

A few defects exist in the code, and they can potentially cause serious harm to the program. These defects are:

+ On line 12, username is assigned to be the same pointer as the **argv[1]** variable. On line 16, we have altered the content of the memory provided by the **username** variable. However, since **username** is the same pointer as the **argv[1]** variable, we have inadvertently also changed the **argv[1]** variable. This change might not be desirable.

+ The variable **firstname** is defined to have the size of 20 on line 4. However, on line 18, the **strncpy()** function did not check to make sure the first name of the user name is less than 20 characters. This defect can cause a potential buffer overflow of the **firstname** variable.

+ On line 16, the return of **index()** is not checked for NULL. It is possible that the user of the program forgot to specify to put a space between the first and last name. Under this scenario, the program will attempt to set a NULL to a NULL pointer.

♦ On line 18, **strncpy()** does not copy the NULL character to terminating the **firstname** character array. Therefore the content of the **firstname** variable after this line may not be correct.

♦ On line 19, the pointer **ptr** is incremented without regard to the validity of such an increment. For example, if the user enters the following name as the command line argument: Joe , the name would cause the ptr to be incremented to a nonsensical part of the memory.

♦ On line 21, the last name should be allocated with one extra character than the value returned by **strlen(ptr)**.

♦ On line 22, the validity of the **lastname** variable after the dynamic allocation using **malloc()** is never checked. If **malloc()** failed, the subsequent assignment will cause a bug.

♦ The **lastname** variable is never explicitly free. We know that once the program exits, the memory allocated to the **lastname** variable will be deallocated. But this is a bad habit, why stick with it?

There are other potential defects, too. For example, the program does not strip away leading and tailing white space characters. But the requirements for the program might not specify that the program needs to handle leading and trailing white spaces, and it is difficult to fault the code for adhering to the requirements.

Chapter 12

Presumably, somewhere in the client code, there is a function or a method that is implemented to retrieve a list of categories from the server. The function that retrieves the categories can conceivably be part of the client–side API. On the GUI there are two ways to display the list of categories. Instead of retrieving the data once using the function and populating the left–side category list and pull–down category menu with the same retrieved data, the GUI simply calls the API on an as–needed basis. This resulted in two identical requests to the server.

On the surface, this does not appear to be a serious problem. Why worry about two identical server requests? It is inefficient, but what's the big deal?

Imagine that the client is a Web browser, and every time the page is loaded, two requests are made to the server when one request would have been enough. On the Internet, millions of requests and users can hit your server all at once. From the systems perspective, this inefficiency has literally cut the system capacity in half. By simply designing the client side a little better, it would be possible to handle twice the number of loads using the same number of machines.

Chapter 13

In this case, the solution was actually presented in the problem statement itself. When the macro is expanded, it results in an expression that is parsed differently than the developer might have envisioned. The desired result is:

```
random() % (j-i+1);
```

The result which is actually generated is equivalent to:

```
(random() % j) - i + 1;
```

The solution is to simply make sure that it happens the way we want. To do this, just modify the macro to do things in a guaranteed order:

```
#define Random(n) random() % (n)
```

Sometimes, it is the paranoid approaches to life that work out best.

Chapter 14

The crux of the matter here is the reason for the growth of the development team. There are two reasons for adding new developers: to create new applications and to maintain existing applications. If the additional 20 developers that your company is hiring are asked to create new applications, then your nagging feeling might be unfounded. Because you need people to maintain existing applications, additional developers are necessary to work on new applications.

On the other hand, if all 30 developers are working on maintenance tasks, then it becomes important to understand the type of maintenance tasks that they are working on. In Chapter 14, we have classified maintenance tasks to three categories, so let us look at what it means for each category:

♦ They are mostly working on adaptive maintenance tasks. In other words, they are porting the applications. This is similar to having new developers working on new applications. There might not be a problem.

♦ They are mostly working on perfective tasks. The additional developers are adding new features and changing the design to make the system run faster and more robustly. These are not bad things to work on.

◆ They are mostly working on corrective tasks. This is the case where your nagging feelings could turn out to be correct and things may not be as rosy as it can be. When new developers are needed to help fix bugs, this means that your development team is creating bugs faster than they can fix them. The increased bug rate can be caused by many reasons. It could be caused by the increasing number of clients and increasing volume that your applications are experiencing. With more clients and more traffic, there is more chance to expose defects and for programs to break. The increasing bug rate can also be attributed to the maintenance changes to the applications. You add a feature, and a host of bugs is introduced. You fix a bug, only to see another one cropping up. So you are running behind, and in order to keep the applications stable, more bodies are added to help find and fix bugs. But with more developers, you also increase the chance for errors that are the results of communication, conceptual, and process problems. This is an inherently unstable and unscalable situation and is a symptom of unmaintainable software. It is only a matter of time before a critical error is introduced and the whole system crashes down on you. Also, from a business perspective, the unmaintainable system is also reducing potential profit of the company—think about the cost of having 10 people maintaining the software versus 30 people.

In the real world, it is likely that some new developers would be working on perfective tasks, and some would be working on corrective maintenance tasks. The only way to accurately assess the situation is to monitor the tasks and to track change requests and bug reports to find out what people are working on and to plan accordingly.

Chapter 15

When you think through the problem, you are likely to miss the real issue. The flaw in the reasoning is quite simple. Phone numbers aren't unique at all. We just think of them that way. In most major companies, there is a single main number, with a PBX system that sends the calls to the various extensions. Each one of those extensions, however, has the same basic number.

When major corporations sign up for the service, they use the main number of the company as their user name. This was true for each and every employee of that company that signed up. When each one used the same phone number, the system simply replaced the previous entry with the new one. Why? Because the phone numbers couldn't be duplicated according to the very logic of the application. Since there could be no duplicates, the programmers had simply forced an update if a user added the same phone number again, figuring that they had forgotten their password and were re-creating the account.

Appendix B
Additional Reading

We have touched upon many different subjects relating to bugs and debugging. Due to the complexity of the subject matter and the scope of this book, we had no choice but to gloss over many important topics and ideas. In this appendix, we list some of the books and journals that might help you gain more appreciation and understanding for some of the topics discussed in this book.

Bug-Related Incidents

Neumann, Peter G. *Computer Related Risks*. Addison-Wesley, New York, New York, 1995.

Peterson, Ivars. *Fatal Defect: Chasing Killer Computer Bugs*. Vintage Press, New York, New York, 1995.

Design

Brown, William H., et al. *AntiPatterns*. John Wiley and Sons, New York, New York, 1998.

Gamma, E., Helm, R., Johnson, R., and Vlissides, J. *Design Patterns*. Addison-Wesley, Reading, Massachusetts, 1995.

Programming

Kernighan, Brian W., and Pike, Rob. *The Practice of Programming*. Addison-Wesley, Reading, Massachusetts, 1999.

Maguire, S. *Writing Solid Code*. Microsoft Press, Redmond, Washington, 1993.

McConnell, Steve. *Code Complete*. Microsoft Press, Redmond, Washington, 1993.

Meyers, S. *Effective C++: 50 Specific Ways to Improve Your Programs and Designs*. Addison-Wesley, Reading, Massachusetts, 1998.

Inspection

Gilb, T., and Graham, D. *Software Inspection*. Addison-Wesley, Reading, MA, 1993.

Wheeler, D. A., ed., Brykczynski, B., ed., and Meeson, R. N., ed. *Software Inspection: An Industry Best Practice*. IEEE Computer Society, 1996.

Maintenance

IEEE Standard 1219-1992. *Software Maintenance Standard*. Published by IEEE Standards Office, P.O. Box 1331, Piscataway, New Jersey, 08855-1331.

Pigoski, T. M. *Practical Software Maintenance: Best Practices for Managing Your Software Investment*. John Wiley and Sons, New York, New York, 1996.

Smith, D. S. *Designing Maintainable Software*. Springer-Verlag, 1999.

Methodologies

Beck, Kent. *Extreme Programming Explained*. Addison-Wesley, Upper Saddle River, New Jersey, 2000.

Meyer, Bertrand. *Object–Oriented Software Construction.*, 2d ed. Prentice-Hall PTR, Upper Saddle River, New Jersey, 1997.

Rumbaugh, J., et al. *Object–Oriented Modeling and Design*. Prentice-Hall, Englewood Cliffs, New Jersey, 1991.

Requirement Engineering

Robertson, Suzanne, and Robertson, James. *Mastering the Requirement Process*. Addison-Wesley, Reading, Massachusetts, 2000.

Weigers, K. E. *Software Requirements*. Microsoft Press, Redmond, Washington, 1999.

Reuse

Jacobson, I., Griss, M. and Jonsson, P. *Software Reuse: Architecture Process and Organization for Business Success*. Addison-Wesley, Reading, Massachusetts, 1997.

Karlsson, Even-Andre, ed. *Software Reuse: A Holistic Approach*. John Wiley and Sons, New York, New York, 1995.

Szyperski, C. *Component Software: Beyond Object–Oriented Programming*. Addison-Wesley, Reading, Massachusetts, 1999.

Software Engineering

Arthur, L. J. *Rapid Evolutionary Development: Requirements, Prototyping & Software Creation*. John Wiley and Sons, New York, New York, 1992.

Boehm, B. *Software Engineering Economics*. Prentice Hall, Englewood Cliffs, New Jersey, 1981.

Florac, W. A., and Carleton, A. D. *Measuring the Software Process, Addison-Wesley, Reading MA, 1999*.

Gilb, T. *Principles of Software Engineering Management*. The Bath Press, Avon, Great Britain, 1988.

Jones, Capers. *Assessment and Control of Software Risks. (Yourdon Press Computing)*. Prentice Hall., Upper Saddle River, NJ., 1994.

Kan, Stephen H. *Metrics and Models in Software Quality Engineering*. Addison-Wesley, Reading, Massachusetts, 1995.

Putnam, Lawrence H., and Myers, Ware. *Measures for Excellence: Reliable Software on Time, within Budget*. Prentice-Hall, Englewood Cliffs, New Jersey, 1992.

Testing

Beizer, Boris. *Software System Testing and Quality Assurance*. Van Nostrand Reinhold Electrical/Computer Science and Engineering Series, Pennsauken, New Jersey, 1984.

Kaner, Cem, Nguyen Hung Quoc, and Jack Falk. *Testing Computer Software.*, 2d ed. John Wiley and Sons, New York, New York, 1999.

Maguire, Steve. *Writing Solid Code*. Microsoft Press, Redmond, Washington, 1993.

Software Process

Florac, William A., and Carleton, Anitas D., *Measuring the Software Process*. Addison-Wesley, Reading, Massachusetts, 1999.

Humphrey, Watts S. *Managing the Software Process*. Addison-Wesley, Reading, Massachusetts, 1989.

Index

80/20 rule, monetary cost of bugs, 68

A

Abnormal terminations, 129
Abort statement crashes telecommunications system, 57–58
Acme DotCom Works Corporation, bug puzzle, 464–465, 476
Ad hoc inspections, 337
Adaptive maintenance, 424
Advance strike debugging, 175–176
ADW Corporation, bug puzzle, 464–465, 476
Aeronautics and space travel. *See also* Ariane 5 explosion;
  Mars Climate Orbiter loss; NASA.
  Boeing flight control software, 70
  Challenger disaster, 13–14
  Mariner Venus probe loss, 100
Algorithms
  testing, 403–405
  understanding, 277–279
Allocation/deallocation errors, 139–141
Anderson, Rick, 290
ANSI/IEEE P104-1994 Standard..., 110
Antivirus software crashes system, 221–222
Application templates, 189
Application types, debugging. *See also* Debugging, methods;
  Debugging, techniques.
  distributed, 301–305
  embedded, 299–301
  large-scale standalone, 295–297
  mid-size client/server, 293–295
  mid-size standalone, 292–293
  real-time, 297–299
  simulated, 305–306
  small-scale standalone, 288–291
Architects, in prebugging, 364
Ariane 5 explosion, 31–33, 49, 50, 50
Assert statements, 198, 380–383
Assumptions, questioning, 268–270
AT&T outages, 1990
  causes of, 48–49, 50, 100–101
  description, 40–42

AT&T outages, 1998
  causes of, 49, 50
  description, 42–44

B

Back doors, 296
Baggage handling system, 65
Binary file corrupted by new guy, 156–157
Blob anti-pattern, 59
Boehm, Barry, 362
Boeing flight control software, 70
Boolean bugs, 159–161
Bottom-up testing, 388, 409–410
Boundary conditions, 262–264
Breakpoints, 10
Buffer overflow
  case studies and examples, 314
  Microsoft Outlook, 44–49, 50
Bug classifications. *See* Taxonomy of bugs.
Bug fixing. *See* Debugging.
Bug puzzles. *See also* Case studies and examples.
  Acme DotCom Works Corporation, 464–465, 476
  ADW Corporation, 464–465, 476
  bugs vs. design flaws, 162–163, 470–471
  C preprocessor, 420, 475
  C string bug, 324, 473–474
  debugging process, 239–240, 474
  GUI performance problems, 390–391, 474
  holistic debugging, 185, 471
  instant messenger hangs, 74–75, 469
  maintenance, 445, 475
  Partition Full Error, 162–163, 470–471
  post debugging, 324, 473–474
  print utility fails, 307, 473
  reusing code, 390–391, 474
  stock quoting system, 10, 467–468
  telephone numbers as passwords, 464–465, 476
  tools, 203, 471–472
  unexplained performance variance, 107–108, 469–470
  Web page loads incorrectly, 51, 468–469

Web server security risk, 286, 473
Web site database bugs, 239–240, 474
Bug reproduction environment, 361
Bugs. *See also* Software defects.
  cost of. *See* Cost of bugs.
  defect rates, 66, 88
  definition, 5, 53–56
  ignoring, 388
  importance of. *See* Cost of bugs.
  and language choice, 70–71
  misdiagnosing, 207–208
  origin of term, 8–9
  predicting, 175–176
  private, 103
  public, 103
  reproducing. *See* Reproducing bugs.
  severity, 5, 122–123
  similarities, 69–71, 218–220, 247–248, 311–312
  and software development cycle, 71–72
  stable systems vs. buggy systems, 72–73
  tracking, 199–200, 321–322, 334–335
  vs. design flaws, 162–163
  vs. problems, 206–208
Bugs, causes
  changes. *See* Changes, as bug causes.
  complexity. *See* Complexity, as bug cause.
  context coupling, 81
  cost constraints, 87
  documentation. *See* Documentation/as bug cause.
  feature creep, 92–93
  human factors. *See* Human factors, as bug causes.
  multithreaded applications, 80–81
  requirements documents too long, 79
  specifications inadequate, 93–94, 106
  testing environment inadequate, 106–107
  time constraints, 86–87
  tools. *See* Tools, as bug cause.
Bugs vs. design flaws, bug puzzle, 162–163, 470–471
Build bugs, 118–119
Built-in debugger, 176–177
Built-in diagnostics, 196–198

C

C assert statements, 198, 380–383
C preprocessor, bug puzzle, 420, 475
C string bug
  bug puzzle, 324, 473–474
  case studies and examples, 311–312
Callback functions, 95–97
Capability Maturity Model (CMM), 330

Case studies and examples. *See also* Bug puzzles.
  abort statement crashes telecommunications system, 57–58
  allocation/deallocation errors, 140–141
  antivirus software crashes system, 221–222
  Ariane 5 explosion, 31–33, 49, 50, 51
  AT&T outage, 1990, 41–43, 49–50, 52, 100–101
  AT&T outage, 1998, 43–45, 50, 51
  back doors, 296
  binary file corrupted by new guy, 156–157
  Boeing flight control software, 70
  Boolean bugs, 160–161
  buffer overflow, 314
  bug similarities across programmers, 69–71
  bugs, misdiagnosing, 207–208
  business information, 17–20
  C string bug, 311–312
  Challenger disaster, 13–14
  coding errors, 129–130
  Company X, 17–19, 49, 50
  Company Y, 15–17, 49
  computer chip arithmetic error. *See* FDIV bug.
  conditional errors, 136–137
  confidential NATO documents exposed, 26
  connectivity checking, 279–280
  conversion errors, 152–153
  core files, 280–281
  crashing when saving files, 207–208
  currency, as floating-point values, 314
  database crashed by date discrepancy, 116–118
  database users denied access, 279–280
  date discrepancy crashes database, 116–118
  DCOM settings, 304
  death and injury
    Challenger disaster, 13–14
    East Texas Cancer Center, 22
    Kennestone Regional Oncology Center, 21
    Ontario Cancer Foundation, 21
    submarine sunk by own torpedo, 31–32
    Therac-25 radiation therapy machine, 2, 20–26, 49, 50, 51
    Yakima Valley Memorial Hospital, 21, 23–24
  distributed application errors, 146–147
  DLLs incorrect, 115–116
  East Texas Cancer Center, 22
  e-commerce, 17–20, 372–378
  edge cases, 263
  electronic books formatted incorrectly, 288–289
  English/metric incompatibility. *See Mars Climate Orbiter.*
  error conditions, failing to check for, 228
  exception handling, 229
  fail-over strategy failure, 17–20, 227

FDIV bug, 26–31, 51

financial report server crashes, 15–17

fingerprint database, 4

floating point division error. *See* FDIV bug.

hard coded lengths/sizes, 154–155

inappropriate reuse bugs, 158–159

infinite loops, 134–135

instant messenger parsing HTML, 53–54

integration errors, 151

Intel Pentium processor error. *See* FDIV bug.

Internet bugs
    business information and e-commerce, 17–20
    fail-over strategy failure, 17–20
    financial report server crashes, 15–17

JAR file not deleted, 85

Kennestone Regional Oncology Center, 21

lack of tool understanding, 100–101

logic errors, 128

loop errors, 134–135

maintainability, designing for, 91–92

Mariner Venus probe loss, 100

Mars Climate Orbiter loss, 36–39, 50, 51, 52

memory, negative allocation, 280–281

memory allocation error, 280–281

memory corruption bug, 58

memory leaks, 126

memory overruns, 131–133

MFC library, inappropriate reuse of, 158–159

Microsoft bugs
    buffer overflow, Outlook, 44–49, 50
    MS Office deletes legitimate e-mail as spam, 33–34
    spam filter deletes legitimate e-mail, 33–35
    virus exposure, Outlook, 44–48

mid-size standalone application, 292–293

money, as floating-point values, 314

MPEG video goes blank, 208–209

MS Office deletes legitimate e-mail as spam, 33–35

multithreaded errors, 142–143

Northeastern University, 2

Ontario Cancer Foundation, 21

Outlook, buffer overflow, 44–49, 50

Outlook, virus exposure, 44–48

Pentium processor error. *See* FDIV bug.

pointer errors, 138–139

point-of-sale data corrupted, 292–293

point-of-sale simulation, 306

process control, 85–86

process errors, 115–118

questioning assumptions, 268–270

ratings lock failure, 219–220

real-time system overwhelmed, 227

reputation damaged by bugs, 2, 26–30

resistors, analogy to reusing code, 346–347

sales tax calculation, 278–279

satellite TV box crashes, 144–145

satellite TV receiver shows blank screen, 263

satellite TV recording failure, 217–218

social security numbers, running out of, 120–121

software filters get confused, 33–35

spam filter deletes legitimate e-mail, 33–35

storage errors, 149–150

strcopy() function, 311–312, 314

strlen() function, 312

submarine sunk by own torpedo, 30–31

Super Bowl XXXIV mistaken for porn site, 34

telephone bugs
    AT&T outage, 1990, 40–42, 48–49, 51, 100–101
    AT&T outage, 1998, 42–44, 49, 50
    trench collapses, 38–39

telephone numbers, running out of, 121

television bugs
    ratings lock failure, 219–220
    satellite box crashes, 144–145
    satellite receiver shows blank screen, 263
    satellite recording failure, 217–218

Therac-25 radiation therapy machine, 2, 20–26, 49, 50, 51

timing errors, 144–145

Titanic, sinking of, 105–106

trench collapses, 38–39

understanding algorithms, 278–279

user perspective, 288–289

versioning bugs, 156–157

Web server crashes, 231–234

Web server displays wrong page, 296

wrapping functions, 314

Yakima Valley Memorial Hospital, 21, 23–24

Year 2000 bug, 120–121

Categories of bugs. *See* Taxonomy of bugs.

Causal analysis, 332–335

Causes of bugs. *See* Bugs, causes.

Challenger disaster, 13–14

Changes, as bug causes
    debugging process, 220–221
    defect rates, 66
    environment changes, 87
    external content changes, 296–297
    recent changes, 264–265
    requirements changes, 80
    software changes, 89–93
    system changes, 87

Chunking, 80, 351–353

Classifying bugs. *See* Taxonomy of bugs.

Client/server applications. *See* Mid-size client/server.

CMM (Capability Maturity Model), 330

Code. *See also* Programs.
  commenting, 247–248
  eliminating during debugging, 250–251
  inspection time, 452–454
  turnover time, 454–455
  unexpected behavior, 127–129, 136–138, 140
Code coverage analysis, 200–201
Coding errors
  definition, 128–130
  and hypothesis formation, 225
Coe, Tim, 28
COM wizard, 83
Command line debuggers, 9
Commenting code. *See also* Self-documenting code.
  bug tracking, 334–335
  as a debugging technique, 247–248
  for maintenance, 431
Commercial off the shelf components (COTS), 343
Company X case study, 17–19, 49, 50
Company Y case study, 15–17, 49
Compilers
  bugs in, 202
  as debugging technique, 257–258
  implementation phase, 384–385
  language extensions, 202–203
  swapping, 260–261
  verifying messages, 201–202
  warning levels, 201
  warnings, 129
Complexity, as bug cause
  of code, 78
  measuring, 81
  of people, 84–85
  of problems, 78–80
  of processes, 85–86
  reducing and managing, 80, 349–354
  of solutions, 80–81, 94–97
  symptoms of, 79–80
  and testing, 397
  of tools, 81–83
Conceptual entropy
  definition, 97–98
  and maintenance, 430
Conditional errors, 135–137. *See also* Loop errors.
Configuration testing, 410–411
Conflict errors, 112
Connection errors, 302–303
Connectivity checking, 279–280
Context coupling, 81
Conversion errors, 151–153
Copy and paste errors, 167–168
Core dumps. *See* Core files; Snapshots.

Core files, 280–281
Corrective maintenance, 424
Cost
  of NASA software, 88
  prebugging, 362
  reusing code, 345–346
Cost of bugs. *See also* Case studies and examples; Death and injury; Monetary cost of bugs; Reputation damaged by bugs.
  morale, 61–62
  by software maturity level, 73
COTS (commercial off the shelf components), 343
Crashes. *See also* Symptoms.
  as bug symptom, 129, 137–138, 146
  coding errors, 129
  distributed application errors, 146
  pointer errors, 137–138
  random, 125–126, 140
  recovery, testing, 411–413
  regular, 131
  when saving files, example, 207–208
Cross-indexing, 194–195
Currency, as floating-point values, 314
Cyclomatic complexity measure, 81

D

Data dependency checking, 282–284
Database bugs, examples
  database users denied access, 279–280
  date discrepancy crashes database, 116–118
  fingerprint database, 4
  Web site database bugs, 239–240, 474
Date discrepancy crashes database, 116–118
DCOM (Distributed Common Object Model) settings, 304
Dead code detection, 195, 200–201, 265–268
Deadlock conditions, 143
Death and injury
  Challenger disaster, 13–14
  East Texas Cancer Center, 22
  Kennestone Regional Oncology Center, 21
  Ontario Cancer Foundation, 21
  submarine sunk by own torpedo, 31–32
  Therac-25 radiation therapy machine, 2, 20–26, 49, 50, 51
  Yakima Valley Memorial Hospital, 21, 23–24
Debuggers (human). *See* Debugging, profession of.
Debuggers (software)
  command line, 9
  as debugging technique, 253–254
  multithreaded, 10
  pros and cons, 195
  symbolic, 9

Debugging. *See also* Diagnostics; Post debugging;
  Prebugging; Symptoms; Tools.
  bugs attract more bugs, 67–68
  bugs beget more bugs, 67
  definition, 57–60, 166
  embedded systems, 301
  history of, 8–10
  holistic. *See* Holistic debugging.
  saving bug data. *See* Suites of/past bugs; Tracking/bugs.
  time estimates, 235
  whole-system view. *See* Holistic debugging.
Debugging, methods. *See also* Application types, debugging;
  Debugging, techniques.
  diagnostics, 175–176
  intuition, 174–175
  leaps of faith, 175
  scientific method, 173–174
Debugging, pitfalls
  component thinking, 19
  failing to follow procedures, 20
  ignoring clues, 19, 50
  inadequate monitoring tools, 20, 50–51
  inappropriate reuse of software, 50
  second guessing clues, 19
Debugging, process
  bug puzzle, 239–240, 474
  bugs vs. problems, 206–208
  environment information, 221–223
  failed test suites, 218
  hypotheses, forming, 223–230
  hypotheses, simplifying, 251–253
  hypotheses, testing, 230–234
  hypotheses, verifying, 234–235
  identifying the problem, 205–206
  log files, 213–216
  personal observations, 216–217
  problem similarities, 218–220
  programs, determining actual operation, 209–211
  programs, determining intent of, 208–209
  recent changes, 220–221
  regression testing, 238
  solutions, 235–237
  symptoms vs. root causes, 217–218
  user descriptions, gathering, 211–213
Debugging, profession of
  code inspections, 452–454
  code turnover, 454–455
  design phase, 451
  learning debugging, 379–380, 448–451
  requirements phase, 452
  traits of a debugger
    detective skills, 457–458
    ego, 460

engineering/scientific methodology, 459–460
    paranoia, 326–327
    patience, 456–457
    perseverance, 461
    stress management, 458–459
    tact, 456
  a typical day, 461–464
Debugging, techniques. *See also* Application types,
  debugging; Debugging, methods; Intrusive techniques;
  Long-term techniques; Non-intrusive techniques;
  Short-term techniques.
  instrumentation, 243
  for production environments, 244–245
Debugging application types. *See* Application types,
  debugging.
Debugging tools. *See* Tools.
Decision tables, 405–406
Defect rates
  in changed code, 66
  NASA software, 88
  post debugging, 320–321
  reusing code, 341, 342
Delocalization, 430, 433
Denver International airport, 64
Deployment bugs, 119–120
Design bugs, working around, 440–441
Design choice risks, 368–371
Design documents, 355–356
Design phase
  bugs, 112–113
  prebugging. *See* Prebugging, design phase.
  role of professional debugger, 451
Designers, in prebugging, 364
Detective skills, 457–458
Deterministic errors, 302
Diagnostics. *See also* Debugging; Symptoms; Tools.
  built-in, 176–177, 196–198
  description, 175–176
  displays, 173, 179–180
  error handling, 197
  hidden diagnostic screens, 179–180
  input, 197
  logging objects, 177
  postconditions, 197
  preconditions, 196–197
  saving bug data. *See* Suites of/past bugs.
  side effects, 197
  tracing objects, 177–179
Distributed application errors, 145–147
Distributed Common Object Model (DCOM) settings, 304
Distributed systems, 301–305
Divide and conquer, 255–256, 298

DLL problems
  example, 115–116
  small-scale standalone applications, 290
Documentation. *See also* Self-documenting code.
  as bug cause, 90
  as debugging technique, 247
  design documents, 355–356
  designers vs. implementers, 355–356
  effectiveness of, 428–429
  FAQ style, 356–357
  feature entry points, 432
  high-level, 431
  lack of incentives for, 84–85
  maintenance changes, 440
  misleading, 90
  missing, 90
  overviews, 356
  pictures, 356
  post debugging results, 315–317
  recording project history, 357–358
  self-documenting code, 358
  test programs, 358–359
  tutorials, 358–359
  vs. code behavior, 428–429
  wrong audience, 90
Documentation bugs, 122
Dumps. *See* Core files; Snapshots.
Dvorak, John, 97
Dynamic loading, 430
Dynamic tracing, 431–432

E

East Texas Cancer Center, 22
Ebay auction crash, 2
E-commerce, 17–20, 372–378
Edelman, Alan, 29
Edge cases, 263
Educating debuggers. *See* Learning debugging.
Ego
  as a bug cause, 105–106
  debugger trait, 460
Egoless debugging, 327–328
Egoless programming, 268
Electronic books formatted incorrectly, 288–289
Embedded systems, 299–301
Emulators, 301
Encapsulated hardware interface, 305
Engineering/scientific methodology, 459–460
English/metric incompatibility. *See Mars Climate Orbiter.*
Enhancements causing bugs. *See* Changes, as bug causes.
Environment information, 221–223

Error handling. *See also* Exceptions.
  definition, 197
  explicit error checking, 383–384
  failing to check error conditions, 227–229
Error messages
  from compilers, 201–202
  implementation bugs, 113
  odd or unexpected, 146, 172–173
Error rates. *See* Defect rates.
Error returns, 305–306
Error seeding, 256–257
Examples. *See* Case studies and examples.
Exceptions. *See also* Error handling.
  case studies and examples, 229
  disadvantages of, 378
Experience levels, as bug cause, 88
Explicit error checking, 383–384

F

Fail-over strategy failure, examples, 17–20, 227
FAQ (Frequently Asked Question) style documentation, 356–357
FDIV bug
  contributing causes, 51
  description, 26–30
  monetary cost, 64
  monetary cost of, 64
Feature creep, 92–93, 353–354
Feynman, Richard, 13–14
Filters get confused, 33–35
Financial report server crashes, 15–17
Flight control software, 70
Flow testing, 398–400
Formatting errors
  electronic books, 288–289
  small-scale standalone applications, 291
Frameworks for problem, 434–435
Freezes, 133–134
Frequently Asked Question (FAQ) style documentation, 356–357
Function definitions, 432
Functions, wrapping, 314
Future planning bugs, 120–121

G

Global variables
  definition, 168–169
  maintenance, 433
Graphical user interfaces (GUIs). *See* GUIs (graphical user interfaces).

Guessing. *See* Leaps of faith.
GUIs (graphical user interfaces)
    errors associated with, 113
    history of debugging, 10
    performance, bug puzzle, 390–391, 474

H

Hager, Fritz, 22
Hand waving, 354
Hangs, 133–134, 146
Hard-coded lengths/sizes, 153–155
Hardware/software contention, 298
Heisenberg's uncertainty principle, 195–196
Helper routines, 193
Heterogeneous paired inspections, 339
History of debugging. *See* Debugging/history of.
Holistic debugging
    bug puzzle, 185, 471
    copy and paste errors, 167–168
    diagnostic displays, 173
    global variables, 168–169
    side effects, 170–171
    unexpected messages or results, 172–173
Holistic thinking, 258–260
Homogeneous paired inspections, 339
Hopper, Grace, 8–9
Human factors, as bug causes
    planning and decision making, 78
    poor comprehension, 90–91
    programmer errors, 89, 97–99
    reducing and managing complexity, 80
    seven-concept limit, 79
    team communication, 84–85
    tunnel vision, 91–92
Hypotheses
    forming, 223–230
    simplifying, 251–253
    testing, 230–234
    verifying, 234–235

I

Implementation phase
    bugs, 113–114
    prebugging. *See* Prebugging, implementation phase.
Inappropriate reuse bugs, 157–159
Infinite loops, 134–135
Information repositories, 304
Inheritance
    effects on maintainability, 97–99
    maintenance, 432–433

multiple, 430
    risks, 370–371
Injury caused by bugs. *See* Death and injury.
Input verification testing, 401–403
Input/output errors, 291
Inspecting your own work, 338
Inspections, 335–340, 453
Instant messenger
    hanging, bug puzzle, 74–75, 469
    parsing HTML, 53–54
Instrumentation, 243
Integration errors, 150–151
Integration testing, 408–409
Interface design
    limiting flexibility, 372–373
    minimizing ambiguity, 373–377
    self-documenting code, 378
    software modules, 371–372
Internet bugs. *See also* Web bugs.
    business information and e-commerce, 17–20
    fail-over strategy failure, 17–20
    financial report server crashes, 15–17
Interrupt suppression, 299–300
Intrusive techniques
    commenting code, 247–248
    core files, 280–281
    debuggers (software), 253–254
    definition, 242–243
    eliminating code, 250–251
    error seeding, 256–257
    looking for similar problems, 247–248
    Mutex, 273–275
    mutually exclusive objects, 273–275
    playback capability, 284–285
    reductionism, 251–253
    tracing, 282
    variables, changing one at a time, 261–262
Intuition, 174–175
Invariants, 271–272
Iterative methodologies, 364

J

JAR file not deleted, 85
Jones, Capers
    data processing budget, 4
    survey of bug costs, 63–64
Journals, as debugging technique, 246. *See also* Logging.

K

Kennestone Regional Oncology Center, 21

L

Language extensions, 202–203
Languages
  avoiding obscure features, 385–386
  effects on bugs, 70–71
  misusing features of, 379
Large-scale standalone applications, 295–297
Laziness, 102–103
Leaps of faith, 175
Learning debugging, 379–380, 448–451
Levenson, Nancy, 20–26
Linear code, 432
Load testing, 417–419
Lockups, 133–134
Log files, 213–216
Logging. *See also* Journals.
  description, 190–191
  objects, 177
Logic analyzers, 301
Logic errors
  description, 127–128
  and hypothesis formation, 226–227
Logs, tracing, 359–361, 383–384
Long-term techniques
  boundary conditions, 262–264
  checking recent changes, 264–265
  commenting code, 247–248
  comparing to stable versions, 276–277
  compiler checks, 257–258
  compilers, swapping, 260–261
  connectivity checking, 279–280
  core files, 280–281
  data dependency checking, 282–284
  dead code removal, 265–268
  definition, 243–244
  documenting the code and process, 247
  error seeding, 256–257
  holistic thinking, 258–260
  invariants, 271–272
  looking for similar problems, 247–248
  memory usage, 272–273
  mirroring production systems, 285
  Mutex, 273–275
  mutually exclusive objects, 273–275
  numerology, 262–264
  operating systems, swapping, 260–261
  playback capability, 284–285
  question your assumptions, 268–270
  tracing, 282
  understanding algorithms, 277–279
  untested code analysis, 270–271

  user involvement, 245–246
  visualization, 275–276
Loop errors. *See also* Conditional errors.
  description, 133–135
  improperly exited loops, 133
  off-by-one loops, 133
  for vs. **while,** 94–97, 99

M

Macro capability. *See* Playback capability.
Maintainability
  characteristics of, 433–434
  designing for, 91–92, 433–436
  inheritance and, 97–99
  one-off solutions, 435–436
  problem frameworks, 434–435
  processes, 435–436
  and testing, 397
  vs. performance, 94–97
Maintenance
  adaptive, 424
  bug puzzle, 445, 475
  categories, 424
  challenges of, 425–426
  comprehensible software, 427–433
  corrective, 424
  definition, 424
  degradations resulting from, 426–427
  design bugs, working around, 440–441
  documenting changes, 440
  existing software, 438–442
  expense, 63–64
  knowing when to quit, 443–444
  maintenance environment, 437–438
  perfective, 424
  porting, 424
  preventive, 424
  regression testing, 441
  regression testing environment, 436–437
  requirements, working around, 440–441
  steps in, 425
  tracking changes, 441–442
Makefile, 343–344
Mariner Venus probe loss, 100
Mars Climate Orbiter loss
  contributing causes, 49, 50, 51
  description, 35–38
  integration testing, 340–341
  monetary cost of, 64
Mathematical errors, 152
McCabe's cyclomatic complexity measure, 81

Measuring improvement
    causal analysis, 332–335
    metrics, 320–321
    personal defect analysis, 334–335
    post debugging, 320–323
    testing, 419
Memory
    allocation errors, 137–138, 140, 280–281
    decreasing over time, 125–126, 140
    errors, symptoms of, 225
    negative allocation, 280–281
    overruns, 131–133
    usage, as debugging technique, 272–273
    usage, increasing over time, 225
Memory corruption bug, 58
Memory leaks
    debugging, 272–273
    description, 125–127
    detecting, tools for, 192–194
    and hypothesis formation, 225
Mentoring, 379–380
Messages. *See* Error messages.
Methodologies for debugging. *See* Application types,
    debugging; Debugging, techniques.
Metric/English incompatibility. *See* Mars Climate Orbiter.
Metrics, 320–321. *See also* Measuring improvement.
MFC (Microsoft Foundation Class) library, inappropriate
    reuse of, 158–159
Microsoft bugs
    buffer overflow, Outlook, 45–50, 51
    MS Office deletes legitimate e-mail as spam, 34–36
    virus exposure, Outlook, 45–49
Microsoft Foundation Class (MFC) library, inappropriate
    reuse of, 158–159
Middleware errors, 301–302
Mid-size client/server applications, 293–295
Mid-size standalone applications, 292–293
Mirroring production systems, 285
Missing functionality, 114
Monetary cost of bugs
    80/20 rule, 68
    Capers Jones survey, 63–64
    data processing budgets, 4
    Denver International airport, 64
    in design phase, 112
    by development stage, 71
    ebay auction crash, 2
    FDIV bug, 64
    maintenance expense, 63–64
    Mars Climate Orbiter, 64
    per lines of code, 88
    quality assurance processes, 103–104
    in requirements phase, 111

Money, as floating-point values, 314
Monitoring
    symbol usage, 194–195
    system usage, 295
MPEG video goes blank, 208–209
MS Office deletes legitimate e-mail as spam, 33–35
Multiple inheritance, 430
Multithreaded applications
    as bug cause, 80–81
    error description, 141–143
    and hypothesis formation, 229–230
Multithreaded debuggers, 10
Multiuser testing, 415–416
Mutex, 273–275
Mutually exclusive objects, 273–275

N

Naming conventions, 432
NASA. *See also* Aeronautics and space travel.
    cost of producing software, 88
    Web site URL, 100
NASA bugs. *See also Mars Climate Orbiter* loss.
    Challenger disaster, 13–14
    Mariner Venus probe loss, 100
NATO documents exposed, 26
Nicely, Thomas, 26–30
Non-intrusive techniques
    boundary conditions, 262–264
    checking recent changes, 264–265
    commenting code, 247–248
    comparing to stable versions, 276–277
    compiler checks, 257–258
    compilers, swapping, 260–261
    connectivity checking, 279–280
    core files, 280–281
    data dependency checking, 282–284
    dead code removal, 265–268
    definition, 242–243
    divide and conquer, 255–256, 298
    documenting the code and process, 247
    holistic thinking, 258–260
    invariants, 271–272
    keeping a journal, 246
    looking for similar problems, 247–248
    memory usage, 272–273
    mirroring production systems, 285
    numerology, 262–264
    operating systems, swapping, 260–261
    question your assumptions, 268–270
    simplifying hypotheses, 251–253
    simplifying reproducibility, 248–249

simplifying test cases, 248–249
simplifying the problem, 249–250
understanding algorithms, 277–279
untested code analysis, 270–271
user involvement, 245–246
visualization, 275–276
Northeastern University over-enrollment, 2
Numerology, 262–264
NVP (N-Version Programming), 69–70

O

Object-oriented designs
maintenance, 432–433
risks, 370–371
Objects become NULL, 225
Omission errors, 112
One-off solutions, 435–436
Ontario Cancer Foundation, 21
Outlook
buffer overflow, 44–49, 50
virus exposure, 44–48

P

Paranoia, 326–327
Parsing, risks, 369
Partition Full Error, 162–163, 470–471
Path testing, 398–400
Patience, 456–457
Perfective maintenance, 424
Performance
GUI problems, bug puzzle, 390–391, 474
testing, 417–419
unexplained variance, bug puzzle, 107–108, 469–470
vs. maintainability, 94–97
Perseverance, 461
Personal defect analysis, 334–335
Personal observations, 216–217
Personality traits of debuggers. *See* Traits of a debugger.
Personnel, 328–332
Pictures in documentation, 356
Playback capability, 284–285
Pointer errors
debugging, 272–273
description, 137–139
stray pointer problem, 251
Pointer issues, 386–387
Point-of-sale, case studies and examples
data corrupted, 292–293
simulation, 306

Polymorphism
maintenance, 430, 432
risks, 370–371
Porting, 424
Post debugging. *See also* Debugging; Prebugging.
bug puzzle, 324, 473–474
bug tracking, 321–322
commenting out scaffolding code, 317–320
creating new tools, 315
defect rates, 320–321
document results, 315–317
finding similar bugs, 311–312
future design implications, 314
measuring improvement, 320–323
metrics, 320–321
preventing reoccurrences, 313–314
previously hidden bugs, 312–313
purpose of, 309–310
saving test cases, 313
understanding causes, 313
Postconditions, 197
Postmortem log analysis, 304–305
Power failures, testing, 411–413
Pragma statement, 202–203
Pratt, Vaughan R., 28
Prebugging. *See also* Debugging; Post debugging.
assembling a team, 328–331
backup personnel, 330
bug reproduction environment, 361
causal analysis, 332–335
chunking, 351–353
commenting code, 334–335
complexity, reducing and managing, 349–354
definition, 326
egoless debugging, 327–328
evolution vs. revolution, 331–332
feature creep, 353–354
hand waving, 354
inspections, 335–340, 453
introducing process elements, 331–332
isolating chaotic elements, 331
matching people to environment, 330–331
paranoia, role of, 326–327
personal defect analysis, 334–335
process, value of, 349–350
project continuity, 329
replacing team members, 332
requirements phase, 362–367
reusable components, 343, 346–348
reusing code
cost of, 345–346
COTS, 343

defect rates, 341, 342
in early development stages, 344–345
encouraging, 348–349
Makefile, 343–344
resistance to, 341–342
risks, 349
without modification, 342–343
simplifying problems, 350–351
snapshots, 359
systematic errors, 333–334
team incentives, 332
tracing logs, 359–361
Prebugging, design phase
design choice risks, 368–371
interface design, 371–378
Prebugging, implementation phase
asserts, 380–383
bottom-up testing, 388
compiler checking, 384–385
explicit error checking, 383–384
ignoring bugs, 388
language, 379
mentoring, 379–380
obscure language features, 385–386
pointer issues, 386–387
testing as you go, 387–389
tools, 378–379
top-down testing, 388
tracing logs, 383–384
Preconditions, 196–197
Preventive maintenance, 424
Print utility fails, 307, 473
Private bugs, 103
Problem decomposition, 429–430
Problem frameworks, 434–435
Problem similarities, 218–220
Problems
similarities, 69–71, 218–220, 247–248, 311–312
vs. solutions, 363
Problems, simplifying
debugging technique, 249–250
prebugging technique, 350–351
simulated systems, 306
Process bugs, 115–118
Process of debugging. *See* Debugging, process.
Processes
and maintainability, 435–436
value of, 349–350
Professional debuggers. *See* Debugging, profession of.
Program crashes, 114
Programs. *See also* Code.
determining actual operation, 209–211
determining intent of, 208–209

Project continuity, 329
Protocol errors, 300
Prototyping, 364–365
Public bugs, 103
Putnam, Larry, 4

Q

QA testing, 396–397
Quality assurance. *See* QA.

R

Radiation overdose. *See* Therac-25 radiation
therapy machine.
Real-time systems, 227, 297–299
Reasons for bugs. *See* Bugs, causes.
Recording actions. *See* Playback capability.
Recursion, risks, 369–370
Reductionism, 251–253
Registry problems, 304
Regression testing
description, 238
environment for, 436–437
and maintenance, 441
Reproducing bugs
data dependencies, 181–182
difficulties in, 65–66, 104
gathering observations, 182–183
simplifying, 248–249
statistics and metrics, 183–184
symptoms vs. root causes, 182
test cases, 181
in testing, 105
Reputation damaged by bugs
customer resentment, 62–63
Intel Pentium processor, 26–30
Northeastern University, 2
Requirements, and maintenance, 440–441
Requirements documents, excessive length, 79
Requirements errors, and hypothesis formation, 227
Requirements phase
bugs, 111
prebugging. *See* Prebugging, requirements phase.
role of professional debugger, 452
Requirements verification, 365–367
Resistors, analogy to reusing code, 346–347
Resource leaks, 125–127
Return values, failing to check, 227–229
Reusable components
buying, 343
designing, 346–347
simplifying, 347–348

Reusing code
  Ariane 5 explosion, 32–34, 50
  bug puzzle, 390–391, 474
  copy and paste errors, 167–168
  cost of, 345–346
  COTS, 343
  defect rates, 66, 341, 342
  in early development stages, 344–345
  encouraging, 348–349
  inappropriate reuse bugs, 158
  Makefile, 343–344
  resistance to, 341–342
  reused code acts differently from original, 158
  risks, 349
  without modification, 342–343
Risks
  design choices, 368–371
  inheritance, 370–371
  inspections, 340
  object-oriented designs, 370–371
  parsing, 369
  polymorphism, 370–371
  recursion, 369–370
  reusing code, 349
  sorting algorithms, 368
Rubin, Howard, 4

S

Sales tax calculation, 278–279
Scaffolding code
  commenting out, 317–320
  definition, 189
  saving for reuse, 317–320
Scalability, 9
Scattered information, 430, 433
Scenario-based inspections, 337
Scientific method, 173–174
Security
  errors, 303–304
  testing, 413–415
  Web server, bug puzzle, 286, 473
Self-documenting code. *See also* Commenting code;
  Documentation.
  as documentation, 358
  interface design, 378
Seven-concept limit, 79
Severity of bugs, 5, 122–123
Short-term techniques
  changing one variable at a time, 261–262
  commenting code, 247–248
  debuggers (software), 253–254

  definition, 243–244
  divide and conquer, 255–256, 298
  eliminating code, 250–251
  error seeding, 256–257
  invariants, 271–272
  looking for similar problems, 247–248
  memory usage, 272–273
  Mutex, 273–275
  mutually exclusive objects, 273–275
  question your assumptions, 268–270
  reductionism, 251–253
  simplifying hypotheses, 251–253
  simplifying reproducibility, 248–249
  simplifying test cases, 248–249
  simplifying the problem, 249–250
  untested code analysis, 270–271
Side effects, 168–171, 197
Silver-bullet problem, 4
Simulated systems
  definition, 305
  encapsulated hardware interface, 305
  error returns, 305–306
  simplifying the problem, 306
Simulator problems, 299
Slowdowns, 125–126, 140
Small-scale standalone applications, 288–291
Snapshots, 359
Social security numbers, running out of, 120–121
Software defects, 56–57. *See also* Bugs.
Software development cycle, 71–72
Software Engineering Economics, 362
Software filters get confused, 33–35
Software maintenance. *See* Maintenance.
Software Testing Techniques, 110
Solutions
  proposing, 235–237
  testing, 237
  verifying, 237
  vs. problems, 363
Sorting algorithms, risks, 368
Source codes, searching, 429
Space travel. *See* Aeronautics and space travel.
Spam filter deletes legitimate e-mail, 33–35
Specifications, inadequacy, 93–94, 106
Stack corruptions, 137–138, 140
Stack overflow, 369–370
Standalone applications. *See* Large-scale standalone;
  Mid-size standalone; Small-scale standalone.
State machine analysis, 406–408
Statistics and metrics
  bug tracking, 199–200
  gathering, 183–184

Stock quoting system, 10, 467–468
Storage errors, 148–150
Strategies for debugging. *See* Application types, debugging;
  Debugging, techniques.
strcopy() function, 311–312, 314
Stress management, 458–459
strlen() function, 312
Studies. *See* Case studies and examples.
Submarine sunk by own torpedo, 30–31
Suites of
  past bugs, 180, 189–190
  tests, 188–189
Super Bowl XXXIV mistaken for porn site, 34
Swiss Army Knife anti-pattern, 59
Symbolic debuggers, 9
Symptoms. *See also* Crashes; Debugging.
  abnormal terminations, 129
  allocation/deallocation errors, 140
  Boolean bugs, 159–160
  and bug determination, 124
  code behaves unexpectedly, 127–129, 136–138, 140
  coding errors, 129
  compiler warnings, 129
  conditional errors, 136
  conversion errors, 152
  distributed application errors, 146
  errors in production but not unit test, 150–151
  errors occur only when multithreading, 142
  errors occur regularly, 144
  errors occur when input changes, 154
  formatting unexpectedly bad, 152
  freezes, 133–134, 146
  hangs, 133–134, 146
  hard-coded lengths/sizes, 154
  inappropriate reuse bugs, 158
  integration errors, 150–151
  lockups, 133–134, 146
  logic errors, 127–128
  loop errors, 133–134
  mathematical errors, 152
  memory allocation failure, 137–138, 140
  memory decreases over time, 125–126, 140
  memory errors, 225
  memory leaks, 125–126
  memory overruns, 131
  memory usage increases, 225
  multithreaded errors, 142
  objects become NULL, 225
  odd error messages, 146
  output incorrect, 152
  pointer errors, 137–138
  previous code versions fail, 156
  process terminates unexpectedly, 133–134

repeatedly displaying same data, 133–134
resource leaks, 125–126
results are opposite of expected, 159–160
reused code acts differently from original, 158
slowdowns, 125–126, 140
stack corruptions, 137–138, 140
storage errors, 148–149
timing errors, 144
unable to find resources, 148–149
values mysteriously change, 131, 137–138, 140
versioning bugs, 156
vs. root causes, 182, 217–218
Syntax errors, 114
Systematic errors, 333–334

T

Tact, 456
Taxonomy of bugs
  allocation/deallocation errors, 139–141
  ANSI/IEEE P104-1994 Standard..., 110
  Boolean bugs, 159–161
  build bugs, 118–119
  coding errors, 128–130, 225
  conditional errors, 135–137
  conflict errors, 112
  conversion errors, 151–153
  deadlock conditions, 143
  definition, 109
  deployment bugs, 119–120
  design bugs, 112–113
  distributed application errors, 145–147
  documentation bugs, 122
  error messages, 113
  future planning bugs, 120–121
  GUI errors, 113
  hard coded lengths/sizes, 153–155
  implementation bugs, 113–114
  importance of, 161
  inappropriate reuse bugs, 157–159
  integration errors, 150–151
  logic errors, 127–128, 226–227
  loop errors, 133–135
  memory leaks, 125–127, 225
  memory overruns, 131–133
  missing functionality, 114
  multithreaded errors, 141–143, 229–230
  omission errors, 112
  pointer errors, 137–139
  process bugs, 115–118
  program crashes, 114
  requirements bugs, 111

requirements errors, 227

resource leaks, 125–127

Software Testing Techniques, 110

storage errors, 148–150

syntax errors, 114

timing errors, 143–145, 229–230

translation errors, 112–113

versioning bugs, 155–157

Teaching debugging. *See* Learning debugging.

Telephone bugs. *See also* AT&T outages.

telephone numbers, running out of, 121

trench collapses, 38–39

Telephone numbers as passwords, 464–465, 476

Television bugs

digital recorder runs out of space, 172

MPEG video goes blank, 208–209

ratings lock failure, 219–220

satellite box crashes (example), 144–145

satellite receiver shows blank screen (example), 263

satellite recording failure, 217–218

Test cases

reproducing bugs, 181

result states, 188–189

saving for reuse, 313

simplifying, 248–249

Test drivers, 202

Test harnesses, 189

Test plan development, 367

Test programs as documentation, 358–359

Testers, in prebugging, 366–367

Testing

algorithmic, 403–405

all possible code paths, 78

a back-end database, 294–295

bottom-up, 409–410

and complexity, 397

configuration, 410–411

costs of, 103–104

crash recovery, 411–413

decision table, 405–406

failed test suites, 218

failure to catch bugs, 103–107

flow, 398–400

input verification, 401–403

integration, 408–409

load, 417–419

and maintainability, 397

measurements and statistics, 419

multiuser, 415–416

nonreproducible bugs, 104

path, 398–400

performance, 417–419

political/marketing decisions, 104

power failures, 411–413

QA, 396–397

regression testing, 238

security, 413–415

small pieces of code, 189

state machine analysis, 406–408

third-party tools, 415

time constraints, 104

top-down, 409–410

transactional, 400–401

unit, 393–395

unrealistic schedules, 104

verification testing, 395–396

as you go, 387–389

Testing environments

description, 187–188

desirable properties of, 106–107

inadequacy, 106–107

Therac-25 radiation therapy machine, 2, 20–26, 49, 50, 51

Time constraints

as bug cause, 86–87

testing schedules, 104

Time estimates for debugging, 235

Timing errors

description, 143–145

and hypothesis formation, 229–230

Timing issues, 298–299

Titanic, sinking of, 105–106

Tools. *See also* Debugging; Diagnostics; Symptoms.

application templates, 189

assert statements, 198

bug puzzle, 203, 471–472

bug tracking, 199–200

built-in diagnostics, 196–198

code coverage analysis, 200–201

COM wizard, 83

comparative programming languages, 83

compilers, 201–203

complexity of, 81–83

cross-indexing, 194–195

dead code detection, 195, 200–201

debuggers, 195

Heisenberg's uncertainty principle, 195–196

helper routines, 193

inappropriate use of, 101–102

lack of understanding, 100–101

language extensions, 202–203

logging, 177, 190–191

memory leak detection, 192–194

pragma statement, 202–203

prebugging, 378–379

scaffolding code, 189

suite of tests, 188–189

test cases, 188–189
test drivers, 202
test harnesses, 189
testing, third-party, 415
testing environment, 187–188
tracing, 177–179, 191–192
usage monitoring, 194–195
user feedback, 198–199
Tools, as bug cause
    complexity of, 81–83
    inappropriate use of, 101–102
    lack of understanding, 100–101
Top-down testing, 388, 409–410
Torpedo sinks own submarine, 31–32
Tracing
    as debugging technique, 282
    description, 191–192
    dynamic, 431–432
    logs, 359–361, 383–384
    objects, 177–179
Tracking
    bugs, 199–200
    changes, 441–442
    maintenance changes, 441–442
Training in debugging. *See* Learning debugging.
Traits of a debugger
    detective skills, 457–458
    ego, 460
    engineering/scientific methodology, 459–460
    patience, 456–457
    perseverance, 461
    stress management, 458–459
    tact, 456
Transactional testing, 400–401
Translation errors, 112–113
Trench collapses, 38–39
Troubleshooting. *See* Debugging; Symptoms.
Tunnel vision, 91–92
Turner, Clark S., 20–26
Tutorials as documentation, 358–359
Types of bugs. *See* Taxonomy of bugs.

U

Unexplained performance variance, 107–108, 469–470
Unit testing, 393–395
Untested code analysis, 270–271
Upgrades causing bugs. *See* Changes, as bug causes.
Users
    feedback, as a debugging tool, 198–199
    involvement, as debugging technique, 245–246
    perspective of, 288–289
    problem descriptions from, 211–213

V

Values mysteriously change, 131, 137–138, 140
Variables, changing one at a time, 261–262
Verification testing, 395–396
Versioning bugs, 155–157
Virus exposure, Outlook, 45–49
Visualization, 275–276

W

Watchdog timers, 300–301
Web bugs. *See also* Internet bugs.
    page loads incorrectly, 51, 468–469
    server crashes, 231–234
    server displays wrong page, 296
    server security risk, 286, 473
    site database bugs, 239–240, 474
Windows Registry problems, 304
Wolfe, Alexander, 27–28
Wrapping functions, 314

Y

Yakima Valley Memorial Hospital, 21, 23–24
Year 2000 bug, 120–121